Britannica
Review
of Foreign Language
Education

Britannica Reviews in Education

Advisory Board

Britannica Review
of Foreign Language Education

Edited by Emma Marie Birkmaier

Volume 1, 1968

Sponsored by the American Council
on the Teaching of
Foreign
Languages

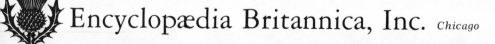

Encyclopædia Britannica, Inc. *Chicago*

William Benton *publisher*

Britannica Reviews in Education

American Council on the Teaching of Foreign Languages

John M. Evans
Director

David G. Hays
Editor-in-chief

Editorial Board

Clara W. Ashley
ACTFL Executive Committee

Frank M. Grittner
Wisconsin Department of Public Instruction

F. André Paquette
Executive Secretary (ACTFL)

Charles James
Research Associate

Julie Archer
Secretary

List of Contributors

Bela H. Banathy
Far West Laboratory for Educational Research and Development
Berkeley, California

Emma Marie Birkmaier
University of Minnesota
Minneapolis, Minnesota

Robert J. DiPietro
School of Language and Linguistics
Georgetown University
Washington, D.C.

James W. Dodge
Brown University
Providence, Rhode Island

John P. Dusel
State Department of Public Instruction
Sacramento, California

Percy Fearing
Minnesota State Department of Education
Saint Paul, Minnesota

William N. Hatfield
Purdue University
Lafayette, Indiana

Leon A. Jakobovits
Center for Comparative Psycholinguistics
University of Illinois
Urbana, Illinois

Charles James
University of Minnesota
Minneapolis, Minnesota

Albert W. JeKenta
Beverly Hills Unified School District
Beverly Hills, California

Edith M. A. Kovach
University of Detroit
Detroit, Michigan

Dale L. Lange
University of Minnesota
Minneapolis, Minnesota

Walter F. W. Lohnes
Stanford University
Stanford, California

Richard J. McArdle
Cleveland State University
Cleveland, Ohio

H. Ned Seelye
Illinois Office of Public Instruction
Springfield, Illinois

Horacio Ulibarri
University of New Mexico
Albuquerque, New Mexico

Rebecca M. Valette
Boston College
Boston, Massachusetts

Preface

Information is essential to decision making, but intelligent decisions can be made only if information has been properly accumulated, catalogued, and interpreted. Foreign language learning and teaching will improve to the extent that those interested in its advancement can communicate information effectively so that learners, parents, school boards, teachers, and researchers can make well-informed decisions.

In June 1966, the Modern Language Association of America initiated the development of a "data bank" on foreign language teaching by agreeing to operate an ERIC (Educational Resources Information Center) Clearinghouse on the Teaching of Foreign Languages for the United State Office of Education. In October 1967, ACTFL (American Council on the Teaching of Foreign Languages) began publication of its Annual Bibliography and in May 1968 published *A Selective Bibliography on the Teaching of Foreign Languages, 1920–1966,* by Emma M. Birkmaier and Dale L. Lange. Dr. Lange is editor of the ACTFL Annual Bibliography and Dr. Birkmaier served as ACTFL President in 1968.

Early in 1968, Encyclopædia Britannica proposed to President Birkmaier that ACTFL sponsor the preparation and publication of a Review of Foreign Language Education as part of the Britannica Reviews in Education. The ACTFL Executive Committee responded enthusiastically to this proposal and decided to make the *Britannica Review of Foreign Language Education* one of the benefits of Comprehensive Membership in ACTFL for 1969–70.

Through the cooperation of government (the MLA/ERIC Clearinghouse), educators (the ACTFL Annual Bibliography), and private enterprise (the *Britannica Review of Foreign Language Education* sponsored by ACTFL) foreign language teachers are being provided with the tools essential to improved foreign language teaching.

F. ANDRÉ PAQUETTE
Executive Secretary, ACTFL

American Council on the Teaching of Foreign Languages

Officers for the Year 1968

President
Emma Marie Birkmaier
University of Minnesota

Vice President
Leo Benardo
New York City Public Schools

Executive Secretary
F. André Paquette

Treasurer
Kenneth W. Mildenberger

Executive Committee

Clara W. Ashley
Newton South High School
Newton Centre, Mass.

Kai-yu Hsu
San Francisco State College

Gail Hutchinson
Atlanta Public Schools

Elizabeth Keesee
United States Office
of Education

Joe Malik, Jr.
University of Arizona

Barbara Ort
Michigan State Department
of Education

Jack Stein
Harvard University

Constituents

Alabama Association of Foreign Language Teachers

Alaska Foreign Language Association

Arizona Foreign Language Association

Arkansas Foreign Language Teachers Association

California Council of Foreign Language Teachers' Associations

Colorado Congress of Foreign Language Teachers

Connecticut Council of Language Teachers

Modern Foreign Language Section, Delaware Education Association

Greater Washington Association of Teachers of Foreign Languages

Florida Foreign Language Association

Classical and Modern Foreign Language Association of Georgia

Hawaii Association of Language Teachers

Idaho Foreign Language Teachers' Association

Illinois Foreign Language Teachers' Association

Indiana Foreign Language Teachers' Association

Iowa Foreign Language Association

Kansas Foreign Language Association

Kentucky Council of Foreign Language Teachers

Louisiana Foreign Language Teachers' Association

Foreign Language Department, Maine Teachers' Association

Maryland Foreign Language Association

Massachusetts Foreign Language Association

Michigan Foreign Language Association

Minnesota Council of Teachers of Foreign Languages

Mississippi Modern Language Association

Missouri Association of Teachers of Foreign Languages

Montana Foreign Language Teachers Association

Nebraska Modern Language Association

Nevada State Foreign Language Teachers' Association

New Hampshire Association for the Teaching of Foreign Languages

New Jersey Foreign Language
Teachers Association

New Mexico Foreign Language
Teachers Association

Modern Language and Latin
Sections, North Dakota
Education Association

Ohio Council on the Teaching
of Foreign Languages

Oklahoma Foreign Language
Teachers' Association

Department of Foreign
Languages, Oregon Education
Association

Pennsylvania State Modern
Language Association

Rhode Island Foreign
Language Association

Association of Foreign
Language Teachers of
South Carolina

South Dakota Foreign
Language Association

Texas Foreign Language
Association

Utah Foreign Language
Association

Vermont Foreign Language
Teachers' Association

Modern Foreign Language
Association of Virginia

Washington Association of
Foreign Language Teachers

West Virginia Modern
Language Teachers Association

Wisconsin Association of
Foreign Language Teachers

Wyoming Language Teachers'
Association

Affiliates

American Association of
Teachers of Arabic

American Association of
Teachers of German

American Association of
Teachers of Italian

American Association of
Teachers of Slavic and East
European Languages

American Association of
Teachers of Spanish and
Portuguese

American Classical League

American Philological
Association

Association of Teachers of
English as a Second Language
(NAFSA)

Association of Teachers
of Japanese

Chinese Language Teachers
Association

Classical Association of the
Atlantic States

Classical Association of the
Middle West and South

Classical Association
of New England

Classical Association of the
Pacific States, Central Section

Classical Association of the
Pacific States, Northern Section

Classical Association of the
Pacific States, Southern Section

Department of Foreign
Languages, National Education
Association

Linguistic Society of America

Middle States Association
of Modern Language Teachers

National Association of
Language Laboratory Directors

National Association of
Professors of Hebrew in
American Institutions of
Higher Learning

National Council of State
Supervisors of Foreign
Languages

Northeast Conference on the
Teaching of Foreign Languages

Pacific Northwest Conference
on Foreign Languages

Rocky Mountain Modern
Language Association

Société des Professeurs
Français en Amérique

South Central Modern
Language Association

Southern Conference on
Language Teaching

Teachers of English to
Speakers of Other Languages

Foreword

The idea of a review or yearbook that would survey the existing state of foreign language learning and teaching annually for an organization such as the American Council on the Teaching of Foreign Languages (ACTFL) has occurred to several members of the foreign language profession ever since 1960. Many felt the need especially when teaching graduate courses in second language learning and in methodology courses. The need was most poignant when we were working with other organizations outside our field who had a large enough membership to afford such a yearbook.

It was not until Dr. David G. Hays of the University of Buffalo and Editor-in-Chief of the Britannica Reviews in Education, made the suggestion to Dr. Kenneth Mildenberger and André Paquette, executive officers of the newly organized American Council on the Teaching of Foreign Languages, and discussed the idea with me to initiate the *Britannica Review of Foreign Language Education*, that the profession felt a dream had come true.

This volume, in what is hoped to be a useful series for the language profession, is the product of the labor of many people and especially a great deal of faith. Grateful acknowledgment is given, first of all, to Encyclopædia Britannica, and especially to John M. Evans, the Director of the Britannica Reviews, for the patience, encouragement, and support so sorely needed for this venture to be born.

A great debt is owed to the chapter authors, whose contributions are the substance of the book, and to David G. Hays who spent many hours with the Editor to talk about various approaches to the Review until we came up with the present format. Dr. Hays, in addition, also gave generously of his precious time in reviewing many of the chapters. Without the Editorial Board of the American Council on the Teaching of Foreign Languages, who provided guidance and assistance with the individual chapters, the Editor would have been in a real quandary. Particular thanks must be given to André Paquette for his support in some of the darkest days of deadline meeting, at a time when the Editor was overseas working in an EPDA Institute.

The writing of the chapters would have been considerably more difficult and taken more time if it had not been for the indulgence of Dale Lange, the editor of the ACTFL Annual Bibliography, in taking the risk of allowing my research associate, Charles James, to make copies of carefully edited and alphabetized cards of the 1968 bibliography for sending to the chapter authors during the early part of the month of February. The Editor is also grateful to Mr. James for taking on the burden of the correspondence necessary in such an effort. My secretary, Julie Archer, provided valuable assistance in checking and arranging the references for each chapter.

The Editor also owes a special debt of gratitude to Carlos A. Cuadra, the Editor of the Annual Review of Information Science and Technology, for conducting an afternoon's workshop at Encyclopædia Britannica headquarters on the problems, tribulations and blessings of editing a review.

The American Council on the Teaching of Foreign Languages and I would like to express our sincere appreciation to Encyclopædia Britannica, Inc., for its willingness in committing itself to a most important venture in the language teaching field, knowing that any innovation of this kind will have many problems from its beginnings to the final production.

Emma Marie Birkmaier
University of Minnesota

Contents

1
Introduction

Purpose of the Review

Emma Marie Birkmaier

University of Minnesota

In the 20th century oral communication has become as important as written communication. Science and invention have catapulted the world into a new situation of face-to-face or electronic contact. In an age of growing nationalism, internationalism demands that we communicate more freely if man is to survive.

Up to ten years ago, the foreign language profession usually concentrated on teaching literature in the narrow sense, neglecting to study the learning of a second language as a human activity, the strategies to be used in assisting the learner with this task, and the content that would enable the student to behave rationally and emphatically with his fellowman in the 20th century.

Business and government have asked us to teach foreign languages in the way the communication of the future requires; they have called our attention to the great need for large pools of language specialists and linguists as well as experts in other cultures. The National Defense Education Act of 1958 (NDEA) allocated millions of dollars to education in mathematics, science, and foreign languages. The result has been acceleration of inquiry in foreign language learning and teaching.

Foreign language pedagogy draws on many fields and disciplines. The behavioral and physical sciences, technology, the arts, and instructional methodology have much to offer. However, our field is not merely drawing from wherever it can, but emerging as a discipline in its own right.

The growth of foreign language education was recognized in 1967 by the organization of the American Council on the Teaching of Foreign Languages (ACTFL), sponsor of this Review and publisher of *Foreign Language Annals*. Bibliographic aid is provided through the *Annals* and by the ERIC (Educational Resources Information Center) Clearinghouse on the Teaching of Foreign Languages, which is supported by the U.S. Office of Education and operated by the Modern Language Association of America.

The need for critical reviews

The literature in our field has been growing rapidly. The Birkmaier-Lange Selective List for 1920–66 includes 1,255 items; the 1967 ACTFL bibliography lists 942 items; that for 1968, 1,333 items. For government officials, educators, parents, school board members, teachers, and researchers these bibliographies alone are not enough. They need periodic analyses, and assessments of progress and problems. The *Review of Educational Research* has devoted a chapter every three years to foreign language education. Handbooks and encyclopedias, which appear even less frequently, treat our field among others. And from time to time, surveys have appeared such as that by John B. Carroll, "Research in Foreign Language Teaching: The Last Five Years," published in the 1966 Northeast Conference Report, *Language Teaching: Broader Contexts*.

The analytic surveys of our field have appeared infrequently or irregularly, have sometimes covered only a small portion of the field, and have sometimes catered to a specialized clientele, excluding the classroom teacher and curriculum specialist.

Foreign language specialists are usually reasonably aware of what is happening in their particular areas of interest, but they are often unable to make the investment in time, money, and energy to keep up with the areas that touch their interests, but more lightly.

This Review is intended to serve educators, and especially classroom teachers and curriculum specialists in the field of foreign language education. Appearing regularly, and covering the field comprehensively, it attempts to describe and appraise all the important work of the year.

We hope that the Review will also prove useful to researchers and professors of education. Many of them, we believe, will be pleased to find a source that unifies information from various disciplines related to foreign language education. We intend the Review as a guide for the orientation of newcomers in the field, as well as a report of new work for the refreshment of experts. We hope that it will stimulate more inquiry as well as better performance in classrooms.

Design of the Review

The scope and organization of the Review follow rather closely the plan of the ACTFL bibliography. In this first volume, some content of potential interest is treated lightly or left out entirely. For instance, the teaching of English as a foreign language will not receive full coverage until Volume 2. On the other hand, some topics covered in detail in this volume will not require as complete examination next year. Each year, certain topics will demand emphasis because of rapid progress.

The authors of this volume come from several different working environments; their diversity broadens the perspective of the Review. Some are university teachers, others are in school systems, and still others conduct research projects or serve as consultants.

All of the authors were chosen because of their grasp of their subjects, their habit of keeping informed, and their willingness to make objective judgments about the merit and implications of the work they report. We have not asked them to be impartial; absolute detachment, if it were possible, would result in a totally uninteresting presentation. But the diversity of authors provides a kind of balance within this volume, as can be seen when different authors review a study from different points of view. In the longer term, balance comes by inviting authors with different perspectives to succeed each other over the years in writing on each topic.

The chapters of this Review cluster in two major divisions. The first deals with the content and organization of foreign language learning; the second, with the theory and practice of foreign language teaching and learning. In addition, a chapter is devoted to the teaching of Latin and Greek, and one to surveys and reports of foreign language enrollments.

The first division: substance

Linguistics (Chapter 2) is expanding and changing rapidly, and has drawn into closer contact with psychology and sociology. Semantics is receiving new emphasis, contrastive analysis keeps its strong place in the field, and the transformationalists continue to play *the* dynamic role—but DiPietro stresses the need for experimentation with alternative linguistic theories. Much linguistic research seems at first glance irrelevant to the teacher and his problems in the classroom, yet its findings do ultimately affect the general view of language. If linguists expect to be truly successful in helping with the methodology of language teaching, according to DiPietro, they must find more effective ways to make the data on student performance avail-

Linguistics

able for theoretical analysis. As Dwight Bolinger says, "Language teaching is no more linguistics than medicine is chemistry. Yet language teaching needs linguistics as medicine needs chemistry." In reading this chapter the teacher will want to consider how well existing and planned curricula appear to take into account what this field offers.

Rather frequently one gets the disturbing impression that few people, including foreign language teachers, know how the study of a foreign language fits into the total educational experience of the student. Foreign language classes can meaningfully contribute to specific, realizable, and educationally sound objectives. In Chapter 3, Seelye notes that foreign language curriculum guides often regard an understanding of foreign cultures as the most important objective of foreign language study; he deplores the failure of actual classroom practice to work toward this objective.

Sociocultural context

Culture is defined in many different ways; Seelye discusses some definitions, and the various levels of culture described by Nelson Brooks. The most widely accepted definition is that culture embraces all aspects of the life of man. When the student has learned enough of a foreign language to study the productions of creative artists, he needs a knowledge of the patterns of everyday life to appreciate these. Seelye shows, in many ways, that the study of language cannot be divorced from the study of culture.

Language and culture can be brought together for the student in several ways. Language courses can be matched with special courses in the culture and civilization of the people who speak it. Language teaching can be made interdisciplinary. The foreign language teacher can immerse himself in a foreign culture through training programs abroad. Instructional strategies that can be used in the classroom include the new simulation techniques, sensitivity training, culture capsules, semiotic approaches, and audiovisual aids.

A student's knowledge of a foreign culture should go beyond geographic and historical data, yet only those are usually tested. To know something about a foreign culture is not the same as to behave competently when confronted with it. Testing how the student is likely to behave when he goes abroad requires sophisticated techniques. Feeble attempts to devise suitable tests are being made, according to Seelye, but they are likely to be unsuccessful until we agree on a taxonomy of behaviors from which to develop test items and evaluation procedures.

Most foreign language departments in colleges and universities look upon the analysis of literature as art as the only reason for their existence. They teach in order to produce more literary scholars. Lohnes, in Chapter 4, challenges us to make the study of literature play a vital role in the liberal education of the student, by illuminating the human experience. The relevance of literature to the happenings of the 20th century is exciting to contemplate. Much research must still be done to establish the right conditions for introducing literature into the language curriculum and to find ways of teaching the literature of a foreign country that will make its relevance clear to students. In addition, the results of the research must be incorporated in training programs for teachers.

Literature

Chapters 5 and 6 span the broad field of curriculum from elementary school through the university. Banathy, in Chapter 5, defines curriculum making as design, development, and management; these are decision-making operations that require structure and strategy—a systems approach. Banathy looks at the curriculum as consisting of components interacting to form an integrated whole for the attainment of educational goals that the learner has accepted. Once behavioral objectives are defined, curriculum makers develop learning tasks through which the student can attain them, taking into account the human and technological resources at hand. Evaluation is built into the learning process at every step, to inform the student exactly where he is and what he has accomplished toward the achievement of his goals. Whenever necessary, the student goes back over what he has not learned well until he masters it. The curriculum itself undergoes constant scrutiny.

The systems approach to curriculum

Banathy criticizes what is happening in the foreign language programs of colleges and universities in terms of his model. His chapter is thought-provoking; undoubtedly controversial, it is nevertheless in keeping with the advanced concepts of curriculum makers today.

JeKenta and Fearing, dealing with the curricula of elementary and secondary schools in Chapter 6, break the systems approach down and spell it out in greater detail. They report new programs and major curriculum innovations, which should ease the problem of the long-sequence in foreign language education. JeKenta and Fearing describe and evaluate individual components of the curriculum—modular scheduling, team teaching, grouping, individualized instruction, and new types of learning tasks including machine-aided instruction.

In summary, these two chapters on curriculum analyze how the subject matter discussed in Chapters 2, 3, and 4 can be encapsulated within a curriculum framework to attain the behavioral goals that need to be fulfilled if a foreign language program is to continue as a major component in the general education of the student.

The second division: theory and practice

Reviewing the physiology and psychology of second language learning in Chapter 7, Jakobovits finds that our field suffers on account of two paradoxes. Teachers tend to seek justification of their practices in psychological theories that often are questionable and rigidify classroom practices. Secondly, although we have enjoyed a breakthrough in technology, the success of foreign language programs in our schools is extremely limited. The profession must try to achieve a correct balance between what educational technology can promise and what students wish to attain. Individualization, and computer-based instruction with a variety of strategies fitted to learners' needs, may make the balance possible. The process must reckon with the specific needs, interests, and aptitudes of the students involved, the time available for study, the age of the learners, the overall foreign language curriculum and its cumulative effect, the social support of the community, and the particular language. Most of all, teachers must recognize that different aptitudes mean the attainment of different goals.

The physiology and psychology of language learning and teaching

Global comparisons of methods of instruction are unrealistic, Jakobovits believes. Each method includes a large variety of instructional activities that are usually not defined or observed in global comparisons; the learner makes his own contributions to the teaching-learning situation, and these cannot be added to the "method" studied.

The sociopsychological meaning of language study needs more attention. The problems of bilingualism are to be understood in this way. We need adequate definitions about language competence (knowledge about a language) and performance (use of a language); once we have defined these concepts, we need ways of evaluating students' competence and performance. Students, parents, the public, and even teachers have mistaken assumptions and expectations about language that we need to correct.

All in all, Jakobovits takes a self-critical view of our profession, and exhorts us to strive continuously for better solutions.

Our writers on linguistics, culture, and psychology touch on various aspects of bilingualism. In Chapter 8, Ulibarri reviews a series of studies made in the Southwest over a period of years. These studies bring out the ramifications of a serious problem for education and the country in general: the federal government is supporting large programs that presume to alleviate the problems of bicultural and bilingual students.

The children Ulibarri discusses learn English out of social necessity. They are usually looked upon as inferior in IQ, academic achievement, physical growth, and emotional development. Today we see more clearly how the problems attendant upon minority-group membership, lower economic status, and forced conformity with the values of the majority inhibit the development of these children.

Bilingualism and biculturism

Ulibarri discusses the process of acculturation, by which the individual acquires the standards and patterns of behavior of a new group; this process goes through stages of diffusion, assimilation, acceptance, adaptation, and reaction. Acculturation of the child's family benefits him in the school and ameliorates the confrontation of two value systems in devious ways.

Bilingual education programs use the child's first language as well as that of the majority group. Certain questions arise: *(1)* Do bilingual programs move the bilingual, bicultural child faster into adequacy in English and help his progress in school? *(2)* What aspects of the curriculum are best taught in each language? *(3)* Is the end goal to have bicultural, bilingual children conform to the middle-class, white, Anglo-Saxon, Protestant ethic, or is he to have adequate facility to function in two languages and *sociologically* in two cultures?

Ulibarri contends that a bicultural, bilingual program cannot be a remedial program. It must help children develop in areas that have been neglected, without penalizing them in other areas of growth and development. The major purpose of the program must be to develop in the child a positive self-concept that will help him function effectively in a multilingual, multicultural world.

Reviewing progress in the education, qualifications, and supervision of teachers since the publication of Paquette's guidelines and MacAllister's report, McArdle (Chapter 9) finds that progress has been made, but much still has to be done. In view of the new curricula reviewed in Chapters 5 and 6, it seems that almost complete reform in teacher education and supervision is needed. Twenty-three states are now changing their procedures for teacher certification, but we do not yet know enough about these changes to say whether they are for the better or for the worse. The NDEA Institutes have provided a model, but even institutes grow rigid and exclude new developments. College language departments, although some of their professors have directed such institutes, have done very little about changing their own departmental structures to facilitate the teacher-training function. A systems approach to teacher training could help execute what Paquette so succinctly outlines. Any program to train foreign language teachers must integrate subject matter and professional development, general education, and teaching experience. Most of the experimentation going on today is in the areas of supervision and practice teaching, where the videotape recorder, interaction analysis, and microteaching are assuming important roles.

Teacher education

The word "method" is misused when only nebulous definitions and descriptions are provided. Lange, in Chapter 10, limits himself to classroom procedures, techniques, or strategies. He analyzes in detail a number of "broad comparison" studies that compare audiolingual and cognitive-code theories in practice, or compare the fundamental-skills approach, using electromechanical equipment, with traditional methods. He deems broad comparison of one method with another ineffective, and deplores the money, time, and energy spent on such studies when learning psychology is already moving in other directions. We would do far better to study various strategies more closely in order to discover how they can complement one another in promoting learning.

Methods and strategies of instruction

Lange finds more value in smaller studies and experiments that go to narrow problems such as the presentation of a drill, the semantic component in pattern practice, the efficacy of drills of a more communicative type, and the like. Not every small study produces the information the researchers were looking for, but these studies reveal the complexities of foreign language learning and produce more questions for research to answer. For example, programmed instruction has a certain degree of effectiveness in helping the linguistically underprivileged reach learning goals such as discrimination among sounds. However, we do not know enough to say exactly what roles programmed instruction should play in instruction. Again, we know something – but not yet enough – about how the student's native tongue interferes with acquisition of a second language, about the use of time in foreign language programs (massed versus spaced learning), and the strategies for foreign language teaching that can be extracted from bilingual programs. Lange asks us to be clear about priorities and goals for further research, and to present a unified front in securing private and public monies for research to make foreign language learning more efficient.

The National Association of Language Laboratory Directors, when speaking of electromechanical-optical equipment, prefers to use the term "machine-aided language learning." We adopt this term for the title of Chapter 11, by Dodge. According to him, the medium most frequently used by the foreign language teacher is the tape recorder in its basic form or in the complex versions of the language laboratory. Next comes the filmstrip projector and the 16 mm motion-picture projector. The overhead projector is used by 61 percent of elementary and high school teachers. This device can be compared favorably with the blackboard, but not too much commercial material is available yet: the teacher must use his own or his students' creative efforts. Teachers also favor more and better color TV programs to assist them in classroom instruction. The benefits of color TV have not yet been shown by research, but many of the educational TV channels use color. Dodge reminds us that many TV films can be obtained and become an asset in language learning through combination of a single film with multiple sound tracks.

Machine-aided learning

Dodge sees the motion-picture film as another extension of the teacher. Several popular language-learning systems for French, German, and Spanish include short films constituting a systematic approach to the whole course. Use of 8 mm and Super 8 film projectors is growing, and the casette tape recorder has become popular. Short single-concept cartridges have been developed for the Technicolor 8 mm sound cartridge projector; they can be very effective for individual instruction.

The videotape recorder is now cheap enough for schools and colleges to use it in instructor training, preservice education, microteaching, and classroom procedures such as the development of cultural miniskits as well as presentation of supplemental, prerecorded materials.

The language laboratory still presents a continuum of equipment, from the simplest recorder through three levels of audio-active and recording capabilities to remote-control, dial-access, video-complemented student positions. Reduction of funds in 1968 made both administrator and teacher think more cautiously about purchase of equipment. The electronic classroom has again become popular. Dodge speaks of the need for equipment that would be more responsive to student performance and interact more in speaking drills. Research on the language laboratory has not yet adequately assessed the real values of this machine aid. The 1968 Pennsylvania Studies, only partially concerned with the language laboratory, give as a sole conclusion that language-laboratory systems, as employed twice weekly, had no discernible effect upon language instruction as measured by the project's testing program.

Computer-assisted instruction (CAI) has taken the greatest forward strides in 1968. Despite the many arguments against CAI in foreign language teaching, a true Socratic dialogue is attainable. Many psychologists of foreign language learning look toward CAI as a key to better understanding of the process that takes place within the individual as he acquires another language. But Dodge still finds few good programs on the market.

Innovative developments in testing (Chapter 12) and evaluation (Chapter 13) are reviewed by Valette and Hatfield, respectively. Recent books by Lado, Upshur and Fata, Davies (writing about British work), Mackey, and Valette will help the teacher and researcher with problems of testing, evaluation, and experimental design.

Testing serves two distinct purposes: prognosis and measurement of achievement. Prognostic testing should not be used for deciding which students should be allowed to study a foreign language. Nor can achievement testing be of any value until specific behavioral goals have been established. The difference between testing competence and testing performance is coming to be seen; the preparation of tests of competence challenges the test makers. The national batteries of foreign language tests are being reevaluated, and the appropriateness of techniques in use for testing the four basic skills is being studied. Testing the cultural aims is a relatively new field; testing the literature aims has been ineffective since no specific terminal goals have been formulated. Kinesics has not been the concern of test makers, or even – until recently – of language teachers.

The function of good teaching is to reduce the correlation between prognostic scores and achievement scores. The use of criterion-referenced measures, which specify what items a student should be able to perform correctly after a unit of work, can help both teacher and student. The criteria give the teacher positive expectancies. The student is helped because he sees what

Testing

he must master before going on to the next unit in the cumulative process of language-learning. As yet, criterion-referenced foreign language tests have not been developed on a commercial scale. In Chapter 12, Valette provides a table for use in developing foreign-language objectives, and a model to be used for a criterion-referenced battery of tests.

Work in program evaluation usually consists of theory and little empirical research. Many reports are simply statements of what an individual or an organization believes effective teaching and learning situations ought to be. Those who believe in an audiolingual approach incorporate into the evaluation such *Evaluation* things as the language laboratory and how it is used, the audiovisual materials at hand, the extent to which drills are used, and the performance of the students in the oral and listening skills. Those who prefer other approaches set up other criteria. Paucity of research and empirical data prevents us from developing criteria against which different types of programs could be evaluated. Hayes and his associates have been the first to attempt the necessary kind of research on foreign language pedagogy. Hatfield reviews the research he found on (1) student achievement, (2) classroom instruction, (3) analysis of program characteristics, and (4) systems analysis. He describes what has been done in evaluating school and college programs as well as teacher-training programs.

A Center for the Study of Evaluation of Instructional Programs has been established at the University of California at Los Angeles. It will work toward theoretical clarification of this area, giving special attention to the ways different types of instruction interact with individual students and teachers in certain learning situations.

Although the preceding chapters include Latin among the languages they discuss, the unique and crucial position of Latin and Greek warrants a special chapter (14, by Kovach). She analyzes the status of classical studies in public, parochial, and independent schools. The exemplary, innovative studies take place in the public schools, where the Latin programs are proportionately smallest. The profession is divided on the length of the program; some propose a three-year sequence in grades 10, 11, and 12, others a longer sequence beginning in the elementary grades and including an introduction to Italian. Kovach des- *The Classics* cribes new programs in large city school systems that begin in the third or seventh grade.

The Advanced Placement Program in Latin continues to be an

11

example of enlightened study of literature in a broad sense. Special enrichment programs parallel those discussed in Chapter 6. The classicists have developed CAI programs for both Latin and Greek. Kovach reports a trend toward the use of oral Latin, and a vigorous growth in Latin teacher-training institutes and in-service programs for the new approaches to Latin teaching, especially the linguistically oriented approach used in Waldo Sweet's program. Much is being done with visual aids.

The Review closes with an examination of surveys and reports on foreign-language enrollments (Chapter 15). Dusel finds many of them inadequate and inaccurate. Studies have been quite regular since 1958, except for the years 1966 and 1967. The Modern Language Association of America compared 1960 and 1965 enrollments in detail. Dusel notes that conducting a census is a difficult enterprise, and that precise sampling can give more accurate results. Tallying or a few generalizations can in any case be misleading; whatever facts are gathered, their significance is to be understood only by detailed examination.

Enrollment data are rarely put to diagnostic use; the profession pays attention only when enrollments fall or a program is dropped. Dusel suggests two techniques for the study of enrollment decreases: fault-tree analysis and Program Evaluation and Review Technique (PERT). By these methods, areas of responsibility can be specified. Department heads and supervisors should gather and maintain enrollment data to analyze why students from the elementary schools tend not to sign up for foreign language in high school, why high school students discontinue their language study after a year or two, why they do not carry on in college with the language they studied in school.

Enrollment surveys and needs

The rate of attrition in foreign language programs revealed in these surveys might be reduced if we had the results of research on some fundamental problems. Better instructional procedures might encourage students to keep on with study of a language once begun. More information about pupil-teacher interaction would help. Knowledge of the attitudes about foreign languages and cultures held by the student, his family, his school, and his community could be used to advantage. We need to understand CAI and machine-aided instruction better. We need to know why so many students are underachievers. We need to understand the obstacles to smooth articulation from level to level. We need to know more about the roles of aptitude and motivation.

With more information on all these issues, we should be able to reduce attrition in the best possible way: by making the study of a foreign language more rewarding.

Context and Organization of Foreign Language Learning

2
Linguistics

Introduction

Every linguist is aware of the rapid expansion of his field and its newly found rapport with other areas of inquiry as disparate as computational studies, sociology, and psychology. With interest growing in the "interface" fields which result from this expansion, the year 1968 saw significant work done in sociolinguistics (Fishman, 28), especially in matters concerning urban language (Labov, et al., 61; Shuy, et al., 93), and in psycholinguistics (Rosenberg & Koplin, 89). Some theorists who concentrated their efforts on situating linguistics within a larger theoretical framework ventured to call it a branch of cognitive psychology (Chomsky, 19). Despite the broad spread of linguistic research, language teaching continued in 1968 to be the favorite recipient of its activity, as witnessed by the many pertinent bibliographical items cited at the end of this chapter. We have provided here a general survey of the field because we feel that the reader whose primary interests in linguistics lie in its relationship to language teaching will need some acquaintance with the activity in the other branches, for example, in psycholinguistics, in order to identify the sources of many practical applications of theory and to see these applications in their proper perspective. Although it may not seem to be so at first glance, the research conducted on any aspect of language ultimately affects in some way the general view of language and, as a consequence, the theories of how languages are learned. As a matter of fact, it is clear that the principal endeavor of the past year centered on the development of theory (Postal, 86; Bach & Harms, 4).

In an effort to overcome the dearth of sufficient vehicles for publishing articles and reports, the years 1967 and 1968 witnessed the founding of two new journals (*Glossa*, 36; *Language Sciences*, 68) concerned directly with linguistics, five others treating linguistics as it is related to language teaching (*Language Teaching Abstracts*, 69; *Journal of English as a Second Language*, 55; *CCD Language Annual*, 15; *Foreign Language Annals*, 32; *TESOL Quarterly*, 99), and one devoted to the dissemination of information (*Bulletin of the ERIC Clearinghouse for Linguistics*, 12). Universities continued to in-

Robert J. DiPietro

Georgetown University

The focus is on language teaching

Thanks are due Frederick J. Bosco for reading this chapter in manuscript form.

crease their course offerings in linguistics and at least one American university (Western Michigan) established a new department of linguistics in 1968. (Several other universities have set up departments in the recent past, such as the University of Connecticut at Storrs.)

Roberts (88), in an article in the *Linguistic Reporter*, discussed the great problem of information flow which has resulted from the recent expansion of linguistics. According to Roberts, the Center for Applied Linguistics of Washington, D.C., which serves as a clearinghouse for linguistics and language study, has identified approximately 2,000 periodicals throughout the world that deal with the language sciences in one way or another. Narrowing the number to those journals edited by linguists, we would have to identify 400 of them as "core" linguistics journals, with another 200 handling closely related materials. Since *New journals* 1964 the Center for Applied Linguistics has provided several very useful bibliographies, such as *Information Sources in Linguistics* (52) and the *Bibliography of American Doctoral Dissertations in Linguistics: 1900–1964* (6). Roberts, who is associate director of the center, has himself headed the *ERIC Bulletin*, mentioned above, which lists work done on the neglected languages. Other bibliographies, e.g., the *MLA Bibliography* (77), the *International Linguistic Bibliography* (53), and the recently started *ACTFL Bibliography* (1), are concerned to varying degrees with linguistic research and its applications. A useful book dealing with the dissemination of information published late last year is Freeman, et al. (33). The chapters by Garvin (34) and Bright (10) deal specifically with the problems of information flow. Those of us who have a professional responsibility to keep abreast of what is being done in linguistics may well concur with Bright in asking the following questions of our colleagues:

1 Why are the compilers of current bibliographies not joining *Problems in the dissemination* forces? *of information*
2 Why can't more of the money spent on linguistic research be diverted to the dissemination of information?
3 Why can't greater use be made of microfilm and microfiche for publication?
4 What can be done to reduce the current flood of publication, especially in serial publications?

Not only are the problems of information flow reaching epidemic proportions but also the lag between writing and publication in linguistics worsens. For example, McCawley's review

(74) in *Language* of Volume III of the important *Current Trends in Linguistics* series, which was published in 1966, did not appear until September 1968. A spread of two years between publication and review may not be significant in some fields, but in linguistics new ideas and insights are literally born overnight. In an effort to provide some historical perspective to the rapid development of linguistic thought, *Language*, the most prestigious of linguistic journals published in the United States, has taken to indicating, after each published article, the date of its submission to the editor. We need, however, more than stopgap measures or token recognition of the problem. The backlog of articles submitted to journals but yet unpublished continues to grow and the ominous word "forthcoming" appears far too frequently in the footnotes and bibliographies of writings in the field.

In view of the situation, it would be impossible in one short chapter to give a detailed coverage of all the live issues of linguistics in 1968. We would easily risk obscuring the "forest" of linguistics among its many "trees." Instead, we shall touch upon the major topics of discussion as we see them and the ramifications of linguistics with psychology, sociology, and language teaching. Since computational linguistics, which subsumes in itself a sizable body of literature, has already been incorporated in the chapter on automated language processing by Salton in Volume 3 of *Annual Review of Information Science and Technology* (90), we shall do nothing more than cite the publication in 1967 of Hays's *Introduction to Computational Linguistics* (48) for those readers who would like some basic information on the subject.

Description and classification

The description of the world's languages and their classification into family groups have traditionally occupied central positions in linguistics, and there was no noticeable decrease in these endeavors during the past year. A number of periodicals regularly publish descriptive analyses of languages, e.g., *International Journal of American Linguistics, American Anthropologist, Anthropological Linguistics, Language*, and *Studies in Linguistics*. The Summer Institute of Linguistics remains very active in its investigations of the nonliterate languages (see, for example, its series on American Indian languages in Bolivia, 40). In such work linguistic theory is not a major issue, although this is not to say that theoretical developments do not arise from

Descriptive analysis of language continues

the urgency of description. The linguist involved in description is usually oriented toward anthropology and uses a structural framework or, sometimes, a tagmemic one. In her review of Broadbent's monograph on Southern Sierra Miwok (11), Jane Hill (49) characterizes the entire survey of Californian Indian languages at Berkeley as one being done in solid structural tradition. Although still negligible, the impact of recent advances in linguistic theory is felt in some studies (as in Grimes, 42). Doubtlessly the training of descriptivists will involve questions of theory and descriptive adequacy far more in the future than it has in the past.

Several doctoral dissertations of a descriptive nature were written during the past year on the major languages of the world, e.g., Phillips (83) on Spanish as spoken in Los Angeles and Popov (85) on the semantic structure of Russian diminutives. Numerous articles describing various parts of languages appeared last year. As an example, we cite only the one by Kelley (56) on the application of the transformational approach in the

		26 d	Rhaeto-Romance	
26	ITALIC & OTHER ROMANCE	26	Raeto-Romance (Rhaeto-Romance)	
		26	Retoroman (Rhaeto-Romance)	
26	Catalan	26	Rheto-Romance (Rhaeto-Romance)	
26 d	Dalmatian			
26 d	Faliscan	26	Romansch	
		26	Romansh	(Romansch)
26	Friulian	26	Rumauntsch	(Romansch)
26	Ladin	26 d	Sabellian	
		26 d	Aequian	Sabellian
26 d	Latin	26 d	Marrucinian	Sabellian
		26 d	Marsian	Sabellian
		26 d	Paelignian	Sabellian
26 d	Lepontic	26 d	Sabine	Sabellian
26 d	Ligurian	26	Sard	
		26	Sardinian	(Sard)
26 d	Oscan	26	Campidorian	Sard
		26	Gallurese	Sard
26	Provencal	26	Logudorese	Sard
26	Langue-d'Oc (Provençal)	26	Logudorian	(Logudorese)
26	Raetic	26	Sicilian	
		26	Sur-Silvan etc.	

FIGURE 1. Sample display of language and dialect names.

treatment of Latin nominal phrases.

As far as classification and collation are concerned, we draw the reader's attention to the work of the Archives of the Languages of the World at Indiana University which was being published as a series of fascicles in the journal *Anthropological Linguistics*, from March 1964 on. LINCS (Linguistic Information Network and Clearinghouse System) of the Center for Applied Linguistics moved ahead in its compilation of a linguistic thesaurus of language names and linguistic terminology. Charles Zisa, a research associate in the project, states that so far approximately 18,000 entries have been made in the computer-assisted inventory of language and dialect names. The data are arranged in columns and cross-referenced according to family grouping (by number), principal language or dialect name, and alternative names and spellings. Varieties now extinct are marked with the letter "d" (see Figure 1). In order to avoid duplication of work, the information gathered for the Archives of the Languages of the World has been incorporated into LINCS.

A linguistics thesaurus

The development of theory

The transformational-generative theory of linguistics continued its rapid development in 1968, with published works by its developers far outnumbering those of its adversaries. Hockett's *State of the Art* (50), representing the major critical work of the year, was most important for the stature of its author as a linguist and for the illuminating background information he provides about the development of linguistics in the first half of the twentieth century, above all the structuralism of Leonard Bloomfield (see also, Hall, 44, especially Chapter 5). It seems unlikely, however, that the theoreticians of today will take Hockett's advice and return to a stage of pristine Bloomfieldianism. Transformationalists are, as a rule, of a younger generation than their critics and so continue their theoretical studies with unbridled vigor. More importantly, the transformational-generative theory is far more productive than any alternative yet suggested. The journal *Foundations of Language*, published by the D. Reidel Company of Dordrecht, Netherlands, has become the forum for many articles, pro and con, on the new theory. The contents of Volume 4 (1968) contains important studies by Chafe (16), Fillmore (26), Kiparsky (58), Lakoff (63), and McCawley (73) on various aspects of deep and surface grammar, the organization of

Hockett's "State of the Art"

The transformationalists are producing

the base component in a grammar, and the role of semantics in a transformational grammar.

Investigations of universals in language had a special prominence last year with the publication of *Universals in Linguistic Theory*, edited by Bach & Harms (4). It is believed that the features held in common by all languages of the world are either formal (i.e., rules concerning the nature of grammatical processes) or substantive (elements which could be roughly termed "noun," "verb," "adjective," etc.) A major problem in uncovering universals is deciding which ones are essential and which are just the results of historical accident (such as the extinction of a language or language family). The search for universals is an important part of the mentalistic philosophy that underlies contemporary theory and is bound to intensify in the future. As a contribution to the place of linguistics in modern thought, Chomsky (19) published three lectures he gave at the University of California (at Berkeley) in 1967. In these three lectures, entitled "Past," "Present," and "Future," Chomsky prophesies a uniting of linguistics, psychology, and philosophy in the study of language problems that reoccur in each. In fact, he identifies linguistics as the branch of "cognitive" psychology that deals both with the universal properties of language as part of human intelligence and with the specific ways in which humans develop particular grammars. The attention of researchers is directed to a new study of linguistic competence that cannot be achieved via the stimulus-response techniques used in the past.

Contemporary linguistic theory seeks the universals of language

These remarks have, of course, a direct bearing on foreign language instruction. Chomsky is attacking the very behavioristic foundations of the currently popular audiolingual method. He goes on to say that if the normal use of language is innovative, i.e., not simply a repetition of what the speaker has heard before, it is erroneous to assume that languages are learned through constant repetition or analogy. Nor can the apparata of learning be explained away by invoking "habit" or "conditioning" or "natural selection." The basis of language learning may be an innate representation of universal grammar. If this is so, we are on the verge of extensive revisions in the theory behind our strategies of instruction. Most assuredly the future preparation of language teachers will have to include more work than presently is being done in grammatical theory and cognitive psychology.

Linguistics: a branch of cognitive psychology

To answer the need for basic texts in generative-transformational grammar, Jacobs & Rosenbaum published their *English*

Transformational Grammar (54), and Langacker's *Language and its Structure* (65) went into a second printing. Harms's *Introduction to Phonological Theory* (47) is moderately technical and directed to the student who already has a firm basis in linguistics. Postal's *Aspects of Phonological Theory* (86) is definitely not for the beginning student nor for the intermediate one. The book is highly polemical in tone and primarily concerned with pointing out the discrepancies of autonomous phonemics. The most innovative part of the book is the discussion of sound change, and we shall have more to say about it later on.

Basic texts the language teacher should read

Perhaps the most outstanding book-length study of 1968 is that of Chomsky & Halle, *The Sound Pattern of English* (20). While the title of the book might suggest that its authors were primarily concerned with describing the phonological component of English, their real interests lay in expounding general linguistic theory and conjecturing about the nature of those mental processes related to language. No apology is considered necessary for slighting some aspects of English (such as the gradation of aspiration in stop consonants) and emphasizing others (e.g., the stress contours). There are four major sections to the book: I. General Survey, II. English Phonology, III. History, and IV. Phonological Theory. In the first part, Chomsky & Halle

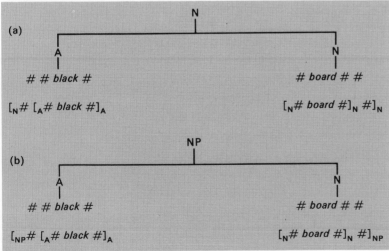

Key to Symbols:
  N — Noun
  A — Adjective
  NP — Noun Phrase
  # — marker indicating the boundary of a lexical category
  [ ] — brackets marking off the strings and substrings within them. Each bracket is identified as to the lexical category of the string it encloses. For example, [N]N identifies the enclosed string as a Noun.

FIGURE 2. Surface structures with labeled bracketing (from Chomsky & Halle [20, p. 16]).

provide the reader with a general orientation to contemporary theory. They discuss in some detail the difference between linguistic competence and performance, pointing out that many factors apart from a speaker's knowledge of the grammar of his language affect his performance; e.g., memory restrictions, inattention, and distraction. Following along the same line of thought as Bach & Harms (4), Chomsky & Halle distinguish between accidental universals of language and those innately endowed, and between formal and substantive ones. Care is taken to locate the phonological component of English within the general theoretical framework of the language and to show how the labeled bracketing of the surface structure determines phonetic representations. In the placement of stress, for instance, a transformational cycle of rules operates according to the syntactic categories indicated in the surface structure. The compound word *blackboard*, with primary stress on *black*, and the phrase *black board*, with primary stress on *board*, are used as illustrations (see Figure 2).

Whereas all monosyllables in English are assigned primary stress by a general rule, e.g.:

$$\text{(a)} \quad [_N \# \# \overset{1}{black} \# \# \overset{1}{board} \# \#]_N$$

$$\text{(b)} \quad [_{NP} \# \# \overset{1}{black} \# \# \overset{1}{board} \# \#]_{NP}$$

(the superscript number 1 signifies primary stress) the weakening of stress wherever it is appropriate is achieved by reapplying the primary stress rule at different places, depending on the layering in the surface structure. In the case of strings labeled as nouns, reapplying primary stress on the first vowel causes the stress on the second vowel to weaken by one degree, yielding:

$$\text{(a)} \quad \# \# \overset{1}{black} \# \# \overset{2}{board} \# \#.$$

Those strings labeled as noun phrases, however, receive the reapplication of primary stress on the second vowel which then weakens the stress on the preceding vowel:

$$\text{(b)} \quad \# \# \overset{2}{black} \# \# \overset{1}{board} \# \#.$$

Finally, primary stress is reapplied once more to the first vowel of the compound noun in order to weaken the second vowel one more degree:

$$\text{(c)} \quad \# \# \overset{1}{black} \# \# \overset{3}{board} \# \#.$$

Part II goes into greater detail on the phonological rules of English which were outlined in Part I. Both the transformational cycle and word-level phonology are covered. The authors consider vowel alternations to be of greatest interest in the formation of the word in English and consequently give the consonants brief treatment.

The discussion about historical change is, like Postal's (86), truly innovative. The usual explanation of language change by "sound law" is rejected in favor of change originating in the child's selection of alternative interpretations of the linguistic performance of others. The competence that the child builds (i.e., the grammar he constructs) may differ from that of an adult while being able to account for the same data (i.e., able to generate the same sentences). The child's choice of grammar will always be according to his personal scale of evaluation. Thus, the performance of each generation of speakers is slightly different from the preceding one. Illustrations of consonant tensing and the adjustment of rounding in vowels in English are given through the examination of writings by John Hart (1551–79), John Wallis (1653–99), Christopher Cooper (1697), and T. Batchelor (1809).

Chomsky and Halle: a milestone in the development of generative theory

The final part of the book is a recapitulation of the discussion in the first and second parts, with greater detail of the basic principles of phonology. This book marks a milestone in the development of generative theory and should be read by every responsible linguist. Since the new orientation to phonology deriving from the studies of this type is bound to bring about extensive changes in the sections on phonetics in foreign language textbooks, the provident foreign language teacher would do well to acquaint himself as much as possible with the necessary theoretical background as represented in the work of Chomsky & Halle.

Also to be studied carefully are the papers by Fillmore (25), Bach (3), McCawley (75), and Kiparsky (57) published in Bach & Harms (4). In the words of the editors, "It is no longer of any interest to describe one after another language 'anyhow' without regard to the relevance of the facts to general linguistic theory" (p. vi, Preface). We must always be concerned with how the grammar of a particular language sheds light on our notions of the general design of languages. Fillmore's paper concerning underlying case relationships in language is the most developed and served as the inspiration for at least one doctoral dissertation written last year (Goldin, 37). McCawley wrote about se-

Is there a general design in language?

mantics and argued convincingly for considering the semantic component as the place from which selectional restrictions on syntactic transformations must originate. In this way Chomsky's notion of complex symbols in syntax is done away with. Bach's proposal concerned nouns and noun phrases, and Kiparsky's paper dealt with universals in linguistic change.

Two survey-type studies are worthy of mention: Volume IV in the *Current Trends in Linguistics* series (91) and Langendoen's (66) critical review of the Firthian school. The *Trends* volume surveyed linguistic studies in the Caribbean and Ibero-America. *Surveys* Sebeok was ably assisted by Lado, Saporta & McQuown in the compilation of chapters. There are four general headings: I. General and Ibero-American Linguistics, II. Linguistics of Non-Ibero-American Languages, III. Applied Linguistics, and IV. Sources and Resources. Langendoen's book is largely a criticism of the English linguists who were the followers of Firth.

Before passing on to historical studies, we take note of L. A. Murray's translation of Trubetzkoy's *Introduction to the Principles of Phonological Descriptions* (101), a classic by one of the founders of the Prague School, and *Language and Symbolic Systems* (17), an introductory text by a long-respected scholar Yuen Ren Chao.

The historical development of specific languages

In the second part of his *Aspects of Phonological Theory* (86), Postal presents what he calls the mentalistic character of so-called sound change. Holding that linguistics is inherently a mentalistic discipline, Postal rejects much of the work done in the neogrammarian tradition of historical studies. This, in turn, means that the mass of research done for almost a century is open to reconsideration. A concise review is made of the historical work of important linguists such as Dyen, Gleason, and Martinet. The review is followed by a set of illustrations showing how changes in the phonological rules of a language may originate in the deep structure. Borrowing is discussed, and it is pointed out that languages may acquire phonological rules in their entirety from other languages. *New tendencies in analysis are incorporated reluctantly*

Historical studies of specific languages continued to appear in 1968, but the impact of the thinking of theorists such as Postal and Chomsky is yet to be felt. Some orientation from transformational theory can be discerned, as in the article by Weinstock

(105). Distinctive features and generative rules are implemented to account for consonant lengthening in Germanic. Meanwhile, Leonard (72), in the very same issue of *Language*, handles lengthening of consonants in the Romance languages with a purely structural approach, taking no heed of the new tendencies in analysis.

The effort to reconstruct a prototype for the Polynesian languages continues (Polynesian, incidentally, has long been a favorite with structural linguists). Wolff's review of Walsh & Biggs's *Proto-Polynesian Word List I* (106) is favorable although it, too, does not incorporate the theoretical implications for historical change made by generative grammar.

Mathiot (76) indicates possible directions for a study of cognition in language. Universals of cognition are extrapolated from an investigation of specific language themes.

Sociolinguistics

Language studies that have to do with the sociological and political problems of our times have just recently been united under the heading of sociolinguistics. Specifically, sociolinguistics comprises work in standard language planning, creole and pidgin languages, bilingualism (in its societal sense), and in the social stratification of language. The last-mentioned area covers a body of growing research in what has been called urban or nonstandard urban speech. Because of its relevance to the immediate needs of a large segment of the population of our cities, urban language study has attracted the attention of many persons. Writers in sociolinguistics have been extremely active in the past few years, and especially in 1968. A key work is Labov's *Social Stratification of English in New York City* (60). Developing the notion of "linguistic variable," Labov surveys the usage centering around five phonological features: (*1*) [r] in postvocalic and preconsonantal position; (2) the vowel in words like *bad, ask, dance, had, cash;* (3) the stressed vowel in *awful, coffee, office;* (4) [θ] in *thing* and *thin;* and (5) [ð] in *then* and *the.* The outcome of the study is that variations in speech patterns can be brought about by socioeconomic conditions and these variations show that American society is socially stratified.

1968 sees a tremendous growth in sociolinguistics research

Fishman also enjoyed prominence in the general area of sociolinguistic research in 1968. His *Readings in the Sociology of Language* (28) provides a number of papers to the reader who wishes a general introduction to the area. Together with Ferguson and Das Gupta (30), he also edited the proceedings of a conference on the language problems of developing nations which was held at Warrenton, Va., in November 1966. He and his collaborators also completed a two-volume study of Spanish-English bilingualism entitled *Bilingualism in the Barrio* (29), submitted as a final report to the U.S. Office of Education which funded it. In this study, Fishman makes a plea for meaningful and thorough studies of performance factors of language through their societal contexts. He criticizes linguistics for being "too parochial" in its treatment of multilingualism as a study in interference. Foreign language teachers are called to task for being insensitive to the "communicative appropriateness" of the languages they teach. Labov, et al. (61) also submitted to the Office of Education a final report on the nonstandard English of Negro and Puerto Rican speakers in New York City. Labov extends his use of the linguistic variable as a measure of stratification to include grammatical features, especially the use (or nonuse) of the copula *be*, as in "he sick" and "he be sick." A study of Negro speech in Detroit was also conducted in 1968 by Shuy (92) and Wolfram (107). Together with Riley, Shuy and Wolfram also published (93) a manual of field techniques to be used in such investigations. The manual is actually a report on the methods and the questionnaire used in the Detroit project by Shuy and his associates. Having a record of the procedures used in past sociolinguistic inquiries should be of valuable assistance in the development of more efficient techniques in the future. Shuy is now general editor of the "Urban Language" series, in which was published not only the field manual but the earlier Labov study (60) as well. Without a doubt, the series will contain many more works of vital interest in sociolinguistics.

Fishman's challenge to teachers

Urban language and dialects, new sources of study

Stewart, a linguist who has done pioneering work in the study of pidgin and creole languages, continues to be productive in examining the relationships of American Negro dialects to the creole languages of the Caribbean and Africa (96). The study of Negro (or "Black") speech has attracted the attention of teachers and school administrators. Programs directed to the problems of teaching standard English to nonstandard speakers were held at various institutions. The experienced-teacher fellowship program at Georgetown University which started in the fall of 1968 and is continuing through 1969 is one example. Some of the aspects of language teaching in "disadvantaged" communities are reported by Bailey (5).

Psycholinguistics

What definition is given of psycholinguistics depends largely on the researcher. Generally speaking, studies which relate the processes of language production with the other mental processes come under this heading. This can include research in those learning processes which are implemented in foreign language instruction, research in the acquisition of speech in the child, and the study of aphasia and other language-related mental disorders. A bibliography of psycholinguistics was compiled by Walters (104) in 1965, but unfortunately has not been updated.

Definition

Lenneberg's *Biological Foundations of Language* (71) is monumental in its survey of physiological and psychological correlates to language acquisition and language disorders. As a result of his investigations, Lenneberg concludes that "language is the manifestation of species-specific cognitive propensities" (p. 374), and that man's cognitive function is basically a process of categorization and extraction of similarities observed in his environment. As the child matures he passes into a stage of what Lenneberg calls "language-readiness," at which time he is able to form his personal linguistic competence from the language he hears spoken around him. The full impact of Lenneberg's work is yet to come, but the support it gives the theorists of the generative school is clear, especially with regard to language universals and the organization of deep and surface structure.

Lenneberg gives support to the generative school

The style of publication in this field seems to be predominantly that of collecting individual papers together in anthologies. Rosenberg & Koplin (89), for example, is a series of papers contributed by a number of researchers on native-language acquisition (Griffin, 41), second-language learning (Lane, 64), language learning in the deaf (Blanton, 7), aphasia (Goodglass, 38), schizophrenic language (Cromwell & Dokecki, 21), and the language of retarded children (Spradlin, 95). In like manner, Zale (108) edited the proceedings of a conference on language and language behavior. Smith & Miller's *Genesis of Language* (94) went into its third printing last year. The work of Fodor, Bever, & Garrett (31) is an effort to develop models for speech recognition. Goodman (39) deals specifically with the reading process.

Reports on various manifestations of language behavior

Psychiatrists, often without formal training in linguistics, continued in 1968 to publish observed speech abnormalities in their patients. Walsh's article (103) in the *Psychoanalytic Quarterly* on the identification of stops and spirants as being universally associated with cathexis is suggestive of the wealth of material awaiting the researcher properly trained in linguistics as well as in psychiatry.

Linguistics applied to language teaching

While ever mindful of the relevance of linguistics to many fields, we feel that linguistics has most to offer to the methodology of language instruction. Almost every operation engaged in by the language teacher somehow involves linguistic theory: the construction of language tests, the organization of grammar, and the interpretation of theories of language learning are but a few of these operations. In fact, there is much the linguist himself can learn simply by observing students engaged in learning a language. Regrettably, the theorist is often cut off from such practical experience and any data of linguistic performance that gets to him is usually lost in a maze of nonlinguistic variables. The contrastive analysis of the students' native language with the language they are learning should provide the teacher with some very useful guidelines for the presentation of the material to be taught. Yet the explanatory and predictive power of this type of analysis is diminished by the great difficulty in filtering out nonrelevant factors such as attention span and personal motivation.

How linguistics helps the language teacher

Linguists' need for observing

Since several other chapters in this book treat testing and language learning in detail, we shall limit ourselves to drawing the reader's attention to some key works published in 1968 and then concentrate on the activity in contrastive analysis. The language teacher should peruse at least four books written during the past year by experts in linguistics and language teaching: *Linguistics and Language Teaching* by Hughes (51), *Teaching German* by Politzer (84), Finocchiaro's new edition of *Teaching English as a Second Language* (27), and Hall's *Essay on Language* (44). Politzer's book is the most recent addition to his series which includes *Teaching Spanish* and *Teaching French.* No major change has been made by the author in either the linguistic orientation or its psychological basis. Apparently Politzer feels that any teacher who must work with more than one of the three languages will welcome the similarities in presentation and theoretical commitment. Titone's *Teaching Foreign Languages: An Historical Sketch* (100) provides some useful background information.

To add to the language teacher's professional library

The efforts of theoretical linguists to develop the semantic component is paralleled to some extent by the applied linguists' attempts to add semantic depth to existing instructional strategies. Two articles appearing in the same issue of *International Review of Applied Linguistics in Language Teaching* deserve to be mentioned in this light. Both discuss the inadequacies of structural drills that are not accompanied by situational contexts. The article by Newmark & Reibel (80), however, makes unsupported claims about similarities between the adult's learning of a second language and the child's learning of his first language. Furthermore, the authors question the value of contrastive analysis. Their objections appear to stem from expecting contrastive analysis to explain more than it should. In their criticism they make no serious effort to separate competence from performance, which may explain their inability to see the value of this type of analysis. The other study, by Oller & Obrecht (82), also questions the value of exercises lacking a semantic context, but their claims are far more modest and thus more credible. An experiment is reported in which two groups of students were taught the same set of structural exercises. One of the groups had the benefit of situational reinforcement while the other did not. The result was that the group with reinforcement learned the exercises better than the group without reinforcement. Rather than make a frontal attack on contrastive analysis, which is tantamount to saying that knowledge of how the native and the target languages differ is irrelevant, Oller & Obrecht neatly isolate one of the variables that hinders the acquisition of competence in the target language.

There is a need for the semantics component in language teaching

Another pair of companion articles is that of Bolinger (9) and Hanzeli (46). This time, both articles are effective in making their point. Recognizing the rapid changes in linguistics as reality, they direct the language teacher to adapt what he can and not worry about the rest. To paraphrase Bolinger, language teaching is no more linguistics than medicine is chemistry. Yet language teaching needs linguistics just as medicine needs chemistry. Implementation of innovations deriving from linguistic research may be profound but it is more often superficial (see, for example, Molina, 78).

Advice to the language teacher on linguistics

English retained its central importance as one of the languages (either native or target) involved in contrastive analysis, as illustrated by Strain's article (98) on Persian and English, and Cheng's treatment (18) of Chinese tones and English stress. The contrastive study of languages not including English was represented by the book-length study of Russian, Czech, and German phonology by Kučera & Monroe (59). Nickel & Wagner (81) reaffirmed the position that contrastive analysis is highly relevant to language teaching, while regretting the present lack of a unified theory to support the claim.

It was in the light of the language teacher's need for contrastive studies that Georgetown University's School of Languages and Linguistics devoted its Nineteenth Annual Round Table Conference entirely to contrastive analysis. Papers on various aspects of theory and pedagogical implications were read and the complete set of papers was published as Monograph No. 21 in the Georgetown Monograph *Series on Linguistics and Language Study* (Alatis, 2). In the first paper of the conference, Stockwell (97) discussed some of the adverse opinions held about contrastive analysis. He reminded the audience that the great theoretical upheaval in linguistics was also felt in its applications to contrastive analysis. Stockwell suggests that contrastive studies can be viable objectives for their own sake. Such studies, when well done, can reveal much about the languages contrasted that is useful to the teacher.

Contrastive analysis: the controversy goes on

The papers by Gleason (35), Moulton (79), DiPietro (22), and Lado (62) dealt with various aspects of procedures and the model of language design. Ferguson (24) spoke on contrastive analysis and child language development, Carroll (13) discussed the relevance of interference theory to contrastive analysis, and Hamp (45) formulated in a stimulating way the ideal goals of contrastive analysis. Rivers (87) and Hall (43) discussed the application of contrastive analysis in the writing of textbooks. Catford's opinion (14) is that contrastive analysis is better suited to explaining language errors than to predicting them. Both Hall (43) and Lee (70) pointed out the need to use many different types of devices in good language teaching. Finally, Twaddell (102) predicted that the well-made contrastive analysis will outlast the changing trends in linguistics and even act as a safeguard against the blind acceptance of dogma in linguistic theory.

The expansion of linguistic activity abroad

During the past year, various European countries, as well as Canada, a few Ibero-American countries, and Australia continued the expansion of their linguistic activities. The newly founded British Association for Applied Linguistics had its first meeting in September 1968 in Edinburgh. Australia established its linguistic society this last year and the Società Linguistica Europaea entered its second year of existence, having had its first annual meeting in Brussels in April 1967. In Italy, several university chairs were set up for linguistics and the Società Linguistica Italiana, as in the case of the larger European society, was in its second year. Toronto continued to grow as a center for linguistic studies in Canada under the leadership of Joos, Gleason, and other linguists from the United States who have recently located there. Meanwhile Canadian linguists and psycholinguists continued their research at other universities such as Laval and Montreal. The University of Kiel in Germany is also expanding in linguistics and has attracted several well-known American linguists such as Haugen, Pike, and Hoenigswald to spend time there as exchange professors. As reported in Sebeok, et al. (91), linguistics is still in its early naissant period in Latin America. A good sign that it will grow, however, is the Inter-American Symposium on Linguistics and Language Teaching which is held every 18 months and attracts linguists from many countries.

The growing interest among Europeans in contrastive analysis was shown at the tenth triennial congress of the Fédération Internationale de Professeurs de Langues Vivantes, held in Zagreb, Yugos., April 5–9, 1968. A series of papers was read on contrastive analysis and ten guidelines were drawn up to guide future work in the field. It was suggested that an international symposium be established on both theoretical and applied aspects of contrastive analysis.

Generally speaking, the future for linguistics is a very bright one, notwithstanding certain problems to be discussed below.

Trends and desiderata

Highly desired in this rapidly growing field is the establishment of efficient means to disseminate information not only about published work but also about the many papers written for special projects that now circulate hand to hand among colleagues. From all appearances, the trend is happily toward that end (Roberts, 88). In addition to the generally shared problem of information retrieval, there are a number of desiderata and trends pertinent to the specializations that have been discussed in this chapter:

The hidden school

1 In theoretical linguistics, greater articulation must be made of the difference between competence and performance. Also of vital importance is the work on the semantic component and its function in the design of language. The question is

31

whether semantics should be thought of as generative (i.e., as the instigator of syntactic transformations) or as interpretive of syntactic rules. The trend of the next decade will certainly be toward the establishment of universals. Some disagreement is already growing as to the general nature of these universals. Are they to be viewed as formal only (Lenneberg, 71) or as both formal and substantive (Bach & Harms, 4; Chomsky, 19)?

Competence and performance

2 New ideas about theoretical design and generative grammar should be incorporated into the description and classification of languages. Yet, work in description must continue even with the lag between theoretical advancement and its applications. It is especially important to investigate the nonliterate languages of the world. Although some are threatened with extinction, many of them have acquired economic, social, and strategic importance beyond their national boundaries and are being taught formally. Description of these previously ignored languages is of great importance in providing the bases for instruction. One good illustration is the case of Swahili in the United States. If adequate texts are to be written, tapes to be prepared, and teachers to be trained in this language, both the applied linguist and the methodologist will need all the descriptive material they can find.

New ideas must be incorporated in the work of linguists

3 Much new work needs to be done in historical linguistics. Generally held notions about sound change should be reconsidered in the light of the attacks on them by Postal (86) and Chomsky & Halle (20). Linguists who are interested primarily in the origins of language change will also have to examine the findings of Labov (60) with reference to the role played by social stratification in language change. Although historical linguistics has had to make room for synchronic studies in the curricula of most foreign language majors, those who have had exposure to the principles of reconstruction in their professional preparation will find the new approaches very stimulating. Along with the historical linguist, the foreign language teacher will also benefit from Labov's study of social stratification. At present, few foreign texts present social levels of style in any systematic way.

Regeneration of historical linguistics

4 Psycholinguists now have the opportunity to experiment within the framework of alternative linguistic models. Perhaps the next decade will see advances in providing clear psychological support for the way the linguist orders his rules or the foreign language teacher presents them and the ways in which the speaker-hearer applies them in producing or understanding speech.

The need for psychological support

32

5 The sizable body of data on linguistic performance and its societal features must be related to a theory of competence. In other words, closer rapport must be established between the psycholinguist and the sociolinguist in the description of speech communities and individual members of the community.

Language is spoken in a community

6 In applied linguistcs, much research is already in progress (see *Language Research in Progress*, 67) on memory retention, aptitude, perceptual learning, etc. More effective ways to make the data on student performance available for theoretical analysis are greatly desired. There is good reason to believe that ways will be found. Already at the State University of New York (Stony Brook), a computer-assisted program of instruction is being used to teach German. In this program, the number and kinds of errors made by the student can be filed and recalled at will. This sort of data holds great promise, especially in the validation of contrastive analysis.

How students perform in language learning is crucial

References, Linguistics

1 ACTFL Bibliography. Foreign languages annals, fascicles I, II in 1:i (October 1967) 87–90; fascicles III, IV 1:ii (December 1967) 179–181; fascicles V, VI in 1:iii (March 1968) 270–280; fascicles VII, VIII, IX in 1:iv (May 1968) 371–387; 2:iv (May 1969) 487–530.

2 Alatis, James E., ed. Report of the nineteenth annual round table meeting on linguistics and language study (Georgetown University Monograph Series in Languages and Linguistics, no. 21). Georgetown University Press, Washington, D.C., 1968, 224 p.

3 Bach, Emmon. Nouns and noun phrases. In: Bach, Emmon; Harms, Robert T., eds. Universals in linguistic theory. Holt, Rinehart & Winston, New York, 1968, p. 91–122.

4 Bach, Emmon; Harms, Robert T., eds. Universals in linguistic theory. Holt, Rinehart & Winston, New York, 1968, 210 p.

5 Bailey, Beryl Loftman. Some aspects of the impact of linguistics on language teaching in disadvantaged communities. Elementary English, 45 (1968) 570–577.

6 Bibliography of American Doctoral Dissertations in Linguistics: 1900–1964. Compiled by P. R. Rutherford, Center for Applied Linguistics, Washington, D.C., 1968, 139 p.

7 Blanton, Richard L. Language learning in the deaf. In: Rosenberg, Sheldon; Koplin, James, eds. Developments in applied psycholinguistic research. Macmillan, New York, 1968, p. 121–176.

8 Bolinger, Dwight. Aspects of language. Harcourt, Brace & World, New York, 1968, 326 p.

9 Bolinger, Dwight. The theorist and the language teacher. Foreign Language Annals, 2:i (October 1968) 30–41.

10 Bright, William. Questions on the information problem in linguistics. In: Freeman, Robert R.; Pietrzyk, A.; Roberts, A. Hood, eds. Information in the language sciences. American Elsevier, New York, 1968, p. 53–55.

11 Broadbent, Sylvia M. The Southern Sierra Miwok language. University of California Press, Los Angeles, 1964, 355 p.

12 Bulletin of the ERIC Clearinghouse for Linguistics. Washington, D.C., published six times a year. First issue: November 1967.

13 Carroll, John B. Contrastive analysis and interference theory. In: Alatis, James E., ed. Report of the nineteenth annual round table meeting on linguistics and language study (Georgetown University Monograph Series in Languages and Linguistics, no. 21). Georgetown University Press, Washington, D.C., 1968, p. 113-122.

14 Catford, J. C. Contrastive analysis and language teaching. In: Alatis, James E., ed. Report of the nineteenth annual round table meeting on linguistics and language study (Georgetown University Monograph Series in Languages and Linguistics, no. 21). Georgetown University Press, Washington, D.C., 1968, p. 159-173.

15 CCD Language Annual. Center for Curriculum Development, Chilton Books, Philadelphia, Pa. Annual (December). First issue: December 1967.

16 Chafe, Wallace L. Idiomaticity as an anomaly in the Chomskyan paradigm. Foundations of Language, 4:ii (May 1968) 109-127.

17 Chao, Yuen Ren. Language and symbolic systems. Cambridge University Press, Cambridge, Eng., 1968, 240 p.

18 Cheng, Chin-Chuan. English stresses and Chinese tones in Chinese sentences. Phonetica, 18:ii (1968) 77-88.

19 Chomsky, Noam. Language and mind. Harcourt, Brace & World, New York, 1968, 88 p.

20 Chomsky, Noam; Halle, Morris. The sound pattern of English. Harper & Row, New York, 1968, 470 p.

21 Cromwell, Rue L.; Dokecki, Paul R. Schizophrenic language: a disattention interpretation. In: Rosenberg, Sheldon; Koplin, James, eds. Developments in applied psycholinguistic research. Macmillan, New York, 1968, p. 209-260.

22 DiPietro, Robert J. Contrastive analysis and the notions of deep and surface grammar. In: Alatis, James E., ed. Report of the nineteenth annual round table meeting on linguistics and language study (Georgetown University Monograph Series in Languages and Linguistics, no. 21). Georgetown University Press, Washington, D.C., 1968, p. 65-80.

23 ERIC Selected Bibliography in Linguistics. ERIC Clearinghouse for Linguistics. Washington, D.C., November 1968 (for 1967-68) 71 p.

24 Ferguson, C. A. Contrastive analysis and language development. In: Alatis, James E., ed. Report of the nineteenth annual round table meeting on linguistics and language study (Georgetown University Monograph Series in Languages and Linguistics, no. 21). Georgetown University Press, Washington, D.C., 1968, p. 101-112.

25 Fillmore, Charles J. The case for case. In: Bach, Emmon; Harms, Robert T., eds. Universals in linguistic theory. Holt, Rinehart & Winston, New York, 1968, p. 1-88.

26 Fillmore, Charles J. Lexical entries for verbs. Foundations of Language, 4:iv (November 1968) 373-393.

27 Finocchiaro, Mary. Teaching English as a second language. 2nd ed., revised & enlarged, Harper & Row, New York, 1968, 478 p.

28 Fishman, Joshua A., ed. Readings in the sociolo-gy of language. Mouton, The Hague, 1968, 808 p.

29 Fishman, Joshua A.; Cooper, Robert L.; Ma, Roxana; et al. Bilingualism in the barrio. Final report no. OEC-1-7-062817-0297, Washington, D.C., August 1968.

30 Fishman, Joshua A.; Ferguson, C. A.; Das Gupta, J. Language problems of developing nations. John Wiley & Sons, New York, 1968, 521 p.

31 Fodor, J. A.; Bever, T. G.; Garrett, M. The development of psychological models for speech recognition. MIT Press, Cambridge, Mass., 1968.

32 Foreign Language Annals. American Council on the Teaching of Foreign Languages, F. André Paquette, ed. Published quarterly.

33 Freeman, Robert R.; Pietrzyk, A.; Roberts, A. Hood, eds. Information in the language sciences. American Elsevier, New York, 1968, 247 p.

34 Garvin, Paul L. What is linguistic information. In: Freeman, Robert R.; Pietrzyk, A.; Roberts, A. Hood, eds. Information in the language sciences. American Elsevier, New York, 1968, p. 33-40.

35 Gleason, H. A., Jr. Contrastive analysis in discourse structure. In: Alatis, James E., ed. Report of the nineteenth annual round table meeting on linguistics and language study (Georgetown University Monograph Series in Languages and Linguistics, no. 21). Georgetown University Press, Washington, D.C., 1968, p. 39-63.

36 Glossa. Published by the Glossa Society, Simon Fraser University, Vancouver, B.C. Biannual (April & October). First issue: April 1967.

37 Goldin, Mark G. Spanish case and function. Georgetown University Press, Washington, D.C., 1968, 83 p.

38 Goodglass, Harold. Studies on the grammar of aphasics. In: Rosenberg, Sheldon; Koplin, James, eds. Developments in applied psycholinguistic research. Macmillan, New York, 1968, p. 177-208.

39 Goodman, Kenneth S., ed. The psycholinguistic nature of the reading process. Wayne State University Press, Detroit, Mich., 1968, 343 p.

40 Gramáticas Estructurales De Lenguas Bolivianas (3 vol.). Summer Institute of Linguistics with the Ministerio de Asuntos Campesinos and the Ministerio de Educación y Bellas Artes, Riberalta, Bolivia, 1965.

41 Griffin, William J. Children's development of syntactic control. In: Rosenberg, Sheldon; Koplin, James, eds. Developments in applied psycholinguistic research. Macmillan, New York, 1968, p. 19-65.

42 Grimes, Joseph. The palatalized velar stop in Proto-Quichean. International Journal of American Linguistics, part 1, vol. 35, no. 1 (January 1969) 20-24.

43 Hall, Robert A., Jr. Contrastive grammar and textbook structure. In: Alatis, James E., ed. Report of the nineteenth annual round table meeting on linguistics and language study (Georgetown University Monograph Series in Languages and Linguistics, no. 21). Georgetown University Press, Washington, D.C., 1968, p. 175-183.

44 Hall, Robert A., Jr. An essay on language. Chilton, Philadelphia, 1968, 160 p.

45 Hamp, Eric P. What a contrastive grammar is

not, if it is. In: Alatis, James E., ed. Report of the nineteenth annual round table meeting on linguistics and language study (Georgetown University Monograph Series in Languages and Linguistics, no. 21). Georgetown University Press, Washington, D.C., 1968, p. 137–147.

46 Hanzeli, Victor E. Linguistics and the language teacher. Foreign Language Annals, 2:i (October 1968) 42–50.

47 Harms, Robert T. Introduction to phonological theory. Prentice-Hall, New York, 1968, 142 p.

48 Hays, David G. Introduction to computational linguistics. American Elsevier, New York, 1967, 260 p.

49 Hill, Jane H. Review of Broadbent, Sylvia M., The Southern Sierra Miwok language. In: Language, 44:i (March 1968) 181–185.

50 Hockett, Charles F. The state of the art. Mouton, The Hague, 1968, 128 p.

51 Hughes, John P. Linguistics and language teaching. Random House, New York, 1968, 143 p.

52 Information Sources in Linguistics. Compiled by F. Rice & A. Guss, Center for Applied Linguistics, Washington, D.C., 1965, 42 p.

53 International Linguistic Bibliography. Permanent International Committee of Linguists. Spectrum, Utrecht-Antwerp, 1967 (for year 1965).

54 Jacobs, Roderick; Rosenbaum, Peter S. English transformational grammar. Blaisdell, Waltham, Mass., 1968, 294 p.

55 Journal of English as a Second Language. Chilton Books & the American Language Institute of New York University. Semiannual. First issue: December 1967.

56 Kelley, David H. Transformations in the Latin nominal phrase. Classical Philology, 63:i (January 1968) 46–52.

57 Kiparsky, Paul. Linguistic universals and linguistic change. In: Bach, Emmon; Harms, Robert T., eds. Universals in linguistic theory. Holt, Rinehart & Winston, New York, 1968, p. 171–202.

58 Kiparsky, Paul. Tense and mood in Indo-European syntax. Foundations of Language, 4:i (1968) 30–57.

59 Kučera, Henry; Monroe, George. A comparative quantitative phonology of Russian, Czech, and German. American Elsevier, New York, 1968, 113 p.

60 Labov, William. The social stratification of English in New York City. Center for Applied Linguistics, Washington, D.C., 1966, 655 p.

61 Labov, William; Cohen P.; Robins, C.; Lewis, John. A study of the non-standard English of Negro and Puerto Rican speakers in New York City. Final report, cooperative research project 3288, U.S. Office of Education, Washington, D.C., 1968.

62 Lado, Robert. Contrastive analysis in a mentalistic theory of language learning. In: Alatis, James E., ed. Report of the nineteenth annual round table meeting on linguistics and language study (Georgetown University Monograph Series in Languages and Linguistics, no. 21). Georgetown University Press, Washington, D.C., 1968, p. 123–135.

63 Lakoff, George. Instrumental adverbs and the concept of deep structure. Foundations of Language, 4:i (1968) 4–29.

64 Lane, Harlan L. Research on second-language learning. In: Rosenberg, Sheldon; Koplin, James, eds. Developments in applied psycholinguistic research. Macmillan, New York, 1968, p. 66–117.

65 Langacker, Ronald W. Language and its structure. Harcourt, Brace & World, New York, 1968 (2nd printing), 260 p.

66 Langendoen, D. Terence. The London school of linguistics. MIT Press, Cambridge, Mass., 1968, 123 p.

67 Language Research in Progress, Report 7. Center for Applied Linguistics, Washington, D.C., 1969.

68 Language Sciences. The Research Center for the Language Sciences, Indiana University, Bloomington. Published occasionally. First issue: May 1968.

69 Language Teaching Abstracts. Published by Cambridge University Press, Cambridge, Eng. Quarterly. First issue: January 1968.

70 Lee, W. R. Thoughts on contrastive linguistics in the context of language teaching. In: Alatis, James E., ed. Report of the nineteenth annual round table meeting on linguistics and language study (Georgetown University Monograph Series in Languages and Linguistics, no. 21). Georgetown University Press, Washington, D.C., 1968, p. 185–201.

71 Lenneberg, Eric. Biological foundations of language. John Wiley & Sons, New York, 1967, 489 p.

72 Leonard, Clifford S., Jr. Initial alternation in Proto-Romance. Language, 44:ii (June 1968) 267–273.

73 McCawley, James D. Concerning the base component of a transformational grammar. Foundations of Language, 4:iii (August 1968) 243–269.

74 McCawley, James D. Review of current trends in linguistics, vol. III. In: Language, 44:iii (September 1968) 556–593.

75 McCawley, James D. The role of semantics in a grammar. In: Bach, Emmon; Harms, Robert T., eds. Universals in linguistic theory. Holt, Rinehart & Winston, New York, 1968, p. 125–169.

76 Mathiot, Madeleine. An approach to the cognitive study of language. International Journal of American Linguistics, part II, 34:i (January 1968) 224 p.

77 MLA Bibliography. Publications of the Modern Language Association of America, 83:iii (June 1968) 519–966.

78 Molina, Hubert. Transformational grammar in teaching Spanish. Hispania, 51:ii (May 1968) 284–286.

79 Moulton, William G. The use of models in contrastive linguistics. In: Alatis, James E., ed. Report of the nineteenth annual round table meeting on linguistics and language study (Georgetown University Monograph Series in Languages and Linguistics, no. 21). Georgetown University Press, Washington, D.C., 1968, p. 27–38.

80 Newmark, Leonard; Reibel, David A. Necessity and sufficiency in language learning. International Review of Applied Linguistics in Language Teaching (IRAL), 6:ii (May 1968) 145–161.

81 Nickel, Gerhard; Wagner, K. Heinz. Contrastive linguistics and language teaching. International Review of Applied Linguistics in Language Teaching, 6:iii (August 1968) 233–256.

82 Oller, John W.; Obrecht, Dean H. Pattern drill and communicative activity: a psycholinguistic experiment. International Review of Applied Linguistics in Language Teaching, 6:ii (May 1968) 165–174.

83 Phillips, Robert N. Los Angeles Spanish: a descriptive analysis. University of Wisconsin Ph.D. dissertation, 1967, 773 p.

84 Politzer, Robert. Teaching German: a linguistic orientation. Blaisdell, Waltham, Mass., 1968, 178 p.

85 Popov, Elisabeth Angela. The semantic structure of the Russian diminutives. Stanford University Ph.D. dissertation, 1967, 98 p.

86 Postal, Paul. Aspects of phonological theory. Harper & Row, New York, 1968, 326 p.

87 Rivers, Wilga M. Contrastive linguistics in textbook and classroom. In: Alatis, James E., ed. Report of the nineteenth annual round table meeting on linguistics and language study (Georgetown University Monograph Series in Languages and Linguistics, no. 21). Georgetown University Press, Washington, D.C., 1968, p. 151–158.

88 Roberts, A. Hood. International information flow in linguistics. Linguistic Reporter, 10:vi (December 1968) 1–3.

89 Rosenberg, Sheldon; Koplin, James, eds. Developments in applied psycholinguistic research. Macmillan, New York, 1968, 311 p.

90 Salton, Gerard. Automated language processing. In: Cuadra, Carlos A., ed. Annual review of information science and technology, vol. 3., Encyclopaedia Britannica, Inc., Chicago, 1968, p. 169–199.

91 Sebeok, T. A.; Lado, R.; McQuown, N. A.; Saporta, S., eds. Current trends in linguistics, vol. IV. Mouton, The Hague, 1968, 659 p.

92 Shuy, Roger W. Detroit speech: careless, awkward and inconsistent or systematic, graceful and regular? Elementary English, 45:v (May 1968) 565–569.

93 Shuy, Roger W.; Wolfram, W. A.; Riley, W. K. Field techniques in an urban study. Center for Applied Linguistics, Washington, D.C., 1968, 128 p.

94 Smith, Frank; Miller, George A., eds. The genesis of language. MIT Press, Cambridge, Mass., 1968 (3rd printing), 400 p.

95 Spradlin, Joseph E. Environmental factors and the language development of retarded children. In: Rosenberg, Sheldon; Koplin, James, eds. Developments in applied psycholinguistic research. Macmillan, New York, 1968, p. 261–290.

96 Stewart, W. A. Continuity and change in American Negro dialects. Florida Foreign Language Reporter, 6:i (Spring 1968) 3–4, 14–16, 18.

97 Stockwell, Robert P. Contrastive analysis and lapsed time. In: Alatis, James E., ed. Report of the nineteenth annual round table meeting on linguistics and language study (Georgetown University Monograph Series in Languages and Linguistics no. 21). Georgetown University Press, Washington, D.C., 1968, p. 11–26.

98 Strain, J. E. A contrastive sketch of the Persian and English sound systems. International Review of Applied Linguistics in Language Teaching. 6:i (1968) 55–62.

99 TESOL Quarterly. Teachers of English to Speakers of Other Languages. Muncie, Ind., published in March, June, September, and December. First issue: March 1967.

100 Titone, Renzo. Teaching foreign languages: an historical sketch. Georgetown University Press, Washington, D.C., 1968, 128 p.

101 Trubetzkoy, Nikolaj S. Introduction to the principles of phonological descriptions. Nijhoff, The Hague, 1968, 46 p. [trans. by L. A. Murray].

102 Twaddell, W. Freeman. The durability of "contrastive studies." In: Alatis, James E., ed. Report of the nineteenth annual round table meeting on linguistics and language study (Georgetown University Monograph Series in Languages and Linguistics, no. 21). Georgetown University Press, Washington, D.C., 1968, p. 195–213.

103 Walsh, Maurice N. Explosives and spirants: primitive sounds in cathected words. Psychoanalytic Quarterly, 37:ii (1968) 199–211.

104 Walters, Theodore W. The Georgetown bibliography of studies contributing to the psycholinguistics of language learning. Georgetown University Press, Washington, D.C., 1965, 125 p.

105 Weinstock, John. Grimm's law in distinctive features. Language, 44:ii (June 1968) 224–229. 224–229.

106 Wolff, John U. Review of Proto-Polynesian Word List I, by D. S. Walsh and Bruce Biggs. In: Language, 44:iv (December 1968) 903–906.

107 Wolfram, Walter A. A sociolinguistic profile of Detroit Negro speech. To be published by the Center for Applied Linguistics, Urban Language Series, 1969.

108 Zale, Eric M. Preceedings of the conference on language and language behavior. Appleton-Century-Crofts, New York, 1968.

3

Analysis and teaching of the cross-cultural context

There are probably not many, if any, foreign language courses that do not attempt to justify their existence to a considerable extent by claiming that an understanding of the foreign culture is an outgrowth of language study. How do language teachers define culture? How do they teach culture? Does what is taught in the name of culture lead to an appreciation or understanding of people with different life styles? In what direction has the thinking of the profession been developing? These are some of the questions this chapter will discuss. Papers read at conferences have not been reviewed in this chapter unless they were subsequently published, and in only infrequent instances have pre-1966 publications been reviewed. An annotated bibliography of sources published between 1945 and 1964 relevant to the teaching of culture is available in Nostrand, Foster, & Christensen's compilation (81, p. 292–307). This chapter is divided into four sections: (1) the scope of culture in foreign language classes; (2) the knowledge, skills, and attitudes to be developed; (3) activities and materials for achieving cultural communication and understanding; and (4) a survey of the status of measuring cultural achievement.

H. Ned Seelye

Illinois Office of Public Instruction

Scope of culture in foreign language classes

What is culture?

Is culture a da Vinci handsomely reposing in the marble hallways of the Louvre, or is it the technique a workman employs to brush his teeth? Does it concern itself with the stirring notes of a de Falla symphony, or is it more interested in the feudal routine of a Spanish peasant?

The first really contemporary effort to define culture was exerted by anthropologists. Culture, they reasoned, was what their science was all about. It was, therefore, imperative to define it precisely. How else, theoretical-minded anthropologists were prone to ask, could valid research be accomplished in the area. It seemed logically evident that to talk about culture one has to know what culture is. But each anthropologist had his own definition of it. Prompted by a desire to isolate the common denominator in the many diverse definitions of the term, two well-known anthropologists, Kroeber & Kluckhohn, almost two decades ago examined approximately 300 definitions in a study entitled *Culture: A Critical Review of Concepts and Definitions* (59). However, a precise common denominator was not found. Instead, if one were pressed to abstract the catholicity of the concept it would be that culture is a very broad concept embracing all aspects of the life of man (and a few other primates as well). The anthropologist White (114) concludes a recent article on this problem by quoting Alfred North Whitehead: "It is a well-founded historical generalization that the last thing to be discovered in any science is what the science is really about."

Culture: the anthropological dilemma

Language teachers have been slow to accept "culture" as a broadly defined concept. For much of the profession, culture has been defined almost exclusively in terms of the fine arts. This narrow definition of culture, unfortunately, does not fully prepare a student to understand other peoples. An understanding of the way of life of a foreign people is important to survival in a world of conflicting value systems, where the boundaries that formerly isolated and protected man from alien ideas have been eroded by advances in the technology of communication, or struck down by the angry clamor of the downtrodden in their search for a better life. How is one to liberate one's ideas from the stagnant recesses of ethnocentrism, from what Francis Bacon called the Fallacy of the Tribe, if not through a study of other cultures? And to penetrate another culture, knowledge of the foreign language is imperative. Elitism—restricting the study of foreign languages to the academically gifted and disciplined, while divorcing the cultural content from those aspects of life that concern most people most of the time—is responsible for much of the dry rot of abject boredom current in too many language programs today.

Culture: the FL teacher's dilemma

Brooks (12), who has been so influential in having the profession recognize the importance of culture, finds (at an arbitrary level of abstraction) five different types of culture: biological growth, personal refinement, literature and the fine arts, patterns for living, and the sum total of a way of life. Brooks stresses the importance of never losing sight of the individual when we talk about culture as it is relevant to language classes. The type of culture that Brooks identifies as most appropriate for beginning language classes is "patterns for living," a concept

Five levels of cultural study

defined as ". . . the individual's role in the unending kaleidoscope of life situations of every kind and the rules and models for attitude and conduct in them" (12, p. 210). It is these patterns that enable the individual to relate to "the social order to which he is attached." Literature and the fine arts and the "sum total of a way of life" should be worked into the curriculum "as can reasonably be added as the learner's competence increases" (12, p. 212). Culture should be broadly sampled. As Brooks says, culture in the classroom "must not only answer the question: Where is the bookstore? It must also answer the question: Where is the bathroom?" (12, p. 210)

Culture and literature

Some professors dedicated to an analysis of literary style claim that literature affords the best tool to teach about the life of the people. Here we need to be cautious, Nostrand (78, p. 16) advises, "in generalizing from literature. Many Russians of today have formed their idea of the American businessman and of Wall Street partly from American novels such as *Babbitt* which reflect a hostile attitude on the part of one subculture in the United States, the writers, toward another subculture, the businessmen." Lewald (66, p. 303), in an article that expertly reviews the problems associated with teaching about culture in language classes, comments on the use of fiction to illustrate a target culture by observing that this "has been defended on the grounds that all art is based on a conscious or unconscious contact with social reality and cultural patterns, present in the mind of the creative writer. Here the problem arises of determining which types of literature or art forms are most suitable to elicit cultural patterns or indicators. A case might be made for those forms that strongly reflect an outer reality." Lewald goes on to suggest that the contribution of psychological, surrealistic, or experimental writing would be questionable. It might be added that if the interest is in contemporary culture rather than in a preindustrial historical period then the number of qualifying documents shrinks greatly.

Which type of literature best reveals a culture?

One writer (Imhoof, 55), cognizant of the cultural biases endemic in reading selections designed for use in foreign language courses, sees the necessity for controlling the cultural variations that appear in the materials. However, in emphasizing the universal aspects of culture one should avoid sidestepping the contrastive manifestations of the target culture. While literary works become important as they develop themes of universal interest, in order to understand a culture's uniqueness study must also be directed to the local, nonuniversal cultural patterns.

Even in situations where the legitimate objective of the language course is the study of fine literature, a knowledge of culture is not an irrelevant digression. One writer whose sympathies were definitely literary in nature came to the conclusion through teaching a course in English as a second language that in the study of literature the whole area of cultural comprehension is more likely than language to cause difficulty (Povey, 87, p. 44). Another writer who reached the same conclusion sees harm in attempting to rely too heavily on cultural generalizations abstracted from literature. Yousef (116, p. 228–229), in describing the experience of some teachers involved in teaching adult Arab employees of an American company, recounts that "it was clear to the teachers that literary values were not universal. These students of English as a foreign language would never be able to reach an understanding of the people and the culture of the United States by studying American literature. Instead, the study of American literature actually seemed to increase misunderstanding and confusion. It was apparent that the students would need pertinent cultural orientation before they could attempt any meaningful literature course." Beaujour & Ehrmann (5, p. 154) maintain that in itself, the study of culture is a humanistic discipline, which must recognize and develop its own tools. It cannot be dealt with as a series of disconnected footnotes to literature.

The quarrel is not with the value of literature or paintings as a means to illustrate how the foreign people live, but rather with the restrictive inroad fiction offers as the major source of information. Since many language teachers feel uncomfortable dealing with concepts and data of the social sciences, they tend to rely too heavily on literature to teach culture. Consequently, the common dual descriptor "literature and culture" has itself become suspect: it too often means a little culture and a lot of literature. On the other hand, "the study of culture and that of literature, which must be clearly separated, are neither irreconcilable nor antagonistic" (Beaujour & Ehrmann, 5, p. 154).

Marquardt (70), to whom credit is due for preparing those portions of the American Council on the Teaching of Foreign Languages (ACTFL) bibliography on culture that deal with Teaching English for Speakers of Other Languages (*Foreign Language Annals* 2:iv, May 1969: 499, 500), suggests the value of certain carefully selected literary works as an aid to teaching cross-

Does literature clarify or confuse cultural understanding?

cultural communication. A doctoral dissertation completed by Christian (21) combined his analysis of 25 Latin American contemporary novels, and tape recorded interviews with 15 novelists, with both social scientific and literary studies of Latin America in an effort to assess the reaction of members of different Latin American social classes to modern urban middle-class values. Christian's interpretation of both empirical and "mystical" data was especially sensitive. Literary approaches such as Marquardt's and Christian's do much to rekindle hope for an eventual rapprochement between those interested in Culture with a big "C," and those interested in viewing it more broadly with a little "c." Literature can best be seen, in the present context, as illustrating the cultural patterns of a society once the patterns have been identified by the methods of the social sciences: social science as source, literature as example.

Literature: a third dimension

Folklore, an ideal compromise?

Morain (72) convincingly argues that folklore offers a logical bridge to service language teachers trained in literary analysis who are interested in getting closer to an anthropological understanding of culture but who are not equipped by disposition or background to deal with the empirical orientations of the social scientist. Morain takes as her definition of folklore the comfortably loose description by Taylor (107, p. 34): "Folklore is the material that is handed on by tradition, either by word of mouth or by custom and practice. It may be folksongs, folktales, proverbs, or other materials preserved in words. It may be traditional tools and physical objects like fences or knots, hot cross buns, or Easter eggs; traditional ornamentation like the walls of Troy; or traditional symbols like the swastika. It may be traditional procedures like throwing salt over one's shoulder or knocking on wood. It may be traditional beliefs like the notion that elder is good for ailments of the eye. All of these are folklore."

Definition

Morain argues that when it comes to mirroring the attitudes of large groups, folklore is superior to literary writing. The very durability of folktales, proverbs, slurs, and jests is an indication of the validity they have for a given people. Therefore, it would seem logical that a study of carefully selected folk materials could illuminate some of the important cultural themes that underlie a country's thought and action (72, p. 676). While Morain's examples are taken from the French, Campa (14) demonstrates how an analysis of folklore can illuminate the main themes of Hispanic culture. One-line proverbs, brief verses, nar-

Folklore mirrors attitudes

rative ballads, and riddles all afford lively illustrations of such themes as the "picaresqueness of the Spaniard," or his sense of "self assurance."

Appearing in *Soviet Education*, an article by Khanbikov (58) advances a communist appraisal of the value of basing educational philosophy in general on the best of the mores and customs, folk knowledge, folk law, literature and art, religious faiths, games and toys, and so forth, which the working people have traditionally transmitted to their children. Khanbikov calls this "folk pedagogy." He goes on to say that this folk pedagogy is of a democratic nature; it is the result of the creative contribution of many generations of working people to spiritual culture, its inalienable component. Many thousands of folk philosophers, psychologists, and educators have worked on its creation. It is the expression of the ideals of the toiling majority, and it puts forward, in correspondence with the needs of the people, the most humane and democratic ideals in the education of the rising generation, rejecting everything that contradicts these ideals (58, p. 39). This Marxist willingness to place faith in the culture of the masses contrasts interestingly with the reluctance of some "democratic" language teachers to discuss in sympathetic terms the life styles of the French, Spanish, or German workers.

"Folk pedagogy"

It is a great disappointment for many students, who have developed fluency in the language after 4 to 12 years of sequential study and have passed the advanced placement test, to go on to advanced classes only to discover in college that if they are to continue taking courses in their second language, they have to study literature or "advanced grammar." Even the somewhat isolated "Civilization and Culture" course usually bases itself "solidly" on literature. If a student wants to satisfy any of the many interests he was led to expect from his high school language teachers, he must often leave, or avoid altogether, the college foreign language department, for frequently it is easier to locate professors who are both fluent in the foreign language *and* interested in its culture in departments other than the language department. Perhaps folklore is the door through which more culturally pertinent materials can be introduced into the rather arid college offerings.

Culture must become the business of an FL department

Knowledge, skills, and attitudes to be developed

In 1967, the American Council on the Teaching of Foreign Languages (ACTFL) began compiling an annual bibliography on a number of areas that pertain to language teaching. Brooks was appointed head of the section on culture, and his bibliography was subsequently published in the December 1967 issue of *Foreign Language Annals* (*FLA*). Nostrand was assigned the responsibility for the 1968 compilation which appeared in the May 1969 issue of *FLA*. These ACTFL bibliographies (to be published yearly in the May issue of *FLA*) offer an excellent, up-to-date listing of articles and books that treat culture. The bibliographies include both content-oriented reference works written by social scientists and historians, and publications that attempt to apply cultural knowledge to the teaching of culture in foreign language classes. Some of the languages for which helpful reference sources were listed include Arabic (Pietrzyk, 86), Chinese (Hucker, 52), French (Pemberton, 85), German (8), Greek (Arnott, 3), Japanese (Silberman, 103), Latin (Crook, 23), Portuguese (Sayers, 93), and Spanish (Adams, 1).

ACTFL Bibliography

Besieged by an endless procession of cultural studies, the language teacher must ask himself what knowledge is relevant and what skills should be developed in students. Nostrand (78) proposes that language teachers concentrate upon just two basic purposes in teaching about a foreign way of life: cross-cultural communication and understanding.

Cross-cultural communication

Since the basic aim of a language class is to have the student learn to communicate in the foreign language, it is obvious that if fairly common emotions and thoughts cannot be understood apart from their cultural referents then these referents must be taught in the language classroom. Some interesting examples of difficulties in cross-cultural communication that arise from ignorance of the target culture are recounted in several articles.

Cultural referents in language

Barrutia (4), in an article that discusses the relation of language development to cultural barriers, illustrates one type of cultural problem by contrasting near synonyms in English. The possible social consequences of a loose interchange of role-linked terms would be amusing to observe—in someone else. Barrutia supplies a verse to dramatize the sex connotation of many common words.

A woman has a figure, a man has a physique;
A father roars in rage, a mother shrieks in pique;
Broad-shouldered athletes throw what dainty damsels toss;
And female bosses supervise, male bosses boss.

Lads gulp, maids sip;
Jacks plunge, Jills dip;
Guys bark, dames snap;
Boys punch, girls slap;
Gobs swab, WAVES mop;
Braves buy, squaws shop.

A gentleman perspires, a lady merely glows;
A husband is suspicious; a wife, however, knows.

Besides sex and social class referents, whether an object is recognized at all depends greatly on an understanding of the extralinguistic cultural referents. The writer (95) had an advanced Spanish literature class in college that considered a paperback from Mexico defective because the pages were not cut. Although the students had presumably mastered the linguistic aspects of *libro*, ignorance of the nonlinguistic referents of the word impeded their recognition of the perfectly normal object. Debyser (26), in a translation of an earlier article appearing in French, offers examples from the French to illustrate how the extralinguistic referents of common terms and phrases can be taught on the elementary level. It is not enough, Debyser shows, to know the words denoting the various members of a family (mother, child, uncle), for example. To be able to use the words with impunity one must also know the specific social context within which each can be employed. The word *maman*, for instance, may be used by a person when he talks to his mother, but would rarely be used by him when talking about her to others.

Extralingual cultural referents

Much misunderstanding among the profession concerning the degree to which an attempt should be made to get the student to act like a native is the result of confusing the *ability* or skill to communicate accurately and the *attitudes* toward man and beast dictated by the foreign mores. There should be no controversy about the aim of accurate communication, and this includes understanding the culturally based mores of the target people but does not necessarily include professing or internalizing the mores.

Acting like a native?

Understanding

Nostrand's second basic purpose in teaching the foreign culture—understanding—raises questions of delineation that the objective of cross-cultural communication does not, for understanding implies a restructuring of our "sacred" cognitive patterns. Nostrand includes under the rubric of understanding, for example, such intangibles as "the psychological capacity to be magnanimous toward strange ways" (78, p. 5–8). In the final analysis, no matter how technically dexterous a student's training in the foreign language, if he avoids contact with native speakers of that language, and if he lacks respect for their cognitive patterns, of what value has his training been? Where can it be put to use? What educational breadth has it inspired?

Unfortunately, some teachers themselves do not feel comfortable in the presence of native speakers of a foreign language. In part, this is because the teachers have not learned to follow speech at conversational speed, have not learned what things to talk about and what to avoid, have not accustomed themselves to the amount of space separating them from the native (Hall, 47, 48), or to the rules governing eyeball to eyeball contact, have not learned to share the target sense of humor or their songs, have not learned the cultural referents to the topics of discussion, and have succumbed to a regrettable tendency to underestimate ethnocentrically the intelligence of a member of another culture. The enlightened teaching of selected cultural elements can do much to prepare a student both to understand and enjoy a native speaker of the language. There is no enjoyment in listening to someone one can't understand, and one can't understand someone if his cultural referents, his view of the world, and his linguistic forms are novel. It is the language teacher who can build bridges from one cognitive system to another (Freeman, 34). Some ways to accomplish this are mentioned in the following section on activities and materials for achieving cultural communication and understanding.

Understanding and personal contact

One naive assumption occasionally made by language teachers is that a mastery of the linguistic patterns of a foreign culture leads in itself to "thinking like a native." As Lewald (66, p. 302) properly points out, this belief is unwarranted. Unless the student is learning the language in the target culture, the cultural referents necessary to understanding a native speaker must be *additionally* learned. Jay argues the point in pertinently broad terms:

"Thinking like a native"

It should be made crystal clear, however, that bilingualism itself does not insure *ipso facto* a respect for other cultural patterns. The traditional hostility between France and Germany has been until recently a bitter reality, even though the language of each was commonly taught and understood by the

45

other . . . . Bilingualism is not in itself the answer to cultural understanding among people. An indispensable asset, it must be fortified by the strongest possible sensitivity education. With knowledge of the language must exist a similar knowledge of the social, religious, and economic attitudes of a people (56, p. 85–86).

Interdisciplinary approaches to culture

Part of understanding consists of developing an awareness of the principles and phenomena governing the cultural system of the foreign country and of culture in general everywhere. It was this level of understanding that prompted the superintendent of a city school system to complain to the writer during an evaluation of his language program that when foreign language teachers are asked to justify the existence of their department in the curriculum, "they cry 'cultural understanding' to high heaven." This superintendent felt that the place to teach cultural understanding is in the social studies department. Are language teachers imperialistically encroaching upon the domain of the social studies teacher, teaching in a haphazard and amateurish way what history teachers are better equipped to handle?

Where does "cultural understanding" belong?

Educators have long recognized the danger inherent in compartmentalizing knowledge into separate academic disciplines. It seems that the average student experiences considerable difficulty in integrating what he learns from one course with what he learns from another. Academicians should rejoice when important areas of shared interest among departments arise, for this presents an opportunity to integrate meaningfully the insights born of different methodological approaches to common problems. The question concerning who should teach about culture should focus on how the social studies department and the foreign language department can complement each other in bringing the student to an understanding of the nature of culture and how it is manifested in the world's societies.

Social studies and foreign language get together

Social studies courses generally approach a study of foreign societies from a cross-cultural perspective. The focus remains for a brief time on one society, then turns to another. In the better courses, cultural systems are compared at critical points with the view of elucidating both the universal principles of man and the particular systems of selected societies. The contribution of language to the development of a society rarely receives attention in social studies courses on the secondary school level. On the college level, on the other hand, the study of linguistics de-

46

veloped out of the anthropology department and did not originate in its modern American form in the foreign language department. Paradoxically, then, secondary school social studies programs largely ignore the role of language in human affairs while the most significant studies of language occur not in departments of foreign language but in the college social science programs.

Language classes, in contrast to social studies classes, concentrate on understanding one particular culture, or at the most, a number of related subcultures. At their best, language classes offer a student the linguistic and cultural skills he needs to function in the foreign culture, and in addition attempt to provide an intellectual grasp of the cultural and linguistic forces that mold *A paradox* the unique culture he is studying. While the language teacher is more apt than his social studies counterpart to have lived in the culture he describes, a broadly-based, cross-cultural perspective is not included in language classes.

The cross-cultural method of social studies classes and the in-depth inquiry of language classes would seem to complement each other, the one affording a check against the generalizations of the other. It is difficult to conceive of a serious student of culture who does not comprehend the nature of language, and one is reluctant to accord confidence in the pronouncements of a person who knows but one culture. Singer (104) further argues that one cannot understand a second culture without first understanding one's own. However, the reverse logic is equally appealing: the only way to understand one's own culture well is to understand another culture first.

There have been several recent publications that have interest for both language and social studies teachers. One attempt to explore the area of interest shared by both disciplines was published by the Illinois Office of Public Instruction (Seelye, 101). Although it missed several logical areas of cooperation such as team teaching and common development of course objec- *Integrating disciplines* tives, it did suggest a reorganization of topics of some importance, largely anthropological and historical, that the language teacher could profitably develop in his classes. The basis for the proposed reorganization is argued in a succinct review essay by Esteves (31), and further elaborated in another article (Seelye, 99), where it is claimed that subject matter content should be regarded as a means to an end, and that content should not be learned for its own sake. Content itself has no intrinsic value if it does not develop new attitudes and skills. The

essence of the approach argued by Esteves and other contemporary educators is that one should not guide students into a solution of teacher-presented problems, but rather stimulate students to formulate questions that then can be brought into
sharper focus through a manipulation of content. Esteves points
out that problem-solving often leads to pat prefabricated solutions to problems that are problems precisely because they do
not have easy solutions. This approach to teaching skills "would
replace the role of teacher as [know-it-all] lecturer, with the role
of research assistant to an interested student" (99, p. 7). To contribute to an atmosphere of organized learning, rather than an
air of anarchy, some model construct of the culture could be utilized, such as the one developed by Taylor & Sorenson (108)
based on Mexican patterns, or the one by Nostrand (77) based on *New teacher and student roles*
French patterns. The writer (99) has claimed that much of the
problem of student interest improves when the student is offered
a choice among topics that are themselves important. To this
end, a bibliographic index of 30 or so recent books on Latin
America, organized under 23 "key ideas" of Latin American culture, has been developed.

The prior availability of these "key ideas" further emphasizes
the advantage to be gained from an interdisciplinary study of
culture. They were developed for social studies teachers by the
Latin American Curriculum Project of the University of Texas *"key ideas"*
in Austin, directed by Gill & Conroy (38, 42), and are quite useful
to the teacher of Spanish or Portuguese. Conversely, the Foreign
Language Innovative Curricula Studies project in Ann Arbor,
Mich., directed by James McClafferty, is producing multimedia
units on French culture, and materials to aid the teaching of
Hispanic culture to Mexican-American children, which may
well interest social studies teachers. This whole area of cross-
pollination and cooperation between departments of social
studies and foreign languages holds much promise for the future.

Teachers interested in reviewing the findings of the social sciences will find the encyclopedic summaries prepared by Berelson & Steiner (7) to be a good place to begin. Hymes' mammoth
reader in linguistics and anthropology (53) is an exceptionally
valuable source although some of the articles are difficult to follow. A recent compilation of some of the outstanding articles of *Reference works in*
the last decade written by anthropologists (Manners & Kaplan, *sociolinguistics*
69) has two sections of special interest to the teacher of foreign
languages: Culture and Personality, and Ideology, Language,
and Values. An anthology of 45 articles (Fishman, 33), each by

a different author writing about the rapidly emerging area of the sociology of language, contains sections on language in small-group interaction, in social strata, plus a number of other categories that treat language as a cultural event. It will be surprising if this area, the sociology of language, does not become increasingly important to foreign language teachers.

Language and thought

Some years ago, Benjamin Lee Whorf (cf. Carroll, 17), citing the earlier work of Sapir (90; also in Mandelbaum, 68), theorized that the world-view of a speech community is reflected in the linguistic patterns they use. The implication was that the way "reality" is categorized in the underlying patterns of a language is an indication of how speakers of that languge view the world; and, inversely, how they view the world depends on the language system they have. The proliferation of Eskimo words for snow, according to what was to become known as the Sapir-Whorf hypothesis, reflects the importance snow has in Eskimo culture. Similar instances are the Trobriand Islanders' multiplicity of terms for yams, the basis of their economy, and the truck-loads of terms to designate automobiles current in contemporary U.S. culture. Colors, kinship relations, perception of space and time, all differ from language to language and from culture to culture. The trick is to demonstrate an association between the two, language and culture. (It may be recalled that Whorf advocated contrasting languages such as Navaho and English, or French and Chinese, and not languages within the Indo-European family.) Off-the-cuff pronouncements on the relation between language and culture are the rule in language classes. The fact that the linguistic structure of some languages enables the speaker to become the object of the action ("the glass broke on me") instead of the subject of the action ("I broke the glass"), to take an example, does not in itself demonstrate the speaker of the first example to view nature as an active agent and man as a passive one. To draw a cognitive conclusion from purely linguistic data is to while away the hours in tautology. To legitimately draw a behavioral inference from an analysis of language structure it is necessary to empirically associate a language pattern with a behavioral pattern.

That the Sapir-Whorf hypothesis has been accepted as truth by so many language teachers is an interesting example of the tendency toward wish-fulfillment. The theory is exciting, there is some corroborative evidence (and, perhaps inevitably, a body of

The Whorfian hypothesis

contradicting evidence also), the idea has been around long enough for most teachers to have forgotten its highly speculative nature, and, last but not least, if the theory were true it would imbue language courses with new-found importance. Unfortunately, few writings by linguistic specialists are, at this stage in the science's struggle for respectability, comprehensible to most classroom language teachers, and few down-to-earth language teachers have shown enough familiarity with the linguistic literature. Consequently, our acceptance of the Sapir-Whorf hypothesis must await either more empirical evidence or improved communication with linguists. Some of the fairly recent books that treat this area include Hoijer (50), Carroll (17), Romney & D'Andrade (89), Gumperz & Hymes (46), Hammel (49), Hymes (53), Greenberg (45), Landar (64), Witucki (115), Mathiot (71), Manners & Kaplan (69), Fishman (33), and Niyekawa-Howard (75).

One probe by the writer (100) into the relation between language structure and cognitive preferences took three instances in Spanish where the speaker could choose either an active or passive linguistic form, then set up six different social situations and asked 50 Guatemalans to make a choice between the active and passive forms within the context of each situation. The writer tentatively concluded that contrary to popular belief   (1) the Spanish passive may not be "generally preferred,"   (2) the passive is not used "to get rid of blame," but   (3) the election of the passive depends on the context of the situation in a more complex way than usually has been acknowledged. This study reported, for example, that in some circumstances the sampled Guatemalans selected either the passive or active form to balance the verb forms when one or the other form had been exaggeratedly used. This level of linguistic preference is clearly stylistic and not cognitive. Other examples did, however, seem to exemplify cognitive preferences.

The case of the Spanish passive

Another study effected a semantic comparison of Russian and English words, with the objective of "determining whether one language tends to operate at an overall level of abstraction which is either higher or lower than that of the other language" (Oppenheimer, 83). Oppenheimer selected a few English words at random and compared their level of abstraction — the extent to which details and characteristics are omitted — to their Russian counterparts. He found that the English words generally appear to be at a higher level of abstraction than the corresponding Russian words. While Oppenheimer advances several interpreta-

Language and levels of abstraction

tions and explanations of this, he is properly cautious about projecting any importance to the cognitive world of the speaker of either language. Articles of this type are productive in that they suggest hypotheses that a more controlled study might advantageously pursue.

The cultural nature of language

Dewey's famous essay, "My Pedagogic Creed" (28), appeared in an education journal in 1897. In it, Dewey observed that "language is almost always treated in the books of pedagogy simply as the expression of thought. It is true that language is a logical instrument, but it is fundamentally and primarily a social instrument." If language is "primarily a social instrument," how can it be divorced from the society that uses it? Writing over 70 years after Dewey, Chao (19) in his recent study of language emphasizes that "action and speech are thoroughly mixed." Chao further observes that language is not even usually in the form of connected discourse such as sentences, paragraphs, etc. (19, p. 112–133).

Dewey: language as a social instrument

There is probably considerable correlation between linguistic change and social change. When for one reason or another members of one language community are forced to functon either within or alongside another language, both their language and way of life inevitably change. Ilbek (54) offers an interesting discussion of the effect of English on the native language of the French-speaking minorities of the U.S. Ilbek gives examples of shifts of meaning caused by the presence of cognates in the language, direct borrowing of lexical items to designate new things, borrowing of patterns through translation, and borrowing of fixed forms directly or through translation. However, instead of using these data to arrive at insights into the nature of linguistic change or biculturation, the author disappointingly concludes that "as teachers of French we are pledged to fight this kind of interference and to keep our language pure. . . ." (54, p. 376).

Linguistic and social change

Many teachers make this same mistake. While intrigued with the cultural implications of linguistic data, they get hung up on the *form* and fail to reach a cultural comprehension of the data beyond an assessment of its snob appeal. Despite two decades of descriptive linguistics, there is still much of the normative puritanism in our souls. Chao correctly characterizes language when he says that "there is no complete uniformity in any speech community; there is always mixture of dialects in the

Linguistic purism

51

same locality; there is class difference; there is difference in speech reflected by different personalities for the dialect or same class; above all, there is difference in style in the same individual" (19, p. 123). Chao adds that besides talking with people, and hearing them talk with you, one should *overhear* them talk among themselves to learn to understand the nonstandard dialects (19, p. 132–133).

Sensitivity training

Referring to West Indian children faced with learning Standard English in school, Jones (57) states that it is unscientific and detrimental to the mental health of the child to attempt to eradicate his home language. Jones suggests that teachers should strive to produce a student who can switch dialects as the situation demands.

Nonstandard dialects have been anathema to many language teachers. The writer recently visited a large school system containing many Mexican-American students, very few of whom were enrolled in any foreign language classes. When the language chairmen were asked why these Spanish-speaking students were not enrolled in advanced Spanish classes, the writer was told that they were poor language students who were not even able to do the work and pass the tests of beginning Spanish courses, let alone advanced classes. When the writer suggested that perhaps this was an indication that the "work" and the "tests" of the beginning Spanish classes had little relevancy to learning to communicate in the language, he was told that the home language of the students was dismally substandard and — to add insult to injury — the students militantly resisted being corrected. And what was the nature of these resisted corrections? In many cases, through ignorance of the wide variety of linguistic forms that educated people employ in the score or more of countries where Spanish is spoken, the teacher was simply incorrect in his statement that a given form was substandard. In other cases, where the form was definitely nonstandard, rather than instill pride in a student of humble origins who knows richly archaic forms — forms that Cervantes may have used — or forms that illustrate imaginative borrowing, the student was made to feel embarrassment because he did not know the comparatively lifeless form that the teacher had learned in some textbook. Minor differences in the way to pronounce some words or sounds caused disproportionate friction between stu-

Nonstandard dialects

dent and teacher. A cultured ex-student of the writer, and a native speaker of Spanish from Guatemala City, almost flunked a Spanish course at a large Midwestern university because the teacher "didn't like his accent." Many teachers seem to pounce on the mistakes, often minor, of their Puerto Rican or Mexican (or Pennsylvania German or French Canadian) students in "retribution" for the teacher's lack of ability to understand them. Sadly, even Mexican-American or native teachers are occasionally hostile toward these children who so much deserve sympathetic nurturing. The fact remains that after unsympathetic teachers have exhausted their repertoire of horror stories about the classroom performance of students who speak Spanish (or French or German) at home, there is still a strong correlation between the best students of a language and those who speak it at home (Carroll, 16, p. 137–138). Teachers who think that American students ignorant of the foreign language can learn it better than students who have been speaking it all their lives —in *whatever* dialect—need to have their goals examined. The testimony of Gaarder (35) before a Senate Subcommittee on Bilingual Education, and an article by Howe (51) on the education of minority groups, contain reasoned pleas for a sensitive and sensible approach to teaching children whose only claim to wealth rests with the rich culture their forebearers have passed on to them.

Negative attitudes of teachers

At the base of much of the tension between a student from an economically deprived background and a teacher who wears his college degree as a middle-class merit badge is a conflict of cultures. A manual has been prepared by an anthropologist, Burger (13), who suggests ways for teachers to increase their effectiveness with groups whose culture differs from the teacher's by first understanding better the student culture (relevant descriptions are presented of Mexican-Americans, Negroes, Pueblos, and Yankees), and then by applying certain values of that culture to the lesson one wants to teach. If, for example, the teacher desires to transmit the idea that "cleanliness is next to godliness," the teacher may find that the "unscrubbed masses" take meticulous care of their "wheels." Basing himself on the student-accepted value that bikes and cars should be washed frequently, the teacher would have a means to communicate cross-culturally on cleanliness, a matter of value belief. Burger's manual is a fine introduction to the type of sensitivity education that language teachers can appreciate.

Being aware of cultural differences in the classroom

Lawton (65) reviewed the psychological and anthropological literatures in the field in an attempt to assess the importance of linguistic differences that exist between various social groups. He then examined a sample of English working-class subjects who were identified as underachievers in school and paid particular attention to their linguistic and cognitive processes, the latter especially as it related to the group's attitudes toward education. Lawton came to the conclusion that there was a great deal of evidence to support the view that an inadequacy of linguistic range and control is a very important and definitive factor in scholastic underachievement, that the linguistic difficulties these underachieving groups have are closely related to wider questions of motivation and culture, and in order to widen the student's control over language the social structure of the school must change considerably to admit greater possibilities of developing new role-relations (65, p. 156–158). While Lawton sees legitimacy in the schools' attempts to transform their pupils into middle-class children, he makes the suggestion that teachers should become more sensitive to the kind of analysis that would enable them to distinguish in the so-called middle-class culture what is of cognitive importance and do away with everything that is irrelevant to the educational process (65, p. 159). Among the "trivial" aspects of middle-class culture Lawton mentions "etiquette and social conventions."

Inadequacy of language affects achievement

While there are cultural advantages to be gained from retaining and even emphasizing subcultural linguistic and behavioral patterns in foreign language classes, care should be taken to develop courses that interest students who come from language and cultural traditions other than the target one. When a language course largely attracts students whose parents or grandparents are or were native speakers of the language, the drawing power of that language often suffers after the first or second generation passes, e.g., Polish, Yiddish, Swedish. Fishman (32) reports there are more teachers and students of Italian whose near ancestors were native speakers of the language taught than that of any other commonly taught language in the U.S. However, he also sees two distressing trends. On the one hand, lower enrollment is anticipated as fewer students associate themselves with their ethnic past, and, on the other hand, as Italian teachers lose their familiarity with their regional language and customs, the cultural content of Italian courses is bound to weaken. Thus there is a constant challenge for all language teachers to reassess the role of culture in their courses.

The "generation gap" and language learning

Activities and materials for achieving cultural Communication and understanding

There are a number of reasons why foreign language classes often omit the teaching of culture. Debyser (25, Part 1) mentions lack of time, the idea that language and culture are one and the same, the belief that students will get it later, and the view of language as a communication skill divorced from social concerns. Debyser rejects these reasons. Cultural concepts must be implemented by specific measures in the classroom if they are to be taught. While many teachers see culture as merely providing the background to matters of linguistic concern—for example, using a trip to the market or a visit with a French family to introduce new vocabulary or structural patterns—he points out that unless this is very well done one should not put great hope in the efficacy of this method (25, p. 24).

Reasons for omitting culture from language classes

There is much the teacher interested in culturally meaningful language commonly accomplishes by insistence on authentic speech patterns and dialogue situations, by describing the cultural significance of words and phrases and gestures, by teaching the songs, games, rhymes, and popular maxims of the culture, and by discussing some of its main themes. Opportunities for cultural instruction often overlooked are listed by Brooks (11, p. 82–96) in the form of specific questions pertaining to some 64 different topics. Questions such as: "In what ways are age, provenance, social status, academic achievement, degree of formality, interpersonal relations, aesthetic concern, personality, reflected in . . . speech?" "What common words or expressions in English have direct equivalents that are not tolerated in the new culture, and vice versa?" "What objects are often found decorating the bureau and walls of a young person's bedroom?" "What careers have strong appeal for the young?" Other sources for the teacher interested in culture include Lado's excellent book (61), and the listing of source materials by Chamberlain (18).

Questions on cultural topics for the classroom

Specifying instructional objectives

Before a teacher can begin to select techniques to teach cultural understanding he must know what *specific* cultural objectives he wants to reach. Objectives of communication and understanding should be dealt with separately, and not lumped together in some all-embracing super-goal. Each set of goals should probably include specific objectives relating to recognition of cultural patterns, comprehension of how patterns function as an interrelated system of mutually supportive forms, an appreciation of how strange or novel patterns work—and consequently are valued—in the target culture, and a sympathetic interest in members of the target culture. General assistance in designing realistic objectives of any type is available in Mager (67). After deciding on the particular set of cultural goals he wants to teach, the instructor must then modify techniques to suit the interests and maturity of his students, keeping in mind the materials available to him. Since maturity levels generally correspond to the traditional designations of primary school, middle school, high school, college, and graduate school, some sort of cooperative division of labor with a view to minimizing costly duplication of effort and to maximizing an intelligent articulation from language level to language level is obviously desirable.

Objectives, techniques, maturity

Defining cultural levels

Divisions can be made along several lines, depending upon one's understanding of the learning process. If the theory that any concept can be taught at any level is credited, then the methodological task becomes one of identifying examples and exercises that are at a level readily understandable by a given age group to illustrate the concepts. If, on the other hand, it is believed that effective teaching of a concept depends on assessing its difficulty and then presenting it to an age group that has reached the requisite level of maturity to comprehend it, then the problem becomes one of arranging cultural concepts into a hierarchy of relative complexity. Certainly *how* a concept is presented to a student will depend on his maturity and educational background. An eclectic scheme that suggests which cultural items are to be presented at various sequential levels was developed by a 1968 committee of the Pacific Northwest Conference on Foreign Language Teaching (Nostrand, 79). The committee, chaired by Nostrand, based its efforts on the previous work of Ladu (62).

Defining cultural levels at Pacific Northwest Conference

The committee's report calls for both behavioral and verbal responses to cultural stimuli at the first level. The student is expected on Level I (a level does not necessarily equal a year) to demonstrate physically how to behave in a number of situations including greetings, introductions, leave-taking, eating, and conduct "toward persons of one's own and of higher social sta-

Level I: behavior in a number of situations

tus." Likewise, he must also be able to describe in English two or more common leisure-time activities of adolescents in the foreign society, as well as to learn a poem and some songs. Some minor adaptations to this proposal for Level I could easily be made to accomodate integration of pre-adolescent FLES (foreign language in the elementary school) programs into the outline. Of course, students beginning study of a foreign language in secondary school will miss the enriching substance of the riddles, games, songs, rhymes, and the way the child of the target culture views his world; students beginning language study at more advanced ages will miss "adolescent culture" as well. On the other hand, much of "adult culture" awaits the persevering curiosity of the developing student, not because a secondary student lacks the intellectual capacity for understanding the preoccupations of the middle-aged and over, but because he is justifiably more interested in his own concerns.

A practical elaboration of the proposed standards for cultural levels is developed in the committee's outline for Level II. Here, two sets of standards are presented: a "minimal standard" and a "desirable standard." Since some schools will be able to teach more than others no matter how uniformly definitions of levels are drawn, it seems wise to elaborate ambitious standards that superior programs are encouraged to cover in addition to minimal standards that any accredited language program should cover. Somewhat disappointingly, however, neither minimal nor desirable activities on Level II require the student to do anything on a nonverbal level. The student is asked to "state orally" insights into literature, the family, education, cultural themes, etc. Although this verbal activity is to be accomplished in the target language, the proposed standards do not show enough awareness of the many language-connected ways in which the language reflects the culture, such as nonlinguistic cultural referents necessary to understanding the spoken word, dialect variations, and ability to follow disconnected discourse. Nor do the proposals imaginatively explore the realm of nonverbal cultural skills. The standards display some bias in expecting children to understand a relatively small segment of most countries, "a middle-class person of the foreign society." Many American children might prefer to identify with another class segment of the target culture. (An age bias also found in the outline seems pedagogically more justifiable.) Another class bias is evident in the statement that one should learn how to conduct oneself "toward

Level II: "stating orally" various insights into family and educational systems

Disregard for nonlinguistic cultural referents

Problem of class and age bias

persons of one's own and of higher social status." When are we going to learn to talk with most of the world's inhabitants, the poor?

While the most detailed sections of both Levels II and III use literature to illustrate the main cultural themes, with Level III the social structure belatedly receives more direct attention beyond the previous emphasis on the family and educational systems. Level IV outlines more balanced expectations but it is very briefly developed. A discussion of how literature can be effectively used to illustrate cultural aspects of a society was published earlier by Nostrand (80). It might be noted at this point that any instruction that requires the use of English can be taken care of in homework, more or less in programmed form, so as not to interfere with the virtually exclusive practice of the foreign language during class time.

Level III: social structure beyond family and education

Level IV?

Cultural themes

Nostrand (77) has been instrumental in developing a conceptual model of those aspects of a foreign culture to which language teachers could most profitably devote their talents. He proposes that the essentials of the target cultural system be organized under headings of a structured inventory which he calls the "Emergent Model." In it, some 30 headings are grouped under the four large rubrics of the Culture, the Society, the Individual, and the Ecology. One of the strengths of this inventory is that it is an outgrowth of integrating Murdock's famous anthropological inventory (74) with the priorities of the language classroom.

Nostrand's Emergent Model

Nostrand's "Emergent Model"

I. *The Culture.* — value system, ethos, assumptions about reality, verifiable knowledge, art forms, language, paralanguage, and kinesics.

II. *The Society.* — organized under institutions: familial, religious, economic-occupational, political and judicial, educational, intellectual-aesthetic, recreational, communications, social proprieties, stratification and mobility, conflict and conflict resolution.

III. *The Individual.* — integration of the personality, organismic level, intrapersonal and interpersonal valuation, status by age and sex.

IV. *The Ecology.* — attitudes toward nature, exploitation of nature, use of natural products, technology, settlements and territorial organization, travel and transportation.

Nostrand suggests that this organization of the life style into four component systems can best be taught by organizing the substance of a given life style under its main theme—a theme being a value that is more fully defined in terms of its underlying assumptions and applications in human relations, personality structure, and interaction with the physical and subhuman environment.

Applying Nostrand's Emergent Model to the French and Hispanic cultures, Ladu (63) has developed a highly commendable book appropriately titled *Teaching for Cross-Cultural Understanding*. In this work she interprets many of the cultural aspects of each of the four major categories of the Emergent Model. An informative discussion of the thematic approach to cultural understanding, along with an analysis of the major themes of North India, was effected by the sociologist Opler (82). Mathiot (71) draws a distinction between those aspects of the cognitive system that are reflected in language and those reflected in nonlinguistic behavior. Consequently, she separates themes of the language from themes of the culture. This study infers the themes of language (Uto-Aztecan) by relating the semantic distinctive features of a given aspect of language to a postulated underlying concept found in the related cognitive contents.

A detailed description of how songs may provide the basis for illustrating the main themes of a culture is presented by Damoiseau & Marc (24). The authors pass over the two most frequent uses to which songs are subjected in language classes (as a literary text for linguistic analysis or as a vehicle for the study of the target poetry) in favor of a cultural objective: the different aspects of the daily life of the target culture as illustrated in song. Compositions should be selected from writers who are involved with the daily life of the target society as seen through their thesis songs of social commentary. The main social problem treated in the song would be the first concern of the class. A linguistic analysis of the coexistence of both urban and more traditional vocabulary with a view to illustrating the direction of social change is suggested by the authors. They make the suggestion that each thematic point could itself be carefully illustrated by a series of slides that show, for instance, the effect of urbanization of life on the target culture. Damoiseau & Marc also expand in considerable detail how lesson plans can be developed on this principle. The examples, as is the language of the article, are French.

Song as a reflection of target culture

59

Semiotic analysis

The methodological apparatus of semiotics, the study of signs, is suggested by Beaujour & Ehrmann (5) as a means to systematically analyze the extralinguistic cultural referents found in "newspapers, movies, recordings of all kinds . . . interviews, confessions, dialogues, opinion polls, etc." They suggest limiting the time scope to be studied to "signs" found in sources of the last 10 or 15 years, although earlier events may be analyzed if they appear in contemporary productions. Referents to linguistic units (ethnosemes) and nonlinguistic or paralinguistic behavioral signs (what the writer [98, p. 35] calls "ethnomorphs") are both grist for a semiotic analysis. The authors give examples of two analyses in French, the first bases itself on data secured via interview, the second on data obtained from a magazine advertisement.

Ethnomorphs

In the first example, a "young person" is asked: "Are you a nationalist?" The authors then psychologically interpret the paragraph or so of oral reply in terms of a cultural determinist frame. They conclude that the informant used nationalism to compensate for individual inadequacies. The second example takes an ad for a vacation club as raw material for semiotic analysis. Through the choice of words and pictorial associations, the ad embodies a composite of paradisiacal values (happiness, freedom from want, liberty) strengthened by pictures that can be identified with the basic values (sun, sea, fish, bather). The simple vacation life is contrasted to the frenzy of industrial life: civilized self versus natural self. Step by step the student is led to understand the cultural referent of each term and picture, and then allowed to see how the fragmented parts illustrate a larger basic theme of the target culture.

When to begin teaching culture

Cultural instruction should begin with the first week of the first year of language learning. There is no need to wait for any linguistic fluency to use culturally authentic pictures and objects to illustrate aspects of the foreign culture. On the first day of class students are usually taught some form of greeting. To be culturally authentic, the greeting should use the forms the students would use in the target culture, or forms that the clearly identified roles the students are asked to assume would use. Graphic illustrations of the target people engaged in greetings are utilized — not nondescript stick figures, but real-looking peo-

No delay!

60

ple from the foreign culture, be they tall, dark, and handsome, or short, white, and ugly. It is desirable to have the students recognize, from the way a person greets another, whether that person is addressing a social equal or whether he is showing deference, where the speaker comes from, whether he is indicating his social class background in the greeting he has chosen or in the way he pronounces it, and whether he is conveying any special information through his intonation (the suprasegmental phonemic structure).

Helpful materials to aid the FLES teacher develop cultural understanding in her students are described in Donoghue's book (30). There are lists of films, filmstrips, pictures, slides, tapes, foreign language radio programs, periodicals, both teacher's and children's books in English about the target culture, and sources of pen and tape pals, which the teacher of French, German, or Spanish can utilize in classes. Bishop (9) describes games and lists verses and songs of interest to the FLES student of Spanish. An annotated guide pertaining to instructional materials for teaching about Latin America is available in Gill & Conroy (39). A similar guide for the secondary school teacher was prepared by the same editors (40); they have also prepared a critique of the treatment of Latin America in social studies sources (41). Chamberlain (18) has gathered together source materials that teachers of various languages can utilize.

FLES materials for the teaching of culture

Illustrations

Some texts are much more adept than others at portraying culturally authentic situations. Many contain mostly pictures of the kind a travel bureau might want displayed at a tea party. Churches, a few tall buildings, a "quaint" Indian or peasant, pretty girls in regional costumes, inspiring mountains and sunsets on the horizon all absorb the space that could be used to display people in social interaction. Many texts fail to integrate the illustrations with the book's content. Illustrated magazines from the foreign country, especially if several periodicals appealing to different social classes are included, afford an excellent and inexpensive way to bring the foreign people into the classroom.

Integration of picture and content

Illustrations chosen with some care can be an important source in conditioning students to react familiarly to situations that affect language use in the target culture. Much of the latitude of communication, both interpersonal and intergroup, is determined by the person's social class background. The teacher

61

can assist students in recognizing the signs that the target culture considers indicators of social class by asking questions such as: Which people in this picture seem to be visiting the city from a rural area? Would this girl's occupation be that of a maid or of a secretary? Aside from the wrinkles on their faces, how can you tell the older men from the younger? While few texts available for use in Spanish, Portuguese, or French classes indicate an awareness of the presence of the Negro in the life or literature of their countries, use of popular magazines can help the teacher overcome this regrettable void. Some urban ghetto schools have found it profitable to begin foreign language instruction with culturally oriented pictures. The illustrations are used as a point of departure for discussions in English about the target peoples. As interest and curiosity are awakened, the instructor begins to teach the students words and phrases that are relevant to their interests. Thus, little by little, the initial cultural emphasis shifts in favor of linguistic considerations.

Four categories of audiovisual materials are mentioned by Nostrand (76): the still picture, the sound film, the sound alone, the silent motion picture. Using the Emergent Model as a construct of the cultural universe to be taught in foreign language courses, Nostrand gives examples of the kind of audiovisual material that can be employed to illustrate the various aspects of the target society. To illustrate the expressive art form of folk humor, for example, stills or brief motion pictures showing various types of humor might be employed. A multimedia approach to courtship and marriage, childhood and birthdays, education, recreation, religion, old age, and death in Mexico has been prepared by Savaiano & Archundia (92) as a culture unit for the American Association of Teachers of Spanish and Portuguese (AATSP).

Four categories of audiovisual materials

Contextual notes

Another common technique for teaching nonlinguistic cutural referents (what the concept of "progress" means to a Latin American, for example) involves the explanation of a cultural item in a note within the text. Perhaps the best example of this is found in the *Condorito* materials for Spanish classes (Extracurricular Programs, University Station, Provo, Utah). Condorito is the hero of a Chilean comic strip who frequently voices utterances that the textbook-oriented Spanish teacher often "overlooks" in his classes. Also badly needed are sophisticated studies of the cultural referents to the most common words and expressions of each popularly taught language. Studies of cultural referents that indicate the age, sex, place of residence, and social class of the speaker of the target language are as yet nonexistent.

Gestures

An introduction to French gestures is available in two articles (Brault, 10; Nostrand, 77, section I.F.2). Green's gesture inventory of Spain (44) should help Spanish teachers create an authentic and animated cultural backdrop for their classes. The AATSP has developed a unit on gestures that includes 35 color slides and taped commentary in either English or Spanish, available to members (Canfield, 15).

Culture capsules

The usefulness of an article by Taylor & Sorenson (108) is attested to by its recent reappearance as a reprint. The article suggests that teachers prepare brief "culture capsules" for presentation during the last five or ten minutes of a class period. (Students could just as well prepare the capsules themselves.) The authors stress that the subject of the capsules should contrast one minimal difference between the culture of the U.S. and the foreign country. They suggest the text of each capsule be illustrated and that questions be directed to the class after the formal presentation. A theoretical matrix of some detail is presented, based on Mexican culture, which would be adaptable to any culture.

Contrast a "minimal difference"

The Taylor & Sorenson (108) and the Beaujour & Ehrmann (5) insistence on contrasting the cultural elements of the native and target countries appears to differ markedly from the Nostrand proposal that "the first three Levels should avoid contrastive analysis as far as practicable, in order to assure first that the learner overcomes the ethnocentric view of the foreign as eccentric. . . ." (79, p. 22). While it is certainly desirable to avoid having students view the foreign culture as eccentric, perhaps what Nostrand's article refers to is the problem of determining the *level* of contrast. It is important to present the view that what the target individual does makes sense, that the efficacy of a given cultural pattern depends on how it fits into the complex whole of a culture. When the teacher takes everyday examples of target life and tells the class that "we do it this way, but they do it that way," he is doing the culture a disservice. One should not lose sight of just what the functional significance of a

The function of a "behavior pattern"

behavioral pattern is in terms of a more abstract value or theme. Getting inside, cognitively speaking, another value system is a difficult matter. Singer (104) argues that one can never understand another culture in its own terms, but always "through the eyes of the observer. . . . Every effort at understanding another culture involves an interaction between one's own culture and that other culture" (104, p. 21).

Folklore

The stimulating articles by Morain (72) and Campa (14) have already been mentioned. Campa observes that the refinements of civilization provide to some extent a common ground for international communication because culture in this sense is a common denominator for a small segment of the peoples of the world, but seldom do such refinements provide an understanding of what makes a Spaniard, a Peruvian, or a Mexican a distinct and individual personality. The folk song, however, from Spain to Argentina, not only reveals what Hispanic people sing about but also why they sing (14, p. 1–2). Morain (72, p. 680–681) explains that most folk materials are ideally suited for the language class. "Tales and legends are usually short. Even the student who grasps the foreign text slowly can read a selection at one sitting without losing the full impact of the terror, the sly smirk, or the guffaw that the original teller intended to arouse. The style is often conversational, providing examples of natural dialogue that can be easily converted into skits by the students, or reworked into oral drills for teaching grammatical structures." The author goes on to exhort the teacher interested in using folklore materials in his classroom to make two stipulations: "The materials used should be authentic, not watered-down 'fakelore'; and they should be used to present valid cultural themes, not generalizations that are more picturesque than profitable." While folk materials designed especially for the language class have usually taken the form of brief verbal vignettes, the AATSP has prepared an illustrated unit on the folk arts of Mexico (Savaiano & Archundia, 91).

Folk music

Simulation

An especially exciting technique for teaching an understanding of the complex way decisions affect the interaction of different forces in a society is to assign different students specific roles (labor leader, student, large land owner, military officer, etc.) and then to introduce the role players to a problem they react to. A book on simulation by Scott, Lucas, & Lucas (94) discusses four different types: (1) simulation of the developmental processes of a hypothetical nation ("Simuland"); (2) simulation of an actual developing nation (Brazil) in terms of its politico-economic conditions; (3) simulation of a political system (Chile) where neither the goals nor the key issues were specified; and (4) simulation of an urban (Durham, N.C.) political system. A simulation of a Latin American *golpe de estado* was demonstrated at a National Defense Education Act workshop in 1968, and an article briefly (and somewhat technically) describing this was published (Parker, Smith, & Whithed, 84). Political scientists have been foremost in developing simulation as a pedagogical technique, but language teachers are beginning to follow their example. Gomez (43) discusses the usefulness of simulation in what he calls "the total immersion approach." Gomez also suggests the construction of a plywood chamber for stimulus presentation and response inforcement based on various experimental contingencies. The contingencies would focus primarily upon a number of problem and conflict situations and would lend itself to the utilization of concepts and techniques from "games theory" (43, p. 303). Gomez does not detail either the hardware or software components of such a teaching device.

A total immersion approach

Language laboratory type and culture

Mueller & Wiersma (73), in an article entitled "The Effects of Language Laboratory Type upon Cultural Orientation Scores of Foreign Language Students," describe an empirically-based study. Unfortunately, while the study's sample size in the various categories was a healthy 637–691 students, the conclusions the investigators were able to draw are not helpful. They conclude that the cultural attitudes of students were better (i.e., more favorably disposed toward Germans or French or Spanish) where students did not have recording facilities in the lab. There were too many variables to enable the investigators to tell why this was so. One variable, for example, was that the nonrecording group studied an average of two hours less per week than the recording group (?). Slight positive correlations (.20 to .50) between disenchantment with one's own culture (anomie) and fondness for the target culture (phylophilia) were reported.

Student research-directed activities

Some examples of how to develop in students the skill of "finding out" about people and places have been given by the writer elsewhere (99). One suggestion is that students develop bibliographic indexes relevant to a problem of importance, and that they be taught to skim the material in a search for answers to pertinent questions that the student has formulated with the help of the teacher. It is of relatively little importance what particular problem is chosen since the general skills in delimiting topics and doing background research are common to most problems. The intrinsic motivation of the student who defines a problem within his own area of interest will lead him to other areas of intrigue. Thus, eventually an integrated understanding of the target culture may emerge.

Travel and study abroad

Perhaps the most powerful technique the teacher can marshall to increase the student's knowledge of the foreign culture and language is for the teacher to inspire, cajole, threaten, or bribe the student into spending some time abroad. Carroll's study speaks of the development of language skills when it reported the following findings, but its implications for the study of culture are not difficult to envision:

> Time spent abroad is clearly one of the most potent variables we have found, and this is not surprising, for reasons that need not be belabored. Certainly our results provide a strong justification for a "year abroad" as one of the experiences to be recommended for the language majors. Even a tour abroad, or a summer school course abroad, is useful, apparently, in improving the student's skill. The obverse of this finding may be rather humbling for the foreign language teaching profession; those who do *not* go abroad do not seem to be able to get very far in their foreign language study, on the average, despite the ministrations of foreign language teachers, language laboratories, audiolingual methods, and the rest" (16, p. 137, italics removed).

What it does for the teacher

Of utmost interest to language teachers is a knowledge of the factors that affect a student's adjustment to a foreign culture. Many of these factors will be outside a teacher's area of influence—personality traits, reception in the host country, health considerations, etc.—but others will suggest ways that the classroom experience can be made more meaningful to cross-cultural understanding.

One study concluded that males and females "have similar attitudes toward associating with members of other ethnic groups" (Zaidi, 117, p. 105). On the darker side, however, the investigator reported that his sample of elite Pakistani university students exhibited considerable reluctance to live with non-Muslim, non-Asiatic groups. (They were especially reluctant to associate with Russians, Indians, British, and Americans; however, they rather liked the idea, comparatively speaking, of associating with Germans.) Whether the sample would actually behave in accordance with their attitudes was not evaluated. A study by Becker shows that the attitudes both to the home and host country in the initial phase of adjustment are a function of the social and cultural distance between the United States and the home country: the greater the distance, the greater are the difficulties of adjustment to the new environment, both because of the student's own reaction to the sociocultural gap and because of the reaction of others to his being different (6, p. 439).

Student adjustment to a foreign culture

Yousef (116, p. 231), in an article on cross-cultural testing, discusses mistakes students made on multiple-choice tests that resulted not so much from misunderstanding the target culture as from mistrusting it and unconsciously refusing to endow the target culture with any shreds of similarity to the native culture. Yousef calls this phenomenon "the resistance reaction." The author goes on to suggest that one of the reasons for this repressed resentment may have been "that in many situations where Americans and Middle-Easterners intermingled, the social intercourse often backfired because of cultural conflict." Unless a student is favorably disposed toward a language and its culture, little learning can occur (116, p. 233). He concludes his article by saying: "Overcoming cultural prejudices must therefore be a major aim of language teaching."

The resistance reaction

Gezi (37) studied 62 Middle-Eastern students in 11 colleges in California and found that:

1 There was a highly significant association (.001) between the students' pre-arrival attitudes toward the U.S. and their subsequent adjustment.

2 While the length of time the students had spent in the U.S. was not significantly associated with their adjustment, the amount of interaction they had experienced with Americans was found to be significantly associated with their adjustment.

Effect of cultural prejudices

3 The association between "the students' perceptions of how Americans rated the students' homelands and their adjust-

ment in the United States" was significant.

4 The students' success in college and their adjustment to the U.S. reached a highly significant level of association.

The implication is clear: a teacher should try to impart a sympathetic view of the target culture. One such attempt was reported by Choldin (20). She describes a cooperative program sponsored by the Chicago Board of Education and the University of Illinois Circle Campus where summer day houses have been set up to accommodate city children who volunteer for the program. Much of the value of this summer instruction is seen in the cultural enrichment it offers the children. A recent study conducted by Gardner & Taylor investigated the effect of message content and social pressure on attitude toward a member of a stereotyped group. One of the study's conclusions states that when a subject is provided with more information about the target person than mere group identification he will tend to make use of this information even though his stereotype about the ethnic group influences his ratings (36, p. 275). There is empirical encouragement, then, to hope that a person's attitude toward a member of another culture can be positively affected by providing the student with the right kind of information.

Providing students with correct information

The desirability of gaining easy access to a fund of cultural information collected through international cooperation is expounded by van Willigen (113). Several somewhat theoretical studies of difficulties obstructing international communication due to the noncorrespondence of linguistic forms from one language to another are developed from the viewpoint of the philosopher (Cohen, 22), the social scientist (van Loon, 112; Singer, 104), and the social psychologist (Szalay & Brent, 106).

Noncorrespondence of linguistic forms causes problems

By way of concluding this section, Decaigny (27) emphasizes the necessity of rethinking basic objectives of cultural study. He also stresses the desirability of employing a multimedia approach in the realization of cultural objectives. To prevent even a multimedia approach from becoming routine, the author says, it should be used experimentally.

Multimedia approaches

Measuring cultural achievement

The present state of affairs with culture tests is especially appalling. The endemic absence of behaviorally-stated culture objectives in written courses of study is symptomatic of an ignorance of the role of culture in foreign language classes. How does one know when an objective has been reached if it has not been stated in measurable terms? If the objectives of a program of study are to be inferred from the areas that are tested, then we must conclude that there is little sincere interest in teaching about culture in foreign language classrooms. Even if the purpose of testing is viewed solely as a device to enable teachers to evaluate how they themselves are doing with culture, the conclusion is inescapable that teachers do not know how they are doing. How can they know? The few tests of the target culture that do get administered largely contain items of fact whose authenticity is often suspect and whose relevancy to objectives of cross-cultural communication and understanding is usually tenuous. Some large projects charged with developing curricular materials in the area of a foreign culture have consciously avoided responsibility for test development because of the controversy over what to test and the lack of knowledge of how to test.

Lack of valid testing instruments

What to test

The abstract objectives of cross-cultural communication and understanding are too general to be of much utility in devising individual questions (items) for a test of culture. The writer has, on a former occasion (97, p. 32), suggested seven questions that the teacher could profitably ask himself in regard to tests of culture:

1 To what extent is the cultural pattern evident to a [member of the target culture]? (Does it represent an implicit or explicit pattern?)
2 To what social, sex, residential, and age groups would the pattern apply?
3 Are the limitations implied in the above two questions reflected in the way the item is worded?
4 [What documentation has the teacher required to back up the "right" answer?]
5 Is the answer to the question either too difficult or too facile for the intended testees?
6 What is the pedagogical justification for testing the item?
7 Can the item be recast to test a skill rather than a fact?

Questions to ask for the improvement of culture tests

The list can be extended to include other important considerations:

8 Exactly what kind of communication is to be tested?

9 What specific cultural referents are to be included in the test?

10 To what extent is understanding to be measured in terms of an abstract comprehension of major cultural themes and to what extent is it to be measured in terms of knowledge of how to function in the target culture?

11 What specific themes or "functional" situations are to be included in the test?

12 If test items from a number of different objectives are to be included in the same test, in what proportion is each to be represented?

13 Does each item measure just one cultural element?

14 Does test achievement indicate knowledge of the target culture or does achievement depend mostly on some extraneous skill such as language or reading ability, general intelligence, or imitating the opinions of the teacher?

15 Can the test be objectively evaluated?

16 Are *attitudes* that are conducive to cross-cultural understanding measured?

17 Will the items be stated in English or in the target language? (See No. 14 above.)

These questions are not meant, of course, to be either exhaustive or especially systematic, but are presented as examples of the type of question that can be asked by teachers interested in improving the content of their culture tests.

The designer of a cross-cultural test begins by defining his specific objectives. He then proceeds to elaborate on the various areas of culture that bear upon the stated objectives. This elaboration consists of mapping out the thematic character of the "universe" of relevant test items. Will the test objectives support items concerned with art and literature, for example? Will the items have to be tied directly to linguistic units? The most common items appearing on culture tests can be correctly answered by a superficial familiarity with geographical and historical facts. A few of these items have a certain practical value, since ignorance of elementary toponyms and history tends to provoke resentment in the target culture-bearer. (The writer asked the local telephone operator for assistance in calling Guatemala City, and she responded, "That's in Mexico, isn't it?"). However, most test items should probe more revealing areas of the culture.

One report (Seelye, 98) of a testing program designed to mea-

A universe of relevant test items

sure the biculturation of the American colony in Guatemala divides test items into two major categories: (1) items that are associated with the ability to function in a society, and (2) items that measure knowledge not significantly associated with functioning in the society. Falling into the latter category are items based on abstract patterns of which the native is not aware (implicit patterns), erudite academic knowledge, and patterns for which there is not wide concordance in the target culture (patterns peripheral to the core culture). In addition, ideal patterns of belief that, in reality, do not occur frequently (false patterns), and patterns that present a cultural anomaly in that they deviate from a major value of the culture (dysfunctional patterns), should probably be avoided unless they are clearly

Items of competence and of performance

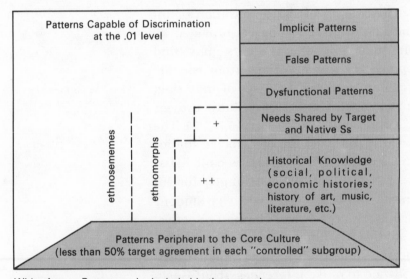

Patterns Capable of Discrimination at the .01 level

Implicit Patterns

False Patterns

Dysfunctional Patterns

Needs Shared by Target and Native Ss

Historical Knowledge (social, political, economic histories; history of art, music, literature, etc.)

ethnosememes

ethnomorphs

\+

\++

Patterns Peripheral to the Core Culture (less than 50% target agreement in each "controlled" subgroup)

White Area: Patterns to be included in the test universe.
Shaded Area: Patterns to be excluded from the test universe.

\+ products of cultural mislearning or other such factors leading native subjects (Ss) to expect a contrastive pattern where one does not exist.

\++ historical knowledge which fulfills two requisites: (1) general agreement among target Ss from native Ss. That is, knowledge which is part of the popular culture, as opposed to the shaded portion representing knowledge which is associated with the upper intellectual classes.

The test universe.

identified in the test as anomalous patterns. The ability to use the target cultural patterns to satisfy societal conventions can be measured through items based on the folklore (popular culture), and patterns in general that have been shown to differentiate empirically the cultural stranger and the target native (discrimination at the .01 level). The figure (taken from 98,

p. 38) suggests graphically what general areas should be excluded from the content of a test that attempts to measure the ability to function in a second culture.

Ultimately, of course, the answer to the question of what to test in the classroom is that the teacher tests what he professes to teach. Sometimes, to be sure, it is difficult to test directly an intangible such as "understanding" and one has to test something more specific that is but indirectly associated with the real objective of the test. Ideally, a wide range of cultural skills and knowledge would be the object of systematic testing in the foreign language classroom.

How to test

An instructive, succinct discussion of the preparation of instructional objectives—the key to good testing—is provided by Mager (67). An example that language teachers may find suggestive of the development of test questions from specific student-oriented objectives can be found in a set of materials developed by the Anthropological Curriculum Study Project under the direction of Malcolm Collier (ACSP, 2, p. 77–91). The multimedia materials concern the teaching of a social studies unit on prehistory, and the accompanying booklet is called *History as Culture Change: An Overview*. An example, for instance, can be taken from the unit that seeks to develop student ability to interpret evidence in the area of early human societies. The Bushman culture is studied via filmstrips, site maps, readings, etc. A number of specific student objectives are identified: "Use imagination and evidence to make inferences about Bushman way of life"; "Identify factual evidence to support an inference"; "Challenge others' inferences if evidence or reasoning suggests an alternative inference"; etc. For the last of the three mentioned objectives, several measurement techniques are suggested. "One way of assessing this objective is to keep a record during regular class of which students do challenge other's inferences." Another way to test the objective is by presenting the student with a question such as: "The Kalahari Bushmen eat only meat and other animal products. Can you tell by what evidence this is known?" The proper student reaction to this question would be to challenge the statement and give contrary evidence, e.g., nutshells (2, p. 82).

Another example, taken from the unit on "Culture as Adaptation to Complex Social Systems: Peasants," asks the student to study a sheet of dialogue typical of a peasant (examples from

Where to go for help in developing test items

Examples

India and Italy are given). The class is divided into thirds, and each is assigned a different situation. One student from each group is selected to play the role of peasant and another the role of outsider. "First they read given lines, then ad lib as long as they can, trying to say kinds of things (and in a manner) typical of part played." The student-oriented objective of this is: "Recognize two or more ways in which peasants usually adapt to outsiders and persons who control their lives and explain how they are adaptive: close-knit family, deference, shrewdness, caution, suspicion, humble appearance" (2, p. 52). The following test item (2, p. 90) is suggested for measuring achievement of the student objective:

Various test formats

Suppose a stranger entered a peasant village and told the first man he met that he was a new government official whose duty was to help the villagers find better ways to farm their land. Which of the following reactions would you expect from the peasant? (Choose three)

_____ Asking the stranger for his credentials

_____ Claiming that he already had the best farming methods in the village

__✔__ Showing a lot of respect for the stranger's authority

_____ Inviting the stranger home for dinner

__✔__ Caution in answering the official's questions

_____ Volunteering information about how lucky the village had been in its crops recently

__✔__ Appearing interested in the official's advice on farming

Other examples of different test formats can be found in Lado (60), Valette (111), and Seelye (97). These foreign language teachers seem to prefer objective, multiple-choice techniques. One example, given by the writer (96, p. 81), which was not successful because women tended to answer it differently than did men, is offered below:

A pretty young woman is waiting for a bus on a busy street corner [in Guatemala City]. A man comes up behind her and pinches her. She would:

a tolerate it, but only during carnival time

b call a policeman any time of the year

c laugh and feel proud

d pretend nothing had happened so people would not notice

(Guatemalan men answered d while women checked b.)

The problem of controlling the cultural boundaries of a pattern, as the above example illustrates, was dealt with in the same article. The following conclusions were drawn:

In developing a cross-cultural test which evaluates an American's knowledge of target cultural patterns by asking him to recognize patterns which target subjects generally identify as native, there is a need to pretest the questions with both target and American groups. Pretesting with target subjects avoids the pitfall of including patterns which masquerade as native when in reality they are not widely recognized as common behavior by the target natives. Pretesting Americans who are ignorant of the target culture assists in identifying questions which discriminate knowledge of the target patterns rather than general intelligence. Additional pretesting in countries within the same cultural family as the target culture facilitates identification of those questions which discriminate knowledge of the specific target (sub-) culture (Guatemala) from those which test recognition of a more universal culture (Latin America). While age and residence controls were forced upon us by circumstance, it was thought desirable to control for the variables of sex and social class. By controlling for these factors it was possible to select those questions which were answered alike by the target natives, regardless of sex or social class, thus minimizing the test biases (96, p. 85).

Need for pretesting items with natives of the target culture

A critique of the rationale contained in this article (96) was prepared by Upshur (110). Upshur questions the consistency with which the writer developed test items that were cross-culturally contrastive to the cultural patterns of the American student. The writer's rejoinder is available (98).

Whenever a test item goes much beyond the "What is the capital of France" level, methods of item validation become important. Besides the technique described in the preceding paragraph, which would be unwieldy to apply to the classroom, and the frequently abused technique of using the classroom authority of the teacher, the writer has suggested that the students pay particular attention to evaluating the authority of experts. A scoring system to grade the level of authority of a report is presented (97, p. 30) that takes into consideration such variables as source proximity, length of time spent in the target culture,

explicitness of the report, and familiarity with the language. *Using experts*
Unfortunately, the evaluative system suggested needs more development for it to be really practical.

It is especially difficult to test attitudes since we are not certain which attitudes are relevant to cultural understanding. Furthermore, sophisticated testing in this area is limited by the availability of sociological and psychological tests. Shaw & *Attitudinal scales*
Wright (102) have prepared a compendium of attitudinal scales, along with examples and evaluations of each. There are sections devoted to the nature of attitudes, methods of scale construction, social practices, social issues and problems, international issues, abstract concepts, political and religious attitudes, ethnic and national groups, and social institutions.

Finally, there are some excellent sources prepared by language teachers to assist the teacher in the technical aspects of test construction. A wonderfully succinct (37 pages) introduction to teacher-made tests is available free from the Educational Testing Service in Princeton (Diederich, 29). Lado's book (60, p. 275–298) on language testing contains two chapters of interest to readers of this section. Valette's testing manual (111, p. 163–167) also briefly mentions cultural testing.

An overview

Nostrand (78) began his excellent 1966 article by observing that "enlightened language teaching today shows gratifying progress in all its component parts except one: the teaching of the foreign cultural context." While the intervening years have seen the advent of a number of encouraging publications, the profession is still probably some years away from substantially changing Nostrand's sobering pronouncement.

The most widely accepted usage now regards culture as a broad concept that embraces all aspects of the life of man. Even a few articles concerned with teaching about the older concept of culture as the limited but praiseworthy production of creative artists, are recognizing to an increasing degree the importance of a knowledge of the patterns of everyday life as a prerequisite to appreciating the fine arts. There are even encouraging signs that augur an eventual harmony between teachers whose major interest is literary and those who are primarily concerned with the other aspects of culture (Marquardt, 70; Christian, 21; Damoiseau & Marc, 24; Campa, 14; Morain, 72; for example). In short, it is becoming increasingly apparent that the study of language cannot be divorced from the study of culture.

There is a need for specific cultural objectives in developing empathy toward people of different life styles. Too often, the cultural content is irrelevant to building a meaningful understanding of other peoples. For example, the writer visited a white, segregated suburb of Chicago where an able German teacher was discussing a critical historical period with his students: the causes and characteristics of Hitler's rise to power. At one point, students were shown some descriptors of educational and governmental objectives in Nazi Germany. In this presentation, some of the objectives were "indoctrination," "building nationalism," "acquiring more land," "discouragement of foreign travel," and "freeing Europe of Jews." Then, rather than have the students think of ready parallels in our own culture to all of these points, the teacher concluded by saying, "And these objectives are obviously the farthest thing imaginable from our own!" How much better it would have been for these students to have seen in their own lives the stirrings of the dark, destructive forces of Nazi Germany. Somehow, we must encourage students to identify with both the problems and successes of the target people.

Most language teachers have not had enough training to effectively teach cross-cultural communication and understanding. Culture should be considered more than spice added here and there in a class to keep up student interest. In fairness, however, it must be recognized that many teachers in an unorganized, intuitive way are able to inspire a sympathetic interest in a second culture through infectious enthusiasm often supported by firsthand anecdotes.

In this day and age there is no reason why practically all foreign language teachers who want to go abroad cannot do so. Recently, the writer visited two large FLES programs in neighboring towns. In one town only five of the 20 teachers had been in the target culture – the plea of poverty was the usual excuse – while in the other nearby town of the same socioeconomic character, *all* of the teachers had been abroad, usually for a year or more. Anyone who has taught two years should have found the time to spend at least a summer in the target culture. Even a very limited amount of time is much better than no time at all. Two excellent sources full of the particulars of study abroad (105) and teaching abroad (109) are published by UNESCO.

In talking with language teachers one often gets the disquieting impression that few know how the study of foreign languages fits into the total educational experience. Yet there are specific, realizable, and educationally sound objectives to which foreign language classes can meaningfully contribute. Many of these objectives are cultural in nature.

It is hoped that in the future the profession will have less to say about the need to teach culture, and more to say about ways to effectively teach and test it. While there will still be a place for general articles exhorting teachers to "teach culture," there needs to be a drastic increase in articles of more substantial content.

There is a growing literature that supports the reassuring premise that, by and large, language teachers teach what they set out to teach. Rather than fuss about the theoretical semantic differences of "society," "culture," and "civilization," the single most productive deployment of energies will be expended in defining specific cultural objectives in operational and measurable terms.

References, The cross-cultural context[1]

1 Adams, Henry E., ed. Handbook of Latin American studies: No. 29: social sciences. University of Florida Press, Gainesville, 1967.
2 Anthropological Curriculum Study Project (ACSP). History as culture change: an overview: teaching plan. Macmillan, New York, 1968.
3 Arnott, Peter. An introduction to the Greek world. Macmillan, London, 1967.
4 Barrutia, Richard. Overcoming cultural barriers. FORUM 6 (December 1967). Available from: ERIC Documentation Service, U.S. Office of Education, Washington, D.C. [ED 019 901]
5 Beaujour, Michel; Ehrmann, Jacques. A semiotic approach to culture. Foreign Language Annals, 1 (1967) 152–163.
6 Becker, Tamar. Patterns of attitudinal changes among foreign students. American Journal of Sociology, 73 (January 1968) 431–441.
7 Berelson, Bernard; Steiner, Gary A., eds. Human behavior: an inventory of scientific findings. Harcourt, Brace & World, New York, 1964.
8 Bibliography of paperback books translated from the German and of works on Germany. 2nd ed. Inter Nationes, Bonn, 1965.
9 Bishop, Dorothy Sword. Hablan los niños. The Spanish for Young Americans Series: Book 1. National Textbook Co., Skokie, Ill., 1968.
10 Brault, Gerald J. Kinesics and the classroom: some typical French gestures. The French Review, 36 (1963) 374–382.
*11 Brooks, Nelson. Language and language learning: theory and practice. Rev. ed. Harcourt, Brace & World, New York, 1964.
12 Brooks, Nelson. Teaching culture in the foreign language classroom. Foreign Language Annals, 1 (1968) 204–217.
*13 Burger, Henry G. Ethno-pedagogy: a manual in cultural sensitivity, with techniques for improv-

1 The entries preceded by an asterisk (*) are especially recommended to the classroom teacher of foreign languages.

ing cross-cultural teaching by fitting ethnic patterns. Southwestern Educational Laboratory, Albuquerque, N.M., 1968. Available only from ERIC Documentation Service, U.S. Office of Education, Washington, D. C. [SP 001 971]

*14 Campa, Arthur L. Teaching Hispanic culture through folklore. ERIC Focus Report No. 2. MLA/ACTFL Materials Center, New York, 1968.

15 Canfield, C. Lincoln. Spanish with a flourish! American Association of Teachers of Spanish and Portuguese (AATSP) Cultural Unit I, 1968. Consult issue of Hispania for nearest ordering point.

16 Carroll, John B. Foreign language proficiency levels attained by language majors near graduation from college. Foreign Language Annals, 1 (1967) 131–150.

17 Carroll, John B., ed. Language, thought, and reality: selected writings of Benjamin Lee Whorf. Massachusetts Institute of Technology Press, Cambridge, 1956.

18 Chamberlain, Jane S. Source materials for teachers of foreign languages. National Education Association, Department of Foreign Languages, Washington, D.C., 1968.

19 Chao, Yuen Ren. Language and symbolic systems. Cambridge University Press, New York, 1968.

20 Choldin, Hannah W. Foreign language day houses. The Modern Language Journal, 52 (1968) 88–89.

*21 Christian, Chester C. Literary representation and sociological analysis: social class in Latin America. Dissertation Abstracts, 28 (1967) 2239A (Texas).

22 Cohen, Maurice. Reflections on the role of philosophy in studying other cultures. Culture, 29 (September 1968) 240–251.

23 Crook, John. Julius Caesar and Rome. English University Press, London, 1968.

*24 Damoiseau, R.; Marc, E. La chanson moderne: étude de civilisation et de langue. Le Français dans le Monde, 47 (1967) 40–44.

25 Debyser, Francis. Le rapport langue-civilisation et l'enseignement de la civilisation aux débutants. Le Français dans le Monde, 48 (1967) 21–24 [Part 1]; 49 (1967) 16–21 [Part 2].

26 Debyser, Francis. The relation of language to culture and the teaching of culture to beginning language students. Language Quarterly, 6:i,ii. Chilton Books, Philadelphia, Pa., 1968.

27 Decaigny, T. L'approche des cultures etrangeres dan les cours de langues vivantes. Revue des Langues Vivantes, 34:iii (1968) 277–293.

28 Dewey, John. My pedagogic creed. The School Journal 54 (1897) 77–80. Reprinted in: Gezi, Kalil I.; Myers, James E., eds. Teaching in American culture. Holt, New York, 1968, p. 408–411.

29 Diederich, Paul B. Short-cut statistics for teacher-made tests. 2nd ed. Educational Testing Service, Princeton, N.J., 1964.

30 Donoghue, Mildred R. Foreign languages and the elementary school child. Brown Company, Dubuque, Ia., 1968.

31 Esteves, O. P. A problem-finding approach to the teaching of social studies. In: Seelye, H. Ned, ed. A handbook on Latin America for teachers: methodology and annotated bibliography. Office of Public Instruction, Springfield, Ill., 1968, p. 3–5.

32 Fishman, Joshua A. Italian language maintenance efforts in the United States and the teacher of Italian in American high schools and colleges. Florida Foreign Language Reporter, 4 (Spring 1966). Available from: ERIC Documentation Service, U.S. Office of Education, Washington, D.C. [ED 014 928]

33 Fishman, Joshua A., ed. Readings in the sociology of language. Mouton, The Hague, 1968.

34 Freeman, Stephen A. Let us build bridges. The Modern Language Journal, 52 (1968) 261–268.

35 Gaarder, A. Bruce. Statement. . . . Before the Special Subcommittee on Bilingual Education of the Committee on Labor and Public Welfare, United States Senate, Thursday, May 18, 1967 . . . TESOL Newsletter, 2:i,ii (January, March 1968) 21–22, 28.

36 Gardner, Robert C.; Taylor, Donald M. Ethnic stereotypes: their effects on person perception. Canadian Journal of Psychology, 22:iv (1968) 267–276.

37 Gezi, Kalil I. Factors associated with student adjustment in cross-cultural contact. California Journal of Educational Research, 16 (May, 1965) 129–136. Also in: Gezi, Kalil I.; Myers, James E., eds. Teaching in American culture. Holt, New York, 1968, p. 254–261.

38 Gill, Clark C.; Conroy, William B., eds. The social scientists look at Latin America: six position papers. Latin American Curriculum Project, Bulletin 3. University of Texas, Austin, 1967. Available from: ERIC Documentation Service, U.S. Office of Education, Washington, D.C. [ED 012 365]

39 Gill, Clark C; Conroy, William B., eds. Teaching about Latin America in social studies instructional materials. Latin American Curriculum Project, Bulletin 1. University of Texas, Austin, 1967. Available from: ERIC Documentation Service, U.S. Office of Education, Washington, D.C. [ED 012 832]

40 Gill, Clark C.; Conroy, William B., eds. Teaching about Latin America in the secondary school: an annotated guide to instructional resources. Latin American Curriculum Project, Bulletin 2. University of Texas, Austin, 1967. Available from: ERIC Documentation Service, U.S. Office of Education, Washington, D.C. [ED 012 833]

41 Gill, Clark C.; Conroy, William B., eds. The treatment of Latin America in social studies instructional materials. Latin American Curriculum Project Bulletin 5. University of Texas, Austin, 1968.

42 Gill, Clark C.; Conroy, William B.; Cornbleth, Catherine. Key ideas about Latin America. Latin American Curriculum Project Bulletin 4. University of Texas, Austin, 1967.

43 Gomez, Samuel. The teaching of other cultures. In: Roucek, Joseph S., ed. The study of foreign languages. Philosophical Library, New York, 1968, p. 293–309.

44 Green, Jerald R. A gesture inventory for the teaching of Spanish. Chilton Books, Philadelphia, Pa., 1968.

45 Greenberg, Joseph H., ed. Universals of language. 2nd ed. Massachusetts Institute of Technology Press, Cambridge, 1966.

46 Gumperz, John J.; Hymes, Dell, eds. The ethnography of communication. Special Publication of American Anthropologist, 66:vi, part 2, December 1964.

47 Hall, Edward T. The hidden dimension. Doubleday, New York, 1966.

48 Hall, Edward T. The silent language. Doubleday, New York, 1959. Fawcett World, 1961 [Paperback].

49 Hammel, E. A., ed. Formal semantic analysis. Special publication of American Anthropologist, 67:v (October 1965) Part 2.

50 Hoijer, Harry, ed. Language in culture: conference on the interrelations of language and other aspects of culture. University of Chicago Press, 1954.

51 Howe, Harold, II. Cowboys, Indians, and American education. TESOL Newsletter, 2:iii (May 1968) 3–6.

52 Hucker, Charles O. China, a critical bibliography. University of Arizona Press, Tucson, 1962.

53 Hymes, Dell, ed. Language in culture: a reader in linguistics and anthropology. Harper and Row, New York, 1964.

54 Ilbek, Jacques. A case of semantic interference. The French Review, 41 (1967) 368–376.

55 Imhoof, Maurice. Controlling cultural variations in the preparation of TESOL materials. TESOL Quarterly, 2 (1968) 39–42.

56 Jay, Charles. Study of culture: relevance of foreign languages in world affairs education. In: Castle, Pat; Jay, Charles, eds. Toward excellence in foreign language education. Office of Public Instruction, Springfield, Ill., 1968, p. 84–92.

57 Jones, J. Allen. English language teaching in a social/cultural dialect situation:(1). English Language Teaching (London), 22:iii (1968) 199–205.

58 Khanbikov, Ia. I. Folk pedagogy. Soviet Education, 9:i (1967) 32–41.

59 Kroeber, Alfred L.; Kluckhohn, Clyde, eds. Culture: a critical review of concepts and definitions. Random House, New York, 1954.

60 Lado, Robert. Language testing: the construction and use of foreign language tests. McGraw-Hill, New York, 1961.

61 Lado, Robert. Linguistics across cultures: applied linguistics for language teachers. University of Michigan Press, Ann Arbor, 1957.

62 Ladu, Tora T. Draft of new guidelines for foreign language teachers. Presented for discussion at State Conference of Foreign Language Teachers, Department of Public Instruction, Raleigh, N.C., December 1967.

*63 Ladu, Tora T.; et al. Teaching for cross-cultural understanding. Department of Public Instruction, Raleigh, N.C., 1968.

64 Landar, Herbert. Language and culture. Oxford University Press, New York, 1966.

65 Lawton, Denis. Social class, language and education. Schocken Books, New York, 1968.

*66 Lewald, H. Ernest. A tentative outline in the knowledge, understanding, and teaching of cultures pertaining to the target language. The Modern Language Journal, 52 (May 1968) 301–9.

67 Mager, Robert F. Preparing instructional objectives. Fearon Publishers, Palo Alto, Calif., 1962.

68 Mandelbaum, David G., ed. Edward Sapir: culture, language and personality, selected essays. University of California Press, Berkeley, 1962.

69 Manners, Robert A.; Kaplan, David, eds. Theory in anthropology: a sourcebook. Aldine Publishing Co., Chicago, 1968.

70 Marquardt, William F. Literature and cross-culture communication in the course in English for international students. The Florida FL Reporter, 5:ii (1967) 9–10.

71 Mathiot, Madeleine. An approach to the study of language-and-culture relations. Dissertation Abstracts, 27 (1967) 3765B, Catholic University of America, Washington, D.C.

72 Morain, Genelle Grant. French folklore: a fresh approach to the teaching of culture. The French Review, 41 (April 1968) 675–681.

73 Mueller, Klaus A.; Wiersma, William. The effects of language laboratory type upon cultural orientation scores of foreign language students. The Modern Language Journal, 51 (1967) 258–263.

74 Murdock, George P.; et al. Outline of cultural materials. Human Relations Area Files, Inc., New Haven, Conn., 1950. [Rev. ed., 1964]

75 Niyekawa-Howard, Agnes. A psycholinguistic study of the Whorfian hypothesis based on the Japanese passive. Educational Research and Development Center, University of Hawaii, Honolulu, 1968.

76 Nostrand, Howard L. Audiovisual materials for teaching the social and cultural context of a modern foreign language: their bearing upon pre-service education. The Department of Foreign Languages (DFL) Bulletin, National Education Association, 5:iii (May 1966) 4–6.

*77 Nostrand, Howard L. Background data for the teaching of French: final report of project OE-6-14-005. Part A: La culture et la société françaises au XXe siècle, 2 vols.; Part B: Exemples littéraires; Part C: Contemporary culture and society of the United States. Department of Romance Languages and Literature, University of Washington, Seattle, 1967.

*78 Nostrand, Howard L. Describing and teaching the sociocultural context of a foreign language and literature. In: Valdman, Albert, ed. Trends in language teaching, McGraw-Hill, New York, 1966, p. 1–25.

79 Nostrand, Howard L. Levels of sociocultural understanding for language classes. In: Seelye, H. Ned, ed. A handbook on Latin America for teachers: methodology and annotated bibliography. Office of Public Instruction, Springfield, Ill., 1968, p. 19–24.

80 Nostrand, Howard L. Literature in the describing of a literate culture. The French Review, 37 (December 1963) 145–157.

81 Nostrand, Howard L.; Foster, David William;

Christensen, Clay Benjamin. Research on language teaching: an annotated international bibliography, 1945–64. 2nd rev. ed. University of Washington Press, Seattle, 1965.

82 Opler, Morris E. The themal approach in cultural anthropology and its application to North Indian data. Southwestern Journal of Anthropology, 24: iii (1968) 215–227.

83 Oppenheimer, Max, Jr. Do languages seek their own level of abstraction? The Educational Forum, 32:iv (1967) 478–490.

84 Parker, John R.; Smith, Clifford Neal; Whithed, Marshall H. Political simulation: an introduction. In: Seelye, H. Ned, ed. A handbook on Latin America for teachers: methodology and annotated bibliography. Office of Public Instruction, Springfield, Ill., 1968, p. 25–28.

85 Pemberton, John E. How to find out about France: a guide to sources of information. Pergamon Press, Oxford, 1966.

86 Pietrzyk, Alfred; et al. 1960–67 selected bibliography of Arabic. "10. Language and Culture," p. 46–50. Center of Applied Linguistics, Washington, D.C., 1968.

87 Povey, John F. Literature in TESL programs: the language and the culture. TESOL Quarterly, 1:ii (1967) 40–46.

88 Renard, Colette; Heinle, Charles H. Implementing "Voix et Images de France" in American schools and colleges. Part 1. Chilton Books, Philadelphia, Pa., 1968. [Preliminary ed.]

89 Romney, A. Kimball; D'Andrade, Roy Goodwin, eds. Transcultural studies in cognition. Special publication of American Anthropologist, 66:iii (June 1964) Part 2.

90 Sapir, Edward. Language: an introduction to the study of speech. Harcourt, Brace & World, New York, 1921.

91 Savaiano, Geraldine; Archundia, Luz María. The folk arts of Mexico. American Association of Teachers of Spanish and Portuguese (AATSP) Cultural Unit III, 1968. [Consult issue of Hispania for nearest ordering point.]

92 Savaiano, Geraldine; Archundia, Luz María. The life cycle in Mexico. American Association of Teachers of Spanish and Portuguese (AATSP) Cultural Unit II, 1968. [Consult issue of Hispania for nearest ordering point.]

93 Sayers, Raymond S., ed. Portugal and Brazil in transition. University of Minnesota Press, Minneapolis, 1968.

94 Scott, Andrew M.; Lucas, William A.; Lucas, Trudi M. Simulation and national development. Wiley, New York, 1966.

95 Seelye, H. Ned. Culture in the foreign language classroom. Illinois Journal of Education, 59:iii (March 1968) 22–26. Available from: ERIC Documentation Service, U.S. Office of Education, Washington, D.C. [FL 000 947]

96 Seelye, H. Ned. Field notes on cross-cultural testing. Language Learning, 16:i,ii (1966) 77–85.

97 Seelye, H. Ned. Item validation and measurement techniques in culture tests. In: Seelye, H. Ned, ed. A handbook on Latin America for teachers: methodology and annotated bibliography. Office of Public Instruction, Springfield, Ill.,
1968, p. 6–14.

98 Seelye, H. Ned. Measuring the ability to function cross-culturally. In: Seelye, H. Ned, ed. A handbook on Latin America for teachers: methodology and annotated bibliography. Office of Public Instruction, Springfield, Ill., 1968, p. 34–43.

99 Seelye, H. Ned. Pertinency in Latin American studies. In: Seelye, H. Ned, ed. A handbook on Latin America for teachers: methodology and annotated bibliography. Office of Public Instruction, Springfield, Ill., 1968, p. 6–14.

100 Seelye, H. Ned. The Spanish passive: a study in the relation between linguistic form and worldview. Hispania, 49:ii (May, 1966) 290–292.

* 101 Seelye, H. Ned, ed. A handbook on Latin America for teachers: methodology and annotated bibliography. Office of Public Instruction, Springfield, Ill., 1968.

102 Shaw, Marvin E.; Wright, Jack M. Scales for the measurement of attitudes. McGraw-Hill, New York, 1967.

103 Silberman, Bernard S. Japan and Korea: a critical bibliography. University of Arizona Press, Tucson, 1962.

104 Singer, Milton. On understanding other cultures and one's own. The Journal of General Education, 19 (1967) 1–23.

105 Study Abroad, 17th Edition, 1968–70. The UNESCO Publications Center, New York, 1968.

106 Szalay, Lorand B.; Brent, Jack E. The analysis of cultural meanings through free verbal associations. The Journal of Social Psychology, 72 (1967) 161–187.

107 Taylor, Archer. Folklore and the student of literature. In: Dundes, Alan, ed. The study of folklore. Prentice-Hall, New York, 1965.

108 Taylor, H. Darrel; Sorenson, John L. Culture capsules. The Modern Language Journal, 45 (December 1961) 350–354. Reprinted in: Seelye, H. Ned, ed. A handbook on Latin America for teachers: methodology and annotated bibliography. Office of Public Instruction, Springfield, Ill., 1968, p. 15–18.

109 Teachers Abroad. The UNESCO Publications Center, New York, 1966.

110 Upshur, John A. Cross-cultural testing: what to test. Language Learning, 16:iii, iv (1966) 183–196.

111 Valette, Rebecca M. Modern language testing: a handbook. Harcourt, Brace & World, New York, 1967.

112 van Loon, J. F. Glastra. Language and the epistemological foundations of the social sciences. Report of the Fifteenth Annual (First International) Round Table Meeting on Linguistics and Language Studies. In: Stuart, C. I. J. M., ed. Monograph series in languages and linguistics, No. 17. Georgetown University Press, Washington, D.C., 1964, p. 171–185.

113 van Willigen, Daam M. International cooperation in foreign language teaching. Contact, 9 (December 1966) 18–27. Available from: ERIC Documentation Service, U.S. Office of Education, Washington, D.C. [FL 000 529]

114 White, Leslie A. On the concept of culture. In: Manners, Robert A.; Kaplan, David, eds. Theory in

anthropology. Aldine Publishing Co., Chicago, 1968, p. 15–20.

115 Witucki, Jeannette Renner. Personal references and personal security: an experiment in language and culture research. Dissertation Abstracts, 27 (1966) 1707B, University of California, Los Angeles.

116 Yousef, Fathi S. Cross-cultural testing: an aspect of the resistance reaction. Language Learning, 18:iii, iv (December 1968) 227–234.

117 Zaidi, S. M. Hafeez. Students' attitude toward living with different ethnic groups. The Journal of Social Psychology, 72 (1967) 99–106.

4

Teaching foreign literature

Is literature relevant?

Walter F. W. Lohnes
Stanford University

This question is raised in a brief but significant article by Shoben, entitled "Texts and Values: The Irrelevance of Literary Education" (18). Shoben prefaces his article with the following quotation: "Literature must be taught as a part of liberal education, not as a series of exercises in literary scholarship," and his arguments center around the two poles of this quotation: liberal education and literary scholarship. His thrust is not directed against literary scholarship as such, that is, against scholarly disciplines that are the domain of specialists in their respective fields, but rather against the use (or misuse) of the methods of literary scholarship in the literary education of nonspecialists.

Literature is hard to define as a discipline. Shoben, in fact, asks, "In what sense *is* literature a discipline?" and goes on to say,

> One can certainly identify literary history as meeting the criteria, and linguistics and philology just as surely fall within the class. The sociology of literature, or the explication of literary works as revelatory of the *Zeitgeist* of a period, probably lies within the definition, and at least certain types of literary criticism and formal analysis, like those of I. A. Richards or R. P. Blackmur, conceivably are admissible. While one is entitled to doubts about psychobiographical approaches to literary study, it is not necessary here to argue the point. The central issue for the present is whether *literature* can be meaningfully conceived as a discipline. Where, without the invocation of history, linguistics, sociology, can one specify the coherent body of knowledge and the distinctive methods of inquiry that define the *literary* (in contrast to the historical, linguistic, sociological) discipline? To suspect that there are none is not at all to denigrate the role of literary history, the study of language, the sociology of literature, of formal aesthetics in either culture or education. One can assume a highly positive posture toward these enterprises and still be concerned about their distance from the fundamental literary experience and its humanizing values.

Is literary study a discipline?

Shoben then speaks of the two basically different ways in which we acquire knowledge: "One is through controlled observation of the world around us," as most highly developed in the sciences.

The other mode of knowing lies less through controlled observation than through participation. In our most intimate experience, including our relationships with others, we discover the meaning of fear, the qualities of desire, and the value of friendship by entering directly into life's impingements on people. By identifying with others, we enlarge our knowledge of ourselves as human beings; by reflecting on the various degrees of our identifications, we learn something about what we individually are—highly socialized isolates, intensely dependent on our interpersonal environment and inextricably involved with it, yet unique and alone as unduplicable personalities. This route is the route to self-knowledge and to that continuously criticized and revised body of value commitments which define a large and significant segment of the examined life.

Literature: a way of knowing

It is this latter mode of knowledge that literary education must provide. "In the opportunities for vicarious but authentic participatory experience that literature offers and in the reflections on its meaning that the imaginatively conceived classroom provides, a special and crucial educational function is served." Shoben, presumably, has the college English curriculum in mind, but his case can be made just as easily for the teaching of English literature in secondary schools and, above all, for the teaching of foreign language (FL) literatures. Thus, the 1967 Northeast Conference Report (15, section 4.2.2.) strikes a very similar note:

The student must make an effort, with whatever encouragement the teacher can provide, to recharge the words with human, not merely lexical, meaning. He must go beyond what the text means as words to what it represents. The only way to have this happen is for the student and the teacher to appeal to their own experience. We realize that one's own experience is not only a help but a limitation; what any person can bring to a work is not what one a few years older or younger will bring to it. That is not the point; what matters is that the student have a "direct and personal confrontation" with the work. Some sense of the analogies between what is said in it

Recharging words with human meaning

and what one knows at first hand must be awakened and cultivated even if, at a later moment, one is led to distinguish one's own experience from that of the author. And so interpretation requires two *phases*: one lexical or linguistic, the other experiential; language habits, grammar books, and dictionaries help us in the first, but our own history, knowledge, and values must provide the basis for the second.

Again, in section 4.3.2., the authors of the same report state: "When we speak of 'experiencing the work,' we must distinguish between two extreme possibilities: an immediate reaction or response on the one hand, and something much deeper and more pervasive on the other. In the former case, we become acquainted with the work; in the latter, we connect it in a vital way with our being; we assimilate it." The question is, do we practice such principles in our literature courses? Shoben (18) has his doubts: "In many, if not most American college classrooms, these requirements are by-passed in favor of enterprises that conform more closely to the canons of technical scholarship," and he sees a major difficulty in "the gulf that lies between professional literary scholarship and the direct literary experience."

Technical scholarship or literary experience?

Obviously, these are not arguments against the legitimacy of technical scholarship. As disciplines, the history of literature, literary criticism, linguistics, etc., are part of a student's professional training and thus properly belong to the realm of graduate study.

All of these approaches to literature, however, when they dominate the teaching-learning scene for undergraduates, tend to minimize participation and to maximize the kinds of knowledge to be gained by controlled observation. To the extent that this statement is accurate, it suggests that humanistic scholarship has grown less humanizing as it has become more scholarly, that the interests of faculty members and the interests of students in literary documents are likely to be so different as to imperil educative communication, and that an intrusive devotion to literary research can inhibit students from discovering the humane relevance of literature for their own development (Shoben, 18).

We inhibit students

Relevance, in these days of campus unrest, has become a catchword, eagerly espoused by some, and violently rejected by others. Yet, clearly, at any given time some works of literature are more relevant than others, especially "in an age whose *Leitmotif* is technologized science." ". . . The power of various works to promote the examined life and to evoke more searching habits of reflection may vary markedly with time and audiences. In this sense, it is highly probable that the *Faerie Queene* can no longer speak provocatively to sophomores, that Scott's novels and narrative poems must be read in early adolescence or not at all, and that Milton is less capable of launching undergraduates on a spiritual quest than are Paul Tillich, C. S. Lewis, or Harvey Cox" — and we might add, Camus and Brecht seem more relevant to young students of French or German than Molière and Lessing.

Relevance

It is ill considered and unrealistic to expect "close readings" by students of material which is seldom read except in the most professional of contexts by their professors and which retains its place in the course of study simply because it has always been there. If the aim of literary education is to excite and give form to the "passion to win experience of the world and of human vice and worth," then the time is overdue for a winnowing and reconstituting of the curriculum in the light of that objective (Shoben, 18).

Shoben considers the possibility that the way the academy presents literature may be one of the reasons for the "decline over the past decade, especially among men, in the proportion of undergraduates either majoring or widely electing work in such fields as English and comparative literature."

Clearly, then, the reconstitution of the curriculum of which Shoben speaks must consider breaking away from established ways in order to reach young people for whom all the excitement today lies in the sciences, in mathematics and physics, in computer science, and in space medicine. It makes no sense for us to close our ears to what these young people are saying: the frontiers of today's knowledge do not lie in the interpretation of a Baudelaire poem or in Shakespearean scholarship or in an Old High German glossary. They are both right and wrong, of course, but we must listen to them carefully if we want to convince them that Western civilization did, indeed, begin before 1945. We must understand that to a high school senior or a college sophomore the contemporary German scene looks much more familiar than French society during the Ancien Régime or Shakespeare's England. If we do, we will later be able to convince these students of the "relevance" of Büchner's *Woyzeck* or Grimmelshausen's *Simplizissimus*.

Reconstitution of the curriculum

The discontinuation of the language requirement in many of the nation's colleges and universities is a clear signal to remind us that, at least for a while, we have to go it alone and that we have to prove our worth through the quality of our offerings. We may not be able to increase the number of undergraduate majors in English or the foreign languages during the next decade, but we may serve the cause of liberal education by teaching, through literature, something about the human condition, which is always relevant in any age. Liberal education, understood in this sense, may even help to keep our age of technologized science from being dehumanized.

Quality teaching may improve the cause of liberal education

What is literature?

If the teaching of literature is indeed relevant, then the question of what *is* literature is legitimate and crucial to the success of literary education. In the opening statement of the Latin section in the College Board's *Advanced Placement Course Descriptions 1968-70* (1), the examining committee states, "As in all courses in Latin beyond the elementary level, the basic objective is progress in the ability to read, understand and interpret Latin literature in the original language." The committee uses the term Latin *literature*, even though the course descriptions list not only courses in Vergil, Comedy, and Lyric, but under the heading Prose require either Cicero's *Tusculan Disputations*, *De Senectute*, and *Somnium Scipionis* or Livy, Book I and Book XXI; in other words, works that in the parlance of modern literatures would be considered nonliterary, expository prose. In addition, the committee assumes "some acquaintance with Roman social, political, and literary history." The committee thus takes cognizance of the general position of its discipline: "Both traditionally and in current practice, classical literature has included not only poetry and the drama but also history, oratory, the essay (in the form of letters), and some philosophy, especially Plato. In fact, classical literature as a literature and an influence on modern Western literature would be sorely impoverished were we to omit the 'non-imaginative' genres from its canon" (Northeast Conference Report 1967, 15).

The Latin perception of literature

Thus, the Latin committee takes a stand quite different from the modern language committees of the Advanced Placement Program. The French reading list ranges from selected poems by Villon to Camus's *L'Etranger*, though it does include selected *Pensées* by Pascal and Rousseau's *Discours sur les sciences et*

The French and Spanish

les arts. The German committee requires only literature "im engeren Sinne," from Goethe to Kafka, and its second list of suggested further readings, from Lessing to Aichinger and Grass, also contains solely *belles lettres*. The Spanish examiners, finally, provide a list of 19th and 20th century authors, ranging from Alarcón to Unamuno, but also "strongly recommend the reading of works by authors of other periods, particularly the Golden Age."

The problem that becomes apparent from this brief overview is not new. The discussion of what should properly be considered as "literature" has been going on for decades. The Germans have been speaking of "Literatur im engeren Sinne" and "Literatur im weiteren Sinne," which latter includes a wide range of *The German perception* writings, but by no means everything that has ever been written in German. German departments in the United States, however, have always tended to look at literature in a very narrow and restricted sense. Classics departments, on the other hand, do not seem to feel restricted by such considerations; they range far afield and include the essay, historical and biographical writing, and philosophy, as do, as a matter of fact, the departments of older German and English literature (or philology, as they used to be called until medieval literature came into its own *qua* literature).

An additional area that has to be considered, especially in the teaching of foreign literatures, is what has in recent years been subsumed under the general heading of "culture." Spanish and French departments have generally been more aware of the necessity of "teaching the foreign culture" than have their German counterparts. But are cultural readings part of the foreign *Culture vs. literature* literature? If they are not, is then literature not part of the foreign culture? The crux of the matter is the definition of that often vague and nebulous term "culture" which is all too frequently used as an excuse for the mediocre teaching of insignificant facts. On the other hand, nobody could possibly quarrel with the inclusion, in the curriculum of a department of German language and literature, of an undergraduate major in German *Geistesgeschichte*, which "introduces the student to the continuum of German intellectual and cultural history, and its relationship to the intellectual life of the other nations of Europe from the 18th century to the present," and in which "emphasis is given to authors whose ideas have had a significant influence on shaping the thinking of our modern world," such as Sigmund

Freud and C. G. Jung (Stanford University Bulletin, Courses and Degrees 1969/70).

Position of the Northeast Conference

The 1967 Northeast Conference Report on Literature is one of a long series of reports on the subject, which goes back to the first Report in 1954. The Conference has shown its concern with the teaching of literature in ten previous Reports of the Working Committees:

1954: "The Teaching of Literature"
1955 and 1956: "The Role of Literature in Language Teaching"
1957: "Materials and Methods for Teaching Literature in Secondary School in Preparation for Admission to College with Advanced Standing"
1958: "The Ghosts in the Language Classroom"
1959: "A Provisional Program to Implement the Report of Committee I: A Six-Year Sequence from Grade Nine through the Second Year of College"
1963: "Reading for Meaning"
1964: "Foreign Languages in the Secondary School"
"Foreign Languages in Colleges and Universities"
1965: "From School to College: The Problem of Continuity"
1966: "Wider Uses for Foreign Languages"

Northeast Conference Reports on Literature

Naturally, not all these reports deal with the topic at length, since, as the titles of some indicate, their main concern goes beyond the teaching of literature. But in one way or another, they all deal with the subject from varied perspectives (15).

The 1967 Report differs from the earlier ones in that about half of it "is theoretical, sometimes very abstract, and not subject to practical application." This theoretical part of the Report, however, provides much food for thought on the subject of literary education, and deserves to be used as the basis for further inquiry that will eventually lead to practical application. Quite naturally, it also deals with the problem of defining literature (sections 1.3 and 2).

"A consideration of the process of defining what is meant by the term 'literature' is essential not only to the development of our Report, but even more so to the further development of a professional consensus that will do away with the confusion that still exists in many quarters with regard to the essential objectives and means of FL instruction."

The authors of the 1967 Report take exception to several statements made in earlier reports, most notably to the 1954 and 1955 committees' warning "against the limited conception of literature as *belles lettres*." "We believe," the 1967 committee states, "that by definition true literary values are found only in *belles lettres*." The authors cite the authority of Wellek & Warren in their book, *Theory of Literature* (20), to back up their point:

They (Wellek and Warren) begin by rejecting the broad definition of literature as practically everything in print, on the grounds that "the identification of literature with the history of civilization is a denial of the specific field and the specific methods of literary study." They also reject the concept of literature as a collection of "great books," which, regardless of subject matter, are to be singled out on account of their esthetic worth. In other words, an esthetic criterion is not sufficient. "The term 'literature' seems best if we limit it to the art of literature, that is, to imaginative literature." It is the work of imagination, infused with a dominant esthetic intent which *Wellek & Warren* constitutes a literary work of art. This conception of literature is descriptive, not evaluative, since the authors believe that "classification . . . should be distinguished from evaluation."

The report, however, takes exception to Wellek & Warren's limitation, "imaginative," stressing the fact that the traditional definition of classical literature goes beyond "imaginative." "These same considerations apply to Hebrew and Chinese literature. We believe it would be equally unwise to exclude the essay from consideration in *modern* literature. We do not feel that this broader definition goes counter to Horace's ideal of *dulce* and *utile*; rather, it is to a large extent the source of his ideal."

If teachers of foreign languages and literatures will accept insights concerning the function and nature of literature which distinguish literature from other types of language effectively used and if we will accept valid and independent objectives of FL instruction, we shall be able to do justice both to language learning and to the study of literature. Once we have accepted these distinctions, it will be possible for us to adopt policy decisions and take practical steps that will enable us to teach language efficiently and effectively and to undertake the study of literature without betraying its true nature and without debasing the literary experience (15).

Three German points of view

The first two of the articles reviewed in this section (8,19) deal with the teaching of German literature in German schools; the third with the teaching of literature in foreign language classes (16).

Hegele (8) reiterates a number of points made above. "It seems to be a matter of course that literature is to be an essential part of German instruction [in German schools]. But what belongs to this literature and what doesn't?"[1] A discussion of the term "literature" seems all the more essential, "since the theory of literature does not belong to those disciplines that are characterized by an exceptionally clear terminology." Hegele eliminates the definition of literature as "the totality of all written documents," but, he asks, where is the dividing line between "Literatur im weiteren Sinn" and "Literatur im engeren Sinn"? *No consensus* Unfortunately, not even scholars like Käte Hamburger and Roman Ingarden have given satisfactory answers to the question, since the logic of their theories fits dime novels (*Groschenromane*) and puberty poems as well as Thomas Mann's novels and Goethe's lyrics. "On the other hand, there are prose texts, especially in the areas of rhetorics and the essay, which cannot be defined with the categories of imaginative (*fiktionale*) literature, but which, nevertheless, have a higher degree of esthetic qualification than many works of fiction." Thus, not only *Dichtungslogik*, but *Dichtungswertung* (evaluation) determine which writings can be considered to be "literature." The trouble is that there are many different *Literaturauffassungen*, all subjectively valid, but in competition with one another. As far as literary education in the schools is concerned, there is an additional complication because of didactic considerations.

Hegele criticizes, on the one hand, those who consider literary education solely as *Lebenshilfe*, as an aid to living. The formula "Dichtung als Lebenshilfe" has been used for extraliterary motives, therapeutically, as it were, to achieve moral, pseudoreligious, and culture-critical goals. He rejects, on the other hand, those who, following Wolfgang Kayser's *Die Wahrheit der Dichter*, regard only those works as "real" literature that do not have any didactic intentions whatsoever and that lead the reader out of reality instead of into it. Hegele calls for a middle position: "What we need is a concept of literature which is broad

1 All translations from the German in this section are the chapter editor's.

enough to include all kinds and forms of literary texts, but which, on the other hand, is also narrow enough to permit only esthetically qualified texts from the vast mass of written documents." This concept must not be didactically prescriptive and one-sided, but should show the student that literature is a wide field, in which many different and even opposing literary forms have a right to coexist.

Ulshöfer, in an article on "Language and Literature in the Age of Technology" (19), adds another dimension to the discussion. The article contains a number of references to other writings on the topic, as well as a fairly long list of literary works dealing with the problems of modern technology. He lists novels, essays, biographies, dramas, and lyric poetry, in that order. The authors listed range from Döblin to Brecht to Enzensberger and the poets of the German Democratic Republic; all the works listed "are useful as an introduction to the problems of our time."

An age of technology demands a new point of view and a new type of teacher

Ulshöfer pleads for greater use of texts dealing with modern industrial society, but warns against the teaching of nonliterary subject matter by nonspecialists, that is, by German teachers. "The teacher must not be primarily oriented toward the [nonliterary] subject matter, nor should he choose literary works because of their current relevance [*Aktualität*], but rather because of their high literary value and linguistic teaching potential." Ulshöfer cites a number of reasons for the necessity of discussing the subject of "Technology and Industrial Society" in literature classes:

(1) Germany is no longer "das Volk der Dichter und Denker," but rather a country with a highly developed industry and a highly differentiated social order. (2) The language of today is no longer the language of Schiller or Stifter, but the sober, matter-of-fact language of automation. (3) Young people's interest in classical literature is not great; it can only gradually be developed. Brecht, Benn, Böll, Eich, Enzensberger and Broch belong next to Goethe, Mörike, and Raabe; Schiller's *Kunstprosa* must be contrasted with the *Sachprosa* of sociologists, psychologists, and natural scientists. We must make use of the students' interest in these subjects and enlarge this interest to include linguistic and literary phenomena. (4) The focal point of our teaching is the present. Even in the discussion of older literature we need contemporary texts for comparison and illustration as well as contrasts.

Finally, Ulshöfer discusses the necessity for the teacher of literature to have at least some knowledge of such fields as physics, psychology, sociology, and politics in order to be able to interpret contemporary literature to students who are apt to be well versed in these nonliterary fields.

The background needs of the teacher of literature

The article by Ross, the director of the Goethe Institut, was first given as a lecture in 1965 (16). Ross starts with the worried question, "How much longer will literature be part of foreign language instruction?" "The new teaching methods are oriented toward speaking, toward the spoken language which has not become 'littera,' letters." Ross feels that there are good and practical reasons for this: the shrinking world, traveling and commerce, scientific texts for which the formula basic German plus specialized vocabulary is sufficient. But: "Wo bleibt da die Literatur?" Literature as a *Lebensnotwendigkeit,* as a necessity for life, is being replaced by comic strips, film, and television, Ross feels; and where young people still encounter literature, in the classroom, there is a constant demand for contemporary authors: Hemingway vs. Shakespeare, Anouilh *contre* Molière, Bert Brecht *statt* Schiller *und* Goethe. But contemporary authors pass like the latest fashion: "der letzte Schrei wird schnell der vorletzte"; and it is bad to run after fads, even literary fads.

Goethe Institut

It is doubtful whether the young Germans of whom Ross speaks would agree with him. Peter Schneider, a young Berlin writer, said in a much talked-about speech of May 5, 1967, in which he criticized the teaching of literature in German universities, "Did we ever make it clear that we first need to know something about Bert Brecht and Peter Weiss before we can pay attention to C. F. Meyer and Theodor Storm, and not the other way around? We did not. So why are we amazed that our lectures on modern literature deal with nothing but dead men and old men [*von lauter Toten und Greisen*]? Did we ever say anything in our examinations and seminars that even approached our anger? We did not" (quoted in *Der Spiegel,* 23:27, June 30, 1969).

"dead men and old men"

The College Board's Advanced Placement Program

The Advanced Placement (AP) Program in foreign languages has been the most systematic nationwide effort at literature teaching over the past 15 years, offering examinations to high school seniors in French, German, Latin, and Spanish for college credit. The history of the program has typified the problems and dilemmas of the teaching of foreign literatures ever since its inception. The program developed during the heyday of the audio-lingual method, hence there was objection to high school courses devoted largely to the foreign literature. "With the audio-lingual method [school people said] more time is needed to pre-pare students for college-level work; therefore, even if we disregard the difference in maturity between high-school seniors and college juniors, the teaching of literature is definitely the task of the colleges" (Lohnes, 11). But Advanced Placement courses are, by definition, college-level courses; they are "spe-cifically designed to stimulate secondary school students and teachers to higher achievement and, then, to help eliminate the wasteful and depressing duplication of studies at college by providing professional descriptions of college-level courses and the results of the examinations based on these courses to the colleges of the students' choice" (Advanced Placement Course Descriptions 1968-70, 1, p. 13).

AP courses should inspire

In many disciplines, the term "college-level course" is quite easy to define: it simply means the course typically taken by freshmen. In the foreign languages, however, it took a number of years before the term was defined as the first college litera-ture course, that is, normally, a college junior course (see Han-son, 7; Lederer, 10). Thus, the foreign language AP Program focuses precisely on the area this chapter deals with: literary education, but not specialization in literature. "The course is *not* designed as a course in literary history, nor in literary criticism. It is intended to be a course in literary understanding" (Lederer, 10). This is a point worth noting, because it resolves the dichotomy between school and college teaching, or between language and literature. "The Advanced Placement Program has to serve two masters, the schools and the colleges. In this role, the pro-gram has become a mediator between two groups whose ideas and attitudes have at times been diametrically opposed. If the program is successful, then its beneficiaries are not only the students who take Advanced Placement courses, successfully pass their examinations and receive college credit for them, but also the school teachers and university professors who prepare and receive these students" (Lohnes, 11). The colleges clearly do not have the kind of course in mind that they offer their majors in the last semester before graduation, but rather the kind of course Shoben (18) speaks of. Ryder (17) puts it this way, "It is my deep conviction that the restoration of writing and of litera-

AP program serves two masters

ture to the high school curriculum is near the top of our corporate agenda. I do not mean translation in either direction, or any other return to the bad old days – although allow me to say that translation is per se no sin. We are now, in the longer sequence of foreign language instruction, at a point where the very level of competence in language cries out for a further, more 'educating' use of that competence. One use is the reading of literature."

The AP committees of examiners in foreign languages all seem to agree; they all express an "up-and-out" direction, based on a thorough knowledge of the four skills. The *French* committee (1) speaks of "a course designed to provide the competent student with a challenging and stimulating context in which to develop his intellectual potential through advanced study of French literature and language."

"Language" must not be neglected

The *German* committee (1) states: "A German course leading to advanced placement should encourage superior students to achieve a high degree of competence in the language skills – understanding, speaking, reading, and writing German – and to develop their ability to read and interpret German literature."

"The aims of the four Advanced Placement *Latin* courses – Vergil, Comedy, Lyric, Prose – are in general conformity with those of corresponding courses taught in American colleges and universities. As in all courses in Latin beyond the elementary level, the basic objective is progress in the ability to read, understand, and interpret Latin literature in the original language."

Finally, the *Spanish* committee has this to say: "To be eligible for a course in preparation for the Advanced Placement Examination in Spanish, the student should have a basic knowledge of the language and culture of the Spanish-speaking peoples. He should have attained proficiency in listening comprehension, speaking, reading, and writing. He should be able to read modern Spanish of moderate difficulty without the aid of a dictionary and, using a dictionary, be able to read any given selection from classical or modern Hispanic literature. Finally, he should be prepared, through the study of selected works of acknowledged literary value, to appreciate and discuss varied aspects of expression, such as style, imagery, and structure."

The AP courses

The AP Course Descriptions (1) show a surprising degree of agreement among the several committees; in fact, their descriptions could almost be interchanged from language to language.

The primary objective of the French course is the development and application of a discriminatory appreciation of the French language and some of its literary expressions. This appreciation includes the following:

A. Proficiency in the fundamental language skills to a degree that enables the student

    1 To understand what an educated native speaker of French is saying when he speaks at a normal speed and at some length on a subject of a nonspecialized nature

    2 To read with comprehension at sight, prose and verse passages of moderate difficulty and mature content

    3 To express in speech and in writing, mature reactions, *French* opinions, and sound critical judgments phrased in correct contemporary French

B. A knowledge of selected major works representative of the principal genres and major trends and periods in French literature. This knowledge should include an understanding of events in the life of the author or in the period in which he lived or about which he wrote to the extent that is essential to the comprehension of the work involved. Students are not expected to have an extensive knowledge of literary history, nor should the course in any way be understood to be a general survey of French literature.

The description of the German course is very similar: "Ideally the preparation of Advanced Placement students should begin in the first-year course in order to achieve the highest possible degree of language proficiency. By the time they start their last year of German in secondary school, candidates should [have a basic mastery of the four skills]. Beyond the acquisition of these basic skills, Advanced Placement candidates should develop an *German* increasing familiarity with the German language as a mode of expression distinctly different from English, and a capacity for literary interpretation and critical analysis of representative works by major German authors."

The reading lists for each language have already been discussed briefly above. It is interesting to note that the committees, besides requiring or suggesting certain works, leave the teacher considerable latitude to teach these works as he sees fit. Most important, they do not require that all classroom discussion be in the foreign language, a fact that has repeatedly been used to criticize the program. Of course, this attitude merely reflects the feeling of most college teachers that on this level of instruction ideas are more important than inconsequential and imperfect expression in the foreign language. This does not mean that the AP committees are averse to the use of the foreign language in the classroom; on the contrary, there is hope that eventually it will be possible to teach literature exclusively in the foreign language. This situation prevails particularly in German, where the sequence leading to the AP examination is generally shorter than in either French or Spanish.

The committees recommend that reading in depth be accompanied by reading in breadth, that "representative readings be selected from several different genres [Spanish]," and that "the student should also master the basic terms and techniques of literary analysis of both prose and verse [French]." "The starting point for any interpretation should be the language of the work itself, leading to a discussion of style, imagery, symbolism, techniques, and aesthetic qualities [German]." *Spanish*

The AP examinations

The examinations are prepared by committees of school and college teachers appointed by the College Board, and produced by the Educational Testing Service. New examinations are written every year and the format is changed gradually. Both courses and examinations are described in a biennial publication: *Advanced Placement Course Descriptions*, published by the College Entrance Examination Board, New York; the current syllabus is for the years 1968-70. The following is a brief résumé of the French, German, and Spanish examinations as described, with examples, in the Course Descriptions (1).

French. The examination begins with a recorded lecture, followed by multiple-choice questions, to test listening comprehension. After another multiple-choice section to test reading comprehension follows a French essay on *one* of a series of literary topics, for example: "Par quels moyens Voltaire arrive-t-il à *French test item* unifier les aventures disparates de Candide?" Finally, there is a section on literary interpretation in which "the student is asked to read several short passages from the works on the reading list and answer in French the questions following them, as, for example, on a passage of Racine's *Andromaque*, 'Expliquez la situation dans laquelle Pyrrhus prononce ces paroles "Qu'est-ce que le langage de Pyrrhus nous apprend sur son caractère? Quelles seront les réponses d'Andromaque à cet ultimatum"?'"

German. The German examination also tests listening comprehension at the beginning, but not reading comprehension per se.

97

Foreign literature/Lohnes

"Candidates may be asked to write a short composition in German on an assigned topic. For example, candidates may be asked to read a brief prose passage or poem and to comment in German on certain aspects, such as content and form. Candidates may be asked to answer a number of multiple-choice questions based on the works and authors from the first reading list. For example: 'Hier traf er, da bald darauf ihre erschrockenen Frauen erschienen, Anstalten, einen Arzt zu rufen, versicherte, indem er sich den Hut aufsetzte, dass sie sich bald erholen würde, und kehrte in den Kampf zurück.' Dem Stil nach zu urteilen, stammt dieser Satz von (A) Kafka, (B) Keller, (C) Mann, (D) Kleist." After this test of literary "facts," candidates may be given a literary passage or two and will have to answer questions like the following: "These two passages precede and follow the turning point of the story. How does the language of these passages reflect the changes that have taken place?" To test what the students can do without preparation, they are given two poems or prose passages with which they are presumably not familiar and are asked questions like, "In each poem, the turning point is introduced in the fourth stanza by the words *und dennoch*. Show how their conclusions differ." Finally, the students are asked to write an essay, in German or English, on a literary topic they can relate to the works they have read.

German test item

Spanish. After listening to a recorded lecture, "the student is asked to read two poems and answer a series of questions about them. He may write in English or in Spanish." Sample question: "Compare o contraste los dos poemas teniendo en cuenta, por ejemplo, versificación (características formales como métrica, forma de estrofa, etc.), imágines y efectos sensoriales, presencia del poeta, importancia de pensamiento o sentimiento, etc." In the next part, there are ten selections, one for each author on the required reading list. The candidates are asked to select some of these and to answer, in Spanish, the two accompanying questions. Finally, the student is asked to write a composition in Spanish on a topic such as, "La tragedia surge del choque entre el hombre y alguna fuerza que no puede dominar; de hecho, no gira en torno a caprichos o accidentes triviales."

Spanish test item

Complete AP examinations have been reprinted in the *German Quarterly* (September 1965), the *French Review* (December 1965), and *Hispania* (September 1967). The September 1965 issue of the *German Quarterly* and the 1969 autumn issue of *Die Unterrichtspraxis* are largely devoted to articles on German Advanced Placement.

Future developments of foreign language AP

The number of students taking foreign language AP examinations is very small, just as the number of high school seniors taking foreign language courses is only a fraction of those taking first-year courses. The same situation exists in the colleges where the number of students taking introductory literature courses represents perhaps 10 percent of those taking introductory courses. Obviously, most students are not interested in what we have to offer.

Students are not interested

In order to improve literary education in both school and college, several measures are urgently needed. Course content must be updated to fit the needs and issues of our time. The German AP committee has recently taken this step by introducing a new required reading list, ranging from Büchner's *Woyzeck* to Dürrenmatt's *Die Physiker*. "The German committee felt a strong obligation to have the German Advanced Placement Course reflect the growing trend at colleges and universities throughout the country to select for their introductory courses in literature works of genuine social significance and impact, and at the same time to make the Advanced Placement course at the secondary school more attractive and meaningful to students and teachers alike" (Lederer, 10).

Motivation

The following suggestions were recently made at the AP Conference at the University of Wisconsin in June 1969.

Perhaps, the most important long-range measure is to encourage teacher-training institutions to include the teaching of literature. This is as important for future college teachers as it is for high-school teachers. Teaching assistants at the college level should be involved in advanced second-year and in third-year courses. One possibility would be to assign one teaching assistant to help the regular professor with each third-year literature course. The assistant could be asked to help work out the schedule, prepare a bibliography, and to work up and teach certain segments of the course under supervision. Such courses are too often turned over to inexperienced new assistant professors, fresh from advanced seminars and graduate courses, who have difficulty adjusting to this level of work. The same thing can happen to the new high-school teacher, just coming, perhaps, from graduate work in literature. Courses in methodology, at all levels, should, therefore, contain training in the methods of teaching intermediate

Teacher training

literary courses (i.e., at the AP level), beyond the introductory language phase. A whole new methodology is needed here to obviate the present necessity of "muddling through."

This would be a long-range solution, but what immediate relief can we offer to teachers already in the field? It is suggested that such established teachers be provided with effective *materials*, in the form of a series of teacher's manuals to accompany each title on the *must* list. By providing all necessary background information (including interpretations — possibly in translation —, biographical material, other secondary material) these manuals would save the teacher time and energy, and effectively boost his morale. Perhaps these manuals could be produced at future EPDA institutes by having five or six specialists in German literature collaborate with institute students to produce the first set, based on the new reading list. Such manuals would also be helpful for introductory literature courses on the college level (Lohnes, 12).

Teaching aid: the manual

But no matter what, "we must face the fact that a majority of our students simply are not interested in German literature and can be attracted into upper-level courses only if we broaden the scope of our offerings."

Conclusion

In conclusion, we shall briefly consider a number of articles dealing largely with the how, when, and to whom of teaching literature.

Cassirer & Hollmann (4) are concerned with bridging the gap between language teaching and literature teaching. "Students . . . complain not infrequently that they forget their active knowledge of the language when they begin taking literature courses, and the high schools and the colleges alike deplore this lack of continuity in a foreign language program that stresses audiolingual training in its initial stages."

The authors' concern is not so much with the language of literature as with the use of the foreign language in literature classes. Thus, they contribute once more to the old debate as to whether literature should be used to teach language. (See Northeast Conference Report 1967, 15; Ryder, 17.)

The old debate

The authors describe a series of 30-minute tape programs used in conjunction with an introductory (fifth semester) German literature course meeting three times a week. The second program described consists of the following exercises: (*1*) listening to the text (a selection from Keller's *Romeo und Julia auf dem Dorfe*), (*2*) pronunciation: *k, ck,* (*3*) the suffix *-ig*: pronunciation and word formation, (*4*) stylistic analysis, (*5*) grammar, (*6*) grammar: relative clauses, (*7*) repetition, and (*8*) questions on the text.

While this type of program is an admirable supplement to language teaching on the level of introductory literature courses, it does not deal sufficiently with the language of the literary work itself and with the uniqueness of literary genius. Linguistic description of poetic intuition is the topic of Ohmann's article on "Mentalism in the Study of Literary Language" (14). Ohmann suggests that every author, of both prose and poetry, has a literary intuition that goes beyond the *Sprachgefühl* of the total population and that dictates his particular style. Beyond literary conventions, "there is a residue of literary intuition – a larger or smaller residue, depending on how conventional the work is – whose source is not in culture, but in the writer himself." "The choices that result in a style may or may not strike the writer *as* choices while he is making them. If he is aware of choosing, his awareness probably extends no farther than the particular passage at hand. Certainly he does not choose an entire style in full consciousness of every structural subtlety it entails. Rather, I imagine, he has an intuition as to how it should sound, what view of things it should reflect, and he writes accordingly."

Ohmann demonstrates his thesis first with an example from Gibbon's *Decline and Fall of the Roman Empire*, in which he shows a preponderance of passives not only in the surface structures but also in the deep structure. Ohmann writes, "a simple – though admittedly inelegant – rule for the main stylistic feature of this passage: 'for every transitive verb the passive transformation is obligatory if the subject of the verb refers to one or more of the early Christians, unless the verb undergoes a transformation that blocks the passive transformation.' It seems likely, given the evidence at hand, that this rule sums up Gibbon's intuition of the form the passage was to take; certainly the particular distribution of passives and actives here seems a matter of more than chance, though it could hardly have been the consequence of *conscious* planning."

Ohmann's next example is taken from Saul Bellow's *Herzog*, where he shows a predominance of postnominal modifiers, "a compact and efficient form within which to house incidental or supplementary information . . . Bellow seems impelled to admit

101

a generous quota of contingent circumstances, as if in wry ac-
quiescence to their plenitude and oddity, to the way things are."

Other examples are taken from Henry James's *The American
Scene*, from Yeats, Keats, and Richard Wilbur. Ohmann's conclusion deserves quoting:

> For a long time now it has been common for critics and criti-
> cal theorists to say that the only legitimate focus for literary
> study is the *work itself*, and to mean by that the *text*: the self-
> contained structure made of words. That was, and perhaps
> still is, a salutary doctrine, as against the always present tend-
> ency of criticism to drift off into biography on one side or into a
> solipsism of the sensitive reader on the other. But whatever its
> strategic virtues, the position is strictly speaking untenable.
> The text in itself, without the background system of the lan-
> guage, is simply marks on a page, or noises. And the locus of a
> language is the minds of its speakers. Quite literally, the struc-
> tures and forms in a literary work can only *be* forms—be real-
> ized as forms—in some mind. It follows that literary criticism
> is the study of mental structures, and that the sense of objec-
> tivity one may get from insisting on the "real" work, out there,
> the work-in-itself, is illusory, in the same way that the comfort
> of an objective corpus was illusory in linguistics.

*"the locus of a language is the
minds of its speakers"*

A few more articles should be mentioned here that have a
bearing on the topic at hand. In 1966, Davison (5) published a
brief piece in *Hispania*, entitled "¿Lengua o literatura?" There
were many replies and replies to replies, the most recent being
McKay, "Literature and the Choice of Language" (13), which
takes issue with some of the earlier replies; Bolinger, "Literature Yes, But When?" (2), who argues against the attempt to
make the transition from language to literature too early and
against discussing literature in the foreign language before the
students are ready for it; Esler, "The Teaching of Literature: to
Whom?" (6), who agrees with Bolinger that "the firm establishment of the audiolingual skills [be] a prerequisite for serious literature study," but who also argues that literature study should
not be the only application of the student's linguistic skills. The
student's goal might well be the study of history or sociology
rather than of literature.

student goals

Finally, I would like to call attention to two articles that are of
practical value to the teaching of Spanish literature. Holby,
"Beginning Literature in the Foreign Language Program"
(9), discusses the question of when the student is ready to read

literature, then makes a number of very practical suggestions.
Cárdenas, "Introduction to Literary Analysis: Its Place in the High School Curriculum" (3), discusses selection and presentation of reading material, then elaborates his technique by using the poem "Dédalo" by Jaime Torres Bodet.

To sum up: a great deal of research still needs to be done to establish optimum conditions for the introduction of literature into the language curriculum; to find ways of teaching literature as language rather than, or in addition to, language through literature; to attract today's generation of students to literature as a vital and "relevant" part of the human condition. Last, but not least, teacher training programs must begin to consider the training of literature teachers as equally important to the training of language teachers.

References, Teaching the foreign literature

1 Advanced Placement Course Descriptions 1968–70. College Entrance Examination Board, New York, 1968.
2 Bolinger, Dwight. Literature yes, but when? Hispania, 51 (1968) 118–119.
3 Cárdenas, Daniel N. Introduction to literary analysis: its place in the high school curriculum. Hispania, 51 (1968) 395–401.
4 Cassirer, Sidonie; Hollmann, Werner. The teaching of literature and the language gap: tape programs for initial literature courses. German Quarterly, 40 (1967) 234–252.
5 Davison, Ned. Lengua o literatura? Hispania, 49 (1966) 300–302.
6 Esler, Richard C., II. The teaching of literature: to whom? Hispania, 51 (1968) 847–849.
7 Hanson, Harlan P. The view from one seat in the boat. German Quarterly, 38 (1965) 427–435.
8 Hegele, Wolfgang. Literaturauffassung und Literaturunterricht. Wirkendes Wort, 17 (1967) 47–61.
9 Holby, Dorothy J. Beginning literature in the foreign language program. Hispania, 51 (1968) 476–479.
10 Lederer, Herbert. Advanced placement in German: crisis, challenge, and opportunity. In: Switzer, Richard, ed. Advanced placement conference in foreign languages. University of Wisconsin, Madison, 1969, p. 31–38.
11 Lohnes, Walter F. W. Advanced placement and the future of German teaching. German Quarterly, 38 (1965) 415–426.
12 Lohnes, Walter F. W. Reflections on the future of German AP. In: Switzer, Richard, ed. Advanced placement conference in foreign languages. University of Wisconsin, Madison, 1969, p. 27–30.
13 McKay, Douglas R. Literature and the choice of language. Hispania, 51 (1968) 116–118.
14 Ohmann, Richard. Mentalism in the study of literary language. In: Zale, Eric M., ed. Proceedings of the conference on language and language behavior. Appleton-Century-Crofts, New York, 1968, p. 188–212.
15 Paquette, F. André; et al. The times and places for literature. In: Bird, Thomas E., ed. Foreign languages: reading, literature, and requirements. Reports of the Working Committees, Northeast Conference. MLA Materials Center, N.Y., 1967, p. 51–102.
16 Ross, Werner. Literatur im Fremdsprachenunterricht. In: Jalling, Hans, ed. Modern language teaching: papers from the 9th F.I.P.L.V. Congress, Oxford University Press, London, 1968.
17 Ryder, Frank G. Literature in high school – a college point of view. German Quarterly, 38 (1965) 469–479.
18 Shoben, Edward Joseph, Jr. Texts and values: the irrelevance of literary education. Liberal Education, 53:ii (1967) 244–251.
19 Ulshöfer, Robert. Sprache und Literatur des technischen Zeitalters im Deutschunterricht. Deutschunterricht, 17 (1965) 5–13.
20 Wellek, René; Warren, Austin. Theory of literature. Harcourt, Brace and World, Inc., New York, 1949.

5

Current trends in college curriculum: a systems approach

Introduction

Bela H. Banathy

*Far West Laboratory
for Educational Research
and Development*

In preparing this chapter, professional journals, research reports, surveys, and other sources published in 1968 have been studied. Classroom texts were not included. Statements and sources, both general and specific to higher education, have been considered. There will be a certain overlapping with other chapters.

In developing the chapter topic by topic, a brief review of trends and developments – prior to 1968[1] – will introduce the discussion.

Curriculum is an organized attempt to respond to such inquiries as what to teach, to whom, and why; how to teach, with what, when, and where; and how to organize, evaluate, and improve instruction. According to this, the design, development, and management of curriculum are decision-making operations requiring a structure and a strategy. A framework within which this curriculum view can be expressed, and within which a review of literature on current curriculum developments can be presented, has been found in the systems concept. According to this concept, curriculum is a deliberately designed entity, assembled of components, forming a coherent and integrated whole for the attainment of an educational goal. Curriculum components are selected based on their potential to provide for educational functions that will best facilitate the proposed learning. Goals, resources, and constraints are the input that comes from the environment, and curriculum is built to produce an output that meets the needs and requirements of the learner and of the environment.

*Circulum as a systems
concept*

The framework

The plan by which a system is built is the systems paradigm. It is the systems paradigm that is adopted here as the organizational plan or framework of this review.

---

1 A more detailed account of earlier curriculum developments can be found in three recently published anthologies: *Trends in Language Teaching* (103), *Foreign Languages and the Schools* (35), and *Approaches to Foreign Language Training: A Survey of Current Practices* (19).

The environment of a curriculum system is Society. Certain *needs* might emerge in the society that can be conceptualized as educational *requirements*. An analysis of these requirements might indicate the necessity of formulating new educational *goals*. These goals, with the resources required for their attainment and with certain given *constraints*, constitute the curriculum input. This input, introduced into the system, produces the kind of curriculum by which the goals can be met and the needs satisfied.

Needs of a society translated into educational goals

Input

Curriculum production involves a set of operations that need *theoretical bases* upon which to make decisions. The first operation transforms the educational goal into a detailed *statement of objectives* describing the expected performance of the learner (output). An analysis of these specific objectives leads to the identification of *learning tasks* that the student masters to be able to perform in the way described by the specific objectives. Then the *content* is selected and organized into *learning tasks* and *learning experiences* that communicate the content to the learner. The components, which include human resources and educational media, need to be considered and selected on the basis of their potential to provide good learning experiences. All these operations and components have to be *scheduled* and organized into an *integrated* whole. *Pretesting* will lead to revision and finally to *implementation*. Continuous *assessment* evaluates the operating curriculum and *changes are introduced by design* to *improve* the system.

Output

Continuous assessment

The systems paradigm as described above furnishes us with the curriculum decision-making structure adopted as the framework of the chapter (see diagram).

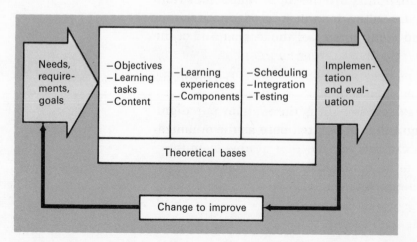

Curriculum is goal-directed. New curriculum is developed in response to new educational goals. Curriculum is changed if its outcome does not meet existing goals. To know what *goals* are, then, is essential. Educational goals emerge as new requirements are expected of the school. These requirements, thus, have their origin in the needs of the society.

Relevant to goals in foreign language education, the 1968 literature shows several trends. A continuing main goal is to serve international understanding through the learning of foreign languages. Another recognizes the vital role of culture. The third one is a reexamination of the audiolingual goal.

Trends in 1968

Examining the needs in a worldwide context, van Willingen (105) notes that the selection of what language to teach and for what purpose is determined by various factors. In the newly emerging countries, for example, English and French are being taught as tools for scientific and technological progress. In other countries, the same languages are the key to Shakespeare, Milton, Dickens, Racine, Voltaire, Rousseau, and others. Utilitarian and literary aspects, however, are not mutually exclusive, but are complementary. Language thus can be conceived as a tool, a vehicle, as well as an intellectual endeavor.

Rivers (91) presents a rather comprehensive picture of goals when she suggests that language teachers generally recognize six classes of goals: (*1*) to develop the intellectual powers of the individual by involving him in the study of foreign languages; (*2*) to enrich his personal culture through a study of literature and philosophy; (*3*) to increase the learner's understanding of how language works and thus also increase his awareness of his own native language; (*4*) to teach the reading of the foreign language with literary and research aims in mind; (*5*) to increase cross-cultural understanding and appreciation; and (*6*) to teach the skills of communication. The accomplishment of this last objective will enable the learner to communicate orally and to some degree in writing with speakers of the target language. Rivers notes that throughout the years one or more of these goals have come into focus and dominated language teaching. It might also be said that at any given time any one of these goals might be considered as a viable goal to students of foreign languages who might have different reasons or rationales for foreign language study.

Rivers' 6 classes of goals

The changing role of this country in the context of the international scene has defined new values. Allen, Glenn, & Otto (4) maintain that it has become a matter of national interest to educate Americans who can communicate with others. Foreign languages today are considered to be more than a discipline in the humanities; they have become a tool by which to improve communication with others and by which to develop better international relations. As a result, foreign language credits for admission are required by one-third of the nation's colleges and 90 percent require language for graduation. In addition, there is a definite trend to teach many languages that have not been taught before.

In order to enhance our capabilities to build bridges of international understanding, Freeman (40) proposes that we should not be satisfied with the acquisition of the language skill for practical use, but should also press for a progressive experience in the foreign culture. The cultural experience should become a central core of foreign language curricula. Yousef (108) found that, if the development of cross-cultural understanding is an educational goal, then overcoming cultural prejudices must become a major objective of foreign language teaching. He reached this conclusion while teaching American literature to foreigners. His students interpreted literature in terms of their own native cultural background. Lewald (58) wonders how much of the cultural system can be attained by a foreign language student who can hardly operate even with a limited scope of the target language. Should we teach our student to be able to act and behave according to the rules of culture, or just understand and learn to appreciate these rules? Should it be an end in itself, or just a means to understanding literature and language better? Should it aim toward dealing more successfully with representatives of the target culture? Recognizing the complexity of the cultural system, is it a realistic goal to teach the student to think in the target language?

Goals for language study are many

As a reaction to some of the excessive claims of audiolingualism, several statements indicate a shift of goals from an audiolingual approach toward more reading and literature. Burling (21) suggests that those who want only to learn to read should not be forced into compliance with a single approach. They should be allowed to follow a course that would most effectively teach reading. Suther (99) finds that the audiolingual approach does not prepare the student for advanced language study. A program limited by the audiolingual scope is a watering-down of higher education. Korfmacher (55) finds it patently difficult to

Reactions to the audiolingual approach

achieve the goal of fluent speech within the scope of the college curriculum and with the mass of foreign language students. He believes, however, that such a goal is a valid one *prior* to the college experience. Foreign language study with reading as the primary goal should be required at the undergraduate level. If such requirement is abandoned, our educational programs "will have descended to a cultural insularity and provincialism unique in the world scene." Members of the Colby College Conference (20) give priority to the goal of reading foreign literature and maintain that the emphasis on the audiolingual approach devalues the student's ability to read. To overcome this handicap they suggest that the order of priority should be: reading, listening comprehension, speaking, and writing. Clark (26) presents an analysis of 1,604 returns on a questionnaire on graduate school foreign language requirements sent to department chairmen of various disciplines. In the natural and social science departments, reading comprehension in one's specialized field was the most highly rated; in the humanities, this goal was outranked by a recognition knowledge of grammatical patterns. The ability to speak, understand the spoken language, and write was rated as the lowest in all three departments.

Colby College conference

Graduate school FL requirements

There might be an underlying reason in the demand for a shifting of emphasis away from audiolingualism. At some places, teaching in the "new key" was at best only tolerated and signs of unfulfilled goals were signals to the representatives of the traditional approach to restore old ways of teaching.

Against this background of uncertainty of purpose for teaching foreign languages, a synthesis is indicated in some new developments in England and in the emerging concept of "liberated expression." Craven (30) reports on new modern language programs that cater to contemporary environmental requirements and at the same time provide for an intellectually "satisfying" education. Biggs (13) gives an account of the development of degree-level modern language courses in which the context of courses has been changed from a strictly literary orientation to vocational and other areas of the students' interest. Languages are studied in the context of real life. The Working Committee of the 1968 Northeast Conference (36) proposes that one of the goals of foreign language students is to reach the stage of liberated expression. "Liberated expression" means a behavior that no longer responds to the control of the teacher, but to those aspects and stimuli that constitute the foreign language and culture. Having reached this stage, the student can go on in improv-

Curricula in England

ing his foreign language performance on his own without the aid of teachers and media. The goal of liberated expression is reached through the process of "habit formation, control, recognition, understanding, freedom of expression, and literature."

In conclusion, a synthesis of the professional dialogue on goals is proposed. Rather than yielding to demands for exclusion of goals, singleness of purpose, denunciation, or an either-or position, the profession now witnesses the emergence of a constructive development. Inclusion, rather than exclusion, is indicated as we extend our goals toward cultural learning. Pluralism, rather than singleness of purpose, is implied as we realize that a foreign language program may serve both pragmatic, vocational purposes and intellectual, literary pursuits. Finally, rather than denouncing audiolingual goals, the profession can grow toward building on and reaching beyond them.

FL curriculum serves many masters

Theoretical bases

If this review had been written a couple of years ago it would have presented a solid front representing the theoretical bases of the audiolingual approach as a behavioristic orientation to learning. During the last few years, however, the monologue has been transformed into a dialogue. Preceding 1968, representative samples of this dialogue were Saporta's (94) exploration of applied linguistics and generative grammar, Carroll's (23) discussion on the audiolingual habit forming theory versus cognitive-code learning, Ausubel's (6) statement on adults versus children in second language learning, and Gagné's (42) book presenting a set of different kinds of learning.

Dialogues among experts

Politzer (86) says that the language teaching profession can benefit from a better understanding of what the descriptive-structuralist school of linguistics can offer for application, and at the same time it can explore transformational-generative applications. Based on a distinction between kernel sentences and derived structures, this exploration may lead to a better sequence of presentation and to operational distinctions between deep and surface structures. According to Molina (66), language teachers have three choices: (1) to ignore the transformationalist, generative grammar view of language; (2) to attempt to follow it blindly; or (3) to put some of the transformationalist's principles to the test in the classroom. Ignoring it would mean a denial of a potential opportunity to have more alternatives in solving learning problems. Transformational analysis,

Alternative in solving learning problems

110

however, has not yet reached the point where it can support a pedagogical theory in itself. Thus, the testing of certain transformationalist principles in the design and implementation of learning offers the attractive alternative.

Rivers (89) identifies two levels of teaching-learning: (1) the level of manipulation within a closed system of limited variation, and (2) the level of expression of personal meaning of infinite variations. The first level requires an inductive and analogical process and the second a deductive and analytical one. Even though the second level is the more advanced, it should not be delayed until the learner has acquired all features on the manipulative level. Thus, depending upon the nature of learning, there will be an interplay of analysis and analogy and induction-deduction. Bolinger (16) draws our attention to the polarization that has taken place in linguistics over the last decade and the effect of this on language teaching. He suggests that the importance of language theory to foreign language teaching is probably less than it is made to appear. We should retain those aspects of audiolingualism that have been proved successful in the classroom and recognize values that were mistakenly discarded. *Language teaching is a profession in its own right*; it should not be dictated to by others, but *it can profit* by the choices offered by conflicting points of view presented by relevant disciplines.

Interplay of analysis and analogy

Language teaching: a profession in its own right

Ney (75) reviews the current debate on the adequacy of the audiolingual habit theory and finds that the practicing language teacher "has been doing much better than his critics would allow." It appears that at present the transformationalists have no workable alternative to the audiolingual approach, although their influence might be felt in textbook writing, particularly in the domains of order and manner of presenting grammatical structure. On the other hand, in light of our understanding of learning, and particularly language learning, the oral approach is in need of reappraisal and revision. Del Olmo (34) calls upon the profession not to allow abstraction to distort the pragmatic evidence accumulated during the last 20 years. The real issue is not audiolingual versus cognitive-code, but effective and efficient teaching versus the approach that fails to teach the language well. We should examine the strategies of the audiolingual approach and see how they work in the classroom. There is a whole set of inquiries that need to be processed, such as the problem of meaning in audiolingual teaching, the use of translation and English, the behaviorist orientation, the primacy of

The practicing teacher is doing much better

The real issue: effective teaching

speech, the question of time lag between skills, and the role of grammar. Frey (41) suggests that an observation of classroom practices reveals the presence of two principal coexisting theories: audiolingual-habit formation, and cognitive-code learning. The two theories need not be regarded as mutually exclusive in their application to language teaching. Much more should be known about language and language learning before a solution can be suggested to this dilemma.

The psycholinguist is concerned with the acquisition of language. Carroll (24) notes that even though theoretical and empirical work in psycholinguistics has grown abundantly, the exploration of the application of psycholinguistic findings to the teaching of foreign languages is only now beginning, and that specific problems need to be defined, and competent and interested researchers trained before such applications can have a true impact. Jakobovits (51) challenges the habit view of language learning and the significance of the role of environmental reinforcement in learning languages. He emphasizes the developmental nature of language acquisition and rejects imitation, practice, and reinforcement as theoretically unproductive. He would replace the shaping type of pronunciation drills, sound discrimination, and pattern drills with transformation exercises at the various linguistic and semantic levels.

Environmental reinforcement

Lewald (58) examines a set of theoretical approaches to the teaching of culture. He finds that the structural approach, a comparative and contrastive technique, has the advantage of having its points of departure in the native cultural experience of the learner. The semantic approach attempts to construct a system of cultural signs and signifiers and then explain the meanings of linguistic, conceptual, and visual symbols. It maintains that values, beliefs, and attitudes typical to a culture can be derived through semantic analysis. The sociolinguistic approach recognizes cultural subgroups and that membership in those groups goes along with corresponding differences in outlook and in language use. The methodological-imitative approach would lead the student to operate on the imitative-habit drill level, using techniques similar to audiolingual drills. This approach would leave unsolved vital sociopsychological factors. The use of area studies would present sociological, political, economic, historical, and geographic-demographic information as a way to acquire knowledge about the culture. The use of cultural anthropology would provide for a systematic analysis of the behavior and value system of the particular culture con-

Different approaches to culture

cerned. The pluralistic approach would allow the teacher to operate within the framework of his experience and select eclectically any cultural material for analysis. This, however, would lack consistency and continuity.

Having considered statements that reflect a struggle with the problems of interpretation and application of various theories coming from different sources, the question of just what is the appropriate relationship between language teaching and its source disciplines comes into focus. Hanzeli (46), reviewing the relationship between the linguist and the language teacher, finds that on the negative side, the excessive claims of some linguists and the servile imitation and misunderstanding on the part of some language teachers have tainted this relationship. On the positive side, however, there are encouraging signs that an understanding is developing on both sides as to the theoretical and practical implications of language and language learning, and that hostility or servility will be replaced by cooperation. Twaddell (101) suggests that findings of linguistics and psychology cannot be used automatically in foreign language education. A delay in application is helpful, since it can protect foreign language teaching from the faddisms that appear at times in these disciplines. The language teaching profession, says Mackey (59), has to "fish out from the oceans of human experience and natural phenomena only the elements it needs, and ignore the rest." Neither applied linguistics nor applied psychology is capable of solving the problems of foreign language teaching. The science of language teaching will emerge from an elaboration and synthesis of relevant findings in disciplines such as phonetics, descriptive linguistics, psycholinguistics, semantics, pedagogy, psychometrics, and others, which will service the theories and practices developed by an autonomous discipline.

A science of language teaching

The last few statements show a trend toward seeking synthesis, rather than promoting dichotomy. What seems to emerge in the domain of theoretical rationale is the position that the language teaching profession is no longer just a recipient of information and direction conveyed to it by the linguist, psychologist, and anthropologist; not even an interpreter of findings generated by these disciplines. It appears that the profession has reached the stage when it can—and wants to—evolve its own theoretical rationale. Such a theory is neither deduced nor inductively generated from the theories constructed by our allied disciplines. As the language teaching field theorizes about foreign language curricula, it explores and uses relevant theoretical

113

statements made by scholars in various disciplines, but ultimately builds its own theory.

Objectives and learning tasks

Goals of a foreign language program are formulated in response to needs and requirements that the program is called upon to satisfy. Goals are usually stated in general terms and thus need to be analyzed and transformed by a process of gradual and continuous specification into a detailed statement of objectives. A high degree of specification of objectives enables the construction of criterion tests by which to measure the degree to which objectives have been attained, to conduct an analysis of the learning tasks and to provide an inventory of learning tasks.

There are two kinds of alternative procedures to follow in formulating objectives. In the case of a job-related training program, such as teacher training, a detailed description of the job performance will become the requirement and thus the basis for objectives (14). In the case of a general kind of foreign language program, such as one in which most college students are involved, we should first assess the general need to which we want to respond and then formulate the goal. The objectives can then be derived from the goals.

Ways of formulating objectives

Brown & Fiks (19) report on a survey of several universities, special language training programs, and government-affiliated university programs. Of the 19 programs reviewed, it was found that in 16 the primary emphasis was placed on the acquisition of the audiolingual skills, and reading and writing were only secondary. In the domain of performance standards, a slightly greater emphasis was placed on accuracy than on fluency. The majority of the programs have not developed specific cultural objectives. Statements in the 1968 literature generally deal with performance descriptions on the goal level, and only a couple of sources treat objectives on the level of specificity described above. An example of specificity is provided by Banathy (8) for an objective in speaking proficiency. It states: (1) the context in which the student is expected to operate, (2) the kinds of language features to be acquired, (3) the degree of accuracy and fluency, and (4) the types of tasks the learner is expected to perform.

Writing objectives on levels of specificity

The four aspects mentioned above are demonstrated in the following example:

1 At the end of the period the student will carry on a conversation with a speaker of the language in the environment of five kinds of objects.
2 These will be used in the singular and plural forms, as appropriate, also making reference to their nearness or farness as implied by the situation.
3 Eight out of ten times the student is expected to perform grammatically correctly with a speed of response characteristic of him. Fluency should be of the degree enabling the speaker to maintain nativelike intonation and stress patterns. The length of the utterances used is not expected to be more than nine to ten syllables. With the exception of some sounds that will be permitted to be transferred from English — and that will be specified later — the pronunciation of the learner should also be nativelike.
4 The student will speak and name an object or objects; designate its distance (near or far); give native designation; answer questions; ask questions; provide a sequence of utterances cued by a set of pictures; and engage in conversation and freely generate utterances within the linguistic and situational constraints described above.

Example

Banathy (7) also suggests that statements describing objectives of the language acquisition in a foreign language teacher education program should first and foremost describe the performance expected of the teacher in the classroom. He provides sample objectives for listening comprehension that (1) specify the particular stimuli that evoke the behavior of the teacher, (2) state the expected performance on observable and measurable terms, and (3) spell out the conditions and constraints of the performance.

Once the specific performance expected of the learner is identified, the teacher can consider what the student has to learn to be able to perform successfully. He will develop an inventory of the features of sound, form, and arrangement, lexicon, and cultural and attitudinal features that will constitute the learning tasks to be mastered. Of course, a student of foreign language enters into his learning with already existing language and cultural capabilities, some of which are relevant and thus transferable to his new learning. A contrastive analysis of the two languages involved will indicate both the transferable features and those that become learning tasks. The current literature is rather rich in statements discussing the pedagogical implications of contrastive linguistic analysis. Moulton (70) pro-

Inventory of learning tasks to be mastered

115

poses a general model for contrast constructed of four levels: (1) the semantic level, and connected with it (2) a hierarchically ordered grammatical structure, (3) the linearly ordered grammatical structure, and connected with it (4) the phonological structure. Within this model phonological difficulties can be predicted quite successfully. There will be far less success in predicting semantic difficulties. Success in predicting grammatical difficulties will be somewhere in between. Politzer (84) notes that contrastive linguistic findings point to similarities and differences between two languages. The teacher can use these findings by maximizing positive transfer, by reinforcing those patterns that are identical, and minimizing negative transfer by concentrating on the teaching of those points at which such transfer is likely to occur. Rivers (88) notes that although the relevance of contrastive linguistics to language teaching has long been recognized, it has been rarely realized in textbook construction or in classroom practices. She makes a distinction between difference and interference. Differences can be learned as new items of acquisition, while interferences should be attacked through contrast. Carroll (22) suggests that the type of interference that the learner of a foreign language has to cope with is caused by native language habits interfering with the acquisition of foreign language habits. Thus contrastive information is useful not only as a source of predicting learning problems, but the information on points of potential interference enables the student to direct his own learning in overcoming the interference effect of the native language. In the same way, similarities between the two languages, if known by the student, might facilitate his learning. Strain (97) says that the mastery of the sound system is to be acquired on both the psychological level (signals of meaningful contrasts) and the physiological level (contrasts of muscular responses). Predictions of differences and interferences should be made on both levels.

Contrastive linguistics rarely used in textbook construction

Differences, interference, and similarities

However several scholars point out certain limitations of the pedagogical application of contrastive studies. One of such limitations, Lado (56) maintains, is that these studies have dealt with the comparison of languages on the level of surface structure. Generative grammar now directs our attention to another level where deep structures can be compared. An exploration on this level would allow the formulation of new teaching strategies that would lead the learner from the identical deep structures toward the different surface structures, thus reducing the interference effect. Ritchie (87) finds that conventional phonem-

Comparing deep structures

ics and contrastive analysis at times do not offer satisfactory explanations of interference between the native and target languages. Generative phonology provides more promising solutions. He expects that an explanation of interference will facilitate the elimination of interference behavior. Lee (57) notes that it is not only the native language of the learner that becomes a source of interference, but that interference, inherent in internal differences, develops within the target language. Another major source of difficulty might be what the learner has mislearned. The assumption that what is different is more difficult, and what is similar is easier, is often challenged by findings in the classroom. Furthermore, different learners cope differently with a given problem. In spite of these limitations, Lee says that the findings of contrastive analysis reveal not only learning difficulties, but also some of their causes and may also suggest ways of overcoming the difficulties. Nickel & Wagner (76) note that next to a detailed description of differences, the contrastive analysis should also establish a hierarchy of differences. It is at this point, however, that we run into another limitation of the pedagogical use of contrastive analysis. Singh (95) reports that an analysis of error-scores data of multiple-choice intelligibility test words in four languages (Hindi, English, Arabic, Japanese) indicated an inverse relationship between error frequency, the number of distinctive differences, and the extent of phonemic differences. Simply, the contrastive data cannot reliably quantify the learning problem. To overcome this limitation, Hamp (45) would start with a careful and detailed analysis of the errors made in the classroom, based on which increasingly predictive statements can be made. These statements will have a direct bearing on what goes on in the classroom whereas formally arrived at contrastive statements relate only indirectly to classroom practices. In agreement with Hamp, Stockwell (96) says that sources of interference between two language systems can be found by collecting errors made by the learner and describing the conflicts between the languages that give rise to the error, or by conducting a systematic comparison of the grammatical points of the two linguistic systems, on which basis, then, errors can be predicted.

Detailed analysis of errors made facilitates the teaching task

As seen above, the learning tasks of a foreign language program constitute patterns of language and culture that the student has to master in order to be able to perform in the way described in the objectives. The greater the degree of specificity of objectives, the more accurately we can measure their attain-

Learning tasks become bases for selecting content

ment and the earlier we can arrive at the analysis of learning tasks. Contrastive analyses of the languages and cultures concerned and error analysis provide the data, on which the actual task of learning is based. The learning tasks, then, become the bases for selecting content.

Content

Content means the language and cultural "stuff" by which the learner can confront the learning tasks. Learning tasks are abstract things, such as: sounds, grammatical signs, word order, behavioral patterns, etc. These tasks cannot be learned in themselves; they have to be represented by actual language and cultural materials. These materials, called the content, are to be selected and organized in a way that best facilitates the mastery of the learning. In the 1967 literature, this domain was treated in some depth by a theoretical statement on the selection and organization of content in foreign language curricula (10), and in the earlier literature Mackey (60) offered a most inclusive statement on the various aspects of content selection in foreign language curricula.

Content-actual language and cultural materials

According to Mackey (61), the content of a language course can be improved by findings of research. There is a growing collection of mostly vocabulary counts in the various languages, based on frequency and range. Most of these are word counts based on printed documents. Recently, however, there has been an increase in making frequency counts based on samples of spoken language. In determining the "value" of words as items of content (37), we should go beyond frequency rates and range coefficients of words and consider also the frequency and the range in the topic and the genre, and also between the topics and genres. Peck (81) comments on another aspect of sequence when he says that language learning begins with understanding meaning in the context of an utterance first, and later the usage of the utterance is extended into numerous meaningful situations.

More than word counts needed

As to the organization of content, Mackey (61) suggests that there is no dichotomy between structural and situational gradation, as these concepts are mutually compatible. Structure, situation, and the semantic and cultural content can all be coordinated, graded, and integrated, since these are embedded in each other. Politzer (83) reports on a set of experiments in learning French and Spanish, in which he tests the sequencing of presen-

Structural and situational gradation compatible

tation of contrasting and parallel structures. The experiments showed: (1) a trend toward the superiority of treatment using contrasting structure over that of parallel, (2) a recency effect in favor of the structure last taught, and (3) that contrasting structures are more difficult to learn when the structure to be learned involves word order. Belasco (12), commenting on sequencing, takes the position that the key to speaking proficiency is proficiency in listening comprehension, and the same relationship exists between writing and reading. The language learning process can be conceived as having three stages: (1) the prenucleation stage with which we associate the current audiolingual method and the use of so-called contrived materials; (2) the postnucleation stage, in which we assign controlled materials in the form of listening and reading comprehension exercises representing real incidents and texts; and (3) the liberated stage of real life situations in which are used original or "liberated" materials. Burling (21) makes what he calls "the outlandish proposal" for a course in which foreign language features would be introduced gradually into the native language, changing the proportions of the two languages progressively until the native language is eliminated. Newmark & Reibel (74) maintain that the type of organization of linguistic data which the course writer usually does can be accomplished by the learner who can organize and store a wealth of structurally diverse input data for future language use. The organization of materials based on situational simulations is recommended as being more efficient than a structurally graded presentation. They propose the abandonment of structural grading and ordering of learning sequences.

Sequencing and organizing problems

On the selection and organization of literary content, Arthur (5) notes that if we want to make literature a useful vehicle for language teaching, it should be perceived first by the learner as a literary experience. In order to enhance such perception and use, works are to be selected that will evoke a literary response in the student. The grammatical and lexical stock of the work should not be overwhelmingly difficult and nonverbal clues to meaning should support the text. Holby (50) suggests that selected literary works can help the learner gain insight into the way of life of a people. To cope with such literary texts, students who have learned by the audiolingual method will need to acquire certain reading skills and an understanding of literary style. Other prerequisites include adequate acquaintance with structure and lexicon used in the selection, in order to gain pleasure

Selecting literary content

from reading, ability to understand the concept (message) of the theme, and getting acquainted with comparable English literary texts. Ryding & Sareil (93) note that while in the first year literature can play a very limited marginal role and in the third year its use is solidly established, in the second year the traditional approach has been a grammar-centered program with dialogues, illustrative sentences, and cultural reading on the one hand, and a book of readings of literary materials on the other. Many teachers feel uneasy about this dichotomy. They suggest that the application of principles of transformation grammar enables the use of literary texts for pedagogical purposes. This could bridge the gap between language and literature.

With regard to the content of special programs, two sources deal with the new English college level foreign language programs. Van Abbe (104) notes that these programs prepare for language careers other than teaching of language and literature, such as careers in business, arts, science, etc. The main thrust is to develop optimum ability in the language skills of a *primary* language and have four years of intensive work in a *second* language. Linguistics and language teaching theory and teaching English as a foreign language are part of the curriculum, as well as the history, geography, economics, and social institutions of the countries concerned. At the University of Aston (30), which has a core program consisting of German, philosophy, and mathematics, contemporary language is the essential feature, including journalism, criticism, communication media, and imaginative literature concerned with human and social aspects. The legal, economic, and some other areas offer further options for exploration. In the domain of philosophy, the great number of German philosophers allow for a wide scope of content selection. The mathematics area involved statistical and computational studies, numerical language, and information retrieval.

Eclectic contents in the FL curriculum in England

The content of cultural programs receives special attention from three writers. According to Morain (67), an increasing tendency can be observed to bring culture into the classroom (besides literature) by introducing history, art, and the social sciences. New insights into the culture are sought from cultural anthropology. The fusion of all the above can be attained by using folklore as a vehicle to carry into the classroom peoples' culture, their humor, wisdom, and attitudes toward life. Brooks (17) notes that even though there is an agreement that we should teach culture in a language course, there is disagreement be-

Cultural content and the folklore of a people

tween scholars of scientific versus humanistic orientation as to what culture to teach and how to teach it. Of the five meanings of culture— (1) biological growth, (2) personal refinement, (3) literature and the fine arts, (4) patterns of living, and (5) the sum of the total way of life—it is the fourth that seems to be most and immediately useful as context for cultural learning. The third and fifth meanings come into focus as language competence develops. In search of content that can bring into the classroom vital aspects of the target culture, Lewald (58) considers several types of materials. Validated information provides verified data that, however, are rather technical in nature and limited in scope. Works of social scientists present adequate coverage on a scholarly level. Such work, however, is often not available in terms of the target culture. Cultural commentaries presenting individual interpretations and a speculative point of view may be thought-provoking, but the question of validity often arises. Fiction is often a good expression of a given culture. Here the question of selection of the type and form most suitable becomes a matter of concern. Literature as a source of cultural information also has its critics, as social scientists are skeptical of the use of literary examples as valid cultural indicators. If cultural interpretation is arrived at based on semantic and linguistic analyses, then of course the nature of the source becomes less important, but the issue of the validity of interpretation comes into focus.

There is an almost infinite amount of language, cultural, and instructional material from which to select content. What criteria to use for such selection is a critical question. An answer suggested here is that we should select such content that best facilitates mastering the learning tasks. More specifically, once we have identified the actual set of learning tasks that the learner has to master in order to be able to perform as described in the objectives, the problem is to select content through which the learner can most efficiently and economically confront the learning task. On the other hand, the exploration and identification of the sequence most conducive to the learner and his learning task is probably the best clue for the organization of content.

Challenging content facilitates learning

Learning experiences

Learning experiences are events, activities, happenings, arranged in the environment of the learner through which the content is mediated and communicated to him. The first set of experiences should ensure the engagement and involvement of the learner in learning. The learning environment needs to provide experiences that facilitate relevant recall and that stimulate, present, display, or otherwise communicate the content to the learner. We inform the learner about the responses he is expected to make, specify how these responses should take place, and facilitate the transfer of what has been learned into later experiences. These experiences also involve the adequate preparation of the learner for the learning experience and his management of it throughout the learning process. Finally, there needs to be provision for the continuing assessment of the learner's progress and for communicating this assessment to the learner.

Learning tasks must involve the learner

In the earlier literature Birkmaier (15) provides a comprehensive description of learning experiences cast in the contemporary mode. Hok (49) and Rivers (90) discuss several kinds of audiolingual learning experiences. Brown & Fiks (19), in their survey, describe general characteristics of foreign language training and find that the majority of schools surveyed provide for learning experiences based on the audiolingual rationale.

The review of the current literature is presented according to the following sequence: (*1*) an overview of general approaches to learning experiences, (*2*) report on research relevant to learning experiences, (*3*) comments on drills, (*4*) programmed instruction, (*5*) experiences on the intermediate and advanced levels, and (*6*) some comprehensive recommendations.

General approaches

Rivers (91) offers the most comprehensive statement of the year about the various strategies (methods) of providing for learning experiences. She assesses the strengths and weaknesses of the various methods by asking such questions as the following: (*1*) whether the objectives of the method used are compatible with the teaching situation of a given program; (*2*) whether the techniques used are the most economical ways to achieve the objectives; (*3*) if they are capable of evoking and maintaining the student's interest and involvement in learning; (*4*) if the techniques used are appropriate to all students; (*5*) and if they are not overdemanding or too taxing for the teacher. Rivers pays equal attention to the four language skills, emphasizes their interdependence, and believes that training in listening and speaking is prerequisite to fluency in reading and writing.

Criteria for assessing learning experiences

Research relative to learning experiences

At Purdue three Spanish sections were selected to follow the audiolingual approach, and three sections the cognitive-code learning approach (25). Inductive presentation and manipulation of structure and a listening, speaking, reading, writing sequence characterized the audiolingual program. In the cognitive approach, deductive explanation preceded practice, and language skills were treated simultaneously. Materials and methods used were selected to fit the two different approaches. It was found that imitative ability was the only factor in which there was a significant difference in performance in favor of the audiolingual group. The cognitive group was significantly better in reading. There was little difference in the ability to speak. Differences in listening and writing favored the cognitive group. Mueller & Niedzielski (72) tested the influence of auditory discrimination training on pronunciation. The experiment conducted at the University of Kentucky included a group of 180 students who received no discrimination training and another group of 63 students who did receive training in sound discrimination. Sequences of random correct and incorrect utterances were presented in the language laboratory to be evaluated by the student as correct or incorrect. Quantitative and impressionistic evaluation of pronunciation were used. Both evaluations indicated the superiority of pronunciation of students who received discrimination training. Oller & Obrecht (77) conducted an experiment to test the assumption that a purposeful and constant relating of pattern drill to communicative activity significantly enhances the value of the drills. Using the same language materials the same number of times, one group had only listening, repetitive, and manipulative drills and was informed of meaning only once. The other group was constantly aware of the meaning and was involved in communicative activity in the form of question-answer and directed dialogues. The outcome indicated that relating pattern drills to communicative activity significantly enhances learning. Politzer (84) conducted an experiment with four Spanish and four French classes to compare the effectiveness of early versus late introduction of grammatical explanation. Although it appeared that early explanation is a more effective treatment, findings also indicated that class differences turned out to be more important than treatment differences. Fantini (38) reports on a three-week, six-days-a-

Learning to do by doing

week intensive multilanguage program that was conducted prior to a stay in the particular countries. The emphasis was on oral communication. Positive results indicated the significance of this intensive training. Upshur's (102) findings suggested that if the foreign language is taught in the foreign language environment, the most efficient learning is informal and is acquired when language is used on the communication level, rather than by pedagogical exercises. It was also found that sequential presentation of language materials is not a necessary condition in an intensive language program. Wajskop-Hianne & Rankin (106) report on the testing of two methods of teaching French to university students. One group completed a 240-hour course, most of it in the language laboratory, consisting mostly of dialogue repetition. The other group had only 200 hours of language lab program which, in addition to dialogue repetition, also included morpho-syntactic pattern drills. An end-of-course test indicated that both groups improved by almost the same extent; thus, inasmuch as the course time of the second group was shorter, it can be said that the dialogue repetition exercises, if used in combination with pattern drills, yield better results than when used alone.

Intensive training in oral work

Computer-assisted instruction (CAI)

Performance of an introductory German section using computer-assisted instruction (CAI) was compared with students using the conventional language laboratory (68). At the end of the first semester the performance of CAI students was significantly better; at the end of the second semester, however, there was no significant difference. On the other hand, by the end of the second semester, the attrition rate of the CAI group was much lower, as 77 percent of this group finished the program, while in the non-CAI group, only 60 percent survived. The Modern Language Association (MLA) Cooperative FL (foreign language) Test was administered to both groups around the end of the second semester. Test results of both groups were compared to the test standardization group. On speaking, both groups were higher than the standardization group; on writing, the CAI group was the best; and on reading, the control group the weakest. Also reporting on this experiment, Ruplin & Russell (92) disclosed that the conventional non-CAI language program consisted of three contact hours and two 50-minute lab sessions a week. The CAI replaced these lab sessions. The CAI program

Results of a study comparing CAI with non-CAI instruction

was designed to lead to a mastery of reading, writing, and grammar translation. The system provided for display of the material and it instructed the learner what to do, supervised his responses, and evaluated his performance. CAI clearly helped the poorer students and the CAI group was markedly superior in writing. The development of other skills was similar to the non-CAI group.

Programmed instruction

Several sources commented on programmed instruction. Brown (18) describes two programming techniques that provide for communication experience. "Simulated tutoring" was developed by recording a live tutorial session of a brief pronunciation dialogue between a linguistically-trained language teacher and a student. Only the tutor's utterances were recorded and pauses were left for student responses. When a student uses this lesson for instructional purposes, he has the illusion of being tutored by a live teacher. The basic notion of the "simulated conversation" technique is a confrontation of the learner with unpredictable communications from a recorded source, such as a conversation between him as a buyer and a clerk in a shoe store. This technique is used once the learner has become familiar with language features that he will encounter. Jernudd (52), conducting a cost-effectiveness analysis on the comparative value of self-instructional versus traditional foreign language programs, found that self-instructional teaching is profitable. A number of self-instructional programs were surveyed and analyzed. Aspects of the cost-effectiveness study were: overall time, cost, equipment acquisition and maintenance cost, and teacher cost. Some of the specific advantages of programmed instruction include: (1) the possibility of standardizing the instructional program; (2) to provide for alternatives in learning experiences; (3) to differentiate and match the learning rate of each individual; (4) to isolate and assess the cost of the various teaching components; (5) to avoid students being exposed to embarrassment while making errors; (6) possible decrease of learning time; and (7) lower teacher cost. Disadvantages include: (1) programmed instruction may not suit all learners; (2) the introduction of the program is costly; (3) adjustment to the program may not be easy; (4) the fatigue factor (of the student). McKim (62), discussing programmed instructional techniques and programs, presents criteria for their evaluation,

Simulation

Advantages and disadvantages of programmed instruction

namely: (1) there must be behaviorally stated, detailed objectives, (2) sequences must be carefully graduated, (3) students proceed at their own speed, and (4) students receive immediate reinforcement. Mueller (71) suggests that programmed instruction particularly helps the linguistically underprivileged. The program he reports on is organized in minimal steps, spaced to match the individual's learning rate, and provides immediate reinforcement by both audio and oral confirmation. Drill sessions are conducted in the language laboratory. At home, the student works with a programmed book that provides for both drills and explanations. Class hours are display sessions where the student demonstrates what he has learned through student-teacher, student-student interaction. The teacher motivates, corrects, and helps; his main role is to see that the student will apply in actual communication what he has learned. An analysis of results as measured by the MLA Cooperative FL Test indicated that the average student taking the programmed course performed as well as those with much higher aptitude and the below-average student can reach average performance level. Retention ratio of the programmed course was significantly better than that of the conventional college course. Sweet (100) finds that programmed instruction cannot provide optimally for all learning experiences. Integration of programmed materials with other media, however, offers a good solution. He describes his Latin program, which provides for an integrated use of programmed and conventional text, recorded materials, reference notebook, printed visuals, reader, filmstrip, and films. The task appears to be the proper proportioning of programmed material with other components. Ornstein (78) provides an overview of the issue of programmed instruction. Reviewing a decade of development of educational technology in the FL field, he notes that following earlier overzealous attempts that rendered magical powers to programming, a second phase is emerging. Marked by a more cautious attitude, a productive nucleus of language programmers are at work who are adopting experience-based new views and approaches. Rather than promoting total programming, the current direction appears to be eclectic and pragmatic, as it considers programming or other kinds of learning experiences based on the nature and the requirements of the task at hand. Thus, a judicious and varied application of both live teaching and programmed instruction appears to be the emerging trend.

The role of the teacher in programmed instruction

Integrating programmed materials into a regular course of instruction

Drills

In the domain of drills, Frey (41) finds much reliance on pattern drills as a means of teaching phonology and grammar. Although often there is a variation of nomenclature, four categories seem to be in use: repetition, substitution, transformation (construction), and translation drills. The repetition drill is considered effective in teaching sounds, particularly when negative transfer is expected. However, the repetition drill is inadequate for teaching grammar. Item substitution drills aim to develop in the learner the capability of automatic correct pattern selection. The expectation, often questioned, is that this capability will be carried over into a communication situation. Transformation (construction) drill focuses on the correct use of syntactic patterns. This practice is being linked up with transformation theory. Translation drills frequently used for testing are often overworked when few or no correspondences exist, but are often overlooked as a means to teach near equivalence in the target language. Ways must be found for the effective use of pattern drills in spite of such inherent shortcomings as monotony, poor pacing, and lack of reality in communication. Cook (29) suggests that drills might be examined in terms of input-output relationships or in terms of the relationships of a sequence of outputs. In designing drills four alternatives in output sequences should be considered. We can design drills that are: (1) noncontextual, (2) partially contextual, (3) fully contextual, and (4) situational. Considering input-output relationships, four types of drills can be distinguished: (1) substitution, when the output is a variation of the input by item substitution; (2) mutation, when the output changes the input structure; (3) repetition; and (4) addition. Strain (98) suggests that the mim-mem type of drills employ sociocultural-meaning-based situational utterances, while pattern practice drills are grammatically based. In both types, lexical meaning is secondary. In the mim-mem type, lexical variation serves the purpose of shifting the learner's attention from the mechanics of production to the meaning of the whole utterance. In pattern practice, the same goal is served, as lexical variation is used to shift attention away from the conscious manipulation of grammar. Thus, a third type of drill — the merging of the two drill methods — is proposed for theoretical speculation and for experimentation. Mathieu (63) finds that the best designed pattern drill might fail as a teaching instrument if not used prop-

Advantages of different types of drills

The Semantic component in a drill

erly. Before using a drill, the teacher should know the kind (mi-micry, mutation) and the nature (transformation, substitution, completion, etc.) of the drill, its grammatical objective, and the nature and kind of response expected of the student (imitation and/or change).

Intermediate and advanced levels

Learning experiences germane to the intermediate and advanced levels have received attention by several authors. Reading-based language laboratory exercises are employed at Ohio State (64) with the purpose of testing the student's comprehension of the material read, of providing him with an opportunity of hearing foreign utterances relevant to what he has read, and thus increasing his familiarity with specific language features, as well as improving his speaking skill. Questions on the tape are so stated that the learner is compelled to respond in a way corresponding to the recorded answer. Questions are yes-no and either-or type, followed by simple information questions relevant to the same topic. Thus, the learner has a triple exposure to a set of language features. With carefully prepared and programmed tapes, with appropriate preparation of the student for the lab session, and with adequate follow-up in the classroom, better comprehension and greater fluency in speaking can be attained. Munnich (73) proposes a set of different kinds of questions as being applicable to guiding discussion of literary reading matter on the intermediate level. The control question can test the completion of an assignment, the collective question allows more than one answer, the general question covers a larger section, the thought question asks for explanation, the guiding question directs the student, the factual question searches for specific information, the point-for-point question is a series of control questions, the opening question is broad in nature, the background question probes into prior historical or cultural knowledge, the suggestive question evokes opinion (as does the rhetorical question), the stimulating question invites the student to take a stand, the retarding question is a way to probe into whether what has been covered is really understood, and the decisive question requires a yes or no answer. Rivers (88) sees special value in translation as an exercise in language contrast, but only on the advanced level when the learner has already acquired enough knowlege in depth of the functioning systems of both languages to explore the full range of contrast and to find equivalents of segments of discourse larger than a single

Using the lab for reading

Types of questions to use in reading

Translation

128

sentence. King (54) recommends adopting audiolingual techniques in the third and fourth year college classes by (1) a lecture summary and question-answer period conducted in the target language as a review of major points made earlier in English; (2) controlled lecture presentation with the use of media; (3) periodic essay assignments in the foreign language; and (4) tests developed in the foreign language. Such a program would provide an opportunity for the student not only to maintain, but also to improve his speaking, reading, and writing skills. Hatfield & Stein (47) define the (literary) seminar as meaning a group of about a dozen graduate students who, under the guidance of their professor, carefully examine a well-chosen limited area of literary research, and prepare a well-documented scholarly paper. A set of three sequential seminars are reported on, each dealing with a single author, a single stage of an author, or with a single work. Students are informed about the topic before the beginning of the semester. At the first meeting they are introduced to the proposed topics and resources in detail. The first three to four weeks are taken up with getting a good start on the individual subjects. Sources are explained, suggestions exchanged. The second phase of the seminar is taken up with oral program reports and discussion on these reports. The third phase is the presentation of the finished papers.

Audiolingual techniques at advanced levels

The seminar

Comprehensive view of language learning experiences

A comprehensive view of learning experiences is given by Hall (44) who notes that at present memorization and drill are often overemphasized and analytical cognition disregarded. He suggests four steps in learning: (1) the memorization of a group of utterances, (2) the overt analysis of patterns inherent in the utterances, with particular attention paid to contrastive differences, (3) practice of the patterns through an extension of their use, and (4) the freer use of patterns learned. Not only linguistic, but also cultural, material should be presented from the beginning, and the situational context should be lifelike and immediately useful. Edgerton (36) maintains that the goal of liberated expression cannot be achieved suddenly at the end of a long training program. It should evolve from the beginning of instruction and it is reached through the progressive process of "habit formation, control, recognition, understanding, freedom of expression, and literature." Materials aiding this progression move from dialogues or basic sentences through structured pattern drills, to increasingly freer variations and recombinations,

Principles of psychomotor skills learning

always leading to communication in natural situations. Hodge (48) introduced a paradigm for a basic foreign language course, which can be presented as a formula:

$$BC = PS + AP$$

$$
\begin{aligned}
PS &= GOU^x & AP &= GPU^x \\
GOU &= Eg + N + D & GPU &= BS + N + V + C \\
& & V &= BS^1 + BS^2 + BS^3 \\
& & C &= \frac{(CD)}{(CN)} + Q
\end{aligned}
$$

A basic course (BC) is composed of a prespeech phase (PS) and an active phase (AP). The PS phase consists of X number of grammatical outline units (GOU^x); each unit (GOU) provides examples (Eg) with explanatory notes (N) and drill (D). The active phase (AP) is organized in grammatical point units (GPU), each of these having a basic sentence (BS), grammatical notes (N), variations (V), and comprehension drill (C). The variations (V) are alternatives of the basic sentences in view of the grammatical point in question. The comprehension section (C) has either a dialogue (CD) or narrative (CN) text, followed by questions (Q). The prespeech phase (PS) is based on the belief that familiarity with the phonological and grammatical features on the comprehension level will make production easier. An experiment conducted at the Intensive Language Training Center in Indiana tested this belief and found that students who had prespeech training learned to speak Russian more quickly and had better control of the sound system than did students who began their training with oral drill. In the active phase (AP), each set of basic sentences presents one grammatical point, followed by grammar and–if necessary–cultural notes. In the variation part (V), each set of basic sentences was varied six times with no restriction on vocabulary. The comprehension drill (C) is recorded and it provides an opportunity to review structure and vocabulary that have been previously learned. It also provides a basis for class discussion in the language.

Paradigm for a basic FL course

To summarize this section, a wide range of curriculum aspects has been presented that is subsumed under the label of learning experiences. Learning experiences are various designed activities, events, happenings, arranged in the environment of the learner, that aim to mediate the content for the learner and provide for ways by which the learner can best interact with the content and thus master the learning tasks.

Human, media, and other resources—employed to provide for learning experiences—are the components of a foreign language program. They are selected because of their potential to carry out and participate in specific learning experiences. The question of who or what should be selected is answered on rational grounds. Questions pursued include: What are specific functions that can best be carried out by the learner, by the teacher, or by others in the learning environment? What media, what books, what audiovisuals, learning laboratory, or other hardware, should be considered? What is the cost-effectiveness balance? And then, what kind of arrangements and integration of the various human and material components will best facilitate mastering the learning tasks?

How are learning tasks distributed?

Inasmuch as Chapter 11 deals with media in depth, earlier developments will not be commented on here. In developing this review, the role of human resources will be examined first, followed by reports on media utilization and concluded with an exploration of the concept of integration.

Role of human resources

The role of the teacher as a component of a foreign language program was commented on in a few sources in the 1968 literature. Otto (79) suggests that foreign language teaching teams can be organized to provide for more effective and greater variety of learning experiences than is possible with individual teachers. Small group and individualized instruction become more feasible, evaluation of student performance and meaningful communication in the target language are more frequent. Teachers have more opportunity to plan for and implement innovative classroom techniques. Advanced foreign language students working under the supervision of teachers can well augment the teaching team. Parent (80) suggests that, rather than making the successful learning of foreign languages a proposition of survival of the fittest only, the teacher should develop a greater sensitivity to the learner's position in his progress and guide him accordingly. The teacher should be able to diagnose the problems of the student and provide properly sequenced learning materials by which to overcome the problems. Lewald (58) says that without adequate training in such disciplines as anthropology, sociolinguistics, semantics, etc., even the native teacher can be hardly more than a native informant. In the case

The teaching team

Sensitivity

of the nonnative teacher, ethnocentricity, of course, compounds the problem. Haile (43) questions the notion of conflict between teaching and research roles. If the teacher is to go beyond the books, and if he is to be a source of establishing facts and organizing them in meaningful context, then, inasmuch as these processes are those of research, no real conflict can exist. If advanced research requires the maintenance of a meaningful contact with the developing civilization, then the best source of contact of the literature professor can be evolved through the teaching of undergraduates. A change in teacher and student roles is indicated in a classroom laboratory instructional system (CLIS) (11). This system makes available specially designed learning experiences by the integrated involvement of the learner, the teacher, a classroom laboratory, and other media. The proficiency of the students who used this system throughout five years was significantly better than those who did not use it. In CLIS, rather than just being the source of information and a conductor of drills, the teacher's main roles are those of a manager of the learner and his learning style, and a decision-maker as to the time and the way to use the electronic media. He is tutor and guide to the learner, and monitors both the progress of the student and the adequacy of the recorded program. In CLIS, the student becomes more actively and frequently involved, and at the same time he can get more individual assistance from the teacher.

Conflict between teaching and research roles

The classroom laboratory instructional system

Media resources

Of the media references reviewed, Adams, Morrison, & Reddy (2) suggest that computer-assisted instruction (CAI) can present language materials to which the student can respond; it can supervise, monitor, record, and evaluate performance, and summarize performance data. The mastery of conventional language learning tasks is enhanced by the unique features of CAI as a system to mediate content to the learner. It is especially useful when mastery of written language is important, as it can quickly process complex language materials and provide immediate remedial information to the student. The learner is to make constructed responses, his errors are corrected immediately, and he is provided with individualized practice until he masters the task. The student-machine interface is enhanced by brief but clear messages. Instructions are minimal and the mechanics of communication simple most of the time. It is the student, rather than the machine, who is active. Adams (1)

CAI facilitates writing

132

views pedagogy as the designing of a learning environment that embodies the aspects of content, media, and program control. The media mediate between the learner and the program. Program control monitors the progress of the learner and informs him accordingly. The computer can assume both the mediation and program control functions. Dannerbeck & Koenig (32) report that at the U.S. Naval Academy a videotape component is integrated into first and second semester German programs in order to present a variety of native conversation, to provide an opportunity for students to participate in the conversation by speaking with those appearing on the screen, and to enhance the student's motivation and interest. Phillips (82) finds that the teacher might correct and respond to written compositions by the use of the tape recorder, recording the corrected version of the theme by commenting on errors and making a summary evaluation of the paper. This method will make corrections and improvement highly personal. Coleman (28) reports that at Northeastern Illinois State College a set of films is used in the form of film teaching units once a week as an integral part of the third trimester Spanish class. The films, 11 to 21 minutes in length, offer informative material on different Spanish-speaking countries, are narrated in Spanish, and are of value in building active vocabulary. The script of the narration is handed out to students well ahead of time and is used in classes once or twice as a basis for exercise and discussion prior to the showing. Following such preparation, the film is shown to the class and discussed in depth. It was found that this approach was an effective, informative, and interest-generating supplement to advanced conversation and composition classes. Cole (27) suggests that pictorial visuals might be used as a means of: (*1*) getting the meaning, (2) providing mental acknowledgement or retention of meaning, and (*3*) evoking stimulus or motivation. The first usage at times might lead to a misinterpretation, rather than correct conveyance of meaning. On the other hand, letting the learner work out the meaning for himself rather than giving it to him, e.g., through translation, appears to be a sound inductive approach. The second usage is often employed in memory work and it is believed that pictorial visuals can support the retention of meaning. Mackey (61) makes a distinction between visuals as aids or as media. Visuals might aid the teacher in increasing the student's interest, or they may actually teach the language. Research is needed in both the motivational and semantic functions of visuals, but particularly in the latter,

Roles the computer can play

Video tape as a component in FL programs

Tape recorder and composition work

Films

Advantages of pictorial materials

More research needed

since on this kind of media may depend the learner's acquisition of correct meaning. The integration of the tape that presents the form of language and visuals that present the meaning is very much of a current trend.

Integration occurs on several levels. The term "multimedia" projects a level on which the various media, employed to mediate content to the learner, are integrated into a coherent scheme. On a higher level we can talk about the integration of both human and media components. On another level the integration of the different content domains of a foreign language program might take place. As an example of integration on the media level, Sweet (100) describes his program, which provides for an integrated use of programmed and conventional texts, recorded materials, reference notebook, printed visuals, reader, filmstrip, and films. The task appears to be the proper proportioning of the various components. According to Fleming (39), pattern drills conducted without sensory clues are often too mechanical and fail to communicate meaning. An integration of visual and situational stimuli with pattern drills can resolve this problem. Deeken (33) notes that the technological explosion has provided the profession with a wide range of media, and the challenge is how to use these appropriately and creatively. The appropriate use, of course, depends upon the availability of effective teaching materials. Printed materials, self-instructional programs, coordinated tapes, laboratories, electronic classrooms, visuals, material resource centers, and evaluative devices can all be employed in a way to allow for individual differences in learning rate and style. The classroom laboratory instructional system, mentioned earlier (11), is a powerful example of integration. In this system the learner, the teacher, the electronic media, the textbook, visual and other components, are all interrelated in a planned way and are integrated into a unified scheme. Media are not used as aids or supplements, but as essential components without which the system cannot operate in the expected way. Interacting components provide for the mediation of specially designed, semiprogrammed materials, and this facilitates the mastery of the learning task. Kalivoda (53) points to a need for integration on the subject-matter level. He observes that in lower division instructional programs a contradiction arises between what the method course conveys and what the undergraduate student experiences in the classroom, as the typical undergraduate foreign language class fails to demonstrate the teaching principles advocated by the methods

Integration

Media as essential components, not aids

Undergraduate classes must demonstrate good teaching practices

134

course. A way to overcome this is by integrating the teaching of languages with the teaching of methods and thus creating a coherent curriculum and freeing the department from contradictory practices. In order to achieve a successful integration of relevant subject matters in a college-level foreign language education program (10), we need to do more than just cross borderlines existing between disciplines; we need to transcend them. We need to do more than just correlate interests traditionally vested in various departments; we have to integrate them. We need to design a comprehensive framework—a new instructional, curriculum, administrative, multiresource, and multidisciplinary program of foreign language education.

A review of the literature on components and their integration has indicated new trends. New teacher and learner roles are emerging and the concept of multimedia is increasing. The resources used in an instructional program are elevated from an "aid level" to the "component level." They are selected based on their capability to facilitate a particular instructional program.

Quality control

Quality control consists of a set of operations that guard the attainment of objectives and facilitate the improvement of the effectiveness and economy of an instructional program. Even before the installation of a program, two such concurrent operations, pretesting and the *training* of components, should take place. The continuous evaluation of the student and the ongoing assessment of the program provide information that is to be used to improve the program design and to achieve better student performance. Two chapters of this review treat teacher training and foreign language testing. Attention here will be limited to suggestions on program improvement.

In the earlier literature, Wallace (107) suggested three areas whose exploration would produce major payoffs in the improvement of foreign language programs. Based on an analysis of the second language competences used and needed in our society, first we should ask the question: What is worth learning? Second, we should investigate the least expensive way to learn whatever is worth learning. Finally, we are to find out the most productive way to pay for whatever learning is to take place. At the University of Illinois (3), a placement and proficiency system was developed with flexibility that enables the system to respond to changes in the curriculum and to the type and quality

How to improve FL programs

135

of incoming students. Findings of the study indicated a need to: (1) change the one high school year and one semester equivalency as bases for credit and proficiency decisions; (2) take into account the numbers of intervening years when no language was taken; and (3) possibly to use such additional predictor variables as high school language grades and types of high schools. Moskowitz (69) suggests that pupil-teacher interaction analysis is an effective tool to use toward the improvement of foreign language programs. Training in such analysis resulted in (1) more favorable attitudes toward teaching; (2) the use of more indirect teaching patterns; (3) an increase of favorable pupil reaction; and (4) a critical attitude toward those colleagues who are not using the analysis. The continued use of the system influenced teachers to make desirable changes in their instructional programs and it generated a feeling of more confidence and competence in classroom interaction. Crowley (31) shares his findings on the Peace Corps language program. He suggests that: (1) the experience gained in language instruction should be systematically collected, recorded, and evaluated; (2) those who coordinate the program should meet regularly and exchange their findings; (3) feedback from volunteers should be systematic; (4) the theoretical bases upon which the programs are built should be studied, described, and reviewed regularly; (5) private notions about language training should be tested out before adoption; (6) text materials should be developed from the close cooperative effort of the experts in the target language and the linguists experienced in the development of language materials; and (7) project directors should accept the judgment of professionals on matters of pedagogy.

College placement

Pupil teacher interaction analysis

Contributions of the Peace Corps language program

Banathy (9) notes that evaluation should continuously monitor the foreign language program and also test the adequacy of the performance of its learner. Monitoring discloses aspects that are lacking or that functon less than expected; it eliminates that which serves purposes other than what the objectives imply; and it provides clues for better integration and for improved economy. Performance testing, on the other hand, provides for the assessment of the input performance of the learner, for the testing of his progress throughout the program, and for the measurement of his terminal performance. The information accrued from monitoring and performance testing is analyzed to bring about changes and adjustments in the design of the program.

Monitoring and performance testing

The purpose of this chapter was twofold. The obvious one, explicitly stated in the introduction, was to present an overview of the literature in developments in general and college-level curricula. The second purpose was to help the reader to understand the emerging systems view of curriculum design and management.

References, current trends in college curriculum

1 Adams, E. N. Use of CAI in foreign language instruction. IBM Research Center, Yorktown Heights, N.Y., 1968.
2 Adams, E. N.; Morrison, H. W.; Reddy, J. M. Conversation with a computer as a technique of language instruction. Modern Language Journal, 52:i (January 1968) 3–16.
3 Aleamoni, Lawrence M.; Spencer, Richard E. Development of the University of Illinois' foreign language placement and proficiency system and its results for fall 1966 and 1967. Modern Language Journal, 6 (October 1968) 355–357.
4 Allen, Edward D.; Glenn, Leona M.; Otto, Frank. The changing curriculum: modern foreign languages. NEA Association for Supervision and Curriculum Development, Washington, D.C., 1968.
5 Arthur, Bradford. Reading literature and learning a second language. Language Learning, 18:iii–iv (December 1968) 199-210.
6 Ausubel, David P. Adults versus children in second-language learning: psychological considerations. Modern Language Journal, 48:7 (November 1964) 420–424.
7 Banathy, Bela H. The design of foreign language teacher education. Modern Language Journal, 52:viii (December 1968) 490–500.
8 Banathy, Bela H. Instructional systems. Fearon Publishers, Palo Alto, Calif., 1968, p. 33–40.
9 Banathy, Bela H. The systems approach. Modern Language Journal, 51:v (May 1967) 281–288.
10 Banathy, Bela H. A theory of the selection and organization of content in foreign language curricula. University Microfilms, Ann Arbor, Mich., 1967.
11 Banathy, Bela H.; Jordan, Boris. A classroom laboratory instructional system (CLIS). Foreign Language Annals, 2:iv (May 1969) 466–473.
12 Belasco, Simon. Developing linguistic compet-

ence. In: Banathy, Bela H., ed. Proceedings of the 1967 MLA Conference on Applied Linguistics. Modern Language Journal, 52:iv (April 1968), 213–215.
13 Biggs, Patricia. Languages and contemporary studies. Modern Languages, 49:ii (June 1968) 75–78.
14 Birkmaier, Emma. Evaluating the foreign language program. The North Central Association Quarterly, Winter 1966.
15 Birkmaier, Emma. A state of turmoil and evolution. In Donoghue, Mildred Q., ed. Foreign languages and the schools. Wm. C. Brown Co., Dubuque, Ia., 1967, p. 9–21.
16 Bolinger, Dwight. The theorist and the language teacher. Foreign Language Annals, 2:i (October 1968) 30–41.
17 Brooks, Nelson. Teaching culture in the foreign language classoom. Foreign Language Annals, 1:iii (March 1968) 204–217.
18 Brown, George H. Providing communication experiences in programmed foreign language instruction. Professional Paper 35–68. Human Resources Research Office, George Washington University, Alexandria, Va., 1968.
19 Brown, George H.; Fiks, Alfred I. Modern approaches to foreign language training: a survey of current practices. Technical Report 67–15. Human Resources Research Office, George Washington University, Alexandria, Va., 1967.
20 Bundy, Jean D., et al. The Colby College Conference on the undergraduate major in French. French Review, 42:i (October 1968) 66–73.
21 Burling, Robbins. Some outlandish proposals for the teaching of foreign languages. Language Learning, 48:i,ii (June 1968) 61–75.
22 Carroll, John B. Contrastive analysis and interference theory. In: Alatis, James E., ed. Monograph series on language and linguistics, no. 21.

College curriculum/Banathy

Georgetown University Press, Washington, D. C., 1968, p. 113–122.

23 Carroll, John B. The contributions of psychological theory and educational research to the teaching of foreign languages. In: Valdman, Albert, ed. Trends in language teaching. McGraw-Hill, New York, 1966, p. 93–106.

24 Carroll, John B. Memorandum: on needed research in the psycholinguistic and applied psycholinguistic aspects of language teaching. Foreign Language Annals, 1:iii (March 1968) 236–238.

25 Chastain, Kenneth D.; Woerdehoff, Frank J. A methodological study comparing the audio-lingual habit theory and the cognitive code-learning theory. Modern Language Journal, 52:v (May 1968) 268–279.

26 Clark, John L. D. The graduate school foreign language requirement: a survey of testing practices and related topics. Foreign Language Annals, 2:ii (December 1968) 150–164.

27 Cole, Leo R. The psychology of language learning and audio-visual technique. Modern Languages, 49:iv (December 1968) 166–171.

28 Coleman, Ben C. A clinical report of the use of motion pictures in foreign language teaching. Hispania, 51:ii (May 1968) 291–294.

29 Cook, V. J. Some types of oral structure drills. Language Learning, 48:iii,iv (December 1968) 155–164.

30 Craven, S. Modern Languages with a difference—at the University of Aston. Modern Languages, 49:v (December 1968) 161–165.

31 Crowley, Dale P. Learning the hard way about language learning. Trends, 1:ii (September 1968).

32 Dannerbeck, Francis J.; Koenig, George H. Closed circuit TV. German Quarterly, 41:iv (November 1968) 773–774.

33 Deeken, Hans W. The advancement of the teaching of German in the United States. National Carl Schurz Association, Inc. and American Association of Teachers of German, Inc., Philadelphia, Pa., 1968.

34 del Olmo, Guillermo. Professional and pragmatic perspective on the audiolingual approach: introduction and review. Foreign Language Annals, 2:i (October 1968) 19–28.

35 Donoghue, Mildred R., ed. Foreign languages and the schools: a book of readings. Wm. C. Brown Co., Dubuque, Ia., 1967.

36 Edgerton, Mills F., Jr.; et al. Liberated expression. In: Bird, Thomas E., ed. Foreign language learning: research and development. Reports of the Working Committees, Northeast Conference (RWCNEC), MLA Materials Center, New York, 1968, p. 77–115.

37 Engles, L. K. The fallacy of word-counts. International Review of Applied Linguistics (IRAL), 6:iii (August 1968) 213–231.

38 Fantini, Alvino E. The experiment in international living's multi-language programs. Foreign Language Annals, 2:i (October 1968) 12–18.

39 Fleming, G. Sprachpsychologische Erwägungen zu der Erarbeitung einer Bildgrammatik des Französischen. International Review of Applied Linguistics (IRAL), 6:ii (May 1968) 111–126.

40 Freeman, Stephen A. Let us build bridges. Modern Language Journal, 52:v (May 1968) 261–268.

41 Frey, Herschel J. Audio-lingual teaching and the pattern drill. Modern Language Journal, 52:vi (October 1968) 349–355.

42 Gagné, Robert M. The conditions of learning. Holt, Rinehart and Winston, Inc., New York, 1966.

43 Haile, H. G. Teaching and basic research in literature. Modern Language Journal, 52:vi (October 1968) 362–366.

44 Hall, Robert A., Jr. Contrastive grammar and textbook structure. In: Alatis, James E., ed. Monograph series on language and linguistics, no. 21. Georgetown University Press, Washington, D.C., 1968, p. 175–183.

45 Hamp, Eric P. What a contrastive grammar is not if it is. In: Alatis, James E., ed. Monograph series on language and linguistics, no. 21. Georgetown University Press, Washington, D.C., 1968, p. 138–147.

46 Hanzeli, Victor E. Linguistics and the language teacher. Foreign Language Annals, 2:i (October 1968) 42–50.

47 Hatfield, Henry C.; Stein, Jack M. Graduate seminars in German literature: some procedures. Die Unterrichtspraxis, 1:i (Spring 1968) p. 77–81.

48 Hodge, Carleton T. BC = PS + AP. Language Sciences, No. 3, Indiana University, Bloomington, December 1968, p. 17–20.

49 Hok, Ruth. Oral exercises: their type and form. Modern Language Journal, 48 (April 1964) 222–226.

50 Holby, Dorothy J. Beginning literature in the foreign language program. Hispania, 41:iii (September 1962) 476–479.

51 Jakobovits, Leon A. Implications of recent psycholinguistic developments for the teaching of a second language. Language Learning, 48:i,ii (June 1968) 89–109.

52 Jernudd, Bjorn H. Is self-instructional language teaching profitable? International Review of Applied Linguistics (IRAL), 6:iv (November 1968) 349–360.

53 Kalivoda, Theodore B. The methods course and lower-division instruction. Hispania, 51:i (March 1968) 124–125.

54 King, Janet K. The use of audio-lingual techniques in the third and fourth-year college classroom. Foreign Language Annals, 2:ii (December 1968) 185–194.

55 Korfmacher, William C. Alleged language studies lag. Classical Bulletin, 44:iv (February 1968) 56.

56 Lado, Robert. Contrastive linguistics in a mentalistic theory of language learning. In: Alatis, James E., ed. Monograph series on language and linguistics, no. 21. Georgetown University Press, Washington, D.C., 1968, p. 123–138.

57 Lee, W. R. Thoughts on contrastive linguistics in the context of language teaching. In: Alatis, James E., ed. Monograph series on language and linguistics, no. 21. Georgetown University Press, Washington, D.C., 1968, p. 185–194.

58 Lewald, H. Ernest. A tentative outline of problems in the knowledge, understanding, and

teaching of cultures pertaining to the target language. Modern Language Journal, 52:v (May 1968) 301–309.

59 Mackey, William F. Language didactics and applied linguistics. Vuosikirja 4 Suomen uusien kielten Opettajien Litto, 1968.

60 Mackey, William F. Language teaching analysis. Longmans, London, 1965.

61 Mackey, William F. Trends and research in methods and materials. International Center for Research on Bilingualism, Cité Universitaire, Quebec, Can., 1968.

62 McKim, Lester W. Recent trends in foreign language teaching techniques and materials. Audiovisual Instruction, 13:v (May 1968).

63 Mathieu, G. Bording. Teaching procedures for pattern practice: a self test. Die Unterrichtspraxis, 1:i (Spring 1968) 46–53.

64 Meiden, Walter; Murphy, Joseph A. The use of the language laboratory to teach the reading lesson. Modern Language Journal, 52:i (January 1968) 23–25.

65 Michel, Joseph, ed. Foreign language teaching, an anthology. Macmillan, New York, 1967.

66 Molina, Hubert. Transformational grammar in teaching Spanish. Hispania, 51:ii (May 1968) 284–286.

67 Morain, Genelle Grant. French folklore: a fresh approach to the teaching of culture. French Review, 41:v (April 1968) 675–681.

68 Morrison, H. W.; Adams, E. N. Pilot study of a CAI laboratory in German. Modern Language Journal, 52:v (May 1968) 279–287.

69 Moskowitz, Gertrude. The effects of training foreign language teachers in interaction analysis. Foreign Language Annals, 1:iii (March 1968) 218–235.

70 Moulton, William G. The use of models in contrastive linguistics. In: Alatis, James E., ed. Monograph series on language and linguistics, no. 21. Georgetown University Press, Washington, D.C., 1968, p. 27–38.

71 Mueller, Theodore H. Programmed language instruction – help for the linguistically 'underprivileged.' Modern Language Journal, 52:ii (February 1968) 79–84.

72 Mueller, Theodore H.; Niedzielski, Henri. The influence of discrimination training on pronunciation. Modern Language Journal, 52:vii (November 1968) 410–419.

73 Munnich, Udo. The question of the question. Die Unterrichtspraxis, 1:i (Spring 1968) 65–69.

74 Newmark, L.; Reibel, D. A. Necessity and sufficiency in language learning. International Review of Applied Linguistics (IRAL), 6:ii (May 1968) 145–164.

75 Ney, James J. The oral approach: a re-appraisal. Language Learning, 18:i,ii (June 1968) 3–13.

76 Nickel, Gerhard; Wagner, K. Heinz. Contrastive linguistics and language teaching. International Review of Applied Linguistics (IRAL), 6:iii (August 1968) 233–255.

77 Oller, John W.; Obrecht, Dean H. Pattern drill and communicative activity: a psycholinguistic experiment. International Review of Applied Linguistics (IRAL), 6:ii (May 1968) 165–174.

78 Ornstein, Jacob. Programmed instruction and educational technology in the language field: boon or failure? Modern Language Journal, 52: vii (November 1968) 401–410.

79 Otto, Frank. Individualizing instruction through team teaching. Hispania, 51:iii (September 1968) 473–475.

80 Parent, P. Paul. Minimizing dropouts in the foreign language program. Modern Language Journal, 52:iv (April 1968) 189–191.

81 Peck, A. J. Teaching meaning. International Review of Applied Linguistics (IRAL), 6:i (February 1968) 23–25.

82 Phillips, Robert. Using the tape recorder to correct student compositions. Hispania, 51:i (March 1968) 126–127.

83 Politzer, Robert L. An experiment in the presentation of parallel and contrasting structures. Language Learning, 18:i,ii (June 1968) 35–43.

84 Politzer, Robert L. The role and place of the explanation in the pattern drill. International Review of Applied Linguistics (IRAL), 6:iv (November 1968) 315–332.

85 Politzer, Robert L. Teaching German: a linguistic orientation. Ginn/Blaisdell, Waltham, Mass., 1968.

86 Politzer, Robert. Two schools of linguistics and foreign language teaching. In: Banathy, Bela H., ed. Proceedings of the 1967 MLA conference on applied linguistics. Modern Language Journal, 52:iv (April 1968) 211–213.

87 Ritchie, William C. On the explanation of phonic interference. Language Learning, 18:iii,iv (December 1968) 183–197.

88 Rivers, Wilga M. Contrastive linguistics in textbook and classroom. In: Alatis, James E., ed. Monograph series on language and linguistics, no. 21. Georgetown University Press, Washington, D.C., 1968, p. 151–158.

89 Rivers, Wilga M. Grammar in foreign language teaching. In: Banathy, Bela H., ed. Proceedings of the 1967 MLA conference on applied linguistics. Modern Language Journal, 52:iv (April 1968) 205–219.

90 Rivers, Wilga M. Listening comprehension. Modern Language Journal, 50 (April 1966) 196–204.

91 Rivers, Wilga M. Teaching foreign language skills. University of Chicago Press, 1968.

92 Ruplin, Ferdinand A.; Russell, John R. A type of computer-assisted instruction. German Quarterly, 41:i (January 1968) 84–88.

93 Ryding, William W.; Sareil, Jean S. Literature in second-year college French: the use of transformations. Modern Language Journal, 52:iv (April 1968) 191–194.

94 Saporta, Sol. Applied linguistics and generative grammar. In: Valdman, Albert, ed. Trends in language teaching. McGraw-Hill, New York, 1966, p. 81–92.

95 Singh, Sadmand. A distinctive-feature analysis of responses to a multiple-choice intelligibility test. International Review of Applied Linguistics (IRAL), 6:i (February 1968) 37–53.

96 Stockwell, Robert D. Contrastive analysis and lapsed time. In: Alatis, James E., ed. Monograph series on language and linguistics, no. 21. George-

town University Press, Washington, D.C., 1968, p. 9–26.

97 Strain, Jeris E. A contrastive sketch of the Persian and English sound systems. International Review of Applied Linguistics (IRAL), 6:i (February 1968) 55–62.

98 Strain, Jeris E. Drilling and methodology. Language Learning, 18:iii, iv (December 1968) 177–182.

99 Suther, Judith. Anti-intellectualism in modern language learning. French Review, 41 (May 1968) 849–862.

100 Sweet, Waldo E. Integrating other media with programmed instruction. Modern Language Journal, 52:vii (November 1968) 420–423.

101 Twaddell, W. Freeman. The durability of contrastive studies. In: Alatis, James E., ed. Monograph series on language and linguistics, no. 21. Georgetown University Press, Washington, D.C., 1968, p. 195–201.

102 Upshur, John A. Four experiments on the relation between foreign language teaching and learning. Language Learning, 18:i,ii (June 1968) p. 111–124.

103 Valdman, Albert, ed. Trends in language teaching. McGraw-Hill, New York, 1966.

104 Van Abbe, Derek M. A new type of language degree course—a report from the United Kingdom. Foreign Language Annals, 1:iv (May 1968) 301–311.

105 van Willigen, Daam M. Present trends in the teaching of modern languages. In: Donoghue, Mildred R., ed. Foreign languages and the school. Wm. C. Brown Co., Dubuque, Ia., 1967, p. 3–9.

106 Wajskop-Hianne, M.; Renkin, A. Semi-programmaction et controle psycho-pedagogique. International Review of Applied Linguistics (IRAL), 6:i (February 1968) p. 63–86.

107 Wallace, H. An exercise in an application of a systems approach to second language learning. In: McClafferty, James, ed. Foreign language innovative curricula studies, report no. 3. Ann Arbor, Mich., 1967, p. 125–146.

108 Yousef, Fathi S. Cross-cultural testing: an aspect of the resistance reaction. Language Learning, 18:iii, iv (December 1968) 227–234.

6

Current trends in curriculum: elementary and secondary schools

Introduction

Albert W. JeKenta
Beverly Hills Unified School District

Percy Fearing
Minnesota State Department of Education

In increasing numbers Americans are hearing foreign languages overseas and within this country. Technicians and specialists are being sent to all parts of the globe. Representatives from the U.S. to other countries are not all college graduates. Therefore educational systems must seriously consider the development of a variety of foreign language programs in the elementary and secondary schools of the nation.

The last decade has witnessed a tremendous growth and interest in the field of foreign language study (3). Not only do enrollment figures indicate this phenomenal growth but also the new developments in programs, curricula, and materials. Some communities now offer 8- to 12-year sequences in foreign language study. The two- or four-year high school foreign language programs have been affected by the widespread interest in foreign language in the elementary school (FLES) as well as the new developments in school administration such as flexible scheduling, team teaching, grouping, and individualization of instruction. The authors will discuss some of the various developments, materials, and programs in foreign language study in both elementary and secondary schools.

Growth

Within the past decade foreign language learning has stressed the fundamental skills with primary emphasis on *using* the language. The learning process follows a definite progression—listening, speaking, reading, and writing. The time differential in the introduction of the reading and writing skills depends upon the age level of the learner. This approach to language learning requires that the materials and strategies used in the classroom be organized in a manner that permits first the presentation of authentic models of that corpus of language the learner is to master. These models must be understood lexically, structurally, and socioculturally, as well as mastered through imitation and memorization. The student then proceeds to manipulate the structures in many contexts and forms to the point where he can begin to express his thoughts and aspirations freely. Thus he finally attains the stage of liberated expression where he can listen and read with ease and with very little use of the dictionary,

The approach to FL study

and where he can make himself understood in speaking and writing with some degree of facility.

The complexity of the language learning process as seen in the above statements entails more than one or two years of foreign language study offered in grades 10 and 11 or 11 and 12 in our high schools. As a result, the late 1950s and early 1960s began to see the expansion of the foreign language programs into the elementary school.

Foreign languages in the elementary schools (FLES)

In December 1967 foreign languages were offered to elementary school students by approximately 95 percent of the large public school systems with 100,000 or more students, 75 percent of the average school systems with 50,000 to 99,999 students, 60 percent of the low.average school systems with 25,000 to 49,999 students, and by 50 percent of the small school systems located in towns with a population of 12,000 to 24,999 students (National Education Association, 57).

FLES enrollment

Programs at the elementary school level are so varied that no one format could begin to describe them. The approaches range from the specialist to the strict use of media with no follow-up instruction (Otto, 59). Elementary foreign language instruction is possibly the weakest link in the development of strong 8- to 12-year sequential programs. Being relatively new in elementary education, the field is faced with a myriad of problems while seeking its place in the education of our youth. It is faced with financial problems, lack of sufficiently trained language teachers, a sometimes unsympathetic unilingual audience, and a lack of well-developed sequential foreign language materials. Although foreign language teachers are very well acquainted with reasons for introducing foreign languages into the elementary schools (Rivers, 65; Penfield, 60; Donoghue, 25), many foreign language programs have fallen by the wayside because of inadequate planning. Nevertheless, there exist today many good foreign language programs in the elementary schools. A few of these will be mentioned, each because of certain unique features.

Programs are varied

FLES research studies

Academic and language achievement. Since 1965 more than a dozen research studies show that the addition of a foreign language to the elementary school curriculum has helped children in their general achievement, language progress, high school language work, and mental maturity (Donoghue, 27). A two-year study of 120 intermediate grade children in Minnesota showed that the addition of Spanish to the school day did not interfere with achievement in reading vocabulary, reading comprehension, language skills, or arithmetic understanding as measured by the Iowa Test of Basic Skills administered at the beginning and end of each school year. The students also progressed significantly in oral skill in Spanish as measured by the Common Concepts of Foreign Language Test administered at the end of each school year (Wayne Smith, 70). Potts (62) reports a one-year study at a New York campus school showing no differences in general school achievement or reading proficiency between children who had French daily and those who had not. A three-year study in Florida (Gaarder & Richardson, 32) with children in the primary grades studying either English or Spanish showed no significant differences between the FLES and the non-FLES pupils on the Stanford Achievement Tests in the language arts and arithmetic, and the children made good progress in learning the respective languages. In Albuquerque, N.M. (Talley, 76), out of a group of 123 fourth- and sixth-grade students, an experimental group was given intensive Spanish language instruction for six months, whereas the control group had none. The results on the California Test of Mental Maturity given at the beginning and end of the study indicated that the experimental group made a significantly greater gain, with pupils in grade six making greater gains than those in grade four.

Scheduling. In three classes of third and fourth graders in Pennsylvania, children received one hour of instruction weekly. One grade studied French daily for 12 minutes, while the other grade studied twice a week for 30 minutes. Testing was done on the listening and speaking skills. Teachers, materials, and techniques were equated, and none of the children had had any language before. Any significant differences favored the group that studied everyday (Cornfield, 19). Muller & Muller (55) report an experiment involving 137 beginners in which one hour was allotted to the study of Spanish. One group was exposed to four 15-minute sessions weekly, the other to two 30-minute sessions. The students were from all three grade levels (primary, intermediate, junior high), using the same materials and having the same teacher. After one semester two longer periods were found to be as effective as four shorter ones in the teaching of the lis-

Minnesota

New York

Florida

New Mexico

Effects of spaced learning

tening skill. However, they were not as effective in teaching pronunciation and intonation. None of three grade levels was more apt than any other grade at either of the two time-spacing arrangements for beginning FLES.

Language learning. Mace (51) divided 108 primary school children (grades one, two, and three) learning French in a Los Angeles public school into four groups:

1 Group I received massed training in speaking followed by massed training in listening;

2 Group II received massed training in listening followed by massed training in speaking;

3 Group III received listening and speaking lessons concurrently, with speaking training first in each lesson;

4 Group IV received concurrent lessons, with listening training first in each lesson.

Effect of various treatments on listening comprehension

At the end of ten days and at the end of an additional two weeks, Group I, the speaking first group, consistently excelled on a listening comprehension test. Since recency might have affected the performance of the first group, the study was replicated. After one month and three months, Group I still excelled (Keislar, Stern, & Mace, 46). Sixty-four children studying Russian were divided into two groups matched by scores on the California Test of Mental Maturity, the California Achievement Test, and by classroom performance (Asher & Price, 5). The experimental group listened to the teacher and acted along with him. The control group listened and watched the teacher perform. On the retention tests the experimental group acted individually, the control group wrote English translations. The result showed spectacular differences in retention favoring children with the active response treatment. Humphrey (38), using 20 boys and girls in grade three, equated two groups in order to develop language understanding. One group used active games; the other, workbook exercises. Four-fifths of the children working with active games had a greater percent gain than those working with workbooks.

Total involvement and FL learning

FLES influence on high school performance. Vocolo (80) found in a group of 62 students in three high schools in Buffalo, N.Y., who were taking intermediate French, some who had had four years beginning with grade five. These students were designated as the experimental group; the others, the control or non-FLES group. The latter had had only one year of French. The two groups were matched in IQ, achievement, sex, and instruction received. The posttest used at the end of the intermediate course was the Modern Language Association (MLA) Cooperative French Test Battery, Level LA. On all four tests the FLES group received a higher mean score than the control group significant at the .05 level in listening, speaking, and writing. It was also found that the FLES experience was especially valuable for the boys.

Boys do better

The public schools of Fairfield, Conn., have offered French and Spanish in the elementary schools beginning in the third grade for more than a decade. A three-year study was made of the high school language progress of the ex-FLES students who had studied language continuously since the elementary school and the more recent arrivals to the city's public schools who began their language study of French or Spanish in high school. Scores on the MLA Cooperative Foreign Language Test Battery, Forms LA, MA, or MB, given to 913 students showed that in listening and speaking the high school sophomores studying French or Spanish continuously from grade three on equaled or excelled students in grade 12 who began their language in high school; in the reading and writing skills, the students with the FLES program equaled students one grade ahead of them who began their language study in high school. It was also found that those high school students with a strong FLES program may be expected to display favorable attitudes toward their elementary school foreign language program. They are also more likely to elect foreign language study in high school (Oneto, 58).

The Fairfield, Conn., study

The research literature on foreign languages in the elementary school shows the effects of good instruction to be favorable. Such programs do not lessen general achievement but rather show an increasing mental maturity, motivation, and promotion of the pupils' language progress. Short daily sessions of instruction were found to be more effective with beginning students in the elementary school, especially with regard to increasing their speaking skill. At the elementary school level, training in speaking preceding training in listening seemed to get better results. Physical involvement in learning tasks produced greater listening comprehension. FLES programs also resulted in broader and more comprehensive achievement in high school study.

Innovative programs in FLES

The Beverly Hills Unified School District. The Beverly Hills Unified School District (JeKenta, 42) operates a multilanguage program beginning in grade one and continuing to the end of grade 12. The 12-year sequence is offered in French and Spanish,

145

the seven-year sequence in German and Latin, and the four-year sequence in Chinese, Hebrew, and Russian. The elementary program, grades one through eight, is coordinated by an elementary school department chairman; the secondary school program, by a high school department chairman. The elementary program is compulsory for all students; the secondary, elective. The district operates four K-8 elementary schools and one four-year high school. Each child entering first grade or any grade up to the end of the eighth grade must take a foreign language. The pupil is allowed to choose French or Spanish; German in two schools beginning in the sixth grade; and Latin in a third school beginning in the sixth grade. Students are encouraged to remain with one language throughout their foreign language experience. A second language becomes optional only at the secondary level (grade nine). The program is staffed by a team of specialists traveling to either two, three, or four schools offering 20 minutes of daily instruction to first through fifth grade and 30 minutes daily to the sixth through the eighth grade.

Compulsory FLES program

Staffing

Major problems occur with the transfer or new student with no foreign language background, the scheduling of the traveling teachers, curriculum development, the transition in curriculum and methodology from the elementary to the secondary school program, the recruitment of elementary school trained foreign language specialists, and the cost factor (see also Otto, 59).

Problems

To solve the transfer student problem the program has moved in the direction of the *ungraded classroom* for foreign language instruction. All students at various grade levels study foreign language at the same time so as not to disrupt the regularly scheduled disciplines in the elementary school. Such scheduling results in only one interruption for the regular elementary school teacher. The divisions decided upon were primary (first and second graders), intermediate school (third, fourth, and fifth graders), and middle school (sixth, seventh, and eighth graders). This allows for the formation of a beginning language class in each group for all new arrivals, and for the possibility of homogeneous grouping and student progression through all levels of achievement. The schedule provides for special remedial help classes for the below-average achiever as well as acceleration for the above-average student. Although this approach greatly reduced the transfer problem and the lockstep approach which prevents the advancement of the fast learner, other problems arose. The maturity and interest levels of the students became a problem. Not all third graders can function harmoniously with

Scheduling causes only one interruption

Adjusting

146

fifth graders, etc. This meant further curriculum adjustments to meet student needs. In the school year 1968–69, an experiment in residential staffing was conducted, which necessitated greater individualization of instruction. Experimental classes were conducted using programmed instruction and individualization of instruction through the use of the Information Retrieval Center (dial access) in the Resource Center of each elementary school. With 80 percent of the elementary students continuing the same language at the high school level, problems in articulation between the elementary and secondary school language programs appeared. The District developed the use of "articulators." A teacher is released two teaching periods from the high school. One of these periods is spent daily teaching and working with eighth grade students and teachers; the other is devoted to articulation problems at the high school level. The latter includes placement problems, interpretation and explanation of the elementary school objectives, and the development of a high school curriculum that provides for a smooth transition.

Dial access

80% continue

"Articulators"

The Birmingham, Mich. program. In 1963, 80 percent of the citizens of Birmingham held the opinion that foreign languages should be taught in the elementary school. A report recommended the introduction of a language from the sixth grade downward to the third grade (Couture, 20). The program, initiated in 1964, chose French since two-thirds of the foreign language enrollment in grades seven through 12 was in French and two-thirds of the fifth grade students' parents selected it as their choice.

The program employs a foreign language coordinator, requires all students at a given grade to participate, makes the program an integral part of the curriculum, exposes students to a daily 20-minute session, advises parents of student progress, and provides for coordination with the secondary school foreign language program and for continuous evaluation in terms of the objectives to be achieved.

Planning

Through fall meetings of the teachers at the different levels, efforts are made to provide articulation horizontally and vertically, to establish properly paced schedules of materials for each level, to maintain a master plan of materials taught at the FLES level and the first level in the junior high school, and to provide for districtwide and departmental FLES tests as well as to administer the MLA Cooperative Foreign Language Tests at designated levels. The teachers produce level charts and observe classes by teachers, department heads, and supervisors. Orienta-

Articulation

tion is provided for new teachers (prior to school opening), a continuous in-service training program is conducted as well as a districtwide teacher evaluation program. The FLES teacher meets ten groups of children of three grade levels each day, tutors new students and students who need assistance, and deals with classroom teachers of varying personalities and with varying attitudes toward the FLES program.

The community is informed of student progress through parent-teacher conferences, report cards, PTA meetings, class demonstrations, invitations to visit classes, special programs, board reports, bimonthly highlights of the board report in the local newspapers, and a pamphlet to all parents that describes the program. *Community involvement*

In the Birmingham program, in the self-contained classroom, the regular teacher's task is to assist the program by showing a positive attitude toward language study. Students of similar ability in the foreign language are grouped together regardless of grade level. Grouping is done on the basis of each individual's needs and abilities. The FLES teacher explores the facilities for large and small group instruction, the use of media and other *The team* activities that help to provide individualized learning activities. Team teaching, in stressing the use of the specialist teacher, allows for relatively few problems in incorporating FLES into this type of organization. Special attention is given to students in a small group situation. They can be combined into larger groups for special activities, and through team planning the learning of the language is integrated with other areas of the curriculum, e.g., language arts, social studies, art, music, arithmetic, physical education, and science.

The Calgary, Can., FLES program. In 1960 the Calgary Public School Board was requested to introduce a TV French program since this was the only way to meet a shortage of competent language personnel. The *Parlons Français* program with Ann *TV becomes part of a team* Slack as the master TV teacher was chosen; a supervisor was added to the staff to coordinate the program. CHCT-TV, channel 2, offered its facilities for the first three years of the experiment to test the hypothesis that a competent television teacher, a supervisor, and a team of classroom teachers with a minimum of matriculation, three years of high school French, would do an effective job of instruction (Davies, 22).

During the past eight years the program has grown from 1,500 pupils in 42 classrooms to 27,000 in approximately 900 classrooms. The results showed a need for teacher training. The regular classroom teachers meet with the supervisor once a week. These meetings are in-service training courses that have become an integral part of the program using the teacher preparation films for the TV series. Lessons are previewed and follow-up techniques practiced and taught. With the help of the international phonetic alphabet, pronunciation is improved and expressions and commands drilled. Techniques for the use of visuals and dramatization to avoid translation are stressed. A total of 15 two-hour lessons gives teachers a base from which to work. Additional in-service courses have been added and teachers now get in-service credit for five different courses in "Parlons français."

Teacher training

A close liaison was established between the city's Separate and Public School Boards and the University of Calgary. The university has designed a special course for the program. It has become a regular part of the university curriculum and includes laboratory periods and film preview sessions that enable teachers to see and work with all three levels of the TV program. A 15-minute televised in-service training program before the school day begins allows teachers to view the lesson material, teacher preparation films, demonstrations, and discussions. Questions raised by the teachers are read during the telecasts and dealt with informally.

The university enters the picture

The television station also provides a series of local monthly TV programs entitled "On parle français à Calgary," based on the material already presented in *Parlons Français*. Each month a different school selects a dozen students and a script is written to involve them in scenes that they have already seen and learned in the previous lessons. The purpose of the local program is threefold: to review expressions and dialogues presented in *Parlons Français*; to stimulate student and parent interest; and to demonstrate student progress to the public.

An educational supplement

Two consultants help the supervisor. These specialists go from class to class to assist the teachers. They are thoroughly familiar with the program and know from personal experience the problems of the regular classroom teacher.

The necessity of articulating with the junior high school brought about the selection of a new audiovisual program to dovetail with the FLES program, namely, *Voix et images de France*, based on the vocabulary in "Le français fondamental" which is also used in *Parlons Français*. The close work between the two elementary and high school supervisors who visit each other's programs and work together as a team in adapting the

Articulation through using two systems based on the same vocabulary count

149

secondary school program to the needs of the elementary students with three years of FLES has proved successful. The secondary school teachers are pleased with the accomplishments of the FLES graduates, particularly in their oral-aural readiness and in their enthusiasm for continued audiolingual training. The students are confident and secure in their pronunciation of a limited but nevertheless useful vocabulary, and a mastery of the sound system of the language.

The Georgia State Department of Education FLES program. Keaton (45) describes a Spanish series, *Viva Nuestra Amistad*, aired on the Georgia educational television (ETV) network. In this program the TV teacher is assisted by a number of native speakers playing supporting roles. The multiplicity of voices extends the program's values. The program was inaugurated in 1967 as a Title III Elementary and Secondary Education Act (ESEA) Exemplary Program of the Cartersville city schools. The course begins in grade three. In 1968–69 the second step was introduced in grade four, with steps three and four being planned for grades five and six in 1969 and 1970. In 1969–70, 116 schools with 13,700 elementary school children were involved in the program. The major developments of the program are adequately qualified instructors and a sound sequence with the addition of reading and writing skills to the audiolingual base.

Using the native speaker

Only schools prepared to follow definite prerequisites are allowed to install the program. Basic is the employment of a Spanish teacher for two follow-up sessions a week per class. This instructor might be itinerant working in several elementary schools or have a program including FLES as well as junior and senior high school classes in his schedule.

Introducing reading and writing

The concept of the team approach (ETV teacher, Spanish specialist, classroom teacher), each doing what he can do best, has been operating successfully in Cartersville for two years (Rise, 64). The special abilities of each teacher are combined effectively in the interests of the pupils. The ETV teacher, using effective techniques in television, presents scenes from everyday life and portrays Spanish and Spanish-American culture. The classroom teacher is not expected to learn Spanish, but acts as a coach in encouraging the pupils to learn, explains in English what is going to happen on each TV sequence as well as points out interesting facets of the culture. The material is in manual form with detailed lesson plans. This frees the Spanish specialist to spend his time in actual language practice. In grades three

The classroom teacher motivates

to six a week's activity brings a 15-minute daily contact with the language. On two days television presentations are given with the classroom teacher preparing the pupils with a two-minute readiness period in English prior to the telecast. This increases anticipation, allows attention to be focused on cultural features, and lays the foundation for class rapport. On two days the Spanish teacher follows up the program with the necessary practice to assure the actual manipulation of the structures and to establish accuracy in pronunciation and intonation. Opportunity for real communication is therefore available. The fifth session finds the classroom teacher again assuming the major role as he employs tape recordings with visuals to solidify the learning. He also administers taped tests to verify the achievement of his group. The advantages of using TV in this particular FLES program are described in detail by DeWright (24).

The "twinned classroom" approach. A novel experiment in the teaching of beginning French to second graders is described as the "twinned classroom approach" by Jonas (44). The program works with two classes: one, the experimental group, and the other, the control group, in two schools located near the College of Mt. St. Joseph-on-the-Ohio, in suburban Cincinnati. The program twins an experimental group of children in this country with a class of boys and a class of girls of their own age in France.

Second graders create their own materials

The twinned groups form the matrix out of which the basic materials originate, which consist of correlated tapes and transparencies made "on location" by the French children under the direction of their teacher who follows a sequential program of language and culture units designed by the program director. The units usually take the form of situational dialogues that highlight similarities and contrasts in the cultural patterns in the daily life of French and American children while emphasizing basic conversational speech patterns.

Both the experimental and the control groups in the U.S. use the audiovisuals from France as stimuli in the learning process. The variable factor is the kind of relationship established between the children in the two American classrooms and the persons they see and hear in the instructional materials from France. The children in the experimental group engage in authentic interpersonal dialogue with the children in France, sending self-recorded and illustrated messages in reply to the earlier pictorial and spoken statements from their French "classmates." To allow for linguistic mastery and cultural understand-

Authentic interpersonal dialogue

151

ing of the contents of a message from France, two or three weeks usually elapse before the children in the experimental group prepare their response. This is done in French, since French children do not begin their study of English before the age of 10 or 12.

The same instructional materials from France are used with the control group. These children do not know the persons seen or heard in the audiovisuals as real persons and potential friends with whom one enters into a two-way dialogue. They know them only as figures in a slide-and-tape set like a commercially produced, impersonal teaching device used in scores of classrooms. As the culminating activity of a unit with the control group, there is no question of preparing recorded, illustrated replies as part of a transatlantic dialogue.

The twinned classroom project operates on two assumptions: the normal person, not excluding the young person between six and nine years of age, prefers authentic, interpersonal relations to make-believe ones, and children communicate more willingly with their peers than with adults. The intensity of the attitudes motivating the language learner is affected by bona fide personal encounter and age compatibility.

Personal encounter with peers increases learning

At the end of the eight months a survey was made of the language achievement and the motives and attitudes, insofar as this was possible to do with extrovert seven- and eight-year-olds. Aural comprehension tests showed no significant difference between the experimental and the control groups although the median and mean scores of the experimental group were slightly higher than those of the control group. The oral production test showed a marked difference in the speed and accuracy with which the children in the two classes made their replies to oral clues. The experimental group with fewer incorrect responses completed the exercises in half the time required by the control group.

Regarding pupil attitudes, the children of both classes indicated a liking for French with a higher percentage of the experimental group indicating that they would feel very bad if they never got to meet a French boy or girl. In the case of the parents there is not only the disappearance of a neutral attitude toward foreign language in both groups, but there is a sharp rise in enthusiasm on the part of the parents in the experimental group as compared to a slight increase registered by the parents of the control group.

Parental involvement

The only known controllable variable in the twinned class-room project is the relation of the experimental and control groups with the children seen and heard in the audiovisual instructional materials. Though it would be rash to offer as conclusive any arguments based on the data gathered thus far, the difference in speaking proficiency and attitude of parents and children serve as supporting evidence for the working hypothesis that proficiency, pleasure, and perseverance in a long foreign language sequence can be affected by the presence or absence of immediate or near immediate dialogue with peers who speak the target language.

Proficiency, pleasure and perseverance affected by dialogue with peers in the target culture

Articulation between elementary and secondary programs.

The problem of articulation is a crucial one when FLES pupils move into the secondary school foreign language program. Children who have had a successful experience with a foreign language in the elementary school and who continue with the same language in the junior high school need to be grouped together in the same class. Students who begin their foreign language experience at the seventh grade level need to be in separate classes. This requires a multitrack system with separate grouping in both the junior and senior high school programs. Differences between these groups should be evident; otherwise the programs are inadequately structured and taught and badly articulated.

Separate groups

A language program at the elementary school cannot be equated with the junior high school program in terms of units, pages in a book, and skills tests. What a foreign language sequence does for the elementary school child, especially with the new types of audiovisual programs can in no way be equated with what is done at the junior high school level, just as that which can be done successfully at the junior high level cannot be equated in terms of courses, units of instruction, and concepts with the senior high school (Birkmaier, 9). A carefully articulated and exciting elementary school sequence taught with the use of culturally authentic films, filmstrips, cineloops, and cartoons, with accurate modeling and control of the basic sounds, structures, and vocabulary, allows children to grow up as part of the peer culture of another country. Such programs cannot be duplicated at any other time in a child's life.

Programs cannot be equated

As we have seen, some school systems provide coordinators for the development and maintenance of well-articulated programs.

Time is provided for teachers to work on materials and activities and on the coordination of the program both vertically and horizontally. Teachers visit each other's classes and are given the opportunity to visit good teachers in other schools.

With the evolution of new organizational concepts in the American school system such as the *middle school* the articulation problems between FLES and the junior high school can be alleviated to a great degree (Brandt, 10; Batezel, 7). Middle schools (grades five, six, seven, and eight or grades six, seven, and eight) strengthen the seventh and eighth grade programs, which have been the never-never-land of the American school system. In the foreign language field the middle school allows a four-year language program starting with grade five and a greater use of the foreign language specialist. In the language learning situation itself the middle school concept can promote a better integration of language proficiency (use) with language competency (understanding). However, there is little experimentation going on with middle school organization. A hopeful sign for foreign languages in middle schools is that publishers are already rewriting and publishing new materials appropriate for the middle school student's characteristics.

The middle school practices may lead to better continuity

Foreign languages in the secondary schools

FLES has had to struggle to prove that foreign language experiences can enrich and implement a child's elementary school experiences. Studies have been made and good programs are flourishing. Developments such as the middle school, cooperative studies with other disciplines, curriculum specialists and administrators, and the establishment of new teacher training programs for FLES will undoubtedly bring about new changes even in the good programs of today.

The foreign language program in the secondary schools, however, suffers from a lack of rigorous experimentation. Large-scale studies have been made (Smith & Baranyi, 68; Smith & Berger, 69). The design of such studies are always open to question because of the many uncontrollable variables with which the experimenter has to cope. Long-term projects such as the Indiana Language Project, the Washington State Project (Bird, 8), and the Foreign Language Innovative Curricula Studies in the state of Michigan (McClafferty, 50) have revitalized programs, increased foreign language enrollments, and developed new materials and new concepts in foreign language education.

Since these are long-term ongoing projects, an evaluation of what is being accomplished, as a total picture, still needs to be put on the drawing boards. Some of the innovations from these projects will be discussed below.

New innovations in the total secondary school curriculum emanating from administrators and general curriculum specialists are also making an impact on the secondary school foreign language curricula. These will also undoubtedly exert a beneficial effect on the learning environment for students who are enrolled in foreign language classes.

Curriculum problems in the foreign language field are still with us. Some are being solved, but new ones arise as other disciplines and new developments in the American school systems affect the foreign language field (Bird, 8; Donoghue, 26; Mueller, 54).

New designs in scheduling and instructional procedures

Eighty percent of the junior and senior high schools still adhere to rigid scheduling with curriculum patterns based on five hours per week. However, more and more schools are beginning to use different time allotments and instructional procedures to provide for a better learning environment. One of these variations gaining great momentum is flexible or modular scheduling. A school faculty selects a time module of between 15 and 30 minutes. These modules are then combined to establish classes of various lengths. Just as modules of time can be varied so can the instructional procedures—large group instruction for listening, viewing, and testing, small group instruction for interaction and communication, and independent study for self-directed learning (Bush & Allen, 13).

Providing better arrangements to promote learning

The potential of flexible scheduling and varying instructional procedures upon the learning of a foreign language has not been subject to much careful investigation. Allen & Politzer (2) made a study of how flexible scheduling was utilized by comparing five foreign language programs in flexible scheduled schools with five similar but traditionally scheduled schools to determine what problems were created, solved, or left unsolved in the flexible scheduled program. The focus was on the scope and sequence, schedule, use of the language laboratory, individualization of instruction, materials and methods of instruction, evaluation of the program and student progress, and staffing.

They found that flexible scheduling had little impact on foreign language education; articulation between elementary, junior, and senior high schools continued to be a major problem; total contact time with the language was reduced; the proper utilization of large group instruction was unsolved; the language laboratory was scheduled independently of class time, which necessitated careful planning; and laboratory supervision and interesting taped materials were adjusted to the age level and interests of the students. Small group meetings and individual conferences did offer more individualization of instruction. Upper levels of instruction were made available. However, the lack of materials for individualization of instruction was made glaringly apparent. In methods and evaluation there was still the lockstep progression and no evidence of measurement in terms of performance criteria. A movement toward differentiation of staff was evident by the introduction of laboratory assistants and teacher aides.

Flexible scheduling found to have little influence on the FL program

The study was followed up by a conference of experts who recommended a careful development of specific behavioral objectives; a study of alternatives in grouping arrangements and time patterns, motivation and holding power, and teacher training programs for this type of innovation. Multiple-level tracks and various types of teaching strategies must be explored (Hernick & Kennedy, 36) and minimum criteria for entry into each level of instruction established. Further study of the use of differentiated staffing as well as appropriate activities for large groups, small groups, laboratory and independent study, the development and use of materials, strategies of instruction, media and programmed materials was stressed by the conferees. The conference participants also recommended large amounts of contact time at the first and second levels of instruction to insure correct language skills and habits; various types of pacing and recycling of students; and different types of elective courses within the program to break any lockstep and satisfy the students who have a great many other reasons for foreign language study than just the study of literature. In a nutshell, to make these scheduling designs and instructional procedures beneficial to a foreign language program that needs to develop more individualization of instruction, the model of the systems approach to learning a foreign language as set up by Banathy (6) and described in the preceding chapter must become a reality.

Recommendations

The flexible scheduled program at Nova Junior-Senior High School. To accomodate the philosophy of permitting each student to progress at his own rate, the Nova School in Fort Lauderdale, Fla., introduced a modular schedule in the fall of 1966 (Brown, 11). The school offers six years of French, German, Latin, Russian, and Spanish. Emphasis is placed on the student's oral performance in the language. Teacher evaluation of student achievement is done through both oral and written testing.

The school day is broken into 30-minute blocks of time. The foreign language department utilizes a multiple-type schedule varying from two mods (short for a modular block of time and equivalent to two 30-minute blocks of time or one hour) scheduled per week to five mods of scheduled class time. In addition to scheduled class time there is the independent study time. These two types of time combined yield eight mods or four hours of required time per week for each student. *Time schedule*

The student is assigned to a group according to his ability and motivation. There are three basic groups: Group A with two mods of scheduled class meetings and six mods in the laboratory; Group B with four mods of scheduled class time and four mods in the laboratory; Group C with five mods of scheduled class time and three in the laboratory. There are two types of laboratory situations—the language laboratory, and the "quiet" study laboratory under teacher supervision. The study time provides the opportunity for students to do their writing assignments and/or obtain individual help. Combinations of blocks of time vary depending upon the individual's needs. *Grouping*

The individual student progresses through a sequence of units developed by the teachers, at a rate calculated to achieve mastery. For example, certain students will complete three or four levels in less than two years whereas others may take three years to complete two levels of work. An independent study program is available to those students who qualify by being granted teacher and department head approval. These students are not required to attend classroom instruction; they meet with the teacher periodically to clear up any questions or to engage in conversation in the target language. *Mobility*

There is a 50-station audio-active language laboratory that provides four listening channels. Programs can be dialed from the Television Control Center or played directly from the teacher's console in the laboratory. In addition to the laboratory, there are listening carrels in the Resource Centers located in the different buildings. From these, the student dials any program available in the language laboratory. Tapes have been rerecorded onto the four-track cartridges utilized by the dial-access retrieval system. A number of tape recorders supplement these *Use of technological media* facilities. These are used primarily by students working independently or taking listening comprehension tests. Students also check out the recorders from the Resource Centers for individual use in the conference rooms.

The Language Arts Resource Center has sets of practice records for student checkout, long-playing records with filmstrips dealing with cultural material (English-speaking sound track), and a selection of literature in the foreign language, as well as books dealing with the culture of each of the countries whose language is being studied and magazines in the various languages that provide the student with up-to-date information and serve to increase motivation and interest.

Resource centers

Team teaching in the Ford Junior High School. Foreign language instruction adapts itself readily to the use of team teaching, particularly the use of the native teacher aides working with master teachers in small-group instruction and in the laboratory as monitors. However, teacher aides are only effective when carefully trained for their duties to implement the program by the master teachers. Stough (74), foreign language department head of the Ford Junior High School in the Berea School District of Cleveland, O., reports a team teaching approach incorporated with modular scheduling. The school has 26 16-minute modules per day. Mondays are used for large groups with an attendance varying from 65 to 90 students, depending upon the individual schedules. The large group meets for two modules or 32 minutes. Activities in these large groups include presentation of cultural materials in films, filmstrips, lecture presentations, special projects developed by the students, music, and group singing.

Native teacher aides

Large group activities

A team of three teachers is assigned to the large group, thus allowing it to be broken into three smaller groups if desired. Students are able to receive remedial help during the time the majority of the students are involved in the large group activities.

On the other four days the students are grouped into classes of 15 to 20 with an individual teacher for two mods or 32 minutes. In these groups the basic dialogues and the language drills are worked with. The same group meets with the same teacher each day. Stough reports that having a block of 40 to 50 students assigned to the three teachers at the same time would enable regrouping from day to day or week to week to meet better the individual needs and to provide more variation and depth for the faster students and more drill for the slower students.

Simultaneous scheduling of teachers

In addition to the large groups and class groups, students are assigned to the language laboratory three times a week for one 16-minute module under the supervision of a teacher. Laboratory activities are devoted to overlearning the structural patterns, intonation, and quick reponse drills. Students practice and receive help from the laboratory teacher. Each student is evaluated orally four to six times per six weeks.

The Oxon Senior High School program. The Oxon Senior High School in Prince George's County, Md., piloted a two-year experiment to show that a modified multilevel grouping with built-in flexibility for intergroup movement of students is more successful than the conventional lockstep arrangement in motivating and retaining students (Hernick & Kennedy, 36). Forcing students to move too rapidly for their learning rates creates not only failure but also negative attitudes toward school and other cultures. One of the major findings was that students who operated in the below-level groups were ready for on-level courses by the time they entered the third year of their language study. Although total school enrollment decreased by 85 students, the foreign language enrollment increased by 61. Students are remaining in the program. The success of the third-year below-level courses enable students to remain in the sequence. If foreign language experiences can be of benefit to and enrich the lives of the disadvantaged student (Hubbard, 37), then innovative programs such as the Oxon Senior High, the Ford Junior High, and the Nova Junior-Senior High programs must be encouraged to develop.

Multilevel grouping

Technological media in the curriculum

Technological media have had a profound influence in the foreign language curriculum. The tape recorder, the electronics classroom, and the language laboratory have been widely accepted as an integral part of the language learning process. The number of language laboratories in the secondary schools has grown from a dozen in 1959 to well over 8,000 in 1967. However, there has been much controversy about the use and misuse of this medium and the Pennsylvania Studies (Smith & Baranyi, 68; Smith & Berger, 69) are having considerable impact on the educational hierarchy. These studies have been adequately described and evaluated by Lange in Chapter 10.

Most of the highly publicized studies manage to say that language laboratories do not increase the competence of the student. However, upon careful scrutiny of these studies one finds

Use and misuse

that they disregard the crucial aspects of a learning situation which are: what is effective material to be put on the tape and how long does it take a student to learn this material in a laboratory situation as compared to a classroom situation with the teacher, what is the economy of time and effort, etc.

After a number of years of good and bad publicity the language laboratory is still found to contribute considerably toward better foreign language instruction. But it is not worth the expense incurred when it is misused. It can make the difference between mediocrity and excellence if its capabilities are understood and incorporated in proper perspective into the curriculum (Hutchinson 39, 40).

Before the purchase of a language laboratory it is very important that the administrator and the foreign language teachers understand the basic principles involved in audiolingual instruction. The language laboratory, no matter how simple or complex, is only an aid, an excellent one at that, that enables the foreign language teacher to do a more effective job of teaching. It provides for the active participation of all students whether they work individually or in a group, provides equal listening conditions regardless of the distance between teacher and students, enables the teacher to work individually with each student while the entire class is in session, and provides native voices as constant and untiring models for students to imitate. It plays an extremely important role as an aid for the student in a programmed learning course (Strasheim, 75; Stack, 73).

What the lab does

At the advanced levels in particular, it can be utilized to enrich the classroom in the cultural offerings of the people who use the foreign language, especially when the teacher makes tapes available of poems, dramatic presentations, and newscasts and commentaries. The student can now work on the refinements of the language that he was not able to perfect in the elementary and intermediate levels of his language study (4). The language laboratory also becomes an important vehicle or medium for individualizing instruction in the modular and flexible scheduled programs and in the foreign language learning systems that feature programmed units of instruction. For example, during an independent study period the student goes to the laboratory or to a carrel in the language resource center to work on a particular aspect of the language either for remedial purposes, as a regular assignment, or for enrichment. Single-concept or single-structure programmed materials as well as programmed reading and listening materials are used in the

Labs provide for presentation of cultural materials at advanced levels

laboratory to allow the student the freedom he needs for mastering language.

Hutchinson (75) expresses doubt as to the value of the audio-active-record laboratory as opposed to the audio-active and listening laboratory at the secondary school level. The greatest advantage he sees in the audio-active-record laboratory in high schools is the capability of recording a speaking test that he feels can be done in other, less expensive ways. He maintains that multiple electronic classrooms in a school alleviate scheduling problems that arise from a single stationary laboratory. He goes on to describe various installations, one of them at the Burris Laboratory School in Muncie, Ind., which has both the electronic classroom and the stationary laboratory, and the Evansville, Ind., North High School with its series of electronic classrooms. It seems apparent that the electronic classroom equipped with good earphones and microphones can be used as a multipurpose room. It is able to do away with booths and is much cheaper, therefore allowing for a much greater number of positions and more time for interesting audiolingual work at a time when it is needed.

The electronic classroom makes a comeback

Gibson recommends that any textbook adoption committee pay particular attention to complete programs with integrated teaching materials composed of taped materials, text, workbooks, teacher's manual, audiovisual aids, and tests since the teacher has not the time to develop materials of his own. She maintains that the *language laboratory program* can be no more effective than the total foreign language program of which it is a part. Like any other tool – blackboard, overhead projector, wall map, etc. – it can be evaluated only in terms of its use and efficacy in the total teaching situation (Strasheim, 75, p. 16). Part III of the Indiana bulletin on language laboratory teaching (Strasheim, 75, pp. 21–31) goes into detail on teaching techniques in the language laboratory with sample lessons and testing techniques to be used. Birkmaier & Hallman (4) find that a language laboratory must include film, slide-filmstrip, and overhead projectors. Each foreign language classroom should include these as well as a tape recorder. No teacher will use technological equipment unless it is readily at hand. Some of the modern high schools already have audio-video dial access study carrels in their laboratories or in their foreign language materials resource centers.

Taped material must be integrated with the total instructional system

Regenstreif, director of the learning laboratory program, in the Michigan Foreign Language Innovative Curricula Studies

161

(FLICS), is developing learning carrels that contain a flexible configuration of audio and visual equipment. These are located in non-classroom areas and used during study hall, lunch, outside of regular class hours, and on Saturdays. The materials are of a cultural nature, two-year minicourses that consist of short episodes on slides, tapes, or films surveying the range of French and Spanish art, music, and history (McClafferty, 50).

Flexible learning carrels

The language laboratory as the profession knew it some ten years ago has undergone changes over the years. Teachers now know what media they need to make their teaching more effective and with the aid of electronics specialists and materials developers are devising new combinations of technological media for foreign language learning. Nevertheless, the wide dissemination of poorly conducted research and the widespread poor management of language laboratories, not to speak of the cheap hardware that was sold the profession, are of serious concern to the language teaching profession.

Programmed instruction

Individualization of instruction through programmed learning materials has had a major impact on the teaching of foreign languages. The profession has had to agree with two factors: students can learn a language at their own learning rates, and properly constructed programs do teach (Mueller, 54; Valdman, 79). Premature emphasis on the teaching machine, however, served to distract attention from the *value of the teaching program*.

Students can learn FLS at their learning rates

The advantages of using programmed materials, whether as short units in a system of instruction or as a complete self-instructional program, are that the course objectives are specified in detailed behavioral terms, the material is presented as a graduated sequence of small items (frames) leading to the objectives, and that the student responds actively to each frame at his own pace with a low probability of error and receives immediate confirmation after his response.

Before a school chooses a program, the goals of instruction of the particular language course must be determined (Banathy, 6). The content, the media, and the strategies used to reach the specific goal should be agreed upon and studied by the foreign language department. The basic questions the teachers must ask are:

1 Is the material intended for individualized instruction and completely self-contained?

2 Is it to be remedial?

3 Is it to be for enrichment purposes only?

4 Is the content and vocabulary appropriate to the learner's level?

5 How has the program been tested and what results have been found by other schools using these materials?

According to Shulze, Arendt, & Rainey (67), the novelty of a complete programmed learning course can wear off. The authors found that the pairing of students in the language laboratory when working on programmed materials seems to have a beneficial effect on learning. Motivation is improved by students working in pairs for dialogue and other audiolingual practice. This idea, according to the authors, should be pursued since not all students work well in isolation. Valdman (78) and Morton (53) also discuss the necessity of display sessions in a communications situation such as is required in the learning of a foreign language. Shulze, Arendt, & Rainey maintain that teamwork permits studying, planning, and assignment development, reporting and testing in pairs, and allows for a more realistic communications situation.

Team learning

Morton (53) lists four problem areas encountered by language programmers and students of language programs in the development and use of programmed self-instructional learning materials:

Problems encountered in the development of self-instructional materials

1 The problem of a change of behavior on the part of the student as he works through a program;

2 Behavior maintenance throughout the programs and its reshaping into minimally new behaviors;

3 A lack of systematization of procedures of direction, analysis, and evaluation of student response during the program workthrough; and

4 Technological breakdowns.

Detailed descriptions of the application of the principles of programmed instruction to foreign languages exist (Spodak, 72; Valdman, 78, 79; Lane, 48; Carroll, 16; Mueller, 54). Fiks (29) lists 48 programs with 17 in French, 15 in Spanish, 6 in German, 3 in Russian, 3 in Latin, and 4 in other languages. He includes title, publisher, author, price category, student level, course objectives, the mode of student response, special devices needed, format, completion time in hours, numbers of frames or responses, and the atomy (number of frames per hour). However, it must of necessity be said that none of the programs have the motivating appeal for the junior and senior high school student

Courses now available

unless the teacher incorporates the program into *his* instructional system.

Administrators and teachers should acquaint themselves with the literature on programmed instruction and with the various uses and types of programmed materials. The trend as of the present seems to be toward programming units as part of the instructional component of a foreign language course that incorporates various media and strategies of instruction for a better learning environment for the student.

Be aware!

Continuity in the foreign language curriculum

Despite millions of federal dollars having gone into local foreign language programs the percent of students continuing into fourth-level courses has remained low. Average fourth-year continuation of all languages falls well below 7 percent when first-year students in 1962 are compared with all fourth-year students in 1965: Spanish, 4.5 percent; French 7.9 percent; German, 6.9 percent; and Latin, 3.4 percent (Teague & Rütimann, 77). The same report indicates large increases in enrollment at the junior and early senior high school levels. More than 90 percent of the students discontinue the study of foreign language at the end of the third year. The pressure of required courses in the high school curriculum tends to reduce advanced course enrollments in the foreign languages, since it is usual to drop a course if enrollment is less than four in some school systems and as high as 15 in others.

Attrition rate high at advanced levels

This condition results in long periods of time when language skills lie dormant before the students resume their study of them in college. As a result, the student does poorly in his college classes. Many times he drops the language he learned in high school and starts another one.

The National Council of State Supervisors of Foreign Languages (56) recommends that foreign languages be offered in an *uninterrupted sequence* from wherever they are introduced into the curriculum through grade 12. To alleviate this serious condition Grittner (34) suggests the offering of three credits for language work done in grades seven through ten, three-fifths of a credit for a course meeting three times per week in grade 11, and two-fifths of a credit for a course meeting twice a week in grade 12. But such innovations are rare. The big problem is still how to maintain language skills during the years when regular foreign language courses are no longer available at the advanced level.

Languages should be given an uninterrupted sequence

In order to study the situation more carefully a questionnaire was sent to foreign language consultants of 50 states; 46 responded. Of these, 39 indicated that large numbers of students were terminating their language study at grades 10 and 11; 39 also indicated a great need for maintaining language skills but there was no agreement as to how such a program should be structured. Seminar meetings held a few times weekly with or without credit (11 states), self-study projects (12 states), pen pals and tape pals (7 states), language clubs, summer programs, foreign travel, auditing of advanced classes, language laboratory attendance, working as teacher aides, and outside reading were reported as ways of keeping the students in contact with the language. Seventeen states said that such programs existed; 24, that no such programs existed; 11 states had no such available information.

Innovative programs and courses to curb attrition

According to Grittner programs maintaining language skills assume that the student has control of the basic phonology, morphology, syntax, and vocabulary and that activities pursued are so dramatic in some cases that they provide an incentive for students at the beginning and intermediate levels to persevere through the more tedious aspects of language learning to become eligible for the maintainance of skills (MOS) programs. To make these programs successful evaluation procedures must be tight. The most common approach is the contract system, where activities are summarized on a contract form signed by the student, teacher, and administrator. According to Grittner, some activities that have great potential are audiovisual productions, correspondence, clubs, newspaper and other student publications, directed reading or writing in a chosen area, guided free expression, self-study topics, and summer programs. Programs are limited only by the creativity of the language department. Included in the report is a list of general sources of books and materials.

Nongraded foreign language classes. During the past ten years the foreign language profession has spoken of levels instead of grades. This was to imply that a certain flexibility was taking place in the foreign language curriculum. But foreign language classes of 30 students moving together in lockstep through a year's work is still a common pattern. Some 40 percent of the students are out of step. These are the academically talented as well as the students who learn more slowly than others. Students are told that a foreign language has something to offer to all and that success is possible, but the attrition rate in the foreign language program is still exceedingly high.

40 percent are out of step in an FL class

165

Nongraded classes are being introduced to give the necessary flexibility and release from pressure that is so necessary for the student to achieve at his optimum rate (Bush & Allen, 13). But, according to Fearing (28), foreign language curricula have been and still are written for mass instruction at both elementary and secondary school levels, taped drills have been one-channel systems, and listen-repeat choral responses have become standard procedure in the foreign language classroom. Multichannel language laboratories have to defer to inflexible schedules, to lack of supervisory staff, and to scarcity of programmed materials for use by the individual student. The antiquated marking system and fear of criticism on the part of the foreign language teacher from colleges and universities and other language teachers who might get his students prove also to be obstacles for the teacher to accept the nongrading organization of schools.

What we are up against

Nongraded classes, according to Fearing, have many important implications for small high schools with small foreign language enrollments. A great variety of programmed materials together with basic and supplementary materials for the four language skills must be provided. Nongraded classrooms must of necessity be small. Some students may be working on advanced levels in speaking and listening but with elementary materials in reading and writing. Regrouping is a continuous process. In a nongraded classroom each student keeps a daily plan that is incorporated into the teacher's master plan so that he knows what each student is doing at all times. Melbourne High School in Florida (Brown, 11) offered an additional five new languages besides the usual Latin and Spanish after it had ungraded its curriculum. The West Bend School District (82) drafted a program for a nongraded 7 through 12 foreign language program in which all beginning students are kept together in a large-group instruction situation for a predetermined number of units to insure a proper introduction into the language learning process and to give a sound background in the audio comprehension skills as well as training in learning procedures that the student needs later in his own private study program. A Science Research Associates bulletin (66) indicates that teachers are not trained for this type of teaching, and that learning materials are not adequate for such programs. Once these programs are accepted by the profession there will be another avenue in which to provide for advanced language study, a crucial factor in today's language programs (Grittner, 34).

Nongraded classes solve problems in the small schools

Need for specialized teacher training

New type courses in the foreign language curriculum

Subject matter courses. Besides the typical language course that concentrates on literature there is a growing movement toward the teaching of subject matter courses in the foreign language (57). These courses are usually offered at the advanced levels of foreign language instruction, although there are greater possibilities of correlation in subject matter areas and foreign language in FLES programs.

An advanced geography course taught in French, using French textbooks and French and social studies teachers working as an interdisciplinary team, has been developed at the *Geography* Cleveland High School in St. Louis, Mo. A world history course is taught in French and Spanish in two Virginia secondary schools for selected fourth- and fifth-level students. The instructors hold teachers' certificates with a double major in the foreign language and social studies. The content parallels that of the world history course offered simultaneously in English. In Utah and California, biology courses were taught in German and Spanish on an experimental basis. Students increased their skills in the language to a greater degree than those who took the regular *Biology* language course, and skills and knowledge in biology were increased. In Sussex, Wis. (47), an experiment involving three groups, one experimental and two control, was undertaken to determine the extent to which the coordinate study of German and history can be more effective in the rapid mastery of the German language. The experimental group devoted one hour to a world history course taught in German and another hour to the regular German II class. The first control group was enrolled in second year German and served as the control in language competency against which the achievement in German of the exper- *World history* imental group was measured. The second control group pursued the traditional world history course and served as the control in history. The results showed that the experimental group gained in language competency over the first control group and did not show any appreciable loss of knowledge of historical influence in relation to the second control group. Graphs in the research study show comparative achievement of the three groups at different stages of the experiment, tables of relevant data, and class reactions to the experiment. The 1968 Northeast Conference Report (Bird, 8) goes into extensive detail on such innovative programs.

Humanities courses in foreign languages. The Foreign Language Innovative Curricula Studies (FLICS) project of the state of Michigan has been and still is developing an extensive program in humanities in foreign languages under the directorship of George Eddington (McClafferty, 50). In conjunction with co-operating schools, program staff, consultants, and Michigan teachers, the broad goal of developing French and Spanish curricula has shifted the literary emphasis of advanced foreign language instruction. The new materials are called *Humanities in French* and *Language and Area Studies in Spanish.* The unit topics have been based on the interests of students. These year-long curriculum courses remain open-ended since the subject of humanities and the culture of a people are vast. This flexibility will encourage a teacher to use the new materials to improve his own courses. The cognitive goals of the new programs are the perfection of the foreign language skills and knowledge of humanistic achievements, as well as significant features of the countries studied. These include geographic and socioeconomic attributes, contemporary values, and behavior patterns. New cultural tests in French and Spanish, using audiovisual items, have been developed. French results, the only complete data available so far, show substantial student achievement in the humanities and achievement as well or better in the language skills as measured by the MLA foreign language battery of tests.

FLICS: Humanities courses taught in French; area studies in Spanish

Examples of the content are units in French on values and technology, an area study of French West Africa and one on French Canada; in Spanish there are sociocultural units focusing on Middle America and its Hispanic culture and history. Many new instructional materials based on the art, music, and way of life of French- and Spanish-speaking areas of the world have been developed.

Content

These courses are to be used at levels III and IV. Demonstrations and pilot programs are in operation in the Michigan schools and in those of other states. During 1968–69, the two-year French sequence, "Introduction to the French Humanities" for the 11th grade, and "Highlights in French Humanities" for the twelfth grade, are being offered at Grosse Pointe High School, Mich.

Such programs enable the student to progress beyond the language per se. Language becomes the tool for further learning in the various disciplines and widens his horizons as well as expands his working capabilities.

Advanced placement courses. The advanced placement program, which has become considerably more common during the last decade, is a means of helping the student benefit in his college education by granting him recognition for his effort and success during his secondary school career (Campbell, 14). A word of caution is needed with regard to the advanced placement program. It requires a well-qualified near-native language teacher. Otherwise the program can vitiate the progress of the student trained in the functional-skills approach to language learning, for the course can easily turn into a watered-down college course, a series of lectures in English on literary history accompanied by the students' laborious decoding of selections from the great masterpieces. The advanced placement program should follow a good four years of intensive language training in the language as it is spoken and written today, with an immersion into the exciting literature of the present century. When an advanced placement program is installed, there should be an alternative program provided at these levels (Deeken, 23).

A word of caution

Summer language programs

Increasingly the profession is realizing that summer schools and language camps provide an excellent opportunity for foreign language study. Such programs are one of the fastest growing areas in the foreign language field. Haukebo (35) discusses various advantages of such programs: they are intensive; the overcrowded academic curriculum does not interfere with and inhibit concentration on the foreign language and culture; there is a greater reservoir of foreign language teachers and other aides at hand; and educational facilities, equipment, and resources are more readily available.

Advantages

A survey made during the summer of 1968 among foreign language leaders in state departments of education found that in 31 states there were such programs, many of them federally funded. Innovative were such programs as the Summer Foreign Language Day Houses in Chicago (Choldin, 17) where high school students of French, German, and Spanish met four hours daily during a period of eight weeks for intensive language practice. In addition, the students made field trips, attended concerts, ate at foreign restaurants, and prepared skits, newspapers, and other related activities. The Jefferson County (Colo.) Schools offer cooking, art criticism, sports, music, nature study, and architecture (studied in the language) as components of their summer school programs in French and Spanish. Many summer

Language Day House

169

schools give the students a chance to study Russian, Chinese, and Japanese. Some colleges will accept high school students in their regular summer school courses.

Greenville High School in North Carolina has a six-week Latin-American Studies Center for high school students with three years of Spanish. The curriculum includes Latin-American civilization, geography, government, literature, as well as Spanish conversation and composition.

The Beverly Hills program (JeKenta, 43) at the elementary school level sponsors a Colegio Español and Le Petit Lycée for pupils in grades four through seven. Although wide use is made of visiting resource people, each school is staffed with three teachers working as a cooperative team. These cultural islands are held in schools separate from the regular summer school sessions, reducing the possibilities for the students to hear and speak English. A serious effort is made to include up to ten native French- and Spanish-speaking children from the surrounding area. These children, ages 9 through 12, are an integral part of the program. Their inclusion helps maintain the cultural island of the schools and the experience is also beneficial to them.

The foreign language camp. The foreign language camp idea is becoming more and more widespread. Thirteen state consultants (Haukebo, 35) reported at least one language camp in operation. The programs are offered to children whose ages span the elementary and secondary schools. Sessions last from two to eight weeks and are held in French, Spanish, German, Norwegian, and Russian. Cultural immersion is behind the language camp concept. Haukebo describes in detail one of the pioneer language camps conducted by Concordia College in Moorhead, Minn. The two-week camp accepts its students by sending them "passports" and other documents. New foreign names are adopted and foreign money is exchanged. Students live in cabins identified by the name of a region or province of the foreign country. Language learning is reinforced by camp store, post office, radio communication, folk dancing, and many other activities that lend themselves to learning language in a near authentic situation. The staff is headed by a camp dean who is a master language teacher. Other experienced teachers form the core with graduate students and superior high school students aiding in the program. Other language camps vary in plan and purpose. The School for International Training in Brattleboro, Vt., provides six weeks of cross-cultural studies followed by two weeks in Mexico and Canada. The students live with host families. The

Minneapolis Board of Education operates a summer language camp for culturally disadvantaged students from the junior high schools that offer little foreign language instruction. Federally subsidized, it attempts to determine whether children from core schools could be stimulated into further study of a foreign language.

Foreign study for high school students. Thousands of high school students travel to foreign countries for periods of six to ten weeks of study. According to Leamon (49) these programs fall into three categories: (*1*) national or regional service type programs, (*2*) programs organized by an individual or a school, and (*3*) commercial programs. There are few students in cate- *Types* gory 1. The program includes a well-qualified staff and linguistic orientation. In category 2 the quality of the programs varies considerably. The third category sends abroad the majority of high school students. In the latter the programs range from well run to carelessly operated. The Leamon report includes a reading list for teachers and schools who contemplate programs abroad and gives a few suggestions. Goals should be realistic, the target language must be used, travel should take place at the end of the study program, the students should live with families, a local representative who is in good standing with the community should help develop the program, the staff must be carefully selected, there should be a good insurance program and clear-cut rules to insure the students' physical and moral well-being, the academic program should be intensive, opportunities for group activities with their peers should be promoted, and, finally, the evaluation should be done carefully.

There is little evidence as to advantages of programs abroad. Carroll (15), in a nationwide testing program conducted in 1965 of the proficiency levels attained by college majors in a foreign language, found that the time spent abroad was one of the most potent factors in increasing the language skills. The Indiana Language Project Honors Program in Foreign Languages for high schools students, which is held abroad, showed positive increases in skills and also a considerable attitudinal change (Jantzen, 41; Meessen, 52). Clark (18), in evaluating a foreign *Advantages* program with 27 high school participants in Aachen, Ger., using the MLA Cooperative Classroom Tests, Forms MA and MB, found that 10 scored over the 90th percentile in the Listening Comprehension Test at the beginning and 25 at the end of the program. At the beginning none were over the 99th percentile, at the end 15 participants were. In reading, 10 scored over the 90th

171

percentile at the beginning and 24 at the end of the program; in writing 16 scored over the 90th percentile at the beginning and 21 at the end. In oral expression the MA form was administered at the beginning but due to technical malfunctioning the speaking portion of the MB form did not record on the tapes.

The American Council on the Teaching of Foreign Languages Study Abroad Committee plans to establish well-run model programs in 1970 with careful evaluation included. An important document for any administrator, parent, and teacher who plans to send high school students abroad for study should make it a point to examine the document on "Criteria for Evaluating Foreign Study Programs for High School Students" (Freeman, 31).

ACTL Study Abroad Committee

Articulation between high school and college

The problems encountered in articulation between the high school foreign language program and the college one are perhaps the most crucial in the foreign language articulation field at the present moment. Students arrive with various competencies, patterns, and number of years of language study. Many wish to continue this study.

Colleges need to find out what these students are capable of doing before they can place them intelligently into the proper courses. Equating one year of high school study with one semester of college study has proved invalid according to studies made at the University of Illinois and the University of Washington (1, 71, 63). Walsh (81) suggests that the college must either prepare local tests in the four skills or use the MLA Cooperative Tests or the College Board Achievement or Advanced Placement Tests. These they must first of all administer to their own beginning and intermediate students to obtain local norms and compare them with the national norms if they are national proficiency tests. These tests should be given to incoming freshmen during freshman week. The decision as to what scores on each of the tests should entitle the student to placement in an intermediate or advanced course must then be made.

Equating is invalid

Need for comparative studies to determine proficiency levels for incoming college students

Colleges and universities will find it more and more necessary to provide courses or programmed materials to accomodate the incoming student or devise other means by which they can help strengthen the weaknesses a student may have in certain skills but yet allow him to go on with the skills in which he is strongest.

The above demands a continuous dialogue between the secondary school teachers and their college couterparts. High school teachers should know the foreign language curricula of

Need for a continuous dialogue between teachers at all levels of instruction

those colleges the majority of their students will be attending. Likewise colleges should take an interest in the high school programs (Frank, 30; Gougher, 33). In any placement system a certain flexibility must be maintained in order to respond to any additional information that may be made available with regard to course structure, curriculum, type and quality of freshmen, etc. (Rabura, 63). The possibility exists of using high school language grades and types of high schools in the prediction equations of success in college language study.

Articulation must of necessity be structured horizontally as well as vertically to minimize the disorientation at the crucial points in the foreign language curriculum—grades 7,10, and 13. It is needed in content and in personnel. A foreign language teacher should know what his colleagues are doing in his school system. He should investigate what is going on in the foreign language courses more elementary than his and those more advanced. He should also know what other teachers are doing at his level. A citywide consultant or head of a foreign language department can be of enormous help in the articulation process. In addition, a person appointed as coordinator of the college language program should work at coordinating language instruction in the college and communicate with the schools as to the weaknesses and strengths of their products (Walsh, 81). The problems in articulation are by no means solved. Perhaps the new type programs as they appear both at the high school and college levels can alleviate the situation through the emphasis on the individualization of instruction.

Horizontal articulation is as important as vertical

The college coordinator

Conclusion

This chapter has made no attempt to discuss materials such as curriculum guides, texts, audiovisual materials, and other resources in detail. That would be an impossible task. Reports on these items can be found in *Foreign Language Annals*, published by the American Council on the Teaching of Foreign Languages, under the section called "Selected Recent ERIC FL Accessions." The December 1968 issue contains 741 items, many of which are listings of the above materials under the title "ERIC Documents on the Teaching of Foreign Languages: List no. I".

The curriculum field is a vast one. It is the focal point of all educational endeavor. The reader can readily see that all other chapters in this review of foreign language education investigate areas and disciplines that assist in the development of a more efficient foreign language curriculum at the elementary, secondary, and college levels.

The profession is taking another look at foreign language in the elementary school since it got off to a bad start in the '50s. The good programs are flourishing and various patterns are emerging that will have a vital role to play in the development of new FLES programs. However, with new organizational formats and curricula in the elementary school, foreign language teachers need to work closely with the leaders in the elementary school field to evolve new types of foreign language programs in collaboration with the other disciplines and thus enrich the learning environment of the elementary school child, especially in the inner-city schools. This child is able to learn a language and is a tabula rasa for new and vital experiences he can get through learning about a new culture and using a new language.

Foreign language programs at the secondary school level are as varied as they are in the elementary school, if not more so. Although the profession speaks of long sequences such as nine-year, six-year, and four-year sequences, few schools can actually carry them through in the traditional type curriculum. It is the new organizational pattern such as flexible scheduling, team teaching, grouping, and individualizing instruction that will assist foreign language departments in carrying out a long sequence. The nongraded school, the maintainance of skills (MOS) program at the advanced levels, innovative single courses, and summer language programs are helping to maintain the continuity of foreign language programs.

The language laboratory concept has changed into a learning carrel in the foreign language materials resource center plus a foreign language classroom equipped as an electronic classroom. Visual media are incorporated in both the carrel and the classroom. In other words, the language laboratory, when it fulfills its original function, that of helping to individualize instruction and give the student a chance to learn language at his own pace, is beginning to find its real place in the foreign language curriculum.

At the secondary school level programmed instruction is becoming a part of the learning system. Programmed units of work rather than complete programmed courses are evolving as part of the new materials. A programmed language course encounters many problems when used in the school curriculum unless it is backed up with display sessions and the continuous guidance of the teacher. This area has been under severe scrutiny by the programmers themselves during the past year and shows evidence of more exciting breakthroughs for language learning at the secondary school level.

The foreign language curriculum is establishing its own identity and independence at the secondary school level by showing greater flexibility through the many innovations in different types of courses, such as the humanities courses in the different languages, subject matter courses being taught in the foreign language, intensive summer school programs, called area and language studies, and more and more study-abroad programs. The curriculum is no longer focused solely on college entrance requirements or a purely college preparatory curriculum. It is now beginning to serve the student in attaining his own objectives in the area of cross-cultural communication.

The articulation problem, which plagues the profession to a greater degree than ever before because of the long language sequences, is being explored thoroughly by the profession. There now exists a real dialogue between the college and high school teachers; coordinators of programs are working together and alleviating a very serious problem in the field. There is a mutual respect for what each level of foreign language instruction is trying to do. National placement examinations are also playing a greater role in the placement of the high school student in the right college course.

The past year has brought greater insights into the problems of language learning. The learner rather than the subject matter has become the focus of our efforts in solving the learning problems of a very complex field. Innovative work of all types, in curriculum, in courses, in instructional strategies and learning media, or combinations thereof, are slowly breaking the lockstep of the traditional foreign language program, be it grammar-translation or audiolingual.

References, Current trends in the elementary and secondary curriculum

1 Aleamoni, Lawrence M.; Spencer, Richard E. Development of the University of Illinois foreign language placement and proficiency system and its results for fall, 1966 and 1967. Modern Language Journal, 52 (October 1968) 355–359.

2 Allen, Dwight W.; Politzer, Robert L. Flexible scheduling and foreign language instruction: a conference report. Modern Language Journal, 51 (1967) 275–281.

3 Allen, Edward D.; Glenn, Leona M.; Otto, Frank. The changing curriculum: modern foreign languages. Association for Supervision and Curriculum Development, National Education Association, Washington, D. C., 1967.

4 American Association of School Administrators. Curriculum handbook for school administrators. National Education Association, Washington, D.C., 1967, p. 71–95.

5 Asher, James J.; Price, B. S. The learning strategy of the total physical response: some age differences. Child Development, 38 (1967) 1220–1227.

6 Banathy, Bela H. The systems approach. Modern Language Journal, 51 (May 1967) 281–289.

7 Batezel, George W. The middle school: philosophy, program, organization. Clearing House, 42 (April 1968) 487–490.

8 Bird, Thomas E. Foreign language learning: research and development: an assessment. Reports of the Working Committees, Northeast Conference on the Teaching of Foreign Languages. MLA/ACTFL Materials Center, New York, 1968.

9 Birkmaier, Emma Marie. Modern languages: a vehicle for the humanities. Educational Leadership, 20 (January 1963) 238–242.

10 Brandt, Ronald S. The middle school in a nongraded system. Journal of Secondary Education, 43 (April 1968) 165–170.

11 Brown, B. Frank. The nongraded high school. Prentice-Hall, Englewood Cliffs, N.J., 1963.

12 Brown, Mary Arnoff. Institute for development of educational activities, Nova Junior-Senior High School, Fort Lauderdale, Fla., Pamphlet, 1967–68.

13 Bush, Robert M.; Allen, Dwight A. A new design for high school education assuming a flexible schedule. McGraw-Hill, New York, 1964.

14 Campbell, Hugh. One solution to advanced placement problems. French Review, 41 (December 1967) 386–389.

15 Carroll, John B. Foreign language proficiency levels attained by language majors near graduation from college. Foreign Language Annals, 1 (December 1967) 131–151.

16 Carroll, John B. Psychological aspects of programmed learning in foreign languages. In: Mueller, Theodore H., ed. Proceedings of the seminar on programmed learning. Appleton-Century-Crofts, New York, 1968, p. 63–73.

17 Choldin, Hannah W. Foreign language day houses. Modern Language Journal, 52 (February 1968) 88–89.

18 Clark, Richard A. The Aachen program: "from I to ich." Die Unterrichtspraxis, 1 (1968) 92–100.

19 Cornfield, Ruth R. FLES: how much time? DFL Bulletin, 5 (October 1965) 3.

20 Couture, Louise. French in the Birmingham (Michigan) elementary schools. Foreign Language Annals, 2:iii (March 1969) 328–335.

21 Dammer, Paul E.; Glaude, Paul M.; Green, Jerald R. FLES: a guide for program review. Modern Language Journal, 52 (January 1968) 16–23.

22 Davies, D. J. E. A comprehensive FLES program without specialists through the medium of television. Paper read at the Northeast Conference, New York, March 1969.

23 Deeken, Hans W. Investigation of the national potential for the advancement of the teaching of German in the United States. Final report, Contract No. OEC-1-7-070901-3907. U.S. Department of Health, Education, and Welfare, Office of Education, Bureau of Research, Washington, D.C. October 1968.

24 DeWright, Yvonne Febres Cordero. Television has value in FLES instruction. Foreign Language Beacon, Georgia State College, Atlanta, vol. 2, no. 1, Fall 1966.

25 Donoghue, Mildred R. Foreign languages and the elementary school child. W. C. Brown, Dubuque, Ia., 1968.

26 Donoghue, Mildred R., ed. Foreign languages and the schools. W. C. Brown, Dubuque, Ia., 1967.

27 Donoghue, Mildred R. Foreign languages in the elementary school: effects and instructional arrangements according to research. ERIC Focus Report on the Teaching of Foreign Languages, no. 3. MLA/ACTFL Materials Center, New York, 1969.

28 Fearing, Percy. Nongraded foreign language classes. ERIC Focus Report on the Teaching of Foreign Languages, no. 4. MLA/ACTFL Materials Center, New York, 1969.

29 Fiks, A. I. Foreign language programmed materials: 1969. ERIC Focus Report on the Teaching of Foreign Languages, no. 7. MLA/ERIC Clearinghouse on the Teaching of Foreign Languages, New York, 1969.

30 Frank, Luella. A pilot project in articulation. German Quarterly, 41 (May 1968) 496–497.

31 Freeman, Stephen A. Criteria for evaluating foreign study programs for high school students. Foreign Language Annals, 1 (May 1968) 288–290.

32 Gaarder, Bruce A.; Richardson, Mabel W. Two patterns of bilingual education in Dade County, Florida. In: Bird, Thomas E., ed. Foreign language learning: research and development. Reports of the Working Committees, Northeast Conference on the Teaching of Foreign Languages, 1968, p. 32–42. MLA Materials Center, N.Y.

33 Gougher, Ronald L. A cooperative effort. German Quarterly, 41 (November 1968) 272–273.

34 Grittner, Frank M. Maintaining foreign language skills for the advanced-course dropout. ERIC Focus Report on the Teaching of Foreign Languages, no. 1. MLA/ERIC Clearinghouse on the Teaching of Foreign Languages, New York, 1968.

35 Haukebo, Gerhard K. Summer foreign language programs for school students. ERIC Focus Report on the Teaching of Foreign Languages, no. 10. MLA/ERIC Clearinghouse on the Teaching of Foreign Languages, New York, 1969.

36 Hernick, Michael; Kennedy, Dora. Multilevel grouping of students in the modern foreign language programs. Foreign Language Annals, 2 (December 1968) 200–204.

37 Hubbard, Louise J. Modern foreign language for the racially disadvantaged. Modern Language Journal, 52 (March 1968) 139–140.

38 Humphrey, James H. Comparison of the use of active games and language workbook exercises as learning media in the development of language understandings with third grade children. Perceptual and Motor Skills, 21 (August 1965) 23–26.

39 Hutchinson, Joseph C. The language laboratory: equipment and utilization. In: Valdman, Albert, ed. Trends in language teaching. McGraw-Hill, New York, 1966, p. 215–233.

40 Hutchinson, Joseph C. The language laboratory: how effective is it? U.S. Department of Health, Education, and Welfare, Office of Education, Supt. of Documents, U.S. Government Printing Office, Washington, D.C., 1964.

41 Jantzen, John B. An analysis of the effectiveness of the Indiana University honors program in foreign languages for high school students. Unpublished Ph.D. dissertation, Indiana University, 1968.

42 JeKenta, Albert W. Annual board report. Beverly Hills Unified School District, California, June 1969.

43 JeKenta, Albert W. A report, elementary summer school. Beverly Hills Unified School District, California, December 1967.

44 Jonas, Sister Ruth Adelaide. A unique use of media: "twinned classroom" approach to the teaching of French. Audiovisual Instruction, 13:v (May 1968).

45 Keaton, Ruth. New FLES program being reached for '67. Foreign Language Beacon, Georgia State College, Atlanta, 2:i, Fall 1966.

46 Keislar, Evan R.; Stern, Carolyn; Mace, Lawrence. Sequence of speaking and listening training in beginning French: a replication. American Educational Research Journal, 3 (May 1966) 169–178.

47 Keitel, Helmut A. Teaching world history in German. Board of Education, Sussex, Wis., n.d.

48 Lane, Harlan L. Programmed learning of a second language. International Review of Applied Linguistics, 2 (November 1964) 249–301.

49 Leamon, M. Philip. Foreign study for high school students: what's going on? ERIC Focus Report on the Teaching of Foreign Languages, no. 5. MLA/ERIC Clearinghouse on the Teaching of Foreign Languages, New York, 1969.

50 McClafferty, James. Foreign language innovative curricula studies. A state-wide Title III, ESEA project sponsored by the Ann Arbor Board of Education and aided by the Center for Research on Language and Language Behavior, University of Michigan, Ann Arbor, 1965.

51 Mace, Lawrence. Sequence of vocal response-differentiation training and auditory stimulus-discrimination training in beginning French. Journal of Educational Psychology, 57 (April 1966) 102–108.

52 Meessen, Lois E. The Krefeld program: "the key is language." Die Unterrichtspraxis, 1 (1968) 87–91.

53 Morton, F. Rand. Four major problem areas in programmed instruction for modern language learning. In: Mueller, Theodore H., ed. Proceedings of the seminar on programmed learning. Appleton-Century-Crofts, New York, 1968, p. 18–37.

54 Mueller, Theodore H., ed. Proceedings of the seminar on programmed learning. Appleton-Century-Crofts, New York, 1968.

55 Muller, Trinidad V.; Muller, Daniel H. A comparison of two time spacing arrangements in elementary school foreign language classes. California Educational Research Summaries, Burlingame: California Educational Research Association, 1967, p. 51.

56 National Council of State Supervisors of Foreign Languages. Modern Language Journal, 49 (February 1965) 93–94.

57 National Education Association. Public school programs and practices: foreign language programs. NEA Research Bulletin, 45 (December 1967) 113.

58 Oneto, Alfred J., project coordinator. FLES evaluation: language skills and pupil attitudes in Fairfield, Connecticut, public schools, bulletin no. 106. Connecticut State Department of Education, Box 2219, Hartford, 1968.

59 Otto, Frank. Alternative approaches to staffing the elementary foreign language program: cost and time vs. achievement and satisfaction. Modern Language Journal, 52 (May 1968) 293–301.

60 Penfield, Wilder. The uncommitted cortex: the child's changing brain. Atlantic Monthly, 214 (July 1964) 77–82.

61 Pillet, Roger A. The impact of FLES: an appraisal. Modern Language Journal, 52 (December 1968) 486–490.

62 Potts, Marion H. The effect of second-language instruction on the reading proficiency and general school achievement of primary grade children. American Educational Research Journal, 4 (November 1967) 367–373.

63 Rabura, Horst. Articulation from high school to college. German Quarterly, 41 (March 1968) 288–290.

64 Rise, Helen. Communication to curriculum leaders in the state of Georgia. Cartersville City Schools, Georgia, April 1969.

65 Rivers, Wilga M. Teaching foreign language skills. The University of Chicago Press, 1968, chapter XIV.

66 Science Research Associates. Teacher education extension service, unit 8, 1 May 1965. Chicago.

67 Shulze, Susan; Arendt, Jermaine; Rainey, Robert G. A two year study of the use of programmed materials for the instruction of French in high school. Minneapolis Public Schools, Minnesota, 1966. Mimeo.

68 Smith, Philip D., Jr.; Baranyi, Helmut A. A comparison study on the effectiveness of the traditional and audio-lingual approaches to foreign language instruction utilizing language laboratory equipment. Project no. 7-0133; Grant no. OEC-1-7-070133-0445. U.S. Department of Health, Education, and Welfare, Washington, D.C., 1968.

69 Smith, Philip D., Jr.; Berger, Emanuel. An assessment of three language teaching strategies utilizing three language laboratory systems. Final report project no. 5-0683; Grant no. OE-7-48-9013-272. U.S. Department of Health, Education, and Welfare, Washington, D.C., 1968.

70 Smith, Wayne H. Linguistic and academic achievement of elementary students studying a foreign language. Dissertation Abstracts, 27 (May 1967) 3882–A.

71 Spencer, Richard E.; Flaugher, Ronald L. A study of an assumption about high school and college equivalency in language training. Modern Language Journal, 51 (October 1967) 331–335.

72 Spodak, Ruth. Selected bibliography in pro-

grammed instruction. Center for Applied Linguistics, Washington, D.C., 1966, 20 p. Available from ERIC EDRS: ED 010 878.

73 Stack, Edward M. The language laboratory and modern language teaching. Oxford University Press, rev. ed., New York, 1966.

74 Stough, Grace. Report, Ford Junior High, Berea School District, Cleveland, O., March 1969.

75 Strasheim, Lorraine A., ed. Language laboratory teaching. A publication of the language laboratory subcommittees of the Indiana State Advisory Committee for Foreign Language. The Indiana Language Program, Indiana University, Bloomington, 1968.

76 Talley, Kathryn S. The effects of a program of special language instruction on the reading and intellectual levels of bilingual children. Dissertation Abstracts, 26 (April 1966) 5796.

77 Teague, Caroline; Rütimann, Hans. Foreign language offerings and enrollments in public secondary schools, fall 1965. Modern Language Association, New York, 1967, p. 14, 23, 32, 58.

78 Valdman, Albert. Problems in the definition of learning steps in programmed foreign language materials. In: Mueller, Theodore H., ed. Proceedings of the seminar on programmed learning. Appleton-Century-Crofts, New York, 1968, p. 50–62, 74–77.

79 Valdman, Albert, ed. Trends in language teaching. McGraw-Hill, New York, 1966, p. 133–158.

80 Vocolo, Joseph M. The effect of foreign language study in the elementary school upon achievement in the same foreign language in high school. Modern Language Journal, 51 (December 1967) 463–469.

81 Walsh, Donald D. Longer and better: the foreign language sequence. Modern Language Journal, 52 (November 1968) 424–431.

82 West Bend (Wisconsin) Public Schools. Continuous progress foreign language program. PL 89-10, Title III project. West Bend Public Schools, Joint District No. 1, Wisconsin, 1967.

Division II Theory and Practice of Foreign Language Teaching and Learning

7

Physiology and psychology of second language learning

Introduction

Leon A. Jakobovits

University of Illinois

The amount of effort that is being expended in the teaching of foreign languages (henceforth abbreviated as FL) in this country has reached considerable proportions. According to various surveys conducted by the Modern Language Association of America, 80 percent of public secondary schools offered FL courses in 1965 and more than one out of every four senior high school students were engaged in the study of a FL (Willbern, 78). Some predictions estimate that by 1970 roughly half of all public school pupils will be engaged in the study of a language other than English. Most of the large universities in the country have either a college entrance requirement in their Liberal Arts and Sciences Schools or a college graduation requirement involving a FL.

There are powerful social pressures for the maintenance of such a large educational investment in the teaching of a second language that go beyond the traditional goals of FL study stated in terms of promoting the "cultured person." According to the 1966 Statistical Abstract of the United States there were in 1960 close to 24 million Americans in the category labeled "native of foreign or mixed parentage," of which almost 10 million were foreign born. Over 18 million Americans claim that their mother tongue is not English (Fishman, 17). Considerable social effort is expended within a non-English medium of communication: over 500 periodicals are published regularly (including 61 daily newspapers); some 1,500 radio stations broadcast in a FL for several hours a week; there are approximately 2,000 ethnically affiliated schools of which more than half offer mother tongue (i.e., non-English) instruction; there exist at least 1,800 ethnic cultural organizations, most of which favor maintenance of their FL (Fishman, 17).

Some reasons for foreign language study

An assessment of the present level of technology for teaching a second language is extremely difficult. Depending on the students involved, the available time for teaching, and the larger social context within which the instruction program is embedded, variable results have been achieved. On the higher end of success, the results are impressive: with preselected students

Different programs produce different levels of attainment

for high motivation and high FL aptitude, placed in an intensive program of instruction involving anywhere from 6 to 14 hours of directed and individual study a day, day after day, meaningful levels of proficiency (e.g., fluent conversation with natives) can be insured within 30 to 40 days according to some lower estimates (Carroll, 12), or six months according to some higher estimates (Mueller, 54). Intermediate levels of success are achieved with FL majors in colleges (Carroll, 8) where after several years of concentrated study audiolingual skills remain generally low. Much more modest levels of success are to be found in the massive educational effort of FL teaching in our high schools where the indications are that most of the students involved do not reach meaningful levels of proficiency.

In one sense the technology of teaching FLs has been solved. Given motivated and talented individuals, we have the "know-how" to expose the individual to an instructional procedure that insures the learning of any FL within a matter of weeks or months. The fact that this success is limited to a preselected sample of individuals should not lead us to minimize this pedagogical achievement. It is far better than we knew how prior to the new techniques developed since the Second World War and it is comparable, and perhaps even superior, to most industrial training programs designed to impart skills of a much lesser complexity.

On the other hand, and from a quite different perspective, our ability to train successfully the multitudes of students in our public schools in the use of a FL is considerably less and by all indications does not compare favorably to the pedagogical achievements of teaching the three Rs. This sobering assessment is apparently shared by members of society at large: parents, students, school administrators, legislators responsible for appropriating educational funds, educators not directly involved in the teaching of FLs, all are increasingly engaged in asking a persistent and disturbing question: Why should so much effort *Gallup Poll Survey* be spent on the teaching of FLs when the results appear to be so meager? In a recent Gallup Poll Survey parents consistently expressed the opinion that FL courses represent the weakest part of the school curriculum and should be the first to go in any curtailment of efforts. There are signs that the largess of federal grant assistance to the FL teaching effort is being tempered along with the general slowdown of federal support for research, and an increasing number of universities are liberalizing their FL requirements, which is to say, reducing them at both the undergraduate and graduate levels. One might say that the FL instruction establishment has been put in a defensive position. It must come up with good answers to the baffling problem that besets it today: How is FL instruction to be made more successful and more relevant to the aspirations of the "New Student" in an educational setting that competes for his attention and time?

College FL requirements reexamined

The responses to this challenge are likely to come along three levels. First, on the technological side, better trained teachers using more advanced techniques (including both "hardware" and "software") are to come on the scene. Second, FLs are to be taught increasingly earlier (cf. FLES [foreign languages in the elementary school] efforts) affording more cumulative time for study. Third, increasing efforts are to be made to improve the motivation of students by recognizing the social-psychological implications of FL study and taking into account the attitudinal and sociological matrix within which FL study and maintenance are embedded in the larger societal, national, and world contexts.

The challenge can be met

This chapter attempts to organize the main facts that have come to be known about the physiology and psychology of FL learning as they impinge upon the three-pronged attack of the problem just discussed. The main issues to be dealt with will be (1) the theory and practice in FL teaching, (2) what is meant by "knowing a language," (3) the physiology of second language learning, and (4) the motivational aspects of FL study.[1]

Main issues

To be examined in the section on the theory and practice in FL teaching is the problem of how research efforts come to influence teaching practices. Several statements by authoritative persons and organized bodies (e.g., The Modern Language Association [MLA]) concerning the state of the art of FL teaching are to be summarized and reviewed. The conclusion that will be presented will stress the fact that most of what we know about teaching comes not from the experimental laboratory but from the teacher's experience in the classroom. Here, as in other areas of education, practical knowledge by far outstrips the specific contribution of organized research. Given the relatively backward condition of social science and educational research, this state of affairs is unavoidable and, though it is pointless to

---

1 The reader who is interested in pursuing in greater detail some of the more technical aspects of the discussion presented in this chapter may do so by consulting the author's articles listed in the reference section as well as the selective bibliographies compiled by Birkmaier & Lange (5), Harmon (20), and Mildenberger & Yuan-Heng Liao (49).

criticize it, the situation should nevertheless be clearly and explicitly recognized.

What it is to know a language poses many problems. Everyone accepts the notion that language is a means of communication, but there is much less agreement about just what is involved in the ability to communicate. The distinction between "linguistic competence" and "communicative competence" is either not explicitly taken into account in the majority of FL courses or it is tacitly assumed that the former must precede the latter in such a way that a certain high level of linguistic competence must be achieved before attempting the functional use of FL. Arguments will be presented that show the harmful consequences of this practice. "Liberated expression" and the practical use of a FL is both desirable and possible at even the very beginning stages of study. A new attitude to the assessment of communicate skills (rather than language skills) is long overdue in the language testing field.

Competence and performance

The section on the physiology of second language learning will look at the current efforts in FLES, often justified on the grounds that there is a biological timetable for language learning that makes it increasingly difficult to learn a second language after puberty, at which time the brain allegedly loses "plasticity." The discussion will question the validity of this argument and will examine other grounds for both the advantages and disadvantages of early versus late FL teaching.

The biological timetable

The importance of the problem of knowing how to motivate the FL learner has been mentioned. This section will examine a number of issues relating to this pressing need: (*1*) the consequences of the fact that becoming bilingual entails becoming bicultural; (2) the attitude of the student towards FL study generally, the goals and purposes that he sees in it.

Motivation

The final section will attempt to summarize the major points that are discussed in this chapter and will offer some thoughts on some possible and desirable developments in the FL teaching field that may take place in the immediate future.

Theory and practice in FL teaching: out of step

Two basic truths about the psychology of human learning are (*1*) that it is amazingly efficient and powerful—by such standards as the learning capacities of other living organisms or man-made automata and (2) that this learning goes on in ways that neither the individual learner nor the educator or social scientist can describe or explicate even in elementary and simplistic terms. Two outstanding instances that illustrate both truths are the learning of a language and the learning of a culture during socialization or acculturation. The concepts, such as "stimulus," "response," "reinforcement," "habit," that social scientists have invented to account for these accomplishments of the individual have such weak explanatory power that even in much simpler learning situations, such as a rat running a maze, they allow for such inadequate and impotent descriptions that psychologists in a narrow field of specialization disagree about them. The weakest aspect about these "scientific explanations" is that they attempt to describe the learning process through concepts that refer to external events (stimuli, responses, schedules of reinforcement, etc.), whereas what obviously accounts for the process is the internal mechanism of the brain, the capacities and workings of the human mind (Jakobovits, 29).

Psychological theories are inadequate

Theories about the mind, theories about knowledge (as distinguished from theories about behavior), theories about capacities, about potentialities and competencies, have been proposed by many writers over the course of modern scientific history, but these occupy the back seat to the leading theories in the social sciences. The most influential and widespread approach to psychological explanation remains in the United States today, in education (cf. programmed instruction), in clinical psychology (cf. behavior modification), in much of experimental psychology (cf. verbal conditioning), that of Skinnerian operant conditioning of behavior. The latter is widely claimed as being "sound" and "tough-minded" in research, while theories of the mind are presented to graduate students and future researchers in a shadowy and not quite respectable light; they are "soft," "nonrigorous," "wishy-washy."

The role of the U.S.

In the field of FL teaching, the trend is notably the same. The recent book by Rivers (66), *The Psychologist and the Foreign Language Teacher*, is often cited as the most advanced scientific achievement in the field. While Rivers herself shows awareness of the theoretical shortcomings of the "habit" approach to language, many language teachers are not so cautious: they take the "habit" notion of the audiolingual approach quite literally, deriving much self-assurance from the "scientific" and "rigorous" pretentiousness of concepts such as stimulus, response, conditioning, and the automatic establishment of habits.

This is a strange situation, indeed. Teachers and therapists are practical people, by necessity, and they ought not to be castigated

for adopting methods that seem to work. The two most nota-
ble and successful accomplishments achieved by the Skinneri-
ans are programmed instruction and behavioral modification,
yet the theoretical foundations from which they have sprung are
simplistic and inadequate in the extreme (Chomsky, 15; Lashley, 41; Lenneberg, 43). This is a curious paradox wherein surely
lies the bankruptcy of the modern social scientific enterprise:
what seems to work best on practical grounds, shouldn't, it
seems, on theoretical grounds, and the theories that appear to be
more sophisticated and more powerful do not enable us to develop effective practical approaches. It would seem to be a be-
trayal of the intellectual spirit to accept that which works when it
shouldn't, yet it would be folly to reject that which works merely
because on theoretical grounds "it ought not."

The relationship between theorist and practitioner

The resolution of this difficulty would seem to lie in a change
of attitude on the part of both the theorist and the practitioner.
On the one hand, today's theorist should give up any claim that
his speculations have the scientific authority whereby he can
make infallible pronouncements about the solution of practical
problems. On the other hand, the practitioner should give up his
attempt to justify his activities in the classroom and clinic by
appealing to competing "scientific" theories often outdated by
the time the practitioner gets hold of them. Careful thinkers
have recognized the abyss that separates theory from practice.
Skinner himself has consistently claimed for over a quarter of a
century that his concern is with behavior, not with theory, and it
is only when he strays into the morass of theoretical justification
(as in some parts of his book, *Verbal Behavior*, 70) that the
shortcomings of his system become so apparent (Jakobovits,
29, 33). One of the most authoritative experts in the area of learning has recently stated that "thus far, there is little empirical
evidence in support of [the] assumption [that] forgetting outside
the laboratory is a function of the same variables and represents
the same processes as are observed in formal studies on inter-
serial interference" (Postman, 64, p. 166). In the area of language, Chomsky (14) has stated that there is no evidence today
in support of the view that the scientific endeavor will ever be
successful in explicating the fundamental facts. Integrity dictates that we clearly recognize the inherent limitations of the
social and behavioral sciences as we know them today and not
to claim for them more than is reasonable.

If this limitation is accepted, as it surely must be, then the
interplay between theoretical and practical concerns can be-

come more honest and possibly more rewarding. Experimenters
can tackle practical problems by relaxing their unrealistic insistence on experimental controls and statistically "adequate"
designs. Practitioners, such as the teacher and the therapist,
need not feel the need to take sides in theoretical controversies
or to justify their practices by appealing to particular theories;
instead, they can adopt a healthy functional attitude concerning
the effects of their methods of approach, *concentrating on developing and constantly using realistic evaluation criteria
that would dictate maintaining or altering their activities in
accord with the results they achieve.* In subsequent sections of
this chapter, such an attitude will be repeatedly advocated.

The audiolingual approach

The most widespread method of FL teaching today, the so-
called New Key approach prevalent since the 1940s, is the audiolingual approach which claims to have largely displaced the
earlier "traditional" method of grammar-translation. The proponents of the audiolingual approach base their claim of correctness on "sound" psychological theory as well as on efficient results. The purpose of this section is to show that both of these
claims are questionable. In the following quotation, an eminent
figure in the FL field questions the first of these claims:

> Let me point out that neither the audiolingual habit theory
> nor the cognitive code-learning theory is closely linked to any
> contemporary psychological theory of learning. The audiolin-
> gual habit theory has a vague resemblance to an early version
> of a Thorndikean association theory, while the cognitive code-
> learning theory is reminiscent of certain contemporary ges-
> taltist movements in psychology which emphasize the impor-
> tance of perceiving the "structure" of what is to be learned,
> without really relying on such movements. Actually, neither
> theory takes adequate account of an appreciable body of
> knowledge that has accumulated in the study of verbal learn-
> ing. Among these facts are the following:
> 1 The frequency with which an item is practiced per se is not
>   so crucial as the frequency with which it is contrasted with
>   other items with which it may be confused. Thus, the learn-
>   ing of items in "pattern-practice" drills would be improved if
>   instead of simple repetition there were a constant alternation
>   among varied patterns.
> 2 The more meaningful the material to be learned, the greater

the facility in learning and retention. The audiolingual habit theory tends to play down meaningfulness in favor of producing automaticity.

3 Other things being equal, materials presented visually are more easily learned than comparable materials presented aurally. Even though the objective of teaching may be the attainment of mastery over the auditory and spoken components of language learning, an adequate theory of language learning should take account of how the student handles visual counterparts of the auditory elements he is learning and help to prescribe the optimal utilization of these counterparts, such as printed words, phonetic transcriptions, and other visual-symbol systems.

Five statements to be carefully weighed by the FL teacher

4 In learning a skill, it is often the case that conscious attention to its critical features and understanding of them will facilitate learning. This principle is largely ignored by the audiolingual habit theory; it is recognized by the cognitive code-learning theory. It would imply, for example, that in teaching pronunciation an explanation of necessary articulatory movements would be helpful.

5 The more numerous kinds of association that are made to an item, the better are learning and retention. Again this principle seems to dictate against the use of *systems* of language teaching that employ mainly one sensory modality, namely, hearing. A recent experiment performed at the Defense Language Institute, West Coast Branch (Army Language School, Monterey, California) seems to show that dramatic facilitation of language learning occurs when words denoting concrete objects and physical actions are associated with actual *motor* performances involving those objects and actions. Thus, the student learns the meaning of the foreign language word for *jump* by actually jumping! Language teaching becomes a sort of physical exercise both for the students and for the instructor whose actions they imitate.

These, then, are a few examples of theory-derived principles that, if further examined and verified, could contribute to more effective ways of teaching foreign languages. It would be trite to say at this point that "more research is needed," although it is obviously the case. Actually, what is needed even more than research is a profound rethinking of current theories of foreign language teaching in the light of contemporary advances in psychological and psycholinguistic theory. The audio-lingual habit theory which is so prevalent in American foreign language teaching was, perhaps, fifteen years ago in step with the state of psychological thinking at that time, but it is no longer abreast of recent developments. It is ripe for major revision, particularly in the direction of joining with it some of the better elements of the cognitive code-learning theory. I would venture to predict that if this can be done, then teaching based on the revised theory will yield a dramatic change in effectiveness (Carroll, 7, p. 104–106).

Carroll's statement agrees with the assessment that theory and practice in FL teaching are out of step but he appears to believe that "contemporary advances in psychological and psycholinguistic theory" are necessarily relevant to FL teaching. As stated earlier, there are no good grounds for such optimism. Note that the five "facts" that he reviews and that he urges the FL teacher to consider are in the nature of empirical generalizations, not theoretically derived principles. His call for "more research" can be welcomed as long as it is understood that this is to refer to efforts in the development of evaluation criteria of the effectiveness of teaching practices in terms of functional or terminal behaviors on the part of the learner. (What can the learner *do* with the knowledge he has acquired?)

Caution must be exercised

Weaknesses of current experimental techniques

There are two principal reasons for the weakness of currently known and practiced experimental techniques: the difficulty (practical impossibility) of controlling a large number of simultaneously varying and interacting factors and the fact that the individual's learning strategy is largely independent of the teacher's manipulative efforts even though it is a factor that greatly influences the learning process.

With respect to the first difficulty, we are confronted with a "double bind": carefully controlled small-scale laboratory experiments yield generalizations whose extrapolation to the real learning situation, where "all things are not equal," is a dubious activity; large-scale experiments on contrasting teaching methods that have, at least potentially, direct relevance for classroom practices leave so many factors uncontrolled that the conclusions are either unconvincing on the strength of the data or the results are more often than not contradictory (Carroll, 10, 11).

Values of experiments

The second difficulty, the contribution of the individual himself to the learning process, is inherent to the nature of the mind as an information processing and storing device about which little of substance is known today. To the chagrin of many teachers, the individual is not a habit forming automaton who can be conditioned by carefully arranging the presentation of stimuli and rewards contingent upon overt responses. Passive learning is immeasurably inferior to active learning and, although we have been able to measure general learning capacities with intelligence tests, these not only represent weak predictors in specific learning situations but are also unenlightening concerning the processes that underlie individual learning strategies and how to influence or manipulate them. The teacher may spend a lot of effort in arranging sequences of materials to be presented at various stages but he has no control over what in fact the individual does mentally with them: how well he remembers them, whether he focuses on just the intended distinction, whether he tries to assimilate the new material to the old, how much of it he will transfer to new situations, whether he inductively arrives at generalizations, and so on.

The learner contributes in unpredictive ways

The development of computer-based programmed instruction in language (such as the PLATO [Programmed Logic for Automatic Teaching Operations] system at the University of Illinois in Urbana) offers the possibility of a real alternative to the present inadequate policy of basing teaching practices on theoretical generalizations gained from laboratory experiments. Computer-based individuated instruction, when fully developed, will not represent a "teaching method" as this is understood today. Rather, it will consist of a conglomeration of many techniques and combinations thereof, fitted to the individual learner in terms of his peculiar learning strategies, learning capacities, interests, and goals. Each student will be taught by a different "method" when one considers the total teaching process from beginning to end, that which is most effective for him and most consistent with the goals he has for learning the language. Until computer-based programmed instruction is a reality for every pupil in the United States we must make do with the present less effective educational means at our disposal. There is much that can be done even during this "stop-gap interval" to render the teaching of FLs more effective. The next section will review some attempts that have been suggested by authoritative figures and bodies in the FL teaching field.

What can computer-based instruction do for us?

The state of FL teaching today

One might begin by presenting an extended statement by Hayes which represents, in his words, "a summary of the state of foreign language teaching in the United States today":

Traditional foreign language instruction in the United States was dedicated to the teaching of reading, approached through the study of the rules of grammar. The basic approach, with only minor variations, was extensive translation. But recent years have witnessed a shift of emphasis, since it has become a matter of national self-interest to increase the number of American citizens who can understand and speak a foreign language. This shift of emphasis is paralleled by recent advances in linguistic science and allied fields, which have contributed to a new view of language and language learning. This view is best characterized as a view of language as spoken communication, as signalling behavior, as a system of habits, which must be acquired to the point of automatic production of, and response to, the structure of the language as isolated by linguistic science, to the point where novel utterances acceptable to a native speaker are freely generated by the learner. Grammar is thus by no means discarded, as is sometimes supposed, but the emphasis is on internalizing it through practice, rather than discussing it. Gaarder (19, p. 171–172) gives a striking point-by-point comparison of language learning with learning to play a musical instrument.

There is reasonably general agreement on the following points in first-level foreign language instruction, although, in practice, procedures vary widely:

The 8 basic tenets of the audiolingual approach

1 Learning proceeds in this order: (*a*) hearing and understanding; (*b*) speaking; (*c*) usually much later—reading; (*d*) writing. The tendency is, therefore, away from "book-centered" materials, and toward extensive audio-lingual practice designed to develop a new set of habits.
2 Instruction proceeds in the initial stages without reference to the printed word.
3 Teaching pronunciation requires extensive *hearing* of the new sounds, preferably contrasted with similar sounds both in the foreign language and the language of the learner, followed by careful drill in their production.

4 Spoken language is initially presented and practiced in what are called pattern sentences or model sentences. Each pattern sentence contains a productive structure, i.e., one which, when mastered, will permit the generation of *new* utterances by substituting new vocabulary; e.g., subject-verb-object in English. Pattern sentences are subsequently manipulated in drills designed to highlight changes in form or order which occur within the structures. Such drills are called pattern drills or structure drills.

5 Pattern sentences may or may not be presented originally in dialogue form.

6 Pattern sentences are practiced to the point of "overlearning," i.e., until they become reflex-like habits.

7 The amount of vocabulary which must be acquired is severely restricted until a large number of structures have been mastered.

8 Translation back and forth between the foreign language and the native language is avoided.

Controversy exists on these points:

1 Ways and means of narrowing the gap between "manipulation" and "communication."

Controversy exists

2 The teaching of "meaning," and the use of English in the classroom.

3 The role of grammatical statements and summaries.

4 The handling of extensive vocabulary acquisition in the later stages of instruction.

A basic tenet of the audio-lingual approach has been the assumption that students so trained will not only be able to understand and speak the foreign language, but will eventually achieve skill in reading and writing at least comparable to and possibly superior to that of students trained by traditional methods. Until recently no experimental evidence existed to substantiate this claim. But now a small-scale experiment by Pimsleur & Bonkowski (62) offers modest support, while a large-scale classroom experiment by Scherer & Wertheimer (68) offers convincing confirmation of this view.

Support for audiolingual training

The language laboratory, an electromechanical installation generally consisting of multiple facilities for student listening and responding to recorded lesson materials, usually on tape, is coming into widespread use, supported in part by funds made available to the several states under Title III of the National Defense Education Act (NDEA). These facilities are *Audiolingual use of the lab* intended to relieve the teacher of some of the drudgery of repetitive drill, and to furnish authentic models for imitation and practice (Hutchinson, 28; Hayes, 23).

The principles of programmed instruction, discussed above, are being applied to the problems of foreign language learning. The resulting programs, designed for presentation through the language laboratory, or through similar audio or audio-visual devices of varying complexity, are thus far only in limited experimental use, and show great promise. Some 35 to 40 research projects are presently active in this field (Hayes, et al., 25).

The teaching of foreign languages in the elementary school (FLES) is spreading rapidly, but is severely hampered (as is the entire field) by lack of qualified teachers and by frequent failure to provide an adequate continuing program for children so trained. For a survey and evaluation of results to date see Alkonis & Brophy (1). The research evidence supporting *FLES* the notion of FLES is extremely slender (Carroll, 9).

Teaching foreign languages by television is receiving strong support, but results have been dubious because of the questionable methodological soundness of certain programs, the impossibility of getting feedback from the learner, and the implication that classroom work following the TV presentation can be handled by teachers with no foreign language training or experience (Reid, 65).

To help cope with the problem of retraining high school teachers to understand and use audio-lingual methods, Summer Institutes have been operated by many colleges and universities pursuant to contracts with the U.S. Office of Education under Title VI of the NDEA. By the end of 1962, some 10,000 such teachers will have attended a total of 216 Insti- *NDEA Institutes vs. universities* tutes. It is chiefly among the products of these institutes that the awakening Miss F's are to be found. Pre-service teacher training programs in colleges and universities are barely in the beginning stages of revision. Two new series of tests, designed to measure teacher proficiency and student achievement respectively, developed under NDEA Title VI auspices, will eventually help training institutions to evaluate their products.

A broadly based program of research in problems of foreign language teaching, as well as the construction of teaching materials predominantly in "critical" but seldom taught languages, Language and Area Centers offering advanced study in such languages, and fellowship awards to students entering upon such advanced study, are likewise supported by Title VI of the NDEA.

The large foundations are providing increasing support for projects involving the teaching of foreign languages or research therein. Serving as a respected neutral intermediary in language matters of interest to government, military, the academic world, the foundations, and industry alike, the Center for Applied Linguistics in Washington, D.C., an arm of the MLA supported by the Ford Foundation, is having an impact which is rapidly becoming world-wide. One of its major interests is the teaching of English as a second language.

The Center for Applied Linguistics

The implementation of audio-lingual teaching has caused an upheaval in the publishing industry, which must now supply and is supplying completely new materials which provide the extensive pattern practice and drills required, plus tapes for the language laboratory and even phonograph records for home practice. It was inevitable that certain publishers should give the impression of "conversion" by offering that certain publishers should give the impression of "conversion" by offering tapes to accompany traditional texts, a confusing and ill-advised practice. A recent publication of the MLA provides criteria for the evaluation of materials (Ollman, 58).

Audiolingual materials

Language teaching in the United States is in a state of transition. Audio-lingual teaching in high schools, variously understood and administered by teachers, is widespread, but commonest in the large urban centers. Thinly disguised traditional teaching clings in many conservative colleges and universities, where the language laboratory tends to provide misleading superficial evidence of change. So radical is the nature of the change in progress, that this situation must be regarded as expected and unavoidable. The pot, however, is boiling. But a more general understanding of language as signalling behavior is a necessary precursor to further progress in cross-cultural communication (Hayes, 22, p. 150–152).

Traditional teaching in disguise

MLA statement on how to study a FL

The Modern Language Association of America sponsored a conference in 1964 which resulted in a statement entitled "Advice to the Language Learner" (51). The 1964 statement was revised "in the light of comments from many teachers and linguists" and thus purports to represent the distillation of knowledge about the state of the art. The following ten claims about the psychology of FL learning have been extracted from the 1966 revised statement.

1 Learning a FL facilitates subsequent learning of another FL thanks to the acquisition of "techniques of FL study." (For some supportive evidence, see Carroll, 12.)

2 "Any intelligent student" can learn a FL provided there are present "hard work," "a good teacher," and "a good text-book." (For a discussion on FL aptitude, see the review by Carroll, 10.)

3 A helpful strategy in learning a FL is to avoid making direct comparisons between it and English. (For a detailed discussion, see Jakobovits, 35.)

4 "Learning a language means learning a whole new pattern of habits . . . a little like learning to play the piano or the violin, except that it is easier." Therefore, it is important to practice, to practice, and to practice still more. Practice should be intensive and enthusiastic, in class and out, silently and out loud, to oneself while reading, and to fellow students. Involve "all your senses as you learn a language by using your ears, mouth, eyes, fingers. Use your imagination. Pretend that you are an actor whose lines you are learning." (For a discussion on "language is a habit," see Jakobovits, 29, 32.)

Claims about the psychology of FL learning

5 "There are three techniques in language learning: imitation, analogy, and analysis." Imitation consists of repeating "what you hear as closely as you can" by listening "carefully to your teacher and the other models." "Learning how to create by analogy is the purpose of pattern drills and other exercises." As one grows older, he begins "to lose [the] capacity for easy imitation" but he gains "the advantage of being able to reason: [to] analyze language." "Information of this sort, given in grammatical explanations or rules, can help you to learn the language faster."

6 Memorizing sessions should be broken up into several intense short periods (15–20 minutes). (For evidence, see Carroll, 12.)

7 Reading and writing are learned more easily if one first learns to speak the language. Even if one is not interested in the spoken language, one "can not learn to read it without using *some* kind of pronunciation, even if it is only a silent one you invent. So, it makes sense to learn the normal pronunciation." (No evidence available.)

8 Practicing to speak should be done right from the start. (This is a matter of controversy.)

9 When reading a FL, one should at first read only what has been previously practiced, and do so out loud. (For a contrary opinion, see Burling, 6.) Later, when reading new materials silently, one should underline new words, pronounce new phrases over and over, later returning to the underlined words.

10 English translations of words or phrases should never be written on the page in the reading book. "Doing so puts the emphasis on the English equivalent and not on the foreign word, which is the word that you must learn." (But, again, see Burling, 6.)

FLES and FLSS programs

Working Committee I of The Northeast Conference on the Teaching of Foreign Languages in 1964 outlined "an ideal FLES program." The statement was reprinted in Michel (48) and the main points made by that influential committee of experts are summarized below. The ideal FLES program is one that:

1 Introduces the FL in grade 3.

2 Has a specially qualified teacher who serves as an excellent model, who motivates the children constantly, who corrects errors immediately.

3 Exposes the children daily to FL instruction: 15-minute periods in grades 3 to 5, longer in grade 6; 45-minute periods, three times a week in grades 7 and 8 or 30-minute periods daily; 45-minute periods, five times a week in grades 9 to 12.

4 Has a coordinated program throughout to insure proper sequencing for continuity.

5 Has proper background support to insure success: parental support, qualified teachers for given languages, adequate budgetary provisions for continuity of program.

Characteristics of the ideal FLES program

6 Uses dialogue and structure drills in combination with careful introduction of new words. The selection of materials and their sequencing are such as to clearly point out some given grammatical principle and to avoid confusion.

7 Devotes the first two-and-one-half years to the listening-speaking skills with no attention given to reading and writing.

8 Is careful to avoid boredom due to repetitious drills.

9 Induces the student to realistically act out dialogues.

10 Makes judicious use of audiovisual aids (especially pictures and tape recorders). (But because of the limited time avail-

able the use of mechanized teaching aids is curtailed.)

11 Introduces reading after two-and-one-half years (in grade 5), and writing after three years (in grade 6). The materials for these should at first consist of items already familiar from the audiolingual training; major emphasis still remains on the speaking-listening skills.

12 Explanation of grammar and its analysis is "rigorously subordinated to the formation of habits" through the use of pattern drills.

To these 12 characteristics of the "ideal" FLES program may be added two further statements on the "ideal" FLSS (foreign languages in the secondary school) program taken from the conclusions of Working Committee II of the 1964 Northeast Conference and also reprinted in Michel (48):

1 The "primary all-important goal of a secondary-school modern foreign language program in the second half of the twentieth century . . . should be to teach as much *language* as possible." By "language" is meant "the four skills of communication: listening comprehension, speaking, reading, and writing." Other goals such as the "development of cultural sensitivity and awareness of humanistic values" are "eminently desirable objectives" but remain nevertheless secondary in importance.

Two further statements on the "ideal" FLSS program

2 Reading skills are important to develop, but "premature preoccupation with [literary studies, such as literary history, analysis, and criticism] constitutes the most discouraging obstacle to the successful teaching of the language skills in high school; . . . reading, in the sense of translation, is not an objective at all. Translation is a special skill which requires special training. It has no place in a secondary-school program. . . . A prerequisite for the *genuine* study of literature is, or ought to be, language proficiency" and "since available time for study is so limited, a preoccupation with literature detracts from the development of the oral-aural skills."

The statements summarized in the last three subsections represent the distilled knowledge of the state of the art in FL teaching today. To ask whether these recommendations are "valid" or not is essentially not a meaningful question. There are two reasons for this. The first is that behind most of the recommendations lie implicit certain assumptions about the value and goals of FL study, and these assumptions stem from larger social and educational premises that are not reducible to true-false considerations. The second reason is that research methodology in education and psychology is too weak to assess unequivocally the truth value of most of the generalizations and recommendations that have been offered. About the only reasonable thing that can be done at this juncture is to point out the fact that there are individuals engaged in research and teaching who disagree with many of the recommendations that have been outlined. For example, Monot-Cassidy argues that "the method advocated in perfecting oral learning goes against the main educational trends of the last two hundred years and, more specifically against the learning patterns instilled in the American child from birth onward. It fails in one fundamental: it does not teach the student to respect the subject-matter of the course. . . . If we want to keep alive the wonderful renewal of interest in foreign languages, we must cease to treat a fifteen-year-old boy as if he were a bright three" (52, p. 16–17). A similar motive, that of introducing adult (rather than childish) content and syntax right from the beginning of FL study, has prompted Burling (6) to make what he calls some "outlandish" proposals whereby reading materials are mutilated in successive steps starting from a mixed English-FL version and gradually replacing the English words and morphemes until, at the final step, the text appears in the original FL version. Others, like Belasco (4), while not subscribing to quite such an extreme method, nevertheless maintain that translation can be useful to convey the meaning of the original and do not hesitate to use it whenever they deem it desirable.

Experts disagree about the above three subsections

"an outlandish proposal"

What is it "to know a language"?

It has been pointed out earlier in this chapter that disagreements about how best to teach a FL cannot be unequivocally resolved by experimental research methods. But the inability of research to solve these practical problems is not the only difficulty to be contended with. There are fundamental differences in what language teachers perceive to be the goals of a specific FL course. Some of the differences pertain to aesthetic considerations, such as, for example, whether or not to insist on "correct" speech, both in the grammatical and phonological areas. This is clearly an aesthetic rather than a functional criterion as indicated by the fact that, first, effective communication is possible without a high degree of accuracy in phonology and syntax, and, second, native speakers of a language do not typically produce grammatical sentences in everyday speech (as a literal transcription of a tape-recorded conversation would show). Other differences pertain to conceptions about the "correct" order of development of language skills; thus, listening comprehension and speaking are considered to be "primary" skills, and reading and writing "secondary" skills; "paralinguistic" features of speech and knowledge about the foreign culture are usually taught after the "basic" linguistic skills are already at a fairly advanced level, the assumption being that these constitute "parallel" knowledge rather than linguistic knowledge per se.

What is effective communication?

These various issues constitute basic and unresolved differences about the fundamental question of what it is to "know a language." Language tests that researchers devise and teachers use are interesting in this connection because they reflect the conceptions one has about what it is to know a language. And what are the constituent elements of most language tests currently used? Vocabulary knowledge, recognition of correct grammatical structure, reading comprehension, dictation, translation, and so on: these may be termed knowledge about the mechanics of language and reflect what some linguists currently call linguistic competence. Linguists like Chomsky (13) argue that the fact that native speakers do not typically speak grammatically is not an indication that their linguistic competence is wanting; he insists on a distinction to be made between linguistic competence and linguistic performance. The latter is influenced by presumably nonlinguistic factors such as inattention, limited memory, time pressure, emotional involvement, and so on, which interfere with the act of speaking and cause disfluencies, false starts, unfinished sentences, lack of grammatical accord, etc. He points out that when native speakers are presented with a written transcription of such sentences or an oral version presented piecemeal, they can recognize the ungrammatical elements and correct them, thereby showing that linguistic performance is not a good measure of linguistic competence.

Linguistic competence and linguistic performance

This argument is quite convincing and seems essentially correct as far as it goes. But it neglects certain crucial facts about how language is used for communicative purposes. An individual who has mastered the mechanics of a language, in short, knows the meaning of so many words, knows the syntactic and phonological structure of the language, and nothing else, would be quite incapable of communicating in that language. Language teachers are well aware of this fact and have sometimes expressed it in no uncertain terms, as the following blunt quotation indicates: "The pedagogues supply ample anecdotal evidence not only that there are students who can perform beautifully on substitution drills, transformation drills, etc., yet with whom communication is virtually impossible; but also that there are students who 'do miserably on your tests, but, hell, we can talk about anything together' " (Upshur, 74, p. 5). Spolsky (72) has documented the fact that nonnative speakers who have attained a certain sufficiently high level of proficiency can perform at almost native level on certain language tests, but as soon as they are presented with artificially mutilated speech (e.g., with background noise on a tape-recorded conversation) they perform much lower than natives, indicating that they have not internalized certain fundamental knowledge about the language. Spolsky refers to this type of knowledge as the "redundancy aspect of language" and includes such things as knowledge of sequential probabilities of phonemes, letters, and lexical items in strings, knowledge about how words are organized semantically in lexical fields, cultural facts (e.g., what is appropriate to say under given situations), and psychological facts (e.g., what an individual is likely to say or think under given circumstances). As Upshur points out, this principle of redundancy "suggests that it will not be possible to demonstrate that any given language item is essential to successful communication, nor to establish the functional load of any given item in communication. Consider the ease with which speakers of different dialects, dialects even with different number of phonemes, manage to converse, or the ways in which speakers constantly handle their forgetting a specific word. All of this suggests then that while a testing of specific linguistic items is likely to be valuable in the control of instruction, the assessment of proficiency in a language must rather be based on functioning in a much more linguistically complex situation than is provided by the one element test" (Upshur, 74, p. 11). (For a similar view, see Jakobovits, 31.)

The redundancy aspects of language and the role they play

Belasco's call for the "total language experience" is motivated by a similar recognition of the independence of various aspects of knowing a language. He points out that a student often has difficulty understanding a spoken sentence that he understands quite easily in print; that it is possible to develop acceptable speaking ability without a concomitant development in listening comprehension; and that a student might control every structure and know the meaning of every word in a reading selection without understanding the selection (4, p. 86).

None of the foregoing remarks are likely to contain any elements of surprise to the experienced language teacher. Yet many of them would insist that mechanical skills are "logically" to be taught separately and prior to communicative skills. But is this truly a logical requirement or an aesthetic preference for which too high a price is being paid when students bored with practicing mechanics end by giving up any real interest and motivation in FL study? And are teachers not placing such an emphasis on the acquisition of mechanical skills partly because currently used proficiency tests measure mechanical rather than communicative skills, thus allowing the curriculum to be guided by available tests rather than the reverse?

Are mechanical skills to be taught prior to communicative skills?

There is evidence that there is developing increasing awareness in the FL field of the importance of teaching communicative competence. Hayes (22), being concerned with teaching "cross-cultural communication," has reviewed the pedagogical perspectives of "paralinguistics" and "kinesics," these terms being defined as "the study of patterned tone-of-voice and body motion aspects of human communication, respectively" (22, p. 152). "Pedagogically," he asserts, "we can expect the paralinguistic frame of reference to broaden considerably the scope of the descriptive component which underlies teaching materials" (Hayes, 22, p. 155). (See also Nostrand, 57.)

As soon as we raise the question of communicative, rather than linguistic, competence, it becomes clear that the traditional fourfold division of levels of skills—listening, speaking, reading, writing—becomes totally inadequate. Fishman has repeatedly emphasized that the FL teacher must make decisions about which communicative skills to teach within a much more complex framework. For example, in a recent article (18) he reviews the "bilingual dominance configuration" in terms of the following factors: (1) What is the desirable level of proficiency in the second language to be encouraged in the various *media* such as listening, speaking, reading, writing? (2) What are the priorities the teacher wants to establish concerning the degree of proficiency to be encouraged in various *roles* such as comprehension, production, and inner speech (talking to oneself, thinking out loud)? (3) Which *formality levels* ought to be emphasized: intimate, casual, formal? ("Each level of formality requires a vocabulary, a sentence structure, and a set of attitudes toward oneself and one's interlocutors quite different from those required by the others" [18, p. 125]). (4) How shall the teacher treat the various *domains* of interaction: art, music, government, religion, business, home, school? As he points out, these

Teachers must determine the "bilingual dominance configuration" they seek to create

201

are contextual factors, and the teacher must arrive at simultaneous decisions concerning all of these. "In doing so, he will have determined the bilingual dominance configuration that he is seeking to create in his pupils" (18, p. 126). This decision cannot be made by default by pretending to teach "general" language skills. "Foreign language teachers are producers of bilinguals" (18, p. 121) and the assessment of the success and relevance of the teaching process which creates "school-made bilinguals" must be made in no less complex and realistic terms than the description of "natural bilinguals" by such a communication framework as that suggested by Fishman or Mackey (46).

The physiology of second language learning

Educators in this country and throughout the world have been concerned with the question of "What is the optimum age of beginning the study of a FL?" (Andersson, 2; Kirsch, 38; Larew, 40). There has been in recent years a definite bias toward the view that FLs should be taught early in childhood, at least before puberty. This view is based on the observation that when children are exposed in a natural setting to two languages during their early childhood they achieve a mastery of both languages (sometimes even three or four languages) that is nativelike in fluency and pronunciation and do so with natural ease and apparently without any special effort. In fact, many people believe that "true bilinguals" are produced only under these conditions of childhood learning. This view was strongly reinforced by statements made by the eminent Canadian neurosurgeon, Penfield, who for many years has argued that the human brain loses "plasticity" after puberty and language learning after that age becomes increasingly difficult.

Arguments for and against FLES

There are, however, opposing views to this argument. Many educators who have examined the effects of the early introduction of a second language in the elementary school curriculum caution against what has come to be known as "the balance effect." This refers to the hypothesis that the more time spent on the second language, the less well one learns the first language, with consequent detrimental effects on the native language, on education, and on the intellectual development of the child.

The purpose of this section is to review the arguments for and against the early introduction of a FL in the school curriculum and to examine the physiological and educational implications that are involved in this crucial question.

Physiological implications

The views of Penfield on the physiology of language learning have appeared principally in two places: in a speech given at the 134th meeting of the American Academy of Arts and Sciences in Boston (Penfield, 60) and in the Epilogue of *Speech and Brain Mechanisms* (Penfield & Roberts, 61), a chapter that has been reprinted by the Modern Language Association and widely circulated (also reprinted in Michel, 48, p. 192–214). A summary of his views is given by the following quotations:

> In 1939 I was asked to give an address at Lower Canada College. . . . "I have long wondered," my talk began, "about secondary education from the safe distance of a neurological clinic. I have wondered why the curriculum was not adjusted to the evolution of functional capacity in the brain. . . .
>
> "Before the age of nine to twelve, a child is a specialist in learning to speak. At that age he can learn two or three languages as easily as one. It has been said that an Anglo-Saxon cannot learn other languages well. That is only because, as he grows up, he becomes a stiff and resistant individualist, like a tree—a sort of oak that cannot be bent in any graceful manner. But the Anglo-Saxon, if caught young enough, is as plastic and as good a linguist as the child of any other race. . . . When you enter [the teaching] profession, I beg you to arrange the curriculum according to the changing mental capacities of the boys and girls you have to teach. . . . Remember that for the purposes of learning languages, the human brain becomes progressively stiff and rigid after the age of nine!"
>
> Again in 1953 I was called upon to address a lay audience. It was at a meeting of the American Academy of Arts and Sciences in Boston. . . . I chose my subject: "A consideration of the neurophysiological mechanisms of speech and some educational consequences." . . .
>
> This aroused far more interest than I could have anticipated. The officers of the Modern Language Association of America heard of it, and, probably because it coincided with their own views, they had it reprinted. It was distributed then to the far flung membership of that Association.
>
> . . . It may well be convenient, for those who must plan the curriculum, to postpone the teaching of secondary languages until the second decade of childhood. But if the plan does not succeed, as they would have it, let them consider whether they

"arrange the curriculum according to the changing mental capacities of the boys and girls you have to teach"

have consulted the timetable of the cerebral hemispheres. There is a biological clock of the brain as well as of the body glands of children.

. . . The learning of language in the home takes place in familiar stages which are dependent upon the evolution of the child's brain. The mother helps, but initiative comes from the growing youngster. The learning of the mother tongue is normally an inevitable process. No parent could prevent it unless he placed his child in solitary confinement!

"the biological clock of the brain"

The brain of the child is plastic. The brain of the adult, however effective it may be in other directions, is usually inferior to that of the child as far as language is concerned. This is borne out still further by the remarkable re-learning of a child after injury or disease destroys the speech areas in the dominant left cerebral hemisphere. Child and adult, alike, become speechless after such an injury, but the child will speak again, and does so, normally, after a period of months. The adult may or may not do so depending on the severity of the injury" (Penfield, in Penfield & Roberts, 61, p. 235–240).[2]

It is clear from this extended quote, and from the rest of the article, that Penfield does not claim any special expertise in FL teaching. One must therefore clearly separate what he says as an expert in neurophysiology from what he says as a concerned Canadian citizen interested in promoting bilingualism in that country. The FL teacher, not being an expert in neurophysiological matters may be quite justified to rely on the expertise of specialists such as Penfield and Roberts. The evidence and arguments they present on the neurophysiological bases of speech development in the infant appears convincing, at least to the non-specialist (Milner, 50). This confidence in their argument is strengthened even more now that it has received further extensive confirmation by the recent comprehensive review of the subject given by Lenneberg (43) in his book, *Biological Foundations of Language*, and elsewhere (Lenneberg, 44).

Relevance to second language learning

The crucial question, however, that which the FL teacher must carefully examine, is just what is the relevance of the neurophysiological evidence for *second* language learning and teaching. It is clear that the learning of language, that is, *first* language, is dependent upon the child's biological mechanisms, that these brain mechanisms develop at crucial time periods, and that

---

2 *Speech and Brain Mechanisms*, by Wilder Penfield and Lamar Roberts (Copyright © 1959 by Princeton University Press). Passage quoted by permission of the publisher.

unless the child is exposed to human speech before the age of puberty he will most likely never speak a human language. Lenneberg presents the argument succinctly:

Primary language cannot be acquired with equal facility within the period from childhood to senescence. At the same time that cerebral lateralization becomes firmly established (about puberty), the symptoms of acquired aphasia tend to become irreversible within about three to six months after their onset. Prognosis for complete recovery rapidly deteriorates with advancing age after the early teens. Limitation to the acquisition of *primary language* around puberty is further demonstrated by the mentally retarded who can frequently make slow and modest beginnings in the acquisition of language until their early teens, at which time their speech and language status becomes permanently consolidated.

. . . Thus we may speak of a critical period for language acquisition. At the beginning it is limited by lack of maturation. Its close seems to be related to a loss of adaptability and inability for reorganization in the brain, particularly with respect to the topographical extent of neurophysiological processes. (Similar infantile plasticity with eventual irreversible topographical representation in the brain has been demonstrated for many higher mammals.) The limitations in man may well be connected with the peculiar phenomenon of cerebral lateralization of function, which only becomes irreversible after cerebral growth phenomena have come to a conclusion" (Lenneberg, 44, p. 246–247; emphases supplied).

Here again it is clear that the neurophysiological evidence is restricted to *primary* or *first* language acquisition. However, Lenneberg, too, sometimes tends to overgeneralize the applicability of his evidence and to make certain claims about second language acquisition that are questionable. For instance, he presents a table of the process of language development throughout the life history of the individual which confounds at one point primary and secondary language acquisition. The table is presented here in a slightly altered form (Lenneberg, 44, p. 248):

Biological aspects of primary language learning

Age	Usual Language Development
Months 0 to 3	Emergence of cooing
Months 4 to 20	From babbling to words
Months 21 to 36	Acquisition of language
Years 3 to 10	Some grammatical refinement; expansion of vocabulary
Years 11 to 14	Foreign accents emerge
Midteens to senium	Acquisition of second language becomes increasingly difficult (?)

The first four entries in the table concern primary language acquisition while the last two deal with second language acquisition. None of the evidence considered throughout his book on "biological foundations" is directly relevant to the learning of a second language. Furthermore, both generalizations are questionable, especially the last. A recent study was designed to "examine some aspects of the commonly held view that young children are better able to learn the phonology of a second language than adults" (Yeni-Komshian, Zubin, & Afendras, 79). The study used only two subjects (ages 5 and 21, respectively) and limited itself to seven hours of training two Arabic phoneme discriminations, and thus the results obtained are to be considered merely suggestive. The authors concluded that the results did not provide any evidence indicating that children are better than adults in acquiring novel speech sounds (79, p. 276). Nevertheless observation indicates that the children of immigrants who are exposed to a second language before their midteens or thereabouts do seem to speak that language with closer native pronunciation than their parents or older siblings. But this difference cannot be unequivocally (or even probably) attributed to neurophysiological factors since (1) children learning a second language in a school setting do not always (or even often) develop native pronunciation, and (2) some adults are capable of acquiring nativelike pronunciation of a FL. The biological timetable that Lenneberg speaks of and the correlated developmental stages of first language acquisition typically follow rigid patterns and do not permit variations of this sort.

Can knowledge about primary language learning be applied to second language learning?

Conflicting evidence

Finally, concerning the last generalization in the table, namely that the acquisition of a second language becomes increasingly difficult after the midteens, there is no evidence to support it. A number of known facts actually contradict it. For instance, a college-level FL course of one semester is typically considered to be the equivalent of a whole year of study at the high school level. Also, some intensive FL courses for adults are capable of imparting a conversational knowledge of the language with nativelike pronunciation in about one thousand hours with an active vocabulary of up to three thousand lexical items (Mueller, 54). This rate of acquisition appears to be at least as good as that of the much younger immigrant child who is immersed in a foreign culture, and is probably superior to it. Although these intensive courses are for "gifted" adults, the number of such people is sufficiently large (up to 33 percent of the population according to one estimate [Carroll, 10]) that a neurophysiological explanation must be excluded.

Educational and intellectual implications

The preceding section attempted to show that there is no neurophysiological evidence to the effect that children are more capable of learning a second language than adults. This section will briefly examine the evidence concerning the educational and intellectual consequences of the early teaching of a FL.

Macnamara's (47) book, *Bilingualism and Primary Education*, is the most extensive review on the subject to date. A large number of studies have been devoted to this question. Macnamara selected 77 of these for detailed analysis, those that seemed to him to have the most adequate experimental controls. The majority of these studies confirmed the balance effect indicating that on the whole children who were required to learn, use, or be educated in two languages had a weaker grasp of either language than monolingual children. Macnamara's own careful study of the "Irish experience" was consonant with this overall pattern. In his concluding chapter, he states:

"the balance effect"

> Yet despite the differences between Ireland and other countries in the conditions relating to the learning of languages the findings of our own study closely parallel those of the majority of papers which have been reviewed. Our own research adds to the already considerable evidence that there is a balance effect in language learning, at least where the time devoted to the second language is so extensive that the time available for the mother tongue is reduced. Native-speakers of English in Ireland who have spent 42 per cent of their school time learning Irish do not achieve the same standard in written English as British children who have not learned a second language (estimated difference in standard, 17 months of English age). Neither do they achieve the same standard in written Irish as native-speakers of Irish (estimated difference, 16 months of Irish age). Further the English attainments of native-speakers of Irish fall behind those of native-speakers of English both in Ireland (13 months of English age) and in Britain (30 months of English age).
>
> Comparisons among groups of Irish children yield results which are also for the most part similar to results obtained in the majority of earlier researches. Teaching arithmetic in

Socioeconomic conditions affect bilingualism

Irish to native English-speakers is associated with retardation in problem, but not in mechanical, arithmetic. The retardation in problem arithmetic is estimated as about 11 months of arithmetic age.

. . . The Irish findings relating to the teaching of other subjects through the medium of the second language are particularly discouraging. For it seems that the teaching of mathematics, at least, through the medium of the second language does not benefit the second language, while it has a detrimental effect on children's progress in mathematics" (Macnamara, 47, p. 135–137).

It ought to be kept in mind that there are a number of studies that, even if they are in the minority, do nevertheless provide a counterargument to the balance effect and to the alleged detrimental educational consequences of the early use of a second language. One recent study, in particular, carried out under the direction of Lambert, an eminent colleague of Macnamara at McGill University in Canada, shows that French-Canadian children in one bilingual setting in Montreal who have developed a good grasp of English are superior in both verbal and nonverbal intelligence to their French-speaking monolingual peers (Peal & Lambert, 59). These authors hypothesize that early bilingualism "might affect the very structure of intellect . . . . a large proportion of an individual's intellectual ability is acquired through experience and its transfer from one situation to another." They argue that bilingual children are exposed to "wider experiences in two cultures" and these will give them "advantages which a monolingual does not enjoy . . . . Intellectually [the bilingual child's] experience with two language systems seems to have left him with a mental flexibility, a superiority in concept formation, and a more diversified set of mental abilities. . . ."

Opposing views

The educator and the FL teacher are likely to experience some confusion and frustration at such seemingly opposing views which these researchers hold, each buttressing their views with hard experimental data. A conclusion stated earlier in this chapter once again comes to mind, namely that research by itself is incapable of providing ready answers to complex and perplexing social and educational problems. It seems pointless to play the "data game" whereby an educator or a politician, having made up his mind in favor of bilingual education or the early teaching of a FL, attempts to "justify scientifically" that his policy is a correct one by quoting those experimental reports that happen to

Can we afford to play the "data game"?

208

agree with his bias. It would be too easy to find experimental reports that show just the opposite. The serious educator must recognize the fact that in complex social and educational settings experimental findings are not easily generalizable: the conditions that hold for any particular setting are likely to be quite different, and significantly so, from any other setting, and his decisions must be made within a complex matrix of interacting factors, educational, social, political, philosophical, etc. Such decisions are always uncertain from the scientific point of view and the latter by itself can never provide a strict and sufficient justification.

This conclusion is supported by a report on an international meeting of experts presented by Stern. The report was published in 1963 by the UNESCO Institute for Education and has as its topic the teaching of foreign or second languages to younger children:

> It is not necessary to justify the teaching of languages in the primary years on the grounds that it is *the* optimum period. What is needed is (1) to show that it is socially and educationally desirable. . . . (2) It must be shown that it is sound from the point of view of the development of children, that, in fact, there are no contradictions on psychological grounds for teaching a language at this stage. (3) If, in addition, it can be demonstrated that the learning of languages in the early years has certain special merits this would add further weight. In other words, instead of searching for the optimum-age-in-general, it should be sufficient to show that the primary years are a good period for beginning a second language, offering certain special advantages . . . (Stern, 73, p. 22).

Other reasons for a FLES program

> Where no immediate urgency dictates a very early start the age to begin language instruction can therefore be decided on grounds of educational expediency . . . . We conclude that the introduction of a language is not simply a matter of curriculum and method, nor one of correct psychological timing. It must also be viewed against the background of aspirations and social attitudes among the population served by the school system" (73, p. 26, 65).

Faced with the necessity of having to make a practical decision concerning the teaching of a second language, the educator must consider all the relevant aspects of the problem and weigh each of them according to the demands of the conditions that hold in his particular setting. In some countries and communities the decision will be dictated by political factors, as was the case with the "Irish experience" (Ferguson, 16). In the United States there are powerful social forces in favor of language loyalty and maintenance (Fishman, 17) by immigrant groups, there are significant political factors in favor of FL study as a means toward international cooperation and understanding, and there are also present traditional cultural views that favor the study of the major European languages. These various motivations are usually primary and take precedence over the more specialized scientific concerns such as the neurophysiological underpinnings and psychological consequences of early or late FL study. A useful role that the latter concerns can play is to help implement whatever decisions were made on the basis of the more general social concerns by discovering the advantages and disadvantages of the policy being followed and showing ways of maximizing the former and counteracting the latter by special or remedial training.

Primary motives in FL learning: social concerns

After reviewing the evidence on the relation between age and FL study, Stern (73, p. 23) presents a summary table of the pros and cons of the early teaching of a second language. The summary is presented in slightly modified form.

1 Age of acquisition: before adolescence (ages 3-10):
  a *Advantages:*
    i Accords with the neurophysiology of the brain. (?)
    ii Easiest and most effective. (?)
    iii Natural good pronunciation.
    iv Leaves richer linguistic memory traces for later expansion.
    v Longer time for language can be allowed.
  b *Disadvantages:*
    i Possible confusion with first language habits.
    ii No conscious acquisition of language learning process.
    iii Time spent not commensurate with results.
2 Age of acquisition: at adolescence (ages 11 to school leaving):
  a *Advantages:*
    i Increased capacity to appreciate many aspects of language and culture contacts.
    ii Still sufficient time to attain high standard.
    iii Improved memory and higher level of intellectual growth.

Stern's summary table of the pros and cons on the early teaching of a second language

iv First language skills well established, hence no con-
　　　fusion.
　b　*Disadvantages:*
　　i More laborious than early learning.
　　ii Success demands tenacity.
　　iii Self-consciousness.
　　iv Possible refusal to memorize.
　　v Experience has shown poor results frequent.
　　vi Already crowded curricula and specialization of studies.
3 Age of acquisition: adulthood:
　a　*Advantages:*
　　i Specificity of purpose.
　　ii Good motivation added to reasons mentioned for ado-
　　　lescence.
　　iii Greatest amount of learning in least amount of time.
　b　*Disadvantages:*
　　i Not enough time.
　　ii Other preoccupation.
　　iii Irregularity of study.

Several of the listings are either in error (e.g., 1ai) or contradictory (e.g., 1aii with 3aiii); others are at best highly controversial. No mention is made of the potential balance effect. However, the summary is useful because it poses the problem of early
FL teaching in terms of relative advantages and disadvantages
rather than in terms of the pseudoquestion of which is *the* best
time.

Motivational aspects of FL study

Bilingualism and multilingualism represent today a major
problem in the world, as they have in the past and undoubtedly
will remain to be in the foreseeable future. In the history of this
planet, there have been periods and situations where people
have stood ready to die for maintaining the use of their language
and resisting the attempt to impose upon them the use of a FL.
In this decade of the 1960s there were times we could read in
the daily newspaper of bloody riots and deaths, of terrorisms and
civil strife associated with language conflicts in India, in Bel-
gium, in Canada, and elsewhere. In all these situations much
more was involved than the language question per se, questions
of national identity, of cultural self-assertion, of social and economic competition, but the language question stood as a symbol

*Language conflicts are
many-sided*

211

for all these and was inextricably tied to them. The language of a people is a living, growing, changing reflection of that people's heart and mind. When we learn a FL we intermingle with a foreign people: language contact is inseparable from culture contact. In a real sense, becoming bilingual entails becoming bicultural. When a person exposes himself to a FL he also exposes himself to a foreign culture. The latter kind of exposure can become for some individuals, we do not know for how many, a threatening experience. Lambert of McGill University in Canada has for the last ten years explored the implications of such a threat. In one article he introduces the issue as follows:

This theory, in brief, holds that an individual successfully acquiring a second language gradually adopts various aspects of behavior which characterize members of another linguistic-cultural group. The learner's ethnocentric tendencies and his attitudes toward the other group are believed to determine his success in learning the new language. His motivation to learn is thought to be determined by his attitudes and by his orientation toward learning a second language. The orientation is "instrumental" in form if the purposes of language study reflect the more utilitarian value of linguistic achievement, such as getting ahead in one's occupation, and is "integrative" if the student is oriented to learn more about the other cultural community as if he desired to become a potential member of the other group. It is also argued that some may be anxious to learn another language as a means of being accepted in another cultural group because of dissatisfactions experienced in their own culture while other individuals may be equally as interested in another culture as they are in their own. However, the more proficient one becomes in a second language the more he may find that his place in his original membership group is modified at the same time as the other linguistic-cultural group becomes something more than a reference group for him. It may in fact become a second membership group for him. Depending upon the compatibility of the two cultures, he may experience feelings of chagrin or regret as he loses ties in one group, mixed with the fearful anticipation of entering a relatively new group. The concept of "anomie" . . . refers to the feelings of social uncertainty which sometimes characterize not only the bilingual but also the serious student of a second language" (39, p. 114).

Attitude toward another group will determine success in learning that group's language

"anomie"

It is not known to what extent ethnocentrism and anomie might represent interfering factors in the study of FLs in the three school systems in the United States today. It is possible, however, that the change in instruction from reading and translation courses to audiolingual speaking courses may have increased the importance and effects of these social psychological factors. Some of Lambert's findings tend to show that students who are integratively oriented towards language study and those who show evidence of anomie are ultimately more successful than the instrumentally oriented students and the psychologically more detached learners, suggesting that the conflicts of anomie may serve as an internal drive and motivating factor. However, our knowledge on this is still very sketchy. Much may depend on how capable the individual is in handling and successfully resolving the conflicts of anomie. If these conflicts become unmanageable and psychologically too threatening, a convenient defense reaction that serves as a protective device might be to slow down progress in the language or eliminate language study altogether (Jakobovits, 30). According to one estimate, up to 20 percent of the student population in high schools and colleges are "beset by a frustrating lack of ability" in FL study (Pimsleur, Sundland, & McIntyre, 63). These students have been labelled "underachievers" in FL study in view of the fact that their grades in FL courses are "*at least* one grade-point lower than [their] average grade in other major subjects." To what extent is this "lack of ability" attributable to motivational problems and conflicts involved specifically with FL study? It is significant for this question that two of the seven subparts of the FL Aptitude Battery developed by Pimsleur and his associates as a means of measuring ability to learn FLs consist of Interest Tests designed to assess the student's attitudes toward FL study. The FL teacher, and the learner himself, ought to be made more aware of the complex psychological issues that may be involved in the study of FLs. The teacher and the student may be aware of a lack of genuine interest in FL study, but to what extent are they aware of the *reasons* behind such a lack of interest? Teachers, educators, parents often ask the question, "How can we infuse more motivation for FL study?" Part of the answer may lie in a recognition of the problems discussed in this section and in finding ways of helping the student manage feelings of anomie and transform it from a conflictual stumbling block into a positive driving force.

Integrative versus instrumental orientation towards learning a language

Student frustration in language learning

The management of anomie may be an important factor in the motivational problem of FL study, but there are undoubtedly additional factors that must be considered: the development of realistic self-evaluation criteria, and the perceived relevance of specific instructional activities.

It is an interesting psychological observation, whose causes are not obvious, that the individual engaged in the study of a FL has some very definite ideas about the progress he believes he is making. Perhaps this pertains to the area of "folk linguistics" which Hoeningswald (26) brought to our attention in a most interesting and perceptive article. People appear to have strong feelings about what constitutes "knowing" a language and who is or is not a "bilingual." A person who is capable of uttering a few mechanical and superficial sentences in a FL with good pronunciation and accurate syntax is a "good bilingual" and "knows the language well" while a person who is quite fluent and is capable of communicating over a wide range of situations, but whose pronunciation is foreign and whose syntax is inaccurate, but perhaps not more so than the conversational speech of the average native, is nevertheless not considered to be a "good bilingual." A student capable of reading advanced materials in a FL but who cannot understand the spoken language may minimize his actual achievement and knowledge of that FL. A student who speaks a FL haltingly and uses stylistic circumlocutions to make up for a lack of vocabulary richness may grossly underestimate his actual knowledge of the language by a tendency to compare this performance to the effortless and automatic expressiveness he experiences in his mother tongue.

"folk linguistics"

It is not known to what extent these kinds of self-generated presumptions affect the student's maintenance of motivation in FL study but it is not unreasonable to suppose that they may sometimes be a source of discouragement and a cause of loss of interest. The FL teacher can help the student develop more objective and more realistic evaluation criteria for assessing progress and achievement. Students can be given some insight into just how complex a system language is by pointing out the amount of knowledge they must have in order to be able to speak their mother tongue as they do and not be misled by the apparent effortlessness with which they speak it. They may thus gain a greater understanding about why it is that learning a FL requires so much effort and perhaps view with greater respect the "modest" achievements they attain at various stages. The

Students should be given insights into the complexities of language learning

FL teacher could further carefully examine his own brand of folk linguistics to see whether he is rewarding meaningful achievement rather than superficialities. Does he insist on an inordinate degree of correct pronunciation and syntax too soon or even at any time? Does he appreciate the student's achievement in terms that are relevant to the latter's ability and effort rather than in terms of some general standard that may be unrealistic or irrelevant for this particular student? Has he realistic expectations about how much progress can be made under the teaching conditions? These are important questions because the teacher is a source of feedback for the student whether this process is made explicit or remains unconscious and unstated.

Finally, the student's parents and their version of folk linguistics may be an influential source of encouragement or discouragement to him. In a recent national poll that was publicized over the news wire services, the majority of parents were reported to have said that they consider FL courses the weakest part of the school curriculum and should be the first to go if anything had to be cut (Wagner, 77). In view of the widespread social, cultural, and political forces in favor of FL study which have traditionally existed in this country, this mounting negativism is both paradoxical and alarming. Much of it can undoubtedly be attributed to a gap between what the parents define as progress in a FL and what their judgment is about how close or how far their children approximate it. Again, are their expectations realistic? Are their evaluation criteria accurate and relevant? These are questions that the FL teacher and the school administrator may find it profitable to discuss at PTA meetings.

To the student, the purpose of the activities in the classroom and the laboratory or the assigned homework may often appear obscure and mysterious and sometimes even irrelevant and silly. Younger children and the more dull among the older children may not question these practices as much as the older and brighter students. But it is a sign of our times that students in our high schools and in our colleges are increasingly demanding that their studies be "relevant" to their goals and aspirations. The teacher and educator can view this age of the New Student either with alarm and worry or with excitement and confidence depending on whether he defines it as rebelliousness or maturity and involvement. Whatever the case may be, this new development in education is affecting the student's attitude toward and motivation for FL study. It must be dealt with.

The "New Student" attitude toward FL study

What is the New Student's attitude toward FL study? A survey conducted at the University of Illinois (Urbana campus) in 1968 by a student committee of the Students Council of the College of Liberal Arts and Sciences (LAS) provides some answers. The survey was planned, executed, and analyzed by the student government representatives entirely on their own initiative. Five thousand questionnaires were distributed to the student body, of which 863 were returned. The questionnaire consisted of 21 questions. The distribution of answers for 13 of these is presented below.[3] (See also Jakobovits, 34.)

University of Illinois student survey

1 Were your grades in language lower than your grades in other courses outside your major field?

        Yes (444)   No (374)   Blank (20)

2 Did you start with a language, then find that you had difficulty with it and then switch to another language?

        Yes (53)   No (785)

3 Do you prefer a language course oriented toward understanding of grammar and reading comprehension rather than a course oriented toward oral-aural comprehension?

        Yes (414)   No (392)   Blank (28)

4 Has the time spent in the language laboratory been beneficial to your study of a language?

        Yes (160)   No (650)   Blank (28)

5 Do you feel that you have to study more for a language course (per credit hour) than for other courses?

        Yes (676)   No (137)   Blank (25)

   If so, do you feel that this is unfair?

        Yes (536)   No or Blank (140)

6 Do you read any material voluntarily in the language you are taking or have taken?

        Yes (233)   No (598)   Blank (7)

7 Has the language requirement [for graduation in LAS at the University of Illinois] prevented you from taking other courses in which you were very interested?

        Yes (514)   No (312)   Blank (12)

8 Do you plan to be able to use the foreign language which you studied to meet graduate school requirements?

        Yes (373)   No (446)   Blank (19)

---

3 Quoted by permission of the Office of the Dean, Liberal Arts and Sciences, University of Illinois, Urbana.

9 Has foreign language helped you to develop discipline or learn better study habits?

> Yes (145)   No (679)   Blank (14)

10 Do you approve of the present foreign language requirement in LAS?

> Yes (199)   No (634)   Blank (5)

Do you think more language should be required, or less?

> More (53)   Less (674)   Blank (111)

11 What is your attitude toward foreign language study?

> Interested   (306)
> Study primarily for the grade   (521)
> Blank   (11)

12 Would you prefer the alternative of taking a two-semester sequence on the literature (in English translation) of the language rather than 103 and 104 of the language? [Note: 103 and 104 are primarily audiolingual courses.]

> Yes (561)   No (261)   Blank (16)

13 Overall do you think that your study of foreign language here has been beneficial or detrimental to you?

> Beneficial (427)   Detrimental (339)   Blank (72)

If the opinions of students at the University of Illinois can be taken to be fairly representative of the national college population, then this survey shows that all is not well with the college FL curriculum. Several of the answers are in fact quite disturbing. While the college curriculum forces everyone to take audiolingual courses, only 47 percent of the students are actually interested in oral-aural comprehension, and 50 percent would prefer grammar and reading comprehension. The evidence for a lack of an intrinsic interest in FL study is clear: only 28 percent read any material voluntarily in the language they are taking; 80 percent feel that they have to work harder in FL courses, a situation that they consider unfair; and for 61 percent of the students this extra work prevents them from taking other courses in which they are interested. Furthermore, 53 percent don't even feel that they would be able to use the FL they studied for meeting graduate school requirements, and 80 percent doubt that FL study is helpful in developing discipline or better study habits. Finally, 76 percent disapprove of the FL requirement and 40 percent feel that FL study in college has actually been detrimental to them.

In considering the significance of these results two important questions pose themselves: Should the school curriculum be

All is not well with the college FL curriculum

217

determined by a majority opinion of students or by the considered professional judgment of educators? And, given a lack of intrinsic interest in FL study on the part of many students, what should be done about it? Let us examine the implications of both questions.

Who determines the school curriculum?

Given the pedagogical philosophy that is prevalent in our society today very few educators would allow the school curriculum to be dictated by a student body vote, and in any event, the students themselves would be just as opposed to such a process. The real issue is not so much who makes the specific decisions[4] as whether the decisions made allow for sufficient flexibility to accommodate individual needs and interests. For instance, it would seem that the insistence on a single goal for FL study is open to question on both educational and philosophical grounds. If roughly half of the college student body is interested in a reading knowledge of a FL is it good educational policy to insist on everyone taking an audiolingual course? Given the low degree of success attained by some students in speaking and reading a FL, would it not be more profitable educationally to allow these particular students to study a foreign culture through the medium of their mother tongue and thus still gain some, if not completely adequate, knowledge of other peoples in the world? Just how useful is it to develop speaking and reading skills in a FL when the educational system fails to provide meaningful opportunities for the use of these skills? It would seem that to make FL study more meaningful to the student it would be desirable to integrate the FL study with the rest of the educational curriculum. For instance, the student could be encouraged to use his FL skills in pursuing projects in other courses in the sciences and the humanities by reading relevant materials in a FL. Travel and study abroad, foreign films and plays, games and play-acting (Lee, 42; Morgan, 53), "The French Club" (Kansas State Teachers College, 37), summer "language camps" (Haukebo, 21), interaction with aliens in this country are all activities that are encouraged and made increasingly available to the students in recognition of this principle, and the more we move in these directions the less we will encounter a "motivational problem" in FL study.

A single goal for FL study open to question

Integrate!

Recent advances in self-instructional FL courses (Valdman, 75) represent another promising development not only because

---

4 But see the interesting suggestion by Rogers (67) that students' motivation would be improved if they were allowed to take a more active role in the planning and execution of classes. See also Holby (27) for some suggestions on how to allow students to evaluate their own work and progress.

of the efficiency associated with programmed instruction but also because these types of courses succeed in eliminating some of the motivational problems discussed in this section. Carroll (11, p. 29) reports certain cases in which "well-developed programs of instruction, particularly of the 'programed' variety, yielded low correlations between [FL] aptitude and performance suggesting that the obstacle of low aptitude may sometimes be surmounted by the use of small-step increment materials that do not challenge language aptitudes." For instance, Mueller & Harris (55) attempted to reduce the high dropout rate in an audiolingual French course in college that a previous survey (Mueller & Leutenegger, 56) had suggested is attributable to the students' disturbance over having to talk too soon and their feeling that too much emphasis was being put on sounds. A reduction in dropout rate was achieved when a special French course called Audio-Lingual Language Program (ALLP) was developed. The course uses programmed instruction techniques and states its terminal goal as the "native-like pronunciation and facility in speaking the language equivalent to that of a seven-year old." The sounds of French are taught with "very little visual support" and sound drills are carried out sometimes without knowledge of the meaning of what is being said. These authors believe that the aversion to the sound emphasis that students often feel is overcome under conditions of programmed instruction where the students are not being overwhelmed, thanks to the step-by-step progression and immediate feedback.

Role of programmed learning

The experienced FL teacher is well aware of the fact that the problem of student motivation is complex and multidimensional and cannot be solved by any one "trick." The solution attempted by Mueller & Harris just discussed seemed to work for them (dropout rate was reduced by 20 percent at the end of the first year of study) but may not be equally successful in other situations and with different students. Its interesting feature was that it first determined what the students found objectionable, then attempted to solve the problem by eliminating the source of dissatisfaction *without changing the original goals of the course.* The FL teacher ought to be aware of the possibility that the explicitly stated objections that students formulate merely represent their personal hypotheses about the dissatisfactions they feel and in these they may in fact be in error. Thus when students state a preference for reading comprehension courses it may reflect a genuine interest in reading over speaking, a reaction against boring drills in the laboratory, a demand for more

The teacher eliminates sources of dissatisfaction

"content," a discouragement with a perceived (real or imagined) lack of progress, or several other possibilities. The solution is not necessarily to change the goals of the course, although that too ought to be considered, but to locate the real source of dissatisfaction and change it. The numerous studies that have been carried out with the purpose of determining which method of instruction is most effective have in general led to disappointing results. It is clear that an important reason for this failure is that the concept of "a method of instruction" actually subsumes a very large number of separate and variable instructional activities in the classroom and laboratory. A much more realistic objective for comparison studies would be to examine the effects of such specific and limited instructional activities. Hayes, Lambert, & Tucker (24) have recently published a check list of several hundred such specific activities associated with FL instruction, and efforts of this kind are more likely to yield real progress than the more traditional monolithic studies on "overall methods."

Let's examine the results of limited and specific instructional activities

Summary and conclusions

The major theme of this chapter has been the exposition of two curious paradoxes that beset the FL teaching field today. The first paradox consists of the widespread tendency on the part of FL teachers to seek justification for their practices in the classroom in originally weak and currently outdated "scientific" theories despite the fact that few experimentalists ever claim for their theories this kind of infallible generalizability to situations outside the laboratory. The most unfortunate consequence of such an outlook has been that classroom practices have tended to become rigidified in the attempt to follow closely the dictates and prescriptions of so-called scientific principles. Thus, the New Key to FL instruction has turned into a mechanistic exercise of rote "habit drills" in which the original goal of liberated and sustained expression, that of communicative competence, has been in practice lost sight of and relegated to a supposedly utopian and unattainable status for the majority of students.

Two curious paradoxes beset the FL field today

The second paradox lies in the fact that although we have achieved in the last 20 years a major breakthrough in the technology of teaching FLs the success of the FL curriculum in our schools has remained extremely limited. Serious dissatisfaction with it is being expressed at all levels by teachers, students, and parents despite the fact that strong social forces remain in this country for the maintenance of an interest in FLs and foreign cultures. Being bombarded by criticisms, from both external and internal sources, the FL teaching field now finds itself on the defensive after enjoying two decades of unparalleled expansion and support.

This, then, is the sobering assessment with which the field is confronted today and the situation from which it must recover. Corrective measures are clearly in order, but what are they to be and which direction are they to take? There is a danger here that must be avoided and lies in the fact that redressive activities that stem from a reaction to the inadequacies of existing conditions tend to overshoot the mark whether it be in the area of politics, legislation, or education. The present shortcomings of the not-so-new audiolingualism may be viewed in part as attributable to the unchecked swing of the pendulum away from the earlier traditionalist emphasis on prescriptive grammar, translation, and the reading of belletristic literature. The danger, now that audiolingualism is on the defensive and students are increasingly demanding "reading" courses, is that the pendulum might be allowed to swing back too far so that we lose sight of the vastly superior instructional technology that we now have at our disposal but was nonexistent in the earlier "dark ages" of FL teaching. We must strive to reach a correct balance between what our educational technology gives us the potential to achieve and what the students are interested in attaining. The key to this balance, (the Newer Key, one might say in jest), lies in individuated FL instruction that is sufficiently flexible to adjust to the particularized characteristics of the individual learner and the learning context. Let us review here the arguments that are presented in this chapter concerning the psychology of second language learning and teaching. These might perhaps serve as guidelines to the corrective measures that are needed.

We must strive to reach a correct balance

1 There is no one single "proper" goal for FL study that can "logically" be demonstrated. There is no proof that speaking is *necessarily* primary or more desirable to reading and, of course, vice versa. Neither can one rationally justify the claim that *all* four skills *should be* the ultimate goal of FL study. We must recognize that students have different interests, needs, and aptitudes and to refuse to accept this fact has the simple and evastating consequence that they shall learn nothing of significance.

Guidelines

Students have different goals

2 The goals of a particular course in a FL program must be clearly defined in specific terms that specify the terminal knowledge and skills to be reached. To purport to teach "general lan-

guage skills" is a retreat from reality in that it ignores the fact of the matter which is that under such conditions a substantial proportion of students fail to derive any demonstrable value from their FL study. The extent of specificity of goals to be defined for any particular course would seem to depend on the conditions that hold for that situation: the specific needs, interests, and aptitudes of the students involved, the time available for study, the age of the learners, the overall FL program and its cumulative effect, the wider conditions of social support and maintenance interests, the particular language and culture involved, and so on. Some examples of such specific goals may be, "to be able to read German literature on chemistry," "to be able to obtain information for travel purposes," "to be able to understand radio broadcasts," "to be able to write business letters," etc. The assessment of FL attainment for degree and requirement purposes should not be in terms of course grade or number of years of study but rather in terms of tests that evaluate such terminal behaviors. In that case, a variety of such terminal behaviors and combinations thereof may be defined for different degree and curricular requirements.

Goals should be specific and adapted to the conditions that hold for certain situations

3 Not only must we recognize variable goals and interests in FL study, but also variable abilities and FL aptitude. In the past, differential aptitude was tacitly recognized by the expectation of a distribution of grades in standard FL courses as well as, more explicitly, by the placement of students in classes being taught at different rates. But what is needed is the recognition that different aptitudes permit the attainment of different terminal goals both in range and degree within the time requirements and opportunities to learn provided by the FL program. Students should be counseled with respect to the specific terminal goals they may reasonably be expected to achieve taking into account their aptitude, the time available for study, and the amount of effort it may require within the context of their motivation and their other educational aspirations and requirements.

Variable abilities and FL aptitudes should be recognized

4 The question of when FLs are to be taught within our educational system is a complex problem that involves political, social, philosophical, and psychological considerations and should not be reduced to a matter of neurophysiology, as it has become fashionable to do in recent years. Since the sociopolitical context varies from place to place, not only on the international plane but also within a particular country, including, of course, the United States, the decision must be considered by each school district in the light of the conditions that prevail within its geo-

When FLS should be taught is not dependent on neurophysiological factors alone

graphic boundary. The knowledge that has accumulated on this matter indicates that there are both advantages and disadvantages to FL study *at any age* compared to any other age. Generalizations about "the optimum age" that fail to take context into account are almost certain to be false.

5 More serious attention must be given to the sociopsychological ramifications of FL study. The proposition that bilingualism entails biculturism has serious implications for both the personal adjustment of the individual and the wider sociocultural character of a nation. There is evidence that it also relates to the type and degree of achievement in FL study and, thus, is an additional important variable that the FL teacher must contend with.

Bilingualism entails biculturism

6 Global comparisons between "methods of instruction" are unrealistic. In general, studies that have attempted such comparisons were unproductive. There are two principal reasons for this. One is that what is usually defined as a "method" actually consists of a large variety of instructional activities, most of which remain undefined and unobserved. The other reason is that the learner makes his own contribution to the learning situation and these learner strategies are to a greater or lesser extent independent of the teacher's activities. What is needed is a more detailed and explicit description of the specific activities of both the teacher and the student in the instructional situation. Once adequate observation techniques are developed, evaluation criteria of effectiveness can then suggest specific changes in instructional activities.

Global comparisons are unproductive; the need is for more precise descriptions of learning tasks

7 It is necessary to take seriously the oft quoted distinction between competence and performance, between knowledge and behavior. Experience has indicated that there are no mysterious transfer effects across various language skills and competencies. Not only is it true that ability to read does not insure ability to speak, and vice versa, but also, ability to function in one communicative context is not necessarily matched in other contexts, and this means that the instructional program that produces school-made bilinguals must take into account the full "dominance configuration" of the natural bilingual. The question of what it is "to know a language" is not yet well understood and, consequently, the language proficiency tests now available and universally used, are inadequate because they attempt to measure something that hasn't been well defined. The tendency to gear the instructional program to enable the achievement of high scores on these tests is thus inappropriate, as is the evalua-

There are no transfer effects across language skills and competencies

tion of the success of the program in terms of these tests. No doubt due to considerations such as these, some specialists in the language testing field are attempting to develop new kinds of tests that are not based on the notion of sampling the surface manifestations of linguistic items and units but rather the underlying potentialities of functionally significant aspects of utterances. These newer efforts take seriously what every FL teacher knows but often neglects in his teaching, namely that learning a FL cannot be separated from learning about the culture for which it is a vehicle.

Present day tests are inadequate

8 The instructional process involved in the teaching of a FL must take proper account of the existence of a "folk linguistics," a term used here to refer to assumptions that individuals hold about language and language acquisition. Students have definite ideas about what it is to "know" a language and use self-generated evaluation criteria to assess their progress. These notions are often unrealistic and tend to underestimate both the complexity of the knowledge to be acquired and the extent of their true achievement. The result is frequently discouragement and a consequent loss of motivation. Likewise, parents may have inappropriate expectations about the rate of progress of their children, minimize their achievement, and, ultimately, withdraw their support and encouragement for FL study. Teachers, too, may not sufficiently differentiate between essential and nonessential features of variations in their students' performance, may not be sufficiently aware of subcultural and idiolectal variations in codes in the language, and may use general standards of evaluating achievement neglecting in their demands to take account of individual capacities. To take proper account of the existence of folk linguistics would involve activities of the following sort: to determine what notions the student has about language and critically discuss their validity with him; to make the student aware of the true complexity of language so that he may appreciate the difficulty of the task he sets for himself; to justify *in terms that are meaningful to the student* the relevancy of the classroom activities and study assignments; to disabuse parents of their unrealistic expectations and make them aware of the cumulative long term impact of FL study; and, finally, to make sure that the teacher himself is knowledgeable about recent sociolinguistic and ethnolinguistic advances.

Folk linguistics held by students, parents, teachers unrealistic

Some activities to counteract wrong perceptions of FL learning

It might be well to end this chapter by reminding the reader that teaching is an art and that there are no sure methods of extrapolating scientific knowledge to the classroom. This review represents the point of view of its author, which is one possible vantage point, and it is safe to say that for every argument presented here one can probably find one or more counterarguments. This is the nature of the beast. But some arguments are more convincing than others, not, hopefully, because of their authoritativeness, but because they may be more rational and their assumptions more likely correct in the light of existing knowledge. As long as decisions about educational matters must be made and ineffective practices corrected, it behooves us to be self-critical about our activities as teachers and researchers and to continually strive for the best possible solutions that available knowledge and logical reasoning can provide.

References, Physiology and Psychology of Second Language Learning

1 Alkonis, N.V.; Brophy, M. H. A survey of FLES practices. In: Reports of surveys and studies in the teaching of modern foreign languages, MLA Materials Center, New York, 1961, p. 213–217.

2 Andersson, Theodore. The optimum age for beginning the study of modern languages. International Review of Education, 6 (1960) 298–306.

3 Belasco, Simon. Nucleation and the audio-lingual approach. The Modern Language Journal, 49 (1965) 485.

4 Belasco, Simon. The plateau or the case for comprehension: the "concept" approach. The Modern Language Journal, 18 (1968) 82–88.

5 Birkmaier, Emma M.; Lange, Dale L. A selective bibliography on the teaching of foreign languages, 1920–1966. Foreign Language Annals, 1:iv (May 1968) 318–353.

6 Burling, Robbins. Some outlandish proposals for the teaching of foreign languages. Language Learning, 18 (1968) 61–75.

7 Carroll, J. B. The contribution of psychological theory and educational research to the teaching of foreign languages. In: Valdman, Albert, ed. Trends in language teaching. McGraw Hill, New York, 1966, p. 93–106.

8 Carroll, J. B. Foreign language proficiency levels attained by language majors near graduation from college. Foreign Language Annals, 1 (1967) 131–151.

9 Carroll, J. B. Foreign languages for children: what research says. National Elementary Principal, 39 (1960) 12–15.

10 Carroll, J. B. The prediction of success in intensive foreign language training. In: Glaser, Robert, ed. Training research and education. University of Pittsburgh Press, Pa., 1962.

11 Carroll, J. B. Research in foreign language teaching: the last five years. In: Mead, Robert G., Jr., ed. Language teaching: broader contexts. Northeast Conference on the Teaching of Foreign Languages: Reports of the Working Committees. MLA Materials Center, New York, 1966, p. 12–42.

12 Carroll, J. B. Research on teaching foreign languages. In: Gage, N. L., ed. Handbook of research on teaching. Rand McNally, Chicago, 1963, p. 1060–1100.

13 Chomsky, Noam. Aspects of the theory of syntax. Massachusetts Institute of Technology Press, Cambridge, 1965.

14 Chomsky, Noam. Language and mind. Harcourt, Brace, & World, New York, 1968.

15 Chomsky, Noam. Review of Skinner's "Verbal behavior." Language, 35 (1959) 26–58. Also in: Jakobovits, L. A.; Miron, M. S., eds. Readings in

the psychology of language. Prentice Hall, Englewood Cliffs, N.J., 1967.

16 Ferguson, C. A. On sociolinguistically oriented language surveys. The Linguistic Reporter, 8 (1966) 1–3.

17 Fishman, J. A. The implications of bilingualism for language teaching and language learning. In: Valdman, Albert, ed. Trends in language teaching. McGraw Hill, New York, 1966, p. 121–132.

18 Fishman, J. A. Language loyalty in the United States. Mouton, The Hague, 1966.

19 Gaarder, A. B. The basic course in modern foreign languages. In: Reports of surveys and studies in the teaching of modern foreign languages, MLA Materials Center, New York, 1961.

20 Harmon, J. T. Annual bibliography on the teaching of foreign languages: 1967. Foreign Language Annals, 1; i, ii, iii, iv (1967–68).

21 Haukebo, G. K. The next best thing to being there: language camps. In: Levenson, Stanley; Kendrick, William, eds. Readings in foreign languages for the elementary school. Blaisdell, Waltham, Mass., 1967, p. 471–473.

22 Hayes, A. S. Paralinguistics and kinesics: pedagogical perspectives. In: Sebeok, T. A.; Hayes, A. S.; Bateson, Mary C., eds. Approaches to semiotics: cultural anthropology, education, linguistics, psychiatry, psychology. Mouton, The Hague, 1964, p. 145–172.

23 Hayes, A. S. Procedures for language laboratory planning. Bulletin of the National Association of Secondary School Principals, 46 (1962) 123–135.

24 Hayes, A. S.; Lambert, W. E.; Tucker, G. R. Evaluation of foreign language teaching. Foreign Language Annals, 1 (1967) 22–44.

25 Hayes, A. S.; Lane, H.; Mueller, T.; Sweet, W. E. A new look at learning. In: Bottiglia, W. F., ed. Current issues in language teaching. Reports of the Working Committees, Northeast Conference on the Teaching of Foreign Languages (RWCNEC), MLA Materials Center, New York, 1962, p. 19–60.

26 Hoenigswald, H. M. A proposal for the study of folk-linguistics. In: Bright, William, ed. Sociolinguistics. Mouton, The Hague, 1966, p. 16–20.

27 Holby, Dorothy J. Self-evaluation and foreign language. Peabody Journal of Education, 44 (1967) 239–241.

28 Hutchinson, Joseph C. Modern foreign languages in high school: the language laboratory. OE-270 13, Bulletin No. 23, U.S. Department of Health, Education, and Welfare, Washington, D.C., 1961.

29 Jakobovits, L. A. The act of composition: some elements in a performance model of language. The National Council of Teachers of English, Champaign, Ill., 1968. Mimeo.

30 Jakobovits, L. A. Dimensionality of compound-coordinate bilingualism. Language Learning (Special Issue No. 3), (August 1968) 29–49.

31 Jakobovits, L. A. A functional approach to the assessment of language skills. Journal of English as a Second Language (Fall 1969).

32 Jakobovits, L. A. Implications of recent psycholinguistic developments for the teaching of a second language. Language Learning, 18 (1968) 89–109.

33 Jakobovits, L. A. Mediation theory and the "single-stage" S-R model: different? Psychological Review, 73 (1966) 376–381.

34 Jakobovits, L. A. Research findings and FL requirements in colleges and universities. Foreign Language Annals, 2 (1969) 436–456.

35 Jakobovits, L. A. Second language learning and transfer theory: a theoretical assessment. Language Learning. (In press.)

36 Jakobovits, L. A.; Miron, M. S., eds. Readings in the psychology of language. Prentice Hall, Englewood Cliffs, N.J., 1967.

37 Kansas State Teachers College of Emporia, Service Bureau for Modern Language Teachers. The French club. ERIC Documentation Service, U.S. Office of Education, Washington, D.C., 1967 [ED-011-184]. (Date uncertain.)

38 Kirsch, M. S. At what age elementary school language teaching? The Modern Language Journal, 40 (1956) 399–400.

39 Lambert, W. E. Psychological approaches to the study of language: II. On second language learning and bilingualism. The Modern Language Journal, 47 (1963) 114–121.

40 Larew, L. A. The optimum age for beginning a foreign language. The Modern Language Journal, 45 (1961) 203–206.

41 Lashley, K. S. The problem of serial order in behavior. In: Jeffress, L. A., ed. Cerebral mechanisms in behavior: the Hixon Symposium. John Wiley, New York, 1951.

42 Lee, W. R. Language-teaching games and contests. Oxford University Press, Eng., 1965.

43 Lenneberg, E. H. Biological foundations of language. John Wiley, New York, 1967.

44 Lenneberg, E. H. The natural history of language. In: Smith, Frank; Miller, G. A., eds. The genesis of language. Massachusetts Institute of Technology Press, Cambridge, 1966, p. 219–252.

45 Levenson, Stanley; Kendrick, William, eds. Readings in foreign languages for the elementary school. Blaisdell, Waltham, Mass., 1967.

46 Mackey, W. F. The measurement of bilingual behavior. The Canadian Psychologist, 7a (1966) 75–92.

47 Macnamara, John. Bilingualism and primary education: a study of Irish experience. University of Edinburgh Press, Scot., 1966.

48 Michel, Joseph, ed. Foreign language teaching: an anthology. Macmillan, New York, 1967.

49 Mildenberger, Andrea S.; Yuan-Heng Liao, Allen. ERIC documents on the teaching of foreign languages: list number 1. Foreign Language Annals, 2 (1968) 1–26.

50 Milner, P. M. Book review of "Speech and brain mechanisms" by W. Penfield and L. Roberts. Canadian Journal of Psychology, 14 (1960) 140–143.

51 Modern Language Association. Advice to the language learner. The Modern Language Journal, 50 (1966) 260–263.

52 Monot-Cassidy, Helene. The new audio-visual student. The Modern Language Journal, 50 (1966) 15–18.

53 Morgan, D. Y. Games and play-acting. English Language Teaching, 21 (1967) 182–185.

54 Mueller, Klaus. The army language school and its implications. In: Levenson, Stanley; Kendrick, William, eds. Readings in foreign languages for the elementary school. Blaisdell, Waltham, Mass., 1967, p. 479–485.

55 Mueller, T. H.; Harris, Robert. The effect of an audio-lingual program on drop-out rate. The Modern Language Journal, 50 (1966) 133–137.

56 Mueller, T. H.; Leutenegger, R. R. Some inferences about an intensified oral approach to the teaching of French based on a study of course drop-outs. The Modern Language Journal, 48 (1964) 91–94.

57 Nostrand, H. L. A shared repertory of audio-visual materials for foreign languages, language arts and social studies? Audiovisual Instruction, 11 (1966) 624–626.

58 Ollman, M. L., ed. MLA selective list of materials. MLA Materials Center, New York, 1962.

59 Peal, Elizabeth; Lambert, W. E. The relation of bilingualism to intelligence. Psychological Monographs, 76, No. 27 (1962). Whole Issue No. 546.

60 Penfield, Wilder. A consideration of the neuro-physiological mechanism of speech and some educational consequences. In: Proceedings of the American Academy of Arts and Science, 82 (1953) 201–214.

61 Penfield, Wilder; Roberts, Lamar. Speech and brain mechanisms. Princeton University Press, N.J., 1959.

62 Pimsleur, Paul; Bonkowski, R. J. The transfer of verbal material across sense modalities. Journal of Educational Psychology, 52 (1961) 104–107.

63 Pimsleur, Paul; Sundland, D. M.; McIntyre, Ruth D. Underachievement in foreign language learning. International Review of Applied Linguistics, 2 (1964) 113–150.

64 Postman, Leo. The present status of interference theory. In: Cofer, C. N.; Musgrave, Barbara S., eds. Verbal learning and verbal behavior. McGraw-Hill, New York, 1961, p. 152–179.

65 Reid, J. R. An exploratory survey of foreign language teaching by television in the United States. In: Reports of surveys and studies in the teaching of modern foreign languages, MLA Materials Center, New York, 1961, p. 197–211.

66 Rivers, Wilga M. The psychologist and the foreign language teacher. University of Chicago Press, Ill., 1964.

67 Rogers, Adrienne. Motivation: the forgotten word. French Review, 39 (1969) 906–909.

68 Scherer, G. A. C.; Wertheimer, Michael. The German teaching experiment at the University of Colorado. German Quarterly, 35 (1962) 298–308.

69 Sebeok, T. A.; Hayes, A. S.; Bateson, Mary C., eds. Approaches to semiotics: cultural anthropology, education, linguistics, psychiatry, psychology. Mouton, The Hague, 1964.

70 Skinner, B. F. Verbal behavior. Appleton-Century-Crofts, New York, 1957.

71 Smith, Frank; Miller, G. A., eds. The genesis of language. Massachusetts Institute of Technology Press, Cambridge, 1966.

72 Spolsky, Bernard. What does it mean to know a language, or how do you get someone to perform his competence? Paper prepared for presentation at the Second Conference on Problems in Foreign Language Testing held at the University of Southern California, Nov. 7–9, 1968. Mimeo.

73 Stern, H. H. Foreign languages in primary education: the teaching of foreign or second languages to younger children. UNESCO Institute for Education, Hamburg, Ger., 1963.

74 Upshur, J. A. Measurement of oral communication. Paper presented at the Second Conference on Problems in Foreign Language Testing held at the University of Southern California, Nov. 7–9, 1968. Mimeo.

75 Valdman, Albert. Programmed instruction and foreign language teaching. In: Valdman, Albert, ed. Trends in language teaching. McGraw-Hill, New York, 1966.

76 Valdman, Albert, ed. Trends in language teaching. McGraw Hill, New York, 1966.

77 Wagner, Grace D. Parental negative reaction to current methods of foreign language teaching: encounter and alternative. ERIC Documentation Service, U.S. Office of Education, Washington, D.C., 1966. [ED-012-546].

78 Willbern, Glenn. Foreign language enrollments in public secondary schools, 1965. Foreign Language Annals, 1 (1968) 239–253.

79 Yeni-Komshian, Grace; Zubin, D. A.; Afendras, Evangelos. A pilot study on the ability of young children and adults to identify and reproduce novel speech sounds. In: Annual report of the neurocommunications laboratory of the Johns Hopkins University School of Medicine, Baltimore, Md., 1968, p. 288–305. Mimeo.

8
Bilingualism

Introduction

Horacio Ulibarri

University of New Mexico

Bilingual means fluency in two languages, including oral communication, the encoding and decoding of written symbols, and the correct inflection, pitch, juncture, etc., commonly called the superimposed structure of a language. Nothing in the term "bilingual" denotes more than this. If the language fluency is all that is assessed as bilingual, it is very obvious that bilingualism is a sterile condition, only a tool to be learned as fully as possible and honed to razor-edge precision.

Unfortunately, or fortunately, *people* are not tools. People are made of flesh and blood with self-images, emotions, intellects, different socioeconomic levels of living, and distinct varieties of physical makeup. Therefore, bilingualism when applied to people must be more than a sterile device. It must be adaptable to people.

Bilingualism, adapted to people, gives the connotation that self-images, emotions, intellects, and different socioeconomic levels of living must be interwoven to the point of amalgamation of language with people. If we deal with two languages, we must take into consideration two language groups of people. If there are two language groups of people, obviously their ways of assessing themselves within their total environments will differ. This then leads to the conclusion that much more than fluency in two languages is our concern. We are, in essence, melding two cultures through the vehicle of languages.

Bilingualism defined as interaction between two peoples and their cultures

The concern of this chapter is bilingualism within the context of foreign language teaching. This places it in the realm of education, and we can begin our look at bilingualism from the standpoint of the bilingual child. Since there are many bilingual-bicultural areas and situations in the United States, and since the purpose is not to analyze the problems besetting each and every one, this chapter will confine itself to one of the largest ethnic groups of non-Anglo people who retain old-country ties and language due to geographic proximity—namely, the Spanish-speaking Mexican-Americans of the American Southwest. This also was done because much of the data and generalizations used were the products of the Bilingual Research Project

A case study

(6) recently concluded. The project's main focus was the Spanish-speaking bilingual of the Southwest. There is no intent, however, to limit the application of the principles, generalizations, and recommendations to the Spanish-speaking bilingual only. Even though the Mexican-American is used as the case group, the implications of the chapter will have application to all bilingual groups in the United States regardless of language or ethnic background.

Nature of bilingualism

The term "bilingualism" lends itself to many interpretations. On the one hand, bilingualism refers to facility in the use of two languages, ranging from a minimal competency in either language to a high level of proficiency in both. Generally, the bilingual person tends to be more proficient in one language than the other even though he may have attained a high level of proficiency in both languages. On the other hand, the so-called bilingual may actually have a very low level of development in both languages, thus making the individual functionally illiterate in both languages (Pryor, 39).

Bilingualism and functionality in two sociocultures are directly related. Generally the level of functionality of the individual in either socioculture determines his level of proficiency in either language. The fact that parents of a given sociocultural background often are more fluent in their native language than in English presents some confusion to the educators. They tend to think that the children are also more proficient in their native dialect than in English. This is not necessarily the case. When one examines the language proficiency of children of minority groups to whom English supposedly is a second language, proficiency in their native language is generally lower than in English, even though their development in either language may be severely retarded. For example, in New Mexico the native Spanish-speaking New Mexican invariably is more proficient in English than in Spanish (6, 36). His level of education and thus his proficiency in English will depend on the educational attainment levels of his parents as well as their socioeconomic status, both factors of acculturation. The same fact was found generally throughout the Southwest (35c).

Bilingualism manifests itself in many ways

On the other hand, in some minority groups whose native dialect is an incomplete language, e.g., Navajo, the children may be as proficient in their native dialect as it is possible to get. This does not mean necessarily that their functionality in the Anglo socioculture increases except that they may be thoroughly functional within the bounds of their native socioculture (McKenzie, 32).

The concepts of bilingualism and biculturism are often mistakenly interchanged. This perhaps is due to the fact that large minority groups in the United States who are bilingual also have a culture that is different from the regular Anglo-American culture (Holemon & Ulibarri, 26). For example, in the Southwest all the bilingual people speak Spanish or an Indian dialect. These native speakers come from a cultural background different from the Anglo-American culture. Hence, in the Southwest bilingualism always connotes biculturism. Little thought is given to the fact that often minority group members, even though bilingual, may not be bicultural. Rather, many of these people are typically marginal persons groping aimlessly and accepting what comes fortuitously from either culture (Herskovitz, 24). Even though interrelated and interdependent, bilingualism and biculturism are two distinct phenomena. Biculturism refers to the cultural elements that may include language but go beyond language. Biculturism is a functional awareness and participation in two contrasting sociocultures (statuses, roles, values). For the sake of greater clarity, it must be stated that it is possible to attain biculturism without bilingualism and bilingualism can be achieved without dual acculturation.

It is rather inconceivable that a person becoming a bilingual with a high degree of proficiency in two languages will fail to absorb any of the culture of his second language. However, it must be noted that any method of teaching a second language that stresses only skills, e.g., the Teaching of English to Speakers of Other Languages (TESOL), is not going to produce a bicultural individual. It is only when the philosophies, emotions, and aspirations of a socioculture are learned both at the conceptual and cathectic level that an individual submerges himself in another culture. Only then does he become a bicultural individual. Perhaps the assumption here is that true bilingualism is better attained when the individual becomes bicultural.

Finally, one must differentiate among bilinguals between those who have acquired a second language as a leisure-time activity and those whose survival depends on learning a second language. Those who have acquired a second language by way of leisure-time learning are relatively few in the United States. Many have developed only the basic essentials of proficiency in

Interrelationships between bilingualism and biculturism

Two types of bilinguals

the second language. Among those who have learned the second language because of social necessity are persons who have spent tours of duty in a foreign country. More numerous, however, are the minority groups in the United States who have a different sociocultural and language background than the typical Anglo-American and have had to acculturate and learn English as their second language for survival purposes. No reliable figures were found to estimate the size of these groups (6) but among these are represented all the nationalities of the world. Perhaps the largest foreign language group is the Spanish-speaking, which includes a large segment of Mexican-Americans, Puerto Ricans, Cubans, and other Latin Americans. The focus of this chapter will be on the bilinguals who have acquired English as a second language because of social necessity and survival purposes.

Growth and development of the bilingual child

In the early days of investigating the bilingual child, it was found that he tended to be inferior in most variables, e.g., intelligence and academic achievement, when compared to the English-speaking child. These discrepancies in favor of the English-speaking child were generally explained in terms of language differences. Today most analyses take into consideration *Handicaps the bilingual faces* the fact that the overwhelming majority of the bilinguals in this country are members of some minority group. Perhaps this factor more than bilingualism or biculturism accounts for the apparent stunted growth in the areas of intellectual, academic, and emotional development among minority group members. Samora (41) explains this by saying minority group members as a whole have less accessibility: (*1*) to the economic base of the nation; (*2*) to the social life of the American people; and (*3*) to the educational opportunities of the schools.

Because of the overwhelming interdependency of American society, no social group can live in isolation. Since the Anglo-American culture is dominant in the United States, all minority groups for survival purposes must function to some degree within the Anglo-American cultural milieu. This is forced conformity *The macro-culture forces* (Ulibarri, 46). The majority group has within its domain the *conformity on the micro-* power to state certain norms for the minority group and to force *culture in adverse ways* them into certain types of behavior according to the preset norms. The fact that the minority group member is operating out of his milieu forces him to behave most of the time in an inferior manner (Marden, 34). At this point the majority group withholds rewards from the minority group and intensifies the acculturation efforts.

The net result generally tends to be that the minority group members, e.g., the Indians and the Mexican-Americans, are relegated to a lower status and are destined to poorer conditions and standards of living than the majority group members (Samora, 41; 35e, a). This condition of poverty initiates the downward spiral of poor education, poor health, less energy, less functionality within the Anglo-American culture, and thus more destitution. As a result one finds today that most minority group members are impoverished and have rather low educational attainment levels.

Poverty begets more poverty

One needs to know what this forced conformity and the characteristic of being poor do to a group of people. No comprehensive study has been made that could give substantive answers to these questions as they relate to bilingual minorities. More attention has been given to the developmental problems of the poor and in recent years to the war on poverty. But a scientifically designed investigation to find where the areas of strengths and weaknesses are among the bilingual-bicultural has not been undertaken.

Regarding physical growth, health, and sickness, there has been no widespread research that has attempted to assess the physical status of the bilingual minority group member, especially as it applies to bilingual education. The general consensus has been that the bilingual is in no respect different from any other group in physical stamina and physical health. What has to be considered is the generally poverty-stricken conditions that characterize the minority groups — including bilingual minorities (35d). More recently, in the McGovern Report (28), a task force has indicated strong evidence that mental growth is affected and arrested by dietary and nutritional deficiencies during the pregnancy period and especially during the first six months of the life of an infant. If the assessment of these studies is correct, it is a frightful consequence that we have to face if poverty is not eradicated from the life of the bilingual-bicultural minorities. It thus becomes possible to have generation after generation of impoverished slow learners among these groups.

The McGovern Report

Intelligence testing

Testing bilinguals has received much attention from researchers for a long period of time. Much of the research has been in comparative studies between bilinguals and monoglots. During the first period when the theory of racial psychology was rampant, it was generally concluded that bilingual-bicultural individuals were inferior in intelligence when compared to monoglot Caucasians. In the second period, when there was considerable doubt about the validity of the testing instruments when applied to bilingual-biculturals, the thrust was to develop culture-free tests, e.g., Davis-Eells Games. The testing results did not improve considerably and this led to the third period where the thrust has been the development of culture-fair tests and the development of local norms instead of relying on the standards of the norming group (6, pp. 33–34).

Three stages in the testing process

The literature is in general agreement that when intelligence tests are applied to bilingual groups, the scores obtained are much lower (about one standard deviation) than the scores of the norming group. It has also been found that when nonlanguage or performance types of tests are administered, the results are more favorable (Bloom, Davis & Hess, 7; Darcy, 15; Eells, et al., 17; Havighurst & Hilkevitch, 22).

These findings have led to the conclusion that the language deficit and/or language barrier is the main causative factor of the low scores of bilinguals on intelligence tests (Henderson, 23; Holland, 27). Some evidence, however, points to the possibility that other variables may enter the picture. When a group of Spanish-speaking students were administered the Stanford-Binet intelligence test both in English and Spanish, the result was that the sample scored higher in the English version than in the Spanish, although the scores in the English version were about one standard deviation below the norms (Keston & Jimenez, 30).

Tests discriminate

Results indicating test discrimination against lower social classes were obtained by Eells et al. (17) in their assessment of the most widely used tests in the Chicago schools when low and high socioeconomic groups were compared. When the Goodenough Draw-a-Man Test was applied to a group of "advantaged" and to a group of "disadvantaged" the results were significantly in favor of the advantaged (Hanson & Robinson, 21). Zintz (50) and others concluded that not only the language and experience barrier but also a culture barrier could not be overcome by most bicultural children.

Nonetheless, intelligence test scores continue to be the best predictors of school success. High correlations are still being obtained when intelligence scores are compared to achievement scores (Cooper, 13; Peters, 38). But since the results in general in the area of achievement testing have been that the bilingual child scores significantly lower than the English-speaking child, the phenomena can be readily understood. (Floyd, 20; Zintz, 50). One must also remember the historical origin of intelligence testing when Binet established the validity for his scales with school achievement scores. Somehow through validation of instruments with other previously established instruments, the vicious circle of the intelligence instrument being validated with school achievement and then becoming the best predictor of school success continues to plague the professional educator in the education of the bilingual.

Origins of the intelligence test affect its validity for the assessment of the bilingual

The overwhelming evidence of the research dealing with the intellectual growth of the bilingual is simply that the bilinguals score at much lower levels than the norming group. No research evidence was uncovered where an attempt was made by some form of treatment to increase the IQ score of the bilingual, e.g., teaching for the test, except one made by Sanchez (42).

The self-concept

Regarding the self-concept of the individual, Palomares (37) and Ulibarri (47) show evidence that the bilingual-bicultural individual tends to be more defensive, to be filled with more anxiety, and to be plagued with more alienation than the English-speaking Anglo-American. This syndrome is not necessarily attributed to bilingualism. Although bilingualism may contribute, the strongest factor may be that most bilinguals are minority groups with all the attendant anomalies.

Besides this defensive syndrome, the bilingual-bicultural individuals, according to Christian (10), tend to experience some confusion and frustration as they move from their native cultural setting into the school setting. This is directly attributed to the lack of facility in the English language and to differences in the cultural setting, especially in the value systems.

Probably the most damaging thing to the self-concept of the bilingual has been the widespread practice in the Southwest of prohibiting Spanish-speaking students to speak their native dialect within the school grounds and the classrooms. This has been done in the name of helping these students to learn English and to reinforce this learning. The results generally have been that the students soon become painfully aware that Spanish is the language of deviancy. It is for this reason that the Spanish-speaking student must be given differentiated treatment (Ulibarri, 46).

Prohibiting the use of the native language can be detrimental

This coupled with the fact that there is a constant influx of lower-class Mexicans in the Southwestern part of the United States (Mexican-American Study Project, 35e, a) has perpetuated the image of the Mexican as an illiterate, lazy, and impoverished individual whose only ambition in life is to become a welfare case. In general, this same orientation has existed in the treatment of the Indians by the Bureau of Indian Affairs (BIA) schools. However, there is some evidence that the inclusion of native language as a vehicle for teaching both subject matter and bicultural factors in a regular school curriculum enhances the development of a positive self-image (Andersson, 2; Arnold, 3).

Achievement

The research literature is in consensus that the bilingual child generally achieves at a lower level and gains at a slower rate than the Anglo-American English-speaking child in all areas of the curriculum when the instruction is done in English. When the instruction is done bilingually, there is a definite gain in language acquisition in both languages by the bilingual. In one study, the bilingual students showed less gain in subject matter areas when compared to students who were not participating in the bilingual program, but were significantly higher in language acquisition (Arnold, 3).

The above findings definitely apply to the Mexican-Americans. Regarding Indian groups, a conclusion drawn in one study was that students who attended off-reservation public schools did better academically than those who attended on-reservation public schools. Similarly students who attended Bureau of Indian Affairs off-reservation schools generally achieved higher than students who attended on-reservation BIA schools (Coombs, 12).

Students achieve better in off-reservation schools than in on-reservation schools

Among the reasons given for this lower achievement has been language interference (Rohn, 40). Generally it has been conceded that the bilingual student, because of his lack of proficiency in the English language, understands less of the teaching in the classroom since it is so highly verbalized. In one study of reading comprehension, the idiomatic expressions used in basal readers were isolated. It was found that a very low level of understanding of these expressions occurred among Navajo and Spanish-speaking children (Dudding, 16; Yandell, 48). Zintz (49) found that the Spanish-speaking students do better on achievement tests in the areas of computation or memorization, such as arithmetic facts and spelling, than they do in the more verbal

A high degree of verbalization in the classroom affects the achievement of bilinguals

236

areas such as the language battery, social studies battery, and the science battery.

Other factors that have been alluded to in the research as having an effect on school achievement by the bilingual are elements not directly evident within the school. These elements have to do with the home and community environment in which the child exists (Caplan & Ruble, 8; Michael, 36). The educational-linguistic backgrounds of the parents have been found to have positive correlations with the achievement of the children in the school. Generally it is argued that the more acculturated the parents are, the better the child will be able to achieve in school. In other words, the more acculturated the parents are, the better they speak the English language, the more they motivate their children, and thus the higher the achievement level attained by the children. It is also assumed that the more acculturated the child is, the better he will be able to achieve in school. These speculations are not supported by research (Cordova, 14). However, in one study Zintz (49) points out that forced acculturation may well have very negative reactions.

The more educated the parent the better the bilingual child's achievement

There is general agreement in the research that culture conflict is directly related to educational retardation (Bergan, 5). This relationship has been found in the areas of science (Charles, 9), English analogies and reading (Condie, 11; Hess, 25), and arithmetic (Ikeda, 29). None of these studies, however, have delineated which are the specific cultural conflicts that intervene in the learning process. Two studies by Zajonc & Wahi (49) and Havighurst & Hilkevitch (22) attribute the cultural norm of conformity and cooperation of Indian children as being the main causative factors of educational retardation among these children.

Culture conflicts affect achievement

Lack of teacher awareness regarding the socioculture of the bilingual-bicultural child has been isolated as a main factor in the educational retardation of Mexican-American and Indian-American children (Caplan & Ruble, 8; Ulibarri, 46). These studies attribute that, because the teachers and administrators are unaware of sociocultural differences, the school curriculum tends to be middle-class, white, Anglo-Saxon, Protestant (WASP) oriented. Because of this lack of awareness and because of the schools' middle-class orientation, the bilingual child tends to feel out of place in the school socioculture. These negative attitudes lead to isolation, defensiveness, and anxiety on the part of the bilingual child and in turn bear on his academic achievement. The teachers, unaware of the chasm between the socioculture of

Teachers must be aware of sociocultural differences to operate effectively in the classroom

the school and the sociocultural background of the children, inflict further wounds by causing culture conflict through their teaching approaches and techniques (Cordova, 14, p. 116–127; Ulibarri, 45).

All of the studies concerned with lack of educational gain among the bilingual explain the phenomena in the terms described above, such as the lack of experiential background, factors of acculturation, lack of teacher awareness of sociocultural differences, the attitude of the children, and the culture conflict. No study was found that attempted to measure the reliability and validity of achievement tests on the market today when applied to bilingual-bicultural children, especially those who come from impoverished conditions.

Relation of bilingualism to minority group status

The prestige of bilingualism is directly related to the status within the larger social setting that the bilingual minority group occupies. This factor became very apparent during World War I with the discrimination leveled at the bilingual German minority. The phenomenon was further reemphasized with the Japanese-Americans during World War II. In the Southwest the bilingual Mexican-American minority has consistently occupied a position of lower status of prestige than the Anglo-American. Only recently has the Spanish language emerged as a desirable second language for the English-speaking majority. Even for the Spanish-speaking Mexican-American, knowledge of the Spanish language has been a dubious asset.

Knowledge of one's native language: a dubious asset

No extensive study of social class stratification has been undertaken of the bilingual minorities in the United States. If one is to use the Mexican-American as an index of the social status of the other minorities in the Southwest, the indications are that

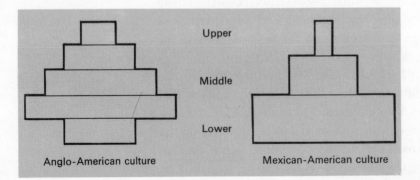

Figure 1.

the minority groups have an undue proportion of their members in the lower classes (Mexican-American Study Project, 35d). Figure 1 represents the disparity between the majority and minority group regarding social stratification (Ulibarri, 47).

Besides the undue proportion of minority group members belonging to the lower class and the culture of poverty, the other phenomenon differentiating them from the Anglo-American is the relative status and prestige accorded them by the majority group. According to Marden (34) the majority group invariably relegates lower status and prestige to the people in the minority group than they do to themselves irrespective of the similarity of criteria for stratification. This is shown in Figure 2 below.

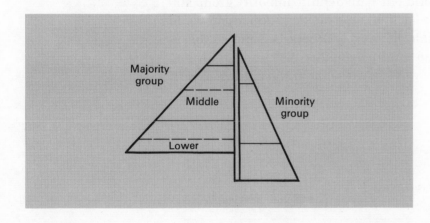

Figure 2.

With respect to self-actualization among minority groups, all of these variables regarding social class spell out one important factor, namely, there are definite limitations or ceilings placed on minority group members. Even though the Anglo world is one of almost unlimited levels of accessibility, the statuses available to the minority group members are definitely limited in level. Accessibility to the statuses they could occupy and the roles they could play is limited because of culturally binding factors. Some of these factors are lack of broad-time orientation, lack of future-time self projection, and lack of competitive drives. It is not sufficient for them to have high aspirational levels. The teaching of the schools that "much hard work," a given amount of "gumption," and a "little bit o' luck" are component parts of unlimited success is at variance with the harsh realities of life. Instead, status and role allocations are determined by the majority group, and only a small number of minority group members are allowed

Aspirations are denied fulfillment by the majority group's attitude

upward mobility (Bendix & Lipset, 4, p. 449–458). The repression of large numbers may be a factor of discrimination, and allowing upward mobility to a small elite may be subconsciously perpetrated to avoid recrimination.

A prolonged history of limited levels of statuses and roles available to minority group members, regardless of individual potential and aspirations, breeds a low motivation to work hard now in order to reap rewards later. Among the Mexican-Americans there is a saying that expresses this factor very succinctly: "You are Mexican; you have to pick cotton." When large numbers of minority group members have tried to move upward and cannot pass this ceiling, they have few choices left. One choice available to them is horizontal mobility under that ceiling still within the Anglo world but with definite minority group status. Another is to bounce back into the Mexican-American world and lead a life of anomic behavior. Others become so disenchanted they succumb to total personality disorganization and exist in the never-never world of abysmia in the culture of poverty (Ulibarri, 47).

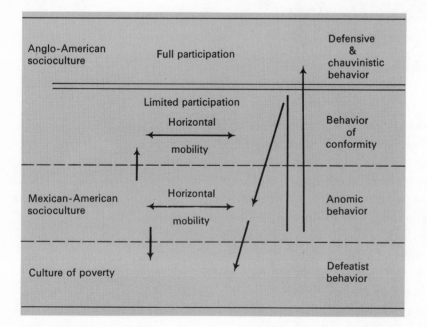

Figure 3.

Even for the elite few who are allowed unlimited upward mobility for the purposes of avoiding recrimination, a high price is exacted. These people have to conform to the nth degree to the

The denial of heritage

WASP ethic. Probably the highest price that these "fortunate" ones have to pay is abandonment and desertion of everything that belongs to their cultural heritage. They are led to believe that the more "Anglo" they become, the more rewards they will reap. This is often the case with the politician at the higher levels of government. If these individuals try to help their own people in a genuine manner, they lose the Anglo vote and thereby their office. Others become chauvinistic in their attitudes regarding their people and with all the power at their command try to erase from themselves anything that resembles their cultural heritage. For example, the Mexican-American who lives in the horizontal mobile world within the confines of the ceiling must at all times attempt to anglicize and cease to be Mexican-American. The teachers are a case in point. They have a definite ceiling placed on them and must perform according to the rules as well as inculcate the WASP ethic according to certain rituals. If they do not perform accordingly, sanctions are brought to bear upon them. From the many who return to the anomic world of their native community, there is a group of individuals with a high potential of a different type. From this group the criminal world will tap a chosen few and these become underground individuals who perform different kinds of roles. They develop a type of bilingualism peculiar to themselves which is incomprehensible to anyone not associated with the criminal world, e.g., the dialect *caló* among the Mexican-Americans.

Role performance exposes itself in devious ways

The limited self-actualization that has been relegated to the minority groups has irreversible consequences. An elite few move beyond the ceiling in the horizontal world, larger numbers settle within the confines of the ceiling, and many fall back or remain in the world of anomia. Large numbers succumb to the world of abysmia in the culture of poverty. All in all, the frustration is great, and the aspirational levels become lower and almost nonexistent. It is a world of disillusionment in which the minority group member lives. The majority find harmony in their lives only by being content with their status as second-class citizens, and in being in complete isolation among themselves.

To the elite few who climb beyond the ceiling, bilingualism is not imperative. Their social functionality is almost entirely within the majority group's socioculture and their primary language is the majority's language. They believe that the better they imitate the majority group in speech the better off they are and that knowledge of their native language is not a particular asset.

The role played affects the attitude toward the native language

To those confined below the ceiling, knowledge of the majority's language is most imperative. Since these people have to *conform*, the presence of an "accent" is used as an index for denial of rewards and the limitation in the allocation of roles. Thus these people overstrive to perfect their English at the expense of their development in their native language. Unless they are in a position of personnel management of people of their own type, knowledge of their native language is of no value to them.

One of the ways in which the minority group member differs from the Anglo-American within his society is in status. When the Anglo-American group is in power, the minority group is at his mercy (Bendix & Lipset, 4, p. 221–239). The Anglo-American has the power to relegate a given status to a minority group and to keep it there. It has within its domain the power to expect given types and qualities of functionality from the minority group member. All of these things the Anglo can do because he controls the economy upon which the minority is dependent. Thus the Anglo-American also controls the reward system of the society as a whole, and can determine which parcels are available to the minority, and which are not. This excruciating circumstance, placed on the minority group member against his will, makes him feel utterly powerless. He is powerless to cope with the never-ending expectations placed on him by the majority group. Yet he cannot do otherwise. If he conforms and performs, he receives his determined rewards. If he does not, he is denied them and actually punished. The minority group member thus becomes more anxious to fulfill his roles properly, but the anxiety developing within himself seldom brings dexterity, and he, because of his anxiety, performs more and more poorly until he finally finds himself in the downward spiral syndrome.

The dominant group sets limit for the operational level of the minority group

The Anglo-American world is caught up in the cult of achievement (Smelser & Lipset, 44). Goal attainment is the objective of all Americans. The minority group is expected to compete despite the foreignness of his native socioculture to that of the Anglo-American world. Because the culturally different minority group member has not internalized the totality of the Anglo-American value system, and because the pressure is so great to succeed, he is not beyond resorting to socially unaccepted means in achieving his goals. This, of course, is classified as deviant behavior by the majority group and punishment is subsequently doled out if the individual is caught.

Deviant behavior

The above patterns are defense mechanisms. Several other patterns of defensiveness can be noted among minority groups such as chauvinistic attitudes and denial of one's heritage. Belligerent and militant attitudes and behaviors are also part of the defenses. Perhaps the last resort of defensiveness is isolation. The minority group members tend to isolate themselves within their own kind. For example, the barrio offers the Mexican-American protective walls against the hostile environment of the *gringo*.

Manifestations of defensiveness

Thus it is within the social context described above that the bilingual minority member often refuses to have his child learn his native language. Historically, all minorities in the United States have within two or three generations after migration lost their sociocultural identity, and thereby their native language.

Minorities intentionally forget their native dialect

With the type of repression described above, the minority group bilingual claims that the cause of his misery is his lack of proficiency in the English language, and that his "accent" is the identifying factor by which he is isolated as a foreigner. In this frame of mind the parent is in no mood to let his children learn his native dialect, "because he will have an accent."

Relation of bilingualism to acculturation[1]

Often the problems associated with minority groups from cultures other than Anglo-American are lumped together under the label "bilingualism." This is done because bilingualism is the most obvious differentiating factor of the minority group member. Poverty, low educational attainment levels, cultural conflict, social disorganization, and personality disorganization are all factors, not so obvious and, therefore, not often taken into consideration (Ulibarri, 45).

Educators tend to think that if the minority group child would acquire proficiency in English, all of the problems of educating that child would be solved. More recently, however, those who have been studying the problems of educating minority group children or bilingual minority group children are fairly convinced that language problems are actually symptomatic of deeper, underlying problems (Bilingual Research Project, 6, pp. 11–13; Leighton, 31). When the TESOL movement came into

TESOL alone does not solve the problem

---

1 Generalizations in this section are primarily drawn from the author's lifetime participation in the Mexican-American socioculture, his prolonged study of minority groups in the acculturation process, and long years of work among minority groups. Not many studies have attempted to relate bilingualism to acculturation and biculturism.

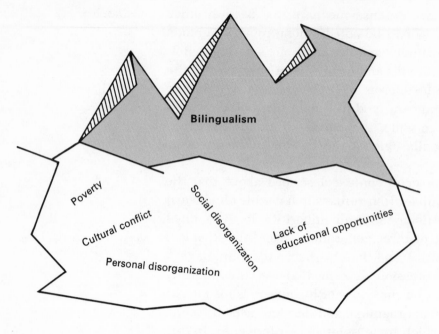

Bilingualism

Poverty

Cultural conflict

Social disorganization

Personal disorganization

Lack of
educational opportunities

prominence, many people were hopeful that this would alleviate
the problems of underachievement and early dropouts among
bilingual minority group children. However, the hopes soon dis-
sipated as the problems of dropouts and low achievement levels
continued to plague the educators of these children.

Some recent studies by Cordova (14, p. 113–115) on acculturation have indicated that there is a low relationship between
acculturation and educational attainment levels. However,
these results may be due to the fact that there are no standardized instruments available for measuring the extent of acculturation. Nonetheless, other spin-offs from the process of acculturation have clearly indicated that there are strong relationships
between the personality development of the individual and the
stage of acculturation in which he finds himself. Cordova related
alienation to acculturation. When he delineated the concept
of alienation into powerlessness, normlessness, purposelessness,
and isolation, he found some strong correlations between these
four factors and several areas in which the individual had acculturated from the native socioculture into the Anglo-American.

Acculturation for the purposes of this discussion will mean the
process by which an individual moves in his behavior from one
sociocultural setting to another. There are several accompanying phenomena that affect the personality of the individual as
he gets involved in the process of acculturation. In one of the
first studies in acculturation, Herskovitz (24) described the

Definition

244

process in terms of diffusion, assimilation, acceptance, adaptation, and reaction. All of these variables play an important part in analyzing the bilingualism problem.

Diffusion is the aspect of cultural change that includes the transmission of techniques, attitudes, and concepts from one cultural group to another. This change can be a two-way process; however, the dominant culture usually undergoes less change, with more selectivity than the minority group culture. *Assimilation* is used to designate the process by which a culture achieves synthesis. In other words, when a value has been assimilated it becomes a functional part of the belief system and is taught through the culture's own process and is reinforced by mechanisms of social control. *Acceptance* occurs when the members of the minority group culture lose most of the values and practices of the old culture and acquire the inner values and behavioral patterns of the culture with which the group has come into contact. *Adaptation* is the condition where original and foreign culture traits are combined so as to produce a smooth, cultural, functional whole. It is achieved by modification of the patterns of the two cultures. There may be the retention of a series of conflicting attitudes and values which are reconciled in everyday life as specific occasions arise (Festinger, 19). *Reaction* occurs because of oppression by the majority group or because of unforeseen consequences in the acceptance of foreign cultural traits. Counteracculturation movements, such as the Chicano movement, develop and the reaction may maintain its psychological force: (1) as a compensation for the imposed or assumed inferiority, and (2) through the prestige which a return to preacculturative conditions may bring the group participating in such a movement (Herskovitz, 24).

Phenomena in the acculturation process

Acculturation is more selective for the adult than for the child. The adult can select from the culture that which has resemblances to the familiar and add his store of new learning as it is needed. In general, the adult can retain his identity in his own ethnic cultural cluster. But for the child who is in the process of learning the social roles, the sociocultural selections create much more stress. He is caught between the culture of his parents and the culture of the school, as well as that of the rest of the community. Thus, he is forever being forced to choose between conflicting sets of values, being rewarded or punished alternately, or simultaneously, by the conflicting cultural systems (Elam, 18).

The dilemma of the bicultural-bilingual child

The individual becomes the victim of the disharmony between

245

the norms of his native culture and those of the socioculture in which he is asked to perform his roles. Even though he may have been able to define the limits of the statuses and the roles he has to play in the majority culture, his tendency is to play them according to the rules under which he was socialized and to disregard or relegate a second level of importance to the rules of the new culture. This tendency exists because of the lack of thorough familiarity with the norms of the majority group as well as his lack of complete emotional commitment to these new rules and norms.

Acculturation can be conceived as a continuum of stages of development (Ulibarri, 45). Starting with the native culture as the point of departure, one can delineate at least four stages up to the time when the individual becomes completely acculturated into a second culture. If the group is in the process of amalgamation, by this time the individual has fully disassociated himself from the native culture. If biculturism is the goal of the group, dual culturization has taken place and the individual becomes emotionally committed to two cultures—his native culture and the second culture.

Four stages in the acculturation process

The first stage of acculturation can be characterized by bewilderment. All the forces of the new culture that beset the individual are for the most part incomprehensible to him and perhaps he may not even be conscious of them. At this level the individual is likely to succumb to the many negative escapes that people undergoing the process of acculturation fall prey to, for example, alcoholism, dope addiction, prostitution, and the like. This perhaps is the lowest level in the process of acculturation to which any individual may fall. Unfortunately, these patterns tend to be widespread among bilingual minorities attending school.

Bewilderment

If the individual is capable of rising from this pit, he then acquires a degree of independence by having acquired greater functionality in the new culture. With more acculturation, that is, learning and internalizing new sociocultural norms and behaviors, the individual finds that the rewards of the new socioculture complex become more readily available to him. At the same time a subconscious, emotional change has been occurring and the rewards that heretofore had been undesirable or incomprehensible now become desirable and meaningful to him.

At this time, he embarks upon the second stage of acculturation, characterized by overcompensation, ultra-proficiency, and conspicuous dexterity in the new socioculture. He feels ashamed of being a member of an ethnic minority and wishes he could *pass* for an Anglo-American. At this stage he becomes ashamed of his native cultural heritage and in compensation degrades the sociocultural practices of his people. He refuses to use his native language even though his level of proficiency in his second language, English, may be poor. *Overcompensation*

The third stage of acculturation can be characterized by deliberate regression of the individual to his native culture. In this stage the individual likes to think of himself as being both bilingual and bicultural. However, the regressions that take place pertain only to the peripheral levels, and do not penetrate into the center-core value area of the culture. The individual will take what he perceives to be the most glaring symbols of his native culture and, parading these symbols, proclaims to the world that he is of such and such a cultural minority, for example, that he is a Mexican-American. At this stage also, the individual valiantly attempts to show the world that he is a bilingual. *Regression*

The fourth stage of acculturation is the stage of biculturism. Here the individual truly understands the major aspects of both sociocultures, and functions wholesomely in both. This aspect will be treated in more detail later. *Biculturism*

In relating bilingualism to the problem of acculturation, one can see that the willingness of the individual to be or not to be a bilingual depends upon the stage of acculturation in which he finds himself. For example, the individual in the first stage of acculturation finds that he does not have command of one of the most valuable tools of the new culture, the English language. In this first stage of confusion, he truly believes that if he would learn the new language, English, all of his problems would be solved (Anderson, 1). This is the reason, perhaps, why so many immigrants in the United States immediately embark on learning English and pin all hope of success on learning the new language.

Further along the continuum, as the individual learns English but retains a given amount of language interference from his native dialect, he is made conscious of the fact that it is not desirable to have a "foreign accent." As he goes into the second stage of acculturation, the intonation patterns of the individual become definitely melodramatic. In this stage, the individual, as he acquires more dexterity in his theatrical mannerisms, is likely to deny any knowledge of his native language or dialect. He becomes overanxious that there be not a speck of an accent either in his private conversation or in his more public utterances. *"a foreign accent"*

247

Bilingualism/Ulibarri

The parents who find themselves in this stage of acculturation decidedly will not permit the children to learn the language spoken in the home. They overaspire to become more Anglo than the Anglo. The children will enroll in second language classes such as French, German, or even Russian, rather than Spanish, as is the case of the Mexican-American in the Southwest. Spanish is too common a language. It is too closely associated with the "bracero" and the lower-class elements that migrate from Mexico. But French is the language of finesse, German is the language of the scientist, and Russian is the language of foreign relations. These are desirable. The parents will excuse themselves with a statement such as: "Anyway, if I want my children to learn Spanish, I can teach it to them myself." However, this rarely happens. And, in addition, the individual rarely becomes bilingual or multilingual through second language classes.

Rejecting one's native language in favor of learning others

As the individual matures physically, mentally, and spiritually, he begins to see that he has been playing a rather confusing, melodramatic, and nonsensical game. He has been able to achieve and overcompensate. He has acquired status in the new society and is content with it. For the first time he begins to look at himself. He takes stock of his accomplishments in relation to the place from which he started. He is proud of himself for having achieved so much. However, mingled with this pride is an uneasy feeling of having left so many "good things" behind – his friends, his parents, and the way of life in his childhood. Nostalgia sets in and overpowers the individual. A sense of often having used almost inhuman means in the achievement of his goal, definitely sacrificing love and abandoning the home, develops extreme guilt feelings in the individual.

"twangs of conscience"

It is in this stage that the individual starts taking stock of the language from which he has tried to disassociate himself for so many years. He starts to redevelop his dexterity in his native language. For example, in the case of the Mexican-American he will begin to listen more to Spanish radio programs. He will start reading more books in his native language, frequently attend theaters and films in his native language, and, in short, start again the process of exaggerating his sociocultural origin. Because of the type of educational opportunities and associations that he has had, and because he deliberately tried to disassociate himself from his native language, the individual finds, much to his dismay, that much of his dexterity in the native language is lost. He will try to carry on conversations with other members of the minority group in his native language, but finds himself

The desire to relearn the native language

unable to do so. Often he cannot even utter complete sentences in the native language. Here he reverts almost identically to the first stage of acculturation, where he found himself in utter bewilderment and, because of his lack of knowledge of the English language, had to mix the native language with English in order to be able to communicate. Now the reverse of this pattern is true. The bilingual individual, because of having forgotten, or because of having stunted his development in his native language, finds himself more proficient in English than in his native language. Thus, most of the time he has to use English mixed with his native dialect in order to communicate.

At this stage of development the parents will also urge their children to start studying the language that was natively theirs but is now a second language to the children. Because the grandparents may not have acculturated to the same extent as the young parents, they may still retain much of the old language. The children associating with the grandparents may have developed their listening facility, mastered the sound patterns, and may understand much of the language system, although they may be unable to use it orally. As a result, these children advance at an accelerated pace in second language classes. They have conquered some very difficult steps in learning a new language even before starting the class. It is only practicing and developing a few new dexterities that they need.

Native language performance becomes an asset

The relationship of bilingualism to biculturism

Unfortunately in the history of minority groups acculturation has actually destroyed and annihilated their native culture. This has been so in the case of all minority groups. Within two or three generations, all vestiges of the native culture and mother language have been lost. As minority cultural groups acculturate, they cease to exist as cultural entities. They immerse themselves in the general milieu of the Anglo-American society, having lost the essence of their culture and language in the process.

Cultural identity ceases, the native language suffers

Generally, the immigrant generation settled within the walls of a ghetto and perpetuated the socioculture of the mother country. The second generation, having had more contact and more education in American schools than the immigrant parents, embarked in the process of acculturation on a wider scale and with greater momentum than the parents. They began to disassociate themselves from some of the elements of the parental culture. They still used the mother tongue to a greater extent than English, and they still retained much language interference. They were desirous that their children not be shackled by the accent of the mother language. Here they deliberately placed obstacles or denied opportunities to their children for learning the mother language. In short, *they wanted their children to become "American."* The loss of the language precipitated the loss of the culture, and the loss of the culture reinforced the loss of the language.

The immigrants coming into America, however, somewhat disassociated from the mother land, had visualized a land of opportunity, and were willing to sacrifice, to shift, and to change both personally and culturally in order to acquire new freedoms in the new country. It was a land of opportunity, and they visualized their children becoming American. While they themselves may be called Italians, for example, and their sons would be called Italian-American, they dreamed of the day when their children's children would be called Americans. They were willing to cast their lot with a new land, a new culture, and a new language.

Immigrant groups differ in the processes of acculturation

This has not been the case with the Mexican-American of the Southwest. Because of the proximity to Mexico and the constant influx from Mexico, these people have maintained their cultural ties with Mexico, and in large part have been able to retain much of their mother language (Shasteen, 43). They have come to the realization that they have been victims of serious injustice and vicious discrimination. This group has tried to amalgamize but all has come to naught. The new approach that this group is pursuing is that of cultural resurgence and identification. These people want the right and responsibility to determine their own destiny.

It is not for this chapter to expound or explicate the minority group movements. The only purpose in mentioning these factors is the impact that native cultural resurgence has on bilingualism and biculturism. This group is developing an esprit de corps based on native cultural resurgence and identification through use of the mother tongue. There is strong sentiment among them to be bilingual and bicultural. Unfortunately, many of the leaders are neither bicultural nor bilingual enough to help their followers into true biculturism and bilingualism.

Can we do the job?

What then is the relationship of biculturism to bilingualism, and what is the bicultural individual? The relationship between biculturism and bilingualism is a natural, intrinsic bond. While it is possible to be bicultural to some extent without knowing the language of the second culture, true biculturism cannot be achieved without high levels of proficiency in the languages of both cultures.

The bicultural individual has had firsthand knowledge of, and acquaintance with, the roles that he is expected to play in the two sociocultures. Not only does he know how to play these roles but he is well versed in and has some emotional commitment to the value systems of both cultures. For example, the bicultural Mexican-American is capable of playing, with high levels of dexterity, the roles that are required of him in the paternalistic, autocratic family of the Mexican-American socioculture. Here he is supposed to be an obedient, respectful son in an intensively cooperative family. At the same time, he is capable of functioning with equal dexterity on the job situation where strong competition, self-acclaim, and high aspirational levels are required. He knows, also, how to use the silent language in playing these roles, as well as the communication system in relating to other members of either socioculture.

The Mexican-American manipulates his roles

Over and beyond being proficient and dexterous in role playing and knowing the communication systems of either culture, the individual has developed within himself a deep sense of perception. He has been able to penetrate into the fantasy roles and idiosyncracies of the value systems of both sociocultures. He has become convinced that both sociocultures are nothing more than stages in which people act and play games. At the beginning of this realization there is an emotional setback and personal dissatisfaction, almost bordering on cynicism. In order to become bicultural, the individual must rise to higher levels where he has the broader perspectives to look at the games people play in either culture. He is able to combine the positive elements of either socioculture into a stronger, broader personality. At all times he remains free in the sense that he knows that even though he is obligated to play roles the roles are nothing more than games. These do not become the end unto themselves as they do for many of the monocultural individuals. Yet, he is able to descend from his higher level of development to play the games of the people, enjoying them to the fullest extent. It must be remembered, however, that many individuals, even though dexterous in the communication system of both cultures, are so emotionally entangled with the idiosyncracies of either or both cultures that they are marginal people instead of true biculturals. They have neither the emotional fortitude nor the spiritual development to become biculturals. In a true sense, they are the

"the games people play"

victims of the conflicts of two sociocultures that spring from two different (and conflicting) ethics.

The bicultural individual has developed a high level of proficiency in both languages. He neither prefers one to the other, but rather uses either one in the appropriate situation. In his leisure time he may use the elements of one socioculture and its language more than the other for certain activities. In short, the truly bicultural individual is one who has mastered the communication system of either socioculture and uses either language as the situation commands.

The truly bicultural know how to use language

Implications for education

The primary thrust of bilingual education, of course, is the inclusion to some degree of a second language other than the official language of the school. On the surface this would seem to be a simple and innocent enough objective. When the educator attempts to implement this objective, however, he finds that there are innumerable problems, repercussions, and implications that have to be considered (Bilingual Research Project, 6, p. 35–52).

One of these is the use to which the second language is to be placed. Is the program going to use the native dialect of the child to move him faster into adequate proficiency in English so as to insure him of normal progress in schooling? Is the program going to attempt to develop equal proficiency in both languages? If so, to what levels? These are decisions that must be made and must be spelled out in behavioral objectives. The program of instruction, of course, must reflect those objectives.

Objectives for learning the native language

Another decision that has to be made is what aspects of the program are to be taught in which language. For the purpose of developing scopes and sequences, it would seem that it makes little difference which language will be used in the instruction of any subject matter. In other words, the development of objectives, whether in English or in the second language, need not present any more difficulty than in a monolingual program. However, by the nature of the language itself, certain subject matter areas will lend themselves to better instruction in one language than in another. For example, it would seem that the sciences would be better taught in English than in Spanish. The reason for this is that more of the recent advances in science have been made in the English-speaking societies than in the Spanish-speaking countries. Thus, the technical vocabularies of

What subject matters are to be taught in which language?

science have been developed in English. To use Spanish would entail awkward translations and Hispanization of technical terms—for example, how to translate into Spanish the term "range finder." On the other hand, the Spanish language is well advanced in the humanities and philosophy. It would seem that this area could very well be taught in Spanish. The same principle would hold true for any set of languages used for instructional purposes.

One factor must be considered, however, in delineating the subject matter areas and the different concepts that are to be taught in one language or another. The bilingual child, because of his psycholinguistic tendencies, would perhaps understand better and become more emotionally committed to certain concepts and principles if taught in one language rather than another. It would seem that the history, literature, and music of a group should be taught in the language of that group. For example, United States history, American literature, and American music should be taught in English. But Mexican history, Spanish literature, and Latin music should be taught in Spanish. Similarly, elements of a culture, such as the Mexican-American family or the concept of American democracy, should be taught in the language of the respective culture.

It would seem that to teach the same concept in two languages, in the long run, would entail a double cost in terms of resources and energies without attaining any substantial gains. For example, if a child adequately understands a certain scientific principle that has been presented to him in English, unless there are extenuating circumstances, little would be gained by reteaching it in Spanish. At the same time there is the danger that this repetition of subject matter in two languages would gradually become boring and stifling to the individual. There is, in addition, the problem of how sensible the program is perceived to be by the individual. For example, it may be all right for the preprimary and primary school child to salute the flag and sing "God Bless America" in both English and Spanish during the same ceremony. But it would seem nonsensical to the upper grade or high school students to go through this double performance just to show their ability to salute the flag in two languages.

Teaching the same subject matter in both languages —ill advised

In establishing a bilingual program perhaps the gravest consideration must be given to the end product that one wishes to have developed through the program. (1) Is the ultimate goal of the program to develop all bilingual children into middle-class

Goals?

WASP models? (2) Is it to develop an individual who can operate in two languages, but whose basic core values are those of an Anglo, middle-class American? (3) Or is it to develop an individual who has adequate facility to function both linguistically and socially in two sociocultures?

The middle-class public in general tends to think that knowledge of a second language is an asset. But they cannot be specific about it. Perhaps it is more a factor of invidious comparison than genuine desire to learn a second language. They look at knowledge of a second language as a quality distinguishing the elite, the refined, or the wealthy. It is a class symbol (the symbol of the class above them) and they would like to attain this symbol. Actually, few parents or children have a strong enough desire to become bilingual and to expend the necessary time and energy in acquiring a second language. Similarly, few parents would like to have their children develop into bilingual, bicultural individuals. Rather they would have their children remain Anglo-Americans who know Spanish or French, or any other language.

Middle class attitudes toward second language learning

About the only time that the middle-class types will learn a second language is when social necessity pushes them into learning one, or when financially it becomes desirable. Thus, until the mood of the American public changes from isolation and ethnocentrism to cosmopolitanism and respect for other cultures, the bilingual in the United States will generally be a minority group member whose culture and language are different from the Anglo-American. These individuals will continue to be the victims of the onslaught of educational systems attempting to acculturate them into middle-class Anglo-Americans. What is the effect on the bilingual-bicultural child of this consistent insistence on middle-class behavior in the school setting? The research is rather scant in this area (Holemon & Ulibarri, 26, p. 5–13). Nonetheless, the educators who have worked with these children for several years are convinced that this system has serious negative effects on the children. Thus, it is not unusual to see the statement: "One of the purposes of the bilingual program is to develop a better self-concept."

The ultimate goals of education are growth and development, which may be similar for all children, whether bilingual or not. In the bilingual program, however, it is possible to take into consideration the special needs of the bilingual children. The children who come from the bilingual or bicultural middle-class home present no special problems to the educator over and be-

Bilingual-bicultural middle-class children present few problems

yond those of middle-class children of monolingual families. The children from the lower classes, however, are a different story. These children have not had the opportunity in the home atmosphere, in the neighborhood climate, and in peer group relations to develop along the lines of middle-class children. The experiential background of children coming from the middle class tends to be much more compatible with the expected behavior in the school program than that of the lower-class children. The lower-class children come from a very restricted geographic area and have parents who in general have a very low educational attainment level. These children have not had the opportunity to develop to their maximum potential in many areas. The bilingual-bicultural program must take these factors into consideration.

This does not mean that the bilingual program should embark on remedial education. Remedial education has been widely misunderstood as being a specialized kind of help, such as, individualized tutoring, by which all children will attain certain levels of achievement. The true spirit of remedial education is quite different, however. The remedial program takes into consideration the given potential of each child, regardless of where he may be and regardless of the goals and standards of the class, and gives him enough help to bring him to up *his potential*. It does not mean that all children can or will attain the same standards of the class. It means rather, that, regardless of potential, children may be in need of remedial help.

Thus, much more important in the bilingual-bicultural program is the concept of compensatory education. Taking the total sociocultural world of the bilingual child, and the sociocultural world in which the child is expected to function one finds that there are gaps in his growth and development. Over and beyond taking the ordinary growth and development patterns for which the schools assume responsibility, the bilingual-bicultural program can attempt *to implement activities and structures whereby these children will blossom out in areas that heretofore had been neglected.* For example, the bilingual-bicultural child coming from an impoverished home should be given the opportunity to learn what the so-called "better things in life" are. He should be given the opportunity to develop emotional maturity. He should be given the opportunity to develop the functional skills of the two cultures in which he will be asked to participate later in life.

In conclusion, a word of warning perhaps is in order concerning bilingual education. Bilingual education should not penalize

A bilingual program as compensatory education

the bilingual child in other areas of growth and development. It must be clearly understood that regardless of how nostalgic or how enthusiastic the program developer of bilingual education may be, there is no merit in learning a new language just for the sake of knowing it. If the bilingual-bicultural program does not do anything to develop an integrated personality and enhance a better self-concept in the bilingual child, perhaps it would be better that bilingual education not be attempted. If the child is going to be penalized in other areas of development for the sake of learning another language without ample justification, careful stock should be taken of the motives of our education. In short, bilingual-bicultural education should open the doors for the bilingual child, broaden his horizons, and enhance a more integrated development of his personality.

References, Bilingualism

1 Anderson, James. Sociocultural determinants of achievement among Mexican-American students. ERIC Documentation Service, U.S. Office of Education, Washington, D.C., 1968. [Ed. 017 394].

2 Andersson, Theodore. Foreign language and intercultural understanding. National Elementary Principal. 36 (February 1967) 32.

3 Arnold, Richard D. Reliability coefficients of certain tests used in the San Antonio language research project. San Antonio Language Research Project, Thomas D. Horn, director. University of Texas, Austin, February 1968.

4 Bendix, Reinhard; Lipset, Seymour Martin, eds. Class, status, and power. The Free Press, New York, 1966, p. 201–239.

5 Bergan, K. Secondary schools and acculturation of Indian people. National Association of Secondary School Principals Bulletin, 43 (October 1959) 115–117, no. 249.

6 Bilingual Research Project: final report. Horacio Ulibarri, director, and James G. Cooper, co-director. College of Education, The University of New Mexico, Albuquerque, 1959, 153 p.

7 Bloom, Benjamin S.; Davis, Allison; Hess, Robert. Compensatory education for cultural deprivation. Holt, Rinehart, and Winston, Inc., New York, 1965, 179 p.

8 Caplan, Stanley; Ruble, Ronald. A study of culturally imposed factors on school achievement in a metropolitan area. Journal of Education Research, 58:i (September 1964) 16–21.

9 Charles, Carol. The Indian child's status in New Mexico's public elementary school science program. Ph.D. dissertation. The University of New Mexico, Albuquerque, 1960.

10 Christian, Chester C., Jr. The acculturation of the bilingual child. Modern Language Journal, 49:iii (March 1965) 160–165.

11 Condie, LeRoy. An experiment in second language instruction of beginning Indian children in New Mexico public schools. Ph.D. dissertation. The University of New Mexico, Albuquerque, 1961.

12 Coombs, L. Madison. The Indian child goes to school. Bureau of Indian Affairs, Department of the Interior, Washington, D.C., 1958.

13 Cooper, James G. Effects of different amounts of

first grade oral English instruction upon later reading with Chamorro-speaking children (Guam). Journal of Educational Research, 58:iii (November 1964) 123–129.

14 Cordova, Ignacio. The relationship of acculturation, achievement, and alienation among Spanish-American sixth grade students. Ph.D. dissertation. The University of New Mexico, Albuquerque, 1968.

15 Darcy, Natalie T. The effect of bilingualism upon the measurement of the intelligence of children of pre-school age. Journal of Educational Psychology. 37 (January 1946) 21–44.

16 Dudding, Christine Glass. An investigation into the bilingual child's comprehension of antonyms. M.A. thesis. The University of New Mexico, Albuquerque, 1960.

17 Eells, Kenneth; et al. Intelligence and cultural differences. University of Chicago Press, Chicago, 1951.

18 Elam, Sophie L. Acculturation and learning problems of Puerto Rican children. Teachers College Record. 61 (February 1959) 259–264.

19 Festinger, Leon. A theory of cognitive dissonance. Row Peterson, Chicago, 1957, 163 p.

20 Floyd, David O. Comparison of standardized test results of Indian and non-Indian in an integrated school system. Journal of American Indian Education, 1 (June 1961) 8–17.

21 Hanson, Earl; Robinson, Alan H. Reading readiness and achievement of primary grade children of different socioeconomic strata. The Reading Teacher, 21 (October 1961) 52–57.

22 Havighurst, Robert J.; Hilkevitch, R. R. The intelligence of Indian children as measured by a performance scale. Journal of Abnormal Psychology, 39 (1944) 419–433.

23 Henderson, Norman. Study of intelligence of children of Mexican and non-Mexican parentage. M.A. thesis. Occidental College, Los Angeles, Calif., 1948.

24 Herskovitz, Melville J. Acculturation. J. J. Augustin, New York, 1938, p. 135–136.

25 Hess, Stephen Grant. A comparative study of the understanding which bilingual students have of the multiple meanings of English words. The University of New Mexico, Albuquerque, 1963.

26 Holemon, Richard; Ulibarri, Horacio. Administration of bilingual education; bilingual research study. The College of Education, The University of New Mexico, Albuquerque, 1969, 17 p.

27 Holland, William. Language barriers as an educational problem of Spanish-speaking children. Exceptional Children, 27 (1960) 42–50.

28 Hurley, Lucille S. The consequences of fetal impoverishment. Nutrition Today, 3:iv (December 1968) 3–10.

29 Ikeda, Hitoshi. The application of the meaning theory in arithmetic in selected third-grade classes. Ph.D. dissertation. The University of New Mexico, Albuquerque, 1960.

30 Keston, J. Morton; Jimenez, Carmina. A study of the performance on English and Spanish editions of the Stanford-Binet intelligence scale by Spanish-American children. Journal of Genetic Psychology, 85 (December 1954) 263–269.

31 Leighton, Roby, ed. Bicultural linguistic concepts in education. Educator's Complete ERIC Handbook, Phase One. Prentice Hall, Inc., Englewood Cliffs, N.J., 1967, p. 42.

32 McKenzie, Taylor. Bilingual problems in the education of the Navajo. Position paper. Conference on Problems of Educating Bilingual-Bicultural Children. Montlores Education Service Center, Cortez, Colo., August 1968.

33 Madsen, William. Mexican-Americans of South Texas. Holt, Rinehart and Winston, Inc., New York, 1964, p. 1–5.

34 Marden, Charles F. Minorities in American society. American Book Co., New York, 1952, p. 32–35.

35 Mexican-American Study Project. Division of Research, Graduate School of Business Administration, University of California, Los Angeles.
  a Fogel, Walter. Mexican-Americans in Southwest labor markets (advance report 10). October 1967, 217 p.
  b Grebler, Leo. Mexican immigration to the United States (advance report 2).
  c Grebler, Leo. The schooling gap: signs of progress (advance report 7). March 1967, 48 p.
  d Mittelback, Frank G.; Marshall, Grace. The burden of poverty (advance report 5). July 1966, 65 p.
  e Moore, Joan W.; Mittelback, Frank G. Residential segregation of minorities in the urban Southwest (advance report 4). June 1966, 40 p.

36 Michael, John A. High school climates and plans for entering college. Public Opinion Quarterly, 25:iv (1961) 585–595.

37 Palomares, Uvaldo. Assessment of rural Mexican-American students in grades pre-school through twelfth. ERIC Documentation Service, U.S. Office of Education, Washington, D.C., April 1967. [ED 013 690]

38 Peters, Herbert D. Performance of Hopi children on four intelligence tests. Journal of American Indian Education. 2 (January 1963) 27-31.

39 Pryor, Guy. Evaluation of the bilingual project of Harendale independent school district, San Antonio, Tex., in the first and second grades of four elementary schools during the 1967-68 school year. Our Lady of the Lake College, San Antonio, Tex., 1968. Mimeo.

40 Rohn, Ramona. Improvement of oral English in the first grade in the Santo Domingo school. The University of New Mexico Press, Albuquerque, 1964.

41 Samora, Julian; et al. The movement of Spanish youth from rural to urban settings. Position paper. National Conference on Problems of Rural Youth in a Changing Environment, White House Council on Children and Youth, Washington, D.C., September 1963, 20 p.

42 Sanchez, George I. Bilingualism and mental measures. Journal of Applied Psychology, 18 (December 1934) 765–772.

43 Shasteen, Amos E. Value orientations of Anglo and Spanish American high school sophomores. Ph.D. dissertation. The University of New Mexi-

co, Albuquerque, 1967.

44 Smelser, Neil J.; Lipset, Seymore Martin, eds. Social structure and mobility in economic development. Aldine Publishing Co., Chicago, 1966, p. 9, 287–298.

45 Ulibarri, Horacio. Acculturation problems of the Mexican-American. Report of Conference on Adult Basic Education. Southwestern Cooperative Educational Laboratory, Inc., Albuquerque, N. M., July, 1968, p. 6–20.

46 Ulibarri, Horacio. Educational needs of the Mexican-American. Position paper. National Conference on the Education of Mexican-Americans, Austin, Tex., April 1968, 20 p. ERIC Center, New Mexico State University, University Park.

47 Ulibarri, Horacio. Sociocultural profile of the Mexican-American. Article submitted to Transaction, George Washington University, St. Louis, Mo., January 1969, 20 p.

48 Yandell, Maurine. Some difficulties which Indian children encounter with idioms in reading. The Reading Teacher, 14 (March 1961) 256–259.

49 Zajonc, Robert B.; Wahi, N. Kishor. Conformity and need-achievement under cross-cultural norm conflicts. Human Relations. 14:iii (1961) 241–250.

50 Zintz, Miles V. The Indian research study: final report. The University of New Mexico, Albuquerque, 1960, 279 p.

9

Teacher education, qualifications, and supervision

Richard J. McArdle
Cleveland State University

A significant step forward in training foreign language teachers was taken in October 1966, with the publication of *Guidelines for Teacher Education Programs in Modern Foreign Languages—An Exposition*, compiled by F. André Paquette (38). This document assessed the state of the profession, pointed up the need for new directions in current training programs, and presented a comprehensive framework within which new programs could be developed.

The publication of this document represented the culmination of years of research, hard work, and cooperation on the part of many individuals and organizations. In this brief space it would be impossible to relate how all of this came about, but much of the story is spelled out in the Introduction and in Part I of the work itself.

Let it suffice to say here that in the past quarter century or so some significant events have happened that left their mark on the language teaching field. The advent of World War II and its effect on language study, the struggle within the profession to establish criteria of excellence, the launching of Sputnik and the National Defense Education Act (NDEA), and the introduction of new materials, and technological advances are just a few.

Contrary to what many believe, the present movement in foreign languages did not begin with Sputnik. The profession was already keenly aware of its problems and was moving toward a carefully considered program of action, albeit slowly (38, p. 329–337). Yet one could hardly underestimate the impact that Sputnik had on the American educational system. Indeed, it gave the entire country a sense of urgency, which might otherwise never have materialized, and spurred the government to action.

The resulting NDEA Institutes have been a great profit to the language profession and have established a whole new model for teacher education (5). These Institutes reinforced what was already apparent to some in the profession; namely, that teachers were being poorly trained in existing undergraduate programs. It was now necessary to pull together the work already being done by various organizations in the area of teacher preparation and put them together in a single package which would serve as a guideline for training institutions.

Part III of Paquette outlines and discusses the major areas that are the basis for a sound teacher education program. These major areas are:

1 The preparation of the American schoolteacher, the general makeup of his program of studies.

2 The modern foreign language teacher in American schools, what's expected of him.

Basic teacher education components

3 Minimal objectives for a teacher education program in modern foreign languages, the tools that the beginning teacher will need in order to perform well.

4 Features of a teacher education program in modern foreign languages, the characteristics of the institution which is training the future teacher. This section is explained in some detail in Part IV.

The magnitude of the problem facing the profession as it attempts to implement these guidelines can be better understood when one realizes the tremendous demands that have been placed on the entire American educational system. Stone (57, p. 3–4) notes that between 1950 and 1960 the number of children enrolled in the elementary and secondary schools in the United States increased some 13.3 million while it had increased only 11.7 million in the entire 50 years preceding this period. Not only was the population increasing but more children were attending school longer. In addition to this sharp rise in enrollments, there was an immense increase in knowledge in virtually all fields, leading to greater demands on teachers.

Population explosion

Knowledge explosion

Naturally this drastic increase in student population and the accompanying knowledge explosion led to a demand for more and better prepared teachers. From 1950 to 1965 the number of teachers increased from slightly over a million to nearly two million, and there was still a deficit in the ranks. Even in the best of circumstances, it would have been difficult to keep the quality at an even pace with the quantity; but the best of circumstances were lacking in teacher training programs.

Lack of teachers

Therefore, Paquette's compilation was a much needed tonic for the profession and was hailed as such by concerned members in and out of the profession. The distinguished William Riley Parker referred to this effort as an "extraordinary—indeed, unprecedented—collection of data." He admonished the lan-

Have the guidelines been implemented?

guage profession, moreover, that it must heed these guidelines and act quickly or face a possibly dismal future (38, p. 324).

The purpose of this chapter will be to discuss the current literature and research in the field concerning teacher education, supervision, and qualifications. In reviewing the work of 1968 and its background, the author has attempted to relate it as much as possible to Paquette's guidelines since they represent the combined thinking of the profession and were published for the express purpose of giving a starting point from which programs and ideas could proceed.

Qualifications

A natural starting point for this chapter seems to be with the qualifications the classroom teacher of foreign languages ought to possess. By stating what kinds of talents the foreign language teacher needs to function well, the profession ought to be better able to develop the type of program that will best develop these talents.

The minimal competencies needed by the modern foreign language teacher are listed in Appendix B of Paquette (38, p. 372). These are broken down into the following seven areas: (*1*) aural understanding, (2) speaking, (3) reading, (4) writing, (5) language analysis, (6) culture, and (7) professional preparation. The *minimal, good*, and *superior* aspects of each of these areas are also described in some detail. Similar guidelines have also been proposed in the classical languages (27).

Seven areas of competency needed by the FL teacher

Appendix D of Paquette (38, p. 377) recommends the procedure to be followed by the respective states in issuing certificates to teach. More and more states are moving toward an approved program approach which involves a cooperative venture on the part of the training institution and the state department of education. This move places most of the burden on the institution to develop a reasonable program that will lead to the above competencies. In many cases the state language associations have led the fight for improved programs of teacher preparation and certification (53).

Cooperation between state departments of education and teacher training institutions

The battery of *MLA Foreign Language Proficiency Tests for Teachers and Advanced Students* was developed precisely to measure the competency of a person in the seven areas mentioned above and is described briefly in Appendix J (38, p. 69). Although this test would seem a natural for evaluating a person for certification, only one state has thus far required it for this purpose; however, some individual institutions make use of part or all of it in recommending a person for certification. Perkins (41) reports the pros and cons of making the test a requirement in Pennsylvania. Among those points in favor of such testing are assuring the hiring agency of at least minimal competencies in its candidates, providing an effective means of screening non-American trained candidates, and forcing certifying institutions to upgrade their programs. Among the problems involved in requiring such a test are determining cutoff points for certification, setting up enough testing centers, and absorbing the costs of the tests.

Pros and cons in testing for certification

From recent surveys it seems evident that most states are working toward improved standards for certification (18). It is also evident that more state language associations are urging the adoption of the *MLA Proficiency Tests* or some similar instruments as a prerequisite for certification (50). All this points up the fact that some progress is being made toward raising standards for foreign language teachers.

Teacher education

In actually developing a teacher training program, an institution will need to become more specific in its certification requirements. Banathy (8) cites the need for a description of the in-class performance of language teachers that will necessarily be more specific than the out-of-class performance stated in Paquette.

These descriptions are not new to the literature and have been attempted to a degree in the past by Andersson (2), Birkmaier (9), Axelrod (3), Paquette (38, p. 20), and Lado (25) to mention just a few. This has also been a feature of some teachers' manuals accompanying audio-lingual texts.

Defining specific in-class teacher behavior

These have been, however, only limited and brief attempts to get at the problem of specificity as called for by Banathy (8). Recently attempts have been made by Politzer & Bartley (44) to describe what the language teacher actually does in specific situations and by Mackey (31) to find and identify specific teacher behaviors.

Politzer & Bartley have produced a minute description of, as well as a rationale for, good language teaching based on the observations of staff members at Stanford who have been involved in the training and supervision of language teachers.

They acknowledge that there is as yet no research evidence to support this model as being the best or even valid, but it does represent a consensus of people working in the field (44). Hayes et al. (20) also advanced some equally impressive evidence along the same line which would support this model in part.

Mackey (31) has worked in a slightly different manner in that he has videotaped examples of specific kinds of teaching behavior and has identified each kind. As the trainee views this specific behavior that has been taped in a real situation, subtitles are flashed on the screen informing him of the type of teacher behavior he is observing.

Videotaping specific teacher behavior

The use of videotape allows for the isolation of specific types of teaching behavior and enables the trainee to view a tape as many times as necessary to identify the type of behavior illustrated.

Both of these programs depend on describing specific behavior although each uses a different approach. The need for specificity is obvious if we are to relate the actual training with the performance of the teacher in the classroom. Norton (36) urges college language teachers to visit the secondary classroom occasionally to see for themselves what is expected of the teacher in hopes that this might lead to their seeing the need for some changes.

The failure to specify has perhaps been due partly to a lack of observational systems that would give an accurate and objective description of the foreign language teacher's behavior. Recent developments in the use of observational systems in foreign languages have enabled teacher trainers to more accurately describe a good teaching model. Work done by Moskowitz using Interaction Analysis (35) and Jarvis (24) using a self-developed observational system for foreign language has shown that an accurate description of classroom behavior can be developed in foreign languages with an objectivity heretofore lacking.

Observational systems

The specific interaction analysis system referred to by Moskowitz (35) was developed by Flanders (15) to describe how teachers use their influence in the classroom, and consists of ten categories. Seven categories are used to describe teacher behavior; two are for student behavior; and one is used to record silence or confusion.

Teacher behaviors are classified as either indirect or direct. When a teacher uses his influence to encourage a student to respond by asking questions or by praising, he is being indirect.

When a teacher uses his influence to limit the student's freedom to respond by lecturing, giving directions, and criticizing, he is being direct.

Student behavior is divided into the kind of activity that occurs as a result of a very direct question by the teacher that allows for only a limited response, and the kind of activity initiated by the student, which is less likely to be predictable.

In using the system, an observer tallies one of the ten categories for each behavior, being careful to record every three seconds even though the same behavior continues to be repeated. The results are then placed on a ten by ten matrix which provides a graphic picture of the interaction that took place between student and teacher. The matrix shows what behaviors preceded or followed other behaviors, the amount of time spent in each behavior, and numerous other details.

The instrument developed by Jarvis (24) is based on much the same principle but is specifically limited to use with foreign languages. This instrument also differs in that it contains categories of nonverbal as well as verbal activities, differentiates between what is called real talk and drill talk, classifies activities as being in the target language or English, and is recorded at intervals of time predetermined by the observer.

The use of observational tools to validate models, such as proposed by Politzer & Bartley (44), is quite feasible and will then allow the profession to describe the kind of specific behavior called for by Banathy.

The need for more work using such systems has already been recognized by some in the profession. Goding (19) and Politzer (43) have both called for more investigation into the use of descriptive devices, especially those dealing with verbal behavior.

Once such an objective description of the classroom behavior of teachers has been accomplished, it may be possible to assess the validity of given models in terms of teacher performance. This indeed has implications both for evaluating methods as well as teachers.

Axelrod (5) points out that one of the major differences between the Institutes and the standard higher education program in American schools is that the tasks laid out for the participants in the Institute are real and not just something they put up with to obtain a degree. In short, the participant of the Institute sees some meaningful relationship between what he is doing and the goals that have been established.

In order to make this possible in standard higher education

programs, a specific task analysis of each objective or performance criterion must be carried out and placed in some logical order. This will involve listing all of the competencies needed for each criterion. After this has been completed, it is then necessary to determine the entry point of the learner. The measuring of this input competency is often overlooked in many existing programs and everyone starts at the same spot or is placed in various spots without any valid evidence.

The value in task analysis

One of the features of a teacher education program called for in Part III of Paquette is a type of evaluation test that can be given to people before they enter the program in order to assure optimum use of their previous training (38, p. 343).

By applying this type of task analysis, it is more certain that what is being done in the program is relevant to the expected outcomes of that program as well as to the needs of the individual in the program.

The depth of the problem of designing programs for teachers that will satisfy the needs of the profession is almost staggering when one confronts all the red tape involved. One of the advantages that the Institutes have over the standard higher education program is precisely their size and unity of purpose.

The relatively small size and common goal of the Institutes have enabled them to develop a "primary group" (5, p. 16), which can come to know one another and work together. Contrast this, if you will, with the typical large university, which according to Axen (6) is already too large for any kind of meaningful dialogue among faculty or between students and faculty.

The quality of any teacher training program must begin in the classroom, and it is an accepted fact that knowledge of his subject matter is a prerequisite for any good teacher. This being the case it becomes quite obvious that the quality of instruction in college language departments must be one of the primary goals of any teacher training program.

The MacAllister report (29) brought to light the depth of the problem and has received wide notice in college ranks. Axelrod's comparison of the NDEA Institutes for Undergraduates with standard higher education programs did nothing to dispel the fear that existing programs are inadequate. Data collected as a part of this study included a questionnaire to the participants in which they were asked to compare the program of the Institute with that on their own campuses. This data indicated that these participants felt the Institute programs were overwhelmingly successful in establishing appropriate goals for teacher educa-

NDEA Institutes vs. higher education programs

tion while their own campus programs were unable or unwilling to use similar means. Axelrod concludes that the difference between the means used by the Institute and the standard higher education programs appears to be "unbelievably great" (4, p. 17).

The reasons for this disparity should be a matter of grave concern. Liedtke (28) points out that the college professors are so absorbed in research they don't have time for undergraduate or graduate teacher preparation. Dalbor (11) finds that most departments are still controlled by individuals who have little sympathy for the new directions in language study.

The heart of the problem centers around the lower-level language classes. The attitude of any language department can be fairly well assessed by examining how it handles these classes. Too often the teaching of the lower-level classes falls upon the shoulders of the teaching assistant who is often the least prepared to cope with them (29).

The enactment of the recommendations of the MacAllister report would go far toward alleviating this problem. There is some indication that progress has been made since the report was published; however, this is probably not sufficient. Piedmont suggests that there is a need to exchange information about successful programs. His report on the Teaching Assistant Training Program at Indiana University (42), the report of Dalbor (11) at Pennsylvania State University, and that of Troyanovich (59) at Kansas University are all quite similar and well within the reach of average language departments.

Quality teaching is needed in lower level college language classes

Each program involves a preservice orientation and training period, an on-going methods course in some form, a controlled teaching experience, supervisory visits, and some observation of other classes. In addition to this, Indiana makes use of videotape and group observation and critiques to improve its program.

There is no doubt that visitations of college classes can be a sticky problem, but this appears to be a necessary step if the quality of the programs is to be regulated and improved. Hayes et al. (20) point out that the feeling that the university classroom ought to be free from any kind of supervision has led to a great disparity in teaching practices.

In addition to the quality of teaching, college programs are faced with the problem of what is to be taught, when, and by whom. Axelrod (5) notes that this problem failed to deter the Institutes because the various disciplines were taught when and where they were relevant to the task at hand, and by whoever was best qualified to handle the chore. He finds that the standard higher education program is often trapped over arguments concerning departmental boundaries or is involved in squabbles between liberal arts preparation and professional preparation. Proof that these problems are not insurmountable can be seen in the program developed at Stanford (44) in which they were apparently dealt with.

Relevancy in an interdisciplinary approach

As noted earlier in discussing Axelrod's findings concerning Institutes for Undergraduates (4), one of the apparent major weaknesses of teacher training programs is the lack of relevance of the program to what actually takes place in the classroom. This charge is equally true of both the academic and professional preparation offered in the typical college program.

Relevance is one of the key points of the Institutes. They have managed to take a new look at the way learning takes place and as a result have implemented entirely new kinds of programs. Meanwhile, however, the traditional college training program has equated teaching with telling, and learning with listening (5) in spite of much evidence to the contrary. By its very nature a teacher training program must involve the trainee in practicing the principles that he has learned. The closer this practice lies to the learning of the principles, the more meaningful it will be.

Flanders (14, p. 260) points out some assumptions about training programs that are often ignored:

First, ideas about teaching and learning must be organized into concepts which have meaning in terms of overt behavior. Ideas about teaching which cannot be related to overt actions are less likely to maintain a consistent meaning when the talking stops and the teaching starts.

Second, concepts about teaching and learning become useful to the extent that they can be applied personally. Concepts about teaching must ultimately be coordinated with one's own behavior. Concepts about pupil behavior must ultimately be applied to one's own class. Concepts about how to use instructional materials must ultimately be explored in one's own classroom.

Concepts must be expressed in performance

Third, insight into principles of effective teaching comes about through personal inquiry. Teaching must be seen as a series of acts which occur with the passage of time. Instantaneous decisions must be made which have immediate consequences. Teachers can learn to recognize decision points, to become aware of more alternatives, to predict consequences accurately a higher proportion of the time, and to develop plans for controlling their own authority.

Politzer & Bartley (44), in the introduction to their practice-centered program for Spanish teachers, point out that training language teachers usually involves, in some form or another, courses in language, civilization and culture, applied linguistics, and methods, followed by some form of practice teaching. These have been traditionally sequential in nature in the standard college program as opposed to the parallel nature of the Institute programs. *The Stanford practice-centered program*

Their proposed syllabus takes on the parallel approach and links each lesson in applied linguistics to a corresponding lesson in language practice and in turn relates this to principles of methodology and finally applies all of this in the teaching of a specific micro-lesson by the trainee.

The program proposed by Mackey (31) is not so completely coordinated with the language program but is a modification of the existing structure in teacher education, and deals with what is traditionally thought of as the methods and practice teaching segments. His program involves three stages: observation, practice, and performance.

The unique thing about Mackey's program is the use of videotape. In the observational period the trainee views short examples of specific teacher behavior on videotape, and by means of subtitles the trainee is at first kept constantly aware of the type of behavior, drill, etc., that he is viewing. After a sufficient amount of time, the trainee is shown a second videotape exactly like the first except for the absence of subtitles, and he is then expected to identify the behavior, type of drill, etc., that is being exhibited. This is followed by more detailed analysis in which the trainee answers a series of questions about the tape he has viewed. Finally, in group discussions the question of why the teacher made such moves is discussed and analyzed. *The Mackey proposal*

The observation period is then followed by a period of planning and practicing. The trainee is expected to develop a plan for the same type of lesson, making use of the demonstration teacher's plan as analyzed on the videotape and from discussions and critiques with his supervisor and his peer group.

Finally, the trainee has an opportunity to perform his lesson under controlled conditions. The use of videotape throughout offers a more nearly optimum use of time and resources than is possible in the traditional practice teaching situation.

A program now in use at the University of Nebraska is also basically a modification of the existing structure, which leaves the methods and practice teaching until last. Both the methods and supervising of student teachers are done in the Secondary Education Department rather than the specific language departments. Although this is not considered to be the most desirable situation (38, p. 354), it becomes a logical solution for many universities and colleges whose departments are not large enough to provide the necessary manpower to do the job adequately.

The approach is based on the system model proposed by Banathy (8) and attempts to integrate as many new approaches to training teachers as possible into a workable package. This leads the student through various phases which include: (1) the learning of Interaction Analysis as an observational tool, (2) training in the use of audiovisual equipment, (3) observation of good teaching models, (4) analysis of audio-lingual principles, (5) exposure to a previously unknown foreign language through audio-lingual techniques, (6) analysis of the psychology of language learning and the language learner, (7) the systems approach to instructional planning, (8) micro-teaching, and (9) practice teaching.

Video and audio tapes are used in both the micro-teaching and practice phases of the program. The two people involved in teaching the methods class also serve as supervisors during the practice teaching phase. This allows for constant feedback and evaluation of the training program (32).

The rationale for each of these three programs seems to be a practice-centered one and is supported by Hough and Amidon (22, p. 307), who found that the key to changing teacher behavior lies in finding ways of helping teachers discover personal meaning in cognitive knowledge regarding the teaching-learning process. According to these two researchers, means must be found by which potential teachers can (1) gain knowledge about principles of teaching and learning, (2) make use of such knowledge in a situation characterized by personal meaning, (3) get immediate feedback regarding the effects of their behavior in the classroom, and thus (4) discover for themselves more effective patterns of teaching behavior.

The micro-teaching referred to above involves scaling down the teaching act to a short time (five to ten minutes), using a small number of students (five to ten), and limiting the material to be taught to a single concept. This enables the trainee and supervisor to focus on one specific skill that is to be practiced by the trainee. Micro-teaching was developed at Stanford under Dwight Allen and has been shown to be a reliable means of training teachers in a much more controlled setting (7).

The use of micro-teaching in language circles has not been widespread but nonetheless is increasing. Mackey (31) has incorporated a slightly different form of it into his proposed training program. He refers to it as a module and is concerned with limiting the time and teaching behavior but not necessarily the students. Micro-teaching has also been slightly modified for use in a recent NDEA Institute (12) and a summer workshop held at the University of Nebraska (33).

Micro-teaching

The advantages of micro-teaching are obvious since it allows the aspiring teacher to advance through a series of planned experiences one at a time. This enables him to gain competence and confidence in handling specific problems and insures that he can practice a single skill until he has reached a prescribed level of proficiency before going to something new. In contrast to the regular student teaching situation, he is never faced with all the problems of teaching collectively until he can handle them individually.

As the language profession moves toward improving the training of teachers, it must be constantly aware of what is happening in the elementary and secondary schools so that the institutions involved in that training may adjust their programs to provide for new needs. Freeman (17), for example, voices some concern over the attitude of the language profession in general toward the slow learner, the disadvantaged, and the adult learner. He sees these as areas that are becoming increasingly important in educational circles but are being somewhat ignored by people in languages. His feeling is that language study has something to offer everyone even if they do not pursue it for long periods of time.

Languages are for everybody

Perhaps this attitude with which Freeman is concerned is brought about partly by the belief in some language circles that only the academically talented should study languages. Roeming (48) points out that somewhere in the rush to develop new materials and methods the student has been left out. The failure to recognize the unique problems of second language learning has made it difficult for many language teachers to deal effectively with above average students as is evident from the high dropout rate among language students. When this problem is compounded by slow or deprived learners, it becomes even more difficult.

So far little has been done to apply in the classroom the theories now being advanced in the field of psycholinguistics and, even though this field is of tremendous importance to teaching a second language, few training programs have made provisions for including it (10).

Since textbooks currently in use often make some questionable assumptions about student attitudes and interests and generally make few allowances for individual or group differences, the burden for doing this is placed on the classroom teacher. This is a problem for all language teachers but an even more serious one for teachers of disadvantaged students. Training programs must recognize the situations their products will face and attempt to provide for them.

Teachers need to be trained for individualization of instruction

The lack of research and writing in the area of the disadvantaged is regrettable, and there is need of involving those working with these students in reporting their activities. Such reports as those by Hubbard (23) indicate that effective jobs can and are being done. The training institution needs to work closely with outstanding teachers already in the field in developing these specialized programs. In this way Roeming's call for an increased use of real classrooms to test the validity of existing theories can be heeded (47).

The development of new programs to adequately prepare teachers for such assignments as working with the disadvantaged may require an approach that is slightly unorthodox. It may be necessary to consider experiences gained through programs, such as those of the Teacher Corps (52), which involve the trainee in much more field experience, specially designed courses, sensitivity training, and social activities designed to orient him to the problems he will face. In this setting, campus courses are constantly questioned in terms of their relevancy to the real situation and become a cooperative search for adequate answers rather than a one-sided exchange on the part of the instructor. In any event, it is not likely that we can continue to avoid this problem if we are to meet our obligations as teachers.

Field experience

Problems in foreign language teacher training are increased when one considers some of the predictions for the future. Technology continues to advance at a breathless pace, and big business armed with technological know-how and supported by large sums of money is constantly probing into educational opportunities. There seems little doubt that the large corporations now entering the education field have the capability to effect a change. The question seems to be whether educational leaders are going to be ready to take advantage of the facilities available to them and control that change (26).

Mildenberger (34) sees the exploration of superelectronic applications to foreign languages as inevitable. A glance at the research being done in languages indicates the degree to which studies involving computers and foreign languages are already being pursued (21).

Are teachers trained in using new technological media?

In addition to knowing how to operate the hardware being considered for use in the near future, the teacher must understand how to get optimum value from these new technological advances. The future might find him playing an entirely different role as emphasis shifts toward dealing with individualized learning styles and working with different types of groupings (51). Goding (19) sees the immediate need for more work in developing leadership potential and in understanding of "group dynamics." Certainly this will become increasingly important as the role of the teacher changes.

Language teachers of the future will have to be prepared to handle all sorts of new problems. Baird et al. (7) point out that teachers in training are not only going to have to be told how to be effective but must experience the best possible instruction themselves. If language teachers are unable to handle even the rather simple electronic devices now in use, they won't find much potential in the more sophisticated ones waiting in the wings. Introduction and innovative use of these devices into college classrooms will assure the future teacher's exposure to them (30).

There is no question that the accomplishment of the goals set forth in Paquette and the new demands that now and in the future will continue to face teachers require new designs in teacher training.

If we are ever to expand such programs as that proposed by Politzer & Bartley (44) into even broader contexts such as the spiral programs proposed by Sorohan (55), in which the general education, the professional education, and the subject area specialization are neatly tied together, we must sooner or later bring together all programs concerned with teacher education and perhaps retool them.

Axelrod's proposed strategy for change involved some such ideas (3). A government-sponsored program which may offer some opportunity to achieve this change is the Triple T (Training the Teachers of Teachers). This relatively new project is aimed at bringing together the three areas most concerned

Triple T (Training the Teachers of Teachers)

with the education of teachers, the public schools and the academic and teacher education divisions of higher education, with the hope that new and creative approaches to training can be found (13).

It is no longer possible or desirable that the training of teachers should take place in a vacuum. Only a concerted effort on the part of everyone in education, however, can bring about the necessary change in order to develop programs that avoid this.

One way of assuring that the profession will be able to keep abreast of the rapid change taking place in education is the establishment of centers for study. Such centers already are in existence, and an excellent example is the Modern Language Center of the Ontario Institute for Studies in Education (OISE).

This center, which was established in the fall of 1968, is somewhat unique in scope and offers an opportunity to cope with all aspects of language teaching in a comprehensive way. It will deal with such things as linguistics, research, content and method, and liaison with teacher training programs.

The Modern Language Center of the OISE

Among the areas of study that the center will undertake is the general study of language teaching, which includes the fundamental disciplines and studies common to all language teaching. This will include theory of language teaching, general linguistics, sociolinguistics, psycholinguistics, language teaching technology, and language testing and assessment. The purpose of this area of study is further explained in the following quotation:

> It should be pointed out that the center is not concerned with the full range of the disciplines represented in these studies. The limiting factor is the relevance of studies to the teaching and learning of languages. The interest is "applied" rather than "pure." It is in this respect that the center distinguishes its work from the study of these fields in other departments and centers of the University or OISE. This restriction of emphasis, however, does not mean that studies are pursued in a narrowly vocational way, unrelated to the basic scholarship. Close contact with the work of scholars, for example, in linguistics, psychology, sociology, educational theory, or communication engineering, will be developed (56, p. 6).

Most of what has been said thus far has been concerned basically with preservice teacher preparation, although programs such as those mentioned earlier can be used in part as a retraining device (44). This, of course, is the whole idea of the NDEA

Institutes whose initial emphasis was aimed at this aspect of teacher training.

However, since it is quite obvious the teacher training process must be a continuous proposition, the idea of in-service programs is one that must be considered as part of the overall teacher training program. Rasmussen (45) found that most participants of NDEA Institutes continued to pursue training in language and teaching competency after completing their first Institute. Although many went on to a higher level Institute, a larger number received further training through in-service seminars. This fact would indicate that more emphasis should be aimed at developing quality programs of the in-service type.

The need for in-service programs

The in-service program is not usually a retraining program but a sort of supplementary approach. Some states such as New York and Minnesota are already initiating in-service workshops which last for a weekend or one day, and are sponsored by the state department of education and the state language association (53). These in-service programs differ from the types of courses usually offered by institutions of higher education and the Institutes. In-service needs often go beyond simply training in language, and such short but more frequent offerings have definite value for the morale and advancement of the classroom teacher.

Obviously in-service needs will vary with individuals and situations, therefore, the colleges and universities must be aware of this and attempt to provide services that will best meet the needs of teachers in their area. Higher education can serve a useful function in in-service training either by working with schools, language associations, and the department of education to formulate the types of short workshops mentioned above, or by providing supplementary kinds of longer and more sophisticated workshops. The local college or university should recognize that it is not always equipped to perform the same service as an Institute, but by careful assessment of the local needs and available staff it can offer a useful in-service program (33).

Supervision

Guideline "D5" (38, p. 354) states that the training institution should provide the trainee with an opportunity to practice teach under expert supervision. There is some general agreement that the opportunity to practice what the trainee has been learning is perhaps the most important aspect of the program. There is also general agreement that the beginning teacher needs to have careful supervision while practicing so he can get immediate feedback concerning his performance.

In implementing this guideline, however, the training institution is faced with at least two immediate problems. The first is the pure logistics of the entire student teaching program which continues to increase in numbers. The second has to do with the quality of the supervisory act and what the role of the college supervisor should be.

The usual procedure in most student teaching programs is to place the student teacher with an experienced teacher for a set period of time. Whether the student teacher spends an entire day at a school for a short period of time, perhaps a quarter, or a part of the day for a longer period of time, perhaps a semester, or two or more quarters, seems to vary widely from institution to institution. A glance at the summary of two studies made by the Modern Language Association concerning teacher training programs (39, 40) gives some idea of the diversity of programs in existence.

Problems in providing field experience for the prospective teacher

In attempting to conduct such a student teaching program as described above, the training institution is faced with the problem of the ever-increasing numbers of student teachers to be placed. Finding a desirable teaching opportunity for these beginners within easy access of the university is becoming more and more difficult, and the trend across the country to close down laboratory schools on campus has not helped. The supervisor's problems have magnified as more and more student teachers are assigned positions farther and farther from the campus.

Because of this, too often the bulk of supervision has fallen on the shoulders of the unsuspecting classroom teacher with whom the student teacher has been placed. The university provides little help as to what "supervising" consists of and so it is interpreted in many ways. As a result, student teaching very often consists of some form of musical chairs in which the regular classroom teacher and student teacher take turns performing.

When the college supervisor finally makes an appearance on the scene, his comments usually fall into one of two categories. If he is from the language department, at the end of class he will present the prospective teacher with a long list of pronunciation and grammar errors duly noted during the entire period. If, on the other hand, he happens to be from the education department, his equally long list will consist of comments on classroom management and possibly methodology. The supervisor then departs after a brief conference not to return again for at least several weeks.

It is not surprising that this traditional model of practice teaching and supervision has recently come under attack from many quarters. Some would shift the responsibility for training teachers out of the hands of higher education and into either the public schools or a new administrative level similar to the NDEA Institutes (58). It is not likely this will happen in the near future, but that does not hide the fact that some way of working closer together must be found by the public schools and institutions of higher learning that will be beneficial to all concerned (54).

Mackey (31) sees traditional student teaching as leaving too much to chance. There is also evidence to show that the amount of time spent in traditional student teaching can be cut drastically without hurting performance (7).

As part of an attempt to overcome some of these flaws in the student teaching and the supervisory function in teacher-training programs, there has been an increasing emphasis on the use of micro-teaching in the preservice programs as noted earlier. Politzer & Bartley's program at Stanford (44) gives the supervision of the practice teaching an entirely new concept. It is no longer a completely separate and unrelated act but an integral part of the entire training program.

The potential of micro-teaching in supervision

Micro-teaching also has the potential of solving at least part of the problem posed by the increasing number of student teachers, since it can cut down or eliminate the amount of time spent in the regular classroom. In addition to this, micro-teaching can insure that the incompetent teacher never reaches the classroom in the first place as so often happens in the traditional student teaching program.

It has been suggested that this type of preservice training may eventually be followed by a year as a teacher-intern with reduced load and continued supervision by someone associated with the public schools. This is entirely possible and perhaps desirable but will probably not take place on any large scale for a long time to come.

Teacher-internships

The actual supervisory function might well be enhanced by the use of the observational systems mentioned earlier (24, 35). Even in a traditional setting of supervision, an observational system offers something tangible to work with. Moskowitz (35) found that there were some positive results achieved by training student teachers and cooperating teachers in interaction analy-

Interaction analysis can bring about change

sis. Jarvis (24) points out that the very use of such systems could be a causal factor in bringing about behavior change.

It would seem reasonable that an accurate and objective description of teacher behavior would be profitable in any kind of supervising situation regardless of size and make up. If we can really identify good teaching models, the possibilities seem endless for statistical analysis. It is entirely possible that in the near future, by means of computer, such things as the matrix referred to by Moskowitz (35) could be tabulated and made available minutes after a teacher's performance, thus providing a statistical "picture" of that performance.

In any event this area has many possibilities for evaluating language teaching and must be explored further in order to realize its potential. The supervision of student teachers, no matter when or where done, is a crucial aspect of teacher training and deserves the most careful consideration of those involved. It must continue to become more relevant to the goals of the overall program if teacher education is to improve.

Supervision is crucial in teacher training

If institutions of higher education cannot or will not provide adequate supervision, perhaps this function should be turned over to the elementary and secondary schools. The colleges and universities can then concentrate on working with the appointed supervisor in each school or language department to develop better ways of supervising and training language teachers. Besides providing needed feedback to the college or university program, this arrangement would have the added advantage of having a trained supervisor in the school who could also be an asset to the regular classroom foreign language teacher.

Summary

Since the publication of Paquette's guidelines in 1966, there has been some progress in the language teaching profession, but the need for more is apparent. At least 23 states are in the process of changing certification procedures (18), a fact that should have a positive effect on the future of teacher education programs.

New and improved types of programs are being tried in various parts of the country, but certain weaknesses that inhibit innovative programs are still inherent in the higher education system. The Institutes have provided a model (5) from which to draw valuable information in developing new programs, but as yet these Institutes have not had the impact it was hoped they would. Part of the problem seems to lie in the language departments' failure to accept the fact that they are in the business of training teachers. Banathy's proposal for a systems approach to teacher education (8) offers a real opportunity to bring Paquette's guidelines to a realization in spite of the problems. Ultimately any program to be effective must combine the three broad areas of teacher education into one program with a clearly defined goal. As it now stands, there is often little connection among general education, professional education, and special subject matter education.

Both preservice and in-service supervision have been neglected areas in teacher training. Supervision of student teachers is often a hit-and-miss affair and adequate supervision of teachers already in the field is practically nonexistent. There seems to be a definite need for some sort of change in this area, but little evidence is available to point the direction of that change.

In short, there is a lack of significant research in all areas of teacher training, and there is a desperate need to test some of the existing theories that now influence our thinking (47). An increased exchange of ideas in all areas is not only desirable but necessary in implementing Paquette's guidelines. The advent of the American Council on the Teaching of Foreign Languages (ACTFL) and the Educational Resources Information Center (ERIC) has given the foreign language profession a much needed boost in this direction.

If the profession is to enjoy the bright future predicted by Freeman (38, p. 327), it must certainly look to the education of foreign language teachers. The existing apathy toward this problem in some institutions of higher education is regrettable and must change if progress is to continue.

References, Teacher education, qualifications, and supervision

1 Allen, Edward D.; Glenn, Leona M.; Otto, Frank. The changing curriculum—modern foreign languages. Association for Supervision and Curriculum Development, Washington, D.C., 1968.

2 Andersson, Theodore. The teacher of modern foreign languages. In: Stabler, Ernest, ed. The education of the secondary school teacher. Wesleyan University Press, Middletown, Conn., 1962, p. 164–190.

3 Axelrod, Joseph. The education of the modern foreign language teacher for American schools.

The Modern Language Association of America, New York, 1966.

4 Axelrod, Joseph. From undergraduate student to professional teacher. An assessment of the NDEA Institutes for undergraduates preparing to become elementary or secondary teachers of modern foreign languages. The Modern Language Association of America, New York, 1967.

5 Axelrod, Joseph. NDEA foreign language institute programs: the development of a new educational model. Publications of The Modern Lan-

guage Association of America, New York, vol. 82, no. 4 (September 1967) 14–18.

6 Axen, Richard. Faculty response to student dissent. In: Smith, G. Kerry, ed., Stress and campus response. Jossey-Bass Inc., San Francisco, 1968, p. 220–231.

7 Baird, Hugh; Merril, David; Bauer, Edith. Teacher education 1984. Proceedings of the Utah Academy of Arts and Sciences, 44, 1 (1967) 214–23.

8 Banathy, Bela H. The design of foreign language teacher education. The Modern Language Journal, 52:viii (December 1968).

9 Birkmaier, Emma. Evaluating the foreign language program. The North Central Association Quarterly, 40:ii (Winter 1966) 263–271.

10 Carroll, John B. Memorandum: on needed research in psycholinguistic and applied psycholinguistic aspects of language teaching. Foreign Language Annals, 1:ii (March 1968) 236–239.

11 Dalbor, John B. A realistic look at the training of college foreign language teachers. The Modern Language Journal, 51:iv (April 1967) 209–214.

12 Dugas, Donald G. Micro-teaching: a promising medium for teacher retraining. The Modern Language Journal, 51:iii (March 1967) 161–165.

13 Engbretson, William E. Curricular relevance in teacher education. In: Smith, G. Kerry, ed. Stress and campus response. Jossey-Bass Inc., San Francisco, 1968, p. 220–231.

14 Flanders, Ned A. Teacher behavior and in-service programs. In: Amidon, Edmund and Hough, John, eds. Interaction analysis: theory, research, and application. Addison-Wesley Publishing Company, Reading, Mass., 1967, p. 256–261.

15 Flanders, Ned A. Teacher influence: pupil attitudes and achievement. Cooperative Research Project no. 397, University of Minnesota, Minneapolis, 1960.

16 Franklin, Mayer J. The preparation of teachers of French and Spanish in southern California secondary schools. Dissertation Abstracts 28: 2580A (U.S.C.).

17 Freeman, Stephen A. Let us build bridges. The Modern Language Journal, 52:v (May 1968) 261–268.

18 Glenn, Leona M. Certification requirements in other states. A report delivered to the National Council of State Supervisors of Foreign Languages, February 1969.

19 Goding, Stowell C. Motivation in language learning: the teacher. Dimension: Languages 68. guage Teaching, Converse College, Spartanburg, S.C., p. 45–55.

20 Hayes, Alfred S.; Lambert, Wallace E.; Tucker, G. Richard. Evaluation of foreign language teaching. Foreign Language Annals, 1:i (October 1967) 22–55.

21 Hayes, Alfred S.; Varley, Joy. Language research in progress. Center for Applied Linguistics, Washington, D.C., August 5, 1967, p. 52.

22 Hough, John; Amidon, Edmund. Behavioral change in student teachers. In: Amidon, Edmund and Hough, John, eds. Interaction Analysis: theory, research, and application. Addison-Wesley

Publishing Company, Reading, Mass., 1967, p. 307–314.

23 Hubbard, Louise J. Modern languages for the racially disadvantaged. The Modern Language Journal, 52:iii (March 1968) 139–140.

24 Jarvis, Gilbert A. A behavioral observation system for classroom foreign language skill acquisition activities. The Modern Language Journal, 52:vi (October 1968).

25 Lado, Robert. Language teaching, a scientific approach. McGraw-Hill, Inc., New York, 1964.

26 Lieberman, Myron. Big business, technology and education. Phi Delta Kappan, 48:v (January 1967) 185–186.

27 Lieberman, Samuel. CAAS seminar on ACL Oxford conference proposals for the training of Latin teachers. Classical World, vol. 62, p. 5–6.

28 Liedtke, Kurt E. H. A common concern: future teachers of German. Die Unterrichtspraxis 1: ii (1968) 76–80.

29 MacAllister, Archibald T. The preparation of college teachers of modern foreign languages. Publications of The Modern Language Association of America, 59:ii (May 1964) 29–43. Reprinted in The Modern Language Journal, 50 (1966) 400–415.

30 Mackey, William F. The new technology of teacher training. Unpublished paper. Université Laval, Quebec, Canada, 1967.

31 Mackey Wiliam F. Practice teaching: models and modules. Unpublished paper. Université Laval, Quebec, Canada, 1967.

32 McArdle, Richard J. A systems approach to language methods. An address delivered to the Nebraska Modern Language Association, December 1968.

33 McArdle, Richard J.; Scebold, C. Edward. Report on workshop seminar held at the University of Nebraska, Summer 1968. The Modern Language Journal, 52:viii (December 1968).

34 Mildenberger, Kenneth W. Prospects for a unified profession. The Modern Language Journal, 51:iii (March 1967) 169–173.

35 Moskowitz, Gertrude. The effects of training foreign language teachers in interaction analysis. Foreign Language Annals, 1:iii (March 1968) 218–235.

36 Norton, Harriet. Teacher training programs. Classical World, vol. 62, p. 7–8.

37 Pap, Leo; Nostrand, Howard L. The foreign language specialist and the beginning teacher. Report on section meeting at the National TEPS Conference, New York City, June 25, 1965.

38 Paquette, F. André, comp. Guidelines for teacher education programs in modern foreign languages—an exposition. The Modern Language Journal, 50:vi (October 1966) 323–425.

39 Paquette, F. André. Undergraduate MFL teacher-training in liberal arts colleges: a survey. The Modern Language Journal, 48:vii (November 1964) 424–431.

40 Paquette. F. André. Undergraduate MFL teacher-training programs in schools and colleges of education: a survey. The Modern Language Journal, 49:vii (November 1965) 414–421.

41 Perkins, Jean A. State certification and proficiency tests: the experience in Pennsylvania. Foreign Language Annals, 2:ii (December 1968) 195–199.

42 Piedmont, Ferdinand. Group observation and the training of teaching assistants. Die Unterrichtspraxis 1:i (1968) 82–86.

43 Politzer, Robert L. Toward a practice-centered program for the training and evaluation of foreign language teachers. The Modern Language Journal, 50:v (May 1966) 253.

44 Politzer, Robert L.; Bartley, Diana. Practice-centered teacher training, Spanish: a syllabus for the training or retraining of teachers of Spanish. Stanford Center for Research and Development in Teaching, Stanford, Calif., 1967.

45 Rasmussen, Alice. An evaluation of the language competence and opinions of secondary language teachers following participation in selected NDEA summer language institutes. Dissertation Abstracts 28 (1967): 2126A–27A.

46 Rexine, John. A proposal for teacher training in the classics. Classical World, vol. 62, p. 43–45.

47 Roeming, Robert F. The Contribution of the classroom teacher to research and knowledge. Foreign Language Annals, 1:i (October 1967) 18–21.

48 Roeming, Robert F. Beyond the limits of our discipline. The Modern Language Journal, 51:vii (November 1967) 411–417.

49 Sadler, Edward J. Certification standards for modern foreign language teachers. Address delivered to the Nebraska Modern Language Association, December 1968.

50 Scebold, C. Edward, comp. Teacher preparation guidelines. Advisory council report to the Nebraska Modern Language Association, December 1968.

51 Shane, Harold G.; Shane, June Grant. Forecast for the 70's. Today's Education, 58:i (January 1969) 29–32.

52 Sharpe, Donald M. Lessons from the teacher corps. NEA Journal, 57:v (May 1968) 21–22.

53 Silber, Gordon R. State organizations and the progress of the profession. Foreign Language Annals, 1:iv (May 1968) 312–317.

54 Smith, E. Brooks. Joint responsibility. NEA Journal, 57:v (May 1968) 18–20.

55 Sorohan, Sister Mary Aloysius. Current guidelines for the undergraduate program for the professional preparation of secondary school teachers of Spanish. Dissertation Abstracts 28 (1967): 2126A–27A.

56 Stern, H. H. A modern language center – scope, activities and plans. The Ontario Institute for Studies in Education, University of Toronto, Ont., October 1968, p. 19.

57 Stone, James C. Breakthrough in teacher education. Jossey-Bass Inc., San Francisco, Calif., 1968.

58 Stone, James C. Reform or rebirth. NEA Journal, 57:v (May 1968) 23–25.

59 Troyanovich, John M. Optimal instructional quality in multi-section teaching. Die Unterrichtspraxis, 1:ii (1968) 69–75.

60 Webb, Clark D., et al. Progress report on an experiment reducing in-class student teaching time and substituting micro-teaching sessions. Proceedings of the Utah Academy of Arts and Sciences, 44:i (1967) 224–228.

10
Methods

Introduction

Dale L. Lange
University of Minnesota

Methods in foreign language teaching or in any subject, for that matter, is a rather nebulous, all inclusive term. For purposes of this review, however, the word will be limited to the meaning of classroom procedures, techniques, or strategies, whichever term the reader would most wish to choose. It may be argued that the term, *methods*, is necessarily vague. This vagueness is largely due to the unpredictability of the situations in which, in this case, foreign languages are taught. Such situations may be directly related to the teacher's personality and training, the characteristics of the students, the goals or objectives of both, as well as the school's environment and the materials used to teach foreign languages. Even though teaching is a highly individualized form of communicating values and culture to students, old or young, as well as an attempt to modify behavior, it is possible for the teacher to share, with others, experiences and/or procedures that "work." This sharing is most likely accomplished by informal means in "shoptalk" sessions at conferences and workshops. But some of it does find its way into the professional literature. This review, then, should be regarded as an attempt to synthesize, communicate, and evaluate the literature concerning methodology of foreign language teaching during the year under consideration, namely 1968.

Methods: What are they?

The review is organized into three main sections: (*1*) information sources in foreign language teaching; (2) research in the methods of foreign language teaching; and (3) general literature in the methods of foreign language teaching. Since it is impossible to carefully discuss each and every journal, article, book, monograph, etc., that has appeared in 1968 in the short amount of space allotted, criteria for the inclusion of those items discussed will be presented in each section.

Information sources in foreign language teaching

This section presents bibliographic sources and discusses new journals that have major import for foreign language teaching and methodology.

Although some of the sources to be discussed in the following paragraphs were available just prior to 1968, they need to be presented here to point up their availability and usefulness since they are relatively new.

Perhaps the most accessible, useful, and current source of information in foreign language methodology is the *ACTFL* (American Council on the Teaching of Foreign Languages) *Annual Bibliography*. This bibliography is an annual compilation of literature on various aspects of foreign language teaching. The literature cited is divided into nine basic categories that are of concern to the foreign language teacher: linguistics, analysis and teaching of the sociocultural context, teaching of the foreign literature, curricular problems and developments, physiology and the psychology of language learning, teacher education and qualifications, methods, equipment, and testing. Methods, obviously, is one of these sections. The bibliography is published each year in the May issue of *Foreign Language Annals*. To provide a foundation for the annual bibliography, MLA/ERIC commissioned Birkmaier & Lange (8) to list the most important documents on the teaching of foreign languages from 1920 to 1966. The *1967 ACTFL Bibliography* (Harmon, 31) and the *1968 ACTFL Annual Bibliography* (Lange, 40) continue this effort. In addition to the annual bibliography, ACTFL will also publish a number of special bibliographies. The first one is on the teaching of Slavic languages and literatures (Birkenmayer, 6). Thus, during the year 1968, the profession received a rather extensive bibliography of mainly published documents, beginning with 1920, concerning foreign language teaching in general and methods in particular.

Bibliographies from ACTFL

The source for many unpublished documents is the ERIC (Educational Resources Information Center) Clearinghouse on the Teaching of Foreign Languages which is housed at the Modern Language Association (MLA). The first of a series of lists of unpublished or difficult to obtain literature (Mildenberger & Liao, 47) represents an effort to assemble documents directly related to foreign language teaching from all 19 ERIC Clearinghouses. The list contains 741 items in such areas of language teaching as programmed learning, use of television, curriculum, teacher preparation, testing, language laboratories, FLES (foreign languages in elementary school), teaching techniques, etc. This series of lists of largely unpublished documents complements the *ACTFL Annual Bibliography*.

ERIC Clearinghouse

The ERIC lists, however, are not the only kind of information available from MLA/ERIC. Each issue of *Foreign Language Annals* contains a section entitled, "ERIC Clearinghouse on the Teaching of Foreign Languages." This section usually consists of three parts: ERIC notes, selected recent ERIC FL accessions, and FL projects in progress. The information, documents, and projects discussed here provide the teacher with a view of the current scene in language teaching.

MLA/ERIC has other projects as well. It has commissioned a series of focus reports and status papers. During 1968 the first two focus reports were published (Grittner, 28; Campa, 13). Grittner's article attempts to cope with the unavailability of advanced FL courses on the secondary school level and with students who have dropped out of advanced courses but who want to maintain their language skills. The Campa article describes the various ways in which folklore as culture is imbedded in Hispanic art forms: novel, folksong, ballad, proverb, *refrán*, folk games. The article contains a rich bibliography of sources for the teacher who wishes information on the teaching of Spanish culture. These focus reports are intended to be short, clear, and concise "helps" for the teacher in meeting everyday classroom problems. The Grittner report seems to meet the objectives set out for the series, but the Campa article presents no major suggestions for solving the problem of how to teach culture, even though it offers a wide variety of content items. *Focus Reports*

The first status study was also published during 1968 (Brooks, 11). It discusses culture from several points of view, suggesting that "patterns of living" is perhaps the most pertinent one for language teaching. Implementation of the idea of culture as patterns of living is suggested in a three-phase program: (*1*) use of culturally authentic language and situations in beginning language courses; (*2*) awareness of culture given to the more advanced student to help explain cultural objectives and aid the student to perceive both a scientific and humanistic interpretation of this awareness; (*3*) systematic study of culture for the advanced student in order to present a more complete profile of it according to specific themes or concepts. Since professional agreement in this area is not generally available, Brooks presents, in addition, nine proposals intended to awaken professional concern for an often discussed but rarely acted upon major element of foreign language learning. *Status study on culture*

In addition to the information sources provided by ACTFL and those that reside in ERIC, several new journals have appeared that relate directly to the area of methods. *Foreign Language* *Foreign Language Annals*

Annals, edited by Paquette (57) and published by the American Council on the Teaching of Foreign Languages, began in the fall of 1967. It is dedicated to the advancement of all phases of foreign language teaching. The first volume published a wide variety of articles from curriculum in a six-year secondary school Latin program, testing in the language laboratory, teaching of culture, teacher training, discussion of the usefulness of pattern drills, to discussions of state FL organizations. In this first volume, the journal has established itself as being of solid reputation.

Language Teaching Abstracts (41), published in England, presents abstracts of important articles in different areas of interest to the teacher, researcher, and coordinator/supervisor. Methods is one of the particular areas into which abstracts are categorized. In addition, each issue also carries a supplement that reviews books related to foreign language pedagogy. The journal carries forward the work of the former *English-Teaching Abstracts* which dealt mainly with the teaching of English as a second language.

Language Teaching Abstracts

The *TESOL Quarterly* (Robinett, 68), published by TESOL (Teachers of English to Speakers of Other Languages), provides a source of information for teachers who teach English essentially as a foreign language. The journal deals with some particularity on matters pertaining to classroom techniques, but also with linguistic and cultural patterns, curriculum, and administration of ESOL programs.

TESOL Quarterly

The American Association of Teachers of German (AATG) and the National Carl Schurz Association (NCSA) are cooperating in the publication of a new journal on the teaching of German, *Die Unterrichtspraxis* (Reichmann, 65). This journal attempts to deal with the pedagogical interest of German teachers on all levels, FLES through graduate school. The articles in the first volume (*UP* began publishing in 1968) reflect this aim. Of special interest are the *UP* columns, including "Methodische Rundschau." The associate editors who write this particular column attempt to bring into focus some of the literature and sources in the U.S. and Germany that pertain to special topics such as programmed learning and testing (Lange, 37, 38; Freudenstein, 26, 27).

Die Unterrichtspraxis

The publication of the bibliographic sources and journals discussed above should awaken the profession to the extent of its commitment to the teaching of foreign languages. The sources show the breadth and depth of the literature in the discussion of foreign language teaching from 1920 through the present. The new journals, in addition to already established ones, provide a platform for the review of current issues and problems. At times one wonders if much difference exists between the past and present, despite all the turmoil surrounding foreign language teaching at the present moment. The sources and new journals may provide some interesting comparisons and contrasts in that regard.

Research in foreign language methodology

This section reviews research on the classroom strategies, procedures, or techniques of second language learning. The criterion for inclusion of a study in this section is similar to that of Carroll's statement in a 1966 review (16), namely that a study must exhibit a valid experimental design in order for the interpretation of the results to be accomplished with a maximum of clarity. Thus, only the literature that meets this criterion will be discussed in the following paragraphs.

The criterion

The section is divided into two parts, one part dealing with broader comparative studies and a second part reviewing the smaller, more discrete studies and newer developments (computer, etc.).

Broad comparisons

The studies chosen for discussion in this section attempt comparisons of different methods or approaches in the teaching of foreign languages. The length of the discussions reflects this author's concern that the most important details and the resulting critical comments concerning these studies be understood because of their pertinence to the present foreign language teaching-learning scene.

What do broad comparisons have to offer?

Audiolingual vs. cognitive code language learning theories. Chastain (19) and Chastain & Woerdehoff (20), reporting on the same study, attempt to contrast an audiolingual habit theory and a cognitive code theory in a study with college students of Spanish at Purdue University. A randomly assigned final sample of 99 students in four sections received treatment according to either a cognitive code or audiolingual habit theory for one academic year. The audiolingual habit theory is described as containing basically three characteristics: (*1*) study and manipulation of language structure; (*2*) presentation of new language material through induction; (*3*) maintenance of

Experiment at Purdue University with college Students

the natural order in which skills are learned (listening, speaking, reading, writing). The cognitive code theory is contrasted with the audiolingual habit theory and is said to possess the following characteristics: (1) exercise activities designed to teach grammatical understanding; (2) deductive explanation prior to practice with structural patterns; (3) practice with all language skills from the beginning of the course.

Although initially students were randomly assigned to six sections totaling 169 students, the final sample contained 99 students in four sections, two cognitive code and two audiolingual. Seventy students were lost to the study for various reasons. The final sample indicated no significant differences, using T tests of significance, in aptitude, intelligence, motivation, preference of learning modality (auditory or visual), and previous language experience. The groups thus seemed similar in character.

After one year of instruction according to the ground rules set down in the definition of either theory, the four groups were tested with the MLA/ETS Cooperative Tests in Spanish, Form LA. The results based on analyses of variance indicated the following for the four skills:

Results of A-L and C-C Groups

1 No statistically significant differences could be inferred between the audiolingual and cognitive code students in listening comprehension achievement, although the authors suggest a direction of difference toward the cognitive code students.

2 No significant differences could be inferred between the audiolingual and cognitive code students in speaking achievement, although a direction of difference was noted in favor of the audiolingual students who did significantly better in repetition of phrases.

3 In reading, the cognitive code groups achieved significantly more than the audiolingual groups.

4 In writing, the results seemed to favor the cognitive code students.

The areas of aptitude, motivation, modality preference, and method, in addition to previous language experience and instructor factors, were related to the achievement results of the four language skills by factorial analysis as a part of the design of data analysis. The results indicated:

1 There were no significant differences between audiolingual and cognitive code groups in relation to the four skills in modality preference, in the instructor variable, or in prior language experience, although significant speaking and writ-

ing results were found in favor of the audiolingual groups for this latter variable.

2 In language learning aptitude and achievement in the four skills a significant difference was found in favor of the cognitive groups.

The authors concluded that the results of the study favor the cognitive code learning theory because it proved as effective for listening, speaking, and writing as the audiolingual habit theory and more effective for reading. The authors also interpolate from the results that:

Cognitive code approach more effective than audiolingual approach

1 A deductive presentation of language patterns is superior to an inductive one.
2 Language analysis is superior to the use of analogy.
3 Practice with language structure stressing understanding is superior to pattern practice.
4 The use of all senses to assimilate language material is superior to the natural order of presentation.

While it is possible to criticize this study in its design, the way in which the final sample was obtained, the imprecise definitions of audiolingual and cognitive code theories, the way in which these theories were applied to the classroom, the evaluation of student achievement according to the definitions, the rather specific conclusions that the authors drew from quite limited measures, and the implied application of these conclusions to a wider population, namely to all of language teaching, there is a more fundamental question that the authors ignored in considering the execution of this study. Are these two so-called theories mutually exclusive or are they complementary, that is, can cognition and habit formation be considered part of a broader but as yet incomplete theory of language learning? Doesn't language learning require habit formation as part of psychomotor skills development *and* cognitive awareness of language structure as an aid to skills learning so that originally learned and understood language material might be the basis upon which new language may be generated?

Are the concepts cognitive code and audiolingual mutually exclusive?

Carroll (14) began the controversy by defining the two theories, suggesting that they exist independently one from the other and that they should be evaluated in a comparative study to determine which one to be the most effective. In the light of the little we know about learning a foreign language, it seems that some cognitive processes must be used in order to make efficient use of time allowed for second language learning in schools and colleges as well as to take advantage of the desire of most adolescents and adults to use cognitive processes in learning almost anything. The tendency to make these two aspects of language learning therefore mutually exclusive is an unfortunate step backward in language learning because of the interrelationship between these two elements in the learning process.

In that regard the study described above perpetuates the polarization in language teaching around traditional and contemporary approaches to language learning, which is accomplished by a set of final conclusions that were reached not as a result of data analysis, but *were* based upon extrapolation rather than statistical inference and that also tend to reveal the authors' biases. Perhaps the only conclusion to be drawn from this study is that because of the lack of significant differences between the two theories, which may actually indicate a relationship between them, there may be now, more than ever, a firmer basis for asking those questions that may lead to the examination of the contributions of both "theories" to a broader understanding of language learning.

Language competence and performance can use both concepts

Studies by Lusetti (43) and Sprague (77) indicate some of the same general results obtained by Chastain. In a study on the junior high school level, Lusetti found that the cognitive code theory of instruction proved itself as effective as the audiolingual theory of instruction for the learning of Spanish. Sprague attempted to compare audiolingual, eclectic, and traditional approaches in the evaluation of student achievement with factors of intelligence, language learning aptitude, and powers of critical thinking. Language learning in any of the skills did not seem to be affected by intelligence or powers of critical thinking, but language learning aptitude did have a significant effect on the speaking skill. The only significant differences between methods of achievement were related to the eclectic approach for speaking and the audiolingual treatment for reading. Both of these studies can be criticized like the Chastain study as examining and comparing elements or methods of instruction that are in reality complementary rather than mutually exclusive.

Junior high school study

Fundamental skills vs. traditional language teaching methodologies. Another and perhaps more important continuing broad comparative series of studies on teaching strategies than that of Chastain is being conducted in Pennsylvania under the direction of Smith. In two reports (Smith & Berger, 76; Smith & Baranyi, 75) three studies on the comparison of the effectiveness of traditional and audiolingual approaches utilizing electromechanical equipment were reported.

The experimentation originally developed as a response to a previous language laboratory study conducted by Keating (35), but was extended to include a replication study and the continuance of the study through a second year. The Pennsylvania Studies, as they have come to be known, attempt to evaluate traditional teaching strategies against fundamental skills and fundamental skills-grammar with three types of language laboratory equipment. The original study examines 25 pre-, mid-, and post-experimental measures and 12 attitude indices on 2,171 students in randomly assigned classes of French and German.

The investigators were extremely careful in setting up this investigation in order to avoid the mistakes of previous studies which have attempted to evaluate teaching strategies and language laboratory arrangements. Provisions were made for: a large enough sample, random assignment of classes, basic definition of language laboratory equipment in the different treatments, adequate definition and coordination of classroom learning materials and their coordination with laboratory practice, teacher preparation, use of valid and reliable standardized tests (with only one exception) for purposes of evaluation, teacher orientation, instructional guidelines, teacher observation and supervision, and extensive pretesting. The design of the study reflects the investigators' careful examination of the experimental conditions.

Design of the Penna. Studies

The results of this initial study, however, are not unlike the general results of the Keating report. After one year of instruction:

General results of the Penna. Studies

1 There were essentially no significant differences between traditional students and the fundamental skills treatment students as measured by listening, speaking, reading, and writing tests.

2 The language laboratory arrangements used twice weekly had no noticeable effect upon either of the fundamental skills treatments.

3 There seemed to be no combination of approach and laboratory arrangement that proved superior to any other.

4 The most reliable predictors of language learning success in the classroom were the MLA Cooperative Foreign Language Listening Test (German and French), the Modern Language Aptitude Test, and the California Test of Mental Maturity.

5 Student learning and attitude factors indicated that females performed better than males and that student attitudes toward a strategy seemed to be independent of it.

6 Students in the fundamental skills treatment classes pro-

ceeded more slowly through learning materials than did traditional students.

7 There was no discernible relationship between the different parts of the MLA Foreign Language Tests for Advanced Students and Teachers given to the teachers and the achievement of the students in their classes in any of the foreign language skills.

Analysis of the data was accomplished by analysis of variance and covariance. The replication study followed the original experimentation with the following exceptions: the tape recorder lab arrangement was eliminated as well as pre- and post-measures from a 25-year-old language achievement examination; speaking and writing measures were not analyzed because of a very small sample. Results of the study confirmed the results of the original study as indicated in the seven points above.

The Replication Study

The second-year study continued the experimentation of the first year, and the replication study with 35 pre-experimental, first year, and final measures taken on 1,090 students. The only new measure was a nonvalidated speech test. After two years of instruction the analysis of the data by means of analysis of variance and covariance indicated nonsignificant differences among the three teaching strategies in listening, speaking, and writing, but a significant difference in achievement for the traditional students in reading. The language laboratory arrangements, used twice weekly, had no discernible effect on any one of the strategies. The most significant predictors of classroom success were prior learning success and the Modern Language Aptitude Test. One of the most elusive elements of this study was student attitudes toward foreign language study which declined throughout instruction but were independent of the learning strategy. Coverage of material throughout the two years was less than indicated by the authors of the textbooks. Students within the fundamental skills strategies who used Holt, Rinehart, Winston texts, *Écouter et Parler—Verstehen und Sprechen*, did significantly better than those who used the Harcourt, Brace and World, *Audio-Lingual Materials*. Although it is possible to consider them a representative sample of students across the nation, the students in these studies did not achieve to the national norms for their grade and experience in language learning. Teacher experience, graduate education, and scores on the MLA Foreign Language Tests for Advanced Students and Teachers were not found to be related to class achievement. Related to the last finding was the fact that no

The Second Year Study

Students did not attain national norms

Teacher competence vs. student achievement

relationship existed between any teacher variable and class attitude toward foreign language study. The sex differences on learning declined in the study of the second level.

As already stated, it would not be extremely useful to criticize extensively the design of these studies because the investigators did make every attempt to apply experimental rigor to the investigations. Actually, these studies are among the most sophisticated and well-controlled experiments with large groups that are available in the area of classroom research in foreign language learning. This statement does not deny a criticism of the studies from several points of view, but rather points to the studies as valid examples of research with educational questions.

The Pennsylvania Studies present an attempt to evaluate a "brand" of the audiolingual approach, fundamental skills, as compared to the traditional approach to language teaching. This broad comparative study may not be capable of evaluating the different strategies that define these two basic approaches. Even though the investigators assembled a group of experts to describe both approaches, the results of such discussions may not have provided the necessary, crucial characteristics that distinguish one approach from the other. As an example, it may be that the similarity in the presentation of grammar with the traditional and fundamental skills-grammar groups was so similar that the evaluating instruments could not distinguish one approach from the other. Other instances of nondistinctive elements between the basic approaches may have provided a sum of poorly defined strategies which resulted in nonsignificant differences. Since no attempt was made to evaluate the defining characteristics of either audiolingual or traditional approaches to language teaching, the Pennsylvania Studies have not provided any new understanding of particular classroom strategies in foreign language teaching, be it from a traditional or modern point of view.

Broad studies do not evaluate all factors which affect FL learning

Another factor relating to the inability of the treatments to distinguish themselves one from the other revolves around the learning materials used in the studies. Although one audiolingual system proved superior to another in fundamental skills treatments, there were still basically no statistically significant differences in achievement between audiolingual and traditional treatments. This fact indirectly suggests that, in spite of built-in controls, the fundamental skills and traditional materials and the way in which they were employed by teachers may also have been nondistinct. The general lack of stimuli to produce the

Treatments not distinguishable

student's ability to generate either spoken or written language in either of the fundamental skills systems of materials directly relates these materials to those of a traditional type which can be criticized for the same lack. Thus, the Pennsylvania Studies indicate that the learning procedures and strategies as reflected in the learning materials of both traditional and fundamental skills approaches are not distinguishable and are therefore related to the lack of difference between the two basic treatments, at least for listening, speaking, and writing.

The success of traditional students in reading is a predictable one after examining the number of units "covered" in the traditional and fundamental skills approach groups. The latter groups finished, on the average, 10-15 units, depending upon the materials used, while the former finished 28-30 units. Valette (82) has indicated this coverage corresponds to 525-650 words for the fundamental skills groups and 1,400-1,500 words for the traditional treatment groups. Thus the traditional groups were exposed to more than twice the vocabulary of the fundamental skills groups, and this difference showed up on test results for the traditional groups. Although the difference between traditional groups and fundamental skills groups in reading is significant, it is small in relation to the number of mean points of difference. Valette indicates this small spread may be related to better vocabulary retention on the part of fundamental skills groups who learned less vocabulary than traditional groups, but retained it better. Thus, the Pennsylvania Studies point out that size of vocabulary is directly related to success in reading skills. And, in addition, they perhaps indicate that fundamental skills trained groups may have better vocabulary retention.

How valid are results for reading?

One of the most important results of the studies indicates that the language laboratory used twice weekly had no effect upon learning with either fundamental skills or fundamental skills-grammar treatment. Furthermore, the traditional students achieved as well in listening and speaking without the laboratory. While these facts seem disturbing, it must be considered that the laboratories were used *only* twice weekly for approximately 60 minutes total. There was no attempt to evaluate other uses of time within the framework of the studies. It is possible to argue that the full potential of the language laboratory for spaced practice in language learning was not evaluated in these investigations. Thus, the Pennsylvania Studies have not added any new understanding of the use of the language laboratory in language teaching and learning.

Full potential of language lab not exploited

The Pennsylvania Studies have not provided any new understanding of either language learning or use of equipment in school language learning. They have mainly confirmed the inappropriate use of electromechanical equipment in language learning and the inability of the profession to define what it means by audiolingual or traditional teaching strategies. Thus they point to the absolute necessity for closer evaluation of individual strategies, procedures, and techniques in second language learning in schools. In that light, these studies are not negative, but rather they point to some of the tasks that still remain ahead of the profession.

Fundamental tasks in language learning still remain to be investigated

In reviews written by Carroll (14, 17), in his book, *The Study of Langue* (18), and in the review of Birkmaier & Lange (7) the usefulness of large comparative methodological studies and small, discrete, carefully designed evaluative studies have been discussed. The general opinion seems to suggest that the smaller, detailed study of specific contributions to the learning process provides more precise information than the large study for the determination of the most effective classroom techniques, procedures, or strategies related to predetermined objectives of second language learning in a school setting. The larger comparative study of one general method against another was not considered productive mainly because of the difficulty of *accurately* defining and determining the characteristics that distinguish one method from another. The large-scale studies reviewed here indicate that the profession is continuing to produce large comparative investigations that for the very reasons stated above have failed in the task set out for them. Thus, the evaluation of audiolingual or traditional approaches to foreign language learning offers little of significance for the classroom teacher who wants to be able to provide his students with an efficient learning program. What he needs is information about specific strategies, procedures, or techniques in fulfilling his objectives. In that regard and until a general theory of second language learning has been formulated, the smaller type studies dealing with techniques, procedures, and strategies may help him obtain the information that is so sorely lacking.

The broad comparison study versus the small experiment

The following section presents some examples of language learning strategies evaluated in smaller, more discrete studies.

Foreign language learning procedures and developments

The studies chosen for discussion in this section present evaluation of teaching-learning procedures as well as some developments that are not necessarily within the teacher group interaction of the classroom, namely the computer.

Drills: with explanations, order, establishment of meaning with, and construction. In a complicated set of experiments, Politzer (60) attempted to answer the questions posed by Carroll (18): Should the grammatical explanation precede the drill? Should it be stated after some language material with the structure has been introduced? Should it be given after the drill has been taught, as a generalization? Should explanation be offered at all? The literature of language learning and learning materials indicates the range of different points of view expressed in these questions. These experimental conditions with six French and six Spanish exercises were accomplished on tape: (*1*) explanation preceding the drill; (*2*) explanation spliced into the tape after the repetition phase of the drill; (*3*) explanation added at the end of the tape; (*4*) no explanation. A posttest for each drill was constructed which consisted of eight English sentences for which the subjects were to write French or Spanish equivalents. By means of ranking the results of four French and four Spanish classes, the results indicated no clear pattern, mainly because of class differences. Thus, the teacher will have to take into consideration the time of day, tiredness of students, student motivation, etc., in completing drill situations. Politzer did offer, however, a general observation from the study that allowed that introduction of a grammatical explanation before drill in the classroom is not advisable and that it is preferable to show the relevancy of new language material in context before explanation takes place.

How should drills be presented

In another study, Politzer (59) examined the order in which the structures of a language ought best be introduced. The order contrasting structure (example: I see him; *Je le vois.*) before parallel structure (example: give me; *donne-moi.*) was examined to provide an answer to the question of which structure should be taught first to make the learning of foreign language structures easier and to avoid problems of interference with the native language. The results of the study with both French and Spanish classes working with syntactic *and* morphologic patterns indicated, as with the study above, that there is no clear-cut answer from the data. The evidence gathered seemed to favor the contrastive structure before the parallel structure treatment (difficult before easy), but only when these two concepts referred to syntactical arrangements involving word order. Although the experiments also dealt with morphological patterns,

Ordering of language structures in instruction

it was not possible to discern a clear pattern of results because of the necessity for students to make compulsory structural (morphological) choices that had no parallel in the native language (example: *avoir* and *être* in the past tenses). Thus the relative ease or difficulty of any pattern of presentation was obscured by the fact that the morphemic compulsory choices may have had more influence on the difficulty of a construction than lexical dissimilarity to the native language.

Oller & Obrecht (55), unconvinced of pure habit formation in using pattern drills, set up two situations to evaluate meaningfulness with, and the application of pattern practice to, communication. In the first procedure the pattern practice sentences were introduced by listening, repetition, and manipulative drills, meaning being given only once. The second procedure used the same basic conditions but with more attention to meaning, extending the situation to include question/answer and directed dialogue activities. Although based on an extremely small sample (two groups of ten each), the results of analysis of response latency and accuracy indicated that the relationship of pattern drills to communicative situations and activities actually produces more acceptable learning toward desired goals. Thus, in this regard, pattern drills need to be made meaningful and tied into actual communication situations, an obvious conclusion from the outset of the study, but a conclusion that needs to be backed up by some evidence, even though it be weak.

Using pattern drills in communication type situations

Newmark & Reibel (53) support the contention of Oller & Obrecht in an article that, though not presenting experimental results, provides support and examples in the use of more communicative drills. They argue against the overemphasis on contrastive drills from the application of linguistic data and in its place substitute observation and exercise of particular instances of language.

The above experimentation does not provide the expected outcomes in all circumstances. Politzer's studies do not supply the information for which he was searching, but they do reveal the complexity of the learning situation and present some of the difficulties of language learning. The studies also relate a kind of latent pessimism about research of this kind which may have been caused by a lack of cautious assumptions about the nature of the final results. Oller & Obrecht's study, although extremely biased, does contribute to the support of evidence for the obvious. Research on the use of pattern drills, their construction, and place in foreign language instruction must be continued in

Smaller research studies need to be continued

order to provide a clearer understanding of and more information on this very widely used technique.

Programmed learning: use with linguistically underprivileged, for discrimination training and as a partial means of achieving learning goals. Mueller (50) conducted an observational study of programmed instruction on college students who had not participated in learning French on the secondary school level and whom he labeled linguistically underprivileged. Both the results of teacher-made semester examinations and the MLA Cooperative French Tests in listening, reading, and writing were used to observe student achievement with the program. The results generally tended to indicate support for the use of programmed instruction with students of this kind. This conclusion, however, is reached by "eyeballing" percentile ratios rather than by using statistical techniques. However useful this technique may be, it has more severe limitations than inference from the results of the application of statistical techniques on collected data. A more carefully designed study could have yielded perhaps more precise indications of why programmed instruction was successful with this type of student.

The linguistically underprivileged can benefit

In another study Mueller & Niedzielski (51) wished to evaluate the interaction of discrimination and pronunciation. They posed the following questions: Does the teaching of discrimination influence pronunciation performance? If so, how? What kind of pronunciation features are affected, sound or intonation features? What role would language aptitude play in the relationship? The questions were tested in a study of 180 students who received no discrimination training and 63 who did. The discrimination training consisted of the presentation of random correct and incorrect utterances to be evaluated either as acceptable or unacceptable. Two-and-one-half hours of discrimination training was used in which the students learned to discriminate intonation features, individual sounds, and finally their graphic representations. The students were tested on repetition of heard utterances and on the recording of a reading passage previously learned orally. Two kinds of results, quantitative and impressionistic, were indicated for seven different variables. Results from the quantitative analysis were basically nonsignificant, indicating little help from the programming of discrimination for pronunciation although the experimental group was better in producing French vowels similar to those of English. The impressionistic evaluation, on the other hand, showed that for the experimental group on pronunciation fea-

The influence of discrimination training on pronunciation performance tures there was little deviation from the French phoneme, that the most common defect was mismanagement of allophonic material, and that fluency and the production of language features were "closer" to French than that of the control group.

The results did indicate that there is a relationship between discrimination training and pronunciation, but an indication of the effects of such training on specific aspects of pronunciation was not clear because of language aptitude differences between groups.

In a study dealing with partial programming of instruction, Wajskop-Hianne & Renkin (83) used two groups of students to contrast different treatments. Group one spent its laboratory time in the repetition of dialogue material, while group two spent its laboratory time practicing phonologic and morphosyntactic drills in addition to dialogue repetition. Group one spent 240 hours learning 32 units of *Voix et Images de France* while group two spent 200 hours with 20 units of the same material supplemented by the semiprogrammed drills in French phonology and morphosyntax. The results indicated no appreciable difference in the comparable learning of the two groups, indicating that a basic program supplemented by the laboratory manipulation of semiprogrammed drills on specific structures is as efficient as a program supplemented by only dialogue repetition in the language laboratory.

Effects of partial programming

The use of programmed instruction in a program of language learning is without doubt extremely useful. However, as has been indicated by Carroll (16), Ornstein (56), and others, the profession has not yet determined its most appropriate use. From the three studies reviewed above it may be possible to suggest that the programming of learning material may be helpful in teaching certain elements of language-discrimination training and control of morphosyntactic patterns. They do not suggest that all of learning can be programmed, an event that is not substantiated in actual use of programmed learning in foreign language instruction. One of its major proponents, Valdman, has begun to look upon programmed learning as capable of performing only certain functions and discusses the technique as only part of language instruction in what he calls guided learning (Valdman, 81). In that regard, language learning for the linguistically underpriviledged might contain some elements of programming but its total or indiscriminate use may not be the most beneficial either in terms of reward mechanisms or efficiency. Thus, the teacher remains an important factor in moti-

Possible uses for programmed instruction

vation and in ability to determine the immediate learning needs of students, functions that a program cannot as yet perform. Further discussion of the pros, cons, and developments in programmed instruction may be found in Mueller (49).

Native language interference. One of the defining characteristics of the audiolingual approach is the presentation of listening and speaking skills before reading or writing to prevent the interference of the native language sounds with the foreign language system which uses the same or very similar written symbols. This procedure has received both positive and negative support from language teachers and learning theorists. Muller & Muller (52) present these pro and con arguments as background information for a study in which they offer a third alternative. Instead of attempting to determine the overall effectiveness of either an extended prereading period or a variation of the same (Lange, 39), the Mullers suggest in a study with the Portuguese language a more precise technique to answer the questions: Does exposure to Portuguese written symbols which are basically those of English interfere with formation of pronunciation habits in Portuguese? If yes, which letters or letter combinations cause pronunciation difficulties in Portuguese? The experiment executed to determine answers to these questions contrasted a group that was not allowed to see the written word for four weeks with a group that was allowed to see written symbols as a means of visual cues for oral material. The results indicated a distinct advantage in pronunciation for the group from which the written symbols were withheld. The situation was further analyzed to see which letters caused the interference. The results of this examination indicated evidence of interference due to the difference of pronunciation represented by the same orthographic symbol as used in the native and target languages. The development of a predicting formula used in this study to examine sound-symbol association in both target and native languages might be applied to other languages to predict points of interference and thus anticipate the interference with appropriate drill and analysis experience before it actually occurs. A reorganization of the prereading experience in language learning could also be related to the results of this study, namely that sound-symbol associations that present few difficulties be introduced before those that present difficulties. Thus the non-order of present practices where all problems of sound-symbol association may be presented at one time can be avoided.

Use of time in foreign language programs: intensive vs.

How should sound-symbol association be treated?

extensive. Williamson (84), noting the lack of methodological studies and surveys regarding the use of intensive programs in foreign language learning, set up a study to evaluate an intensive vs. an extensive approach for the teaching of Spanish on the college level. Nineteen students living in a dormitory for the summer studied Spanish for an eight-week period with four 55-minute instructional periods, four half-hour language laboratory sessions, and two hours of homework as elements of the daily schedule. These men were compared with 196 others, the control group, who had completed two years of Spanish during the years 1965-67. Standardized tests in language aptitude, intelligence, and achievement in Spanish were used to compare the two groups. Results indicated similarity of the background of the two groups. But after eight weeks of intensive instruction, the experimental group of 19 achieved results equal to that of the control group after one year of instruction, while 12 of the experimental group achieved to the level of the control group after two years of instruction. Although there was no definition of approaches other than use of time, and although the sample was quite unrepresentative of the population, the results do suggest further examination of the use of the intensive approach on the college level as a means of achieving a more meaningful and complete language experience within the liberal arts context. Perhaps connecting it to a foreign experience as a culminating event might even increase its usefulness.

An intensive approach to language study at the college level could mean a better learning experience

Intensive summer programs and bilingual programs in subject matter areas. Studies by Elkins (25) and Bolger (9) do not reflect concern with specific strategies, procedures, or techniques of language teaching in the classroom as such, but they do present developments that may be related to, or that may cause, classroom problems.

Summer programs as elements of summer school curricula and in the form of summer language camps seem to be favorite ways of continuing or extending students' knowledge of foreign languages during the so-called dormant summer months. Elkins' study attempted to investigate the influence of a summer intensive program on the learning of German by secondary school students by comparing results of the regular program to the regular program *plus* the intensive summer program by means of achievement measures in German. The findings indicate that:

Maintaining and motivating students in summer school activities

1 Students with one year of German plus a summer program scored significantly higher in listening, reading, and culture

measures than students with two years of German. Writing scores showed no significant differences.

2 Students with two years of German and the summer program showed no significant differences in listening, reading, and writing with students who had finished three years.

3 Students felt the program influenced their listening comprehension the most and their pronunciation the least.

4 Teachers felt the summer program influenced the students' listening and vocabulary most and their writing, pronunciation, and grammatical knowledge the least.

Thus, since intensive summer programs are popular and are greatly increasing, it is appropriate that language teachers understand what they best can do for students who have participated in such programs. Extending the intensive experience into the classroom in matters of placement, method, and perhaps content might be some general strategies toward which teachers could look.

What strategies used in summer activities can be incorporated in the regular FL classroom?

In a study of bilingual language programs related to the teaching of science on the junior high school level to English/Spanish bilinguals, Bolger found that such a program resulted in students achieving differently in science than in conventional programs. Also, the achievement in science was related to the fluency of the instructor, in this case Spanish. The results of the study, though more related to bilingual education, indicate that for advanced language programs that attempt to teach subject matter in the language, the teacher ought most likely to have near native proficiency and that the target language ought to be used most of the time.

Computer-assisted instruction as a technique of language learning. Ruplin & Russell (72), among the first to use CAI (computer-assisted instruction) in foreign language learning, believe that it offers a solution to the unevenness of goal achievement with various teaching methods and the audiolingual approach in particular. They suggest that it provides for the teaching of partial skills—spelling, dictation, translation, vocabulary—for which little time is found under the conventional audiolingual method. CAI, therefore, does not remove the teacher from instruction, but rather aids him in better management of it. CAI goes beyond the conventional language laboratory to provide learning experiences with reading and writing. Tentative impressions of the techniques show that students are motivated to work at the program, that the underachiever or poor student is being helped, and that test results indicate superior achieve-

CAI aids the teacher in management of instruction

ment on national norms for writing and results similar to audio-lingual instruction for listening, reading, and speaking.

Adams, Morrison, & Reddy (1) describe the more technical features of the CAI program which Ruplin & Russell did not report: machines, programming, preparation of materials, execution, pedagogical control, and evaluation.

Morrison & Adams (48) relate in detail a general comparison of audiolingual students and CAI students in a pilot experiment directed by Ruplin. The study indicated, within the similarity of the two groups, that CAI students without conventional classroom experience were similar to audiolingually trained students in acquiring listening and speaking skills, and under the same conditions for reading and writing they either equaled or surpassed the audiolingually trained students. Detailed comparisons were offered for the groups' achievement and attitude. The results point to the use of the computer as a technique of foreign language learning that needs to be further evaluated. It is still highly experimental and controversial. It possesses not only internal problems of program development and materials, but also external problems of cost and most efficient use in a foreign language curriculum. Until some of these questions are answered, this technique should be employed only with great care and preparation.

CAI still experimental

The studies and related literature reviewed here indicate that experimentation is taking place with individual techniques, strategies, and procedures of both a specific and broader nature. The section also includes reviews of studies that point to some of the directions to which language teaching methods will have to adapt themselves, namely advanced language teaching, bilingual education, and use of the computer. It is hoped that even more attention would be given in coming years to experimentation that might elucidate some of the presently used techniques in the average foreign language classroom.

To some degree the whole area of research in foreign language methodology is quite disappointing, mainly because of a lack of general direction. Now that federal funds are difficult to obtain and that that weak organizing factor has largely been removed, it seems that the profession should begin to apply its own ideas and resources to determine priorities and goals for research in foreign language teaching and learning. Possible vehicles for organization do exist. The Standing Committee on Research of the American Council on the Teaching of Foreign Languages could provide leadership in the area. The universities

Need for organization of research in strategies of instruction

301

that now offer Ph.D. programs in foreign language education might offer their pooled knowledge to help determine research priorities and perhaps even support research from some of their own research funds. Since federal funds are no longer plentiful for foreign language pedagogical research, only the presentation of a unified and aggressive front will be successful in securing both private and public monies for the necessary research to make foreign language learning more effective.

New Ph.D. program in foreign language learning

In regard to priorities, Heise (32) has noted a lack of specific information for the learning conditions of the real academic world. As a result he has formulated a set of priorities that might be valuable as a model from which to work. Carroll (15) has also suggested some priorities for investigation in second language teaching. But whether there are one or ten models, the question still remains: Can the profession organize itself to set research priorities and see to the accomplishment of the needed research?

Research priorities

General literature on the teaching of foreign languages

The literature to be reviewed in this section contains specifically nonresearch information, ideas, suggestions for techniques, procedures, or strategies that make a contribution to the teaching of foreign languages. This section is divided into two major parts, one reporting literature that may be considered *general* to all languages and a second section reporting the given literature related to a *specific language*.

General

Perhaps the most important and useful publication during 1968 was that of Rivers (67), a text that contains information about language teaching that is adaptable to all levels of instruction. With each one of the language skills, Rivers outlines a series of steps and procedures that point the student away from very controlled practice with language in what might be called an introductory stage to a less controlled form of language practice that might be called liberated expression for speaking and writing and liberated use for listening and reading. (The reader's attention is drawn at this point to an article by Edgerton [24], which extends the meaning of "liberation" and presents further information regarding the achievement of "liberated expression" in speaking and writing.)

Rivers' book on teaching the four skills moves the profession forward

As an example, in the chapter that concentrates on perhaps the most neglected area of language learning, namely listening comprehension, Rivers dissects the listening skill into four different stages: identification; identification and selection without retention; identification and guided selection with short-term retention; identification, selection, and long-term retention. She then identifies some of the possible strategies for each one of these stages within various levels of instruction (elementary, intermediate, and advanced). These suggestions are not of a theoretical nature, but are actual procedures that can be used to develop students' ability to perform within the various stages of listening.

An important book for the training of teachers

While other skills are treated to the same general analysis, the same specificity of techniques for the development of student abilities is not carefully applied. It is hoped in a future revision of the book that more specific examples would be given of the different reading stages, for example.

In the chapter on the place of grammar, Rivers indicates that there is necessity for both habit formation and rule-governed behavior in language learning. She indicates that the application of this principle to the classroom should thus take the form of grammatical explanation only after the student has had some experience in the operation of a structure. Thus she underscores from practical experience the experimentation performed by Politzer (60).

Other chapters in the book relate to testing, FLES, language laboratories, construction of drills, and an overview of objectives and methods, all of which add completeness to the contemporary view of language learning, making the book an excellent core for an undergraduate methods course in a teacher preparation program.

Bennett (5) and Roucek (71) have also published books in the general area of language learning, teaching, and study, but they do not have the relevance to immediate problems as does Rivers. The only article in the Roucek book that deals specifically with general methodology (Oliva, 54) traces the changes in methods over the past 20 years and suggests some needed areas of research, but adds nothing substantial to the area under review. A similar article by Simches (74) compares the classroom of 1898 with that of 1968, a contrast that indicates the teacher has become the decision maker and manager of the classroom, *the* person in the instructional system who chooses the most appropriate learning strategies for the learner in order to meet the

The teacher as manager and guide

desired objectives. Several questions posed at the end of the article, directly related to learning procedures, suggest the need for further examination of the teacher's role as the manager of instruction.

One of the most generally accepted elements or procedures in second language learning is the use of contrastive analysis for the anticipation of learning problems and the preparation of drill material to overcome them. In a monograph (Alatis, 2) devoted to the definition, evaluation, and use of contrastive analysis in language teaching, Rivers (66) points out that contrastive information for some languages has been available in linguistic form but that it has rarely been realized in classroom materials or teaching procedures. For pedagogical purposes contrasts and differences do not result in the same learning conditions. Differences are taught as new knowledge, and contrasts are dealt with as areas of native language interference. The difficulty of language differences can be estimated by means of the number of contrasts. This difficulty can be reduced if students are prepared for contrastive learning and have access to the active learning of language structures. Translation may seem to be the best means of exercise in language contrast, pedagogically. However, because of the necessity of the student to have a mature grasp of both native and target languages, the technique is usable only at an advanced level of study. These are about the most useful statements from this particular monograph that are directly applicable to the pedagogical situation. Contrastive studies and their *direct* application for the realities of classroom teaching and materials could very well be a subject for another monograph. Other comments concerning the relationship of applied linguistics to language teaching procedures may be found in Banathy (4), del Olmo (22), Bolinger (10), and Hanzeli (30).

Contrastive analysis rarely used in teaching strategies

The one general methodological publication for the teaching of foreign languages on the elementary school level is that of Donoghue (23). The lengthy publication is disappointing in that it deals with the methodology of language teaching before the consideration of the characteristics of children. Although adequate, the book does not really provide the hoped-for strategies for helping the elementary school child through the series of necessary tasks in the learning of foreign languages. The book devotes most of its effort to the description of teacher tasks, instructional resources, and sources for materials to aid program planning, both long range and daily. What is extremely needed

New text on the teaching of FLES

in the area of FLES is an examination of the characteristics of the elementary school child, how he learns and what he learns best, to establish some goals for foreign language learning in the elementary school, and then to examine foreign language teaching procedures, their order and usefulness. A systems approach to FLES might be an extremely worthwhile venture; it might give us useful information about our present strategies in FLES teaching, provide suggestions for new ones, and evaluate both in the process.

Other kinds of general literature on teaching methods, procedures, strategies, and techniques are available. They are indicative of both the far-out thinking and the lack of understanding of present teaching strategies. Burling (12) represents the former in suggesting that to develop reading skill in foreign language learning it may be necessary to omit training in oral skills unless they support the reading skill; reading might be developed more rapidly and thoroughly if the student is not expected to simultaneously learn the writing skill; grammar, phonology, and lexicon may be learned in more separate ways. If these procedures were to be accomplished and evaluated as usable, the usual, very elementary and perhaps childish content of language learning may be avoided for adult learners, thus increasing both motivation and learning.

Reading skills development

Suther (79), who represents the latter point of view, does not wish to criticize modern language learning and teaching, but by her comments reveals her lack of understanding of developments in foreign language learning, the human resources such developments create, and the developments that must still take place.

Specific languages

The following paragraphs relate teaching strategies used in the three major languages taught in schools and colleges in this country, French, German, and Spanish.

French. Marty's book (44), prepared for use with his French learning program, deals with many specific aspects of the teaching of French. Although related to his learning materials, the many individual techniques discussed there could be applied elsewhere: techniques used in directed expression, free expression, group instruction with machines, to give particular examples.

Valuable techniques to be used

For the development of the speaking skill in French and other foreign languages as well, TAVOR (80) has developed the concept of picture writing, a series of pictures whose constant symbols can provide stimuli for the generation of speech and writing as well.

The use of visual stimuli, namely pictures, to support the teaching of grammar is related by Raymond (63). Other uses of these pictures are described by Schertz (73) for helping the visual learner with aural comprehension and oral expression, *and* by Janicot (34) to support the understanding of poetry by employing a combination of pictures and question-answer practice.

Visual cues

In the development of the writing skill, Ropert (69) indicates the success she found with the establishment of a school newspaper by which means her students had an opportunity to review structure and vocabulary and attend to matters of formal writing. The technique is easily turned into a speaking project by means of tape and can then be sent to others as a means of correspondence.

A newspaper

Meiden & Murphy (46) write about the use of the language laboratory in the teaching of reading. They used the laboratory to provide exercise in other skills but with the content of the reading material so as to use that exercise to support the reading skill activities.

The lab and reading

German. As with the teaching of French, Politzer (61) has put together a book that provides examples of the application of linguistics to foreign language pedagogy. The work concentrates particularly on the teaching techniques for, and the teaching of, such language elements as phonology, morphology, syntax, and vocabulary. Standard procedures are presented: contrast, drills of different kinds, use of English, and the like.

Application of linguistics to classroom pedagogy (German)

In attempting to overcome students' problems with clusters and juncture in German pronunciation, Reichmann (64) suggests shorter and shorter pauses in putting together word segments where these problems occur. Such a technique allows for some humor and yet accomplishes a specific task.

Humor in the classroom

In teaching German grammar, Rosenbaum (70) and Holschuh (33) attempt to relate the grammatical structure being drilled to either experience with one's environment or to a game situation. In working with pattern practice for the same reason, Mathieu (45) has developed a series of questions that forces the teacher to understand what the technique is about and how it is used in the teaching of German structure.

Learning is fun

Ratych (62), noticing the difficulty of German programs in this country to include appropriate writing experiences, sets up a series of activities, themes, and exercises that adds up to a program for writing German, beginning with language similar to the spoken language (grammatical exercises, dehydrated sentences, etc.) and building to more complicated and freer types of writing (*Nacherzählung*, monologue, description, report, etc.). In the same vein, Gruenbauer (29) offers the keeping of a diary as a means of stimulating writing on all levels. She indicates especially the flexibility of the technique in terms of topics. Examples of actual diaries from different levels are included in the article.

Writing activities

In a description of the Nuffield Foundation German Teaching Materials, Peck (58) indicates that the materials attempt to teach meaning of lexical material through memorization in context. This memorized material is then manipulated and the meanings extended in what may be called *Unterhaltungen*, attempts to reproduce authentic German situations. Visual materials are very much a part of the establishment of the original meaning.

Unterhaltungen

Techniques for advanced courses in secondary schools or even on the college level are reflected in the suggestions of Lukner (42) and Streng (78). Lukner uses the production of a *Hörspiel* as a means of both understanding the genre, the recording and production problems, and maintaining language skills, especially listening and speaking. Streng's suggestions for the use of newspapers in the language classroom tend to force students to use more than one skill at a time—reading for information gathering, listening for understanding, speaking for explanation, writing for giving resumés.

The radio play

King (36) reminds college instructors of foreign languages and German in particular that audiolingual techniques are usable in third- and fourth-year language study. Extensive use of the foreign language in the classroom through question-answer techniques, resumé of previous class content, controlled lecture with blackboard to facilitate comprehension, short essay and/or listening experience turned into a composition on a weekly basis, and tests in the foreign language are the major points of audiolingual technique carry-over into advanced college courses.

Maintaining the audiolingual in the advanced classes

Spanish. Concerned about the reading process, Arellano (3) relates some of the techniques she uses with FLES students to make sure that students are "ready" to make the transition to reading: familiarity with the sound system through a variety of oral genres, familiarity with the symbols, gradual transition

Transition to reading in a FLES program

from sound to letter, oral reading. Once the transition has been made and the pupil feels comfortable with it, he can begin the process of reading.

Coleman (21) reports that the use of foreign language films, in this case Spanish, served as an important adjunct to advanced conversation and composition courses on the college level. He found the films valuable in four ways: (*1*) they promote interest in the people and their culture; (*2*) they help increase comprehension; (*3*) they give the student an overall view of the geographic location and condition of the Spanish-speaking communities; (*4*) they break up the regular classroom routine.

Use of the film

The techniques, procedures, and strategies reported here both in experimental and nonexperimental literature suggest that during 1968 at least some attention was given to communicating results of classroom and experimental "research" concerning these areas to the profession. It is difficult at times to see how all of this fits together to answer specific questions. But, if nothing else, this review indicates that the search for more efficient learning procedures continues and that progress is being made in answering some of the questions that face the practitioner.

References, Methods

1 Adams, E. N.; Morrison, H. W.; Reddy, J. M. Conversation with a computer as a technique of language instruction. Modern Language Journal, 52:i (January 1968) 3–16.

2 Alatis, James E., ed. Report of the nineteenth annual round table meeting on linguistics and language studies: contrastive linguistics and its pedagogical implications. Georgetown University Press, Washington, D.C., 1968.

3 Arellano, Sonya I. From speaking to reading. Hispania, 51 (1968) 312–316.

4 Banathy, Bela, ed. Proceedings of the 1967 MLA conference on applied linguistics. Modern Language Journal, 52:iv (April 1968) 205–219.

5 Bennett, W. A. Aspects of language and language teaching. Cambridge University Press, London, 1968.

6 Birkenmayer, Sigmund S. A selective bibliography of works related to the teaching of Slavic languages and literatures in the United States and Canada, 1942–1967. MLA/ERIC/ACTFL, New York, 1968.

7 Birkmaier, Emma M.; Lange, Dale L. Foreign language instruction. Review of Educational Research, 37:vi (April 1967) 186–199.

8 Birkmaier, Emma M.; Lange, Dale L. A selective bibliography on the teaching of foreign languages, 1920–1966. Foreign Language Annals, 1:iv (May 1968) 318–353.

9 Bolger, Philip A. The effect of teacher Spanish language fluency upon student achievement in a bilingual science program. Dissertation Abstracts, 28 (1968) 3403A (St. John's).

10 Bolinger, Dwight. The theorist and the language teacher. Foreign Language Annals, 2:ii (October 1968) 30–41.

11 Brooks, Nelson. Teaching culture in the foreign language classroom. Foreign Language Annals, 1:iii (March 1968) 204–217.

12 Burling, Robbins. Some outlandish proposals for the teaching of foreign languages. Language Learning, 18:i, ii (June 1968) 61–75.

13 Campa, Arthur L. Teaching Hispanic culture through folklore. ERIC Focus Report No. 2 on the Teaching of Foreign Languages. MLA Materials Center, New York, 1968.

14 Carroll, John B. Contributions of research to foreign language teaching. Modern Language Journal, 49:v (May 1965) 273–281.

15 Carroll, John B. Memorandum: on needed research in the psycholinguistic and applied psycholinguistic aspects of language teaching. Foreign Language Annals, 1:iii (March 1968) 236–238.

16 Carroll, John B. Research in foreign language teaching: the last five years. In: Mead, Robert G., ed. Reports of the Working Committees of the Northeast Conference. MLA Materials Center, New York, 1966, p. 7–58.

17 Carroll, John B. Research in teaching foreign languages. In: Gage, N. L., ed. Handbook of research on teaching. Rand McNally, Chicago, 1963, p. 1060–1100.

18 Carroll, John B. The study of language. Harvard University Press, Cambridge, Mass., 1953.

19 Chastain, Kenneth D. A comparison of the audio-lingual habit theory and the cognitive code learning theory to the teaching of introductory college Spanish. Dissertation Abstracts, 29 (1968) 830A (Purdue).

20 Chastain, Kenneth D.; Woerdehoff, Frank J. A methodological study comparing the audio-lingual habit theory and the cognitive code-learning theory. Modern Language Journal, 52:v (May 1968) 268-279.

21 Coleman, Ben C. A clinical report of the use of motion pictures in foreign language teaching. Hispania, 51 (1968) 291-294.

22 del Olmo, Guillermo. Professional and pragmatic perspectives on the audio-lingual approach: introduction and review. Foreign Language Annals, 2:ii (October 1968) 19-29.

23 Donoghue, Mildred R. Foreign languages and the elementary school child. William C. Brown, Dubuque, Ia., 1968.

24 Edgerton, Mills F., Jr. Liberated expression. In: Bird, Thomas E.,ed. Foreign language learning: research and development: an assessment. Reports of the Working Committees of the Northeast Conference on the Teaching of Foreign Languages, MLA Materials Center, New York, 1968, p. 75-118.

25 Elkins, Robert J. An evaluation of an intensive summer language program for secondary school students and suggestions for the improvement of future intensive programs. Dissertation Abstracts, 28 (1968) 4373A-4374A (Kansas).

26 Freudenstein, Reinhold. Methodische Rundschau:II Bericht aus Deutschland: Testen, Tests und Testverfahren. Unterrichtspraxis, 1:i (1968) 110-113.

27 Freudenstein, Reinhold. Methodische Rundschau:II. Bericht aus Deutschland: Vier Jahre PL, PI, PU. Unterrichtspraxis, 1:ii (1968) 89-93.

28 Grittner, Frank. Maintaining foreign language skills for the advanced-course dropout. Foreign Language Annals, 2:ii (December 1968) 205-211. (Also published separately as ERIC Focus Report No. 1.)

29 Gruenbauer, Anne K. Tagebuch-technique and writing skill. Unterrichtspraxis, 1:i (1968) 37-41.

30 Hanzeli, Victor E. Linguistics and the language teacher. Foreign Language Annals, 2:ii (October 1968) 42-50.

31 Harmon, John T., ed. 1967 ACTFL bibliography. Foreign Language Annals, 1:i (October 1967) 80-90; 1:ii (December 1967) 178-181; 1:iii (March 1968) 270-280; 1:iv (May 1968) 371-387.

32 Heise, Edward T. Language methodology: an order of priorities. French Review, 41:vi (May 1968) 853-860.

33 Holschuh, Albrecht. "Maus im Haus": Ein Spiel im Dativ und Akkusativ. Unterrichtspraxis, 1:i (1968) 28-30.

34 Janicot, Aimé. La dernière fleur: exercise audio-visuel. Le Français dans le Monde, 55 (Mars 1968) 26-32.

35 Keating, Raymond F. A study of the effectiveness of language laboratories. Institute of Administrative Research, Teachers College, Columbia University, New York, 1963.

36 King, Janet K. The use of audiolingual techniques in the third and fourth-year college classroom. Foreign Language Annals, 2:ii (December 1968) 185-194.

37 Lange, Dale L. Methodische Rundschau:I. The American scene: programmed learning. Unterrichtspraxis, 1:2 (1968) 84-88.

38 Lange, Dale L. Methodische Rundschau:I. The American scene: testing. Unterrichtspraxis, 1:i (1968) 107-109.

39 Lange, Dale L. The pre-reading period for adolescents: an examination. In: Birkmaier, Emma M., ed. Acquiring foreign language reading skills. Minnesota State Department of Education, St. Paul, 1967, p. 1-12.

40 Lange, Dale L., ed. 1968 ACTFL annual bibliography. Foreign Language Annals, 2:iv (May 1969) 483-530.

41 Language-Teaching Abstracts. Ed. by English Teaching Information Centre and the Centre for Information on Language Teaching. Published by Cambridge University Press. (Available from 32 East 57th Street, New York.)

42 Lukner, Roland F. Unser erster Hörspielversuch: Ein Beitrag zum Deutschunterricht mit dem Tonbandgerät. Unterrichtspraxis, 1:ii (1968) 32-35.

43 Lusetti, Walter I. A comparison of approaches to beginning Spanish instruction in grade seven. Dissertation Abstracts, 28 (1968) 3190A (Oregon).

44 Marty, Fernand. Teaching French. Audio-Visual Publications, Roanoke, Va., 1968.

45 Mathieu, G. Bording. Teaching procedures for pattern practice: a self-test. Unterrichtspraxis, 1:i (1968) 46-53.

46 Meiden, Walter; Murphy, Joseph A. The use of the language laboratory to teach the reading lesson. Modern Language Journal, 52:i (January 1968) 23-25.

47 Mildenberger, Andrea; Liao, Allen Yuan-Heng. ERIC documents on the teaching of foreign languages: list number 1. Foreign Language Annals, 2:ii (December 1968) 222-247.

48 Morrison, H. W.; Adams, E. N. Pilot study of a CAI laboratory in German. Modern Language Journal, 52:v (May 1968) 279-287.

49 Mueller, Theodore H. Proceedings of the seminar on programmed learning. Appleton-Century-Crofts, New York, 1968.

50 Mueller, Theodore H. Programmed language instruction: help for the linguistically underprivileged. Modern Language Journal, 52:ii (February 1968) 79-84.

51 Mueller, Theodore H.; Niedzielski, Henri. The influence of discrimination training on pronunci-

ation. Modern Language Journal, 52:vii (November 1968) 410-416.

52 Muller, Daniel H.; Muller, Trinidad. The problem of interference in beginning Portuguese. Modern Language Journal, 52:iv (April 1968) 201-205.

53 Newmark, Leonard; Reibel, David A. Necessity and sufficiency in language learning. International Review of Applied Linguistics in Language Teaching, 6:ii (May 1968) 145-161.

54 Oliva, Peter F. Modern trends in teaching foreign languages. In: Roucek, Joseph S., ed. The study of foreign languages. Philosophical Library, New York, p. 328-338.

55 Oller, John W.; Obrecht, Dean H. Pattern drill and communicative activity: a psycholinguistic experiment. International Review of Applied Linguistics in Language Teaching, 6:ii (May 1968) 165-174.

56 Ornstein, Jacob. Programmed instruction and educational technology in the language field: boon or failure? Modern Language Journal, 52:vii (November 1968) 401-410.

57 Paquette, F. André, ed. Foreign Language Annals. Published by the American Council on the Teaching of Foreign Languages, 62 Fifth Avenue, New York.

58 Peck, A. J. Teaching meaning. International Review of Applied Linguistics in Language Teaching, 6:i (February 1968) 23-35.

59 Politzer, Robert L. An experiment in the presentation of parallel and contrasting structures. Language Learning, 18:i, ii (June 1968) 35-43.

60 Politzer, Robert L. The role and place of explanation in the pattern drill. International Review of Applied Linguistics in Language Teaching, 6:iv (November 1968) 315-331.

61 Politzer, Robert L. Teaching German: a linguistic orientation. Blaisdell, Waltham, Mass., 1968.

62 Ratych, Joanna M. Vom Sprechen zum Schreiben: Versuch einer systematischen Aufsatzlehre für "Composition"-Kurse. German Quarterly, 41:iii (May 1968) 422-432.

63 Raymond, André. Emploi d'un support visuel pour les exercises de fixation. Le Français dans le Monde, 54 (Janvier-Février 1968) 25-29.

64 Reichmann, Eberhard. Tackling cluster and juncture problems in pronunciation drills. Unterrichtspraxis, 1:i (1968) 44-45.

65 Reichmann, Eberhard, ed. Unterrichtspraxis. Available from TAP, 339 Walnut Street, Philadelphia, Pa.

66 Rivers, Wilga M. Contrastive linguistics in textbooks and classroom. In: Alatis, James E., ed. Report of the nineteenth annual round table meeting on linguistics and language study: contrastive linguistics and its pedagogical implications. Georgetown University Press, Washington, D.C., 1968, p. 151-158.

67 Rivers, Wilga M. Teaching foreign language skills. University of Chicago Press, 1968.

68 Robinett, Betty W., ed. TESOL quarterly. Available from Executive Secretary, TESOL (Teachers of English to Speakers of Other Languages), James E. Alatis, Institute of Languages and Linguistics, Georgetown University, Washington, D.C.

69 Ropert, Suzanne. Un journal scolaire au Liban. Le Français dans le Monde, 60 (Octobre-Novembre 1968) 33-38.

70 Rosenbaum, Eric. The reflexive verb story: an experience unit. Unterrichtspraxis, 1:i (1968) 23-26.

71 Roucek, Joseph, ed. The study of foreign languages. Philosophical Library, New York, 1968.

72 Ruplin, Ferdinand A.; Russell, John R. A type of computer-assisted instruction. German Quarterly, 41:i (January 1968) 84-88.

73 Schertz, Pierre. Les vrais faux débutants dans l'apprentissage du français, langue étrangère. Le Français dans le Monde, 59 (Septembre 1968) 33-39.

74 Simches, Seymour O. The classroom revisited. In: Bird, Thomas E., ed. Foreign language learning: research and development: an assessment. Reports of the Working Committees of the Northeast Conference on the Teaching of Foreign Languages. MLA Materials Center, New York, 1968, p. 47-73.

75 Smith, Philip D., Jr.; Baranyi, Helmut A. A comparison study on the effectiveness of the traditional and audio-lingual approaches to foreign language instruction utilizing language laboratory equipment. Project no. 7-0133; Grant no. OEC-1-7-070133-0445. U.S. Department of Health, Education, and Welfare, Washington, D.C., 1968.

76 Smith, Philip D., Jr.; Berger, Emanual. An assessment of three language teaching strategies utilizing three language laboratory systems. Final report. Project no. 5-0683; Grant no. OE-7-48-9013-272. U.S. Department of Health, Education, and Welfare, Washington, D.C., 1968.

77 Sprague, Robert O. Factors in students' abilities which condition effectiveness of teaching methods in Spanish. Dissertation Abstracts, 28 (1968) 4393 (UCLA).

78 Streng, Rosalie. An oral exercise. German Quarterly, 41:i (January 1968) 134.

79 Suther, Judith D. Anti-intellectualism in modern language learning. French Review, 41:vi (May 1968) 849-852.

80 Using picture writing. TAVOR Bulletin, 3:vii (1968) 1-7; 3:ix (1968) 3-7. [TAVOR Bulletin, Tavor Aids, P.O. Box 282, Forest Hills, N.Y. 11375]

81 Valdman, Albert. Programmed instruction versus guided learning in foreign language acquisition. Unterrichtspraxis, 1:ii (1968) 1-14.

82 Valette, Rebecca M. Some conclusions to be drawn from the Pennsylvania Study. National Association of Language Laboratory Directors Newsletter, 3:iii (March 1969) 17-19.

83 Wajskop-Hianne, M.; Renkin, A. Semi-programmation et controle psycho-pedagogique. International Review of Applied Linguistics in Language Teaching, 6:i (February 1968) 63-86.

84 Williamson, Vern G. A pilot program in teaching Spanish: an intensive approach. Modern Language Journal, 52:ii (February 1968) 73-78.

11

Machine-aided language learning

Introduction

James W. Dodge

Brown University

When one attempts to speak of using electromechanical-optical equipment in the teaching of foreign languages, there is a great deal of linguistic confusion. No proper nomenclature has as yet been assigned to this field formed by the union of foreign language teaching and the branch of the applied physical sciences and engineering that so many of us foreign language teachers hastily label "technology." As an example of this confusion one need only look at the profession. The National Education Association (NEA) recently attempted to change the name of its Department of Audiovisual Instruction. The members were offered three simultaneous alternatives: Educational Media Association, Association for Instructional Technology, and American Educational Communication Association (13). The NEA membership rejected all three substitutes. The Northeast Conference on the Teaching of Foreign Languages, planned in 1968, resorted to the literary device of the colon and named its 1969 meeting, whose theme was the use of media in the teaching of foreign languages, "Sight and Sound: The Sensible and Sensitive Use of Audio-Visual Aids" (17). The American Council on the Teaching of Foreign Languages (ACTFL) simply omitted considering this field when it set up committees in areas where it considered professional action most urgently needed. Had it not been for the section of the ACTFL bibliography (6, 28) succinctly named "Materials and Equipment," it would have been forgotten. The National Association of Language Laboratory Directors (NALLD) prefers to use the term "machine-aided language learning" to describe this larger field of which language laboratories are but a small part. It would appear that for the purposes of this chapter the NALLD term would be most fitting. "Language learning" is focused narrowly enough and "machine-aided" is comprehensive enough to account for all of the technological events that happened in foreign language teaching during the year 1968.

It was hinted at above that there sometimes exists a certain antipathy between the two disciplines involved in machine-aided language learning, viz., the applied physical sciences and

Decision: nomenclature

foreign language teaching. This can be understood if one has devoted one's life to language and literature and is called upon to deal with the technicalities of electronics, optics, and mechanical engineering. It is also true that an engineer is seldom able to see all the rationales of foreign language *learning*, let alone teaching. Sadly, the vested interests on both sides frequently attempt to overawe their opposite numbers with their own jargon, exaggerations, and unessential triumphs. For instance, it seems unnecessary that *American School & University* (57) should describe as an "attractive feature" of the New York University language laboratory the "vast surface, easily 25 feet long, with a terrifying array of switches which enable the teacher to play on his students as if he were conducting an electronic symphony." Few classroom teachers of foreign language would care to conduct their students like an electronic symphony, and the one sure way to make an array of switches terrifying is to call it that. On the other hand, the language teacher who couches his conversations to the engineer in behavioral, linguistic, or literary terms is equally appalling. Thus, it is necessary for each side to fight against a communications gap.

Unnecessary antipathies between two fields

Speaking before the 1968 National Convention of the Institute of Electrical and Electronics Engineers, Shelley (69) foresaw an emergence of a humanistic society from what he termed our present industrial society. If it is true that the individual being and humanistic endeavor will become more and more prominent in our lives, then it is perhaps justified for teachers of the humanities (and this includes foreign language teachers in the U.S. since the prime goal of most of their instruction is humanistic) to naturally want to retreat from the inroads that the engineers have been making into foreign language teaching methodology. The teachers feel that Truth belongs to them, and not to the electronic contraptions and optical gadgets that exist as machine aids to language learning. Luckily there is a sufficient number of foreign language teachers who see machine-aided techniques as a way of accomplishing their work more efficiently. An attempt will be made to outline some of the prominent trends of thought that these two groups of independently dedicated people — the engineers and the teachers — produced during 1968.

Machine-aided techniques can enrich teaching the humanities

Media

According to figures released in October 1967 (34) a group of over 1,000 teachers in secondary and elementary education reported the utilization of various media devices shown in Table 1.

Brown & Fiks (8) reported that some 75 percent of the group of foreign language teachers investigated used the tape recorder either in its basic form or in the more complex version of the language laboratory. It should be noted, however, that these data are based on a small sample of 19 university language programs and are not truly equatable to the NEA data in Table 1. They do show agreement in the predominance of the use of the filmstrip projector (67 percent) and the 16-mm motion picture projector (52 percent) as educational media in the foreign languages.

What do we want in the way of technological aids?

TABLE 1. Percentage of elementary and secondary school teachers using various media.

Medium	Percentage of teachers using
Silent film strip projector	81.2%
Phonograph	79.0
16-mm motion picture projector	77.4
Overhead projector	61.5
Tape recorder	53.8
Opaque projector	49.4
Sound filmstrip projector	43.9
TV broadcasts (open circuit)	39.6
8-mm motion picture projector	16.0
Closed circuit TV	7.0
Computer-assisted instruction terminal	1.4

With this exception the percentages in Table 1 are probably also indicative of foreign language teachers' media utilization habits. The underlying reason for these devices to be ranked in this specific order and the reason that far more than half of the foreign language teachers use the tape recorder is due to the availability of materials for classroom use (Martin, 48). There can be little argument that filmstrips, phonograph records, and 16-mm motion picture films are universally available. This puts these three pieces of equipment at the top of the list.

Overhead projector

Another observation that can be made by comparing the NEA data with the Brown & Fiks data concerns the absence of the overhead projector from the university-level foreign language programs while 61.5 percent of the elementary and secondary teachers polled used this device. There are endless amounts of materials available for use on the overhead projector in most subjects; foreign language is the exception. Still the overhead projector is the one machine aid that allows artistically unskilled persons to produce quite professional-looking materials that can be used to good advantage in the classroom. Even though there is no large source of prepared foreign language teaching materials for the overhead projector at the university level, it is a shame that none of the 19 colleges chosen by these researchers for their "advanced techniques of instruction" could muster one overhead projector among the various devices used in their foreign language programs.

More FL materials need to be developed for the overhead projector

An excellent description as well as a fine rationale for using an overhead projector in the foreign language classroom is given by Pond (64). He compares it favorably with the blackboard which, too, is always at the teacher's fingertips and is relatively low in cost. But the overhead projector allows the preparation of visuals before class and a very sophisticated presentation of the visuals during the class. Wrenn (83) describes one use of the overhead projector that is suitable for the machine-aided learning of any language dialogue in addition to the Chinese dialogue in his example. This writer has used Wrenn's technique with success in a German language class. It consists of typing mnemonic letters symbolizing each expression or word of the target dialogue on a sheet of paper for transfer to an overhead projector transparency with any office copying machine that uses a xerographic, thermographic, or photographic process. Such machines have been available for a number of years now, and their clerical usefulness has made them appear in almost every school building in the country.

The projector used as a mnemonic device

The exact gains that might be expected from using an overhead projector in foreign language instruction can be extrapolated from a study by Miller & Colligan (50) who divided a first-year bookkeeping class into a control and an experimental group. The latter students were taught the same material as the former except that all presentations were made with the overhead projector instead of with the conventional chalkboard. It was observed that the use of this machine aid allowed the experimental group to cover the same material more quickly and with no detectable loss of quality. This is the usual gain of machine-aided learning.

Overhead vs. blackboard

Because the overhead projector does not produce nearly as much heat, does not require a darkened room, is easier to carry and work with accounts for the fact that it is slowly displacing the opaque projector in classroom use. Although transparencies

Overhead vs. the opaque projector

must be prepared in advance (instead of projecting original hard copy) this process is quick and inexpensive and can no longer be looked upon as a disadvantage in the choice of the overhead projector over the opaque projector.

Television

While it may be true that teachers will use machine aids to a greater or lesser extent depending upon the availability of materials, it is perhaps more interesting to examine the desires teachers have for new equipment. The same NEA study (34) cited above also inquired what single piece of audiovisual equipment that was not now available the teachers would most like to have in their classrooms. This resulted in the data for a population of 1,145 shown in Table 2.

TABLE 2. Percentage of elementary and secondary school teachers desiring various media.

Medium	Percentage of teachers desiring
TV broadcasts (open circuit)	23.6%
Closed circuit TV	18.3
Opaque projector	7.7
Computer-assisted instruction terminal	7.3
Sound filmstrip projector	7.0
Overhead projector	5.9
Tape recorder	5.6
8-mm motion picture projector	1.9
16-mm motion picture projector	1.5
Phonograph	0.8
Silent filmstrip projector	0.3

Observations pertinent to these data are that what teachers already have is low on their list of priorities, e.g., silent filmstrip projector, phonograph, and 16-mm motion picture projector; also, a device such as the 8-mm motion picture projector for which there are only a very few materials available is ranked low in desirability. Perhaps most important is the large number of classroom teachers who indicated that they would like to have some form of television.

Television fits as logically into the desires of American education as milk does into the school lunch program. It is widely accepted by both youth and adults; it is an accessible medium for the teacher to use in the class without great pains; and it lends a certain prestige to the teacher, the curriculum, and the school.

TV is everywhere, why not use it in the classroom?

315

In short, television is a medium with which both teacher and student can identify in the learning situation as well as outside it. The cries for more and better television teaching materials may be indicative of the inflated growth rate of classroom television spurred on by federal subsidy. However, the wish for improved TV programming is in many ways no different than the desire for more and better printed teaching materials that has been expressed for half a millenium.

The popularization of television as a medium, i.e., as a means of presenting a remote environment, must obviously be credited to the commercial networks. Educational television (ETV), although dedicated, informative, and frequently watched in some homes, is only a very small part of most students' conceptions of television.

The student's concept of TV

Color television

According to the networks approximately 25 percent of the viewing audience in the United States watches color television. When people buy new TV sets, this figure will increase as the price of color receivers drops and the quality of the color picture continues to improve. Thus, within a period of five or six years, which is the time it takes an average family to purchase a new TV set, it would be safe to estimate that over half of the students in our classrooms will be watching color television at home. During 1968 they watched black-and-white television in school almost without exception.

Color TV in the home; why not for the classroom?

The obvious question is whether or not there is any advantage in providing color television for foreign language instruction. At the moment the predominant use of black and white seems to satisfy everyone's requirements. The search is not for color programs but for better programs and better technical quality in black and white. Kanner & Rosenstein (38), working with the U.S. Army, found that color television did not provide any enhancement of student learning when compared with black and white. In the field of medicine it was found that pathologists are able to make diagnoses more accurately by looking at a black-and-white picture than by looking at a color picture. It should be noted, however, that considerable experience on the part of the pathologist is necessary to make any diagnosis at all via televised pictures, but the lack of fidelity in the color image is sometimes misleading in judging tissue conditions.

Certainly the same compensations in our optic senses that make contemporary color television acceptable for home entertainment would apply to the use of color in foreign language instruction. That is, although the reds are somewhat orange in hue, we see them quite acceptably as red. Our dependence upon the true reproduction of the color is not as great as a doctor's looking at an inflammation.

What can be said for the case of color television? It is roughly two to three times as expensive as black and white. It is imperfect in its rendition of reds since it is balanced to make flesh tones appear most natural. It is hard to maintain a balance of color without frequent manual resetting, and this results in either fluorescent orange or bright green faces against a background of purple skies. But color television does have two important advantages. First, it is aesthetically more pleasing to watch than black and white. Although the latter is certainly sufficient, color is more interesting for the viewer and certainly a more fertile medium for the producer. Although we hesitate to compare our intellects with those of childish simplicity, who ever heard of a monochrome Little Red Riding Hood?

Aesthetically more pleasing

The second major point in favor of color is somewhat more tangible. There is more information present in a color picture than in a black-and-white picture. This additional information comes from the fact that in composing a black-and-white picture, the electronic circuits have a very severe limitation known as the gray scale. The extremes of the gray scale are black at one end and white at the other, but in reality no television picture is capable of true black or white—only shades of gray that vary in intensity. Color television, on the other hand, has not only the gray scale but also the three primary color scales, each of which adds to the definition of the picture. To demonstrate this to yourself watch a color TV picture for a short time and then turn the color control off and examine the black-and-white picture. Everything is still there, but appears less distinctly, and shadows have tended to become very confusing where they had hardly been noticeable in color.

More information present in color TV

It is this writer's feeling that color television will gradually displace black-and-white television even in the classroom. The only literature to support this now is, sadly, a paid advertisement for a color television component that declares, "Color gives your television presentations more impact, more dramatic interest and emotional appeal, and of critical importance, it puts more information on the screen." Perhaps the next few years will document this claim and refute those like Kanner (36) who find that color does not appear to provide any important learning cues that are not present in black and white or are not compensated for by the sound track.

Instructional television

Whether it is in color or in black and white, instructional television (ITV) is here to stay. Its application in the foreign language teaching field is epitomized by the *Parlons Français* (62) series for teaching French language (and a good deal of culture) in elementary schools including those that are not fortunate enough to have a full-time French teacher. The series was filmed well. The segments are short, and each attempts to teach just enough for the time allowed.

A popular ITV program

Even though foreign languages in the elementary schools may be growing less popular in some regions, the techniques of using the *Parlons Français* curriculum are worth preserving. First, the producer did not rely on the comparatively poor picture quality of even the finest television equipment but chose color motion picture film which has 10 or 12 times as much information as television. That is, the picture can be projected in very large sizes for big audiences without loss of picture quality. If the series had been produced in videotape its usefulness would undoubtedly have been less.

The color film version

Second, individual school systems were able to purchase the films either in 8-mm or in 16-mm for their own use. A schedule could then be set up for the films to rotate from one school to another. Alternately, schools were also able to utilize the ETV broadcasts if they could fit their other scheduled classes around the station's broadcast time, or local ETV outlets that served the schools more directly were able to tape and rebroadcast the programs at a more convenient time.

Advantages

The amount of classroom follow-up a school gave the *Parlons Français* lesson that came into the classroom by television depended upon its personnel situation. It is without doubt true that the presence of a French teacher in the classroom would be a great advantage. That way television would not be replacing the teacher as it should never be allowed to do. But it is also probably true that many children were given French language instruction that consisted solely of Ann Slack's televised explanation and practice. Thus, there can be an inherent danger in pursuing the goals of instructional television. These are outlined by Tabor (80) of the Santa Ana (Calif.) Unified and Junior College Districts, viz., help strengthen and control the district's curriculum as well as strengthen and control the subject matter

The administrator's zeal to economize can destroy the true value of TV

taught and provide opportunities for team teaching effectiveness and economy in such areas as foreign language, music, etc. The inherent danger is that the administrator's zeal to economize in such areas as foreign languages might prevent him from placing a classroom foreign language teacher in the schools into which he is piping foreign language programs.

In fairness to Tabor and ITV in general the other advantages should also be enumerated. These include the opportunities the system offered for teacher training, the increased communication capability throughout the school district, the exposure of all district students to the expertise of the television teacher, and the opportunity of classroom viewing of any filmed or televised event of the past or present. The Santa Ana ITV classrooms were outfitted with monitors that look very much like home TV sets. The system utilized telephone company cables for the distribution of programs to the individual schools.

Television distribution systems

There are two ways to free oneself from the high expense of leasing telephone lines for the distribution of instructional television throughout a school district. One is to utilize a 2,500-megaHertz television transmission system. This instructional television fixed system (ITFS) is a microwave band capable of providing omnidirectional radiation of a television signal over a line-of-sight path of about 15 miles. Greater distances are covered with the installation of repeaters or relay transmitters. *ITFS* In this manner the school district can transmit any of several programs simultaneously for selective reception by the individual schools. Although this does free one from monthly telephone charges, there is still the necessity of maintaining a rather complex system of transmitters and receivers. Information on ITFS 2,500-megaHertz television for those interested is contained in a well-edited document by Cooper, et al. (12). The technology involved is quite commonplace in the communications industry, and there are at least four large companies that market such equipment on a nationwide basis.

The other alternative to the rental of transmission lines is to work closely with the local licensing of community antenna television (CATV) companies. CATV is presently the subject of considerable public debate in regard to various aspects of its home entertainment service. It appears that the CATV operators are winning their petitions to set up large central antennas and transmit nearly flawless television signals into private homes

CATV can be made to serve the public interest

via their own cables in return for a monthly charge. To be permitted this right, however, the franchise holder must first obtain a license from local authorities. Hill (30) cites Smithtown, N.Y., where a CATV installation must provide considerable public service to obtain a license. Such service includes the free installation of CATV receiving terminals in every public and private school in the town, free use of one channel of the CATV network to any school district lying wholly or partly within the town, and, eventually, free television cable interconnections among all schools and school districts lying wholly or partly within the town. Thus, the private enterprise of CATV is made to serve the public interest. This plan will have its opponents who base their objections on political grounds, but it is one very effective way to lower the cost of transmission of television for instructional use.

A note should be made on the production of materials for foreign language instructional television. Just as foreign language texts are either published by commercial houses on an it-better-make-money-or-we-will-not-publish-it basis or by publicly subsidized efforts (compare the ways that the publication costs of French language texts are paid for to the ways Chinese language texts are funded!), so it is, too, with the materials used on television in foreign language teaching. These include films as well as videotapes.

Television films

The few foreign language courses using integrated films that might be suitable for television transmission are well known to the profession. Less well known is the endless number of supplementary films that can be obtained at moderate expense from distributors, rental libraries, and regional audiovisual centers. The main reason so few of these films are ever widely publicized is that the film industry, like the publishing industry, is more interested in high volume audiences, and foreign language films are seldom popular enough to fall into this category unless they are full-length features.

An endless number of supplementary films can be used in an FL program

In an attempt to promote interest in the humanities the now financially emasculated National Endowment for the Humanities funded a grant to the Boston educational television station, WGBH-TV, for the production of five instructional television films in the humanities. These were all for use at the secondary level. The 63 proposals included nine—that is, about 15 percent—that dealt with language instruction or, perhaps more important, some interdisciplinary form of language study. None of these nine were judged worthy enough to receive a production grant.

Hauser (29) describes a very simple device that is demonstrated in one of the films mentioned above (19). The subject was the use of television for classroom instruction. The device is a four-channel selector and a headset (very similar to the equipment supplied at the listening end of a simultaneous translation installation) that allows the student to choose one of four different sound tracks to accompany the picture. The selection of the channel depends upon the student's individual ability, interest, and motivation. After the presentation of the single-picture/multiple-sound lesson, the teacher attempts to focus the students' thought during a discussion session. The applicability of such a simple device might easily be extended to foreign language teaching. If a school is equipped with a language laboratory, it is a simple matter to use a 16-mm motion picture projector for the picture while listening to any of a number of graded sound tracks over the multiple program channels available in most installations.

Multiple sound track for some film provides flexibility

Although this is as close as the ITV humanities project got to being of use to the foreign language teaching profession, it is one example of what might be done to make television an effective instructional medium. Skinner (73) calls for such properly written materials, especially ones that do not just give facts but leave unanswered questions in the minds of the viewers with the hope that they will be motivated to study further. In commonly taught foreign languages, and even more so in the critical foreign languages, there is a very great need for some bold investment of money and talent to produce filmed materials for television use to replace the limited or inadequate films presently available.

A bold investment of money needed

Videotape recorder

In addition to the ITV and ETV aspects of television there is also another outgrowth of the industry that has made a place for itself in many branches of American education including foreign language teaching. This is the videotape recorder (VTR). Originally this device was used by the networks to allow them to get away from having to broadcast home entertainment programs from a live camera. In doing this their productions were made more flexible and costs were reduced. These machines took magnetic recording tape that was two inches wide. The recording heads were in a configuration referred to as quadra-

Commercial VTR too expensive

plex. They are still used in broadcast television and can be purchased at prices starting at about $40,000. That is approximately what it costs to put three additional classrooms into a new building and is obviously prohibitive for school use except on the most grandiose scale.

Continued research on the part of electronics firms has produced two types of less expensive videotaping equipment that put the VTR within the realm of possibility for a high school or college budget. They start at around $1,000 for camera, recorder, and monitor; color is available at increased cost. Such machines are all known either as helical scan or slant-track; these terms refer to the path that the recording heads describe on the magnetic tape. This tape is either an inch or a half-inch wide; one-inch tape is a middle-of-the-road solution between the extremes of the two-inch quality and the half-inch economy. No helical scan machine is suitable for use in broadcast television. Such programs must be transmitted by sending the tapes through the mail or by messenger. There is also a difficulty one encounters when playing tapes made on a different machine. That is, if one owns brand X, the tapes that are played on it must have been recorded on a brand X machine of the same tape width. Similarly, brand Y machines only play tapes made on brand Y, etc. 1968 saw most of the reputable manufacturers of helical scan VTR equipment providing compatability between their own machines; this had been a problem up to now and might still warrant investigation if one is in the market for an inexpensive VTR.

VTR now within reach of high school and college

Kanner (37) reports that the U.S. Army has increased the number of training bases that use videotape for the distribution of television teaching programs from 10 to 40 in the decade 1958–68. He mentions uses in instructor training, supplemental classroom materials, individualization of lessons because of the replayability of the tapes, and the possibilities of sharing materials produced at other training bases. Interestingly enough, he notes a resistance to the use of instructional materials that were produced outside of each local command on the ground that if it was not made locally, it cannot be any good. Perhaps this all too human quality of vainglory should be taken into account by all who plan to write foreign language teaching materials for use by other schools.

VTR and the U.S. Army

Of the uses for videotape just mentioned, all of them fit into the teaching of foreign languages. Instructor training is perhaps the spot where the VTR is presently most valuable. Gustafson

VTR an important tool in teacher education

(26) suggests it for student-teacher self-evaluation. Politzer (63) describes the use of the VTR at Stanford for microteaching, which is a part of the standard training for foreign language classroom teachers at that school. Although this technique could be utilized independently of the videotape recorder, Politzer compares its importance to that of the language laboratory in the audiolingual approach to foreign language teaching. McDonald & Allen (47), in research carried out for the U.S. Office of Education on the effects of feedback and teaching models, mention that the VTR was the most important device in their experiments because of its ability to immediately replay and feed back the information that it had just recorded. They equate the "instant replay" capability of the VTR with seeing oneself perform.

The videotape recorder is also suited for classroom instructional use. Jaquith (35) sketched a typical high school application. Sherriffs (70) reports on the University of Oregon's use in teaching the acquisition of musical skills. He observes that more information is transmitted in a given amount of time than with conventional teaching techniques. Behmer (5) describes the production of cultural miniskits for foreign language instruction at Wayne State University. These skits are used both in the university as well as outside. Thus, the VTR has replaced a trip outside the school, or, perhaps more simply, it has only replaced the use of a motion picture film, but it is still a useful tool that is becoming more accessible to the classroom teacher of foreign languages. With a lack of materials for general distribution, the main use of this machine will remain that of producing an awareness of good and bad teaching techniques in teachers—at least for the moment.

VTR in regular classroom instruction

Portable videotape recorder

Recently there has been an increase in the number of companies in the United States that market a truly portable videotape recorder (PVTR). The term has long been used to refer to any machine that was not bolted down, with no indication of how many men it took to carry it. But the currently available six-pound camera and 12-pound recorder pack with a shoulder strap constitute a real PVTR. In view of the fact that such PVTRs are battery operated, it might be more appropriate to call them mobile videotape recorders. Such machines use half-inch magnetic tape and cost about the same as other half-inch VTRs.

Gustafson (26) reported in December 1967 on the use of PVTRs for student-teacher training at Michigan State University.

The following month he began a column in *Audiovisual Instruction* on the PVTR (27). It has appeared sporadically ever since. One of the more recent appearances concerned the general outcry for standards in the PVTR industry. Gustafson (25) commented that the absence of industry standards is what accounts for the availability of devices that let one make personal videotape recordings and still cost less than the price of putting a football team on the field for a season. He points out that the use of these machines is mostly limited to local replay, but this does not mean that they have no practical value. If there is a need for the quality one is used to on the home TV set (viz., resolution, stability, and compatability), one should buy a full-sized VTR.

PVTR still backs quality reproduction

Television viewing problems

With open-ended opportunities for utilizing television in some form in the foreign language classroom, attention should be given to the viewing conditions that exist there. We are all familiar with the six-inch and nine-inch personal TV sets that are sold to receive commercial broadcasts. This size of individual monitor is probably the best way of making telecasts completely visible to all students on a one student:one monitor basis. It has the added advantage that different students can watch different programs, but it is also the most expensive way of solving the viewing problem.

Small sets for individualized learning

Conventional television viewing in the classroom is accomplished by using either 21-inch or 23-inch monitors in as many locations as are necessary for everyone to see the tube. These sets can either be permanently attached to the building or wheeled in and out of the room on carts when needed. The actual location of the monitors in the room is somewhat tricky because the further away one is from the set, the less visible the image appears, and at angles greater than 30 degrees from "straight-on" the ability to perceive what is on the screen is greatly diminished. Neal (55) conducted extensive studies which are succintly reported in *Audiovisual Instruction* (56). These show the limitations imposed by screen size, image (i.e., letter) size, off-center viewing angle, and bandwidth of the signal. For instance, the viewer should not be farther away from the set than 12 to 15 times the screen width. Note that there is a difference between the actual width of a television screen and the diagonal measurement by which it is sold in the store and otherwise commonly referred to. Neal's article contains a num-

The Neal study recommendations

Planning a classroom TV installation

ber of graphs which should be of good use to anyone planning a classroom television installation.

The bandwidth of the signal mentioned by Neal is a rather technical expression that can be reduced to a question of just how expensive the VTR was to purchase. Of course, this is an oversimplification, but it is true that if one starts with the cheapest VTR and progresses dollar by dollar up to the most expensive VTR, the bandwidth of the signal will increase with the increase in money. It will not, however, increase linearly. Neal's results indicate that there is no difference in the student's ability to perceive letters of the Roman alphabet, which is dependent upon the bandwidths of the signal available in the low priced VTRs. Although a smaller bandwidth results in a slightly less well-defined picture, the human eye presumably compensates for the irregularities of the image in much the same way as the human ear compensates for aural dropouts. Thus, it would appear that any foreign language project contemplating the purchase of a low priced VTR would not be well advised to consider too heavily the machine's bandwidth.

The human eye compensates

The third way to view television in the classroom is to use a video projector. This is simply a device that produces a video image and projects it optically for mass viewing. Warning! As the size of the picture increases, the apparent resolution of the image and the viewer's ability to define what is on the screen are diminished. Such video projectors are of two types: Schmidt lens and oil film. The Schmidt lens projector costs from $2,000 to $4,000 and is suitable for audiences of a few hundred people in a darkened room. The oil film projector can hardly be bought (they are usually rented for several thousand dollars a day) but are suitable for audiences of two to three thousand people in a moderately lighted room. Color is available in some projectors at greatly increased cost.

Video projector in the classroom: warning

Film

The concept of visual literacy (18) that is so important in the use of television as a classroom medium is equally important in deciding whether or not to use film for instructional situations. If the film itself is in 35-mm or 16-mm format, it could be televised, but to realize the qualities of high resolution, true color, and greatest visibility of the projected image, it is actually necessary to project directly in the classroom without resorting to a video buffer. If the film is in 8-mm format, its value for classroom use is decreased only by the fact that it is hard to project an 8-mm picture large enough for a big audience. Eight-mm, or more frequently today Super-8, is far more useful in groups of 10 to 12 or individually.

8-mm film excellent for small group instruction

When Thomas A. Edison conceived the motion picture projector, he thought of it as a device that one day would replace the teacher in the schools—or at least that is the interpretation that contemporaries attach to his thoughts. It would be a shame to ascribe such a generalization to a man who was so adept at the application of details. The motion picture projector is no different from any other machine aid to language learning in that it is not a substitute for the teacher but an extension of the teacher. Everyone is familiar with the student reaction when they see that a motion picture projector is set up in their classroom and heave a sigh of relief that there will be no need to concentrate on working in class that day. This is a situation where the film has, indeed, become a substitute for the teacher. It has become a null substitute, and such uses of film are to be avoided. The projector in the classroom must mean work to the students.

Visual media an extension of the teacher

It is possible to make film an important part of foreign language teaching. Sanchez (68) and Chamberlain (11) list many sources of films that foreign language educators can take advantage of for very little money. Edgerton (16), Newmark (58), and Dodge (15) describe several ways in which a film can be employed with considerable finesse in the foreign language curriculum without resorting to local production.

Sources for films

How to use a film

8-mm film

The advent of inexpensive, automatic 8-mm cameras also makes it possible to conquer the photographic techniques when local production seems to be the only way to acquire the right teaching materials. Kemp & Szumski (42) report on the steps involved in making one's own simple 8-mm films. Forsdale (22) cinemagraphically describes a number of useful techniques that can be used in making economical and useful 8-mm films within a local school or individual class. The main advantage of making a film as a class project (and it need not be as spectacular as *War and Peace* nor as timeless as *Gone with the Wind*) is that the entire teaching environment is brought to bear against the instructional problems of foreign language. Fearing (20) used the production of a short 8-mm film as a term project in his German language class in Minneapolis. He saw this as a way to make the students recognize the importance of the proper use of

8-mm film production as an FL class project

the target language. The details of production resulted in a continuing and critical assessment of each student's foreign language performance by his peers, and because of the common goal of the film story such criticism did not result in the usual awkward feelings of peer evaluation in the classroom.

The 8-mm film market changed radically in August 1958 when the photographic industry replaced the previously standard 8-mm format with what they called Super-8. This newer format gives more picture area on the same width of film, viz., 8-mm wide, but it is wholly incompatible with the standard 8-mm cameras and projectors. Sleeman & Crosswhite (74) and Kemp & Szumski (41) give detailed accounts of the history and present state-of-the-art in 8-mm and Super-8 equipment. They also mention the development of sound tracks for 8-mm work and explain the various problems associated with it including the lack of compatibility among different manufacturers' standards.

Super-8

Humphrey (31) gives some reasons why there are so few materials available for 8-mm classroom use. His point is that it is not profitable for commercial producers to market short films (Hail Plutus! once again), but since such short films often prove most useful in the foreign language classroom, they are needed. The solution is for producers to make series of short films that constitute, in effect, a systematic approach to an entire foreign language course. This is, of course, the secret of success for those series such as *Parlons Français, Familia Fernández*, the *Guten Tag* series, and a few others.

Short films: a systematic approach to an entire language course

Just as the production of 8-mm films has become simpler so that it is possible to make films in the classroom, the projection of these films is much easier than what many teachers are used to with the 16-mm older brother. In 1960 Technicolor first marketed a cartridge loaded, continuous-loop 8-mm projector. This was followed by the Fairchild cartridge rear screen projector of slightly different design in 1963. In 1968 Technicolor introduced the 8-mm sound cartridge projector. This device is lightweight, handy, easy to load, and not prohibitively expensive.

"Single concept" cartridges for Technicolor projectors

The materials suppliers have already prepared a large number of short, "single concept" cartridges for Technicolor projectors. Very few such films are directly geared to foreign language use, but imaginative use of single concept films from other disciplines can result in an excellent supplemental exercise in any foreign language class. One especially valuable technique is applicable to the teaching of English to speakers of other languages. If, for example, one is to train physicists from abroad in the ability to lecture more fluently in English, it would be quite natural to use several single concept films demonstrating physics experiments (there are many of these available) and provide the sound track in English. If the silent projector were used, the sound could accompany the film by means of a tape recorder, and the same film cartridge could be used with sound tracks of varying complexity and difficulty.

It is possible to load film cartridges with locally produced footage. There is probably no better way to allow for the inexpensive individual drill of language usage in different social situations, for what better way is there to show a nonnative speaker how to apologize for stepping on a person's toe than to show a film of such a situation. Such social contexts are important because the correct response in the instance of stepping on someone's toe depends on many things that are not linguistic, e.g., the person's appearance, the location, etc. Such individual practice in foreign language can easily be handled in most language laboratories without undue alterations; small cartridge projectors make it possible. If a school is lucky enough to have a learning center with study carrels, the ease with which the visual can be implemented is much greater. Regenstreif (66) goes into considerable detail about just how much equipment can be put into a carrel. It is considerable, and 8-mm film offers a workable way of making the advantages of motion pictures highly accessible.

Inexpensive drill of language usage in different social situations

16-mm film

The technique used to apply sound to an 8-mm film is to stripe the developed film with the magnetic oxide that is used on recording tape. This material is dark brown and is what gives tape its characteristic color. When applied to the edge of motion picture film, it can easily be identified. Sixteen-mm film can also be striped for sound even when there is already an optical sound track on it. Thus, any film—even one that has an English sound track—can be made suitable for use in foreign language teaching. In effect, what the teacher does is to take advantage of the photography, write a script, and record a foreign language sound track over which he has complete control of grammar and lexis. This writer has personally edited a discarded fund-raising film produced for the alumni of his university and made a "travelogue" recorded in French for the magnetic sound track. The result was a short film of totally familiar scenes that intermediate French language students could work with productively.

16-mm film striped for sound gives flexibility

Just as television is a valuable tool in the training of foreign language teachers, motion pictures, too, are useful in this application. It is perhaps not as apparent since there are far many more useful foreign language films available commercially than there are television programs, and the use of film in teacher training is secondary to classroom instructional uses. The major disadvantages in using film for instructor training is that there is no immediate feedback from instant replay; the major advantage is that one is dealing with a professionally produced medium that delivers highest picture quality even in color for a moderate price, and the projection of motion pictures can be accomplished in almost any school in the nation. The Northeast Conference on the Teaching of Foreign Languages for 1969, the work for which was done in 1968, used films to transport its 4,000 conferees into a dozen classrooms scattered throughout the nation. Most of the scenes for the Northeast Conference films were unstaged; they were shot on the day that the lesson would have been taught even if the cameraman had not been present. This use of cinema verité proved quite successful, and the footage collected is being edited into a set of films for public distribution (Dodge, 15).

Films for teacher training can be effective

1969 Northeast Conference report

Other excellent uses of 16-mm film in teacher training include the five-reel series produced in cooperation with the Modern Language Association (39) and the 13-reel Henry Lee Smith (44) series produced by National Educational Television. Less important entries which suffer greatly because of their "talking face" qualities include the eight-reel monologue by Cannaday & Gamba (10) and a seven-reel panel-monologue produced by the Center for Applied Linguistics (45).

Recent improvements in the techniques of using the 16-mm motion picture film include innovations in both the projector and the light source. Besides the self-threading projectors, there is now also one that threads just like a tape recorder, i.e., the film drops into a slot and is driven by a capstan instead of sprocket wheels. This was introduced to the profession at the Department of Audiovisual Instruction convention in July 1968, and is described in greater detail in a recent column in *School Management* (59).

Improvements in the 16-mm media

Besides the increased brilliance of projection lamps which have a reflecting mirror enclosed inside the glass (appropriately named proximity reflectors because of the closeness of the reflector to the filament light source) and the extremely natural looking light of considerable intensity produced by quartz lamps (also known as halogen lamps), the major improvement in projection lighting has been the General Electric Marc 300 light source released late in 1967. This is actually an enclosed direct current arc lamp not dissimilar to the type of illumination used in 35-mm theater projectors except that it does not need as much care and feeding. The Marc 300 produces a very intense light with a natural color temperature (i.e., like daylight when the sky is blue) without the unwanted production of excessive heat or overly bulky power supplies. It expands the use of 16-mm film to larger audiences since the picture size can be increased severalfold without loss of brilliance, and it also makes the use of motion pictures possible in rooms that are not darkened.

TABLE 3. Comparison of the advantages and disadvantages between the use of helican scan television equipment and motion picture film.

Television	*Film*
Low to moderate picture quality	Very high picture quality
Color is very expensive	Color is not prohibitively expensive
Immediate feedback by means of "instant replay"	No immediate feedback because of processing delays
High equipment acquisition costs	Moderate equipment acquisition costs
Low tape costs for local production	Moderate film costs for local production of 8-mm; high film costs for local production of 16-mm
Complex equipment needing constant supervision of a technical department	Simple equipment that can be serviced by local firms on a contract basis
Lack of compatability between machines of different manufacturers	Complete compatability of 16-mm sound and 8-mm silent films and film projectors of different manufacturers
Few available foreign language teaching materials available	Considerable number of foreign language teaching materials available
Poor visibility of image in classroom	Good to excellent visibility of image in classroom
Monitors for individual use quite expensive	Projectors for individual use moderately priced.
Transmission possible via broadcast or cable	Transmission limited to sending films by messenger
No supplementary lighting usually necessary for local production of black and white	No supplementary lighting usually necessary for local production of black and white
Bright lights needed for local production of color	Bright lights needed for local production of color
Great ease in editing sound	Considerable difficulty in editing sound
Extreme difficulty in editing picture	Great ease in editing picture

By way of review it would be well to compare the advantages of the two visual-motion media that have just been dwelt upon to such a length. Table 3 points up some rather important comparisons.

Language laboratories

The language laboratory is probably the most familiar machine-aided language learning device to the majority of foreign language teachers. Since its conception at Ohio State University in 1924 and its later development into the form in which it generally exists today by Louisiana State University in 1947, the language laboratory has become a common sight on every college campus and in most of the nation's high schools. Commercial interests have been largely responsible for the development of language laboratory teaching materials and equipment, and copious amounts of federal funds ensured that even the most remote school in the country would be able to finance both hardware and software — for better or for worse.

Hardware and software — for better or for worse

Language laboratories present a continuum of equipment from the simplest listen-only tape recorder setup through the three levels of audio activity and recording capability to the complex extreme of remote control, dial-access, and video complemented student positions. Commercial vendors, recognizing that there was more profit to be had in selling the more expensive installations, tended to oversell their wares. As a result, schools have bought dial-switching equipment for instructional situations that could have just as easily been satisfied with manual switching, schools have bought cartridge players that should have had the flexibility of open reel machines, schools have bought full-record laboratories that could have accomplished the same goal with listen-only equipment, and so forth. The list of oversells on the part of industry is endless, but 1968 is the year in which Uncle Sam finally made administrators resume their proper roles of being fiscal devil's advocates when it comes to equipment purchases.

Goals in the FL program determine the sophistication of the language laboratory

According to the National Audio Visual Association (84) the amount of equipment funding in Title III-A of the National Defense Education Act (NDEA) and Title VI-A of the Higher Education Act (HEA), two large sources for equipment funds, dropped from an allotment in fiscal year 1968–69 of $91.24 million to nothing in fiscal year 1969–70. The portent of this budgetary reduction is not as black as it might seem; any program for which the federal government is still offering subsidy, e.g., bilingualism, poverty, etc., still has access to equipment funds, but the inflated years of the mid-sixties have come to a close. It will probably no longer be possible for school systems, such as Beverly Hills, Calif. (14; Gibson & Higgins, 23), to spend hundreds of

The end of an era

thousands of dollars on an audio-video dial-access system that requires the classroom teacher to call a technician in a central program studio who loads the desired materials and gives the right number to be dialed depending upon which machine he puts them on. And it is probably just as well that we are now in a position to surmise that dial-access will continue to remain a severely limited way of disseminating information even with the sophistication of design typified by the Oak Park and River Forest High School, Ill., learning center system. In this school 30 student positions were given the capability of dialing any of up to 500 language or music programs, and, as the connection was established, the program was very rapidly rerecorded onto individual student equipment. The entire process lasted only a fraction of a minute and gave the student several minutes of exclusive access to the material. This is in contrast to the nonexclusive access of most dial installations where one student starts a program and the next student wanting that program must enter it at whatever point it might have progressed to by that time. There have been no loud cries of success from Oak Park and River Forest, and in their absence one must suspect a lack of success.

Dial-access systems have their problems

Oak Park and River Forest (Ill.)

The Pennsylvania Report

1968 will probably be remembered by language laboratory teachers as the year that the Pennsylvania Report was released. Although several studies (Hutchinson, 32; Keating, 40; Lorge, 46; Mueller & Wiersma, 52) of the effectiveness of the laboratory in foreign language teaching have been released that have made national news, the results of the Pennsylvania teaching strategy assessment published by Smith & Berger (77), Smith & Baranyi (76), and Smith (75) have probably reached more people outside the language profession than any of their predecessors because of the fact that their summarized results were picked up out of context by the press wire services. It is *not* true that the Pennsylvania Project produced statistically significant data indicating that the language laboratory produces no advantage over nonlaboratory curricula. In reality, the study was only partially concerned with the language laboratory, and its sole conclusion that did refer to the laboratory was that those language laboratory systems *as employed* twice weekly in the project schools in Pennsylvania had no discernable effect upon language instruction as measured by the project's testing program. More detailed evaluation of the Pennsylvania Project results

Results of the Penna. Studies quoted out of context

may be found in Marxheimer (49), Valette (81), and forthcoming issues of the *Modern Language Journal* and *Foreign Language Annals*. This writer is inclined to agree with Grittner (24) who questions the validity of the entire concept of evaluating educational strategies as it has been pursued for the past half century.

Tape cassettes

The newest hardware development in the language laboratory in 1968 was the great increase in popularity of the cassette tape recorder designed for the home entertainment market. One must remember that the equipment used in most laboratories is modified from the manufacturer's consumer products lines. It is not usually designed especially for institutional use (as gym lockers and cafeteria tables are!). With this in mind it is possible to predict that the cassette will soon be making inroads in the educational market now that it is inexpensively available to everyone and is being bought by the thousands.

A tool for individualized study

The cassette was originally a patent of Philips, a Dutch electronics firm. Norelco is the trade name used in North America, and licensees have sprung up in Europe, the U.S., and Japan. A cassette recorder may be purchased for $30 or several hundred dollars depending upon the fanciness of the case. Basically the tape transport mechanism is the same, and the tape cassette is exactly the same for all such machines. A narrow (0.15 inch instead of the more traditional 0.25 inch) audiotape is contained in a plastic case or cassette. The main expense of this arrangement is not the magnetic recording tape itself but the plastic housing and the labor of loading it. It is impossible to physically edit, i.e., cut and splice, cassette tape unless one is very highly skilled and extremely patient. The tape is not meant to be removed from the cassette.

Problems

The fidelity or frequency response of the cassette tape recorder is potentially sufficient for foreign language instructional use. Any sound that can be reproduced through earphones — as in the language laboratory — will be reproduced with good fidelity through those same earphones using a cassette machine as the program source, but the built-in speakers are perhaps not quite good enough for the rigors of learning an unknown language.

Fidelity

The main attraction that will probably make the cassette tape recorder popular for foreign language study is the low price and ease in carrying the machine from one place to another. Thus, a school tape library could conceivably check out cassette players as well as tapes for student use at home. This would free those precious minutes from the daily schedule when the students were previously in the language laboratory. This type of study is not, however, a proper replacement for language laboratory study with the teacher present in the laboratory; it is just individual drill done at a more convenient time but without supervision.

It is to be hoped that the use of the cassette machine will grow slowly and with full knowledge of the pitfalls. At present there is only the Philips patent which uses a single-motor tape drive. Two American firms are currently working on three-motor drives, and this should greatly extend the usefulness of such a recorder. Since the present machines are inexpensive they are made to be thrown away after having served their comparatively short useful life; repair is difficult. With some luck the cassette should prove a fair solution to many foreign language teaching problems. For instance, it would serve as well as the magnetic disc in such applications as suggested by Allen (4). In that situation, the disc was used as a way of allowing students to make recordings that could be readily passed on to their instructors for easy correction within a short length of time.

New models promise greater use

Responders

Other technical innovations on the language laboratory scene in 1968 concerned the entrance of a third commercial firm into the production of a device designed to allow the student to hear his response to a stimulus immediately after having made it. This is known as a responder or immediate playback machine. Its popularity will undoubtedly be limited, however, since there is nothing new in its technology. With that as a hypothesis one can conclude that someone should have discovered and successfully marketed it ten years ago if there really had been a need for such a device. Also, it is quite expensive and only useful for drill at the imitation stage of language acquisition.

Electronic classrooms

Finally, there was a resurgence in 1968 in the use of the old term "electronic classroom." This is a conventional school classroom that has been outfitted with equipment similar to that which can usually be found in the language laboratory (Siegel, 71). The student terminals are sometimes contained in the desks, sometimes lowered from the ceiling, and sometimes located around the edge of the classroom. There is seldom the capability of student recording. Regenstreif (65) describes the main

Advantages

advantages of such installations. They are economical because no additional floor space is needed as with the full-size laboratory and readily accessible because the equipment is in the classroom for the teacher's use whenever needed. The latter advantage was confirmed by Smith & Littlefield (79) but later seriously questioned by Smith & Hocking (78).

The future of language laboratories

Since the language laboratory is perhaps the most loved and simultaneously the most despised of the foreign language teacher's machine aids, it is interesting to contemplate whether or not that which has evolved into today's laboratories is really the best thing to get the job done. The "job" is presumably to allow the foreign language student the opportunity to practice the target language. He can practice listening comprehension and discrimination and through the medium of printed materials determine the extent to which this skill improves; he can also practice speaking, but there is considerable technological lack in most laboratory installations when it comes to permitting the student to determine his progress in this skill.

What is needed in the equipment that students use in language laboratories is a greater degree of responsiveness on the part of the equipment and materials to the student's performance. The presence of the teacher or other trained monitor in the laboratory permits such responsiveness to one student at a time, but this is insufficient. With the technology of magnetic recording on media other than tape (e.g., high-speed disc packs as used in data processing equipment) and simple transistor logic no more complex than the device that opens a supermarket door automatically, it would be possible to produce a student learning position that could help make the use of the language laboratory for speaking drill more interactive.

Computer—assisted instruction

There is one instructional medium that utilizes the advantages of the audio from the language laboratory, the visual from television or films, and the logic of the classroom teacher: computer-assisted instruction (CAI) (Rosenbaum, 67). Oettinger (60) advances the idea that computers will have as great a humanistic effect upon the culture of our society as did the perfection of movable type by Gutenberg. He does not, however, see significant progress in the next decade because of the inflexible educational structure and the erratic behavior of technology as it rises and falls under commercial interests. Oettinger also points out that what is being described as individual instruction is really mass instruction administered individually. But students would prefer unindividual attention from a computer rather than neglect from a classroom teacher. With this indictment in mind let us investigate what CAI can do for foreign language teaching and what foreign language teachers can do for CAI.

Silvern (72) describes a CAI system as one in which a computer contains a stored instructional program designed as a source of information and guidance. Further, CAI provides control and evaluation of a student until a predetermined level of proficiency is reached. Two-way communication between the student and the instructional program within the computer must exist. The position of the teacher in such a situation is one of being the director of communication whereas previously he was merely the classroom communicator. The latter chore is taken over by the computer. Notice that this still leaves the teacher in control of the instructional situation.

CAI controls and evaluates until a predetermined level of proficiency is reached

In point of fact CAI demands far more planning and programming of instructional material on the part of the teacher than does conventional classroom teaching. The computer cannot shrug its shoulders unless it is told to do so. What this means is that the creation of learning materials must be handled by a team whose members come from different fields. Besides the authors or instructional programmers (who are presumably teachers of foreign languages), there is also a group of computer programmers. The authors write the exercises and the computer programmers convert them into a form that is meaningful to the

It takes a team to write the program

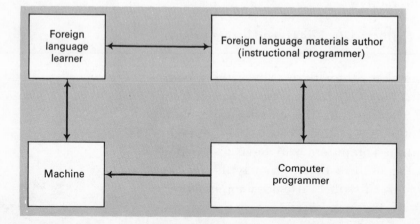

Flow chart of CAI interaction among the learner, author, computer programmer, and machine.

computer machinery. Thus the interaction of learner, author, computer programmer, and machine is shown in the accompanying chart.

Notice that the computer programmer, who we assume is not skilled in anything but programming computers, does not come into contact with the language learner. All results of the computer programmer's efforts that are produced by the interaction of the learner and the machine are fed back to the *author* for reevaluation before being reprogrammed. Thus, the higher echelon of teaching ability is still preserved in a fitting manner, and the author is made continuously aware of the results of the instructional program. *"learner↔author" interaction*

It is not necessarily true that CAI foreign language courses must suffer the weaknesses of programmed instruction such as those pointed out by Ornstein (61). A true Socratic dialogue is attainable; one such is described by Bolt (7); and a two-way i.e., dialogue, foreign language lesson in CAI is set forth in detail by Adams, et al. (1, 2, 3, 51). Also, work by Keller at the U.S. Naval Academy (33) and by van Campen at Stanford (82) is designed to allow the computer to direct the student through various audio drills from prerecorded sources. Audio evaluation, though, remains difficult. *A true Socratic dialogue is possible*

Visual displays are also being implemented in the Roman Catholic diocese in Brooklyn using home television receivers and by many others using local slide presentations (Silvern, 72; Myers, 53). These visual displays are in addition to the printed display that either appears on paper or a cathode ray tube (similar to a green TV tube) at the student terminal. This printed display is the actual student-machine dialogue. *Visual displays*

Present programs in CAI in the foreign languages include the University of Illinois (47) and the State University of New York at Stony Brook (44), as well as Stanford and the Naval Academy. The University of Illinois has named its CAI facility PLATO (Programmed Logic for Automatic Teaching Operations) but not for any fondness for the humanities (Myers, 54). In its 1968 list of PLATO programs there were 80 entries. Three of these were in foreign language: one Latin and two French. At Annapolis there were 18 courses that used the CAI facility in 1968; one was a Russian language course. One reason for this bias of research away from the rather sizable study of foreign language was suggested by Bundy (9) who points out that because of the high costs involved and the usual location of computing machinery in science departments (Featherstone & Bell, 21) there will exist a *Present programs* certain tendency for CAI programs to be scientific in subject matter.

Kopstein & Seidel (43) discuss the economics of computer-assisted instruction. They equate the economic factor of teacher shortages in teacher-assisted instruction with the shortage of instructional programmers (authors) in CAI. They also develop a rather neat financial justification for a university-level CAI installation based on the sharing of the machinery by a number of schools. At the secondary level they conclude that CAI would need an effectiveness ten times what it is today to be economically justifiable.

Financial justification for CAI installation

It is, of course, not essentially necessary that the CAI computers be shared exclusively with other CAI users. It is possible to have one central processing unit (CPU), which is the heart of the system, dividing its efforts among instructional, clerical, and research projects. This sharing concept, known as time-sharing, enables a computer to serve more than one master. For instance, in the time it might take a student to think of a reply to a computer-produced question, the machine could be generating questions to 20 or 30 other students. It is this feature that will eventually make the use of CAI in individually administering mass education a reality.

Conclusion

It is apparent that although foreign language teaching might be in some ways the stepchild of college entrance requirements, the field has an important interest in the technologies of 1968 and of the future. Federal money spurred the growth of language laboratories throughout the country, but further developments will be much slower in coming because of increased difficulty in financing both research and application. With sound basis of those professional language teachers who have shown themselves to be truly interested in the two disciplines involved in machine-aided language learning, it will be possible to slowly integrate media, including television in all its forms as well as the extremely powerful technology of computers, into the humanistic endeavor of studying foreign languages, literatures, and cultures.

References, Machine-aided language learning

1 Adams, E. N. Field evaluation of the German CAI lab. In: Computer-assisted instruction: a book of readings. Academic Press, New York, 1969.

2 Adams, E. N. The use of CAI in foreign language instruction. IBM Research Paper No. RC 2377. Available from Thomas J. Watson IBM Research Center, Yorktown Heights, N.Y. (Oct. 30, 1968).

3 Adams, E. N.; Morrison, H. W.; Reddy, J. M. Conversation with a computer as a technique of language instruction. Modern Language Journal, 52 (January 1968) 3–16.

4 Allen, Robert L. A reassessment of the role of the language laboratory. Journal of English as a Second Language, 3:i (1968) 49–59.

5 Behmer. Note submitted to Portable Video Tape Recorder (PVTR), Gustafson, Kent L., ed. Audiovisual Instruction, 13:vii (September 1968) 740.

6 Birkmaier, Emma Marie; Lange, Dale L. A selective bibliography on the teaching of foreign languages, 1920–1966. Foreign Language Annals, 1:iv (May 1968) 318–353.

7 Bolt, Richard H. Computer-assisted socratic instruction. In: Orr, William D. Conversational computers. Wiley, New York, 1968, p. 90–95.

8 Brown, George H.; Fiks, Alfred I. Modern approaches to foreign language teaching: a survey of current practices. Technical Report 67–15. Human Resources Research Office, George Washington University, Alexandria, Va. (December 1967).

9 Bundy, Robert F. Computer-assisted instruction – where are we? Phi Delta Kappan, 49 (April 1968) 424–429.

10 Cannaday, Robert W.; Gamba, Terry. Film series: successful use of the language laboratory. W. G. O'Connor, Harrisburg, Pa., 1964.

11 Chamberlain, Jane Scott. Source materials for teachers of foreign languages. National Education Association, Washington, D.C., 1968.

12 Cooper, Bernarr; et al. ITFS – instructional television fixed service (2500 megaHertz) – what is it? How to plan. National Education Association, Washington, D.C., 1969.

13 DAVI name change proposals. Audiovisual Instruction, 13:vii (September 1968) 764–772.

14 Dialing for lessons in Beverly Hills. Educational Technology, 8:iii (Feb. 15, 1968) 16.

15 Dodge, James W. Film Series: Sight and sound: media in foreign language teaching. Northeast Conference, Box 881, Madison, Conn. 06443.

16 Edgerton, Mills F., Motion picture film: a demonstration. Northeast Conference (1969). In: Reports of the Working Committees, Northeast Conference (RWCNEC), MLA/ACTFL Materials Center, New York, 1969.

17 Edgerton, Mills F. Sight and sound: the sensible and sensitive use of audio-visual aids. Reports of the Working Committees, Northeast Conference (RWCNEC), MLA/ACTFL Materials Center, New York, 1969.

18 Elements of visual literacy. Eastman Kodak, Rochester, N.Y., 1968.

19 Fass, Martin. Film: Man's ability to search and reason. National Instructional Television, University of Indiana, Bloomington.

20 Fearing, Percy. Using the 8mm film to bridge the gap from drill to creative language use. Unpublished demonstration: Northeast Conference (1969).

21 Featherstone, Richard; Bell, Norman. Space design and equipment for the CAI laboratory. American School & University, 40 (April 1968) 24–26, 51.

22 Forsdale, Lewis. Film: 8mm film in education: its emerging role. National Archives and Record Service, National AV Center, Washington, D.C.

23 Gibson, Dan M.; Higgins, William. New A-V technology meets program needs. American School & University, 40 (March 1968) 43–45.

24 Grittner, Frank M. Letter to the editor. National Association of Language Laboratory Directors (NALLD) Newsletter, 3:ii (December 1968) 7.

25 Gustafson, Kent L. Another look at standards. Audiovisual Instruction, 13:x (December 1968) 1123.

26 Gustafson, Kent L. Portable VTR's for student teachers. Audiovisual Instruction, 12 (December 1967) 1070–1071.

27 Gustafson, Kent L., ed. Portable video-tape recorder (PVTR). Audiovisual Instruction, 13:x (December 1968) 1123.

28 Harmon, John T., ed. Annual bibliography on the teaching of foreign languages. Foreign Language Annals, 1 (October 1967, December 1967, March 1968, May 1968).

29 Hauser, Rick. The ITV humanities project. Audiovisual Instruction, 13:i (January 1968) 31–34.

30 Hill, Roger W., Jr. ITV & CATV: a natural marriage. Audiovisual Instruction, 13:x (December 1968) 1062–1063.

31 Humphrey, John H. Where are we going? Educational Technology, 8:vi (March 30, 1968) 14–15.

32 Hutchinson, Joseph C. The language laboratory: how effective is it? School Life, 46 (January-February 1964) 14–17, 39–41. Also in: Donoghue, Mildred R. Foreign languages and the schools: a book of readings. Wm. Brown, Dubuque, Ia., 1967.

33 Inman, Richard P. Computer-assisted education at the Naval Academy. EDUCOM, 4:ii (March 1968) 3–7.

34 Instructional resources in the classroom. NEA Research Bulletin, 45 (October 1967) 75–77. Also in: Audiovisual Instruction, 13:iii (March 1968) 284–85.

35 Jaquith, Charles E. An old school uses new tools. Audiovisual Instruction, 13:x (December 1968) 1084–1085.

36 Kanner, Joseph H. The instructional effectiveness of color in television: a review of the evidence. Palo Alto, Calif., January 1968.
Available from ERIC Documentation Service, U.S. Office of Education, Washington, D.C.

37 Kanner, Joseph H. Teaching by television in the army – an overview for 1968. AV Communication Review, 16:ii (Summer 1968) 178–187.

38 Kanner, Joseph H.; Rosenstein, A. Television in army training: color vs. black and white. AV Communication Review, 8:vi (Fall 1960) 243–252.

39 Karp, Theodore B.; et al. Film Series: Principles and methods of teaching a second language. Teaching Film Custodians, New York.

40 Keating, Raymond F. A study in the effectiveness of language laboratories. Teachers College, New York, 1963.

41 Kemp, Jerrold E.; Szumski, Richard F. 8mm film. Educational Screen and Audiovisual Guide, 47:vii (July 1968) 12–13.

42 Kemp, Jerrold E.; Szumski, Richard F. So you want to make an 8mm film. Audiovisual Instruction 13:iv (April 1968) 342–344.

43 Kopstein, Felix F.; Seidel, Robert J. Computer-administered instruction versus traditionally administered instruction: economics. AV Communication Review, 16:ii (Summer 1968) 147–175.

44 Language and linguistics. Film series. National Educational Television Film Service, University of Indiana, Bloomington.

55 Language: the social arbiter. Film series. Stuart Finley, Falls Church, Va.

46 Lorge, Sarah W. Language laboratory research studies in New York City high schools: a discussion of the program and the findings. Modern Language Journal, 48 (Novenber 1964) 409–419.

47 McDonald, Frederick J.; Allen, Dwight W. Training effects of feedback and modeling procedures on teaching performance. U.S. Office of Education Report Contract No. OE-6-10-078. Available from: ERIC Documentation Service, U.S. Office of Education, Washington, D.C.

48 Martin, James S. The audio-visual department comes of age. American School & University, 40 (February 1968) 24–25, 58.

49 Marxheimer, Edward. Comments on the Pennsylvania project: challenge for the secondary school laboratory. National Association of Language Laboratory Directors (NALLD) Newsletter, 3:iii (March 1969) 20–22.

50 Miller, Morris; Colligan, Jerome. A study of the effectiveness of the use of the overhead projector as a visualization tool in teaching first year bookkeeping. Office of Educational Research, Board of Education of the City of New York, Brooklyn (September 1956).

51 Morrison, H. W.; Adams, E. N. Pilot study of a CAI laboratory in German. Modern Language Journal, 52 (May 1968) 279–287.

52 Mueller, Klaus A., Wiersma, William. The effects of language laboratory type upon foreign language achievement scores? Modern Language Journal, 51 (October 1967) 349–351.

53 Myers, M. Keith. Essential components of a student CAI terminal. Paper presented at the AAS meeting (December 1968). Available from the author at the University of Illinois, Urbana.

54 Myers, M. Keith; Gilpin, John B. PLATO: the teacher's mentor–dialogues with a computer. Discussion paper. Modern Language Association Conference 39, Annual Meeting (December 1967). Available from MLA/ACTFL Materials Center, New York.

55 Neal, Alan S. Legibility requirements for educational television. Information Display, 5:iv (July 1968) 39ff.

56 Neal, Alan S. Viewing conditions for classroom TV: an objective study. Audiovisual Instruction, 13:vii (September 1968) 707–709.

57 The nearly perfect language lab. American School & University, 38 (April 1966) 26–27, 60.

58 Newmark, Gerald. Use of children's films and other children's materials in teaching foreign languages to adults. Modern Language Journal, 51 (May 1967) 272–274.

59 New product column. School Management (October 1968).

60 Oettinger, Anthony G. The myth of educational technology. Saturday Review, 51:xx (May 18, 1968) 76–77, 91.

61 Ornstein, Jacob. Programmed instruction and educational technology in the language field: boon or failure? Modern Language Journal, 52 (November 1968) 401–410.

62 Parlons Français. Film series to accompany text by D. C. Heath, Boston. Films: Heath de Rochemont, New York.

63 Politzer, Robert L. Micro-teaching: a new approach to teacher training and research. Discussion paper. Modern Language Association Conference 39, Annual Meeting (December 1967). Available from MLA/ACTFL Materials Center, New York.

64 Pond, Karl S. A language teaching tool: the overhead projector. Modern Language Journal, 47 (January 1963) 30–33. Also in: Donoghue, Mildred R. Foreign languages and the schools: a book of readings. Wm. Brown, Dubuque, Ia., 1967.

65 Regenstreif, Harry. The language laboratory vs. the electronic classroom. National Association of Language Laboratory Directors (NALLD) Newsletter, 2:ii (March 1968) 14–17.

66 Regenstreif, Harry. The learning laboratory program of the foreign language innovative curricula studies project. Paper given at the 4th Annual Meeting of the National Association of Language Laboratory Directors (NALLD), Houston, Tex. (March 1968). Available from FLICS, 550 City Center Building, 220 East Huron Street, Ann Arbor, Mich. 48100.

67 Rosenbaum, Peter S. The computer as a learning environment for foreign language instruction. Foreign Language Annals, 2:iv (May 1969), 457–465.

68 Sanchez, José. Films for exotic foreign language instruction. Modern Language Journal, 51 (April 1967) 195–203.

69 Shelley, Edwin F. Toward an individualized education. Paper presented at the 1968 National Convention of the Institute of Electrical and Electronics Engineers, New York (March 18, 1968).

70 Sherriffs, Ronald E. Old ways to solve new problems. Audiovisual Instruction, 13:vii (September 1968) 702–705.

71 Siegel, Ernest. Every classroom an electronic classroom. Audiovisual Instruction, 13:vii (Sep-

tember 1968) 722–723.

72 Silvern, Leonard C. CAI in an expanding universe of educational methodology. In: Orr, William D. Conversational computers. Wiley, New York, 1968, p. 45–89.

73 Skinner, Ray, Jr. A new format for ITV. AV Communication Review, 16:iii (Fall 1968) 287–293.

74 Sleeman, Philip J.; Crosswhite, Vivian. The 8mm film revolution. Audiovisual Instruction, 13:viii (October 1968) 880–882.

75 Smith, Philip D., Jr. How effective the language lab? National Association of Language Laboratory Directors (NALLD) Newsletter, 3:i (October 1968) 5–8.

76 Smith, Philip D., Jr.; Baranyi, Helmut A. A comparison study of the effectiveness of the traditional and audiolingual approaches to foreign language instruction utilizing laboratory equipment. Final Report. U.S. Office of Education Project No. 7-0133 (1968). Available from ERIC Documentation Service, U.S. Office of Education, Washington, D.C.

77 Smith, Philip D., Jr.; Berger, Emanuel, An assessment of three foreign language teaching strategies utilizing three language laboratory systems. Final Report. U.S. Office of Education Project No. 5-0683 (1968). Available from ERIC Documentation Service, U.S. Office of Education, Washington, D.C.

78 Smith, W. Flint; Hocking, Elton. The fallacy of accessibility. National Association of Language Laboratory Directors (NALLD) Newsletter, 3:iii (March 1969) 10–13.

79 Smith, W. Flint; Littlefield, R. L. The language laboratory and the electronic classroom: a comparison. Report to the Indiana Language Program, Indiana University, Bloomington, 1967.

80 Tabor, Glenn D. Instructional TV–what about it? American School & University, 40 (April 1968) 29–30, 33, 52.

81 Valette, Rebecca M. Some conclusions to be drawn from the Pennsylvania study. National Association of Language Laboratory Directors (NALLD) Newsletter, 3:iii (March 1969) 17–19.

82 Van Campen, Joseph. Project for the application of mathematical learning theory to second language acquisition with particular reference to Russian. Project Report U.S. Office of Education Contract No. C-0-8-00120901806. Available from ERIC Documentation Service, U.S. Office of Education, Washington, D.C.

83 Wrenn, James J. The dialogue in the classroom. Journal of the Chinese Language Teachers Association, 3:i (February 1968) 23–26. Also in: Edgerton, Mills F., Jr., ed. Reports of the Working Committees, Northeast Conference (1969). Available from MLA/ACTFL Materials Center, New York.

84 Zero funds requested for National Defense Education Act (NDEA) III, Higher Education Act (HEA) VI-A in president's budget. National Audio Visual Association (NAVA) News, 23 (Jan. 20, 1969) 1–3.

12
Testing

Introduction

In the domain of foreign language measurement and evaluation much research remains to be undertaken and many problems await investigation, but the promise of significant advances in techniques and applications looms on the horizon. The most exciting developments lie in the area of criterion-referenced testing (with pioneer work being undertaken in California) and mastery learning. This review will try to place this innovative work within the perspective of the broader field.

Second language testing falls into two broad categories: the measurement of language aptitude (which precedes the language learning process) and the measurement of language acquisition (which may either parallel or come at the end of the learning process). We shall briefly touch upon the first topic before concentrating attention on the second.

Rebecca M. Valette

Boston College

General

There are two general handbooks on language testing. Lado (27) stresses the need for testing foreign language problems as defined by research in contrastive applied linguistics. The book, which was primarily intended for teachers of English as a foreign language and which draws most of its examples from tests of English designed for speakers of Spanish, presents techniques for testing the elements of language and the integrated skills. Lado also touches on the problem of testing cultural aims. The final section describes technical aspects of measurement with specific references to foreign languages. Valette (63) meets the practical needs of the American teacher of foreign languages. After a short introduction to principles and procedures of classroom testing, the handbook treats the four skills of listening, speaking, reading, and writing, plus the subjects of culture (briefly) and literature. There are copious examples in the commonly taught modern languages. An appendix describes available commercial tests.

Upshur & Fata (61) have edited the proceedings of a foreign language testing conference held at the University of Michigan

Five important books for the FL teacher's library

in September 1967. The papers, which cover a broad spectrum of topics, are accompanied by excerpts from the ensuing discussions.

Davies (22) presents a collection of papers on language testing. The various chapters give the reader a perspective on recent British testing developments and present both practical and theoretical aspects of second-language evaluation. Of particular relevance are Carroll's taxonomies of language test tasks.

Plaister (47) has prepared a bibliography on foreign language testing. Although the emphasis is on English as a second language, most of the references would interest teachers of other languages.

Mackey's analysis (29) of language teaching components provides a useful source of reference for those engaged in testing research.

Aptitude testing

In the area of aptitude testing, the basic research of Carroll (13) and of Pimsleur, Mosberg, & Morrison (45) has not been challenged. Within the foreign language profession there is general agreement on the following statements:

1 Language aptitude is *not* a "special gift" which some possess and others do not. All human beings who have mastered their mother tongue are able to reach a basic level of proficiency in a second language, although some will learn more rapidly than others. The "special gift" myth is still frequently invoked in spite of its lack of substance: the teacher calls on the myth to absolve himself of his failure to teach many of his students *The "special gift" myth* the foreign language, the student (and his parents) finds in the myth an acceptable explanation for failure to learn the language, and administrators looking back on an unhappy language experience are also ready to perpetuate the myth. Carroll (13) equates aptitude with the *time needed* to master a task; in this sense, students with a high aptitude are those who learn more quickly.

2 Language aptitude seems to consist of several factors. In the newer language aptitude tests, for example, subtests measure *Subtests* the student's grammar sensitivity and his phonetic coding ability (the ability to recognize and remember differences in sounds).

3 In the school situation, aptitude is but one aspect contributing

to success in learning. Other variables are student motivation, general intelligence, the effectiveness of the presentation (teacher and materials), and the time allowed for learning (Carroll, 13). Consequently, students should not be excluded from foreign language classes on the basis of aptitude test results.

Aptitude only one aspect

Aptitude tests

At this time there are three aptitude batteries commercially available. The Carroll-Sapon Modern Language Aptitude Test (MLAT) (16) is appropriate for use with high school students and adults. The battery's five subtests are designed to measure the following traits: the ability to learn numbers aurally, the ability to associate sounds and symbols (through phonetic script), vocabulary knowledge via a "spelling clues" section, grammatical sensitivity, and the ability to learn foreign vocabulary by rote. The complete MLAT runs 60–70 minutes, but the short form, containing only the last three subtests, requires only 30 minutes. The Carroll-Sapon Elementary Modern Language Aptitude Test (EMLAT) (15), designed for grades three through six, is an outgrowth of the MLAT. The EMLAT contains four subtests: "hidden words" is a vocabulary test similar to the "spelling clues" section of the MLAT, "matching words" tests grammatical sensitivity, "finding rhymes" is a new section which measures the ability to hear speech sounds, and "number learning" is a simplified form of the number learning section of the MLAT. The EMLAT takes 60–70 minutes to administer; there is no short form.

MLAT

EMLAT

Pimsleur (42) describes his construction of the Pimsleur Language Aptitude Battery (46), designed for use with junior high and high school students. The last four sections of his battery measure vocabulary (word knowledge in English), grammatical analysis (tested without recourse to formal terminology), sound discrimination (recognizing new phonetic distinctions in differing contexts), and sound-symbol association. These subtests are roughly similar to the first four subtests of the MLAT. Pimsleur found that he could improve the correlation of his aptitude battery with success in foreign languages (as measured by a final achievement battery) by introducing two additional factors: grade point average (GPA) and the student's statement of interest (or lack of interest) in learning a new language. The Pimsleur Language Aptitude Battery contains six sections and may be administered in 50–60 minutes; there is not short form.

Pimsleur Language Aptitude Battery

Using aptitude tests.

The diagnostic function of aptitude tests remains to be systematically exploited. Pimsleur, Sundland, & McIntyre (44) discovered that underachievers in foreign language courses were characterized by poor auditory ability. If such students could be identified at the outset of their language learning experience, perhaps intensive help in auditory discrimination and phonetic coding would improve their chances for achievement.

The diagnostic function

Lambert (28), in reviewing research on motivation, points out that students with low measured aptitude and positive attitude can experience success in second language learning.

In a recent experiment, Rosenthal & Jacobsen (50) found that if the teacher expected a child to demonstrate greater intelligence, the child actually increased his intellectual capacity, as measured by IQ tests. It is probable that a similar "Pygmalion effect" exists in the language class. If the teacher assumes that all students will master French pronunciation, for example, they usually do. If the teacher feels that most students will never learn the Spanish subjunctive, they generally don't. This explains the (unfortunately) high correlation between GPA and language grades: teachers have developed expectations about students from their previous academic achievements, and these expectations have a way of fulfilling themselves.

The Pygmalion effect

Summary

Within the American educational framework, prognostic tests have but one legitimate use: to predict success in particular cases where an agency (governmental, industrial, etc.) needs to train a small number of personnel in a foreign language. Under such conditions, budget constraints and time factors demand that every effort be made to find the most suitable "risks," that is, those candidates with the greatest chance of completing the course. Under such conditions, the fact that other equally suited candidates might be excluded due to the imperfections of the prognostic instrument is not a matter of concern since only a limited number of trainees is required in the first place.

Aptitude tests should definitely *not be used to exclude* students from (or select students for) language classes at the grade school, secondary school, or college levels, since aptitude is just one of many factors contributing to student success. Denying students a foreign language on the basis of aptitude test scores is just as indefensible as not teaching the slow readers how to read.

Classifying the aims of foreign language instruction

Objectives must be clearly stated in behavioral terms if the teacher intends to test whether or not these objectives have been attained. This growing emphasis on terminal behavior, that is, on observable and verifiable changes in student behavior, has grown out of research in programmed instruction. Mager's (30) general handbook explains how to prepare objectives and avoid ambiguity. Consider the following examples:

1 The student should read the foreign language easily and with conscious translation.
2 The student will be able to read, without the aid of a dictionary, unfamiliar texts written in *Le Français Fondamental*. He shall demonstrate direct comprehension by answering correctly 95 percent of the related multiple-choice questions, written in French.

How to prepare objectives

The first statement is vague: What texts should the student be able to read? What is meant by "easily"? How can one determine whether the student is consciously translating or not? The second statement is more precise: the desired behavior is specified (reading texts based on *Le Français Fondamental*); the limitations are defined (without a dictionary); and the criterion of acceptable performance is given (95% accuracy on a reading test of direct comprehension, not inferential ability).

Fortunately, there is an increasing concern for appropriate statements of second-language learning objectives. Nostrand (in Seelye, 54) has further developed guidelines that describe level objectives in terms of carefully specified terminal behaviors. Damore (21) in the appendices to his study, presents a system for classifying sentence patterns so that lesson objectives may be clearly specified.

Table of foreign language objectives

Figure 1 presents the content areas and the behavioral objectives in a two-dimensional schematic. The first two principal areas of content are language and culture. Language has been subdivided into spoken language, written language, and body language or kinesics. Culture includes way-of-life culture, civilization (history, geography, etc.), and the arts (or refinement culture). Literature, which brings together language and culture in

347

an artistic form, is the third general area. Communication is a global category which includes all the preceding content areas and combines several behaviors; the participant in a conversation is simultaneously sending and receiving messages at the levels of both surface meaning and deep meaning.

Areas of content	Knowledge and perception				Manipu- lation		Understanding and production					
	A	B	C	D	E	F	G	H	I	J	K	
1. Spoken language 1.1 Vocabulary 1.2 Grammar 1.3 Phonology												Language
2. Written language 2.1 Vocabulary 2.2 Grammar 2.3 Spelling												
3. Kinesics (body language)												
4. Way-of-life culture 4.1 Society 4.2 Culture												Culture
5. Civilization		▨		▨	▨	▨						
6. The Arts					▨	▨						
7. Literature		▨		▨	▨	▨						Literature
8. Communication 8.1 Face-to-face 8.2 Telephone 8.3 Message	▨	▨	▨	▨	▨	▨					▨	Communi- cation

Behavioral objectives

A. Knowledge of elements

B. Ability to differentiate and discriminate among elements

C. Knowledge of rules and patterns

D. Ability to differentiate and discriminate among rules and patterns

E. Ability to reproduce elements and patterns

F. Ability to manipulate elements and patterns

G. Ability to grasp explicit (surface) meaning of utterances or patterns

H. Ability to produce utterances or patterns conveying the desired explicit meaning

I. Ability to analyze utterances or patterns in terms of implicit (deep) meaning

J. Ability to produce utterances or patterns conveying the desired implicit meaning

K. Ability to evaluate a work or phenomenon

Figure 1. Table of foreign language objectives.

The behavioral objectives A through K progress from the simple to the more complex. Objectives A and C entail the simple cognitive act of knowledge: knowledge of vocabulary, declensions, historic dates, names of authors, etc. (A), and knowledge of grammar rules, sentence patterns, sociological trends, literary conventions, etc. (C). The psychomotor behavior of perception (objectives B and D) becomes particularly important with respect to the content area of language: can the student hear differences among phonemes, distinguish among new written forms (scripts, diacritical marks), notice new significant gestures? Objectives E and F often are taught first in the classroom. The student memorizes a dialogue (E) and engages in pattern drills (F) before making generalizations about elements and patterns (A and C). All six objectives A through F are preliminaries for the true aims of second-language study: the communication skills of listening and reading (G and I) and speaking and writing (H and J). Objectives G and H refer to explicit, or direct, surface meaning whereas I and J, which are less frequently attained, stress implied meaning and deep structure. Objective K, evaluation, is emphasized particularly with respect to literature.

In the subsequent sections of this review, we shall make reference to specific cells of this table. The cells will be identified by an Arabic numeral (content area) and a letter (behavioral objective). For example, the student's ability to shake hands as a French student would be classified as cell 3-E.

Competence vs. performance

Chomsky's distinction between *competence* (how much language the student "knows") and *performance* (how the student actually "uses" the language) is beginning to filter into the area of language testing. Carroll (in Davies, 22) develops a chart of linguistic competences and suggests a chart of linguistic performance abilities. Traill (59) points out that bilinguals may hide their lack of competence by using only familiar vocabulary and structure and skirting potential problem areas. He suggests that a test of bilingual competence contain a translation section and a recall section.

Competence and performance

Most current language tests seem to be measures of performance rather than measures of competence. The preparation of tests of competence presents a challenge to testmakers for the student uses performance to signal his competence. Future research is focusing on this area.

Measuring achievement: testing

Having determined which behavioral objectives he expects his students to attain, the teacher must select the appropriate testing techniques. The most useful basic handbooks are those by Lado (27) and Valette (63), described earlier.

Testing the language aims

Content area 1 (spoken language) has risen in prominence since World War II. Since listening tests lend themselves to multiple-choice items and objective scoring techniques, their widespread use and general acceptance has been assured. In his experiments (cell 1-B), Brière (9) has discovered that students find it easier to identify two "same" items than two "different" items. Belasco, et al. (7) emphasizes audio-identification (cells 1-B, 1-D) and insists that then the students must make the shift from audio-comprehension (cell 1-G) of more redundant to that of less redundant forms. To test this new state of expectancy, to ascertain, for example, whether the student has heard and understood the difference between "Il vient manger" and "Il vient de manger" the teacher may employ rapid oral translation. We might note at this point that although it has been the trend to avoid translation on foreign language examinations, Carroll (in Davies, 22) questions whether the use of an English stimulus on some items or the request for an English response might not be a valid testing technique.

Testing listening comprehension

Comprehension of connected discourse, which also falls into cell 1-G, is usually evaluated by having the student answer questions about the passage or conversation he has just heard. In order to measure level of proficiency with respect to a specified knowledge of grammar and vocabulary, Valette (in Upshur & Fata, 61) suggests the following method: a group of contrived selections containing x number of structures and y number of lexical items are recorded so that the first is at careful conversational speed, the second at normal conversational speed, the third at rapid conversational speed, the fourth with much slurring and fast delivery, and the fifth with a regional accent; students demonstrate comprehension by answering multiple-choice questions. Belasco (5) recommends the transcription as a comprehension check: students listen to a live recording, such as a radio interview, and are allowed to stop and replay the taped selection until they have produced a written version of what they are listening to; this is a hybrid technique, utilizing the writing skill, but it provides an excellent measure of comprehension. At present there are no tests that evaluate the student's ability to analyze speech (cell 1-I), either according to levels of meaning or from the point of view of regional, contextual, or stylistic variations.

Speaking tests are much more problematical than listening tests (cf. Perren, in Davies, 22). First, there is the matter of mechanics: administration, recording facilities, and correction time. Even when these questions of logistics have been solved, there remains the question of scorer reliability. Agencies such as the Educational Testing Services (ETS) have been successful by scoring one aspect of speech at a time. In reporting the results of an experiment at New York University, Carton (17) states that individual phoneme ratings were found to be more reliable than more global general impressions. Clark (18) found that judging accuracy is mainly determined by individual differences in sound discrimination ability; whether the judge is a native speaker of English or of the foreign language does not appear to be significant. The matter of scorer reliability is the subject of continuing investigation, one that must be taken into account for each set of test papers and each team of new scorers.

Testing speaking

As we shift our attention to the content of speaking test items, additional factors demand consideration. As a result of his research project, Carton (17) stresses the importance of measuring the mastery of lengthy strings of phonemes, for such behavior is an essential factor in the production of comprehensible speech. He is furthermore concerned with the eventual creation of an instrument that could be used to predict the student's degree of success in communicating with native speakers of the language under consideration. In cell 1-F, Wilkins & Hoffman (66) point out the effectiveness of using lists of cognates in a "reading aloud" test of pronunciation. Knowledge of vocabulary and grammatical forms (objectives A and C) may be tested by having the student identify pictures or complete sentences. Eliciting specific sentences containing predetermined structures (objective F) is trickier: pattern drills may be used, but the student is thus given many of the building blocks that will figure in his response.

In research for a doctoral dissertation, Roy (51) investigated the evaluation of longer speech samples (cell 1-H). He discovered that rate of speech, measured in syllables, correlated well with correctness of grammar and phonology and was most reliable in separating first- or second-year college students of the foreign language from the native speakers. The difference in delivery rate between first- and second-year students was much smaller. Perhaps further research could refine the rate-of-delivery measurement technique for it is much easier to count syllables than to analyze numerous individual errors. Cooper, in Upshur & Fata (61), asserts the need for students to vary the level of speech they use according to the context in which they find themselves (cell 1-J). Techniques to evaluate this complex objective have not yet been developed.

Content area 2 (written language) has been the concern of language teachers over the centuries. Reading tests evaluate student proficiency at the levels of knowledge, comprehension, and analysis (objectives A, C, G, and I). In learning a language with a writing system different from that of English, students are faced with the psychomotor task of recognizing new symbols (cell 2-B). With respect to reading tests, attention of the test-maker is drawn to content analysis (objective testing techniques have assured scorer reliability and the use of printed items assures freedom from contamination by other language skills). Word-matching tests and multiple-choice fill-in-the-blank tests may be used to measure knowledge of vocabulary and verb forms (cells 2-A, 2-C). Completion tests may also require comprehension of the context as a requisite to selecting the proper answer (cells 2-F, 2-G), and occasionally application in questions where the student must select the pronoun appropriate to the context (cell 2-H). Passage items may test comprehension and analysis (cells 2-G, 2-I). Very often, however, passages are followed by items demanding simple knowledge of vocabulary (cell 2-A) at the direct-meaning level. Items of this latter variety, while varying in difficulty according to the frequency of the word being tested, necessitate only the simple cognitive process of recall. An overabundance of such vocabulary items on reading tests results in a "vocabulary bias."

Testing reading

Belasco (6) stresses the need for evaluating the student's ability to handle deep structure (objective I) and suggests the development of item types that would have the student identify embedded structures.

Writing tests are of two sorts. Those items that use the writing skill to measure knowledge (of vocabulary and grammar) and the application of these elements in highly structured situations, such as completions, question-answer, transformations, etc., lend themselves well to objective scoring: they may be used to test behavior in cells 2-A, 2-G, 2-F. Valette (62) discovered that on multiple-choice grammar tests in German, poorer students tended whenever possible to match the ending of the determiner with that of the preceding word; examples: neb*en* d*en*, unt*er* d*er*, hab*e* ein*e*. In the area of foreign languages, objective items are more useful than in tests of writing ability in the native language, the second kind of test, because one of the problems at the early levels is the acquisition of new vocabulary, new grammar, and new spelling habits. Once original compositions are assigned in the foreign language, the matter of scoring must be dealt with: how do you compare the composition written correctly in simple vocabulary and short sentences with the more imaginative composition which exhibits a deeper "feeling" for the flow of the language but at the same time contains several mistakes? Diederich (23) insists that schools cannot significantly improve the grading of compositions until the responsibility for measuring these objectives has been transferred from individual teachers to the department as a whole. This departmental approach might also be effectively applied to testing the speaking skills. Austin and Riordan, at the annual meeting of the American Council on the Teaching of Foreign Languages (ACTFL), Chicago, December 1967, have suggested that correctness is best tested via objective items and that the composition should be judged primarily from the point of view of the monolingual native speaker: in this sense, errors that do not interfere with comprehensibility are judged less severely than errors that reduce or preclude understanding. Spelling mistakes that do not detract significantly from the message are overlooked. Idioms, phrases, and expressions that seem highly appropriate to the context are given extra credit. Brière (10) has demonstrated that the actual subject of the composition does not encourage the student to prefer one part of speech (e.g., nouns, adverbs) over another.

Testing writing

Kinesics (content area 3) has not to this time been the concern of language testers; in fact, it has hardly been the concern of language teachers. At the cognitive level (cells 3-A, 3-C) it is not difficult to devise multiple-choice items asking, for example, where the Frenchman keeps his left hand while eating (questions of this type do occur on the culture section of the MLA Proficiency Tests). Through videotape or film clips it would be possible to measure whether or not a student perceives certain movements (cells 3-B, 3-C) and whether he understands their significance (cell 3-G) and can analyze the conditions under which they were used (cell 3-I). In the absence of a true cul-

Kinesics

353

tural situation, the students could be asked to play roles (cells 3-E, 3-F) and demonstrate their ability to use typical gestures in a natural manner and under appropriate circumstances; e.g., the French handshake and when it is used. Green's inventory of Spanish gestures (25) will prove a valuable sourcebook for the test maker.

Testing the culture aims

The testing of culture aims is a relatively new field for foreign language teachers. True, for decades the New York State Regents Examinations have contained questions on geography, history, and civilization but these have been of the "knowledge" type (cells 5-A, 6-A, 5-C, 6-C). As the attention of teachers is drawn to the area of way-of-life culture, new testing techniques are needed.

Nostrand (in Seelye, 54) describes standards in sociocultural understanding for secondary students. Students recite a poem or describe a cultural theme, for example; almost all the test situations require knowledge and recall (objectives A, C, and E). Occasionally the students are asked to identify a typical gesture (objective D). The most complex behavior occurs in levels 3 and 4: students recognize cultural themes in unfamiliar material or explain why a cartoon or joke is humorous in terms of the second culture (cells 4-G, 4-I).

Upshur (60) warns against the danger of testing intelligence and general knowledge on culture tests. Seelye (53) field tested multiple-choice items of Lado's type and found that it was necessary to validate such items by pretesting them on both American groups and natives of the culture under study (in this case, Guatemala). A longer discussion of validation techniques in culture tests is found in Seelye (54). In this latter article he describes a variety of testing techniques: (1) simulated situations in which each student is given a role (e.g., Latin American student leader, president of Guatemala, peasant, Peace Corps volunteer, etc.) and the group is presented with a problem to solve; (2) objective tests (as in Lado, 27); (3) visual identification of cultural referents in a story (e.g., which of the following pictures shows a lottery vendor); (4) identification of auditory stimuli (e.g., the vendor's harangue); (5) tactile exercises (e.g., handling a knife and fork as the native would). Although many of these techniques test facts (cell 4-A) rather than skills (cells 4-E, 4-F), Seelye feels that the correlation between knowledge about a foreign culture and the ability to function in that

Validation

foreign culture is high. This, however, remains to be corroborated through further research.

In his work with Arab employees of American business enterprises in the Near East, Yousef (67) has found that students may attain fluency in English and accurately acquire facts about American culture and yet refuse to transfer this cultural knowledge in situations where American behavior patterns run counter to Arab etiquette and custom. The situation items Yousef has designed to reveal cultural conflict might be adapted to the testing of student sensitivity to aspects of cultural differences between the United States and France, Spain, Germany, etc.

Tests of student ability to analyze the cultural content of materials (such as articles or advertisements) have yet to be developed and validated. It might be possible to devise tests similar to the teaching materials described by Beaujour & Ehrmann (4). The use of videotape and film as an item stimulus also remains to be investigated. (As a counterpart to the testing of culture, testmakers have the challenge of devising culture-free tests of linguistic ability. Plaister [48] uses stick figures and geometric designs to build a culture-free test for listening comprehension.)

Videotape and film

Testing the literature aims

It is in the area of literature that the role of testing as a clarifier of objectives becomes most prominent. Literature has a queenly role in the language curriculum: literary works rise above ordinary prose and their appreciation demands careful analysis and evaluation (cells 7-I, 7-K). However, the introduction of "literature" courses before the students are linguistically able to cope with intensive reading in a second language has often led to a lowering of objectives. A look at the types of questions that occur on literature tests will point up the kinds of learning that take place.

A heavily used category of questions is that of knowledge (cell 7-A). Items of this type request the student to supply dates, names of authors, titles of works, etc. Other items in this category ask the student to describe romanticism or to discuss the "three unities" of classical French theater. It must be remembered that all questions that have been treated in class discussion and require the student to recall what he wrote in his notes are simple knowledge questions. For example, "Discuss Baudelaire's concept of poetry as it is expressed in *Correspondances*" sounds like a question of analysis (cell 7-I) and would require

Memory

355

analysis if the students were given the sonnet for the first time. But usually the students have discussed the poem in class and the writing of an acceptable exam paper requires primarily memory.

The category of comprehension (cell 7-G) elicits more complex behavior on the part of the student. Here he shows, for example, that he has understood the plot of a short story or the complexities of the intrigue of a play. Comprehension questions are used informally in class to determine whether the students have grasped the major events of a novel or other work. Here the language barrier frequently comes into prominence, for many students have difficulty reading the second language. Often the problem is one of unknown vocabulary (so the teacher returns to cell 2-A). To test comprehension on a formal test, the teacher might give the class a new poem by an author under study and ask for a brief résumé. The résumé of a work discussed in class would require only recall on the part of the student. Another exercise of comprehension is furnished by the items that ask the student to interpret figures of speech.

Comprehension

Literature has earned its renown in academic circles, not because it elicits behaviors on the levels of knowledge and comprehension but because the serious student of literature must engage in analysis (objective I) and critical evaluation (objective K). When the French student reads that the "Enfant de la haute mer" is covered with "taches de douceur," he must know that Supervielle is playing on the expression *taches de rousseur* ("freckles") and is using the new image to heighten the poetic effect of gentleness and a certain other-worldliness. Such analysis presupposes a solid command of the second language, a knowledge of literary conventions, and a comprehension of the overall meaning of the selection. Here the language teachers and the literature teachers join hands, for the student's performance at this level is a product of both linguistic and literary training. This is the French *explication de texte*.

Analysis

Other types of analysis, such as the study of character, themes, and sources, really do not necessitate the knowledge of a second language. In fact, all too often the students would be able to engage in more sophisticated analysis and avoid floundering in a pool of misinterpretation, were they to read the work of literature in their native language. If the aim of literature courses is analysis and evaluation at the extralinguistic level (that is, the analysis and evaluation of those aspects of the literary work that come across in translation), why have the students stumble through the original?

Testing the communication aims

The global category of communication cuts across the areas of language, kinesics, culture, and, to a lesser extent, literature. In evaluating student behavior from this global viewpoint, the examiner tries to measure general performance rather than the correctness of specific elements. The ability to communicate in a real-life situation could be tested in the foreign country by sending the student out to buy, for example, airmail stationery and envelopes. In such a situation the student himself can judge the effectiveness of his communication by seeing how readily he makes himself understood. In a contrived classroom situation, the teacher or a native informant is given a role to play (e.g., agent at a ticket counter) and the student is told to find out when the next train leaves for Munich. Communication has taken place if the student can obtain the required information; if there are items he fails to understand, he may ask questions to clarify his dilemma. This type of communication test is different from the "interview" test where the teacher asks the student questions and evaluates the latter's responses. In the former, the burden of comprehension is placed on the student himself.

A real life situation

The student's success in communicating via transmitted speech (telephone, tapes, etc.) may be evaluated in the language laboratory by indirect means. Marty (31) and Roy (51) have postulated the rate of delivery as a partial measure of speaking ability. Further validating studies must be carried out, for admittedly rate of delivery is an easy factor to measure. Listening comprehension may be evaluated by a modified "cloze" procedure. Spolsky, et al. (Upshur & Fata, 61) have been experimenting with sentences altered through the addition of white noise or static. Comprehension is checked by means of simple transcription. The tests are administered to a control group of native speakers. As the student listens to the various passages, his level of comprehension becomes an index of his listening ability. The more familiar the student is with the second language, the better able he will be to profit from the redundancies of the language to understand what is being said.

Once a group of students has attained a certain level of mastery in the second language, their relative proficiency in reading may be equated with reading speed at a specific level of comprehension. Then the students are given a speed test which is composed of several passages of similar difficulty, and the performance is timed.

The dictation has been shown to be a valid general measure of language proficiency (Valette, 65). If dictations are given rather infrequently in class, the performance on the dictation correlates highly with performance on subtests in vocabulary, grammar, and comprehension via all four language skills.

Dictation

Using tests

In the course of the year language students may take two kinds of tests: those that relate to the material taught in class ("homemade" tests or published tests that accompany the language program) and commercial tests that measure achievement with respect to a broader sample of the language. Both homemade and commercial tests may be divided into two categories according to the manner in which they treat student scores. The *norm-referenced test* enables the teacher to compare a student's performance against that of other students. On classroom tests, scores are given letter-grade equivalents. On commercial tests student results may be reported as standard scores (such as the well-known 200–800 scale used by the College Board), as percentile or norm bands, or as stanines. Norm-referenced tests are often used in research projects where it is necessary to compare the achievement of an experimental group with that of a control group. The *criterion-referenced test* reports the student's proficiency in absolute terms, e.g., student A speaks the language well enough to get around in the foreign country, or student B can handle the present tense but not the past tense. Classroom tests of this type are graded on a pass/fail or mastery/nonmastery basis. (Although Glaser [24] originally stated that a criterion-referenced test would equate scores with a point on a unidimensional learning continuum, the term "criterion-referenced test" is now being applied to all absolute content tests.) Achievement tests often appear as norm-referenced tests; a true proficiency test must by definition be a criterion-referenced test.

Criterion-referenced testing and mastery learning

Just as the emphasis in aptitude testing is shifting from the negative "who will succeed and who will fail" to the positive "how can the course be set up so that all students will succeed," so too is a change underway in the realm of classroom testing. The traditional quiz or unit test had to be difficult enough to provide a broad range of scores so that grades could be assigned with some degree of confidence. This practice of ranking students, either numerically or by means of letter grades, did furnish an incentive for the competition-minded student, but it had a stifling effect on the "C" and "D" student who found that success was consistently out of reach. Even when this student had reached a positive level of achievement in a specific subject, the top third of the class had outdistanced him in terms of material covered and his achievement went unrecognized. Bloom (8) states categorically that the traditional set of expectations (whereby the teacher assumes that one third of the class will adequately learn what he has to teach, that another third will fail or barely get by, and that the others will learn some but not enough) is "the most wasteful and destructive aspect of the present educational system." The new trend in classroom teaching is toward promoting mastery for all the students.

Traditional expectations destructive

In the area of foreign languages, the emphasis on mastery is of greatest importance. Pimsleur, Sundland, & McIntyre (44) in their study on underachievement pointed out the cumulative nature of second-language learning: of the students who get an A the first year, less than half will get an A the second year; more than half of those who get a B the first year will get a lower grade the second year. A serious problem facing foreign language teachers in the United States is the high attrition rate: roughly half the students in a first-year class go on to second year, only half of these progress to third year, etc. Unless the student really learns, unless he *masters* the material presented in the first year (rather than merely "covering" it), he will be unable to succeed in the second-year course.

FL learning cumulative

Newmark & Sweigert, et al. (36) used criterion-referenced tests in a project comparing the effectiveness of three Spanish elementary school programs. The striking—and rather frightening—conclusion was that students were attaining only a small percentage of the stated objectives of the three courses of study. With respect to language testing, this study is of singular importance: (1) it demonstrates the feasibility of criterion-referenced testing within the context of a large-scale research project, and (2) it leads one to question whether the traditional method of evaluating only a small sample of the linguistic course objectives might not obscure serious deficiencies in learning conditions and teaching materials.

Mastery needed

For Bloom (8) the strategy for mastery learning rates rests on the effective utilization of *formative evaluation*. The formative test covers a brief unit of instruction and is graded on a mastery/nonmastery basis. The level of mastery may be set quite high (control over 90 percent of the material presented) but the student is given as many chances as he needs to attain the mastery level. If a student does not pass the formative test, his corrected test shows not only where his weaknesses are (*diagnosis*) but also suggests what he might do (listen to specific tapes, read a related presentation in another text, go over a few pages in the workbook, etc.) to remedy those weaknesses (*prescription*).

Smith (55) reports on a California experiment with sixth-grade students of Spanish: group I was not allowed to proceed from one unit to the next unless 90 percent of the students responded correctly to 80 percent of the items on a formative test of listening comprehension. The teachers of group II classes were informed of unit test results but were free to continue to the next unit at their discretion. Teachers of group III (the control group) were not given the results of the unit tests. At the end of the year, group I, although it had covered less material, showed significantly greater gains on unit pretests and posttests and also performed significantly better than the other groups on the final test. Smith concludes that "teachers who are held responsible for specific objectives (i.e., who must bring the entire class to a specified level of mastery before continuing to the next unit) can be, at least, 1.6 times more effective in their teaching than teachers who are not held responsible." These California criterion-referenced tests are described in Damore (21).

Teachers held for specific objectives

The writer (Valette, 64) has suggested the *core-test concept* which would adapt formative evaluation to the area of foreign languages. All students enrolled in a given language course would be expected to master the core vocabulary and core structure plus the phonetic and morphophonemic systems; those students who assimilate the core material more rapidly would be given supplementary work in reading comprehension and listening comprehension. Since all students would be working on the same core material, group work in speaking and writing would be facilitated. In the place of traditional grades, report cards would indicate the number of units mastered. It is hoped that eventually colleges will word their foreign language entrance requirements in terms of a specified level of mastery rather than in terms of the number of hours (measured in "years") spent sitting in a language classroom. The adoption of such an entrance

Core-test

requirement has been frequently recommended; e.g., Belasco, et al. (7) at the Northeast Conference in 1963.

Available standard tests

At the present time there are, in addition to the secure and constantly revised College Entrance Examination Board (CEEB) Achievement Tests in foreign languages, three commercial standardized tests that reflect the present emphasis on functional skills. (For a listing of other commercial tests, see the appendix to Valette, 63.)

The Common Concepts Test by Banathy, et al. (1) tests comprehension of the spoken language (scripts are in English, French, German, and Spanish) by having the student select the one picture of four that corresponds to the sentence he hears on tape. The test evaluates the skill of understanding at level one, and by extension the author feels that the test provides a measure of overall language proficiency. Switzer & Pederson (58) have been successful in using the test as a component in a placement battery.

Common concepts test

The MLA (Modern Language Association) Cooperative Foreign Language Tests (33) are a battery of 80 tests: two forms at each of two levels (less advanced and more advanced) in the four skills of listening, speaking, reading, and writing for each of five languages (French, German, Italian, Russian, and Spanish). At the time of their publication, these tests represented a significant breakthrough in the evaluation of achievement in foreign languages: all skills were measured and English was used only in the instructions. The norm tables for these tests were developed more than five years ago: changes in instruction since that time would indicate that these norms be revised to keep the tests up to date. Smith & Baranyi (56) have reported new Pennsylvania secondary school norms in German; these norms are lower than those established by ETS at the time of test publication. This Pennsylvania study also showed that the less advanced forms of the French and German MLA Coop Tests are too difficult for students with only one year of study and still rather difficult (especially German) for students with two years of study. Carroll (14) underscored two disadvantages of the tests: "the tests are not adequate as measures of the student's command of the grammar of the foreign language, since rather high scores on many of the tests can be attained through sheer vocabulary knowledge" and "the tests do not yield scores on a single scale of language competence in a given skill." This mat-

MLA Cooperative FL Tests

ter of vocabulary load must be carefully determined for each test. It should be noted that vocabulary knowledge represents the simplest behavioral objective: if students fail to do well on the test because of limited vocabulary, then the test results are no longer a measure of proficiency in a language skill.

In the fall of 1968, the early forms of the MLA Proficiency Test for Teachers and Advanced Students (34) forms A and B for French, German, Spanish, and Russian, and form A for Italian were made available for purchase by accredited agencies and institutions under the new designation of forms HA and HB of the MLA Coop Tests. The relationship between the scores of these tests and the scores of the L and M levels of the MLA Coop Tests was the subject of a study by Paquette, et al. (40). The handbook for the HA and HB forms is in press. At this time there remains only one secure form of the original MLA Proficiency Tests.

MLA Proficiency Tests for Teachers and Advanced Students

The Pimsleur Proficiency Tests (45) in French, German, and Spanish comprise a battery of 24 tests: two levels (A or level one, and C or level two) in the four skills for the three languages. The development of these tests is described in Pimsleur (42). The Pimsleur tests were designed for use with first- and second-year high school students. The reading tests are rather difficult and provide more reliable results if used with students with one or two semesters training beyond the level indicated. About half of the items in the reading tests are inference items: when students miss these items the teacher cannot be sure whether the student understood the surface meaning of the passage and failed to draw the correct inference or whether the student was unable to understand the passage itself. The vocabulary load in this battery remains to be defined.

Pimsleur Proficiency Tests

The College Entrance Examination Board Achievement Tests are developed yearly by a committee of secondary school and college teachers. At present, the students go to the test center and take a one-hour objective-type reading test in the language of their choice (options: French, German, Spanish, Russian, Latin, Hebrew). Subsequently they may take a supplementary achievement test in listening comprehension at their own schools; written supplementary tests are available in Italian and Greek. Within the next few years it is hoped that the listening and reading portions will be combined in a single one-hour examination to be given at the testing center. Norms for these tests, which previously were developed for students with one to four years of high school study, are now being extended to in-

CEEB Achievement Tests

clude students with FLES (foreign language in the elementary school) and junior high experience.

Commercial language tests were originally constructed for a single purpose: to provide comparative data about student proficiency in foreign languages. The College Entrance Examination Board, which has exercised a considerable influence on the form of commercial tests, prepares language achievement tests with one aim in mind: to allow member colleges to compare applicant A's language background with that of applicant B. The 200–800-point scale indicates the applicant's approximate position with respect to high school seniors on a national scale. That the CEEB Tests are norm-referenced conforms to the nature of the College Board program.

If we turn our attention to the other widely-used commercial language tests, we find that they too are norm-referenced. The MLA Coop Test, the Pimsleur Proficiency Tests, and the Common Concepts Test all report scores in comparative terms. By using the manuals that accompany these tests, the teacher can estimate approximately where a student stands with respect to a national norms group and with respect to his classmates or schoolmates (if the teacher follows instructions for developing local norms). But how useful is this information to the teacher? It is necessary to the researcher who, in evaluating different approaches or different techniques, needs to compare group performances, but to the individual teacher such information is merely "interesting."

The criterion-referenced battery and diagnostic tests

What the teacher needs is diagnostic information: Who knows what? Who doesn't know what? How can incoming students be grouped in homogeneous classes? The handbook for the MLA Coop Tests mentions that item data may be used to evaluate programs and students, but no listing of item content is provided. The manuals for the Pimsleur Proficiency Tests state that the tests were not intended for diagnostic purposes, but do provide item-by-item breakdowns of the following points: the sounds *A diagnostic function* tested in Part 2 of the Speaking Test, the grammatical content of the first three parts of the Writing Test, and the abilities (comprehension and inference) measured in the Reading Test. Both the MLA Coop Tests and the Pimsleur Tests do allow the teacher to draw general conclusions about the student's relative proficiency in the four skills. Retired forms of the CEEB Achievement Tests are available to schools for use as placement tests; however, these tests were never designed as placement instruments and the simple sectioning of students by CEEB scores does not take into account the relative strengths and weaknesses of the individual.

The present commercial tests were developed as norm-referenced instruments. Items were selected for inclusion in these batteries for only one reason: they discriminated effectively between the good students and the weak students. The purpose of these tests is to provide a broad range of scores so that conclusions about the comparative proficiencies of students may be made with the best possible degree of reliability. The description of item content simply reflects the final form of the test.

The diagnostic test or placement test, to be most effective, is developed in just the opposite manner. The test designer determines which elements of language must be measured, he writes the items, and then, if desired, he can determine item difficulty and test norms. In other words, the criterion-referenced test requires the prior establishment of a criterion. In a few areas, such as phonology, sound-symbol associations and morphophonemics, languages may have a closed system: it is possible to list all the aspects to be tested and write appropriate items. (See the Valette Listening Discrimination Tests and the Valette Sound Production Tests developed for the Pennsylvania Research Project in Smith & Berger, 57.) Testing of vocabulary, on the other hand, requires sampling techniques. Grammar may be classified in categories; one such system has been established by Damore (21).

Criterion – referenced item writing

Effective placement tests for foreign languages have been developed by institutions whose primary function is teaching a second language to foreigners (for example, the Alliance Francaise and the Goethe Institut). Test C.G.M. 62 (20) has been designed to accompany the Saint Cloud materials (*Voix et Images de France*). The professional language schools use these tests to place incoming students in the sections appropriate to their level of competence.

The typical American college or secondary school, however, does not have the same flexibility as the professional language school. Often the courses are not as tightly articulated. Specific institutions typically develop their own placement procedures based on a variety of factors, such as years of language study, scores on an achievement test, IQ measures, and grade point averages. It is in this context that a criterion-referenced place-

364

ment battery would permit a more effective system of placement.

Valette (Upshur & Fata, 61) has proposed a model for a series of criterion-referenced tests for elementary and intermediate students that would measure both mastery of specific elements and proficiency in the skills.

For example, once the student has demonstrated his knowledge of a predetermined amount of vocabulary and grammar (e.g., point B on Figure 2), he would take skills tests built around that

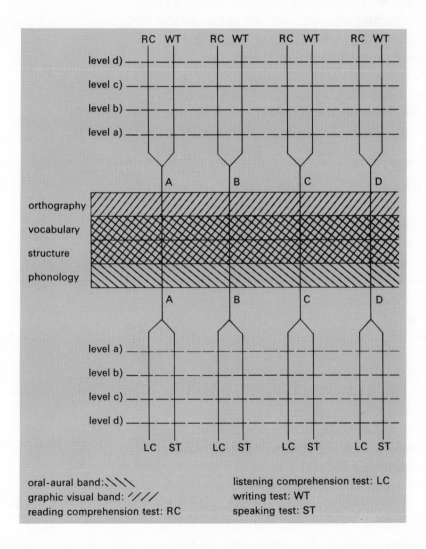

FIGURE 2. Model for a criterion-referenced battery. (Reprinted with permission from *Language Learning*.)

corpus of language. In the area of listening, for example, level (a) would mean that the student could understand the material when it was clearly and carefully enunciated. At a higher level, e.g., level (c), he would be able to understand similar conversations when spoken rapidly. The form such criterion-referenced tests will take remains to be determined. Perhaps packages of "microtests" will prove more efficient for the classroom teacher.

As we emphasize each student's potential for learning a second language, and implement the effectiveness of our classroom instruction with some sort of formative evaluation, we will also need reliable diagnostic and placement tests to improve articulation between grades and between schools. At present the lack of coordination between grades and between schools is one of the reasons for the high attrition rate in foreign languages and explains the existence of such a high proportion of underachievers (cf. Pimsleur, Sundland, & McIntyre, 44). Appropriate criterion- *Articulation* referenced tests accompanied with carefully prepared manuals will contribute to the improvement of foreign language instruction in this country.

The classification of commercial tests and test items

The proliferation of language tests, together with the wide variety of skills and knowledges measured by these tests, has made it necessary for research groups to attempt the classification of test collections. To date the most extensive effort in this direction is being made by the Center on Bilingual Studies at Laval University in Quebec. The basic classification system is described by Mackey (29) and is presented in greater detail by Savard (Upshur & Fata, 61). Carroll (Davies, 22) proposes a system for the classification of language test tasks in a series of three tables.

Summary

In the classroom, the teacher must turn his attention to formative evaluation and use his tests to bring every student (not just those in the top ten percent) to the level of mastery. The current standard tests should be subjected to careful content analysis to determine what biases they contain: it appears that in reading tests undue emphasis is presently placed on vocabulary knowledge, while some speaking tests give too much importance to the ability to produce phonemes accurately. All the current standard tests are norm-referenced tests and provide comparative data on the students. What is needed in the profession is a battery of absolute-content or criterion-referenced tests that can serve as placement instruments and provide objective measures of proficiency.

Testing foreign language requirements in the graduate school

In graduate schools throughout the United States the nature of the foreign language requirement is periodically reexamined and new means of evaluating the requirement are investigated. In 1964, the Educational Testing Service offered the Graduate School Foreign Language Test (GSFLT) to institutions of higher education wishing to test their students' competence in French, German, and Russian. Section I of the test contains multiple-choice questions in the foreign language that measure the student's control of basic vocabulary and structure; Section II contains reading passages followed by multiple-choice questions in English that evaluate the student's grasp of specific content in one of four areas: humanities, biological sciences, physical sciences, and social sciences. In 1967, a Spanish test was offered that differed from the tests in French, German, and Russian in that it did not offer optional sections in fields of specialization. Scores on the GSFLT are reported on a scale ranging from 200 to 800.

GSFLT

Harvey (26) reviews the development of the GSFLT. Whereas the Spanish test will continue in the same format, the French, German, and Russian tests, effective 1968–69, will contain only three optional sections: humanities, natural sciences, and social sciences. Beginning in the fall of 1969, these tests, which were previously administered by participating institutions, will be offered on a national basis at testing centers established by ETS with the cooperation of colleges and universities. The Harvey Report contains the mean scores and minimal cutoff scores reported by 44 graduate schools in the United States. The report also contains the percentile ranks of scores obtained by 900 undergraduate students who had just completed a fourth semester of French or German with a grade of C− or higher; these tables allow institutions to compare GSFLT scores with the performance of students completing an "intermediate" college course.

The Harvey Report

Bartlett (3) presents the results of a detailed study of the foreign language requirement at the University of Colorado. It was found that the passing scores on the GSFLT had been set so low as to make the foreign language requirement a "meaningless hurdle." This article contains the specific recommendations of the study, which were adopted by the University of Colorado in April 1968. The emphasis of the requirement lies on "communi-

Recommendations from the University of Colorado study

cation" skill: all Ph.D. candidates must demonstrate at least second-year college proficiency in one language, either by presenting his undergraduate transcript showing a grade of C or better in a fourth-semester undergraduate course, by registering in such a course as a graduate student and earning at least a C, or by obtaining an equivalent score on the GSFLT. Additional foreign language requirements may be made by individual departments.

Clark (19) surveys the current doctoral-level language requirements and testing practices as reported in questionnaires received from 1,604 graduate school department chairmen in the United States. About half of the chairmen indicated that they used locally prepared language examinations, 25 percent used only the GSFLT, 20 percent used both the GSFLT and a local exam, and about 7 percent apparently used less formal evaluation procedures. The survey also presents the degree requirement status of five common languages (French, German, Italian, Russian, and Spanish), as well as importance ratings by the chairmen of various language learning goals.

Clark's survey of doctoral-level language requirements

It should be noted, in conclusion, that the GSFLT is a norm-referenced test, and hence schools are experiencing difficulties in interpreting test scores. What is needed in this area is a criterion-referenced test, scored on a pass/fail basis or a "fluency" continuum, which would indicate whether the student can read the foreign language well enough for research purposes.

Evaluating teacher competence

Over the past ten years, as foreign language enrollments have risen, the need for competent foreign language teachers has similarly become more acute. Efforts have been made to develop objective measures of teacher competence to supplement, or perhaps even replace, current certification procedures. Our point of departure in this discussion on the evaluation of teacher proficiency is Paquette's *Guidelines for Teacher Education Programs in Modern Foreign Languages: an Exposition* (37). This compilation contains the statement of "qualifications for secondary school teachers of modern foreign languages" and a description of the MLA Proficiency Tests for Teachers and Advanced Students.

The statement of qualifications, since it was to apply to teachers of all languages, is made up of broad statements. Before it will be possible to determine with precision whether such stand-

Guidelines must be translated into behavioral goals

ards have been met, or whether a teacher's qualifications should be classified as "minimal," "good," or "superior," it will be the task of teachers in each language to derive a set of comparable standards stated in behavioral terms (cf. Mager, 30).

At present the only tests that provide a measure of teacher competence are the MLA Foreign Language Proficiency Tests for Teachers and Advanced Students (34). The Commonwealth of Pennsylvania has been the first state to require that all candidates for certification present their scores on these tests (Perkins, 41). Several other states, such as New York, use the tests to certify teachers who have not received formal training in American universities. However, three questions have been raised with respect to this test battery.

MLA Proficiency Tests

The first is the matter of test content. A team of language teachers has reviewed forms A, B, and C of the battery (Paquette & Tollinger, 39). Reviews of the tests have also appeared in Buros (11). Although the tests have been praised because they perform well statistically (the MLA Proficiency Tests are norm-referenced tests) and because they do provide an objective evaluation of teacher proficiency, many questions of detail have been raised. Is listening comprehension effectively measured in the listening test, or are other factors such as retention introduced? Do the many factual questions in the culture test (styles of furniture, names of authors, details of geography, etc.) add up to a measure of "culture"? What is the vocabulary load of the reading test? Does the professional preparation test become too dogmatic in its espousal of "New Key" theories? In an effort to establish the validity of the four skills tests, Battery A (listening, reading, speaking, writing) was administered to native speakers in France, Germany, Spain, South America, etc., in the summer of 1967 (Paquette & Tollinger, 38). It was found that the speaking tapes (especially the mimicry and reading aloud sections) were being scored so rigidly that native speakers received mediocre scores because of allophonic variations in their delivery. Native speakers occasionally received lower scores on the reading comprehension tests because they had difficulty with sections requiring literary analysis.

Content

The second question with respect to the MLA Proficiency Tests is that of scaling. Meyers & Melton (32) studied the relationship between scores on these tests and outside ratings of teacher competence, but no interpretive scale was established. The candidate's performance on these tests is still being reported in the form of raw scores. One of the recommendations of the MLA committee (Paquette & Tollinger, 39) was that these scores be converted to the 200–800-point scale that ETS uses for College Board examinations. It was also pointed out in one of the reports that the MLA tests are not really proficiency tests at all, but rather high-level achievement tests in the sense that the results furnish only comparative information. In a nationwide testing of college seniors majoring in foreign languages, Carroll (12) made a preliminary effort to equate the raw scores of Part A with the criterion-based ratings of the Foreign Service Institute. Although his sample was relatively small, and although his investigation should be duplicated on a larger scale in order to permit a more reliable scaling of raw scores, the results of the study do indicate that the individual tests measure varying ranges of competence.

Scaling

The third question is that of application. Since a prime reason for the development of these tests was to provide states and administrators with an objective evaluation of teacher proficiency, it will be necessary to assess relationship between this measured proficiency and competence in the classroom. As a result of their study of foreign language teaching strategies and the utilization of the language laboratory, Smith & Berger (57) concluded that:

MLA Proficiency Tests and classroom competency

1 Assessment of teacher proficiency by competent observers correlated highly with teacher scores on the MLA Proficiency Test for Teachers and Advanced Students. They did not correlate with teacher self-ratings.
2 There was no significant relationship between scores of 89 French and German teachers on all seven parts of the Teacher Proficiency Tests and the achievement scores, both gross and gain, of their first-year classes in foreign language skills.

Perhaps the teacher's most important role with first-year classes is to stimulate the students' interest in learning the language. Perhaps the teacher's actual command of the language is less important at that level, than at the third or fourth level. After the second level, students' listening ability in French did correlate with teacher scores on the Speaking Test (56). It would be interesting to see what correlation exists between teacher proficiency in language skills and the performance of advanced classes. It is certain that further research in the area of teacher proficiency must try to define which teacher qualities do contribute to enhancing student achievement and then develop instruments that can measure those qualities.

Another step in the direction of providing a measure of teacher competence is the Performance Criteria for the Foreign Language Teacher developed by Politzer, et al. (49) and elaborated by Ryberg, et al. (52). If these criteria, or this series of hypotheses, are to be used for teacher evaluation, their validity and reliability must first be established.

Performance criteria

Moskowitz (35) has applied interaction analysis to foreign language teaching. So far, it has been found that teachers using interaction analysis techniques sense an improvement in their teaching ability and that the students develop more favorable attitudes toward these teachers. Further research in this area might lead the way toward the creation of a measurement instrument whose scores would correlate more highly with measured student achievement.

Interaction analysis

Summary

Much work remains to be done in the area of teacher competence. The descriptions of MLA qualification levels must be translated into behavioral terms if we wish to measure whether these levels have been attained by the candidates. Teacher performance must be carefully examined to determine whether standards can be objectively described and evaluated.

Concluding comments

In the area of foreign language testing, the innovative work of the past three years (1966–68) lies in the domain of criterion-referenced testing. Researchers and teachers are slowly turning away from their preoccupation with prognostic measures and the corresponding norm-referenced achievement tests. Although it was intellectually stimulating to try to rank beginning students according to their probable chance of success in a foreign language course and to test one's prediction against the results of an end-of-the-year standard test that ranked students according to performance, researchers are now focusing on the greater challenge of affording each student a satisfactory language learning experience. In aptitude testing, therefore, the shift is away from prognosis toward diagnosis and the new concern is to reduce the correlation between aptitude and achievement measures to zero (i.e., to enable *all* students to attain a degree of mastery in a second language regardless of initial aptitude). With respect to achievement testing, the new trend is moving in the direction of positive teacher expectancies, mastery tests, and criterion-referenced measures. Research to date has indicated that student learning can be significantly enhanced if teachers focus on specific linguistic objectives and insist that a high percentage of those objectives be mastered before continuing to the subsequent lesson. The existing criterion-referenced tests have, up to this time, been constructed and administered by individuals or districts. Hopefully, the next few years will witness the development and distribution of criterion-referenced language tests on a commercial scale: tests to accompany teaching materials, tests for articulation and placement purposes, tests for teacher proficiency, and tests of specific skills (such as reading knowledge of a foreign language for research purposes).

References, Testing

1 Banathy, Bela; et al. The common concepts foreign language test. California Test Bureau, Monterey, Calif., 1962.

2 Banathy, Bela; et al. The common concepts foreign language test. Modern Language Journal, 46(1962) 363–365.

3 Bartlett, Albert A. The foreign language requirement for the Ph.D.: a new approach. Foreign Language Annals, 2(1968) 174–184.

4 Beaujour, Michel; Ehrmann, Jacques. A semiotic approach to culture. Foreign Language Annals, 1(1967) 152–163.

5 Belasco, Simon. The plateau or the case for comprehension: the concept approach. Modern Language Journal, 51(1967) 82–88.

6 Belasco, Simon. Structure plus meaning equals language proficiency. The Florida FL Reporter, Spring, 1966.

7 Belasco, Simon; et al. The continuum: listening and speaking. In: Reports of the Working Committees, Northeast Conference (RWCNEC). MLA Materials Center, New York, 1963, p. 1–21.

8 Bloom, Benjamin S. Learning for mastery. UCLA Evaluation Comment, Center for the Study of Evaluation of Instructional Programs, 1:ii(May 1968) 12 p.

9 Brière, Eugène. Phonological testing reconsidered. Language Learning 17(1967) 163–171.

10 Brière, Eugène. Testing the control of parts of speech in foreign language compositions. Language Learning, 14(1964) 1–10.

11 Buros, Oscar Krisen, ed. Sixth mental measurements yearbook. Gryphon Press, Highland Park, N.J., 1965.

12 Carroll, John B. Foreign language proficiency levels attained by language majors near gradua-

tion from college. Foreign Language Annals, 1(1967) 131–151.

13 Carroll, John B. The prediction of success in intensive foreign language training. In: Glaser, Robert, ed. Training research and education. University of Pittsburgh Press, Pittsburgh, 1962. (Reprinted by MLA Materials Center, New York).

14 Carroll, John B. Research in foreign language teaching: the last five years. In: Reports of the Working Committees, Northeast Conference (RWCNEC). MLA Materials Center, New York, 1966, p. 12–42.

15 Carroll, John B.; Sapon, Stanley. Elementary modern language aptitude test. Psychological Corporation, New York, 1967.

16 Carroll, John B.; Sapon, Stanley. Modern language aptitude test. Psychological Corporation, New York, 1967.

17 Carton, Aaron S. Rating speech: many considerations, some data. Experimental Teaching Center, School of Education, New York University, New York, 1964. Mimeo.

18 Clark, John L. D. Empirical studies related to the teaching of French pronunciation to American students. Laboratory for Research in Instruction, Graduate School of Education, Harvard University, Cambridge, Mass., 1967.

19 Clark, John L. D. The graduate school foreign language requirement: a survey of testing practices and related topics. Foreign Language Annals, 2(1968) 150–164.

20 CREDIF, École Normale Supérieure de Saint Cloud. Test C.G.M. 62. Didier, Paris, 1962. (Reprinted by Chilton Books, Philadelphia, Pa., 1967.)

21 Damore, Anthony P. Teaching Spanish by being responsible for specific objectives. Stanislaus

County Schools Office, Modesto, Calif., 1968.

22 Davies, Alan. Language testing symposium: a psycholinguistic approach. Oxford University Press, London, 1968.

23 Diederich, Paul B. Cooperative preparation and rating of essay tests. Educational Testing Service, Princeton, N.J., 1967. Mimeo.

24 Glaser, Robert. Instructional technology and the measurement of learning outcomes: some questions. American Psychologist, 18(1963) 519–522.

25 Green, Jerald R. A gesture inventory for the teaching of Spanish. Chilton Books, Philadelphia, Pa., 1968.

26 Harvey, Philip R. Minimal passing scores on the graduate school foreign language tests. Foreign Language Annals, 2(1968) 165–173.

27 Lado, Robert. Language testing: the construction and use of foreign language tests. Longmans, London, 1961. (Reprinted by McGraw-Hill, New York, 1964.)

28 Lambert, Wallace E. Motivation and language learning: psychological aspects. In: Newell, Sanford, ed. Dimension: languages 68. Southern Conference on Language Teaching, Spartanburg, S.C., 1968.

29 Mackey, William. Language teaching analysis. Indiana University Press, Bloomington, 1967.

30 Mager, Robert F. Preparing instructional objectives. Fearon, Palo Alto, Calif., 1962.

31 Marty, Fernand. Teaching French. Audio-Visual Publications (Box 5497), Roanoke, Va., 1968.

32 Meyers, Charles T.; Melton, Richard S. A study of the relationship between scores on the MLA foreign language proficiency tests for teachers and advanced students and ratings of teacher competence. Educational Testing Service, Princeton, N.J., 1964.

33 MLA Cooperative Foreign Language Tests. Educational Testing Service, Princeton, N.J., 1963.

34 MLA Foreign Language Proficiency Tests for Teachers and Advanced Students. Educational Testing Service, Princeton, N.J., 1961.

35 Moskowitz, Gertrude. The effects of training foreign language teachers in interaction analysis. Foreign Language Annals, 1(1968) 218–235.

36 Newmark, Gerald; Sweigert, Ray L.; et al. A field test of three approaches to the teaching of Spanish in elementary schools. California State Department of Education, Sacramento, 1966.

37 Paquette, F. André, ed. Guidelines for teacher education programs in modern foreign languages: an exposition. Modern Language Journal, 50:vi(1966).

38 Paquette, F. André; Tollinger, Suzanne. The MLA foreign language proficiency tests for teachers and advanced students: analysis of the performance of native speakers and comparison with that of NDEA summer institute participants. Modern Language Association, New York, 1968.

39 Paquette, F. André; Tollinger, Suzanne. The MLA foreign language proficiency tests for teachers and advanced students: a professional evaluation and recommendations for test development. Modern Language Association, New York, 1966.

40 Paquette, F. André; et al. A comparison of the MLA foreign language proficiency tests for teachers and advanced students with the MLA foreign language cooperative tests. Modern Language Association, New York, 1966.

41 Perkins, Jean A. State certification and proficiency tests: the experience in Pennsylvania. Foreign Language Annals, 2(1968) 195–199.

42 Pimsleur, Paul. Testing foreign language learning. In: Valdman, Albert, ed. Trends in language teaching. McGraw-Hill, New York, 1966, p. 175–214.

43 Pimsleur, Paul; Mosberg, Ludwig; Morrison, Andrew L. Student factors in foreign language learning. Modern Language Journal, 46(1962) 160–170.

44 Pimsleur, Paul; Sundland, Donald M.; McIntyre, Ruth D. Under-achievement in foreign language learning. MLA Materials Center, New York, 1966.

45 Pimsleur French/German/Spanish proficiency tests. Harcourt, Brace & World, New York, 1967.

46 Pimsleur Language Aptitude Battery. Harcourt, Brace & World, New York, 1966.

47 Plaister, Ted. Language testing: a selected bibliography. Department of English as a Second Language, University of Hawaii, Honolulu, 1968.

48 Plaister, Ted. Testing aural comprehension: a culture fair approach. TESOL Quarterly, 1: iii(1967) 17–19.

49 Politzer, Robert L.; et al. Performance criteria for the foreign language teacher. Stanford Center for Research and Development in Teaching, Stanford, Calif., 1966.

50 Rosenthal, Robert; Jacobsen, Lenore F. Pygmalion in the classroom. Holt, Rinehart, & Winston, New York, 1968.

51 Roy, Robert R. Complexity—a factor of oral proficiency. Manitoba Journal of Educational Research, 3(1967) 45–52.

52 Ryberg, Don; et al. Performance criteria for the foreign language teacher. Upper Midwest Research Educational Laboratory (UMREL), Minneapolis, Minn., 1968. Mimeo.

53 Seelye, H. Ned. Field notes on cross-cultural testing. Language Learning, 16(1966) 77–85.

54 Seelye, H. Ned, ed. A handbook on Latin America for teachers. Office of the Superintendent of Public Instruction, Springfield, Ill., 1968.

55 Smith, Melvin I. Teaching to specific objectives. Stanislaus County Schools Office, Modesto, Calif., 1968.

56 Smith, Philip D., Jr.; Baranyi, Helmut A. A comparison of the effectiveness of the traditional and audiolingual approaches to foreign language instruction utilizing laboratory equipment. U.S. Department of Health, Education and Welfare, Office of Education, Washington, D.C., 1968.

57 Smith, Philip D., Jr; Berger, Emanuel. An assessment of three foreign language teaching strategies utilizing three language laboratory systems. U.S. Department of Health, Education and Welfare, Office of Education, Washington, D.C., 1968.

58 Switzer, Charles A.; Pederson, Walter E. Placement testing: from FLES to high school. West

High School, Bakersfield, Calif., 1967. Mimeo.

59 Traill, A. Concerning the diagnosis and remedying of lack of competence in a second language. Language Learning, 18(1968) 253–258.

60 Upshur, John A. Cross-cultural testing: what to test. Language Learning, 16(1966) 183–196.

61 Upshur, John A.; Fata, Julia, eds. Problems in foreign language testing. Language Learning (1968), Special Issue no. 3.

62 Valette, Rebecca M. Improving multiple-choice grammar tests in German. German Quarterly, 40(1967) 87–91.

63 Valette, Rebecca M. Modern language testing. Harcourt, Brace & World, New York, 1967.

64 Valette, Rebecca M. Testing and motivation. In: Newell, Sanford, ed. Dimension: language 68. Southern Conference on Language Teaching, Spartanburg, S.C., 1968.

65 Valette, Rebecca M. The use of the dictée in the French language classroom. Modern Language Journal, 48(1964) 431–434.

66 Wilkins, George W., Jr.; Hoffman, Lee E. The use of cognates in testing pronunciation. Language Learning, 14(1964) 39–43.

67 Yousef, Fathi S. Cross-cultural testing: an aspect of the resistance reaction. Language Learning, 18(1968) 227–234.

13
Foreign language program evaluation

Introduction

William N. Hatfield
Purdue University

"Program evaluation" is a relatively innocent-appearing term that encompasses a considerable scope of educational activities. As a term it frequently appears in the professional literature and is often heard in faculty curriculum meetings. However, and quite paradoxically so, the behaviors and procedures usually symbolized by the term are much less frequently encountered in the domain of educational activities.

Significant materials from 1968 and early 1969 and relevant documents from the 1965–67 period immediately indicate that there is considerably more theoretical pondering and prescription than true empirical research.

A review of research and related literature must begin with a definition of essential terminology. "Program" is a highly inclusive term referring to all aspects of the teaching-learning process involved in learning a second language in our educational system. Within any program most curriculum theorists distinguish between *curriculum* and *instruction*. The former is the content, or the skills and verbalized knowledge to be transmitted, whereas the latter refers to the efficiency with which the particular arrangement of content is transmitted to the learner. Macdonald (33) in making this distinction accurately points out that curriculum evaluation is frequently conducted at the output point of instruction rather than at the input position. In this way curriculum evaluation is confounded with instructional evaluation. The output evaluation is, in fact, a type of program evaluation. Johnson (30) takes note of the fact that, if one wishes to perform curriculum evaluation rather than program evaluation, differences in instructional effectiveness must be controlled, randomized, or partialled out. Evaluation of extant programs, without consideration for constituent factors, is very feasible through evaluation of the outputs. This approach is discussed in greater detail below.

"Evaluation" implies the collection, processing, and interpretation of data pertaining to an educational program. In an evaluation two major kinds of data are collected: *(1)* objective descriptions of goals, environmental factors, personnel, pro-

Curriculum is . . .

Instruction is . . .

Thanks are due to Gilbert A. Jarvis for his extensive help in developing this chapter.

cedures, and content, and their relationships to outcomes; and (2) value judgments as to quality and appropriateness of these goals, environmental factors, etc.

Stufflebeam (47) lists four questions that must be answered in carrying out any evaluation: (1) What is to be evaluated? (2) What information is to be collected? (3) How will this information be collected, organized, analyzed, and disseminated? (4) How will these activities be accomplished?

Evaluation components

The information collected must be both valid and reliable. Broad considerations are involved in these two simple terms. The information must be representative of the program not only at a single point in time, but also through the continuum of time during which the program functions. For example, information gathered in October must not be contradicted by information gathered in April. Furthermore, before the information can become meaningful, criteria must be established. The criteria determine the ideal to be attained or the degree of approximation that will be tolerated.

The scope of this chapter and relevance to the reader preclude listing individual program evaluations that have been completed. Such information is rarely published and lacks pertinence for those outside the school district or institution. Information about such evaluations is most readily available from the supervisory offices of the educational unit with which one is concerned. A listing of state and local foreign language supervisors and their addresses is maintained by MLA/ERIC (Modern Language Association/Educational Resources Information Center) and was most recently published in *Foreign Language Annals* (13).

Also excluded from individual evaluations are textbooks and programs of commercial publishers. Research comparisons of the effectiveness of various programs generally do not permit objective evaluation of the materials per se because of the confounding of many variables. Guidelines for textbook or materials selection are usually available from state supervisors, from the Modern Language Association Foreign Language Research Center (38, 39) which had committees in each of the languages evaluate over several thousand items. Those found acceptable were rated in various categories and criteria included that show the bases for reaching the judgments. In addition, books are also reviewed in several of the foreign language journals. Most commercially prepared materials remain within the traditional format of a textbook accompanied by various supplementary

Materials evaluation

materials such as audiotapes, films, filmstrips, overhead projection materials, and posters. Gut (25) lists the most commonly used text materials in American colleges and universities for first- and second-year French courses. Fiks (17) identified only 26 programmed courses available for the 1966–67 academic year. There were three each in French, Spanish, and German, and one each in various other languages. More recently Ornstein (42) reviewed the current state of programmed foreign language instruction. He concluded that despite a rather dreary picture that has emerged up to this point, redeeming features and even considerable promise are present in the current programmed materials. Previous failure may be due to unrealistic expectations and inability to identify proper instructional roles for the materials. All materials reviewed were of the linear rather than branching variety. *Programmed courses*

In 1969, after several years of preparation, the first National Assessment of Educational Attainments was scheduled to begin. The overall purpose of the National Assessment is to provide a base line of census-like data on the educational attainments of our population in certain subject areas. The initial areas selected are writing, reading, social studies, citizenship, science, art, music, literature, and vocational education. Finley (18) notes that there has been discussion of developing additional areas once they have been launched and that foreign languages might be among them. Critics of the effort see it as resembling a nationwide individual testing program. They fear, moreover, that it could lead to a national curriculum. Proponents stress the fact that census-like data will be collected rather than achievement scores for individual students and that it will be done only on a sampling basis. *National assessment*

Relevant to the general topic of program evaluation is the establishment of the Center for the Study of Evaluation of Instructional Programs based at the University of California at Los Angeles. The center's basic purposes are (50): to clarify the process of evaluating instructional programs by formulating appropriate theory; to identify, measure, and study variables relevant to the evaluation of instructional programs; and to develop and field test systems for evaluating educational programs and institutions. Special attention is given to the multiple consequences produced by instruction interacting with individual students and teachers in learning situations. *New Center for Evaluation*

The existence of interaction between individual students and the method by which they are taught seems to be a growing concern. Students of differing aptitude seem to learn more (or less) efficiently under different methods. The same method is not equally effective with students of all levels of ability. Chastain (11) offers tentative conclusions from research in college-level beginning Spanish that students not only learn differently but also have predispositions for different approaches to learning, and that these differences can be anticipated. Kelly (31) also found interaction between method and aptitude. Bartley (4) in a pilot study of aptitude and attitude as influences upon the high dropout rate concludes by wondering what part of the instructional process is at fault in the high attrition rate. The conclusion one must draw from this work is that any program evaluation that looks at global aspects, such as mean achievement, does not make use of all the information potentially available. Information is lost, and undoubtedly this is frequently significant information. While this statement is, in a sense, an indictment of all current program evaluation work including the methodologies described below, it must be remembered that practical considerations make summary data an unavoidable and a time-saving technique in evaluation. The processing of all individual bits of information, even if such information were totally valid and reliable, would be an overwhelming task.

Different aptitudes call for different methods

The methodologies employed in program evaluation and their concomitant problems are the central focus of this chapter. The great mass of operations and behaviors that are subsumed under the label "program evaluation" can be abstracted or categorized in many different ways. Goodlad (22), while speaking in the context of evaluating new programs, identifies four different approaches:

1 Observation of whether or not the students appear to be progressing successfully.
2 Casual and systematic questioning of teachers and students involved in the program.
3 Periodic examinations of students by tests designed to cover the new material.
4 Comparative testing of students in "new" and "old" programs.

Various approaches to program evaluation

Grittner (23) discusses three ways of evaluating a contemporary foreign language program. The first involves a tabulation of characteristics relevant to foreign language instruction. Evaluators then determine the state of the program with regard to these characteristics. A second approach involves a careful analysis of teacher and student activities to determine whether or not these activities are consistent with stated course objectives. The third evaluation procedure involves a direct measure of student achievement. Each procedure has, he finds, advantages and disadvantages in terms of the information they yield.

The methodologies for evaluation delineated here resemble those of Grittner, with some modification. They are:

1 Evaluation of student achievement.
2 Evaluation of classroom instruction through direct observation.
3 Evaluation by analysis of program characteristics.
4 Evaluation by systems analysis.

Program evaluation through evaluation of student achievement

Measurement of student achievement can rightly be called the most direct means of program evaluation. The logic of the approach assumes that there are behavioral outcomes that can be identified and measured, and that variations in these outcomes are due, at least in part, to factors in the instructional program.

Basic considerations in testing the acquisition of language skills are treated in Chapter 12 and will not be repeated here.

Worthy of discussion is the question of whether one should accept language skill achievement measures as valid representations of course or program outcomes. Some educators prefer to claim objectives that are more spiritual than material — they are indefinite, unobservable, and immeasurable. While the profession may not have clearly identified all the outcomes of instructional programs, this futilitarian approach seems to lead nowhere. As Ebel (14) very practically indicates, one does have difficulty in demonstrating that the pursuit of such objectives is a good way to spend taxpayers' money. Foreign language teachers have achieved a measure of precision and validity by recognizing the existence of the four distinct language skills. Learning outcomes in these skills are not only amenable to measurement but even to direct measurement, i.e., in order to measure, for example, listening skill, the student is required to listen to a multiple-choice item and to comprehend it. He must perform the very behavior being tested. Much of the language teaching profession readily accepts the language skills as valid outcomes of language study. Other outcomes such as various kinds of cultural information and attitudes are recognized as program outcomes, but seem to be less systematically evaluated. These outcomes

Is testing language skills enough to evaluate an FL program?

have been categorized into taxonomies developed for both the cognitive (7) and affective (32) domains.

Program evaluation through measures of student achievement can be carried out through the use of valid and reliable locally-devised measures, or through the use of commercially prepared, standardized achievement exams. Commonly used tests of the latter type are the Modern Language Association Co-operative Foreign Language Tests (36), the Modern Language Association Foreign Language Proficiency Tests for Teachers and Advanced Students (37), and the Pimsleur Modern Foreign Language Proficiency Tests (43). The latter type of test has the advantages of providing norms outside the local situation and of being of a known quality. The norms provided with such tests provide an indication as to whether or not local students are progressing as well as the average foreign language student in the large sample used to standardize the test. Standardized proficiency tests have the further advantage of being mechanically well constructed and professionally reproduced.

Evaluation through classroom observation

Essentially, classroom observation involves someone making value judgments about the behavior occurring in a classroom. The judgments can be single summary statements or they may be ratings of many individual aspects of the program. The summary rating, particularly of teacher effectiveness, remains the most ubiquitous type of evaluation. It is sometimes called the "eyeball" approach, and, quite evidently, the validity varies with the skill of the evaluator.

An extended inventory of features considered to be important or unimportant in the foreign language teaching-learning process was presented by Hayes, Lambert, & Tucker (27). The aspects of the program covered by the inventory include administration and policy, teachers and teacher competence, course design and materials, classroom procedures, and language laboratory practices. This system represents a large-scale effort to improve evaluation and, when validated, has the possibility of being used in an ongoing evaluation of the effectiveness of a given language program. Each step for validating this approach to evaluation is described in detail by the authors. The system is concerned basically with comparing language principles and procedures with student achievement. These principles and procedures (324 in number) were rated by 364 faculty members of

Inventory of features considered important in FL teaching-learning

the 1965 National Defense Education Act (NDEA) Institutes throughout the country and should be termed "tentatively desirable practices" at the time of this writing until validation studies are completed. By administering pretests to effect matching of treatment groups and posttests to measure achievement, the authors would be able to determine that differences in language proficiency at the end of the training program were due to the differences in teaching procedures. By taking into consideration the weighted judgments of classroom observers, modified by the students' and teachers' judgments of the relevancy of these principles and procedures, the authors, in this validation study, would correlate the results of the posttests and the procedures observed and rated in the classroom. High positive correlations would announce the effectiveness of each principle and procedure and presumably qualify them to be used as validated evaluative criteria for foreign language instruction.

The success of this approach to program evaluation seemingly is based on the predisposition of the evaluators toward a specific set of goals of instruction that include in this instance the development of skills.

While the Hayes, Lambert, & Tucker article might lead an unwary reader to conclude that those principles and procedures (even if validated) were the final word in language teaching, it *A point of view needed* should be pointed out that the ratings were obtained from NDEA Institute faculty who may have been already inclined toward audiolingual practices in teaching and were probably chosen to teach in the Institutes because of their commitment to the method. A sampling of another group of teachers could reveal, obviously, another point of view. While this approach to evaluation has many possibilities, it also has the usual limitation of restricted application and must be applied, not unlike any other good measure of evaluation, to a specific set of preestablished goals.

An improvement upon summary ratings involves an analysis of classroom behavior and course objectives. The behavior observed is judged in terms of relevance and consistency with the course objectives. Several systems for direct observation of student and teacher behavior have been developed.

In these behavioral observation systems an observer in the classroom (or of a video- or audiotape made in the classroom) records the behaviors occurring or a sample of the behavior in terms of a system of categories. Percentages of class time or ratios of amounts of time devoted to various kinds of activities are then compared to the stated objectives. If, for example, the development of speaking skill is a high priority objective, and 90 percent of the class is conducted in English, one has identified an inconsistency. Three recently published systems are designed directly for foreign language instruction. Moskowitz (40) has adopted the well-known Flanders System of Interaction Analysis to the foreign language classroom. The categories primarily reflect various kinds of direct and indirect teacher influence. Jarvis (29) has developed a system of 22 categories that indicate qualitatively different aspects of the practice variable and the skill emphasis in the teacher and student behavior. Grittner (23) includes a behavioral observation system developed by Orrin Nearhoof that resembles that of Jarvis. It has fewer categories and, consequently, looks at fewer aspects of behavior, but it has the advantage of greater simplicity of use.

Behavioral observation systems

The primary difficulty with this approach is the lack of agreement as to how much of each category of behavior is optimum in a particular teaching situation. Nevertheless, such systems do provide the opportunity to describe accurately what is being done in the classroom, either with observation by outside observers or self-evaluation by the teachers themselves through the use of audio- or videotape.

Evaluation by analysis of program characteristics

Program evaluation is sometimes carried out without direct observation of instruction and without direct measurement of student achievement. Evaluators make judgments about the quality of a program on the basis of the desirability of program traits and on the basis of the consistency and logic of these characteristics. Evaluators look at such things as the qualifications and preparation of the staff, length of program, articulation between levels, and availability of equipment and materials.

A theoretical model:

Birkmaier (5) described theoretical ideals in facilities, instructional procedures, student selection, teacher characteristics, and evaluation procedures. Characteristics treated relate most closely to an audiolingual program.

Section D-8 of the *Evaluative Criteria* (16) deals with foreign language program evaluation. The *Evaluative Criteria* has separate sections for evaluating each subject area, the school physical plant, school staff and administration, student activities, instructional materials, guidance services, and health services. The instrument is frequently used in the self-evaluations by

Evaluative Criteria

school faculties which are a part of the accrediting procedures of the regional associations of colleges and secondary schools. Evaluators have the opportunity to indicate the aspects of the program that are satisfactory and those that need improvement. The 1970 edition of the *Evaluative Criteria* is scheduled for completion by summer 1969. Oliva (41) notes that the revision will reflect increased emphasis in the use of audiolingual techniques. (Oliva also includes the current edition of the *Evaluative Criteria* as an appendix in his book.)

Dammer, Glaude, & Green (12) present criteria for the evaluation of elementary school foreign language programs. The carefully prepared guide includes two types of items: those that are primarily informational or data-eliciting, and those that are primarily evaluative. There is no key for "right" answers; hence, faculties doing self-evaluations must be knowledgeable with regard to program considerations. Items deal with program objectives and organization, selection of pupils, administration and supervision of the program, coordination and articulation, instructional staff, methods of instruction, materials of instruction, pupil achievement, and evaluation.

Elementary school FL program

Colleges, through their entrance requirements in foreign languages, have influenced the kinds of foreign language programs in the secondary school. Very slight influence has been exercised by the 39 colleges (out of the 1,155 degree-granting institutions) that require more than two years of foreign language study for admission. Miller (34) points out that this influence is primarily directed by small, Eastern, Catholic colleges and is on preparatory schools whose graduates achieve college credit through advanced placement programs. Professional organizations at all levels have vigorously worked for longer sequences of programs. A greater awareness and concern for non-English speakers within the United States may also influence foreign language programs. The effect of these influences seems to be one of encouraging longer sequences in preparatory and public high schools that have a large number of college-bound students. Negative influences on secondary programs were reported by Zeldner (51). Entrance requirements of two years or less in many institutions of higher learning can be viewed as resulting in less national foreign language study. Since no more than two years of a foreign language are required for entrance, less motivated students have a tendency to drop out of language study. The high cost of education and a growing hostility on the part of taxpayers is a further threat to extended foreign language programs. The

College influence on secondary school FL programs: good and bad

failure of foreign language teachers at all levels to justify second language study to the general public makes the area vulnerable when cutbacks are made in the overall institutional offerings. The result of these influences is a considerable variety in the quality and scope of high school language programs. It is well known that schools that are satisfied to offer only two years of foreign language study seldom produce more than minimal language skill development.

The systems approach to evaluation

The systems analysis approach does include some elements from all the other approaches. Banathy (3) presents an impressive discussion of the concept and its methodology. The systems approach is a method for designing the organization of an orderly whole by analyzing the way the functioning of the parts or components will affect the performance of the whole. Interrelatedness and interaction among the components implies that they do mutually contribute toward the total performance of the system and, at the same time, influence the performance of each other. According to Banathy the structure of inquiry into an instructional system requires the following sequence of elements: *What it is.*

1 Statement of objectives in measurable behavioral terms.
2 Identifications of functions (which are needed for the attainment of learning tasks and objectives).
3 Selection of components that will best perform the functions (e.g., man, media, and other resources). *Components*
4 Distributions of functions to specific components.
5 Scheduling into time and space.
6 Implementation of the system as a whole.
7 Evaluation and planned change.

Program evaluation utilizing this approach requires that one identify the various components and modify on the basis of this identification. Additional information about the systems approach in program evaluation is available in Gagné (21), Heinich (28), Hartley (26), and Entwisle & Conviser (15).

Foreign study programs

The most frequently used means for evaluating foreign study programs appears to be the Freeman criteria (20). The work is a consequence of the great proliferation of so-called study programs offered by hundreds of organizations, private, commercial, or "nonprofit." The criteria consider such aspects as sponsorship, recruitment and selection procedures, group leader selection, where and what the student will study, what academic control is there, how travel is mixed with study, what kind of housing is involved, and what all the financial considerations are. The criteria call attention to the aspects of the program that can create serious problems for the student. They are available through the state foreign language supervisors.

Study abroad needs evaluation

Teacher proficiency

An instructional program cannot exist apart from the teachers who put it into operation in the classrooms. No aspect of the program functions independent of teaching behavior. The profession has yet to devise a completely autonomous program, be it traditional text materials or a complex of mechanical and electronic aids. Consequently, evaluation of teacher competence becomes an integral part of program evaluation.

The general state of research on teaching effectiveness remains relatively unchanged. Few variables consistently hold up as factors in effectiveness regardless of the criterion used. In the teaching of foreign languages, particular concern has been focused upon the teacher's subject matter competence, with emphasis placed on proficiency in the four language skills. Carroll (8), in studying the foreign language skill achievement among college language majors, concludes that his study "has provocative and even disturbing things to say about the attainment of foreign language majors in our colleges. The overall level of attainment of these foreign language students, particularly in the audio-lingual skills, leaves something to be desired when judged against a criterion of what could be reasonably expected of them."

Attainments of the FL major

The three-year Pennsylvania Foreign Language Research Project (45, 46) assessed more than 100 foreign language teachers in 58 Pennsylvania high schools who taught 59 French and 38 German classes using the audiolingual approach, audiolingual plus grammar approach, and the traditional approach. The secondary school foreign language teachers were professionally well-prepared, averaging ten years of teaching experience and at least 45 hours of graduate work. Competent observers found teacher proficiency to correlate highly with the Modern Language Association Foreign Language Proficiency Tests for Teachers and Advanced Students (37). However, there was no

Relationship between teacher competence and student achievement

significant relationship between the scores of the 89 French and German teachers tested and the achievement scores of their classes in foreign language skills after one year. In fact, some of the teachers with the lowest scores had students with the highest achievement and vice versa. However, here again a word of caution is needed. Broad comparative studies of this kind have been criticized as adding little to the understanding of exact strategies, and the *professional* competency of the teacher (Carroll, 9, 10; Birkmaier & Lange, 6).

The "Guidelines for Teacher Education Programs In Modern Foreign Languages" (24) describe expectations of the modern foreign language teacher, minimal language skill proficiencies that should be developed, and essential features of a satisfactory teacher preparation program. Axelrod (1) expands upon needed teacher competencies in urging a prominent role for culture and civilization, relevant professional preparation, and linguistics.

Banathy (2) accentuates what may be a growing and fortunate trend in teacher preparation. He applies a systems analysis approach to teacher training, and, in so doing, takes note of the fact that current statements of objectives of teacher education programs, such as those above, denote out-of-class rather than in-class performance of the teacher. They do not describe classroom performance, but are only a necessary basis for it.

Systems analysis applied to teacher training

Politzer (44), in speaking of teacher proficiency tests, underscores this same distinction between what the teacher actually does in the classroom and assumed correlates of that behavior when he suggests that there is a real need to supplement existing tests with tests that measure, not the teacher's *preparation* for teaching languages, but his actual *performance* in the classroom. This viewpoint would seem to have much to offer to the profession.

Summary

Program evaluation, as written about in most of the literature, focuses on theory and includes little empirical research. "Good" qualities of "effective" teaching appear in the numerous guidelines for language programs. State departments of education, individual school districts, colleges and universities, and national organizations have all contributed to the literature in this respect. Reflected in the guidelines is their individual and collective understanding of what effective teaching is. Those who believe that a fundamental skills approach is the best way to learn foreign languages will incorporate such things as laboratory practice, pattern drills and extensive use of audiovisual materials. Those concerned with the development of only reading and writing skills will likely omit these characteristics and specify other aspects that suit their particular needs. What is evident here and throughout language teaching is the paucity of adequate research that prevents us from scientifically establishing a rationale not only for good teaching practices but also for sequencing them and for reconciling them with developmental changes in the learners in order to best serve most of our students most of the time.

References, Foreign language program evaluation

1 Axelrod, Joseph; et al. The education of the modern foreign language teacher for American schools: an analysis of ends and means for teacher-preparation programs in modern foreign languages based on a study of NDEA foreign language institutes. Modern Language Association, New York, 1966.

2 Banathy, Bela H. The design of foreign language teacher education. Modern Language Journal, 52 (December 1968) 490–500.

3 Banathy, Bela H. The systems approach. Modern Language Journal, 51 (May 1967) 281–289.

4 Bartley, Diane. A pilot study of aptitude and attitude factors in language dropout. California Journal of Educational Research, 20 (March 1969) 48–55.

5 Birkmaier, Emma. Evaluating the foreign language program. The North Central Association Quarterly, 40 (Winter 1966) 263–271.

6 Birkmaier, Emma M.; Lange, Dale L. Foreign language instruction. Review of Educational Research, 37 (1967) 186–199.

7 Bloom, Benjamin S. Taxonomy of educational objectives. Handbook I: cognitive domain. David McKay Co., New York, 1956.

8 Carroll, John B. Foreign language proficiency levels attained by language majors near graduation from college. Foreign Language Annals, 1 (December 1967) 131–140.

9 Carroll, John B. Research in foreign language teaching: the last five years. In: Mead, Robert G., Jr., ed. Language teaching: broader contexts.

1967 Reports of the Working Committees of the Northeast Conference on the Teaching of Foreign Languages. MLA Materials Center, 1967, p. 12–42.

10 Carroll, John B. The study of language. Harvard University Press, Cambridge, Mass., 1953.

11 Chastain, Kenneth D. Prediction of success in audio-lingual and cognitive classes. Purdue University, West Lafayette, Ind. [In press.]

12 Dammer, Paul E.; Glaude, Paul M.; Green, Gerald. FLES: a guide for program review. Modern Language Journal, 52 (January 1968) 16–23.

13 Directory of state and local FL supervisors. Foreign Language Annals, 2 (October 1968) 74–85.

14 Ebel, Robert L. Prospects for evaluation of learning. Bulletin of the National Association of Secondary School Principals (December 1968), 32–48.

15 Entwisle, Doris R.; Conviser, Richard. Input-output analysis in education. The High School Journal, 52 (January 1969) 192–198.

16 Evaluative criteria, 1960 ed. National Study of Secondary School Evaluation, Washington, D.C., 1960.

17 Fiks, Alfred S. Foreign language programmed materials: 1966. Modern Language Journal, 50 (January 1967) 7–14.

18 Finley, Carmen J. National assessment – spring 1968. California Journal of Educational Research, 20 (March 1969) 69–74.

19 FLES evaluation: language skills and pupil attitudes in the Fairfield, Connecticut, Public

Schools. Bulletin No. 106. State Department of Education, Hartford, Conn., 1968.

20 Freeman, Stephen A. Guidelines for the evaluation of foreign study programs for secondary pupils. National Council of State Supervisors of Foreign Languages. (Distributed through the offices of individual State Supervisors) 1965.

21 Gagné, Robert M., ed. Psychological principles in system development. Holt, Rinehart, and Winston, New York, 1962.

22 Goodlad, John I. School curriculum reform in the United States. Fund for the Advancement of Education, New York, 1964.

23 Grittner, Frank M. Teaching foreign languages. Harper and Row, New York, 1969.

24 Guidelines for teacher education programs in modern foreign languages. Publications of the Modern Language Association of America, 81 (May 1966) A-2 and A-3. Also in: Modern Language Journal, 50 (October 1966) 20-22.

25 Gut, Ann F. A survey of methods and materials in French language programs of American colleges and universities. Modern Language Journal, 51 (December 1967) 470-480.

26 Hartley, Harry J. Limitations of systems analysis. Phi Delta Kappan, 50 (May 1969) 515-519.

27 Hayes, Alfred S.; Lambert, Wallace E.; Tucker, G. Richard. Evaluation of foreign language teaching. Foreign Language Annals, 1 (October 1967) 22-44.

28 Heinich, Robert. The systems approach. Audio-Visual Instruction, 11 (June-July 1966) 432-434.

29 Jarvis, Gilbert A. A behavioral observation system for classroom foreign language skill acquisition activities. Modern Language Journal, 52 (October 1968) 335-341.

30 Johnson, Mauritz, Jr. Definitions and models in curriculum theory. Educational Theory, 17 (April 1967) 127-140.

31 Kelly, Leo. A comparison of the monostructural and polystructural approaches to the teaching of college French. Purdue University, West Lafayette, Ind., August 1965. (Unpublished Ph.D. dissertation.)

32 Krathwohl, David R.; Bloom, Benjamin S.; Masia, Berthram B. Taxonomy of educational objectives. Handbook II: affective domain. David McKay Co., New York, 1964.

33 Macdonald, James B. Researching curriculum output: the use of a general systems theory to identify appropriate hypotheses. Paper presented at American Education Research Association (AERA) meeting, February 1965.

34 Miller, Mary R. Possible college influence on foreign language study at secondary level. Modern Language Journal, 53 (May 1969) 329-334.

35 Minnesota State Department of Education. Evaluation of a FL program. In: Donoghue, Mildred, ed. Foreign languages and the schools, William C. Brown Co., Dubuque, Ia., 1967, p. 302-304.

36 MLA Cooperative Foreign Language Tests. Cooperative Test Division, Educational Testing Service, Princeton N.J., 1964.

37 MLA Foreign Language Proficiency Tests for Teachers and Advanced Students. Educational Testing Service, Princeton, N.J., 1962.

38 MLA 1964 supplements to the MLA selective list of materials. MLA Materials Center, New York.

39 MLA selective list of materials for use by teachers of MFLs in elementary and secondary schools. Ollman, Mary J., ed. (French, German, Italian, Modern Hebrew, Norwegian, Polish, Portuguese, Russian, Spanish, Swedish). MLA Materials Center, New York, 1962, p. 143-153.

40 Moskowitz, Gertrude. The effects of training teachers in interaction analysis. Foreign Language Annals, 1 (March 1968) 218-235

41 Oliva, Peter F. The teaching of foreign languages. Prentice Hall, Inc., Englewood Cliffs, N.J., 1969.

42 Ornstein, Jacob. Programmed instruction and educational technology in the language field: boon or failure? Modern Language Journal, 52 (November 1968) 401-410.

43 Pimsleur Modern Foreign Language Proficiency Tests. Harcourt, Brace and World, New York.

44 Politzer, Robert L. Toward a practice-centered program for the training and evaluation of foreign language teachers. Modern Language Journal, 50 (May 1966) 251-255.

45 Smith, Philip D., Jr.; Baranyi, Helmut A. A comparison study on the effectiveness of the traditional and audiolingual approaches to foreign language instruction utilizing laboratory equipment. Project no. 7-0133; Grant no. OEC-1-7-070133-0445. U.S. Office of Education, Washington, D. C., 1968.

46 Smith, Philip D., Jr.; Berger, Emanuel. An assessment of three language teaching strategies utilizing three language laboratory systems. Final Report. Project no. 5-0683; Grant no. OE-7-48-9013-272. U.S. Department of Health, Education, and Welfare, 1968. Also obtainable from ERIC Documentation Reproduction Service, U.S. Office of Education, Washington, D.C. (ED-021-512)

47 Stufflebeam, D. L. Evaluation as enlightenment for decision-making. Paper presented at Working Conference on Assessment Theory, Sarasota, Fla., January 1968.

48 Tanner, Daniel. Curriculum theory: knowledge and content. Review of Educational Research, 36 (June 1966) 362-372.

49 Walbesser, Henry H.; Carter, Heather. Some methodological considerations of curriculum evaluation research. Educational Leadership, 26 (October 1968) 53-64.

50 Wittrock, M. C., ed. Statement of intent. UCLA Evaluation Comment, Center for the Study of Evaluation of Instructional Programs, 1 (May 1968) 1.

51 Zeldner, Max. The foreign language dropouts. Modern Language Journal, 50 (May 1966) 275-280.

14

Classics: The teaching of Latin and Greek

Introduction

Edith M. A. Kovach

University of Detroit

At the turn of the century, the classical languages, Latin and Greek, enjoyed a position of virtual autocracy in the educational institutions of Europe and the Americas.

The period from 1890 to 1925 was characterized in the United States by all-encompassing investigations and authoritative recommendations concerning goals, course content, and methodology for the teaching of Latin and Greek. In recent articles, Carr (14) revitalizes the nature and scope of the classical investigation for a new generation; DeWitt (19) characterizes attitudinal changes since 1925; Shero (90), writing for a British audience, summarizes the role of classics in American education from the beginnings through 1965; and Ganss (29) takes us back to 1556 in his rapid survey of Latin teaching.

Today, however, Greek has almost vanished from the high school curriculum and Latin trails well behind French and Spanish in numbers of students enrolled, at all levels of education. Parker sums up eloquently the rationale for Latin study in American schools: "The subject matter of Latin is the very roots of Western civilization" (77, p. 6); but it is obvious that the role of classics in American education has changed significantly.

What surveys show

Whatever the causes for this change, they appear to exist worldwide. Else (24) presents the candid comments of individual classicists from 15 countries (as diverse as New Zealand, Ghana, Spain, Japan, and Brazil), meeting under the aegis of the Fédération Internationale des Associations des Études Classiques, and in his Foreword (p. v) comments on their mutual "deep concern for the survival and future prosperity of classical studies, seen in global perspective" and on "the similarity of the problems . . . in many places." Elsewhere, speaking equally candidly to his classical confreres in this country, Else (25, p. 1) sums up the challenge: "Our situation—our dilemma—is that the role of the Classics in present-day American life is almost nil, while their relevance is enormous."

Mention of such concerns may seem misplaced and unduly pessimistic as introduction to a survey of the vital and innovative developments in a teaching field as viable and varied as classics, but it is precisely these concerns that explain some recent curriculum developments and many kinds of professional organizational activity.

The status of Latin in the schools

The three sectors of secondary education in the United States, public, parochial, and private or independent, present quite different pictures as regards the role of Latin.

Satisfactory large-scale statistics on annual enrollments are available, albeit at irregular intervals, only for the public schools, and much of the published material concerning current curricular innovation in Latin is concerned with programs that are publicly funded, but the approaches and experiences of the public schools are not necessarily reflected in the practices of either parochial or private schools, which must be considered separately.

Probably the most significant fact is that nationally the public secondary school enrollment in Latin has declined from its peak in 1962. Some apparent external causes for this decline may be summarized as follows:

1 The introduction of one or more modern foreign languages in the elementary school (FLES) has caused a decrease in the number of pupils available to begin Latin at grade nine, the most common starting point, and also a change in the type of student so available: he is more apt now to be a "FLES-dropout" than the traditional "bright" Latin student;

2 The National Defense Education Act (NDEA), passed in 1958, has meant substantial (and exclusive) support for modern foreign language (MFL) programs and extra educational opportunities for modern foreign language teachers, to the exclusion of their classical counterparts; and

Causes for the decline of the classics

3 The shift from Latin to the vernacular in the liturgical activities of the Roman Catholic Church has meant a shift in emphasis on Latin study in Catholic schools and, indirectly, a lessening of the importance of Latin in the public eye.

That there are other, internal causes for the decline is undeniable, however. The Airlie House Conference of 1965 and the Oxford Conference of 1967 (both discussed below) represent attempts on a national scale to examine and resolve them.

Parochial schools

Parochial secondary schools, the majority Roman Catholic in affiliation, have traditionally supported strong programs in Latin, often to the total exclusion of work in MFLs. One justification for such programs lay in the fact that Latin was the liturgical language of the Roman Catholic Church, this despite the fact that liturgical Latin was rarely included in the course of study.

The large proportion of students studying Latin in parochial high schools may perhaps be extrapolated from a recent study (Kovach, 44) of FL backgrounds of randomly selected students entering the freshman class at a single Catholic university in the fall of 1966. Nearly 93 percent of the students entering from Catholic high schools had studied Latin, as compared with some 36 percent of those entering from public high schools.

Strong programs in danger

In effect, until very recently Latin was a compulsory subject for students in college preparatory programs of parochial secondary schools, with the result that, as in all required courses, teaching could be less than inspired with no fear of enrollment drop as a possible consequence.

When the "lid was released" by the changes promulgated by Vatican Council II, which permitted the introduction of the vernacular into liturgical worship, there was a predictable reaction. In the absence of concrete data, an "impressionistic" study of enrollment figures in individual schools and areas indicates a sizable drop in numbers enrolled in Catholic-affiliated high school Latin classes.

Two recent National Catholic Educational Association reports (28, 52) concentrate on the apparent conflict between MFLs and Latin for a position in the Catholic secondary school curriculum, and support the proposal, which has been made elsewhere for other reasons and in other contexts, that Latin be introduced in the grade school. Here, however, despite insistence on the need for careful articulation with the high school program, the reasoning seems to be that Latin should become a subject for the grade school only, rather than part of an extended curriculum.

Some excellent suggestions for the parochial schools are made by Koob (52, p. 1–5) concerning imaginative scheduling; special programs for talented students, including two-week summer workshops and tours to Rome; teacher selection, motivation, and stimulation; extra- and intracurricular motivational activities for students; and the need for administrative officers to stop

New ideas and suggestions

their "drifting" policy, to decide whether Latin belongs in the high school curriculum, and, if so, to promote its vigorous teaching.

New teaching materials and methods are being explored, elementary and junior high school Latin programs are being developed, and vigorous proposals for viable programs in Latin and classical studies are being espoused. However, there has been an undeniable "swing of the pendulum," particularly with regard to the role of Latin and Greek in seminary training for potential priests or other religious, and the current insistence on a probably specious immediate relevance is having a negative effect on the position of Latin in the parochial schools also.

The other church-affiliated schools have much smaller foreign language enrollments generally and presumably have not been affected by the same forces-for-change that have lowered Latin enrollments in the Roman Catholic parochial schools.

Independent schools

In the private or independent schools, on the other hand, a long and strong Latin program continues to flourish. Again, statistics on any large scale are impossible to obtain — a result partly of the independent and, ipso facto, largely unaffiliated nature of the schools themselves — but there is evidence to indicate that Latin continues to occupy a significant position in the elementary and secondary school curriculum. The National Association of Independent Schools (NAIS) annually offers a series of examinations (in English, mathematics, and five foreign languages) *Long sequences typical* to serve as "reliable tests of the general preparation, accomplishment, and ability of candidates seeking admission or promotion to the lower forms or classes of secondary schools" (18, p. 3).

The fact that there are three levels of the Latin examination indicates that it is accepted practice for the Latin program to begin in grade seven or eight or even earlier and to be part of a sequential program continuing throughout the high school years. While many public and parochial school systems are just exploring the possibility of initiating Latin in the elementary and junior high schools, the independent schools have had a long and successful tradition of five-, six-, or seven-year programs, some of which might well serve as prototypes.

It should be remarked, however, that the findings of the NAIS Latin Committee (made available through its chairman, Elizabeth H. Ferguson) indicate that in textbook selection, at least, the independent schools tend to be relatively conservative: of 98 such schools surveyed, 71 use Jenney's revision of Smith-Thompson's *First Year Latin* as their chief Latin text for beginning courses at whatever grade level. They tend also to be sturdily independent: 16 other texts were also named as being used by one or more schools in the group. Use of this relatively traditional text, however, should not be taken as an indication that the Latin curricula in the private schools are unchanging and uncritically old-fashioned: Latin is offered as a subject-in-competition — *par inter pares* — with other languages, and rivals them on its own merits as a subject of modern-day study.

New materials are not apparent

Curriculum development

Latin in the total school curriculum

The first issue of *Foreign Language Annals* had as lead article (58) a discussion on the place of Latin in the curriculum. At the very time when the Oxford Conference participants by their actions and in their report (49) were vigorously advocating elementary and junior high school Latin programs, Levy, the author, while personally disclaiming any understanding of high school scheduling complexities, gave strong support to the notion that Latin study should be channeled into a three-year sequence beginning in grade ten.

Two camps

The proposal is a reactionary one, made significant by the prominence of its place of publication and by the esteem in which the author is held by his colleagues, and reveals, inter alia, the communication and information gap existing between teachers in the schools and their university counterparts. The Oxford and Airlie House Conferences (49, 50) served a valuable function in providing a common forum for competent representatives of both groups.

A later proposal by Latimer & Eaton (51) examines and incorporates most of the current trends in Latin curriculum developments. They dismiss the idea of Latin as a badge of intellectual aristocracy, as a puzzle to be solved rather than a language to be used, and as a static, traditional ("not modern") discipline. They reject as impracticable and generally undesirable the Levy-Brooks proposal (58) that Latin be studied as a second FL and offered chiefly in grades 10 – 12. Instead, they support the rationale of the six-year Latin program, which was the chief concern of the Airlie House Conference in 1965 (50) and of the Oxford Conference in 1967 (49), as well as, implicitly, of all the

Conferences seek unity in the profession

393

federally-funded institutes for Latin teachers. Their proposal incorporates the types of urban programs described later: Latin FLES programs, the Advanced Placement Program (APP) at the other end of the sequence, and opportunity for work in depth and enrichment of every type. They remind the profession: "If it is to be effective, Latinists at every academic level must agree upon it, plan and work toward it, seek all possible aid and support for it."

Innovative program awards

In 1966 the American Classical League (ACL) sponsored a Master Secondary School Latin Teacher and Program Award. One aim of the award was to discover and focus attention upon innovative Latin curricula. Ultimately 32 teachers from the U.S. and Canada were honored as master teachers (Kovach 43, 45), with three singled out as having developed significant new programs: Richard T. Scanlan, for his five-year multitrack program involving the development of new materials, fourth and fifth year advanced placement work, and an introduction to classical Greek and modern Italian; Mrs. Thomas Cutt, for the "Latin Heritage" course, an enrichment program for inner-city students with limited FL experience; and Edward C. Woll (since deceased), for his multisensory approach, with Latin as the language of instruction. The specific emphases implicit in these approaches have become increasingly important in secondary school Latin curriculum development.

Large city Latin and classics programs

Highly significant new programs in Latin and classical studies are being developed in large city school systems where the need for realistic and relevant programs is imperative. Some steps —not necessarily sequential—in the development of such programs have been documented:

Detroit. In 1964 "Latin Heritage," described by Kovach (45, p. 39–40), was first offered to inner-city high school students in Detroit. This is a one-year course, focusing on the student and his needs as the starting point and using Latin and classical culture and their relationship to the student's academic and everyday life as the medium to stimulate him academically, to orient him to language study, and to familiarize him with some of the origins of our civilization.

Latin programs become relevant

The publicity given to Mrs. Cutt's program through the ACL award attracted wide attention and planted many seminal ideas.

Washington, D.C. A lineal descendant of Mrs. Cutt's program was an "Exploratory Latin" course taught in the Washington, D.C., summer school program of 1965 (Hayden, 30). The use of Latin, and sometimes Greek, classical mythology and other aspects of classical studies continue in the development of widespread programs for inner-city students and also for elementary and junior high school students.

Latin for inner-city students

The appointment of Judith LeBovit in 1966 as supervising director of FLs gave new impetus to a rebirth of Latin studies in Washington, D.C., public schools at sixth and seventh grade levels. The program began in the fall of 1966 with two pilot programs. Its growth is revealed in these statistics:

TABLE I. Enrollment in the Washington, D.C., Sixth and Seventh Grade Latin Programs

	1966-67	1967-68	1968-69
Sixth grade			
No. of students	620	1,240	1,484
No. of classes	23	43	51
No. of schools	17	39	50
Seventh grade			
No. of students	259	535	814
No. of classes	10	20	31
No. of schools	5	13	20

Statistics supplied by the Department of Foreign Languages, Public Schools of the District of Columbia.

The sixth grade program has been taught by peripatetic teachers, with 20-minute classes five times per week. The aims are fluency in Latin on a simple oral level, and use of Latin as a tool in English word-building.

The seventh grade Latin program is "general language" in a sense: emphasis is on how languages work, especially English, and word formation from Latin bases in English, French, and Spanish, as well as further work in the Latin language. It is a "bridge" course and students now have an alternative choice for eighth and ninth grade study: either Latin or a MFL. In either case, their FLES Latin courses will serve as a useful complement to all future language work. New materials and a teachers' manual (61) have been developed for these programs by the Foreign Language Department of the Washington, D.C., Public Schools. Reports by Eaton (23), Hayden (32), LeBovit (55, 56), and an unnamed author (54) describe the programs, with fur-

New materials with teachers' manuals developed

ther information available in mimeo from the Office of the Foreign Language Director.

Inner city Latin conferences. In November 1967 the American Classical League, under a grant from the National Endowment for the Humanities and with the cooperation of the District of Columbia school system, held two Inner City Latin Conferences (Hayden, 31). Participants, both Latin teachers and FL supervisors, came from Cleveland, Chicago, Detroit, New York, and Philadelphia, all cities in which interest in such programs was already manifest.

Philadelphia. The School District of Philadelphia is developing new programs in classical languages at all levels. Mascionto-nio (64) reports on the Latin FLES program: over 1,000 students in 28 elementary schools are being taught Latin 20 minutes daily by itinerant teachers using locally developed materials in a course called *Romani Viventes et Dicentes* — How the Romans Lived and Spoke. Emphasis again is on oral Latin, English derivatives, and cultural materials in English, plus liberal use of multisensory media.

Latin in the grade school: objectives

A sixth grade course centering on classical mythology is being developed for the fall of 1969.

At the secondary school level, 12 schools are using the *Artes Latinae* program (97) and two are experimenting with Oerberg's direct method, all-Latin text (75), to accompany which the school district has permission to develop multisensory materials. In prospect is the development of curriculum material on the role of Africans in classical antiquity, to be integrated into the Latin course of study in secondary schools. Staff upgrading to make effective use of these new materials is in progress via (1) workshops held weekly in 1967–68 to acquaint teachers with the *Artes Latinae* materials; (2) preservice and in-service workshops in 1968–69 for the Latin FLES teachers; (3) a brief workshop in summer 1969, to improve the oral skills of Latin teachers; and (4) a full-fledged Latin Institute planned for summer 1970.

Role of Africans in classical antiquity

A Greek Curriculum Committee formed in May 1968 is developing a multisensory classical Greek program for secondary schools involving an audiolingual approach initially, programmed learning for specific portions of the course, horizontal presentation (e.g., all accusative singular forms presented together for all noun declensions, rather than taught individually as each complete noun declension is presented vertically with all its cases), and stress on the cultural and linguistic influence

Classical Greek Program

of Greek. A pilot program in Greek begins in selected high schools in the fall of 1969.

The Magnet Foreign Language Program at South Philadelphia High School provides opportunities for FL experimentation. Instruction in classical Greek has already begun there, and courses in areas related to linguistic specialties are being developed. Related to classical languages are The Classical Heritage Through Films, Greek and Latin in Scientific Terminology, and Blacks in Antiquity. A Model Center for Classical Studies, offering films, exhibits, lectures, books, etc., to the general public is also planned for this site.

The Magnet FL Program in Latin and Greek

The essential elements for such a program are summarized by Masciantonio (62, 63): teachers who are able and willing, suitable instructional materials, and a strengthened and lengthened classical studies program, especially continuing into community and city colleges to which many of the graduates of city public schools will go and from which many potential teachers of classics will come.

Cleveland Heights-University Heights. In the Cleveland Heights-University Heights (Ohio) School District a new program, Cultural Language Study, for seventh and eighth graders will begin in the fall of 1969. Nisius (71) describes the formal machinery under which the program was initiated and Tappenden & Schwartz (100) specify its content and operation.

Cultural Language Study for grades 7 and 8

In imitation of a French-humanities program already initiated in the four junior high schools of the district, this classical language and civilization course is viewed as the foundation for further humanities work, involving as it does linguistic elements and materials designed to help students develop insights into man's universal dilemmas and challenges and his responses to them in antiquity.

The program is two-pronged: for some, it is the start of a five- or six-year Latin or classics sequence, leading to Advanced Placement Program work during the last two years; for all, it will provide a "firm orientation to an interdisciplinary approach to the study of man" (100) as well as a stable foundation in the languages which have been the bases of his own.

Syllabus writing and materials production are in process, with the nearby Humanities Institute of Baldwin-Wallace College making its ample research facilities available. A two-week workshop before the start of school will be conducted by the two project directors for the four prospective teachers and "feedback" sessions throughout the year are projected.

A common denominator in the programs just described (and they serve as representative of other developments elsewhere) is the emphasis on the entire classical field as the subject matter area, rather than on a narrow, purely linguistic approach. This has undeniable advantages from almost any point of view, but prompts one observation: to many purists such programs are not *Latin* programs and, despite an obvious trend toward courses of this nature at all levels from elementary school through college, there are those classicists who—probably injudiciously—refuse to accept or support them.

No narrow linguistic approach

On the other hand, the danger exists that the Latin program may metamorphose into a sort of "general language" program which, though valid under that rubric, will make students feel that they have "had" Latin and grasped its essence, when they have not yet achieved more than a nodding acquaintance with the sounds and a few basic structures of the language.

The trend toward "area" courses in classics is the subject of other proposals by Antczak (3), Christie (15), Morton (66), Shriver (91), and Trent (102). Still other innovative Latin programs variously involving greater depth in literature reading, team teaching of various types, honors programs featuring the teaching of Latin plus a modern foreign language, and enrichment of various kinds are described by Kovach (43, 46), Riddering (83), Scanlan (85), and for the Norwalk, Conn., schools (78).

Latin FLES

Latin FLES programs are increasingly widespread, although usually offered experimentally and on a small scale. An unusual one has been conducted since 1962 by Gardocki (reported by Kovach, 46, p. 152). In 1968–69, over 1,100 elementary school students (fourth-eighth grades) are being taught Latin on Saturdays by "live" teachers in 32 teaching centers of the Cleveland Diocesan Schools and the Garfield Heights Public Schools. In addition, over 500 fourth and fifth grade students are being taught via the diocesan radio network.

Use of radio

By 1967 some 300 students had completed up to four years of work in the Saturday classes and had entered high school. A survey taken by Gardocki reveals that over five-sixths of those surveyed continued Latin in high school. Nearly one-fourth of this group received some sort of advanced placement in high school Latin and of those enrolled in Level One, nearly seven in eight had earned A or B grades.

The Advanced Placement Program

The Advanced Placement Program (APP) of the College Entrance Examination Board (1) continues to flourish. Initiated in 1956 as a means of giving college credit and advanced placement to students completing college level work in any of 11 subject matter areas while in secondary school, it has grown steadily, and in May 1968, Advanced Placement Examinations were taken by some 46,000 students from over 2,900 secondary schools.

It may be instructive to study comparative figures in the various foreign languages included in the APP during the years of its history as revealing the numbers of students seeking advanced credit for foreign languages, the growing numbers involved in the total program, and the relative popularity of the individual languages.

TABLE 2. Number of FL Examinations Taken Under the Advanced Placement Program

	1956	1958	1960	1962	1964	1965	1966	1967	1968
French	201	400	702	928	1,497	1,781	2,077	2,351	2,485
German	–	49	224	307	270	340	302	349	439
Latin	38	144	208	439	862	879	973	882	971
Spanish	40	136	232	398	749	901	1,117	1,198	1,471

Based on statistics furnished by the Advanced Placement Program of the College Entrance Examination Board.

A changed format

The format of the Latin examinations has been significantly changed for 1969 (CEEB, 70; Scanlan, 84). Instead of the two areas examined in three-hour tests as Latin 4 (Vergil) and Latin 5 (lyrics of Catullus and Horace plus either comedies of Plautus and Terence or philosophical works of Cicero and either Livy or Tacitus) in earlier years, four more closely specified areas are covered in one-and-one-half hour examinations in Vergil, Comedy (Plautus and Terence), Lyric (Catullus and Horace), and Prose (Cicero or Livy).

It will now be possible for a student to take one or two examinations each year as a high school junior or senior and to be graded separately on each examination, although the total testing time has not been increased. The number of candidates for the Vergil examination will not be affected by this change of format, but presumably the total number taking the three individual examinations should increase markedly since the course load for fifth-year-level advanced placement work can now be lightened where that seems desirable. Many secondary schools that begin Latin in grades seven or eight now may choose to channel their upper level students into a truly viable Advanced Placement Program.

Kaplan's recent study (40) of the foreign language backgrounds of the 1966 National Merit Scholarship semifinalists found that French had been studied by 47.7 percent of the students sampled; Latin, by 46.5 percent; Spanish and German, by 22.6 percent and 18.8 percent respectively. French was most popular for girls, Latin for boys. French was first choice in public schools, Latin first choice in parochial schools, and in independent schools French was studied by 65.2 percent of the students, Latin by 63.8 percent.

National Merit Scholars and FL study

Special enrichment programs

Among interesting developments in short-term enrichment programs for high school Latin students are the *Castra Latina* (Banks, 7) and programs of at least three universities.

Castra Latina, the Latin division of the Midwestern Music and Art Camp at the University of Kansas, has its third annual session from June 15 to July 25, 1969. The six-week course provides instruction in Latin language and literature; Roman art, archaeology, and history; classical mythology; ancient Greek; and, for advanced students, Roman paleography, epigraphy, and numismatics. In 1968 there were 60 students from 24 states enrolled.

Castra Latina

The Universities of Indiana, Michigan, and, more recently, Illinois, have each been offering one or more classical weeks or Latin conferences for high school students each summer for several years, providing college level instruction in Latin and Greek and various ancillary disciplines, with attendance usually limited to 50 per session.

Summer schools

The number of summer study trips to classical lands for high school students is sizable and increasing. A new trend is the ten-day Easter vacation trip to Rome. At least five school systems or cities, Philadelphia, Washington, D.C., Wichita, Detroit, and Anaheim, Calif., plus groups from New Jersey and Montana were involved in such projects in 1969. The Philadelphia trip, under John C. Traupman, has flourished for many years and involves some 1,200 students annually.

Overseas study trips

The value of such programs in motivating and enriching high school Latin study is incalculable and deserves encouragement and emulation. (Latin teachers too could profit from similarly stimulating opportunities.)

Modular scheduling

Modular or flexible scheduling is a matter of practical concern in many school systems. Warburton and Caffey (103) have some suggestions for Latin, and a Cleveland report (89) includes a four-year Latin program along with six years of MFLs in its planning, but a really definitive program for Latin remains to be written.

Computers and the classics

Computer-assisted research and development in classical fields has proceeded rapidly during the last half decade. A good indication of the rate of progress can be seen in the response of the American Philological Association (APA) to the opportunities provided by the computer, at and after three successive annual meetings.

At the 1966 APA meeting in Toledo, an informal meeting of people interested in projects involving both computers and classics led to the founding of a newsletter, *CALCULI* (13).

A similar session at the time of the 1967 meeting in Boston produced two tangible results: formation of a group called The Friends of Homer and the Computer to coordinate the efforts of individuals analyzing Homeric meter, languages, and composition, partly via an informal newsletter; and establishment of a committee instructed to report to the association on the current status of computer use in ancient studies, uses which are likely to develop, and possible solutions to problems already being encountered.

The use of the computer in ancient studies and research

A third informal meeting in December 1968 was prelude to the announcement of the APA Summer Institute in Computer Applications to Classical Studies, to be held from June 16 to July 26, 1969, at the University of Illinois, Urbana. The institute is intended to introduce classical scholars and graduate students to various computer techniques which may be used in their research and teaching.

APA is being assisted by a grant from the IBM Corporation (for importing visiting consultants and lecturers from North America and Europe) and a grant from the National Endowment for the Humanities (to provide fellowships for participants). It is to be expected that the institute will result in expansion of computer-assisted instruction (CAI) work in Latin and Greek and of scholarly research in classical fields.

Computer-assisted research in classics

The existence of such publications as *CALCULI* (13); *Computers and the Humanities* (17), with its semiannual "Directory of Scholars Active," "Annual Bibliography," and reports on "Computers and the Classics"; *Revue* (80), devoted entirely to international news of computer work in ancient languages; and the SICLASH *Newsletter* (68) have served admirably to report and thus help to coordinate scholarly computer-assisted research in the humanities. The new (1969) *Hephaistos* (34) should also further such efforts.

Scholars in the U.S., Canada, Great Britain, Ireland, the countries of Western Europe, and Australia have reported on and shared results of work on literary texts (e.g., studies of authorship, stylistic traits, and metrics; grammatical, syntactical, and morphological analysis; concordances and *indices verborum*; analyses of Latin vocabulary and sound changes in medieval Latin; word-frequency lists; techniques of literary criticism; production of texts of individual authors in machine-readable form), other linguistic items (work on Minoan seals and Linear A and B, the Etruscan language, Greek and Latin papyruses and their reduction to a machine-readable format, inscriptions), archaeology (study of manufacturers' stamps on *terra sigillata*, astronomical data, vase painting styles), and paleography (catalogue of MSS written before the 16th century in Greek and Latin and other early languages). At least some of this activity should have significant effect on the content of courses in Latin and Greek and classical studies generally. In addition, increasing familiarity with the machines and their potentialities should lead to more use of computers in instructional programs.

Areas of computer based research

The Fifth International Congress of Classical Studies, meeting in Bonn, Ger., Sept. 1–6, 1969, has scheduled one session devoted to Problems in Electronic Data Processing. Titles of the papers indicate that there will be one each in Latin, French, German, and English, which underlines again the international and cooperative nature of present computer-assisted research work in the classics.

Mention should also be made of the fact that the American Council of Learned Societies along with the IBM Corporation offers a limited number of awards up to $10,000 each to support humanistic research involving the use of computers.

Computer-assisted instruction

The number of CAI programs known to exist presently for the teaching of Latin or Greek is diappointingly small. Francis M. Wheeler, Department of Classics, Beloit College, Wisconsin, is developing materials for a CAI course in Greek, processing selected texts of Homer and working on a generalized tutorial program.

Greek

C. W. E. Peckett, the Priory School for Boys, Shrewsbury, Shropshire, Eng., is using computers in the preparation of Latin school texts which will be suitable for use with teaching techniques emphasizing reading and recognition rather than composition.

The editor of *CALCULI*, Stephen V. F. Waite, Dartmouth College, Hanover, N. H., has developed a testing program for elementary Latin, which stores grades and provides a summary of results, including which students missed each question.

Item analysis

Richard T. Scanlan, University of Illinois, Urbana, has helped develop an experimental program in beginning Latin using the Illinois PLATO (Programmed Logic for Automated Teaching Operations) system. To the questions "Can the computer provide individualized instruction?" and "Is there greater efficiency in learning from immediate correction and response to student answers?" the response is "Yes." Whether the system provides better retention remains to be seen.

PLATO and Latin

Scanlan uses a branching program with original material but following the order of presentation in Oerberg (75), and at present involving 20 student stations, each with electronic keyset and TV screen. Students spend three periods per week in a regular class setting and in addition one or more hours per week reinforcing class-taught material in the computer laboratory. There is a wide variety of types of exercises concerned with vocabulary, forms in isolation and in context, substitution and transformation drills, translation, and rapid comprehension. Immediate reinforcement, correction, reteaching, and a printout of the entire lesson are available for the student. The teacher gets information on each student's progress, including a printout of wrong answers only.

By 1973, 4,000 remote stations in and around Illinois are expected to be tied into the Educational Research Laboratory facilities of the University of Illinois, any of which, theoretically, could use such a CAI program for one or more beginning students of Latin. Scanlan demonstrated this project via kinescope at the Northeast Conference on the Teaching of Foreign Languages in New York City, 1969.

Further development of elementary Latin and Greek CAI programs such as these seems highly desirable for use in the proliferating junior and community colleges and other institutions in which full-scale classics programs cannot be mounted for reasons of economy and scarcity of qualified "live" instructors.

Need for CAI in the junior colleges

The case for oral Latin

Nearly every new program in Latin, most of the new texts (for a sampling see Ashley & Lashbrook, 5; Burns, et al., 12; O'Brien & Twombley, 74; Stephens & Springhetti, 93; Towey & Akielaszek, 101), and many new teaching aids involve the use of oral Latin, ranging from simple factual question and answer patterns, to class sessions conducted entirely in the target language. There is a tacit assumption that this is a competency of most Latin teachers, which is not yet the case. The growing availability of tape programs, however, to accompany even quite traditional texts, and the use of teaching materials that build the use of Latin right into the course and teach the teacher in the process of teaching the students; greater emphasis on the oral use of Latin in summer workshops; and, undoubtedly, competition from the oral approach in modern foreign languages are changing the situation.

Are the Latin teachers trained for oral work:

An excellent annotated bibliography by Kobler (42) lists texts, dictionaries, magazines, grammars, etc., written in Latin and designed to aid in producing oral fluency.

Lenard, the creator of *Winnie Ille Pu*, in his report (57) before the Illinois Classical Conference, illustrates his thesis that "to keep Latin alive calls for teaching it as a living language" with facile references to international developments in the use of Latin as a living language by teachers, poets, and hobbyists.

Povsic, another able Latinist, in Latin articles (79) and speeches gives testimony to an old tradition and a newly reviving interest, and Jones (38) stresses the importance of oral reading for understanding classical poetry.

Speeches

Oral reading of poetry

A report on the Pontificium Institutum Altioris Latinitatis, the recently established Latin studies center in Rome, by Lang (48) stresses the stimulating challenge posed by the all-in-Latin courses of study.

Journals in Latin, among them the Vatican *Latinitas*, Spanish *Palæstra Latina*, and French *Vita Latina*, and the international

Journals

Latin competitions (Certamen Capitolinum in prose, Hoefftianum in poetry, and Vaticanum in both) set a high standard of excellence for practitioners of "living Latin."

Three classical conferences scheduled for 1969 will employ Latin as a living language: the IV Conventus Vitae Latinae at Avignon in April will be conducted entirely in Latin; the American Classical League Institute at Oxford, O., in June will have an entire session in Latin; and the Fifth International Congress of Classical Studies at Bonn in September has scheduled one Latin paper.

Conferences

In modern foreign language groups, using the target language is taken as a matter of course. But using Latin orally in the classical field, particularly in this country, serves to point up an important trend.

Teaching methods and teacher training

In December 1959 the Committee on Educational Training and Trends of the American Philological Association sponsored a panel on New Approaches to the Teaching of Latin and Greek. The transcription (59) of papers and remarks of the panel plus comments of some of the over 400 classics teachers present remains still the liveliest and most realistic summary of attitudes, beliefs, and practices of teachers of Latin and Greek.

The outstanding methodology book by Distler (20) is especially useful for its stress on oral work in Latin. Morris (65) is less specific and devoted largely to an endorsement of Sweet's innovative ideas (96), but he also presents a useful picture of Latin teaching in England.

Forbes (27) has produced a useful guide for the in-service training of Latin teachers, relying largely on Distler's work (20).

Needed: national standards, exams, program evaluation

To the crucial questions, "How should Latin teachers be trained?" and "What competencies must be required of them?" there are still no uniformly acceptable answers. Several "clarion calls to the profession" have been issued, notably by Bhaerman (11), Dudek (21, 22), Hitt (35), Norton (72), Rexine (81, 82), the Airlie House Conference and the Oxford Conference (49, p. 19–21), in the hope that a set of national standards for teacher preparation, proficiency examinations, and program evaluation can be agreed upon by a national classical group (logically the American Classical League) and then promulgated and implemented, but definite action has yet to be taken.

In an attempt to revitalize the teaching of Latin in its own area, the Texas Education Agency, under Bobby W. LaBouve, Latin consultant, has undertaken an exemplary in-service teacher education program. Margaret Forbes, now of the University of Texas, has produced a syllabus (27) that is being used to develop teacher-trainers, whose individual task is in turn to conduct multiple series of six in-service sessions in various parts of Texas to acquaint teachers with new modes and materials for teaching Latin. Distler's methodology book (20) and the useful new work on Latin pronunciation by Allen (2) are the chief references; the valuable surveys by Bateman (8, 9, 10) of Latin readers are reprinted; and great stress is placed upon the oral use and manipulation of Latin as an integral step in the process of comprehension of Latin as Latin (i.e., without recourse to translation). This might well serve as a prototype for in-service programs to be conducted on local or state levels throughout the nation.

Syllabus and in-service sessions

Spillenger (92) reports on Latin-centered activities of the New York Bureau of Foreign Languages Education, including in-service workshops (one day or several weeks), production of new materials, public relations activities, etc.

New York efforts

Texas and New York are, at the present writing, the only states with Latin consultants in their state departments of education, although several FL consultants have been giving increasing support to classical matters within their own states and nationally, notably in the form of the recent statement issued by the National Council of State Supervisors of Foreign Languages on "The Role of Latin in American Education" (67).

FL consultants and Latin

Among recent curriculum guides for Latin are those of the Diocese of Cleveland (53), New York City (69), Prince George's County, Maryland (41), and the state of North Carolina (47). Numerous others are in prospect, notably in New York State.

Curriculum guides

The annual listing in the *Classical Outlook* of summer programs for teachers of the classics provides a handy index to available opportunities for in-service training. The 1968–69 account (94) indicates that there are at least 53 summer programs in classics in colleges and universities of the U.S. and Canada, including two federally supported institutes and four short-term Latin workshops, plus seven overseas programs in Greece and Italy.

Summer programs

Federal grants for institutes in classics have been awarded since 1966, chiefly under the aegis of the National Foundation for the Arts and Humanities and, more recently, the Education Professions Development Act (EPDA). In summer 1966 the

Classics Department of the University of Minnesota conducted such an institute for six weeks with 40 junior high school teachers who would be teaching Latin at seventh grade level, using materials developed locally under the name Latin Elementary Enrichment Program (LEEP). In 1967 another grant to the University of Minnesota provided a two-week institute for college personnel who train and supervise potential teachers of Latin. In 1968 a grant to the Classics Department of the University of Illinois for six weeks with 35 participants financed a joint effort with University of Minnesota personnel to continue the work with LEEP and to develop competencies in other aspects of the six-year curriculum of which it is a part. During 1968–69 and again for 1969–70 the University of Minnesota is conducting both Prospective Teacher and Experienced Teacher Fellowship Programs, with stress on reading, oral interpretation, writing, linguistic theory, and teaching methods.

Institutes

The six-year or extended classical curriculum as developed by Minnesota-Illinois has these salient features: learning a related language (Italian, another Romance language, and modern Greek) as an integral part of the classical curriculum; interpretative reading in the target languages; comparative study of Greek and Latin literature with introduction to literary criticism; attention to principles and techniques of language learning for transfer; use of multisensory materials (cf. Erickson's excellent annotated bibliography [26] in this field).

Content

The work of all three institutions – Illinois, Minnesota, SUNY-Albany – is helping to produce a truly viable extended curriculum, every part of which is complete and valid in itself. The humanistic approach, insistence on a high level of linguistic competency, inclusion of other related languages and disciplines, and a thorough, sound presentation of teaching and learning techniques are important, both for teacher-training and the classical programs in the nation's schools. In addition, all three institutions have developed new multisensory materials for the teaching of elementary Latin which are being made available to teachers nationally via the individual institute directors.

Teaching materials

At the outset, special mention must be made of the innovative and pioneering work of Waldo E. Sweet. It is probably no exaggeration to say that he is primarily responsible – directly or through teachers and writers whose thinking he has influenced—for the major changes in Latin teaching techniques and materials that have occurred in the last decade and a half. More detailed accounts of his efforts and achievements are available in *Didaskalos* (95) and a recent report of the Northeast Conference (4). They may be summarized briefly as follows: (*1*) he was among the first to recognize the importance of modern linguistic analysis for the teaching of Latin; (2) almost a score of years ago he began to develop new materials for the teaching of Latin and, more important, was quick to share his discoveries, efforts, and enthusiasms with other teachers, enlisting the aid of 24 "highly qualified" (his phrase) Latin teachers in the development of a package of materials for beginning Latin, consisting of text (98); reader (99), disc and tape recordings, flashcards, and filmstrips, all this with the assistance of two Carnegie Corporation grants to support the University of Michigan Latin Workshop during the summers of 1952 and 1953; (3) he continued experimenting and in 1957 published a new text (96) which uses artfully selected native Latin rather than "made" Latin as the basic text, a structurally oriented description of Latin grammar, and pattern drills and other structural and lexical exercises written almost entirely in Latin; (4) a variety of materials on Vergil and Ovid plus articles explaining his theories and describing his experimentation followed rapidly, some published, some still in mimeograph; and (5) in 1961 Sweet began the development of linearly programmed materials for first and second level Latin, which were tested and revised five times before final publication; other parts of these materials are still under the author's hand.

Waldo Sweet's contributions to the teaching of Latin

Sweet's programmed texts (97) form the core of the *Artes Latinae* program and are enhanced by coordinated drill tapes, filmstrips, tests, graded readers, reference notebooks, study prints, sound films (with narration available in both Latin and English), and teacher's manual and guide. By December 1968 the text materials, in various stages of development, had been used in 31 states and Puerto Rico, at every level from junior high school through graduate school. They represent a radical departure in teaching method, of course, and require creativity and willingness to experiment on the part of teachers employing them, but they provide the best and most obvious means available for individualizing instruction, adapting to flexible scheduling, and satisfying the current interest in objectifying goals and testing the achievement thereof.

Multimedia approach

In addition to the computer-assisted programs described earlier, at least one other published set of programmed materials for Latin (described by Hayes, 33) is available, but the fact that it is based on the Vulgate text of the New Testament limits its usefulness and adaptability. The Greek version, however, structured to teach Koine Greek and including in the second stage the text of St. Matthew's Gospel, can serve as a valuable function for seminary and other highly motivated students who wish to concentrate on the Greek of this period. Third and fourth stages of the two-year program use further biblical readings and then switch to the Attic Greek of Plato. All four stages use printed texts plus tapes to teach both oral and visual reading skills, and both the Greek and Latin programs, plus the similar French one, are designed for independent study.

Programmed learning in Latin and Greek using biblical materials

The McGill University Greek Project, funded since September 1968 by a substantial two-year grant from the Ford Foundation, is developing materials to teach classical Greek, based on the principles of structural and applied linguistics. C. Douglas Ellis (linguistics) and Albert Schachter (classics) are producing text materials, drill tapes, and teacher's manual. The program stresses both directed and free oral and written composition, self-correcting oral pattern drills, and manipulation of basic dialogues, using Plato and Xenophon as basic text materials.

McGill Greek Project

Mention has been made earlier of some of the new teaching materials which stress the use of oral Latin (5, 12, 20, 74, 75, 93, 101). Revisions of more traditional texts and still other new materials, representing every range of the methodological spectrum, continue to appear in gratifying numbers. Among recent important publications in classics that cannot be neatly categorized are the first fascicle of an entirely new Latin-English dictionary (76), a supplement to the most recent edition of the Liddell-Scott Greek-English dictionary (60), a structural grammar of ecclesiastical Latin by O'Brien (73), Horgan's work on testing (36), and two works designed to help students develop techniques of literary criticism by Balme & Warman (6) and Hornsby (37).

New publications

Service organizations for classics teachers

The emphasis here will not be on the purely scholarly activities of these associations but rather on their service functions. Jones (39) gives a more complete account, from a broad historical point of view; *The Classical World* has a most comprehensive and practical list (16).

The American Philological Association (APA) is the oldest of the American classical associations. Its committees on Educational Training and Trends, Greek and Latin College Textbooks, and Classics and Computers and its corporate role at the annual meeting as intermediary between prospective employer and employee are of special importance to classicists as teachers.

APA

The Archaeological Institute of America serves teachers primarily through its lectures before local societies, publications, and sponsoring of films on archaeology.

The American School of Classical Studies at Athens, the American Academy in Rome, and the Vergilian Society through its Villa Vergiliana at Cumae provide summer programs chiefly for secondary school teachers of classics. In recent years liberal support for attendance at these programs has come through Fulbright fellowships as well as the scholarships offered by many regional and local classical groups.

Overseas study

The American Classical League (ACL) through its establishment, with the support of numerous other groups and individuals, of a national office with a full-time executive secretary, John F. Latimer, has assumed the role of coordinator and spokesman for the classics. Services of the League include its publications, *Classical Outlook* and *Classical Action USA*, the executive secretary's newsletter, sale of teaching materials through the ACL Service Bureau at Miami University, Oxford, O., an annual Classical Institute devoted chiefly to matters pedagogical, a Placement Service for teachers, sponsorship of the Junior Classical League (largest classical organization with over 80,000 members and with its own publication *Torch: US*, state conclaves, and an annual five-day national meeting), and the Senior Classical League (for former JCL members), and, most important, with the aid of two federal grants, the sponsoring of two national conferences on classics (reported by Latimer 49, 50) and other supportive activities.

ACL: Spokesman and coordinator for the classics

Eta Sigma Phi is a national fraternal organization for college students of the classics and publishes *Nuntius*.

The regional associations, Classical Association of the New England States, Classical Association of the Atlantic States (CAAS), Classical Association of the Middle West and South (CAMWS), and Classical Association of the Pacific States, sponsor annual meetings, offer scholarships to teachers and prospective teachers, in some cases sponsor summer workshops, and, in two cases, have major publications. The *Classical Journal* (CAMWS) is primarily a scholarly journal but includes the "For-

Regional associations and their journals

um" for pedagogical articles and has useful reviews and other notes. *The Classical World* (CAAS) is an invaluable source of help to teachers, particularly through its annual listings of AV materials (88), textbooks for Greek and Latin (87), and inexpensive books for classical courses (86). "Notes and News," numerous concise reviews of texts and other teaching materials, author bibliographies, and various special listings of, e.g., college faculty rosters, make *The Classical World* an especially useful tool for teachers.

Vigorous state and local classical organizations have been in existence for years and offer many services (meetings, workshops, scholarships, newsletters and other publications, contests, programs for students, public relations projects, and curriculum studies, inter alia).

The formation in 1967 of the American Council on the Teaching of Foreign Languages, of which every eligible classical association has become an affiliate, has given active support to classics teachers and their activities through its publication *Foreign Language Annals*, its annual meetings, and its important FL bibliographies. In particular, the Council's insistence that state FL organizations cannot affiliate with the national group unless they welcome teachers of all FLs to membership has tended to strengthen relationships of teachers of MFLs and state FL supervisors with classics teachers within individual states. *ACTFL*

The Northeast Conference on the Teaching of Foreign Languages similarly, through its attention to the interests of Greek and Latin teachers, has done much to strengthen a sense of solidarity between teachers of all FLs and gives them realistic opportunities to learn from each other. *Northeast Conference*

Epilogue

It is perhaps appropriate to conclude this overview of recent trends and developments in the teaching of classics with some echoes from the recent supportive statement of the National Council of State Supervisors of Foreign Languages concerning "The Role of Latin in American Education" (67).

Like any other foreign language, Latin can serve to break down monocultural and monolingual barriers, but it is uniquely qualified to help the student develop a sense of the significant past by providing a direct contact with the ancient world, to help him develop a deeper understanding of linguistic concepts because its structure is so radically different from that of English, and to help him develop a sense of judgment based on an understanding of the past.

In the judgment of the council, such values come through the competence developed in an extended sequence of study (three to six years). The relevance of such study is enhanced through the use of multisensory materials and methods that are appropriate to the interests and abilities of the students, and the key factor in the success of any foreign language program is the effectiveness of the teaching.

In substance, the council is endorsing the kinds of innovative programs and approaches that have been described in this chapter. If their logic is sound, continued concerted efforts along these lines should reverse Else's gloomy dictum and make both relevance and role of the classics in American life once more "enormous."

References, Classics: teaching of Latin and Greek

1 Advanced Placement Program, 1968–69. College Entrance Examination Board, New York, 1968.

2 Allen, W. Sidney. Vox Latina: a guide to the pronunciation of classical Latin. Cambridge University Press, London, 1965.

3 Antczak, Robert A. Classical studies. Classical Outlook, 45(1968) 64–65.

4 Artes Latinae, an Examination of the Waldo Sweet Latin Program. In: Foreign language learning: research and development: an assessment. Northeast Conference on the Teaching of Foreign Languages, 1968. MLA Materials Center, N.Y.

5 Ashley, Clara M.; Lashbrook, Austin M. Living Latin: a contemporary approach, Bk. I and II (with Ruth Fiesel). Ginn, Boston, 1967 and 1968.

6 Balme, M. G.; Warman, M. S. Aestimanda. Oxford University Press, New York, 1965.

7 Banks, Elizabeth Courtney. Latin camp. Classical Outlook, 45(1967) 40–41.

8 Bateman, John J. Latin readers for high school use. Classical Journal, 60(1965) 306–307.

9 Bateman, John J. More Latin readings for high school use. Classical Journal, 59(1964) 350–354.

10 Bateman, John J. A survey of Latin readers for high school use. Classical Journal, 58(1963) 296–312.

11 Bhaerman, Robert D. Needed: guidelines for "program approval" in Latin. Classical Journal, 63(1967) 70–74.

12 Burns, Mary Ann T.; Medicus, Carl J.; Sherburne, Richard, S.J. Lingua Latina: liber primus and liber alter. Bruce, Milwaukee, 1964 and 1965.

13 Calculi. Department of Classics, Dartmouth College, Hanover, N.H. (A bimonthly newsletter).

14 Carr, W. L. The classical investigation forty years after. Classical Journal, 60(1965) 151–154.

15 Christie, J. T. The study of classical civilization without classical languages? Greece and Rome, 13(1966) 129–138.

16 Classical Societies in the United States 1967. Classical World, 61(1967) 13–16, 21–24.

17 Computers and the Humanities. Queens College of the City University of New York, Flushing.

18 Curriculum Suggestions for Grades Six Through Nine: Latin (with sample examinations). National Association of Independent Schools, Boston, 1968.

19 DeWitt, Norman J. Classical languages. In: Harris, Chester, ed. Encyclopedia of educational research. 3rd ed. Macmillan, New York, 1960.

20 Distler, Paul, S.J. Teach the Latin, I pray you. Loyola University Press, Chicago, 1962.

21 Dudek, Henry X. Guidelines for teacher education programs in Latin. The Classical World, 61(1968) 397–400.

22 Dudek, Henry X. Ideal Latin teacher-training program: teacher opinions. Classical Journal, 63(1967) 10–11.

23 Eaton, Annette. The Washington, D.C., sixth, seventh, and eighth grade Latin programs. In: ACL PR Packet. American Classical League, Oxford, O., n.d.

24 Else, Gerald F., ed. Report of the colloquium on the classics in education, 1965. American Council of Learned Societies, January 1966.

25 Else, Gerald F. The role and relevance of classical education today. In: Latimer, John F., ed. Report of the planning conference to examine the role of classical studies in American education and to make recommendations for needed

research and development. The George Washington University, Washington, D.C., 1967, p. 1–7.

26 Erickson, Gerald M. Selective annotated bibliography for the multi-sensory approach to Latin teaching. University of Minnesota, Minneapolis, October 1967 (mimeo.)

27 Forbes, Margaret. A syllabus for an in-service course in the teaching of Latin. Texas Education Agency, Foreign Language Section, Austin, January 1969 (mimeo.)

28 Foreign Languages in the Catholic High School. (Report of the Advisory Committee on Foreign Languages). Catholic High School Quarterly Bulletin, 21(January 1964) 1–18.

29 Ganss, George E. Changing objectives and procedures in teaching Latin, 1556–1956. Classical Journal, 52(1956) 15–22.

30 Hayden, Hilary, O.S.B. Classics in the inner city school: experiments and proposals. The Classical World, 60(1966) 93–98.

31 Hayden, Hilary, O.S.B. Inner city Latin conference. The Classical World, 61(1968) 178–180.

32 Hayden, Hilary, O.S.B. To speak in thunder. Classical Journal, 63(1967) 77–78.

33 Hayes, Walter M., S.J. Programmed Greek, Latin, and French: an experiment. Classical Journal, 62(1966) 114–116.

34 HEPHAISTOS, a quarterly journal devoted to computer research in the humanities. Office for Humanistic Research, St. Joseph's College, Philadelphia.

35 Hitt, James A. Basic standards for the preparation of Latin teachers. Classical Journal, 59(1964) 248–249.

36 Horgan, Edward D., S.J. Testing Latin structure. Georgetown University Press, Washington, D.C., 1964.

37 Hornsby, Roger. Reading Latin poetry. University of Oklahoma Press, Norman, 1967.

38 Jones, Frank. On reading Latin hexameters out loud. Classical Outlook, 46(1968) 41–44.

39 Jones, W. R. Classical associations in the United States. In: Classics in the U.S.A. (JACT Pamphlet/3). Joint Association of Classical Teachers, London, n.d., 40–46.

40 Kaplan, Rosalyn. Language study of national merit scholarship semifinalists. Foreign Language Annals, 2(1968) 51–53.

41 Kennedy, Dora F., ed. A curriculum guide in Latin. Prince George's County Board of Education, Upper Marlboro, Md., 1965.

42 Kobler, John F., C.P. A bibliography of spoken Latin. The Classical World, 59(1966) 149–157, 172.

43 Kovach, Edith M. A. Admirandi, laudandi, imitandi. Classical Outlook, 46(1966) 40–44.

44 Kovach, Edith M. A. Latin curricula: student attitudes. Classical Journal, 63(1967) 109–114.

45 Kovach, Edith M. A. Ten master teacher and program award programs. The Classical World, 60(1966) 37–47.

46 Kovach, Edith M. A. Triplex acies. Classical Journal, 62(1967) 150–156.

47 Ladu, Tora T.; et al. Latin curriculum guide. North Carolina State Department of Public In-

struction, Raleigh, N.C., 1966.

48 Lang, Frederick R. Impressions of living Latin. Classical Journal, 63(1968) 297–298.

49 Latimer, John F., ed. The Oxford conference and related activities. A report to the National Endowment for the Humanities. American Classical League, Washington, D.C., 1968.

50 Latimer, John F., ed. Report of the planning conference to examine the role of classical studies in American education and to make recommendations for needed research and development. The George Washington University, Washington, D.C., 1965.

51 Latimer, John F.; Eaton, Annette. Latin in secondary schools: a six-year program. Foreign Language Annals, 1(1968) 295–300.

52 Latin–Does it still belong? Catholic High School Quarterly Bulletin, 23(July 1965) 1–32.

53 Latin guidelines for secondary schools. Diocese of Cleveland, Board of Catholic Education, Cleveland, 1966.

54 Latin is not dead. Smith, Mortimer, ed. Bulletin of the Council for Basic Education, 12(February 1968) 7.

55 LeBovit, Judith. Qui timide rogat, docet negare. The Classical World, 61(1967) 37–40.

56 LeBovit, Judith. Sixth and seventh grade Latin in Washington, D.C., schools. In: ACL PR Packet, American Classical League, Oxford, O., n.d.

57 Lenard, Alexander; Drake, Gertrude, eds. Living Latin. Classical Journal, 63(1967) 11–14.

58 Levy, Harry L. The place of Latin in the total foreign language curriculum. Foreign Language Annals, 1(1967) 13–17.

59 Levy, Harry L. Teaching Latin and Greek: new approaches. Classical Journal, 57(1962) 202–230.

60 Liddell, H.G.; Scott, Robert; Jones, H. Stuart. A Greek-English lexicon: a supplement (E. A. Barber, ed., assisted by P. Maas, M. Scheller, and M. L. West). Oxford University Press, New York, 1968.

61 Lingua Latina Pueris Puellisque Exposita (Latin for sixth grade–teachers' manual). Foreign Language Department, Washington, D.C., Public Schools, n.d. (mimeo.)

62 Masciantonio, Rudolph. Latin materials for the inner-city public school. Classical Outlook, 45(1968) 61–62.

63 Masciantonio, Rudolph. Latin's needs in the big city public schools. The Classical World, 61(1969) 390–393.

64 Masciantonio, Rudolph. A pilot project in Latin for the elementary schools. The Classical World, 62(1969) 294.

65 Morris, Sidney. Viae novae: new techniques in Latin teaching. Hulton Educational Publications, London, 1966.

66 Morton, Richard K. Expanding our field. Classical Outlook, 45(1967) 17.

67 National Council of State Supervisors of Foreign Languages. The role of Latin in American education. The Classical World, 62(1969) 293–294.

68 Newsletter of the special interest committee on language analysis and studies in the humanities (SICLASH). Sponsored by Association for Com-

puting Machinery. Edited by Department of English, University of Iowa, Iowa City.

69 New York City Foreign Language Program for Secondary Schools: Latin, Levels I-IV. (Curriculum Bulletin—1967–68 Series, No. 19). Board of Education of the City of New York, 1968.

70 1968–70 Advanced Placement Course Descriptions. College Entrance Examination Board, New York, 1968.

71 Nisius, Ray F. The Cleveland Heights Latin task force. In: ACL PR Packet. American Classical League, Oxford, O., n.d.

72 Norton, Harriet. Teacher training programs. The Classical World, 62(1968) 7–8.

73 O'Brien, Richard J., S.J. A descriptive grammar of ecclesiastical Latin based on modern structural analysis. Dissertation Abstracts, 28(1967): 657A-C58A(Georgetown). [Order from Loyola University Press, Chicago, Ill.]

74 O'Brien, Richard J., S.J.; Twombly, Neil J., S.J. A basic course in Latin, and An intermediate course in Latin. Loyola University Press, Chicago, 1962 and 1964.

75 Oerberg, Hans H. Lingua Latina secundum naturae rationem explicata, Vols. I-IV. Nature Method Language Institute, New York, 3rd ed., 1965.

76 Oxford Latin Dictionary. Fascicle I: A-Calcitro. Oxford University Press, New York, 1968.

77 Parker, William Riley. The case for Latin. Publications of the Modern Language Association, 79(September 1964) 3–10.

78 Pilot Program: Latin in the Seventh Grade. Classical Journal, 63(1968) 346–350.

79 Povsic, Boleslav. De Latinarum litterarum fortuna. Classical Outlook, 45(1968) 100–101.

80 Revue, a quarterly. International Organization for Ancient Languages Analysis by Computer (LASLA), Liège, Belg.

81 Rexine, John E. A proposal for teacher training in the classics. The Classical World, 62(1968) 43–45.

82 Rexine, John E. Teacher training and the classics. The Classical World, 59(1966) 257–260.

83 Riddering, Donald L. A foreign language honors program. In: ACL PR Packet. American Classical League, Oxford, O., n.d.

84 Scanlan, Richard T. Changes in the CEEB AP Latin. The Classical World, 62(1968) 46–47.

85 Scanlan, Richard T. A Latin combo. In: ACL PR Packet. American Classical League, Oxford, O., n.d.

86 Schoenheim, Ursula. Inexpensive books for teaching the classics. The Classical World, 62(1969) 173–186.

87 Schoenheim, Ursula. Textbooks in Greek and Latin: 1969 list. The Classical World, 62(1969) 311–323.

88 Seittelman, Elizabeth E. Thirteenth annual survey of audiovisual materials. The Classical World, 62(1969) 261–275.

89 Sequential Programs in Foreign Language for a Restructured Curriculum, Grades 7–12. Educational Research Council of Greater Cleveland, 1966.

90 Shero, L. R. A historical survey of the classics in the schools and universities of the United States. In: Classics in the U.S.A. (JACT Pamphlet/3). Joint Association of Classical Teachers, London, n.d.

91 Shriver, John R. Why not Greek? The Arch (CMFLA of Georgia Education Association), 8(1966) 1–5.

92 Spillenger, Morton E. Dicta et facta. Classical Outlook, 46(1968) 41.

93 Stephens, Wade C.; Springhetti, Emilio, S.J. Lingua Latina viva II. McGraw-Hill, New York, 1967.

94 Summer Study. Classical Outlook, 46(1968) 89–91.

95 Sweet, Waldo E. The continued development of the structural approach. Didaskalos, 2:ii(1967), 141–159.

96 Sweet, Waldo E. Latin: a structural approach. University of Michigan Press, Ann Arbor, 1957. Revision with Ruth Craig and Gerda Seligson, ibid., 1966.

97 Sweet, Waldo E. Latin: level one and Latin: level two. Encyclopaedia Britannica Educational Corporation, Chicago, 1966 and 1968.

98 Sweet, Waldo E., ed. Latin workshop experimental materials. Book one. University of Michigan Press, Ann Arbor, 1953. Rev. ed. 1956. Second revision in two vols. under new title, Elementary Latin: the basic structures, part I and part II, ed. by G. Crawford, C. Ashley, F. Kempner, University of Michigan Press, Ann Arbor, 1963.

99 Sweet, Waldo E., ed. Latin workshop experimental materials. Book two. University of Michigan Press, Ann Arbor, 1954. Rev. ed. 1957.

100 Tappenden, Jacqueline; Schwartz, Betty L. Cultural language study for grades seven and eight. Cleveland Heights-University Heights, Ohio-1 School District, n.d. (mimeo.)

101 Towey, Cyprian, C.P.; Akielaszek, Stanislaus. Lingua Latina viva I. McGraw-Hill, New York, 1963.

102 Trent, Andrew J. Cultural enrichment. Classical Outlook, 44(1967) 99–100.

103 Warburton, Joyce; Chaffey, Mary. Latin classes in a flexible schedule. Classical Journal, 63(1968) 299.

15

Surveys and reports on foreign language enrollments

Introduction

John P. Dusel

*Department of
Public Instruction,
Sacramento, California*

For many years foreign language educators have investigated student supply and the demand for the inclusion of foreign languages in the curriculum. Others have surveyed the progress of students in colleges and universities and the progress of programs in the elementary schools, and almost annual surveys have been conducted at the secondary school level.

Surveys of national enrollments are frequently compilations of statewide enrollments made by state supervisors of foreign languages for their departments of education. Occasionally a county will survey its supply of foreign language teachers when new programs and additional languages are being considered. They will often find teachers fluent in a foreign language teaching other subjects. School districts often delegate the responsibility of enrollment surveys to the foreign language supervisor or coordinator. An alert foreign language department chairman in a high school may consider that keeping track of fall and spring semester enrollments helps to diagnose potential enrollment problems in his particular school. Sometimes teachers of a specific language report upon the teacher supply as well as the increasing or decreasing number of students electing study of that language.

Need for enrollment surveys

It is the writer's purpose to mention enrollment surveys and reports previous to 1968. Reference will also be made to a major survey to be published in 1969, to list the concerns that exist about foreign language enrollments, as well as to discuss what is being done to solve some of the pressing problems in this area.

The need to report on research done prior to 1968 is obvious since so little has been done in the field even though statistics have been available that graphically demonstrate the existence of problems in the teaching of foreign languages.

Enrollment reports

Eight studies of foreign language enrollments in public secondary schools, grades 7 through 12, have been published from 1958 through 1965 with a ninth study now underway for the fall

1968 enrollments. These national surveys were made by the Modern Language Association (MLA) except for the years 1966 and 1967. Prepared for the U.S. Office of Education pursuant to contracts under the National Defense Education Act, these reports have furnished educators with data on the status of all the languages taught in public junior and senior high schools. Childers reported public secondary school enrollments in 1958, 1959, and 1960 (8, 9, 10), Eshelman & Dershem in 1963 (22), Dershem, Lund, & Herslow in 1964 (13), and Teague & Rütimann in 1965 (48). An abridged report of the 1965 enrollments was provided by Willbern (54) in a recent issue of *Foreign Language Annals.*

The Modern Language Association has conducted surveys of enrollment in nonpublic schools in 1959 (Foreign Languages in Independent Secondary Schools, Fall 1959, and Foreign Language Enrollments in Seventh-Day Adventist and Catholic Parochial Schools, Fall 1959). A comparison of these data was made by Eshelman & Lian (23) in the 1961 and 1962 report.

Highlights of the 1964 and 1965 national surveys, for example, have been widely used in newspaper articles throughout the country to show trends, to pinpoint problems, and to call attention to the number of dropouts in the more popular languages: French, German, and Spanish. Charts in the 1965 report (54) illustrate such things as summary comparison by region, by number of schools, and by language enrollment matched with the 1960 results. In a most professional effort to be honest and accurate the authors of these national surveys further list data missing from certain states, data that have been adjusted from earlier reporting, and data that reflect the previous year's situation. Anyone who has ever made a survey will appreciate the great difficulty in collecting data from 50 states. On occasion the Modern Language Association has had to collect data from school districts in a state where no state supervisor of foreign languages was employed or where the supervisor was not authorized by his superiors to collect the data.

Willbern's comparative survey

Other national surveys have been done by Eaton (21) on 1959 enrollment data; by Breunig (38) on foreign languages in the elementary schools of the United States, 1959-60; by Harmon (38) on foreign languages in independent secondary schools in the fall of 1959; by Childers & Bell (38) on modern foreign language teaching in the junior colleges in the fall of 1959 and 1960; by Vamos, Margulis, & White (38) on modern foreign language enrollments in four-year accredited colleges and universi-

Summary Comparisons, by Region, of Number of Schools, PSS Enrollment, and Foreign Language Enrollments, Grades 7-12: Fall 1960 and 1965

		USA Totals	New England	Mideast	Great Lakes	Plains	Southeast	Southwest	Rocky Mountains	Far West
1		2	3	4	5	6	7	8	9	10
Number of schools	1960	18,613	805	2,062	3,297	3,116	5,189	2,245	726	1,173
	1965	22,527	1,155	2,845	3,606	3,244	6,304	2,180	1,062	2,131
PSS enrollment	1960	11,847,783	572,574	2,606,176	2,215,503	949,467	2,827,434	843,117	390,696	1,442,816
	1965	16,400,895	823,714	3,177,121	3,176,650	1,398,694	3,788,315	1,415,002	494,213	2,127,186
Spanish enrollment	1960	1,037,320	30,138	261,799	155,053	51,787	129,280	160,854	36,650	211,759
	1965	1,833,960	68,917	441,515	319,498	98,676	246,984	221,219	54,433	382,718
French enrollment	1960	853,342	121,170	314,359	121,326	27,501	146,287	19,437	17,648	85,614
	1965	1,586,852	223,697	478,384	279,632	67,013	275,902	48,155	35,459	178,610
German enrollment	1960	162,130	6,209	57,470	36,131	14,492	4,485	5,232	8,022	30,089
	1965	373,771	11,737	100,153	98,298	38,705	17,717	15,568	17,023	74,570
Russian enrollment	1960	10,051	896	3,167	1,928	247	447	189	723	2,454
	1965	32,027	1,698	7,902	13,194	1,583	1,319	663	2,096	3,572
Italian enrollment	1960	21,036	4,018	15,342	446	39	0	0	28	1,163
	1965	29,931	6,339	17,657	4,646	48	75	0	29	1,137
MFL enrollment	1960	2,096,002	163,740	659,811	315,583	95,357	280,499	185,712	63,139	332,161
	1965	3,867,894	313,164	1,051,837	716,085	206,312	542,063	285,675	109,080	643,678
Latin enrollment	1960	678,928	76,715	172,443	157,443	42,338	120,420	37,540	16,069	55,960
	1965	626,199	68,762	170,144	157,960	32,893	112,304	34,454	12,897	36,815
Total FL enrollment	1960	2,775,152	240,532	832,254	473,026	137,708	401,051	223,252	79,208	388,121
	1965	4,494,212	381,995	1,221,951	874,069	239,205	654,375	320,129	121,995	680,493
FL as percent of PSS enrollment	1960	23.4	42.0	31.9	21.4	14.5	14.2	26.5	20.3	26.9
	1965	27.4	46.4	38.5	27.5	17.1	17.3	22.6	24.7	32.0
MFL as percent of FL	1960	75.5	68.1	79.3	66.7	69.9	69.9	83.2	79.7	85.6
	1965	86.1	82.0	86.1	81.9	86.2	82.8	89.4	89.4	94.6

PSS: Public secondary schools Printed with Permission of the editor of *Foreign Language Annuals*, 1:iii (March 1968) 243.

ties. Recent research by Lund & Herslow (36) on foreign language entrance and degree requirements in the colleges and universities during 1966 updates studies done in 1957 by Viens & Wadsworth (53), by Wolfe (57) in 1959, and by Plottel (44) in 1960. The article by Willbern (55) is an abridgment of the study by Lund & Herslow (36). The Wolfe and Plottel studies are used by Remer (45) in her handbook for guiding students in the modern languages.

Other surveys

FLES

A national study done by Gradisnik (28) surveys FLES (foreign languages in elementary school) instruction in cities with populations exceeding 300,000. The report lists information contributed by 31 out of 41 cities to which the questionnaire was sent. It includes such items as the year that the FLES programs began, languages offered, number of days per week of instruction, grade in which the program is begun, number of schools participating, and information regarding the use of television. Although almost four pages are used to report the data, Gradisnik concludes:

> Are the thirty-one cities satisfied with their FLES programs? Fourteen cities reported that they were. This seems to indicate that, despite certain shortcomings, at least some of the established objectives are being accomplished. However, since only nine cities report that they have conducted a formal evaluation of their FLES program, the other cities may not be sharply aware of the areas that need strengthening. This may be the reason why nineteen cities could report that they did not anticipate any major modifications in their programs in the near future.

The Gradisnik report

The reader of the article does not receive the full impact of the data when they are tallied separately without designating the districts involved. The chart in the report indicates that in the Los Angeles City School District, the second largest district reported in the survey, instruction in Spanish is started in grade six through the use of a 15-minute television program in all of the 428 schools having a sixth grade. The report fails to show that no opportunity is given for these pupils to continue their study in grades seven and eight, that the classroom teachers have little or no facility with Spanish, and that supervision of instruction and actual teaching must be done by only 24 visiting

418

teachers who visit the classroom about once every two weeks with little or no chance for warm-up or follow-up of the television instruction, and little or no supervision by qualified teachers. Does this district really have a FLES program? The article does not define what constitutes a FLES program. From the information presented one could not gather that another district reporting, the Long Beach Unified School District, also in Los Angeles County, has an exemplary FLES program. This district offers pupils a *choice* of foreign languages, employs qualified classroom foreign language teachers, provides a foreign language coordinator, groups pupils according to ability, offers a well-coordinated program with television as only one of the components, and *requires* students to continue with the language of their choice in grades seven and eight. A mere tallying of questionnaire data from cities having a population over 300,000 is misleading and really does not reveal the status or effectiveness of foreign language education in city schools, nor does the tally serve to isolate and identify those cities doing a creditable job.

Some states survey foreign language offerings and enrollments in order to diagnose trends and practices. The Massachusetts State Department of Education recently published such data concerning the academic year, 1965-66 (37). The California State Department of Education made a similar comprehensive study entitled *General Observations on the Results of the Survey of Foreign Language Offerings and Enrollments in California Public Schools, Fall 1965* (19). Both elementary and high school districts were included. Surveys of secondary schools have been made annually to study the enrollments brought about since 1965 when legislation mandating foreign language instruction in California public schools in grades six, seven, and eight took effect. The law was repealed in 1968 making such instruction optional in kindergarten and grades one through six. However, districts are required to offer foreign language instruction beginning in grade seven. Total enrollments in the California public secondary schools have nevertheless increased in 1968 over the previous year (18).

Various language groups have made reports on national enrollments, trends, and practices. In most instances the studies are conducted by those language groups that do not lead in enrollments—Chinese, Italian, Latin, and Russian. These language groups are particularly concerned when FLES programs do not allow pupils a choice of language. An imbalance of enrollments

Some unresolved questions in the report

The California law is repealed

419

results. This imbalance continues into the junior and senior high school grades with the result that classes in Chinese, German, Hebrew, Italian, Japanese, Latin, and Russian are hard pressed to stay alive.

Chinese

In November 1967 the Modern Language Association cooperated with the Executive Board of the Chinese Teachers' Association in a survey of the professional status of college teachers of Chinese. Willbern reported (56) from a 25-percent usable return on the college institutions, educational backgrounds and ranks of the faculty, number of courses taught, level of courses, previous teaching experience, salary, summer work, tenure, reimbursement for travel, and benefits. The Chinese Teachers' Association realizes that teacher supply is crucial if enrollments are to be increased.

Italian

Teachers of Italian are also interested in student enrollments and teacher supply. In California, a recent survey of Italian in universities and colleges presented some encouraging conclusions (12). De Petra, the coordinator of the American Association of Teachers of Italian (AATI), found that the number of higher institutions of learning that offer Italian has more than doubled, from 23 in 1965 to 52 in 1968; the number of college students also increased from 3,727 to 5,108. Teachers of Italian are using the results to encourage high school students to begin the study of this language and to show counselors the colleges in which such study might be continued.

Latin

For the past several years teachers of Latin have been deeply concerned over the decreasing number of secondary school students studying classical languages and the increasing number of school districts that have eliminated Latin from the curricular offerings. Goldberg reported (27) the high school enrollment drop for 1964-65 based on MLA reports in *The Classical World*. He strongly urged a nationwide "public relations program" which the American Classical League is vigorously supporting. Latimer's report (32) and his recent article coauthored by Eaton (33) show the comprehensiveness of the plan to attack the serious problem facing all teachers of classical languages. In another article in the same journal Lieberman (35) points out that

Classicists attack their problems

there are increased enrollments in Latin and Greek at the college level. According to Phinney in a speech to the California Action Council for Classics (42), two branches of the University of California reported an increased enrollment in Latin for 1968 over the 1965 figures. The Los Angeles and Santa Barbara branches of the university showed a combined total of 1,517 students studying classical languages in 1965 and 2,020 in 1968. The Action Council in 1969 surveyed enrollments, teacher positions, and textbooks used in Latin instruction and is presently using these data toward the improvement of foreign language programs in the California schools.

Russian

Although Russian enrollments increased almost 175 percent between 1960 and 1965 in grades 9 through 12, teachers of this subject are constantly working to hold their gains. Bockman reported (6) the results of a survey of foreign language supervisory experience with high school programs and the opinions concerning factors affecting enrollment in high school Russian. According to the 1965 returns, the latest complete national tally, only some 32,000 students in grades 7 through 12 were studying this language. A factor that limits continued increase in enrollment is a shortage of well-qualified teachers. Terras outlined the difficulty he encountered in determining the number of college students working toward a major or minor in Russian (49). The second part of his survey, the teaching of Russian in secondary schools (50), can soon be compared with the 1968 MLA survey to determine if enrollment has grown. Mention will be made of partial returns of 1968 enrollments for Russian later in this article.

No well-qualified teacher — no enrollments

Enrollment concern

Some educators such as Dale (11) feel that we have been generous with the time of our language students; in many instances we have wasted their time by questionable pedagogical practices. As we have gone about our teaching we have not known specifically what our objectives were. We have not adjusted our teaching to correspond to the varying abilities of our students. We have tried to "cover" too many grammatical principles, too many lexical items, too many idiomatic expressions without making sure that all of these things have been learned. Only recently has much thought been given to criterion-referenced testing. When students have failed to learn basic concepts, we have often blamed other teachers or the students themselves. We have rarely blamed a so-called sequentially developed set of texts.

Administrators frequently overload beginning classes of foreign languages explaining their apparent poor planning with the rationale that a great number of students have always dropped out after the first grading period. Dale says further:

Let's look at our curriculum: what are we spending our tin on?

> We could save huge amounts of time if we sharpened our focus on the kinds of goals we think are worth spending our time on. We travel day by day in a verbal and social jungle without an adequate map. If you don't know where you're going, the chances of getting there are poor. And unfamiliar shortcuts may turn out to be the longest way home. Have we pledged our time to ends that now seem glitteringly golden but which in the long run may turn out to be dross? To map our lives requires a scrutiny of values. Do our high schools and colleges spend enough time helping students discover what is worth investing time in, worth prizing, honoring, valuing? (11, p. 2)

Who should study a foreign language?

Presidents of nine colleges and universities in the state of Oregon (47) recommend that all students bound for college should take a minimum of four years of a foreign language. These men believe that the study of foreign languages is a basic school discipline of great humane value and practical use in preparing young men and women for college and university studies.

In an extensive research project completed in 1963 by Pimsleur, Sundland, & McIntyre (43) the authors point out that about 10 to 20 percent of all students now studying foreign languages are beset by a frustrating lack of ability to learn them. This problem occurs among the gifted as well as among the average students. The authors proceed to examine reasons why many students underachieve and include actual interviews with underachievers whose IQ scores ranged from 96 to 138. Those students who underachieve and show this by low grades or by dropping the subject altogether could learn a foreign language if certain suggestions were acted upon. These are:

Why the student frustration?

1 That a foreign language aptitude test in combination with the grade point average would help predict a student's foreign language achievement. The teacher is immediately aware

that remedial help is needed.

2 That coordination of teacher's goals, of teaching methods, and of grading procedure is badly needed.

3 That a student's estimation of his facility in each of the basic skills is usually accurate. The teacher should be aware of this estimation in preparing work assignments and in grading.

4 That instruction should be individualized as much as possible to allow for different abilities and varying rates of learning.

5 That students want the teacher to be patient, kind, and understanding. They also want the teacher to push them along in their work.

Pimsleur, Sundland, & McIntyre state further: "It appears — this opinion was formed after sitting in on many classes — that each teacher follows his own judgment, stressing this, passing over that, with the result that students are very unevenly prepared to move on to the class of another teacher" (43, p. 21).

The "Foreign Language Cumulative Report Form" devised by DuFort & Schevill (15) gives attention to the need for record keeping. Keeping track of the results of foreign language aptitude tests, of the use of television in the sequential language program, of progress in various texts, and of the duration and frequency of foreign language instruction are made possible with this report form. Space is also provided so that the teacher can show the student's facility in each of the basic skills as he progresses year by year.

Record keeping

Who should continue the study of a foreign language?

The 1965 statistics supplied by Teague & Rütimann (48) were compared with data obtained in the fall of 1962 to show that 95.5 percent of those students who had begun Spanish instruction in 1962 had discontinued their study by the beginning of the 1965-66 school year. A total of 92.1 percent of the French students had discontinued, and 93.1 percent of those studying German were not enrolled as fourth-year students by 1965. This is a shocking exposé of the state of foreign language programs. There undoubtedly are other reasons for this dropout rate, but Remer (45) points out that in many cases students do not understand the continuous work essential to attain both competency and proficiency in using a foreign language. Much time and effort is involved since language learning is a complicated process. The student forgets that he learned his native language without conscious effort; he has spent years learning it and never really completes the task. He cannot expect to master a for-

Students should know what is involved in learning a language

eign language overnight. The important thing for him in mastering a foreign language is to learn well a small amount each day, practice it regularly, and keep his purpose or goal in mind continuously. Prospective foreign language students should be told this when planning their programs and should not lose sight of these facts.

Reasons for student dropout of foreign language study

A 1961 study reported by Mueller & Leutenegger (40) at the college level included variations in teaching methodology and a follow-up study on the dropouts. The reason for dropping French given by the students who had extensive high school training in reading and writing French was the changeover to the oral approach in college with its accompanying frustrations. The negative aspects of this study resulted largely from an abrupt change in methodology and an emphasis upon the new skills of speaking and listening. High school teachers today could reverse that comment to say that the college people do not recognize the audiolingual abilities of the entering high school graduates.

A later study by Mueller & Harris (39) showed the effect of an audiolingual program on the dropout rate. Again in this study a technique different from the methodology used in high school was used to achieve as its "terminal goal native-like pronunciation and facility in speaking the language equivalent to that of a seven-year-old." The authors found that previous experience with learning French was of no help to the students placed in either experimental or control sections. The type of experimental program was described as follows:

The college dropout problem

> To achieve the stated goals, the [experimental] French Program begins by teaching the sounds of the language with very little visual support. During about forty hours, the student drills sounds, words, and word groups in a number of situations without knowing the meaning of what he says. Meaning is withheld in order to maximize the student's concentration on sound (39, p. 135).

The research found that students with high aptitude dropped out of the experimental section almost as frequently as those with middle or low aptitude and that a dropout rate of 54 percent in the control sections is normal at the University of Akron. Some inquiry needs to be made as to the real reasons why so many students discontinue foreign language study at the college level. In an article by Dusel (20) the tremendous attrition of students who begin foreign language study is discussed and several causes listed: *(1)* teaching methods, *(2)* teacher qualities, *(3)* programming, *(4)* unwise counseling, *(5)* change in student plans, and *(6)* transferring from one school to another. A recent article by the same author (17) encourages the principal, superintendent, or supervisor of foreign languages who wishes to objectively diagnose the decrease in foreign language enrollment to use the questionnaire proposed for this purpose. Not only should the department head or the district supervisor gather and maintain enrollment data in foreign language, but he should know why students from the elementary schools do not sign up for foreign language upon entering high school and why high school students discontinue foreign language study after a year or two.

Reasons for the dropout rate

Newmark & Sweigert (41) reported on the testing of three approaches to the teaching of Spanish in the elementary schools. The specific objectives were *(1)* using absolute assessment procedures to measure the extent to which each of three language courses achieved its own linguistic objectives; *(2)* providing baseline data that would enable a school administrator to relate the advantages and disadvantages of a set of instructional materials to the needs of his local school situation on the basis of his agreement with an explicit statement of objectives, the effectiveness of the materials under specified conditions, the problems and difficulties experienced in using the materials, and the cost; *(3)* providing comprehensive data on student achievement that could be used for diagnostic information on a given student's learning difficulties; determining how students who have had a course should be grouped for subsequent instruction and suggesting modifications of learning conditions, instructional materials, or objectives for the next group of students taking the course.

Objectives must be realistic and realizable?

With the exception of the *Spanish A* programmed course listening-comprehension vocabulary and the *Spanish A* reading vocabulary, the test results showed that all three language courses failed to achieve their basic linguistic objectives under the learning conditions involved in this study. In all three courses there was considerable deviation in classroom procedures from those recommended by the course developers. This was caused in part by problems connected with implementing a new course of instruction. The low scores on most criterion variables and the wide spread in student performance indicated that relatively few students would be prepared to profit from the next course of instruction.

Implications and recommendations of this research can help educators understand why some students may have great difficulty in progressing from one year of foreign language study to the next. Newmark & Sweigert warn teachers that they should not assume that a substantial number of students learn all, or even most, of what is "covered" in a given language course. Substantial modifications of materials and/or learning conditions would be required to achieve the goal of having most students acquire sufficient mastery of the basic language objectives to profit from the next sequence of instruction. In addition, the traditional method of evaluating only a small sample of the specific linguistic objectives of a language course may obscure serious deficiencies in materials and/or learning conditions.

Criterion: pages covered or materials mastered?

Zeldner's article on foreign language dropouts (58) lists several measures to strengthen and make effective foreign language programs. The suggestion to require four years of foreign language in the high school for admission to college would certainly reduce dropouts among the college preparatory students who discontinue language study after the general requirement of two years. However, this implies that the purpose of studying a foreign language is for college entrance. Another suggestion proposes that promising fourth-year students be rewarded with summer travel. Even though travel abroad can be most helpful in the development of foreign language fluency, the proposed solution may be of little help to the great majority that discontinue foreign language study by the end of the first year or so in high school. Zeldner's last suggestion seems to reflect more of the reasons for the dropouts, but it appears questionable that providing tutors for students would remedy the misuse of "cybernetic hardware" or enlarge the supply of "competent licensed teachers."

Together with the designation of a group of students who discontinue foreign language study as dropouts is a group that falls under the term *pushout*. The percentage of students reported by Teague & Rütimann (48, tables 3-F, 4-F, and 5-F) who do not continue into the third and fourth years of language study could be considered as a *dropout* percentage only if the following were confirmed: *(1)* the third and/or fourth years of language study were not offered; *(2)* the student did not care for the alternative of being bussed to one school in the district where the advanced instruction was offered; (3) the student is advised to drop because his minimum college requirements have been met; (4) mixed classes of third- and fourth-year students are essentially repeat courses to the fourth-year students; (5) teachers, administrators, counselors, and parents have the idea that foreign language is only for the intellectually gifted, for the elite.

Fault tree analysis

An interesting technique which may be used to study enrollment decrease is fault tree analysis. This operations research tool has been used in system safety engineering on aerospace projects. According to a report of this technique prepared by George F. Wilkinson, Project Director, and Belle Ruth Witkin, Research and Evaluation Specialist (1), a fault tree provides a concise and logical step-by-step description of the various combinations of possible occurrences within a system that can result in a predefined "undesired event," in this instance a high dropout in foreign language enrollment. The analysis includes a diagram that traces systematically the probable modes of failure leading to the undesired event, the interactions among these modes, and the critical paths.

Techniques for detecting enrollment problems

PERT

A somewhat similar technique in its graphic representation of a task to be accomplished is the Program Evaluation and Review Technique (PERT) which was used in the research by Newmark & Sweigert (41). Both PERT and fault tree analysis techniques use the term *critical path* and plan through an intricate design an economical use of time and a rational system of attack upon the work to be done. Fault tree analysis technique can be used to put all pieces of a problem together into a systematic whole and to pinpoint areas of responsibility.

Retaining students in a foreign language program

Measures can be taken to keep more students in foreign language study for a longer period of time. An assessment of student attitudes and aptitudes, a revision of the rigid scheduling system, and a recognition of the need for improved motivational techniques in teaching will encourage many students to stay in the language program and develop the fluency that comes with years of successful study.

Bartley reports (4) the important role that attitude plays in students who discontinue foreign language study. A preliminary investigation of group and sex differences causes her to speculate that in school districts where the percent of college-bound students is low, the percent of noncontinuing students would be higher. In a similar study involving both aptitude and attitude factors Bartley defines a dropout as one who has studied foreign language since the sixth grade and discontinues the study after grade eight (5). Using the Carroll-Sapon Modern Language Aptitude Test and the DuFort Foreign Language Attitude Scale, she comes to the conclusion that students who in their aptitude test scores appear to lack one or more components of aptitude could undergo remedial training if it could be shown that aptitude itself is subject to training. In addition, by using the attitude scale as a means of detecting low scorers, the reasons for these low scores signaling a poor disposition could then be investigated, thereby helping the student in question.

A student's attitude and aptitude does matter

Lester (34) is attempting to discover significant variables in the field of modern foreign language dropouts between levels two and three, to discover relationships between certain of these variables and, thereby, to lay the groundwork for later more systematic, rigorous testing of hypotheses and field testing of conclusions. Measurements taken in Connecticut secondary schools will assess student attitude toward the teacher and aptitude for foreign language study. Statistical comparisons of numbers of dropouts and continuers to numbers that fall into groups of high or low interest, high or low aptitude, etc., will lead to a determination of the most significant factors that appear to be related to dropout in the second and third years of high school foreign language study.

A number of studies have been made relating foreign language dropout to class scheduling. Convinced that the conventional method of scheduling is outmoded for an age expanding with technological advances, Hoye (31) suggests creative improvements that allow combinations of conventional class periods. In combination with flexible periods, opportunity for individual instruction is also given. The scheduling changes have effected a rise in foreign language enrollments in Minneapolis schools.

Needed: schedules that make room

Grittner explains (29) how foreign language skills may be maintained for the advanced-course potential dropout. His suggestions include flexibility of scheduling in which the high school student continues his study of foreign language into the 11th and 12th grades meeting with the instructor twice or three times a week or on a basis intended to assure that he will maintain his language skills. Grittner's ideas for student activities list types of work that are creative and that put into use the language skills already learned. Audiovisual productions, correspondence with students in the foreign country, language club activities, newspaper projects, directed writing and reading, and advanced conversation sessions are among the types of work possible in such advanced courses.

Individualizing projects

The nongraded system as reported by Fearing (24) allows schools to teach more languages for a longer sequence. Individualization of instruction is made possible after the student's successful completion of an introductory phase. It is hoped that controlled evaluation will be obtained to support some of the premises put forth in the latter two studies.

Nongraded classes

The research completed by Allen & Politzer (2) consisted of (1) an investigation of how flexible scheduling is presently used in the foreign language curriculum and what different experiences have revealed as the advantages, potentials, or even dangers that flexible scheduling may hold in store for the foreign language curriculum, and (2) a conference of specialists in areas of foreign language education, flexible scheduling, and administration who discussed the results of the above investigation. The recommendations for the use of flexible scheduling in the foreign language curriculum and the recommendations for research that the conference of specialists made constitute guidelines that school administrators and teachers could well use for the implementation of flexible scheduling.

Research in flexible scheduling

According to the foreign language specialists flexible scheduling might deal effectively with the present trend toward an early start in foreign language. The early start allows an ever-increasing number of pupils to reach third or even fourth level proficiency by the time they reach the 10th or 11th grade in high school. A system of rigid scheduling leaves these FLES students with the choice of either continuing the foreign language into a fourth or fifth level with a five-hours-per-week exposure or of dropping it. Flexible scheduling, on the other hand, makes it possible to offer a maintenance contact with the language already learned to the pupil whose main interest is either not foreign language or who wishes to study another foreign language.

Flexible scheduling: the answer to articulation with FLES

Allen & Politzer recommend that flexible scheduling be used to offer language instruction with a specific practical or business goal and in this way retain the potential dropout by offering a course to appeal to his specific needs. The effective use of flexible scheduling can prevent the student from being pushed out just because his language grammar course conflicts with some other course.

A multilevel grouping of foreign language students as reported by Hernick & Kennedy (30) has decreased the number of failures and dropouts in a high school district in Maryland. The decrease in total school enrollment in 1968 at Oxon Hill did not reflect a similar decrease in foreign language enrollments; on the contrary, foreign language enrollment increased. The authors of the article attribute the increase to several factors: *(1)* students are advanced according to their ability and not because they have had a certain number of years of study, *(2)* the underachievers have been able to bring up their grades and are remaining in the language program, and *(3)* more of the below-level students are now ready to enter the third-year courses. One of the concluding statements in the article seems especially noteworthy, "The academic diploma, the artificial incentive for taking foreign languages, no longer exists in most states. Students *will* take a foreign language if they find it worthwhile for its own sake—for what it does for them—rather than as an obstacle to be hurdled" (30, p. 204).

Multilevel grouping

"The experienced teacher is indeed one of the most flexible educational instruments that has ever been devised," said Allen & Politzer (2, p. 22). Teachers using creative techniques can motivate students in their language learning. Fearing attributes some of the dropout problem in foreign language classes to boredom (25). The oral drills and other textbook exercises must be augmented by a change of pace and by activities that relieve the monotony and are at the same time part of the planned instruction. Musical versions of fables, homemade 8-mm motion pictures with a tape-recorded sound track, and color slides of students acting out the language lessons bring variety and novelty to the routine hours. Phinney emphasized (42) to teachers of Latin that they must teach it in an interesting way: "My heart goes out to the reckless teacher who chucks all the books and passes out his own hastily typed, dittoed selections, and somehow, in this gaudy, psychedelic, television age, can make students interested in Latin. Heracles never had it so hard." Regardless of this teacher's reckless feeling, variety, color, novelty, practicality, and creativity can add motivation to learning. But careful planning should not be neglected.

The creative teacher

Teachers of Hebrew, Italian, Latin, Norwegian, Portuguese, and Russian are concerned about enrollments. Unless a sizable number of young people sign up for these classes they are usually dropped from the curriculum. It is therefore imperative that problems affecting enrollment be diagnosed early in the student's study of the foreign language. Attitude and aptitude assessment can be done before instruction begins. Cumulative cards containing detailed data on the student's abilities in the basic skills should accompany him as he advances from teacher to teacher and from school to school. An enthusiastic and well-trained teacher who is not aware of scheduling problems, poor counseling, and the needs of his students may find his program floundering regardless of his brilliant teaching.

A cumulative file on each student

National trends in foreign language enrollment

Although the annual report on national enrollments for fall 1968[1] is at this writing incomplete, returns do indicate some general trends. Complete figures from 18 states and the District of Columbia together with partial returns from Alaska (95 percent), Illinois (87 percent), Michigan (60 percent), and Nevada (94 percent) for French, German, Italian, Latin, Russian, and Spanish enrollments will serve as indicators of possible increases or decreases in public secondary school foreign language enrollments.

The sample

Of the 18 states with complete returns 12 show an increase in French, grades 7 through 12; therefore, the national French enrollment will also probably show an increase, although slight.

French

All 18 states show that the increase in German enrollments is still growing, with six of those reporting having made great gains. California will probably lead the states in total German enrollment.

German

Although only eight of the 22 states report any students studying Italian, increases were noted in four. Two states added Italian to the curriculum. This language may show a slight increase or a leveling-off when the tally of all 50 states is in.

Italian

Only the District of Columbia shows an increase in Latin enrollments. Twenty-two states show the decline that has taken place over the past few years. A heroic effort on the part of Latin teachers, counselors, and school administrators can stem the tide that threatens to eliminate this language from the public schools.

Latin

---

1 The writer is indebted to Miss Julia B. Gibson, Research Assistant, Modern Language Association, for the data being collected for the coming publication of 1968 enrollments.

The prediction made for French will probably also hold true for Russian—a slight increase in some states with a leveling-off in others. The states of Washington, Montana, and Kansas show the greatest increase, but the total number for all three is just under 2,000. Eleven of the states show some increase.

Russian

Spanish shows continued gains with 17 states exceeding their 1965 totals. Only North Dakota and Colorado report reduced numbers while four of the 17 states show great gains—Arkansas, California, New Hampshire, and North Carolina.

Spanish

The national percent of increase in student enrollment, grades 7 through 12, will probably exceed the percent of increase in foreign language enrollment since some states report that foreign language enrollments are not keeping pace with the general increase in the student population.

Cautions in evaluating surveys and reports

In a recent article Chastain (7) cautions the reader of research and statistical analyses to beware of the practice of accepting the general conclusions of experiments without questioning the conditions affecting a study. Educators not familiar with research reporting, experimental design, and statistical analyses often turn to the last pages of an article and accept conclusions without examining the content that led to those conclusions. This leads to an acceptance of the results of many studies in the absence of a proper examination of the contents and a true evaluation of the study itself and hinders the progress that should be taking place in the field.

Read the entire document

In surveys made of the number of language laboratories, for example, the term language laboratory is rarely clearly defined. It may be one tape recorder lying on a table in the corner of the classroom or a sophisticated dial-access laboratory.

Lab surveys

Is a teacher who turns on the television set so that pupils may view the foreign language program to be counted as a foreign language teacher? The definition of a foreign language teacher's qualifications should be part of a survey when the number of foreign language teachers is being tallied. Does a district have a FLES program when instruction is offered only 15 minutes per week or once every eight days? Or does a survey establish a minimum number of minutes per week or months per year before a district or school may be included as having a foreign language program?

TV surveys

FLES surveys

Is a student considered a dropout if he does not continue for-

432

eign language study into the third year of high school when the school does not offer a third-year class? How many high school students begin foreign language study in their junior year, and how many of these same students are counted in high school surveys to demonstrate the high dropout rate between the second and third year of foreign language study? Enrollment statistics need qualification by the one who makes the survey, and these same statistics should be questioned by the reader when conclusions are drawn by the authors of enrollment surveys. Unless detailed explanations are given that include just what the statistics do and do not do, the reader should consider that the range of error might well be considerable.

Enrollment surveys

Those who plan to survey a large geographical area (state, regional, or national) or those who plan to use statistics compiled from that area should consider the effect that a large school district has upon such a survey. If, for example, the report of the Los Angeles Unified School District with its 734,809 students is included in a California statewide report for the year 1968 and for some reason is not included for the year 1969, the total enrollment figures as well as the enrollments in each of the languages taught in the state will seem to indicate a drop. This *one* Los Angeles district is about one-sixth of the total kindergarten through grade 12 enrollment of the 4,412,035 public school pupils in California, according to the figures of fall 1968. Even though 99 percent of the districts are included in the annual enrollment returns, the inclusion one year and the exclusion another year of a large district will give a false impression of enrollment trends. It is therefore imperative that when figures from one year are compared with those of another, the number of students should also be known for each year.

Statistics must be carefully examined

In statewide or national surveys more exacting information can be obtained if the returns from the largest districts are examined separately and then included in the total returns. Teachers of German, for example, may believe that enrollment in that language is decreasing in the state when they read from the final results of a survey that fewer students were reported studying German. However, the opposite may be true if it were known that the three largest districts had not sent in enrollment figures for that language.

It has been the writer's experience over a number of years that gathering accurate census-type data is difficult. Questionnaires, form replies, and check sheets are often completed in a rather haphazard manner with incorrect figures and omissions occurring in as many as one out of every three replies. Undoubtedly many more such mistakes are not caught. Sometimes it is possible to correct errors and omissions by telephoning the person who has submitted the form and discussing the possible error. Writing a follow-up letter is time consuming but cheaper than a long-distance call. A personal visit may prove the best way to resolve an incompleted questionnaire or incorrect information; this procedure is perhaps the easiest if field or area assistants can perform the task. If a state department foreign language supervisor is collecting data, he can request help from county foreign language supervisors.

Difficulties in obtaining accurate data

Precise sampling techniques tend to be more accurate than a census-type survey, and a careful projection from precise samples may be a more economical way to gather data and still achieve honest results. Using a random sample will give a high degree of control to a survey and will reduce the error to an acceptable limit.

Sampling

Data use in reports and surveys of language enrollments

The data that has been collected on enrollments has been put to little diagnostic use. Teachers have observed the general trends rising or falling statistics have portrayed. New elementary school programs in foreign language have been viewed as swelling the total enrollment. The introduction of such languages as Chinese, Japanese, and Russian add to the programs and to the general enrollment. However, as enrollments have risen an awareness of the underachiever or the dropout has been slight.

Only when enrollments have slackened, when school district foreign language programs have been dropped, or when a certain foreign language has been dropped from the instructional program has a concern been felt. Occasionally someone expresses regret that so many young people begin language study to discontinue it after a year or at the most two years. Quite often the rationale for dropouts has been, "It's too hard for him." Little else has been given as the cause for the majority of students who fail, become discouraged, and drop, or who remain for the time specified by college requirements and then quietly discontinue their study. In many instances the attitude that foreign language study should be pursued only by the college preparatory student or by an elite scholar has persuaded parents, school

Data can help diagnose

434

administrators, and even teachers to do practically nothing about the great number of students who neither attempt nor remain in foreign language study. The fact that everyone learns *a* language does not seem to convince those with this narrow attitude that almost everyone *can* learn a second language.

Studies should be made that ascertain whether better teaching methods might encourage more students to study foreign language for a longer period of time. An early diagnosis of learning problems may demonstrate to the researcher that many more students can develop fluency in a foreign language if they can proceed at their own rate. Studies should be made to determine how scheduling improvements can help keep students in a foreign language program and enable more to continue into the advanced years of study.

Studies needed

The Working Committee chaired by Simches (46) concluded its report to the 1968 Northeast Conference with several provocative questions:

1 What is it that we need to know about pupil-teacher interaction in the FL classroom? What studies of interaction analysis are available and how can they be applied?

2 How do attitudes toward a foreign language and culture affect the motivation of the FL student in the classroom?

3 How significant a role can new electronic devices and media play in the FL classroom?

4 With all the new techniques and new school environments, why is there still an agonizing number of underachievers? What can be done about it?

Some work is being done to provide answers to the above questions, but much is left to be done to keep elementary school students in foreign language study when they enter secondary schools. Too many FLES programs are just that—elementary school foreign language programs with little relationship to high school study. High school programs that do not build upon the elementary program cause students to wonder why teachers cannot agree on course content and methodology. When objectives and methods differ greatly from school to school, the percent of those who discontinue foreign language study remains high. Bulletins such as the one written by Remer (45), which is intended to be a handbook for guiding students into foreign languages, should be updated and reprinted every two years since they are fine resources for counselors and teachers. Because many states are now discussing the partial or total elimination of the foreign language requirement for entrance into college or

Enlist the counselor

for the baccalaureate or advanced degrees, a greater emphasis must be placed upon the opportunities in the world of work for people who possess fluency in foreign language.

The justification of foreign language in the curriculum as a college preparatory subject may soon be a memory. Teachers should act now to see that their instruction is not based solely on the college requirement premise. Foreign language supervisors and consultants as well as foreign language department chairmen should gather data on the reasons for the high rate of dropout from their foreign language programs. Surveys may disclose that poor teaching is going on. Inflexible schedules may have to be changed, and counselors with bias and incomplete or inaccurate information will need more information. It should be of professional interest to all foreign language educators to isolate the reasons why students do not enter foreign language classes and why they discontinue their study so quickly. Something is definitely wrong if FLES programs give pupils only an earlier opportunity to drop foreign language.

College requirements on the wane

Surveys and reports on enrollments used as an assessment of a foreign language program can indicate trends, needs, or deficiencies. Simply collecting enrollment data is insufficient, and not being aware of problems in a foreign language department allows bad practices to continue unnoticed, irritations to fester, and unhappy situations to escape scrutiny. Warning signs are visible to those who can recognize them: no third- or fourth-year classes in high school, a high dropout rate in beginning classes or during the second year, the number of students changing language upon entrance into high school, and an abundance of low grades in foreign language for otherwise average students.

Is the FL curriculum relevant?

Although excellent state and national surveys have been made almost annually during the past decade, more use should be made by teachers of enrollment figures. Attitude and aptitude assessment can be of real help to counselors and teachers in placement and counseling of students. Variations in scheduling may have a beneficial effect upon performance. Improved scheduling practices have already been shown to exert a positive influence upon enrollment in the advanced language courses. Additional research may show definite relationships between comprehensive evaluation and enrollment, between high interest and continuers, between student aptitude and individualized instruction. The high dropout rate demonstrates graphically that foreign language programs need strengthening.

References, foreign language enrollments

1 Alameda County Pace Center. Fault tree analysis: a research tool for educational planning. Technical Report No. 1. Alameda County School Department, Hayward, Calif., October 1968.

2 Allen, Dwight; Politzer, Robert L. A survey and investigation of foreign language instruction under conditions of flexible scheduling. Contract No. OE 6-14-026, U.S. Department of Health, Education, and Welfare, Office of Education, Bureau of Research, Washington, D.C., September 1966.

3 Ammons, Margaret P. Do we really want students to learn? Foreign Language Newsletter State of Oregon, 4:ii (January 1967).

4 Bartley, Diana E. The importance of the attitude factor in language dropout: a preliminary investigation of group and sex differences. Stanford University, Stanford, Calif., March 1969. (Unpublished paper)

5 Bartley, Diana E. A pilot study of aptitude and attitude factors in language dropout. California Journal of Educational Research, 20 (March 1969) 48-55.

6 Bockman, John F. Results of a survey: FL supervisory experience with high school programs, and opinions concerning factors affecting enrollment in high school Russian. Speech read at Arizona chapter of American Association of Teachers of Slavic and Eastern European Languages (AATSEEL), 1967.

7 Chastain, Kenneth. Let's look at research. Hispania, 50:iii (September 1967) 496-500.

8 Childers, J. Wesley. Foreign-language offerings and enrollments in public secondary schools, fall 1958. Prepared for the U.S. Office of Education pursuant to a contract under the National Defense Education Act (NDEA). Modern Language Association, New York.

9 Childers, J. Wesley. Foreign-language offerings and enrollments in public secondary schools, fall 1959. Modern language Association, New York.

10 Childers, J. Wesley. Foreign-language offerings and enrollments in public secondary schools, fall 1960. Modern Language Association, New York.

11 Dale, Edgar. The time of our lives. The News Letter. Published by the College of Education, Ohio State University, Columbus, 34:v (February 1969).

12 De Petra, Giulio. Italian in California universities and colleges: report of the fall 1968 survey. Unpublished survey conducted by the American Association of Teachers of Italian (AATI) Coordinator for California and tabulated by Giulio C. Cassani, Department of Italian, Defense Language Institute, West Coast, Monterey, Calif.

13 Dershem, James F.; Lund, Gladys A.; Herslow, Nina Greer. Foreign-language offerings and enrollments in secondary schools, fall 1964. Modern Language Association, New York, 1966.

14 Dufort, Mary. Foreign language attitude scale. Alameda County School Department, Hayward, Calif., 1963.

15 Dufort, Mary; Schevill, Karl. Foreign language cumulative report form. California Journal for Instructional Improvement, 7:iv (December 1964) 16-28.

16 Dufort, Mary; et al. A practical handbook for implementation of foreign language programs. Alameda County School Department, Hayward, Calif., 1967.

17 Dusel, John P. Diagnosing the decrease in foreign language enrollment. Tennessee Foreign Language Bulletin, No. 48, Vol. 16, No. 2. (Winter 1969).

18 Dusel, John P. Foreign language offerings and enrollments in public secondary schools, fall 1968. Department of Education, State of California, Sacramento, March 1969.

19 Dusel, John P. General observations on the results of the survey of foreign language offerings and enrollments in California public schools, fall 1965. Parts I and II. Department of Education, State of California, Sacramento, October 1966.

20 Dusel, John P. Why the FL dropouts? Foreign Language Newsletter published by the Foreign Language Association of Northern California, May 1966, p. 5-7.

21 Eaton, Esther M. Foreign languages in public secondary schools, a national survey, fall 1959, interim report. U.S. Office of Education, Government Printing Office, Washington, D.C., 1963.

22 Eshelman, James N.; Dershem, James F. Foreign-language offerings and enrollments in public secondary schools, fall 1963. Modern Language Association, New York, 1965.

23 Eshelman, James N.; Lian, Nancy W. Foreign-language offerings and enrollments in secondary schools public schools: fall 1961, fall 1962 and nonpublic schools: fall 1962. Modern Language Association, New York, 1964.

24 Fearing, Percy. Nongraded foreign language classes. Foreign Language Annals, 2:iii (March 1969).

25 Fearing, Percy. Using creative activities to reduce the dropout rate. From an unpublished paper delivered at Wisconsin State University, Whitewater, March 30, 1968. Obtainable from the Department of Education, St. Paul, Minn.

26 Fulton, J. Renée. The drop-out of students after the second year of language instruction. In: Bottiglia, William F., ed. The language classroom. Reports of the Working Committees, Northeast Conference (RWCNEC), 1957, p. 36-45.

27 Goldberg, Samuel A. High school enrollments in Latin, 1964-65. The Classical World (May 1966).

28 Gradisnik, Anthony. A survey of FLES instruction in cities over 300,000. Foreign Language Annals, 2:i (October 1968) 54-57.

29 Grittner, Frank M. Maintaining foreign language skills for the advanced-course dropout. Foreign Language Annals, 2:ii (December 1968) 205-211.

30 Hernick, Michael; Kennedy, Dora. Multi-level grouping of students in the modern foreign language program. Foreign Language Annals, 2:ii (December 1968) 200-204.

31 Hoye, Almon. Can flexible schedules affect for-

eign language enrollments? Minnesota Foreign Language Bulletin, 6:iv (May 1966).

32 Latimer, John F. The Oxford conference and related activities. The American Classical League, George Washington University, Washington, D.C., 1968.

33 Latimer, John F.; Eaton, Annette H. Latin in secondary schools: a six-year program. Foreign Language Annals, 1:iv (May 1968) 295-300.

34 Lester, Kenneth A. Factors related to dropouts between levels two and three of modern foreign language study in the public secondary schools of Connecticut. From abstract of dissertation in progress. Connecticut State Department of Education, Hartford, 1969.

35 Lieberman, Samuel. College classical enrollments, 1965-66. The Classical World, 59 (May 1966) 295-296, 298.

36 Lund, Gladys A.; Herslow, Nina Greer. Foreign language entrance and degree requirements in U.S. colleges and universities, fall 1966. Contract No. OE-5-14-032, U.S. Department of Health, Education, and Welfare, Office of Education. Modern Language Association, New York, 1966.

37 Massachusetts State Department of Education. Foreign language offerings and enrollments in Massachusetts public secondary schools, academic year 1965-66. Boston, Mass., 1967.

38 The Modern Language Association of America. Reports of surveys and studies in the teaching of modern foreign languages, 1959-61. Modern Language Association, New York.

39 Mueller, Theodore H.; Harris, Robert. The effect of an audio-lingual program on drop-out rate. Modern Language Journal, 50:iii (March 1966) 133-137.

40 Mueller, Theodore H.; Leutenegger, Ralph R. Some inferences about an intensified oral approach to the teaching of French based on a study of course drop-outs. Modern Language Journal, 48:ii (February 1964) 91-94.

41 Newmark, Gerald; Sweigert, Ray L., Jr. Three media in search of their message: a summary of research on three approaches to teaching Spanish. AV Communication Review, 15:iii (Fall 1967).

42 Phinney, Edward, Jr. Report to the California Action Council for Classics. From an unpublished paper delivered at Fresno State College, Calif., March 22, 1969.

43 Pimsleur, Paul; Sundland, Donald M.; McIntyre, Ruth D. Under-achievement in foreign language learning. Final Report. Ohio State University Research Foundation, Columbus. Contract No. OE-2-14-004, U.S. Department of Health, Education, and Welfare, Office of Education, Washington, D.C., 1963. Abridgment available from the Modern Language Association, New York, 1966.

44 Plottel, Jeanine Parisier. Foreign language entrance and degree requirements for the B. A. degree. Publications of the Modern Language Association (PMLA), 75:iv (September 1960) 14-28.

45 Remer, Ilo. A handbook for guiding students in modern foreign languages. U.S. Department of Health, Education, and Welfare, Office of Education. U.S. Government Printing Office, Washington, D.C., 1963.

46 Simches, Seymour O.; et al. The classroom revisited. In: Bird, Thomas E. Foreign language learning: research and development: an assessment. Reports of the Working Committees, Northeast Conference (RWCNEC), 1968, p. 48-73.

47 Statement on foreign language study by nine Oregon Higher Education presidents (January 1967). Foreign Language Annals, 1:iii (March 1968) 197-198.

48 Teague, Caroline; Rütimann, Hans. Foreign-language offerings and enrollments in public secondary schools, fall 1965. Modern Language Association, New York, 1967.

49 Terras, Victor. A survey of the teaching of Russian in the U.S., fall 1966, part I: colleges and universities. The Slavic and East European Journal, 11 (1967) 308-321.

50 Terras, Victor. A survey of the teaching of Russian in the U. S., fall 1966, part II: secondary schools. The Slavic and East European Journal, 11 (1967) 450-463.

51 Vamos, Mara; Harmon, John. Modern foreign language enrollments in four-year accredited colleges and universities, fall 1958 and fall 1959. Modern Language Association, New York, 1961.

52 Vamos, Mara; Harmon, John. Modern foreign language enrollments in four-year colleges and universities, fall 1960. Modern Language Association, New York, 1961.

53 Viens, Claude P.; Wadsworth, Philip. Foreign language entrance and degree requirements for the M. A., M. S., and Ph. D. degrees. Publications of the Modern Language Association (PMLA), 72:iv (September 1957) 22-32.

54 Willbern, Glen. Foreign language enrollments in public secondary schools, 1965. Foreign Language Annals, 1:iii (March 1968) 239-253.

55 Willbern, Glen. Foreign language entrance and degree requirements in colleges that grant the B. A. degree: fall 1966. Foreign Language Annals, 1:i (October 1967) 49-70.

56 Willbern, Glen. Survey of the employment of teachers of the Chinese language, fall 1967. Journal of the Chinese Language Teachers Association, October 1968.

57 Wolfe, Warren J. Foreign language entrance and degree requirements for the B. S. degree. Publications of the Modern Language Association (PMLA), 74:iv (September 1959) 34-44.

58 Zeldner, Max. The foreign language dropouts. Modern Language Journal, 50:v (May 1966) 275-280.

Index

FL enrollment survey 420
Chinese Teachers Association 420
Choldin, Hannah W. 169-70
Chomsky, Noam 20-24, 349
    linguistic competence and per-
      formance 199
    psychology of learning 186
    Sound Pattern of English, The 21
Christian, Chester C. 41
Christie, J. T. 398
Cincinnati, Ohio
    FLES program 151
Clark, John L. D. 109, 351, 368
Class, Social
    middle-class attitudes 254
Classical Association of the Atlantic
    States (CAAS) 410
Classical Association of the Middle
    West and South (CAMWS) 410
Classical Association of the New
    England States 410
Classical Association of the Pacific
    States 410
Classical World, The (CAAS publi-
    cation) 411
Classics (languages) 389-412
Classroom 293, 380
    technological aids 313-38
Classroom laboratory instructional
    system (CLIS) 132
Cleveland Diocesan Schools
    Latin courses 398
Cleveland Heights-University
    Heights (Ohio) 397
CLIS (Classroom laboratory instruc-
    tional system) 132
Cognitive-code learning approach
    123, 285-88
Cognitive psychology 12
    linguistic competence 20
Colby College Conference 109
Cole, Leo R. 133
Coleman, Ben C. 133, 308
College
    articulation between high school
      and college 172
    attrition 425-26
    curriculum 105
    enrollment survey 420-21
    evaluation programs 378
    technological aids 322
    testing 361, 362
    University of Illinois student sur-
      vey 216-17
College Entrance Examination
    Board (CEEB) 399
    Achievement test 361-63
Colligan, Jerome 314
Colorado, University of
    FL requirements for Ph.D. 367
Color television 316-18
Commercial tests 364, 366
Common Concepts Test (Banathy)
    361
Communication 357
    computer-assisted instruction 336

Communicative skills 201
Community antenna television
    (CATV) 319-20
Competence 349
Comprehension 356
Computer-assisted instruction (CAI)
    132, 335-38
    classics teaching 401-3
    German teaching 124-25
    management of instruction 300-2
    University of Illinois 190
    value of 10
Computers and Humanities 402
Concepts: teaching and learning
    performance 267
Concordia College (Moorhead,
    Minn.)
    language camps 170
Conroy, William B. 48, 61
Content 369
    language and cultural materials
    118-21
Contrasting structure 294
Contrastive linguistic analysis 29,
    115-18, 304
Controlled observation 84
Cook, V. J. 127
Cooper, Christopher 23
Cooper, James G. 234
Coop test 363
Cordova, Ignacio 237, 244
Core-test concept 360
Craven, S. 109
Creative teacher 430
Creole language 25, 26
Criterion-referenced test 358, 364-65
Cross-cultural communication 40,
    43
Cross-cultural context 37-77
Crosswhite, Vivian 327
Crowley, Dale P. 136
Cultural anthropology 112-13
Culture, 37, 77, 108
    bilingualism and biculturism
    230-56
    teaching methods 112-13, 283
    testing 314
Curriculum 5, 86, 106, 109
    college 217
    elementary and secondary schools
    141-75
    Latin 393
    program evaluation 375
Cutt, Thomas 394

D

Damoiseau, R. 59
Damore, Anthony P. 360
Dannerbeck, Francis J. 133
Das Gupta, J. 26
Davies, D. J. E. 148
Davis, Alan 344, 351
Debyser, Francis 55
Deeken, Hans W. 134
    advanced placement courses 169
Del Olmo, Guillermo 111-12